157

PRINCIPLES OF SCOTTISH
PRIVATE LAW

PRINCIPLES OF
SCOTTISH
PRIVATE LAW

by
DAVID M. WALKER,
C.B.E., M.A., Ph.D., LL.D., Hon. LL.D., F.B.A., F.R.S.E., F.S.A. Scot.,
One of Her Majesty's Counsel in Scotland,
Of the Middle Temple, Barrister,
Regius Professor of Law in the
University of Glasgow

Volume I

Book I: Introductory and General
Book II: International Private law
Book III: Law of Persons

FOURTH EDITION

CLARENDON PRESS · OXFORD
1988

Oxford University Press, Walton Street, Oxford OX2 6DP
London Glasgow New York Toronto
Delhi Bombay Calcutta Madras Karachi
Kuala Lumpur Singapore Hong Kong Tokyo
Nairobi Dar es Salaam Cape Town
Melbourne Auckland
and associates in
Berlin Ibadan Mexico City

Published in the United States by
Oxford University Press, New York

First published 1970
Second edition 1975
Third edition 1982
Fourth edition 1988

British Library Cataloguing in Publication Data

Walker, David M.
Principles of Scottish private law.—4th ed.
Vol. 1
1. Civil law—Scotland
I. Title
344.1106   KDC330

ISBN 0–19–876215–1

Library of Congress Cataloging in Publication Data
(Revised for vol. 1)
Walker, David M.
Principles of Scottish private law.
Bibliography: p. Includes indexes.
Contents: v. 1. [without special title] — v. 2.
Book IV, Law of obligations.
1. Civil law—Scotland. I. Title.
KDC330.W35   1988   346.411   87-22905   344.1106
ISBN 0–19–876215–1 (v. 1)

Typeset by Graphicraft Typesetters Ltd, Hong Kong
Printed and bound in Great Britain by
Biddles Ltd, Guildford and King's Lynn

PREFACE

The purpose of this book is to provide students and practitioners of the law of Scotland with a plain statement, as concise as reasonably practicable, of the leading general principles and rules and the chief detailed rules of the private law of Scotland, and of the main qualifications and exceptions thereto, systematically set out, and supported by references to the main authorities for the propositions stated. It is hoped that this will provide a useful basis for the study of the original sources of the principles and rules in statutes, judicial decisions, and institutional writings, and of the more detailed textbooks on the particular branches and topics of the private law.

The scope of the book covers the whole of the substantive private law, including international private law, remedies, and diligence, but, save incidentally, excludes the adjective law, namely the subjects of evidence, procedure, pleading and court practice, representation and legal aid, practical conveyancing, and matters of practice. Constitutional, administrative, criminal, and tax law are excluded, save for occasional mentions. Even within these limits the private law steadily grows more voluminous and complicated, and it steadily becomes more difficult to discern general principles in the mass of particular enactments and decisions and to state them accurately. Despite this there is continuing value in a general book which tries to set out the principles and rules of the whole private law systematically, so that the different branches of law can be related one to another as parts of a larger whole and that whole be considered as a rational entity. Since the subject-matter of many groups of chapters, and even of some single chapters, has provided material enough for substantial books on those topics alone, it has been impossible, and no attempt has been made, to deal with every point of detail or matter of dispute or difficulty, nor to cite all the authorities. The older authorities may be found in older books, but I have tried to give a substantial citation of modern authorities. Non-Scottish authorities have been cited only where this seemed necessary. For reasons of space historical, jurisprudential, and comparative discussions have necessarily been excluded.

As in the third edition the book is divided into four separate volumes and all of the material again revised and parts of it rewritten in an attempt to present the law more clearly.

I am indebted to many secretaries who toiled to convert the manuscript into typescript, to the Delegates and staff of the Oxford University Press, and to the printers who have devoted so much skill and care to the printing.

Many of my academic colleagues in Glasgow and in other Scottish universities have given me the benefit of their views on various points, and to them all I offer my thanks. I am, however, alone responsible for the final state of the whole book.

I have sought to state the law as at 1 October 1987, but where possible have noted some later changes.

Department of Private Law,   D.M.W.
The University of Glasgow,
Glasgow, G12 8QQ.

CONTENTS

BOOK I
INTRODUCTORY AND GENERAL

BOOK II
INTERNATIONAL PRIVATE LAW

BOOK III
LAW OF PERSONS

CONTENTS

PART 1

NATURAL PERSONS

PART 2

UNINCORPORATED ASSOCIATIONS

PART 3

JURISTIC PERSONS: INCORPORATED BODIES

CONTENTS OF VOLUME II

BOOK IV
LAW OF OBLIGATIONS

PART 8
OBLIGATIONS ARISING FROM STATUTE

PART 9
OBLIGATIONS ARISING FROM DECREES

CONTENTS OF VOLUME III

BOOK V
LAW OF PROPERTY

CONTENTS OF VOLUME IV

BOOK VI
LAW OF TRUSTS

BOOK VII
LAW OF SUCCESSION

BOOK VIII
LAW OF CIVIL REMEDIES

BOOK IX
LAW OF DILIGENCE

BOOK X
LAW OF INSOLVENCY

TABLE OF CASES

TABLE OF STATUTES

AUTHORITIES AND ABBREVIATIONS

A.A.   Act of Adjournal.
A.Ass.   Act of the General Assembly of the Church of Scotland.
A.P.S.   Acts of the Parliaments of Scotland, 1124–1707, ed. Thomas
Thomson and Cosmo Innes, 11 vols. in 12, 1814–1875.
A.S.   Act of Sederunt.
Anton.   Professor A. E. Anton, *Private International Law*, 1967.
Balf.   Sir James Balfour of Pittendreich, *Practicks: or a System of the
more Ancient Law of Scotland*, 1754 and (Stair Socy.) 1962–3.
Bankt.   Andrew McDouall, Lord Bankton, *Institute of the Laws of Scot-
land in Civil Rights*, 3 vols., 1751–3.
Begg.   J. Henderson Begg, *Law of Scotland relating to Law Agents*,
2nd ed., 1883.
Bell, *Arb.*   J. M. Bell, *Law of Arbitration in Scotland*, 2nd ed., 1877.
Bell, *Comm.*   Professor G. J. Bell, *Commentaries on the Law of Scotland
and the Principles of Mercantile Jurisprudence*, 7th ed., 1870.
Bell, *Conv.*   Professor A. Montgomery Bell, *Lectures on Conveyancing*,
3rd ed., 2 vols., 1882.
Bell, *Dict.*   William Bell, *Dictionary and Digest of the Law of Scotland*,
7th ed., 1890.
Bell, *Prin.*   Professor G. J. Bell, *Principles of the Law of Scotland*, 10th
ed., 1899.
Borthwick.   J. Borthwick, *Law of Libel and Slander in Scotland*, 1826.
Broun.   J. C. C. Broun, *Law of Nuisance in Scotland*, 1891.
M. P. Brown.   M. P. Brown, *Law of Sale*, 1821.
Brown.   Richard Brown, *Sale of Goods Act, 1893*, 2nd ed., 1911.
Burn-Murdoch.   H. Burn-Murdoch, *Interdict in the Law of Scotland*,
1933.
Burns.   John Burns, *Conveyancing Practice*, 4th ed., 1957.
C.   Code (Corpus Juris Civilis).
C.L.J.   Cambridge Law Journal.
Cheshire and North.   G. C. Cheshire and P. M. North, *Private Interna-
tional Law*, 11th ed., 1979.
Clark.   F. W. Clark, *Law of Partnership and Joint Stock Companies*, 2
vols., 1866.
Clive   E. Clive, *Law of Husband and Wife*, 2nd ed. 1980.
Cooper.   F. T. Cooper, *Law of Defamation and Verbal Injury*, 2nd ed.,
1906.

Craig. Sir Thomas Craig, *Jus Feudale*, 3rd ed., 1732, and trs. Lord President Clyde, 2 vols., 1934.

D. Digest (Corpus Juris Civilis).

Dallas. George Dallas of St. Martin's, *Styles of Writs*, 2nd ed., 1774.

Dicey and Morris. A. V. Dicey and J. H. C. Morris, *Conflict of Law*, 11th ed., 1988.

Dickson. W. G. Dickson, *Law of Evidence in Scotland*, 3rd ed., 2 vols., 1887.

Dirleton. Sir George Nisbet, Lord Dirleton, *Doubts and Questions in the Law, especially of Scotland*, 1698.

Dobie. W. J. Dobie, *Manual of the Law of Liferent and Fee in Scotland*, 1941.

Dobie, *Prac.* W. J. Dobie, *Law and Practice in the Sheriff Court*, 1948.

Duff, *Deeds.* A. Duff, *Treatise on Deeds, chiefly affecting moveables*, 1840.

Duff, *Feudal.* A. Duff, *Treatise on Deeds and Forms used in the Constitution Transmission and Extinction of Feudal Rights*, 1838.

Duncan and Dykes. G. Duncan and D. Oswald Dykes, *Principles of Civil Jurisdiction as applied in the Law of Scotland*, 1911.

Encyc. *Encyclopaedia of the Laws of Scotland*, 18 vols., 1926–52.

Ersk. Professor John Erskine of Carnock, *An Institute of the Law of Scotland*, 8th ed., 2 vols., 1871.

Ersk., *Prin.* Professor John Erskine of Carnock, *Principles of the Law of Scotland*, 21st ed., 1911.

Ferguson, *Roads.* J. Ferguson, *Law of Roads, Streets, Rights of Way, Bridges and Ferries*, 1904.

Ferguson, *Water.* J. Ferguson, *Law of Water and Water Rights in Scotland*, 1907.

Forbes. Professor William Forbes, *Institutes of the Law of Scotland*, 2 vols., 1722–30.

Fraser, *H. & W.* Patrick, Lord Fraser, *Husband and Wife according to the Law of Scotland*, 2nd ed., 2 vols., 1876–8.

Fraser, *M. & S.* Patrick, Lord Fraser, *Master and Servant, Employer and Workman, Master and Apprentice*, 3rd ed., 1882.

Fraser, *P. & Ch.* Patrick, Lord Fraser, *Law of Scotland relative to Parent and Child and Guardian and Ward*, 3rd ed., 1906.

Gibb. Professor A. Dewar Gibb, *International Law of Jurisdiction in England and Scotland*, 1926.

Gibb and Dalrymple. *Scottish Judicial Dictionary*, 1946.

Gloag. Professor W. M. Gloag, *Law of Contract*, 2nd ed., 1929.

Gloag and Henderson. Professor W. M. Gloag and Professor R. C. Henderson, *Introduction to the Law of Scotland*, 8th ed., 1981.

Gloag and Irvine. Professor W. M. Gloag and J. M. Irvine, *Law of Rights in Security, Heritable and Moveable, and Cautionary Obligations*, 1897.

Goudy. Henry Goudy, *Law of Bankruptcy in Scotland*, 4th ed., 1914.

Gow.   J. J. Gow, *Mercantile and Industrial Law of Scotland*, 1964.
Graham Stewart.   J. Graham Stewart, *Law of Diligence*, 1898.
Halsbury.   *Laws of England*, 4th ed.
Henderson.   Professor R. C. Henderson, *Principles of Vesting in the Law of Succession*, 2nd ed., 1938.
Hope, *Major Prac.*   Sir Thomas Hope, *Major Practicks*, 1608–33, 2 vols. (Stair Socy.), 1937–8.
Hope, *Minor Prac.*   Sir Thomas Hope, *Minor Practicks*, 1726.
Hume.   Baron David Hume, *Decisions*, 1781–1822, 1839.
Hume, *Comm.*   Baron David Hume, *Commentaries on the Law of Scotland respecting Crimes*, 4th ed., 2 vols., 1844.
Hume, *Lect.*   Baron David Hume, *Lectures on the Law of Scotland*, 6 vols. (Stair Socy.) 1939–58.
Hunter.   R. Hunter, *Law of Landlord and Tenant*, 4th ed., 2 vols., 1876.
I.C.L.Q.   International and Comparative Law Quarterly, 1952–.
Inst.   Institutes (Corpus Juris Civilis).
Irons.   J. Campbell Irons, *Judicial Factors*, 1908.
J.R.   Juridical Review, 1889–.
Kames, *Eluc.*   Henry Home, Lord Kames, *Elucidations respecting the Law of Scotland*, 1777.
Kames, *H.L.T.*   Henry Home, Lord Kames, *Historical Law Tracts*, 4th ed., 1817.
Kames, *Equity.*   Henry Home, Lord Kames, *Principles of Equity*, 5th ed., 1825.
L.Q.R.   Law Quarterly Review, 1886–.
Mor.   W. M. Morison's *Dictionary of Decisions*, 22 vols.
M.L.R.   Modern Law Review, 1937–.
Mackay, *Manual.*   Aeneas J. G. Mackay, *Manual of Practice in the Court of Session*, 1893.
Mackay, *Prac.*   Aeneas J. G. Mackay, *Practice of the Court of Session*, 2 vols., 1877–9.
Mack.   Sir George Mackenzie of Rosehaugh, *Institutions of the Law of Scotland*, 1684.
Mack., *Crim.*   Sir George Mackenzie of Rosehaugh, *Laws and Customs of Scotland in Matters Criminal*, 2nd ed., 1699.
Mackenzie Stuart.   Professor A. Mackenzie Stuart, *Law of Trusts*, 1932.
Maclaren.   J. A. Maclaren, *Court of Session Practice*, 1916.
McLaren.   John, Lord McLaren, *Law of Wills and Succession*, 3rd ed., 1894; Supplement by Dykes, 1934.
Menzies.   Professor Allan Menzies, *Lectures on Conveyancing according to the Law of Scotland*, revised ed., 1900.
Menzies, *Trs.*   A. J. P. Menzies, *Law of Scotland affecting Trustees*, 2nd ed., 1913.
Millar.   J. H. Millar, *Handbook of Prescription according to the Law of Scotland*, 1893.
Miller, *Partnership.*   Professor J. Bennett Miller, *Law of Partnership in Scotland*, 1973.

More, *Lect.*   Professor J. S. More, *Lectures on the Law of Scotland*, ed. McLaren, 2 vols., 1864.

More, *Notes.*   Professor J. S. More, *Notes to Stair's Institutions*, in fifth edition thereof, 1832.

Morris.   J. H. C. Morris, *The Conflict of Laws*, 3rd ed., 1984.

Napier.   Mark Napier, *Law of Prescription in Scotland*, 2nd ed., 1854.

N.I.L.Q.   Northern Ireland Legal Quarterly.

Nov.   Novels (Corpus Juris Civilis).

Paton and Cameron.   G. C. H. Paton and J. G. S. Cameron, *Law of Landlord and Tenant*, 1967.

Q.A.   *Quoniam Attachiamenta.*

R.C.   Rules of the Court of Session, 1965.

R.M.   *Regiam Majestatem*, ed. Skene, 1609, and ed. Cooper (Stair Socy.), 1947.

Rankine, *Bar.*   Professor Sir John Rankine, *Law of Personal Bar in Scotland*, 1921.

Rankine, *L.O.*   Professor Sir John Rankine, *Law of Land Ownership in Scotland*, 4th ed., 1909.

Rankine, *Leases.*   Professor Sir John Rankine, *Law of Leases in Scotland*, 3rd ed., 1916.

Ross, *Lect.*   Walter Ross, *Lectures on the History and Practice of the Law of Scotland relative to Conveyancing and Legal Diligence*, 2nd ed., 2 vols., 1822.

S.L.R.   Scottish Law Review, 1886–1963.

S.L.T. (News).   Scots Law Times, News portion.

Skene, *D.V.S.*   Sir John Skene, *De Verborum Significatione*, 1597.

Smith, *British Justice.*   Professor T. B. Smith, *British Justice—The Scottish Contribution*, 1961.

Smith, *Precedent.*   Professor T. B. Smith, *Doctrines of Judicial Precedent in Scots Law*, 1952.

Smith, *Studies.*   Professor T. B. Smith, *Studies Critical and Comparative*, 1963.

Smith, *Sh. Comm.*   Professor T. B. Smith, *A Short Commentary on the Law of Scotland*, 1963.

Spotiswoode.   Sir Robert Spotiswoode, *Practicks of the Laws of Scotland*, 1706.

Stair.   Sir James Dalrymple, Viscount Stair, *Institutions of the Law of Scotland*, Tercentenary ed., 1981.

Thoms.   G. H. Thoms, *Judicial Factors*, 2nd. ed., 1881.

Steuart.   Sir James Steuart, *Answers to Dirleton's Doubts in the Laws of Scotland*, 1715.

Walker, *Civil Remedies.*   Professor D. M. Walker, *Law of Civil Remedies in Scotland*, 1974.

Walker, *Contracts.*   Professor D. M. Walker, *Law of Contracts and Related Obligations in Scotland*, 2nd ed., 1985.

Walker, *Damages.*   Professor D. M. Walker, *Law of Damages in Scotland*, 1955.

Walker, *Delict*.   Professor D. M. Walker, *Law of Delict in Scotland*, 2nd ed., 1981.

Walker, *Judicial Factors*.   Sheriff N. M. L. Walker, *Judicial Factors*, 1974.

Walker, *Prescription*.   Professor D. M. Walker, *Law of Prescription and Limitation of Actions in Scotland*, 3rd ed., 1980.

Walker, *S.L.S.*   Professor D. M. Walker, *The Scottish Legal System*, 5th ed., 1981.

Walkers.   Sheriffs A. G. Walker and N. M. L. Walker, *Law of Evidence in Scotland*, 1964.

Wallace.   G. Wallace, *System of the Principles of the Law of Scotland*, 1760.

Walton.   F. P. Walton, *Handbook of the Law of Husband and Wife in Scotland*, 3rd ed., 1951.

Wilson.   Professor W. A. Wilson, *Law of Trusts and Trustees in Scotland*, 1974.

Wood.   Professor J. P. Wood, *Lectures on Conveyancing*, 1903.

BOOK I

INTRODUCTORY AND GENERAL

The Introductory and General Book deals with those matters of an introductory character which are necessarily preliminary to the understanding of the rules of any of the particular branches of Scottish private law, and also those principles of wide general application, not falling wholly within any one branch of private law.

CHAPTER 1.1

SCOTTISH PRIVATE LAW: ITS SCOPE, SOURCES, AND LITERATURE

SCOPE OF SCOTTISH PRIVATE LAW

The private law is the branch of the municipal law of Scotland comprising the principles and rules applied in defining and determining the rights and duties of ordinary private persons in their relations with one another, and of the State, and of public and governmental agencies and persons, in their relations with persons, in respects in which they do not enjoy any special position, right, or immunity, by virtue of any rule of public law.[1] The division between private and public law is not clear or rigid nor is it so familiar as in continental legal systems.

Scottish private law has never known the distinguishable, and sometimes conflicting, bodies of rules of common law and of equity, as long did, and to some extent does, English law, nor distinct bodies of civil and of commercial law, applicable respectively to ordinary citizens and to merchants, as do many European systems of law. Equitable principles and rules derived from commercial and maritime customs are woven into the fabric of the private law.

Private law is entirely civil in character, being defined and applied by civil courts under civil procedure, though at many points touching and interacting with principles applied by the criminal courts in dealing, under rules of criminal procedure, with the kinds of conduct legally deemed criminal and punishable, and with principles applied by administrative authorities and tribunals in dealing with disputes arising from matters of public administration, and with the principles applied by courts of special jurisdiction, which are sometimes civil and sometimes criminal in character.

Within private law a distinction exists between rules of substantive law, which state what rights and duties are recognized as applying to persons in various categories of relationships, and what legal remedies exist for infringement or breach thereof, and rules of adjective law which define

---

[1] See also Inst. I, 1, 4; Stair I, 1, 23; Bankt. I, 1, 54; Ersk. I, 1, 29; Articles of Union, 1707, Art. 18; *Gibson* v. *Lord Advocate*, 1975 S.C. 136, 142; Markby, *Elements of Law* (6th ed.), 151; Holland, *Jurisprudence* (13th ed.), 128; Salmond, 533; Pollock, *Jurisprudence and Legal Essays*, Ch. 4; Jones, *Historical Introduction to the Theory of Law*, Ch. 5; Paton, *Jurisprudence* (4th ed.), Ch. 14; Walker, *S.L.S.*, Ch. 5.

the means whereby rights can be vindicated, duties enforced and remedies obtained.

Within private law the most satisfactory classification is fundamentally that of the Roman law, into law of persons, law of things, and law of actions,[2] which was generally adopted by the earlier Scottish institutional writers,[3] by the modern Roman law of the German jurists,[4] and by European codifications.[5]

The arrangement herein adopted substantially follows these models. The General Part[6] deals with matters common to many or all branches of the private law, and that on International Private Law[7] with cases where an issue of private law involves a non-Scottish or international element.[8] The Law of Persons[9] deals both with natural living persons and with juristic persons or corporations.[10] The Law of Things is divided into rights of obligation[11] or personal rights availing only against other particular persons,[12] and rights of property[13] or real rights availing against other persons generally.[14] Distinct branches of the law of things deal with the holding of rights in trust,[15] and the rules as to the disposal of the estate of a deceased person.[16] Consequential on the rules as to various kinds of rights are the secondary rules as to remedies for infringement of primary rights,[17] as to diligence or the enforcement of claims,[18] and providing for the distribution of the property of an insolvent among those entitled thereto.[19] On the substantive rules are dependent the adjective rules of the forms and methods requisite to create, transfer, and extinguish the recognized kinds of rights of a proprietary kind and the rules of civil procedure, practice, pleading, and evidence.[20]

Within each of these main divisions are heads and subheads, mostly derived from Roman law, but necessarily modified by indigenous developments and the progress of legal science, under which the principles and rules can be stated.

---

[2] Gaius I, 8; Inst. I, 2, 12; Dig. I, 5, 1. See further Buckland, 56–9.

[3] Stair, I, 1, 23; Mack. I, 2, 1; Bankt. I, 1, 86; Ersk. I, 2, 1. Bell departed from Roman arrangement.

[4] General Part; Special Part—property, obligations, family law, inheritance.

[5] e.g. French *Code civil*: Persons; Property Rights; Acquisition of Property (including Obligations). German *Burgerliches Gesetzbuch*: General Principles; Obligations; Things; Family Law; Inheritance. But these codes do not deal with rules applicable to specifically commercial transactions.

[6] Book I.   [7] Book II.

[8] Stair I, 1, 16; Bankt. I, 1, 76; Ersk. III, 2, 39.   [9] Book III.

[10] Stair I, 4–6; Mack. I, 6–7; Bankt. I, 5–7; Ersk. I, 5–7.   [11] Book IV.

[12] Stair I, 7–18; Mack III, 1–7; Bankt. I, 4 and 8–24; Ersk. III, 1–7.   [13] Book V.

[14] Stair II, 1–12; Mack. II, 1–13; Bankt. II, 1–12; III, 1–3; Ersk. II, 1–12.

[15] Book VI.

[16] Book VII; Stair III, 4–9; Mack. III, 8–10; Bankt. III, 4–9; Ersk. III, 8–10.

[17] Book VIII.   [18] Book IX.   [19] Book X.

[20] Stair IV; Mack. IV; Bankt. IV; Ersk. IV; These topics are, save for incidental mentions, excluded from this book.

SOURCES AND THEIR EVALUATION

The term 'sources' of Scottish Private Law may be used of at least four sets of materials,[21] namely

(1) historical sources, or the facts, events, ideas, and practices which have, down to the present time, influenced the development, content, and form of the principles and rules of the positive law;

(2) philosophical or theoretical sources, or the presuppositions, beliefs, ideals, and doctrines, religious, moral, social, political, and economic, which underlie and explain the character of various legal doctrines accepted and enacted;

(3) formal or legal sources, or those statements of principles and rules which are recognized by courts and legal advisers as authoritative, and from which rules for the definition of rights and the determination of matters in controversy in particular cases may be discovered.

(4) literary sources, or the books which contain statements of the law and from which knowledge of the law is obtained.

The formal or legal sources alone yield principles and rules which are parts of the positive law and are enforceable. The historical and philosophical sources merely help to explain the form and content of particular rules. The literary sources give information on what the law is or is believed to be.

(1) *Historical sources*

The historical sources of Scottish Private Law are the customary practices of the community, generally accepted as binding and enforceable, ancient statutes and books of law, such as *Regiam Majestatem*, principles of conduct enunciated in the Bible and generally followed in reliance thereon, principles developed in the Civil Law of Rome and accepted in Scotland, usually through the mediation of the writings of French, German, and Dutch jurists from the fourteenth to the eighteenth centuries, the principles of the Canon Law of the Roman Church as developed down to the Reformation and accepted in Scotland, the principles of the feudal law of Western Europe applied in Scottish practice, the principles of the general mercantile and maritime customs of Western Europe, and some principles of the common law and equity of England. Many of these have been adopted in Scots law under the influence of the great systematic writings of the institutional writers.[22]

---

[21] Walker, *S.L.S.*, Ch. 10.
[22] On these sources see the various chapters in (Stair Society) *Sources and Literature* and *Introductory History*. See also Stair I, 1, 6–9, 12–14, 16; Bankt. I, 1, 38–46; Ersk. I, 1, 27–8, 30–6, 41–2.

(2) *Philosophical sources*

The philosophical sources are difficult to isolate. They include above all the ideas of justice generally held at various times by the legally dominant sections of the community, related to the prevailing religious, moral, social, political, and economic views.

They include such principles as a belief in the equality of individuals before the law, and in the freedom of individuals to act as they please, subject only to specified restrictions; acceptance of the Christian notion of marriage and the family; the acceptance of the belief that individuals should be free to bind themselves legally as they wish, and must take care for their own protection, a principle greatly modified in modern times by statutory intervention for the protection of the presumed weaker party; the belief that an individual should have to compensate for harm done to others for which he is morally responsible, to which has been added in certain cases in modern times, the obligation to compensate for harm resulting from a risk created by the individual's activities, or for harm resulting from his failure to implement a statutorily imposed duty; the acceptance of the doctrine of private ownership of property and of the means of production, exchange, and distribution, a principle increasingly qualified, restricted, and subjected to exceptions; the acceptance of the doctrine that, subject to certain limitations, an individual is free to determine the way in which his property will devolve after his death, but that, failing such provision, the law will destine it to certain surviving relatives.[23]

No single body of philosophic thought or beliefs has had a monopoly of influence, but particularly important have been the idea of natural law,[24] and, in modern times, the idea of utility, of serving the greatest good of the greatest number.

(3) *Formal or legal sources*

The formal or legal sources alone yield authoritative statements of principles and rules for the guidance of legal advisers and for application by the courts to the resolution of controversies brought before them.[25] They are of six kinds.

(1) LEGISLATION

Legislation comprises (a) the law of the European Communities, both existing at the date of the United Kingdom's entry into the European

---

[23] cf. Stair I, 1, 18; Pound, *Jural Postulates*, in *Outlines of Jurisprudence* (5th ed.), 168.
[24] cf. Stair I, 1, 6; Ersk. I, 1, 7–17.
[25] See generally Craig I, 8, 1–17; Stair I, 1, 16; Mack. I, 1, 6–15; Bankt. I, 1, 58–86; Ersk. I, 1, 30–60.

Communities[26] and made thereafter, which under the Community Treaties is directly applicable in member states. These comprise certain provisions of the Community Treaties themselves, regulations, and certain directives of the Council of Ministers and of the Commission. Decisions of the Council and Commission are not directly applicable save to those to whom they are addressed. That part of Community law which has direct application takes precedence over the domestic law of each member state, and national courts are obliged to apply it and enforce it when called on to do so.[27] Other parts of Community law are applicable only if enacted by United Kingdom legislation. Any enactment passed or to be passed by the United Kingdom Parliament must be construed and have effect subject to obligations and restrictions from time to time created or arising by or under the Treaties.[28]

Legislation also comprises (b) the bodies of statutes or Acts enacted by the Parliaments of Scotland down to 1707, of the Parliaments of Great Britain from 1707 to 1800, and of the Parliaments of the United Kingdom since 1801, in all cases so far as amended but not repealed by subsequent legislation,[29] and (c) subordinate or delegated legislation.

Statutes comprise public general statutes, of general application throughout the United Kingdom, or one or more of the countries thereof, and local and personal Acts, applicable only to particular localities or to particular bodies or persons. The former are enactments of public bills introduced by the government of the day, or by a private member; the latter are introduced as private bills and the promoters must satisfy a select committee at a hearing of a judicial nature that the statutory powers or authority sought are necessary for their purposes and may properly be granted. Public authorities and private bodies more frequently now obtain parliamentary powers by obtaining from the Secretary of State for Scotland, if necessary after inquiry, a provisional order granting the desired powers, which is subsequently confirmed by the passing of a bill brought in by the Secretary of State for Scotland as a Provisional Order Confirmation Act.[30] Private Acts are of the nature of contracts, sanctioned by Parliament, between the promoters and the public.[31] If an undertaking is established by private Act it can be abandoned only under statutory authority.[32]

---

[26] 1 Jan. 1973.

[27] European Communities Act, 1972, Ss. 2(1), 3(1); *Applications des Gaz SA* v. *Falks Veritas* [1974] 3 All E.R. 51; *Van Duyn* v. *Home Office (No. 2)* [1975] 3 All E.R. 190.

[28] Ibid., S. 2(4). See also *Gibson* v. *Lord Advocate*, 1975 S.C. 136.

[29] See further Erskine May, *Parliamentary Practice*; Craies, *Statute Law*. On Scots Acts see Ersk. I, 1, 37–9.

[30] For procedure see Private Legislation Procedure (Scotland) Act, 1936. In certain cases orders made by Ministers may be given Parliamentary authority under the Statutory Orders (Special Procedure) Acts, 1945 and 1965.

[31] *Milligan* v. *Ayr Harbour Trs.*, 1915 S.C. 937, 949; *Holburnhead Salmon Co.* v. *Scrabster Harbour Trs.*, 1982 S.C. 65.

[32] *Ellice* v. *Invergarry Ry. Co.*, 1913 S.C. 849.

The Crown still has powers, in limited classes of case, of legislation by authority of the royal prerogative, by way of Orders in Council, Letters Patent, or Proclamations. Such powers are almost confined to actings in wartime and to legislation for colonies. It is incompetent to challenge an Act of Parliament as being *ultra vires* or to inquire into the validity of the procedure whereby it was passed;[33] the same applies to regulations or bye-laws declared to have effect as if enacted in an Act.

(c) Subordinate or delegated legislation consists of rules, regulations, and orders made by a minister of the Crown or other person or body to whom or which Parliament has delegated power to issue such legislation, and who or which remains, in the exercise of this power, subject to the control of Parliament. Such legislation was formerly known collectively as Statutory Rules and Orders and since 1947 as Statutory Instruments.[34] Unless expressly declared by the empowering Act to have the force of statute, subordinate legislation may be challenged as *ultra vires*.[35] The chief forms of subordinate legislation are Orders in Council, and ministerial or departmental Regulations, Rules, or Orders,[36] and local authority by-laws.

Certain public authorities and local authorities have delegated statutory powers to make by-laws which have application only within the area of the authority's responsibility. Local authority by-laws normally require the confirmation of an authority such as the Secretary of State or the sheriff.[37] A by-law is open to challenge as *ultra vires*,[38] as unreasonable,[39] or as contrary to the general law,[40] and even though it has obtained the requisite approval.[41] It falls if the authorizing statute is repealed.[42]

Acts of Sederunt are rules of a legislative kind made by the Court of

---

[33] *Hamilton* v. *Fyfe*, 1907 S.C. (J.) 79; *B.R. Board* v. *Pickin* [1974] 1 All E.R. 609.

[34] Statutory Instruments Act, 1946.

[35] *Institute of Patent Agents* v. *Lockwood* (1894) 21 R. (H.L.) 61; *Dunsmore* v. *Lindsay* (1903) 6 F. (J.) 14; *Shepherd* v. *Howman*, 1918 J.C. 78; *Lawson* v. *Torrance*, 1929 J.C. 119; *Sommerville* v. *Langmuir*, 1932 J.C. 55; *Sommerville* v. *Lord Advocate*, 1933 S.L.T. 48. See also *Henderson* v. *Ross*, 1928 J.C. 74, 76.

[36] They are published in annual volumes known down to 1947 as Statutory Rules and Orders and since then as Statutory Instruments.

[37] See Local Government (Sc.) Act, 1973, Ss. 201–4; *Aldred* v. *Miller*, 1925 J.C. 21; *Baird* v. *Glasgow Corporation*, 1935 S.C. (H.L.) 21. On effect of confirmation see *Crichton* v. *Forfarshire Road Trs.* (1886) 13 R. (J.) 99. On sheriff's function see *Glasgow Corpn.* v. *Glasgow Churches' Council*, 1944 S.C. 97.

[38] *Kerr* v. *Auld* (1890) 18 R. (J.) 12; *Eastburn* v. *Wood* (1892) 19R. (J.) 100; *Rae* v. *Hamilton* (1904) 6 F. (J.) 42; *Rossi* v. *Edinburgh Mags.* (1904) 7 F. (H.L.) 85; *McGregor* v. *Disselduff*, 1907 S.C. (J.) 21; cf. *Shepherd* v. *Howman*, 1918 J.C. 78; *Aldred, supra*; *Aldred* v. *Langmuir*, 1932 J.C. 22; *Baird, supra*; *Baker* v. *Glasgow D.C.*, 1981 S.C. 258.

[39] *Saunders* v. *S.E. Ry.* (1880) 5 Q.B.D. 456; *Apthorpe* v. *Edinburgh Street Tramway Co.* (1882) 10 R. 344; *Dunsmore* v. *Lindsay* (1903) 6 F. (J.) 14; *Da Prato* v. *Partick Mags.*, 1907 S.C. (H.L.) 5; *Ronaldson* v. *Williamson*, 1911 S.C. (J.) 102. The court is slow to hold unreasonable a by-law passed by a public representative body; *Kruse* v. *Johnson* [1892] 2 Q.B. 91; *Aldred, supra*; *Baird, supra*.

[40] *Dunsmore* v. *Lindsay* (1903) 6 F. (J.) 14; *Aldred, supra*.

[41] *Lawson* v. *Torrance*, 1929 J.C. 119.

[42] *Watson* v. *Winch* [1916] 1 K.B. 688.

Session under powers conferred originally at its foundation[43] or, in modern times, under the authority of statute.[44] They are now confined to the regulation of procedure in the civil courts. The extant Acts were collected in the codifying Act of Sederunt, 1913, now almost entirely replaced by the Rules of Court authorized by the Administration of Justice (Scotland) Act, 1933.[45] Acts of Sederunt are now normally statutory instruments.[46]

Acts of Adjournal are Acts passed by the High Court of Justiciary under similar powers for regulating procedural matters in the criminal court. They also are now normally statutory instruments.[46]

Acts of Court are directions issued by sheriffs-principal regulating business in sheriff courts. They cannot alter substantive law.[47]

Authority of legislation

Where legislation of any kind is in force in relation to any subject, it is authoritative, in that it is superior to any inconsistent rule of law, however old or well-established, and overrules it,[48] and mandatory, in that it must be implemented, unless it clearly appears to be permissive.

Proof of terms of legislation

Courts take judicial notice of the Community Treaties,[49] of the Official Journal of the Communities,[50] and of any decision of, or expression of opinion by, the European Court. The Official Journal is admissible as evidence of any instrument or other act of any of the Communities or of any Community institution. Evidence of any instrument issued by a Community institution may be given by a certified true copy, by production of a copy purporting to be printed by the Queen's Printer, or where the instrument is in the custody of a government department by production of a certified true copy. In Scotland evidence given in such a manner is sufficient evidence.[51]

---

[43] Ersk. I, 1, 40.
[44] Hence the power falls if the statute is repealed; *Inglis's Trustees* v. *Macpherson*, 1910 S.C. 46.
[45] See *Rules of Court*, 1965. On whether the Court of Session can entertain an action to determine the validity of one of its own Acts of Sederunt, see *Carron Co.* v. *Hislop*, 1930 S.C. 1050.
[46] Law Reform (Miscellaneous Provisions) (Sc.) Act, 1966, S. 10.
[47] *U.D.T.* v. *Stark*, 1981 S.L.T. (Sh. Ct.) 58.
[48] *Gower* v. *Sheriff of Caithness* (1828) 6 S. 650.
[49] i.e. The European Coal and Steel Community Treaty, 1951; The European Economic Community Treaty, 1957; The European Atomic Energy Community Treaty, 1957; The Convention on certain Institutions common to the European Communities, 1957; The Treaty establishing a single Council and single Commission, 1965; the amending Treaty, 1970.
[50] i.e. the *Journal officiel de la Communauté européenne de charbon et de l'acier*, 1952–8; the *Journal officiel des Communautés européennes*, 1958–67, and the latter in two sections, since 1968, containing legislative and other texts respectively.
[51] European Communities Act, 1972, S. 3.

Public general statutes of the U.K. Parliament are judicially noticed and the terms thereof need not to be proved to a court.[52] The text of an Act as printed by the Queen's Printer will be accepted as accurate.[53] The Text of a Scots Act as printed in the Record edition would probably be accepted.[54]

The terms of private acts must be proved to the court, but the Interpretation Act, 1978, S. 3, provides that all Acts are to be public Acts and judicially noticed as such, unless the contrary is expressly provided by the Act, in which case a copy certified by the Clerk of the Parliaments must be produced unless the Act itself provides that a Queen's Printer's copy shall be admitted in evidence.

The terms of statutory instruments may be proved by production of a copy of the London or Edinburgh *Gazette* purporting to contain the order or regulation, or of a copy of the order or regulation, purporting to be printed by the Government printer,[55] or of a copy or extract purporting to be certified to be true by one of the persons statutorily empowered to certify, without proof of the handwriting or official position of any person so certifying.[56]

The production of a copy of a by-law purporting to be made by a local authority under any enactment or by any other authority to whose by-laws the Local Government (Sc.) Act, 1973, S. 201 applies, upon which is endorsed a certificate purporting to be signed by the clerk of the authority stating that the by-law was made by the authority, that the copy is a true copy, that on a specified date the by-law was confirmed by the authority named or was sent to the Secretary of State and has not been disallowed, and the date fixed by the confirming authority for the coming into operation of the by-law, is evidence of the facts stated in the certificate until the contrary is proved, without proof of the handwriting or official position of any person purporting to sign a certificate under this provision.[57] If the empowering statute provides that the by-law is to have the same effect as if it were contained in the Act[58] or to have the effect of an Act,[59] no proof of it is required.[60]

Acts of Sederunt and Acts of Adjournal are statutory instruments[61] and do not require proof.

---

[52] Interpretation Act, 1978, S. 3.
[53] cf. *Aiton* v. *Stephen* (1876) 3 R. (H.L.) 4; *Scottish Drainage Co.* v. *Campbell* (1889) 16 R. (H.L.) 16.
[54] i.e. *The Acts of the Parliaments of Scotland*, ed. Innes and Thomson (12 vols., 1814–75); Scots Acts still in force in 1966 are reprinted in *The Acts of the Parliaments of Scotland* (H.M.S.O., 1966), but see *Kemp* v. *Glasgow Corpn.*, 1920 S.C. (H.L.) 73, 78.
[55] *Macmillan* v. *McConnell*, 1917 J.C. 43; *Herkes* v. *Dickie*, 1958 J.C. 51.
[56] Documentary Evidence Acts, 1868 and 1882.
[57] Local Government (Sc.) Act, 1973, S. 204; see also *Herkes* v. *Dickie*, 1958 J.C. 51.
[58] e.g. *Inst. of Patent Agents* v. *Lockwood* (1894) 21 R. (H.L.) 61.
[59] e.g. *Hamilton* v. *Fyfe*, 1907 S.C. (J.) 79.
[60] *Herkes* v. *Dickie*, 1958 J.C. 51.
[61] Statutory Instruments Act, 1946, S. 1(2); Law Reform (Miscellaneous Provisions) (Sc.) Act, 1966, S. 10.

Application

A statute of the United Kingdom Parliament prima facie applies to the whole United Kingdom.[62] The express exclusion of Ireland suggests the inclusion of Scotland in the area of application.[63] If intended to apply to Scotland only this is stated and the word '(Scotland)' is included in the title. If intended not to apply to Scotland this may be stated expressly, or it may appear from such facts as that the statute is an amendment of an Act from which Scotland was excluded,[64] or is expressed in English technical terms without mention of their Scottish counterparts,[65] or incorporates by reference statutes not applicable to Scotland.[66] If intended to apply in part to Scotland this may be stated expressly or may appear from the existence of parts or sections of the Act applicable in terminology only to Scotland.[67]

Statutes applicable to the United Kingdom are commonly framed in English technical terms with an 'application to Scotland' section giving the equivalent terms to be used when applying sections to Scottish conditions.[68]

Commencement

An Act of Parliament prima facie comes into force on the date on which it receives the Royal Assent,[69] but an Act may provide for the date of its coming into force, or provide that a Minister may, by statutory instrument, bring the Act or parts of it, into force on a date or dates specified by him. Hence an Act, though passed, may be only partly in force, or not in force at all. Effect cannot be given to an Act passed but not yet in force.[70]

Duration

Once passed and brought into force a statute continues in force, even though not applied, until repealed, unless expressly enacted for a limited

---

[62] *Bridges v. Fordyce* (1844) 6 D. 968; (1847) 6 Bell 1; *Perth Water Commrs. v. McDonald* (1879) 6 R. 1050; *Murray v. Comptroller-General of Patents*, 1932 S.C. 726; *H.M.A. v. Burns*, 1967 J.C. 15. Whether it can apply abroad is a matter of interpretation.

[63] *Scottish Drug Depot v. Fraser* (1905) 7 F. 646. 648.

[64] *Westminster Fire Office v. Glasgow Provident Investment Socy.* (1888) 15 R. (H.L.) 89, 94; *Levy v. Jackson* (1903) 5 F. 1170; See also *McLean v. Murdoch* (1882) 10 R. (J.) 34; *Bell v. Mitchell* (1905) 8 F. (J.) 15.

[65] *Levy, supra; Scottish Drug Depot, supra.* But see *H.M.A. v. Holmes and Lockyer* (1869) 1 Coup. 221; *Perth Water Commrs. v. McDonald* (1879) 6 R. 1050; *Dunlop v. Goudie* (1895) 22 R. (J.) 34; *Murray v. Comptroller-General of Patents*, 1932 S.C. 726; cf. *Conn v. Renfrew Mags.* (1906) 8 F. 905; *Wilson v. Kilmarnock Assessor*, 1913 S.C. 704.

[66] *H.M.A. v. Cox* (1872) 2 Coup. 229; *H.M.A. v. Davidson* (1872) 2 Coup. 278.

[67] *Scottish Aviation v. L.A.*, 1951 S.C. 33.

[68] But see *Wan Ping Nam v. Federal German Republic Minister of Justice*, 1972 S.L.T. 220.

[69] Interpretation Act, 1978, S. 4; *Tomlinson v. Bullock* (1878) 4 Q.B.D. 230; *R. v. Weston* [1910] 1 K.B. 17.

[70] *Wilson v. Dagnall* [1972] 2 All E.R. 44.

period only, in which case the Act lapses automatically at the end of the
period, though it may be continued in force by an Expiring Laws Continuance Act or made permanent. Alternatively, an Act may provide that
its duration may be terminated by Order in Council.

Desuetude

Prior to 1707, and subsequently, but in respect of pre-1707 Scots Acts
only, a statute may be held abrogated by desuetude, by great antiquity
together with absence of recent precedent for the application of the Act,
long disregard of it in practice, and its being obsolete and inappropriate
in modern conditions.[71] Since the repeal of much obsolete pre-1707
legislation in 1906 and 1964[72] there is a rebuttable presumption that any
Scots Act not thereby repealed is not in desuetude. Desuetude has no
application to post-1707 legislation.

Amendment

An Act may be amended in any respect and to any extent by any
subsequent Act, either expressly, or by implication arising from the occur-
ence of an inconsistent provision in a subsequent Act.[73] The whole statute
law on one topic must be read together[73] and in case of inconsistency the
latest provision is presumed to supersede earlier ones.

Repeal

An Act, or any part thereof, may be repealed by any subsequent Act,
either expressly, or impliedly, when a subsequent provision is inconsistent
with the earlier one, which is held superseded thereby.[74] The courts are,
however, unwilling to imply repeal in this way.[75] An Act may be repealed
quoad England but be left in force quoad Scotland.[76] The repeal of an Act
wholly obliterates it, and does not revive anything not in force at the time
of the repeal, unless such an intention is disclosed.[77] Nor does the repeal

[71] Craig I, 8, 9; Stair I, 1, 16; Mack. I, 1, 10; Bankt. I, 1, 60; Ersk. I, 1, 45; *Gardiner* v.
Kilrenny Mags. (1826) 4 S. 539; (1828) 6 S. 693; *Bute* v. *More* (1870) 9 M. 180; *Middleton* v.
Tough, 1908 S.C. (J.) 32; *McAra* v. *Edinburgh Mags.*, 1913 S.C. 1059; *Brown* v. *Edinburgh
Mags.*, 1931 S.L.T. 456; *MacCormick* v. *L.A.*, 1953 S.C. 396, 417.
[72] Statute Law Revision (Scotland) Acts, 1906 and 1964.
[73] *Mount* v. *Taylor* (1868) L.R. 3 C.P. 645.
[74] *Kutner* v. *Phillips* [1891] 2 Q.B. 267, 272; *Lang* v. *Munro* (1892) 19 R. (J.) 53; *Ross* v.
Ross (1894) 22 R. 174; *Melville Coal Co.* v. *Clark* (1904) 6 F. 913; *Hendrie* v. *Caledonian Ry.*,
1909 S.C. 776; *Cowdenbeath Mags.* v. *Cowdenbeath Gas Co.*, 1915 S.C. 323; *Moss' Empires* v.
Glasgow Assessor, 1917 S.C. (H.L.) 1; *Angus C.C.* v. *Montrose Mags.*, 1933 S.C. 505.
[75] *Bain* v. *Mackay* (1875) 2 R. (J.) 32; *Dobbs* v. *Grand Junction Waterworks Co.* (1882) 9
Q.B.D. 151; *Kutner* v. *Philips* [1891] 2 Q.B. 267; *Aberdeen Tramways Co.* v. *Aberdeen Mags.*,
1927 S.C. 683.
[76] *Smith's Trs.* v. *Gaydon*, 1931 S.C. 533; *Lindsay's Trs.* v. *L.*, 1931 S.C. 586.
[77] Interpretation Act, 1978, S. 16; *Henderson's Trs.* v. *H.*, 1930 S.L.T. 346; *Moray C.C.* v.
Maclean, 1962 S.C. 601.

of an Act which had repealed earlier legislation revive that legislation unless such an intention is disclosed.[78] A special Act is not repealed by a general Act unless there is express reference thereto or a necessary inconsistency in allowing both to stand.[79] A public Act is not repealed by a private Act unless such clearly appears to be the intention.[80] The repeal of an Act does not affect rights or liabilities acquired or incurred by persons acting under the Act while in force,[81] nor affect any legal proceeding or remedy in respect of any such right or liability, which may be enforced notwithstanding the repeal.[82]

Interpretation of legislation

Interpretation[83] or construction is necessary to ascertain whether a particular statutory provision is applicable to the facts before the court, and, if so, what it prescribes or requires. It is always a question of law for the court, to be determined by consideration of the words used in the light of legal arguments, not one to be determined by evidence, and the question is to ascertain what is the fair meaning and intention of the legislature.[84] A statute cannot be challenged as being *ultra vires* or on the ground that its purpose is illegal.[85]

Literal and liberal interpretation

There may be conflict between the two main judicial approaches to legislation, the literal approach, which stresses attention to the words actually used, and the liberal approach, which stresses the legislative purpose and general intention to remedy defects in the law. The literal meaning ought not to prevail if opposed to the legislative intention appearing in the statute, if the words are sufficiently flexible to admit of another construction by which that intention will be better effectuated.[86] The purpose or spirit of the legislation cannot be given effect to if the words used preclude the court from so doing.[87]

[78] Interpretation Act, 1978, S. 15. For a case of express revival of a repealed Act by a later Act, see Trade Disputes and Trade Unions Act, 1947, S. 1.
[79] N.B. Ry. v. Wingate, 1913 S.C. 1092; Aberdeen Suburban Tramways Co. v. Aberdeen Mags., 1927 S.C. 683, 689.
[80] Russell v. Aberdeen Mags., (1899) 1 F. 792; Balfour, 1909 S.C. 358.
[81] Interpretation Act, 1978, S. 16(1); Smith's Trs. v. Irvine and Fullarton Property, etc. Socy. (1903) 6 F. 99; Moray County Council v. Maclean, 1962 S.C. 601.
[82] Ibid.
[83] See generally Ersk. I, 1, 49–60; Craies on Statute Law (7th ed.); Maxwell on Interpretation of Statutes (12th ed.); Walker, S.L.S., Ch. 10; Report of Law Commission and Scottish Law Commission on Interpretation of Statutes (Sc. L. Comm. No. 11, 1969).
[84] E. Breadalbane v. Lord Advocate (1870) 8 M. 835.
[85] Cheney v. Conn [1968] 1 All E.R. 779.
[86] Caledonian Ry. v. N.B. Ry. (1881) 8 R. (H.L.) 23; Inland Revenue v. Luke, 1963 S.C. (H.L.) 65.
[87] Campbell's Trs. v. O'Neill, 1911 S.C. 188, 196.

When interpreting European Community legislation courts must look to the purpose or intent, not the bare words, and seek to give effect to the purpose.[88]

Liberal interpretation is necessary when construing pre-1707 Scots Acts, which were commonly drafted generally, and as to which greater weight must be given to contemporaneous interpretation.[89] Broad principles should be applied to interpreting Acts giving effect to international conventions.[90]

If the meaning of an Act is plain effect must be given to it without any speculation as to Parliament's intention.[91]

Interpretation Act and interpretation sections in Acts

The Interpretation Act, 1978, assigns meanings to a number of words commonly found in statutes, unless the context of a particular act gives a contrary indication,[92] and many statutes contain their own interpretation sections assigning particular meanings to words for the purposes of that Act. But if defined expressions are used in a context which the definition does not fit, the words may be used in their ordinary meaning.[93]

Failing such assigned meanings the usual dictionary meaning of a word falls to be adopted,[94] and its technical meaning if it has one.[95] A judge, such as the sheriff of a locality affected, does not require to be instructed in the meaning of technical terms used in a local statute.[96]

Relevance of context

A statute must be read as a whole and sections read in the light of one another. Words and phrases must be read in their context and may take on a shade of meaning from the context. This requires that words be interpreted by regard to the whole section or Act in which they appear[97]

---

[88] *Bulmer* v. *Bollinger* [1974] 2 All E.R. 1226, 1236.
[89] *Johnstone* v. *Stotts* (1802) 4 Pat. 274, 283; *Fergusson* v. *Skirving* (1852) 1 Macq. 232; *Thomas* v. *Thomson* (1865) 3 M. 1160, 1165; *E. Home* v. *L. Belhaven & Stenton* (1903) 5 F. (H.L.) 13, 23; *Heriot's Tr.* v. *Paton's Trs.*, 1912 S.C. 1123; *Whatmough's Tr.* v. *B.L. Bank*, 1934 S.C. (H.L.) 51.
[90] *Buchanan* v. *Babco* [1978] A.C. 141; *Fothergill* v. *Monarch Airlines* [1980] 2 All E.R. 696.
[91] *Glasgow Court House Commrs.* v. *Lanarkshire C.C.* (1900) 3 F. 103; *West Highland Ry.* v. *Inverness C.C.* (1904) 6 F. 1052. But see *Caledonian Ry.* v. *N.B. Ry.* (1881) 8 R. (H.L.) 23, 30; *Bradlaugh* v. *Clarke* (1883) 8 App. Cas. 354, 384.
[92] *Colquhoun* v. *Dumbarton Mags.*, 1907 S.C. (J.) 57; *Griffith* v. *Ferrier*, 1952 J.C. 56.
[93] *Strathern* v. *Padden*, 1926 J.C. 9; *Chernack* v. *Mill*, 1938 J.C. 39.
[94] *Vacher* v. *London Compositors* [1913] A.C. 107; *Lord Advocate* v. *Mirrielees' Trs.*, 1945 S.C. (H.L.) 1.
[95] *Clerical Assurance Co.* v. *Carter* (1889) 22 Q.B.D. 444.
[96] *Oliver* v. *Hislop*, 1946 J.C. 20.
[97] *Edinburgh Street Tramways* v. *Torbain* (1877) 3 App. Cas. 58, 68; *Colquhoun* v. *Brooks* (1889) 14 App. Cas. 493, 506.

and even to the whole course of legislation,[98]and with regard to the general scope of the Act.[99]

In particular the maxim *noscitur a sociis* expresses the principle that a word of indefinite meaning takes a shade of meaning from the accompanying words.[1]

The maxim *expressio unius est exclusio alterius* imports that an express mention of one thing or category may be held to imply the exclusion from the statute of the other thing or category of the same kind.[2]

The *ejusdem generis* principle is to the effect that if statute enumerates a number of items or categories belonging to some class or genus of things, any subsequent general words must be held limited to other things of the same class as those enumerated.[3] The principle does not apply if the enumerated items belong to no recognizable genus or have no common factor,[4] nor if the subsequent general words are so general as clearly not to be limited by the context of the items specifically enumerated,[5] nor if the general object of the Act indicates that the general words should not be restricted in meaning by the earlier specific words.[6]

Usage *and* contemporanea expositio

In construing ancient statutes weight may be attached to the interpretation adopted in practice through a long course of time and to contemporaneous decisions of the courts,[7] but these factors are of little value in construing more modern statutes particularly if unambiguous.[8] Even in modern, but not very recent, statutes, *contemporanea expositio* may impart a shade of meaning to an ambiguous word.[9] Where an Act is silent or doubtful, long continued usage may supply the defect.[10] But no usage

[98] *Tennent v. Partick Mags.*, (1894) 21 R. 735; *Antrobus* (1896) 23 R. 1032; *Lord Advocate v. Sprot's Trs.* (1901) 3 F. 440; *Barty v. Hill*, 1907 S.C. (J.) 36; *Campbell's Trs. v. O'Neill*, 1911 S.C. 188; *Hamilton v. N.C.B.*, 1960 S.C. (H.L.) 1.
[99] *Hutchison's Trs. v. Downie's Trs.*, 1923 S.L.T. 49.
[1] *Muir v. Keay* (1875) L.R. 10 Q.B. 594.
[2] *Stevenson v. Hunter* (1903) 5 F. 761; *Inverness C.C. v. Inverness Mags.*, 1909 S.C. 386.
[3] *Henretty v. Hart* (1885) 13 R. (J.) 9; *Walker v. Lamb* (1892) 19 R. (J.) 50; *Caledonian Ry. v. Glasgow Corpn.* (1901) 3 F. 526, 531; *Duncan v. Jackson* (1905) 8 F. 323; *Admiralty v. Burns*, 1910 S.C. 531; *Moss' Empires v. Glasgow Assessor*, 1917 S.C. (H.L.) 1; *Baird v. Lees*, 1924 S.C. 83; *Benzie v. Mickel*, 1945 J.C. 47; *Minister of Pensions v. Ballantyne*, 1948 S.C. 176; *Lord Advocate v. Glasgow Corpn.*, 1958 S.C. 12; *Mortimer v. Allison*, 1959 S.C. (H.L.) 1.
[4] *Crichton Stuart v. Ogilvie*, 1914 S.C. 888.
[5] *Skinner v. Shew* [1893] 1 Ch. 413.
[6] *Powell v. Kempton Park Racecourse Co.* [1899] A.C. 143.
[7] *Clyde Navigation Trs. v. Laird* (1883) 10 R. (H.L.) 77; *Graham v. Irving* (1899) 2 F. 29; *Middleton v. Tough*, 1908 S.C. (J.) 32; *Borthwick-Norton v. Gavin Paul*, 1947 S.C. 659, 693–4.
[8] *Walker Trs. v. Lord Advocate*, 1912 S.C. (H.L.) 12.
[9] *Scottish Cinema and Variety Theatres v. Ritchie*, 1929 S.C. 350.
[10] *Dunbar Mags. v. Dunbar Heritors* (1835) 1 S & McL. 134, 195; *Molleson v. Hutchison* (1892) 19 R. 581, 587.

can prevail against a plain statutory provision,[11] nor can usage under a repealed Act be used to help construe the repealing Act.[12]

Internal and external aids to construction

Assistance in interpretation may be derived from examination of other parts of the Act in question such as the long title,[13] the preamble,[14] headings prefixed to groups of sections or parts of an Act,[15] and schedules,[16] but not the short title,[17] rubric,[18] marginal notes,[19] or punctuation.[20]

Assistance may also be obtained from sources outside the Act under interpretation, such as the prior state of the law,[21] prior statutes repealed or consolidated by the present Act,[22] subsequent Acts in *pari materia*,[23] prior cases in which the precise words or phrase, or the same, or very similar, words or phrases in another Act on a related subject, have been construed,[24] usage and *contemporanea expositio*,[25] and statements in

---

[11] *Dunbar Mags.* v. *Roxburghe* (1835) 3 Cl. & F. 358; *Gorham* v. *Bishop of Exeter* (1850) 15 Q.B. 52, 73; *Walker Trs., supra,* 17.

[12] *Thomson* v. *Bent Colliery Co.,* 1912 S.C. 242.

[13] *Fielding* v. *Morley Corpn.* [1899] 1 Ch. 1, 3; *Fenton* v. *Thorley* [1903] A.C. 443, 447; *Miller & Lang* v. *Macniven and Cameron* (1908) 16 S.L.T. 56; *Vacher* v. *London Socy. of Compositors* [1913] A.C. 107, 128; *Mags. of Buckie* v. *Dowager Countess of Seafield's Trs.,* 1928 S.C. 525; *Ward* v. *Holman* [1964] 2 All E.R. 279.

[14] *Minister of Brydekirk* v. *Minister of Hoddam* (1877) 4 R. 798; *Caledonian Ry.* v. *N.B. Ry.* (1881) 8 R. (H.L.) 23, 25; *Tennent* v. *Partick Mags.* (1894) 21 R. 735; *Renfrewshire C.C.* v. *Orphan Homes of Scotland* (1898) 1 F. 186; *Ellerman Lines* v. *Murray* [1931] A.C. 126; *A. G.* v. *Prince Ernest of Hanover* [1957] A.C. 436; *Anderson* v. *Jenkins,* 1967 S.C. 231.

[15] *Lang* v. *Kerr, Anderson & Co.* (1878) 5 R. (H.L.) 65, 67; *Nelson* v. *McPhee* (1889) 17 R. (J.) 1; *Scott* v. *Alexander* (1890) 17 R. (J.) 35; *Inglis* v. *Robertson & Baxter* (1898) 25 R. (H.L.) 70; *McEwan* v. *Perth Mags.* (1905) 7 F. 714; *Mags. of Buckie, supra; Martins* v. *Fowler* [1926] A.C. 746, 750; *Alexander* v. *Mackenzie,* 1947 J.C. 155; *Brodie* v. *Ker,* 1952 S.C. 216, 225; *D.P.P.* v. *Schildkamp* [1969] 3 All E.R. 1640.

[16] *Ellerman Lines* v. *Murray* [1931] A.C. 126; but a schedule cannot extend or overrule a provision in the body of an Act: *Laird* v. *C.N.T.* (1883) 10 R. (H.L.) 77; *Jacobs* v. *Hart* (1900) 2 F. (J.) 33.

[17] *Re Boaler* [1915] 1 K.B. 21.

[18] *Farquharson* v. *Whyte* (1886) 13 R. (J.) 29.

[19] *D. Devonshire* v. *O'Connor* [1890] 24 Q.B.D. 468, 478; *Nixon* v. *A.G.* [1930] 1 Ch. 566, 593; *Chandler* v. *D.P.P.* [1964] A.C. 763.

[20] *I.R.C.* v. *Hinchy* [1960] A.C. 748; but see *Turnbull's Trs.* v. *L.A.,* 1918 S.C. (H.L.) 88; *Alexander* v. *Mackenzie,* 1947 J.C. 155; *D.P.P.* v. *Schildkamp* [1969] 3 All E.R. 1640.

[21] *Bank of England* v. *Vagliano* [1891] A.C. 107, 144; *Eastman Photographic Co.* v. *Comptroller-General of Patents* [1898] A.C. 571, 575; *L.A.* v. *Sprot's Trs.* (1901) 3 F. 440; *Sharp* v. *Morrison,* 1922 S.L.T. 272; *Avery* v. *N. E. Ry.* [1938] A.C. 606, 612, 617.

[22] *Walsh* v. *Pollokshaws Mags.,* 1907 S.C. (H.L.) 1; *Sharp, supra.* But one enactment cannot be controlled by reference to previous legislation if it is plain: *Sandys* v. *Lowden & Rowe* (1874) 2 R. (J.) 7; see also *Couper* v. *Mackenzie* (1906) 8 F. 1202; *Jack* v. *Thom,* 1952 J.C. 41.

[23] *Re Macmanaway* [1951] A.C. 161; *A.G.* v. *Prince Ernest of Hanover* [1957] A.C. 436.

[24] *Barras* v. *Aberdeen Steam Trawling Co.,* 1933 S.C. (H.L.) 21; *Paisner* v. *Goodrich* [1957] A.C. 65; *Inland Revenue* v. *Glasgow Police Athletic Assocn.,* 1953 S.C. (H.L.) 13; *Hamilton* v. *N.C.B.,* 1960 S.C. (H.L.) 1; *Ogden Industries* v. *Lucas* [1970] A.C. 113.

[25] *Gorham* v. *Bishop of Exeter* (1850) 15 Q.B. 52; *Migneault* v. *Malo* (1872) L.R. 4 P.C. 123; *Welham* v. *D.P.P.* [1961] A.C. 103.

reputable textbooks on the Act or that general field of law.[26] No reference may be made to Royal Commission or other reports on which the legislation may have been founded[27] nor to Hansard, White Papers, or memoranda circulated to Parliament.[28]

Presumptions

Numerous presumptions may be invoked to assist interpretation, in the absence of clear contrary indications. The most important are: that the Crown, its officials and departments are not bound by statute unless that is expressly stated;[29] that fundamental principles of constitutional law or of common law will not be altered by implication;[30] that a United Kingdom statute is not intended to infringe international law;[31] that a United Kingdom statute is to be interpreted uniformly throughout the United Kingdom;[32] that the existing jurisdiction of the courts is not altered;[33] that an individual may appeal to the ordinary courts if aggrieved;[34] that ordinary procedures may be invoked[35] and are not altered;[36] that a word judicially interpreted and later repeated in a subsequent statute has the meaning originally given it by the court;[37] that statutes imposing a penalty or a tax, encroaching on property rights or restrictive of personal liberty, fall to be strictly construed, as applicable only to cases clearly falling within the circumstances prescribed;[38] that a

---

[26] *Bastin* v. *Davies* [1950] 1 All E.R. 1095.

[27] *Salkeld* v. *Johnson* (1846) 2 C.B. 749, 767; *Holme* v. *Guy* (1877) 5 Ch. D. 901; *R.* v. *Hertford College* (1878) 3 Q.B.D. 693; But see *McKernan* v. *United Masons* (1874) 1 R. 453; *Shanks* v. *United Masons* (1874) 1 R. 823. As to international conventions see *Fothergill* v. *Monarch Airlines* [1980] 2 All E.R. 696.

[28] *Viscountess Rhondda's Claim* [1922] 2 A.C. 339; *McCormick* v. *Lord Advocate*, 1953 S.C. 396; *Beswick* v. *B.* [1968] A.C. 58.

[29] *Schulze* v. *Steele* (1890) 17 R. (J.) 47; *Somerville* v. *Lord Advocate* (1893) 20 R. 1050; *Edinburgh Magistrates* v. *Lord Advocate*, 1912 S.C. 1085; *Salt* v. *MacKnight*, 1947 J.C. 99; *Tamlin* v. *Hannaford* [1950] 1 K.B. 18.

[30] *N.B. Ry.* v. *Mackintosh* (1890) 17 R. 1065; *Nairn* v. *University Courts of St. Andrews and Edinburgh*, 1909 S.C. (H.L.) 10; *Central Control Board (Liquor Traffic)* v. *Cannon Brewery Co. Ltd.* [1919] A.C. 744; *Nokes* v. *Doncaster Amalgamated Collieries* [1940] A.C. 1014; *Hynd's Tr.* v. *Hynd's Trs.*, 1955 S.C. (H.L.) 1.

[31] *Mortensen* v. *Peters* (1906) 8 F. (J.) 93.

[32] *E. Breadalbane* v. *L.A.* (1870) 8 M. 835; *Inland Revenue* v. *Glasgow Police Athletic Assn.*, 1953 S.C. (H.L.) 13.

[33] *Tennent* v. *Partick Mags.* (1894) 21 R. 735; *Cameron* v. *McNiven* (1894) 21 R. (J.) 31; *Dunbar* v. *Scottish Investment Co.*, 1920 S.C. 210.

[34] *Dunbar, supra; Chester* v. *Bateson* [1920] 1 K.B. 829; *Pyx Granite* v. *Ministry of Housing* [1960] A.C. 260.

[35] *Portobello Mags.* v. *Edinburgh Mags.* (1882) 10 R. 130.

[36] *Kinnear* v. *Whyte* (1868) 6 M. 804.

[37] *Barras* v. *Aberdeen Steam Trawling Co.*, 1933 S.C. (H.L.) 21. cf. *Nicol's Trs.* v. *Sutherland*, 1951 S.C. (H.L.) 21.

[38] *Johnston* v. *Robson* (1868) 6 M. 800; *Scottish Cinema and Variety Theatres* v. *Ritchie*, 1929 S.C. 350; *I.R.C.* v. *Wolfson* [1949] 1 All E.R. 865; *I.R.C.* v. *Hinchy* [1960] A.C. 748; see also *Edinburgh Life Assce. Co.* v. *Inland Revenue* (1875) 2 R. 394; *Ross and Coulter* v. *Inland Revenue*, 1948 S.C. (H.L.) 1; *I.R.C.* v. *Ruffle*, 1979 S.C. 371.

remedial statute should be given a favourable construction;[39] that an exemption from taxation should be rejected unless clearly conferred;[40] and that where statute creates a crime or offence the commission of the offence requires guilty knowledge or intention and not merely inadvertence; but this presumption is frequently held rebutted by the words used.[41] None of the presumptions is, however, more than an indication of meaning, which may be overcome by indications in the language of the Act.[42]

Private Acts are not construed as conferring any greater powers than are given in plain terms or by necessary inference from the terms used,[43] nor as abrogating general common law rights or public Acts by implication.[44]

Retrospective and prospective operation

Prima facie a statute modifies the law for the future only,[45] but provisions which bear to be declaratory[46] or remedial[47] may be held retrospective also,[48] and any statutory provision may be made retrospective by clear expressions to that effect.[49]

Imperative, directory, or permissive

Prima facie words such as 'must' or 'shall' are imperative,[50] but may be merely directory.[51] Negative and prohibitory words must always be read as imperative.[52] Permissive words normally confer a discretionary power and do not impose an obligation.[53]

---

[39] *Turner* (1869) 8 M. 222; *Robb v. Logiealmond School Board* (1875) 2 R. 417.

[40] *Edinburgh Life Assce. Co. v. Inland Revenue* (1875) 2 R. 394, 398; *Hogg v. Auchtermuchty Parochial Board* (1880) 7 R. 986; *Gillanders v. Campbell* (1884) 12 R. 309; *Renfrewshire C.C. v. Orphan Homes of Scotland* (1898) 1 F. 186.

[41] *Younghusband v. Luftig* [1949] 2 K.B. 354; *Sweet v. Parsley* [1970] A.C. 132.

[42] cf. *Edinburgh Life Assurance Co. v. Inland Revenue* (1875) 2 R. 394.

[43] *Scottish Drainage and Improvement Co. v. Campbell* (1889) 16 R. (H.L.) 16; cf. *Rothes v. Kirkcaldy Waterworks Commrs.* (1882) 9 R. (H.L.) 108; *Bruce v. Whyte* (1900) 2 F. 823, 829.

[44] *Clyde v. Glasgow Ry.* (1885) 12 R. 1315; *Balfour*, 1909 S.C. 358.

[45] *Urquhart v. U.* (1853) 1 Macq. 658; *Kerr v. M. Ailsa* (1854) 1 Macq. 736; *Brown v. Macdonald* (1870) 8 M. 439; *Gardner v. Lucas* (1878) 5 R. (H.L.) 105; *Stuart v. Jackson* (1889) 17 R. 85; *Callander v. Smith* (1900) 2 F. 1140; (1901) 3 F. (H.L.) 28; *Russell v. Assoc. Boilermakers* (1907) 15 S.L.T. 118; *N.C.B. v. McInnes*, 1968 S.C. 321.

[46] *Scott v. Craig's Reps.* (1897) 24 R. 462; *Murray v. Inland Revenue*, 1918 S.C. (H.L.) 111; *Scott v. Aberdeen Corpn.*, 1976 S.C. 81.

[47] *Taylor v. T.* (1871) 9 M. 893; *Wilson v. W.*, 1939 S.C. 102; *Scott v. Aberdeen Corpn.* 1976 S.C. 81; *Bell v. Hay*, 1979 S.C. 237.

[48] See also *Gardner v. Lucas* (1878) 5 R. (H.L.) 105.

[49] e.g. War Damage Act, 1965, cancelling decision in *Burmah Oil Co. Ltd. v. Lord Advocate*, 1964 S.C. (H.L.) 117.

[50] *Pendreigh's Tr. v. McLaren & Co.* (1871) 9 M. (H.L.) 49.

[51] *Kinnear v. Whyte* (1868) 6 M. 804; *Campbell v. Duke of Atholl* (1869) 8 M. 308; *Robertson v. Adamson* (1876) 3 R. 978; *Duchess of Sutherland v. Reid's Trs.* (1881) 8 R. 514.

[52] *Cowper v. Callender* (1872) 10 M. 353.

[53] *Degan v. Dundee Corpn.*, 1940 S.C. 457; *Fleming & Ferguson v. Paisley Mags.*, 1948 S.C. 547; *Gordon D.C. v. Hay*, 1978 S.C. 327; cf. *Lanark C.C. v. East Kilbride*, 1967 S.C. 235.

But even permissive words may be construed as imperative,[54] where the court holds that the power conferred is coupled with a duty on the person to whom it is given to exercise it.[55]

Provisos and qualifications

When an enacting phrase is followed by a proviso, the latter must be construed with reference to the enactment, and, unless the contrary be explicitly declared, cannot extend the enacting words;[56] but it may be in reality a substantive enactment.[57] A proviso does not necessarily fall to be construed on the principle *expressio unius est exclusio alterius*.[58]

(2) JUDICIAL PRECEDENTS

On matters of European Community law, such as the interpretation of the Community treaties or the validity and interpretation of measures taken by Community institutions or national enterprises, judgments of the European Court of Justice are authoritative.[59] But the European Court is not bound by its own previous decisions and may, in another case, give a different ruling, so that its decisions are not binding in future cases.[60] In a British court, if a ruling on Community law is necessary, the House of Lords must, and any other court may, refer the matter to the European Court for a ruling which, when given, is authoritative for that case.[61] Unless the point is difficult and important it is better for the other court to decide the point itself. In reaching that decision previous decisions of the European Court and superior courts in member-states are persuasive.[62]

Principles and rules of municipal law of general future application may be found expressed or implied in the judicial decisions of specific cases heard and determined in the past by the superior courts of Scotland down to date.[63] The bodies of recorded decisions of the superior courts of England and of Ireland are, on certain topics of law, sources of principles having similar but lesser authority than have Scottish decisions,[64] and, on certain topics, the recorded decisions of the superior courts of Commonwealth countries, the U.S.A., and other English speaking countries, such

---

[54] *Lord Advocate* v. *Sinclair* (1872) 11 M. 137; *Gray* v. *Fife C.C.*, 1911 S.C. 266.
[55] *Walkinshaw* v. *Orr* (1860) 22 D. 627; *Julius* v. *Bishop of Oxford* (1880) 5 App. Cas. 214; *Black* v. *Glasgow Corpn.*, 1958 S.C. 260.
[56] *Forster* v. *F.* (1871) 9 M. 397.
[57] *Davidson* v. *Johnston* (1903) 6 F. 239.
[58] *Stevenson* v. *Hunter* (1903) 5 F. 761.
[59] European Communities Act, 1972, S. 3; *Bulmer* v. *Bollinger* [1974] 2 All E.R. 1226, 1232.
[60] *Da Costa* v. *Nederlandse Belastingadministratie* [1963] C.M.L.R. 224; *Bulmer, supra.*
[61] *Bulmer, supra.*
[62] *Bulmer, supra.*
[63] Gardner, *Judicial Precedent in Scots Law*; Smith, *Judicial Precedent in Scots Law*; Walker, S.L.S., Ch. 10.
[64] *Little* v. *H.M.A.*, 1983 J.C. 16.

as South Africa, which have systems of law having some affinities with Scots law are also of some, but lesser authority.

Formerly a uniform series of decisions of the Court of Session was accounted authoritative, as being evidence of the customary law, but individual decisions created no obligation on subsequent judges to follow them.[65] Since the early nineteenth century, however, largely under English influence, it has been accepted that even single decisions, particularly of the appellate courts, may be held to have established principles which must be followed subsequently.

In addition to recording the manner in which a court decided the previous case, and the opinions expressed therein by the judges regarding the applicable law, a reported decision may be held to contain a statement of legal principle applicable to a case subsequently before a court and decisive of it also. The accepted modern Scottish practice is that even a single decision of a superior court on a legal issue may be held to determine that issue for the future and accordingly to be a precedent to be followed. The actual decision binds only the parties to that case, but the principle on which it was decided or the general rule therein laid down may rule subsequent cases raising the same point for determination, unless the circumstances can fairly be said to be distinguishable, or at least it may have persuasive influence on the decision of subsequent cases.

The authority of a decision does not depend on whether it is reported or not,[66] but unauthenticated,[67] brief or inadequate reports[68] are less trustworthy and valuable than those printed in recognized series of reports or in text books.[69] A decision is not of doubtful validity merely because it was decided by a small majority.[70]

Decisions on facts, or reasons for such decisions, are not propositions of law and consequently not precedents.[71]

Whether precedent 'in point' or not

Before a principle of general rule can be extracted from a prior judicial decision, the court before whom the problem now arises must determine, firstly, whether the prior decision is 'on all fours' or 'in point', that is, deals with the same problem of law, or with a point so closely related as to make a ruling on it decisive, or at least a guide as to the decision, of the

---

[65] Craig I, 8, 13–15; Stair I, 1, 16; Mack. I, 1, 10; Bankt. I, 1, 74; Ersk. I, 1, 47.
[66] *Leighton* v. *Harland & Wolff, Ltd.*, 1953 S.L.T. (Notes) 36; *H.M.A.* v. *Burns*, 1967 J.C. 15.
[67] cf. *Rivoli Hats* v. *Gooch* [1953] 1 W.L.R. 1190; *Birtwistle* v. *Tweedale* [1954] 1 W.L.R 190; *Perez* v. *C.A.V.* [1959] 2 All E.R. 414.
[68] *Rivoli Hats, supra; Birtwistle supra; Chapman* v. *C.* [1954] A.C. 429; *Maitland*, 1961 S.C. 291, 294; *McLaughlin*, 1965 S.C. 243.
[69] *Smith* v. *Grayton Estates*, 1960 S.C. 349, 354.
[70] *H.M.A.* v. *Burns, supra.*
[71] *Qualcast Ltd.* v. *Haynes* [1959] A.C. 743.

case now before the court; and, secondly, where the court which delivered the opinion in the prior case stands in the judicial hierarchy as compared with the court in the instant case, which factor mainly determines whether the precedent, if in point, falls to be treated as binding on the court in the instant case, or only persuasive.

If the precedent is deemed to be not 'in point' it can be ignored; if not directly in point it may be 'distinguished' or set aside on the ground of the existence of some difference in material facts and relevant circumstances from the present case which the present court regards as significant; but if directly in point and indistinguishable on the facts it has an influence on the decision of the instant case depending on the standing in the judicial hierarchy of the court which pronounced the precedent, as superior to the court now considering the matter, or equal, or inferior. It may be a binding precedent which the later court must follow and apply, or a persuasive precedent which influences the later court in its decision.

Precedents binding and persuasive

The principles now accepted are:

(a) Decisions in point of the House of Lords pronounced in Scottish,[72] but not English,[73] appeals (except, probably, English appeals on U.K. statutes,[74] matters of general jurisprudence, and matters already decided to be the same in both countries) are generally binding on the House itself in future Scottish appeals, though the House now reserves liberty in exceptional cases to reconsider its own precedents,[75] and are binding on all lower Scottish civil courts; though a Court of Session decision which has determined practice for some time will not lightly be overruled merely because the House disagrees with it;[76]

(b) Decisions in point of the whole Court of Session,[77] or of a larger bench than either Division,[78] are usually regarded as binding on both Divisions of the Inner House and on all the inferior civil courts;

---

[72] *Houldsworth* v. *City of Glasgow Bank* (1880) 7 R. (H.L.) 53, 62; *London Street Tramways Co.* v. *L.C.C.* [1898] A.C. 375; *Oliver* v. *Saddler*, 1929 S.C. (H.L.) 94, 97.
[73] *Glasgow Corpn.* v. *Central Land Board*, 1956 S.C. (H.L.) 1; see also *Virtue* v. *Alloa Police Commrs.* (1873) 1 R. 285; *Orr Ewing's Trs.* v. *Orr Ewing* (1885) 13 R. (H.L.) 1; *Blacks* v. *Girdwood* (1885) 13 R. 243; *Primrose* v. *Waterson* (1902) 4 F. 783.
[74] *Rankine* v. *I.R.C.*, 1952 S.C. 177, 186; *I.R.C.* v. *Glasgow Police Athletic Assocn.*, 1953 S.C. (H.L.) 13; *Glasgow Corpn.*, supra, 9, 13, 17; *Dalgleish* v. *Glasgow Corpn.* 1976 S.C. 32, 52.
[75] Statement by the Lord Chancellor, 26 July 1966, noted in [1966] 3 All E.R. 77; *Dick* v. *Burgh of Falkirk*, 1976 S.C. (H.L.) 1. See also *Fitzleet Estates* v. *Cherry* [1977] 3 All E.R. 996.
[76] *Kirkpatrick's Trs.* v. *K.* (1874) 1 R. (H.L.) 37. On the binding character of such decisions on lower courts in England see *Cassell* v. *Broome* [1972] 1 All E.R. 801.
[77] e.g. *Hutton's Trs.* v. *H.*, 1916 S.C. 860; *Bell* v. *B.*, 1940 S.C. 229; revd. 1941 S.C. (H.L.) 5; cf. *Sugden* v. *H.M.A.*, 1934 J.C. 103.
[78] *Yuill's Trs.* v. *Thomson* (1902) 4 F. 815; *Cochrane's Exrx.* v. *C.* 1947 S.C. 134; *McElroy* v. *McAllister*, 1949 S.C. 110; *Marshall* v. *Scottish Milk Marketing Board*, 1956 S.C. (H.L.) 37, 39; *Smith* v. *Stewart & Co.*, 1960 S.C. 329.

(c) Decisions in point of either Division of the Inner House are normally treated as binding on that Division,[79] and on the other Division,[80] and are binding on judges of the Outer House[81] and on all inferior civil courts.

(d) Decisions in point of single judges in the Outer House are not binding on one another[82] but are generally regarded as authoritative in all inferior civil courts.

(e) Decisions in point of a sheriff-principal or sheriff are not binding, but are generally followed in the sheriff court in the absence of reason to the contrary.

(f) Decisions in point of any court standing lower in the hierarchy than the court presently considering the issue have persuasive influence depending in degree on the status of the court, the personal eminence of the judges, and the consistency of the principle of the precedent with reason and settled general principles of the law, but are never binding.

(g) A decision in point may be disregarded if inconsistent with prior authorities not brought to the notice of the court,[83] or depending on social or other views out of keeping with modern views,[84] or if its *ratio* has been superseded by subsequent legislation,[85] or the point in question was not argued in it.[86]

Overruling power

It is accordingly competent for the House of Lords, a full court, or a Division to overrule as bad law a precedent of the Outer House,[87] and for the House of Lords, a full court, or a larger court to overrule a precedent decided by a Division,[88] and possibly for the full court to overrule a precedent decided by seven judges, though this is contrary to practice.[89]

Precedents from other United Kingdom courts

Decisions of the House of Lords on appeal from England or Northern Ireland on matters of law common to Scotland and the other jurisdiction

---

[79] *Garden's Exor.* v. *More*, 1913 S.C. 285; *Cameron* v. *Glasgow Corpn.*, 1935 S.C. 533; 1936 S.C. (H.L.) 26, 29; *Marshall, supra*; But see *Campbell* v. *West of Scotland Shipbreaking Co.*, 1953 S.C. 173; *Maitland*, 1961 S.C. 291.

[80] But see *Shanks* v. *United Masons* (1874) 1 R. 823, 825; *Earl of Wemyss* v. *Earl of Zetland* (1890) 18 R. 126, 130; *Lord Advocate* v. *Young* (1898) 25 R. 778, where it was indicated that a Division might not be bound by a single previous decision.

[81] e.g. *Fortington* v. *Kinnaird*, 1942 S.C. 239, 244–5.

[82] *Blackwood* v. *Andre*, 1947 S.C. 333, not following *McDaid* v. *C.N.T.*, 1946 S.C. 462.

[83] *Mitchell* v. *Mackersy* (1905) 8 F. 198. See also *Wilson* v. *Chatterton* [1946] 1 All E.R. 431.

[84] *Bowman* v. *Secular Society* [1917] A.C. 406; *Welldon* v. *Butterley Coal Co.* [1920] 1 Ch. 130; *Beith's Trs.* v. *B.*, 1950 S.C. 66, 70.

[85] *Beith's Trs., supra*.

[86] *Aldridge* v. *Simpson-Bell*, 1971 S.C. 87.

[87] e.g. *Lennie* v. *L.*, 1950 S.C. (H.L.) 1, overruling *Goold* v. *G.*, 1927 S.C. 177.

[88] e.g. *Fortington* v. *Kinnaird*, 1942 S.C. 239; *McElroy* v. *McAllister*, 1949 S.C. 110; *Smith* v. *Stewart*, 1960 S.C. 329.

[89] *Yuill's Trs.* v. *Thomson* (1902) 4 F. 815.

concerned, or on questions of general jurisprudence, are binding on Scottish courts,[90] particularly when dealing with a principle common to Scotland and the other country.[91]

Decisions of the superior courts of England and Northern Ireland (Courts of Appeal and High Courts) are not absolutely binding on any Scottish court but are persuasive in a degree proportionate to the status of the court in the judicial hierarchy of the country in question, particularly in cases where the same statute or a similar principle of common law applies in Scotland to that under consideration in the English or Irish case.

Judgments of the Privy Council are never binding on any Scottish court,[92] though they may be highly persuasive if relevant to Scots law.[93]

Precedents from foreign courts

Judgments of the superior courts of Commonwealth countries, of the Supreme Court of the U.S.A. and of courts in foreign countries of equivalent status have persuasive force depending on the similarity of the law in question to Scots law on the relevant matter.[94]

Practice in other civil courts

In other Scottish civil courts the rules of precedent are less rigidly followed. The Inner House sitting as Court of Exchequer may not have the power of reconsidering precedents before a larger court, the court in this capacity having been established on the English model.[95] In the Scottish Land Court previous decisions may be not followed.[96] The Lands Valuation Appeal Court may decline to follow its own precedents,[97] but follows decisions of the House of Lords in English cases where those are applicable.[98]

Finding the ratio decidendi

If the court deciding a case considers that a prior decision is directly in point, or at least sufficiently in point to yield a ruling or guidance for the

---

[90] *Virtue* v. *Alloa Police Commrs.* (1873) 1 R. 285; *Orr Ewing's Trs.* v. *Orr Ewing* (1885) 13 R. (H.L.) 1; *Blacks* v. *Girdwood* (1885) 13 R. 243; *Primrose* v. *Waterston* (1902) 4 F. 783; *Dalgleish* v. *Glasgow Corpn.*, 1976 S.C. 32. cf. *Donnelly* v. *Glasgow Corpn.*, 1953 S.C. 107, disapproved by H.L. in *Davie* v. *New Merton Board Mills* [1959] A.C. 604.

[91] cf. *Hamilton* v. *N.C.B.*, 1960 S.C. (H.L.) 1.

[92] *Brown* v. *John Watson, Ltd.*, 1914 S.C. (H.L.) 44; *Duncan* v. *Cammell Laird & Co.* [1942] A.C. 624.

[93] *Leask* v. *Scott* (1877) 2 Q.B.D. 376, 380.

[94] See *Donoghue* v. *Stevenson*, 1932 S.C. (H.L.) 31; *Walsh* v. *L.A.*, 1956 S.C. (H.L.) 126; but see *A/B Karlshamns Oljefabriker* v. *Monarch S.S. Co.*, 1949 S.C. (H.L.) 1.

[95] *Drummond* v. *I.R.C.*, 1951 S.C. 482, 488.

[96] *Niven* v. *Cameron*, 1939 S.L.C.R. 23; *Georgeson* v. *Anderston's Trs.*, 1945 S.L.C.R. 44.

[97] *Glasgow Assessor* v. *Watson*, 1920 S.C. 517; *Inverness-shire Assessor* v. *Cameron*, 1938 S.C. 360.

[98] *Aberdeen Assessor* v. *Collie*, 1932 S.C. 304.

decision of the instant case, and has also decided whether, having regard to what court pronounced the prior decision, its decision is to be treated as binding and decisive, or only persuasive and influential, the later court must determine what was the *ratio decidendi* of the precedent; the *ratio* is the principle of law underlying and justifying the actual decision, or the proposition of law which can be extracted from it, or the legal ground on which it was decided, for which it is authority, and which must, or may, according to circumstances, be applied to the instant case. A precedent, that is, is binding or persuasive, as the case may be, in respect of its containing a principle which justified its disposal in the way it was decided, and which is capable of application to the case, now before the later court[99] and raising the same point of law. It is only matter necessary for the decision of the precedent which is binding or persuasive in the later case.[1] It is for the later court to determine what it understands to be the *ratio decidendi* of the precedent. Where a case is decided on alternative grounds each is binding in future.[2]

There are no fixed rules or methods for finding or extracting the *ratio decidendi*; it is not necessarily contained in the rubric of the report, nor expressed in any judgment, but is a proposition of law implicit in the actual decision of the case and consistent with the material facts thereof.[3]

If the *ratio decidendi* of a precedent has been superseded or invalidated by subsequent legislation or similar cause that *ratio* ceases to be binding.[4]

Obiter dicta

Judicial observations not part of the judge's *ratio decidendi* are called *obiter dicta* and their weight and value varies with their nature and the eminence of the judge who pronounced them. While never binding, they may be invoked or relied on as persuasive precedents in a later case.

Treatment of binding precedents

If the court holds a precedent to be in point and binding on it, it must follow it, and apply the ratio to the case before the court, unless it can 'distinguish' the precedent as dealing with an issue different in some material respect and accordingly hold it not to be in point,[4] or can regard

---

[99] *Re Hallett* (1879) 13 Ch.D. 696, 712; *Osborne to Rowlett* (1880) 13 Ch.D. 774, 785; *Fortington* v. *Kinnaird*, 1942 S.C. 239, 269; *Beith's Trs.* v. *B.* 1950 S.C. 66, 70; *Douglas Hamilton* v. *Duke and Duchess of Hamilton's Trs.*, 1961 S.C. 205, 229.

[1] *Penn-Texas Corpn.* v. *Marst-Anstalt* [1964] 2 All E.R. 594.

[2] *Miliangos* v. *Frank* [1975] 1 All E.R. 1076.

[3] *Walker, S.L.S.,* Ch. 10; see also *Saunders* v. *Anglia Building Socy.* [1970] 3 All E.R. 961, 963.

[4] *Beith's Trs.* v. *B.*, 1950 S.C. 66.

the *ratio* as not binding, having been superseded by later statute or changed social and legal conditions.[5]

Treatment of precedents not binding

If the court holds a precedent in point but not binding in the circumstances the later court may treat it as persuasive and follow it or may 'not follow' it,[6] or doubt it, or disapprove it.[7]

Other factors affecting evaluation of precedent

Particularly in relation to precedents merely persuasive,[8] a court, in deciding how much weight to attach to a precedent, may consider the age of the precedent,[9] whether it has previously been approved, followed, or applied,[10] or distinguished, not followed, or criticized,[11] the personal eminence of the judges who decided it,[12] whether other judges were consulted,[13] whether the judges were unanimous or not, whether the case was argued on both sides or not,[14] whether any matters were conceded or not argued, whether any relevant statutes or cases were not considered, and whether the report is satisfactory or not.[15]

(3) INSTITUTIONAL WRITINGS

Principles and rules laid down in those books known as institutional writings and traditionally recognized as having high authority, namely Sir Thomas Craig's *Jus Feudale* (1655); (Sir) James Dalrymple, Viscount Stair's *Institutions of the Law of Scotland* (1681); Sir George Mackenzie's *Institutions of the Law of Scotland* (1684); Andrew McDouall, Lord Bankton's *Institute of the Laws of Scotland* (1751); Henry Home, Lord Kames's *Principles of Equity* (1760); Professor John Erskine's *Institute of the Law of Scotland* (1773); and Professor George Joseph Bell's *Commentaries on the Law of Scotland and the Principles of Mercantile Jurisprudence* (1804) and his *Principles of the Law of Scotland*, (1829), may also be decisive. Of these institutional writers Stair, Erskine, and Bell

---

[5] e.g. *Donoghue* v. *Stevenson*, 1932 S.C. (H.L.) 31, 49–56, 65–9; *Hughes* v. *L.A.*, 1963 S.C. (H.L.) 31, distinguishing *Muir* v. *Glasgow Corpn.*, 1943 S.C. (H.L.) 3; *B.R.Board* v. *Herrington* [1972] A.C. 877.

[6] *Beith's Trs.* v. *B.*, 1950 S.C. 66.

[7] e.g. *McDaid* v. *C.N.T.*, 1946 S.C. 462, not followed in *Blackwood* v. *Andre*, 1947 S.C. 333.

[8] e.g. *Cook* v. *Grubb*, 1963 S.C. 1, disapproving *Torbat* v. *T's Trs.* (1907) 14 S.L.T. 830.

[9] cf. *Donnelly* v. *D.*, 1959 S.C. 97, 102, 103.

[10] cf. *Fortington* v. *Kinnaird*, 1942 S.C. 239, 266; *Baird* v. *B's Trs.*, 1956 S.C. (H.L.) 93, 107–8.

[11] cf. *McElroy* v. *McAllister*, 1949 S.C. 110.

[12] cf. *Stewart* v. *L.M.S. Ry.*, 1943 S.C. (H.L.) 19, 38.

[13] As in *Connell* v. *C.*, 1950 S.C. 505.

[14] cf. *Bell* v. *B.*, 1941 S.C. (H.L.) 5.

[15] cf. *Robb* v. *R.*, 1953 S.L.T. 44, criticized in *Hamilton* v. *H.*, 1954 S.L.T. 16.

stand pre-eminent,[16] and it is possibly doubtful whether Mackenzie's *Institutions* and Kames's *Equity* are fully entitled to institutional status.[17]

The authority of a statement in point by any one of the institutional writers is generally accepted as equivalent to that of an Inner House decision to the same effect,[18] but in case of conflict it must yield to any statutory rule or judicial pronouncement. The evaluation of any such statement depends largely upon whether the legal context has changed, whether the passage has been approved or criticized, and its consistency with the law on related topics.

Not all the writings of an institutional writer have institutional standing; his lesser works, or works not finally revised or published by him, are of only lesser authority.[19]

(4) TREATISES AND TEXTBOOKS

The writings of some later jurists have done much to systematize, rationalize, and explain the law in particular branches and on points of doubt and difficulty their views are entitled to weight, rather less than that accorded to the institutional writers, but still substantial and probably as great as that allowed to the decision of a single judge. This weight attaches only to certain writings, treatises which have repeatedly been regarded as authoritative,[20] and not by any means to all textbooks. The standing of, and the weight accorded to statements in, a treatise depends on the regard in which it is held professionally, and may therefore decline with time while newer treatises achieve recognition. Mere textbooks and manuals have no weight.

(5) CUSTOM

Though the common law of the realm declared in the older books and judicial decisions embodies many customs commonly accepted as law

---

[16] On the authority of Stair, see *Drew* v. *D.* (1870) 9 M. 163, 167; on Kames see *Kennedy* v. *Stewart* (1889) 16 R. 421, 430; on Bell's *Commentaries* see *Gardner* v. *Cuthbertson* (1824) 2 Sh. App. 291, 298. See also *Will's Trs.* v. *Cairngorm School*, 1976 S.C. (H.L.) 30, 77, 118, 156.

[17] In Scottish criminal law Mackenzie's *Laws and Customs of Scotland in Matters Criminal* (1678), Hume's *Commentaries on Crimes* (1797), and, probably, Alison's *Principles* (1832) and *Practice of the Criminal Law of Scotland* (1833) enjoy institutional status. On institutional writers and editions thereof, see Walker, *S.L.S.*, Chs. 10 and 11. There are various other older writings on Scots law which are certainly not institutional.

[18] Lord Normand, *The Scottish Judicature and Legal Procedure* (1941).

[19] Erskine's *Principles* and Hume's *Lectures* are not institutional, but still valuable: *Fortington* v. *Kinnaird*, 1942 S.C. 239; but see *Pettigrew* v. *Harton*, 1956 S.C. 67; *MacLennan* v. *M.*, 1958 S.C. 105; *Thomson* v. *St. Cuthbert's Cooperative Assn.*, 1958 S.C. 380, 394, 398; *N.C.B.* v. *Thomson*, 1959 S.C. 353, 383; *Cole-Hamilton* v. *Boyd*, 1963 S.C. (H.L.) 1.

[20] This class includes Fraser on *Husband and Wife* and on *Parent and Child*; McLaren on *Wills*; Gloag on *Contract*; Candlish Henderson on *Vesting*; Dickson on *Evidence*; Rankine on *Landownership* and on *Leases*.

throughout the country, and so settled and notorious as not to require evidence, such as the legal rights of spouses and children, a custom not hitherto so recognized may be held in any particular case, if adequately proved, to have been accepted by the parties as binding and be treated as laying down an authoritative rule for them. Customary law derives its binding force from tacit consent presumed from the inveterate usage of the community.[21] Admiralty law is based on the ancient customs of the commerical nations of Europe.[22]

To be given the force of law in an unprecedented case a custom must be proved by evidence,[23] and shown to be a definite and certain practice,[24] habitually observed in the locality[25] or trade in question,[26] fair and reasonable,[27] generally accepted for so long as to justify the inference that it has long been accepted as a binding rule,[28] and, though possibly an exception to or qualification of the general rules of law of the country, not contradictory thereof.[29] Custom cannot prevail against statute,[30] nor against express words in a contract.[31]

Apart from custom proven as a general rule of law, mercantile custom may be proved to have been an implied term in a particular contract, where parties knew of, and must be held to have contractd subject to, a particular practice or usage of trade.[32]

(6) EQUITY

Principles of equity, of natural justice and right reason, may be resorted to to prevent an unduly rigorous application of strict law from working injustice. Numerous such principles are woven into the fabric of Scots law and are considered as part of the common law.[33] The Scottish courts have

[21] Stair I, 1, 16; Mack. I, 1, 10; Bankt. I, 1, 58–9; Ersk. I, 1, 43–6.
[22] *Boettcher v. Carron Co.* (1861) 23 D. 322, 330; *Currie v. McKnight* (1897) 24 R. (H.L.) 1, 3; *Sheaf S.S. Co. v. Compania Transmediterranea*, 1930 S.C. 660.
[23] *Mackenzie v. Dunlop* (1856) 3 Macq. 22.
[24] *Strathlorne S.S. Co. v. Baird*, 1916 S.C. (H.L.) 134.
[25] M. *Queensberry v. Wright* (1838) 16 S. 439; *Royal Four Towns Fishing Assoc. v. Dumfries Assessor*, 1956 S.C. 379.
[26] *Learmonth v. Sinclair's Trs.* (1898) 5 R. 548; *Holman v. Peruvian Nitrate Co.* (1878) 5 R. 657; *Sagar v. Ridehalgh* [1931] 1 Ch. 310; *Clydesdale Bank v. Snodgrass*, 1939 S.C. 805; *Marshall v. English Electric Co.* [1945] 1 All E.R. 653.
[27] *Bruce v. Smith* (1890) 17 R. 1000; *Cazalet v. Morris*, 1916 S.C. 952.
[28] Ersk. I, 1, 44; *Learmonth, supra; Macome v. Dickson* (1868) 6 M. 898; *Sturrock v. Murray*, 1952 S.C. 454.
[29] *Allan v. Thomson* (1829) 7 S. 784; *Dunbar Mags v. Dunbar Heritors* (1835) 1 S. & McL. 134; *Bruce, supra.*
[30] *Walker Trs. v. Lord Advocate*, 1912 S.C. (H.L.) 12.
[31] *Tancred Arrol & Co. v. Steel Co. of Scotland* (1890) 17 R. (H.L.) 31; *Maclellan v. Peattie's Trs.* (1903) 5 F. 1031.
[32] Bell, *Comm.* I, 465; *Holman v. Peruvian Nitrate Co.* (1878) 5 R. 657; *Strathlorne S.S. Co. v. Baird*, 1916 S.C. (H.L.) 134.
[33] Stair I, 1, 16; IV, 3, 1; Ersk, I, 1, 18; I, 3, 22; Kames, *Equity, passim; Historical Law Tracts*, 228; Walker (1954) 66 J.R. 103.

always administered an undivided system of law and equity. Apart from many cases where discretion may be exercised and equitable considerations are relevant in the application of rules of strict law, the Court of Session retains an ultimate residuary equitable power, the *nobile officium*, to provide a remedy where justice requires it or to intervene where strict law might work injustice.[34] But this power has come to be much restricted and is now exercised only in circumstances for which there is precedent or analogy.[35]

(7) EXTRANEOUS SOURCES

Failing guidance from any of the foregoing sources the courts may turn to such extraneous sources as legal literature[36] or those other systems of law which have in the past been quarries for the materials of Scots law, such as the Roman law, canon law, feudal law, and the law merchant and maritime, and the leading commentators thereon, other modern systems of law, particularly those founded on similar historical bases, such as the Roman-Dutch, and the French and German Codes, with the commentators thereon, and those developed in countries having a similar social and economic structure, such as England, Northern Ireland, Commonwealth countries, and the U.S.A.[37]

The judgments of dissenting judges, *obiter dicta*, and analogies drawn from principles accepted in other contexts may be prayed in aid.

In the last resort a judge may rely on his own conscience, his idea of what justice, equity, and reason demand in the circumstances and his beliefs as to what is fair and right and reasonable in the circumstances, or consistent with the dictates of morality and public policy.[38]

These formal sources determine the general character of Scottish private law. It is largely but not entirely written law, discoverable from printed materials, but still with scope for the derivation of principles from unwritten law, such as custom or moral beliefs. But it is not a systematic written code of law, established as a piece by a lawgiving authority, but rather the product of growth and development over a long period, a growth influenced by numerous factors of different strengths at different times, not always consistent nor logical.

---

[34] Stair IV, 3, 1; Bankt. IV, 7, 24; Ersk. I, 3, 22; Kames, *H.L.T.*, 231; Walker *Remedies* Ch. 65; *Gibson's Trs.*, 1933 S.C. 190, 198.

[35] MacLaren, *Practice*, 100–5; Walker, *Remedies*, Ch. 65.

[36] *Infra.*

[37] See e.g. *Collins* v. *C.* (1884) 11 R. (H.L.) 19; *Purves' Trs.* v. *P.* (1895) 22 R. 513; *Cantiere San Rocco* v. *Clyde Shipbuilding Co.*, 1923 S.C. (H.L.) 105; *Donoghue* v. *Stevenson*, 1932 S.C. (H.L.) 31; *Sugden* v. *H.M.A.*, 1934 J.C. 1; *Drummond's J.F.* v. *H.M.A.*, 1944 S.C. 298; *A/B Karlshamns Oljefabriker* v. *Monarch S.S. Co.*, 1949 S.C. (H.L.) 1; *Walsh* v. *L.A..*, 1956 S.C. (H.L.) 126.

[38] cf. Stair I, 1, 16. See also *Beresford* v. *Royal Ins. Co.* [1938] A.C. 586; *Steel* v. *Glasgow Iron & Steel Co.*, 1944 S.C. 237.

It is fundamentally a body of common law, based on customs common-ly recognized and accepted as binding throughout large parts of the community, recognized and applied by judges in particular cases, and systematized and synthesized with materials from other sources by judges and authoritative text-writers, but increasingly modified, supplemented, and replaced by statements of the presumed general will of the community made by Parliament in the form of statute.[39]

(4) Literary sources

The literary sources are the different kinds of legal literature.

Legal literature includes all writings on and about the law other than legislation, reported decisions, and institutional writings, such as legal dictionaries, encyclopaedias, editorial notes to institutional writings,[40] older non-institutional writings, commentaries, textbooks, academic lectures on law,[41] judge's notes,[42] books on legal history, philosophy, comparative law, and periodical literature.

Legal literature is not an authoritative source of rules of law,[43] but merely exposition or criticism of, or commentary on, various principles, or branches of law, but some individual works of legal literature may come to enjoy a reputation and regard falling not far, if at all, short of being authoritative, depending on the personal eminence and reputation of the author, whether or not he held judicial office, the known quality and value of the work, and the extent to which it has received judicial approval.[44] There was formerly an alleged rule that the work of a living author might not be cited in argument, being unauthoritative, while the work of a dead author might be cited, but this rule has now been largely departed from.[45]

Statements in textbooks may assist a judge by reinforcing his view as to a previous decision,[46] but may be disregarded or condemned as incorrect.[47]

[39] cf. Ersk. I, 1, 30.
[40] See e.g. Fortington v. Kinnaird, 1942 S.C. 239, 265, 276.
[41] On the authority of such works see Kerr v. Martin (1840) 2 D. 752, 776, 792; Fortington v. Kinnaird, 1942 S.C. 239, 253, 265, 276, 277. Reference is also sometimes made by a judge to his own notes of academic lectures: e.g. Kerr, supra, 792; Bute v. More (1870) 9 M. 180, 190.
[42] See Hutchison v. H. (1872) 11 M. 229; Fortington, supra, 277.
[43] Donoghue v. Stevenson, 1932 S.C. (H.L.) 31, 35.
[44] See under Section 2(4) above.
[45] e.g. citation of Gloag on Contract; or Cheshire's Private International Law.
[46] cf. Dempster's Trs. v. D., 1949 S.C. 92, 95; McElroy v. McAllister, 1949 S.C. 110, 135.
[47] e.g. Bell v. Blackwood Morton & Sons, Ltd., 1960 S.C. 11, 23.

DOCTRINES, PRINCIPLES, AND RULES

The whole body of the private law consists of verbal statements of what one may or may not, should or should not, do, in various circumstances and of what consequences follow if conduct does not conform to the required standard. It comprises a number of general doctrines and a much larger number of principles and rules, which are capable of being classified and arranged in a coherent logical structure and of being stated, exemplified, and discussed, and applied to the solution of actual difficulties and controversies.

Doctrines, principles, and rules

While there are no fixed meanings for these terms, the word 'doctrine' is usually used of a very general notion which can comprehend many more specific principles and rules, such as the doctrine of personal bar, to the general effect that no person can be allowed to speak or act in contradiction of an attitude he has already asserted by words or actings. A 'principle' of law is a statement in general terms applicable to a large, and frequently uncertain, range of circumstances, such as: an employer must take reasonable care and precautions for the safety of his employees; while a 'rule' is a statement in narrower and more rigid terms applicable to a limited, and possibly very confined, set of circumstances, such as: an employer must take care that dangerous machinery is adequately fenced. The three kinds of statements are accordingly of different degrees of generality and applicability. To instances of all three kinds of formulations there are frequently exceptions and qualifications, and there are often difficult questions of precisely how a doctrine, principle, or rule should be formulated verbally and of whether the circumstances of a particular case fall within or outwith the application of a particular principle or rule. In general doctrines and principles have been formulated inductively by judges and text-writers as generalizations on the basis of prior particular instances; in general rules have been formulated by judges in particular cases and by Parliament in statutes.

Certain doctrines and principles of law are of wide and general application and common to several branches of the law, and underlie numerous specific rules. Their very generality renders them difficult or even incapable of definition and makes it difficult to state categorically in what cases such a principle will apply.

The doctrine of natural justice

The doctrine of natural justice is more commonly invoked in public than in private law, but has important applications in the latter field also. It subsumes three main principles, that a person judging must hear both sides of the case, or at least give both sides equal opportunities of presenting their arguments,[1] that a person should not be, nor even appear to be, judge in a matter where his own interest is, or may be thought to be, involved,[2] and that justice must not only be done, but be seen to be done.[3]

So too a foreign judgment contravening a principle of natural justice cannot be enforced in Scotland. The cases turn on failure to give the litigant notice of the proceedings,[4] or failure to give him an opportunity of presenting his case to the foreign court.[5]

The doctrine of public policy

The doctrine of public policy[6] or public interest or the accepted morality of the community at the time is a limitation which in many contexts is held to justify treating certain conduct as reprehensible and legally unenforceable, though it may not be positively prohibited or otherwise illegal. 'Public policy is that principle of law which holds that no subject can lawfully do that which has a tendency to be injurious to the public or against the public good in which may be termed the policy of the law, or public policy in relation to the law.'[7] The doctrine is necessarily vague and an unsafe basis for decision save where there is precedent,[8] and there is warrant for the view that the courts can no longer invent new heads of public policy, though they may interpret existing heads in new circumstances.[9]

The doctrine justifies the refusal to enforce agreements to divorce,[10] or collusive agreements,[11] or to recognize promises made *stante matrimonio*

---

[1] i.e. the principle *audiatur et altera pars: Mitchell* v. *Cable* (1848) 10 D. 1297; *Black* v. *Williams*, 1924 S.C. (H.L.) 22; *Barrs* v. *British Wool Marketing Board*, 1957 S.C. 72; *McDonald* v. *Lanarkshire Fire Brigade Joint Cttee.*, 1959 S.C. 141; *St. Johnstone F.C.* v. *S.F.A.*, 1965 S.L.T. 171; *Malloch* v. *Aberdeen Corpn.*, 1971 S.C. (H.L.) 53; *Scott* v. *Aberdeen Corpn.*, 1976 S.C. 81.
[2] i.e. the principle *nemo judex in causa sua: Caledonian Ry* v. *Ramsay* (1897) 24 R. (J.) 48; *Wildridge* v. *Anderson* (1897) 25 R. (J.) 27; cf. *Palmer* v. *Inverness Hospitals Board*, 1963 S.C. 311.
[3] *Barrs, supra*; cf. *Laughland* v. *Galloway*, 1968 S.L.T. 272.
[4] *Rudd* v. *R.* [1924] P. 72.
[5] *Jacobson* v. *Frachon* (1928) 44 T.L.R. 103.
[6] Generally Lloyd, *Public Policy*; Winfield, 42 H.L.R. 76.
[7] *Egerton* v. *Earl Brownlow* (1853) 4 H.L.C. 1, 196; *E. Caithness* v. *Sinclair*, 1912 S.C. 79.
[8] *Richardson* v. *Mellish* (1824) 2 Bing. 229, 252 ('a very unruly horse'); *Re Mirams* [1891] 1 Q.B. 594, 595; *Janson* v. *Driefontein Consolidated Mines, Ltd.* [1902] A.C. 484, 507.
[9] *Janson, supra*, 491; *Fender* v. *Mildmay* [1938] A.C. 1, 23.
[10] *Royle* v. *R.* [1909] P. 24; contrast *Aldridge* v. *A.* (1888) 13 P.D. 210; *L.* v. *L.* [1931] P. 63.
[11] *Lowndes* v. *L.* [1950] P. 223.

to many another,[12] and the refusal to enforce a will the bequests of which are extravagant or wasteful.[13]

The main applications of the doctrine arise in the field of contract where it is held to justify the judicial refusal to enforce certain kinds of contract,[14] such as one with an alien enemy,[15] one for the obtaining of an honour,[16] or benefit from the government,[17] or for promoting a marriage,[18] contracts unreasonably restricting the party's freedom of action[19] or of marriage,[20] contracts in restraint of trade generally,[21] and a rule wholly excluding the jurisdiction of the courts in case of dispute.[22] Similarly there is the rule that a person may not benefit from his own crime.[23]

In international private law British courts have sometimes declined to give effect to rights acquired under a foreign system if the rights or the method of obtaining them was deemed contrary to the British concept of public policy.[24] Thus a contract obtained by coercion or objectionable under a British rule of law cannot be enforced though entered into abroad.[25] An action cannot be founded on a foreign judgment deemed contrary to British public policy.[26] But it is difficult to determine what heads of the British concept of public policy are so material as to justify the rejection of rights otherwise validly acquired.

The doctrine of good faith

A person acts in good faith when he acts honestly, or does not know, and has no grounds for suspecting, the invalidity or illegality of his conduct or of the rights he claims. The doctrine arises in very many contexts.

Thus in the law of persons, where at least one party to a marriage legally void honestly and *bona fide* believed that it was valid, the marriage is designated 'putative' and the children are deemed legitimate.

---

[12] *Wilson v. Carnley* [1908] 1 K.B. 729; contrast *Fender v. Mildmay* [1938] A.C. 1.
[13] *Sutherland's Tr. v. Verschoyle*, 1968 S.L.T. 43.
[14] Ch. 4.5, *infra*; cf. Bell, *Comm.* I, 320.
[15] *Porter v. Freudenberg* [1915] 1 K.B. 857; *Rodriguez v. Speyer* [1919] A.C. 116.
[16] *Parkinson v. College of Ambulance* [1925] 2 K.B. 1.
[17] *Montefiore v. Menday Motor Co.* [1918] 2 K.B. 241.
[18] *Hermann v. Charlesworth* [1905] 2 K.B. 123.
[19] Ch. 4.3, *infra*.
[20] *Perris v. Lyon* (1807) 9 East 170; cf. *Clayton v. Ramsden* [1943] A.C. 320.
[21] Ch. 4.3, *infra*.
[22] *St. Johnstone F.C. v. S.F.A.*, 1965 S.L.T. 171.
[23] *Cleaver v. Mutual Life Assocn.* [1892] 1 Q.B. 147; *In re Crippen* [1911] P. 108; *Beresford v. Royal Insce. Assocn.* [1938] A.C. 586; contrast *re Houghton* [1915] 2 Ch. 173; *Tinline v. White Cross Insce. Assocn.* [1921] 3 K.B. 327.
[24] *Dynamit A/G v. Rio Tinto Co. Ltd.* [1918] A.C. 292, 302.
[25] *Hope v. H.* (1857) 8 De G.M. & G. 731; *Roussillon v. R.* (1880) 14 Ch. D. 351; *Kaufmann v. Gerson* [1904] 1 K.B. 591.
[26] *Macartney v. M.* [1921] 1 Ch. 522, 527; cf. *Masinimport v. Scottish Light Industries*, 1976 S.C. 103.

In the law of obligations, there is a special requirement of good faith in the case of certain contracts, commonly referred to as contracts *uberrimae fidei*, in which each contracting party must make full disclosure of possibly relevant facts to the other. Such are the contracts of partnership, cautionry, insurance, and contracts between persons in fiduciary relationships.[27]

In the law of property, one who honestly and on reasonable grounds believes himself proprietor of subjects which he possesses is deemed a *bona fide* possessor and, though ejected, has some rights with regard to the gathering and consumption of the fruits of his possession, greater than enjoyed by the squatter or *mala fide* possessor.[28] He has a claim for recompense for improvements executed during his possession.

In negotiable instruments the privileges of being a holder in due course attach only to the person who takes in good faith, for value and without notice of any imperfection in the title of the previous holder. Such a holder acquires a good title even though the instrument was acquired from one who had stolen it.[29]

The doctrine of personal bar

In many circumstances a person may be prevented from exercising what is prima facie his legal right by reason of some principle within the general doctrine of personal bar.[30] Stated most generally this doctrine is to the effect that a person cannot be allowed to enforce claims which he has already, expressly or impliedly, repudiated or departed from, or to adopt an attitude inconsistent with his own earlier words or conduct;[31] where A has by his words or conduct justified B in believing that a certain state of facts exists, and B has acted upon such belief to his prejudice, A is not permitted to affirm against B that a different state of facts existed at the same time.[32] Where one or other of the principles which exemplify the doctrine of personal bar applies its effect is conclusively to shut out all pleas and proof contradicting the inference from the earlier conduct.

The general doctrine embraces the principles of *rei interventus*, homologation, ratification, adoption, acquiescence, taciturnity, mora, delay, waiver, standing by, holding out, and similar inference from conduct.

Rei interventus and homologation are normally invoked to prevent a party resiling from a contract which requires to be, but has not been, constituted by probative writings. He may not, however, resile if he has by earlier words or conduct permitted the other party to act on the faith

---

[27] Chs. 4.13, 4.20, 4.21, *infra.*
[28] Ch. 5.6, *infra.*
[29] cf. *Walker & Watson* v. *Sturrock* (1897) 35 S.L.R. 26.
[30] Generally Rankine on *Personal Bar and Estoppel.*
[31] cf. *Graham* v. *G.* (1881) 9 R. 327; *Baird's Tr.* v. *Murray* (1883) 11 R. 153.
[32] *Gatty* v. *Maclaine*, 1921 S.C. (H.L.) 1, 7, per Lord Birkenhead.

of the contract as if it were perfectly constituted (*rei interventus*[33]), or has himself acted in a manner clearly approbatory of the informal agreement (homologation).[34] Homologation applies also to many circumstances where a party seeks to avoid an obligation which he is held to have approbated.[35]

Ratification of the conduct of an agent, servant, or partner by another in the full knowledge that what had been done on his behalf was challengeable is a clear ground for holding him barred from subsequent objection.

Adoption is the acceptance as valid and binding of an obligation which is fundamentally null, such as one constituted by a forged signature.[36] It can be inferred only if the person actually had the knowledge to enable him to repudiate liability, and this knowledge must be actual, and not merely constructive, i.e. attributed to him by law, such as the knowledge of an agent.[37]

Acquiescence consists in intimating, by words or conduct, consent or absence of opposition to what might have been objected to, thereby inducing a person or others to believe that their conduct is being and will be tolerated.[38] It requires knowledge of the contravention.[39] This plea is commonly advanced as a defence to an action for nuisance[40] or interference with a servitude right, or for failure to fulfil contractual obligations,[41] but has been pleaded in defence to actions for matrimonial wrong,[42] and in contract where a member might have challenged a building society's rule,[43] where a party continued to accept services under contract after intimation of increased charges therefor,[44] where clauses were added to draft contracts,[45] where a contract was performed after discovery of grounds for rescission,[46] and in many cases of contravention of rights relative to heritage.[47] Save in special circumstances a singular

---

[33] Ch. 4.4, *infra.*

[34] Ch. 4.4, *infra.*

[35] *Roberts v. City of Glasgow Bank* (1879) 6 R. 805; *Westville Shipping Co. v. Abram S.S. Co.*, 1923 S.C. (H.L.) 68.

[36] *Urquhart v. Bank of Scotland* (1872) 9 S.L.R. 508; cf. *Powrie v. Louis* (1881) 18 S.L.R. 533; see also *McKenzie v. B.L. Co.* (1881) 8 R. (H.L.) 8; *B.L. Co. v. Cowan* (1906) 8 F. 704.

[37] *Muir's Exors. v. Craig's Trs.*, 1913 S.C. 349.

[38] *Cairncross v. Lorimer* (1860) 3 Macq. 827; *D. Buccleuch v. Edinburgh Mags.* (1865) 3 M. 528; *Wylie & Lochhead v. McElroy* (1873) 1 R. 41; cf. *Gatty v. Maclaine*, 1921 S.C. (H.L.) 1, 7.

[39] *Ben Challum, Ltd., v. Buchanan*, 1955 S.C. 348.

[40] *Rigby & Beardmore v. Downie* (1872) 10 M. 568; *Houldsworth v. Wishaw Mags.* (1877) 14 R. 920.

[41] *Johnstone v. Hughan* (1894) 21 R. 777; *Eliott's Trs. v. E.* (1894) 21 R. 858; *Hamilton v. D. Montrose* (1906) 8 F. 1026; *Ben Challum, Ltd., supra.*

[42] *Colvin v. Johnstone* (1890) 18 R. 115.

[43] *Sinclair v. Mercantile Building Investment Socy.* (1885) 12 R. 1243.

[44] *Caledonian Ry. v. Stein & Co.*, 1919 S.C. 324.

[45] *Charles v. Shearer* (1900) 8 S.L.T. 273; *Roberts & Cooper v. Salvesen*, 1918 S.C. 794.

[46] *Boyd & Forrest v. G.S.W. Ry.*, 1915 S.C. (H.L.) 20.

[47] e.g. *Davidson v. Thomson* (1890) 17 R. 287; *Fraser v. Campbell* (1895) 22 R. 558; *Rankine v. Logie Den Land Co.* (1902) 4 F. 1074.

successor is not barred by acquiescence of his predecessor in title from complaining of encroachment.[48]

Taciturnity is mere silence and failure to object. By itself this does not bar any legal claim, as no man is bound at once to voice his objections on pain of otherwise being held barred for the future. But silence may bar a claim if continued and if the other party is thereby induced to act in reliance on non-objection.

Mora, taciturnity, and acquiescence are normally linked,[49] in that mere delay to enforce a claim or make objection to an infringement of right short of the period fixed by a prescription statute does not by itself bar a claim unless it is such as to give rise to an inference of non-objection and acquiescence in the *status quo*, or other parties have been prejudiced by the delay and silence.[50]

Waiver consists in conduct which implies acceptance of the other party's conduct and the giving up of any claim to which it might normally have given rise.[51] Thus where A, in breach of contract with B, bought from C who obtained his material from B, and B claimed damages from A, B was held to have waived his rights under the contract to the extent that he had supplied materials to C.[52] The inference of waiver is not always to be drawn from failure to reserve a claim of damages for breach of contract on settlement of the contract.[53]

Holding out is the principle which prevents a party from denying that one whom he had allowed to appear to be his agent or partner was in fact such agent or partner.[54]

As a general rule a party pleading that the other is personally barred must have been one with whom the other had a legal relationship, so that the other owed him a duty not to mislead him by his express or implied representation. Thus a customer owes a duty to his bank and is barred from pleading his own carelessness in drawing a cheque so that it could be, and was, fraudulently altered[55] but an acceptor of a bill of exchange does not owe a duty to be careful to a member of the public who may subsequently become an indorsee of the bill.[56] Also, the party pleading personal bar must show that in reliance on the other's words or conduct he has changed his position to his detriment.[57]

---

[48] *Brown* v. *Baty*, 1957 S.C. 351.

[49] *Mackenzie* v. *Catton's Trs.* (1877) 5 R. 313. See also *Lees's Trs.* v. *Dun*, 1912 S.C. 50.

[50] *Mckenzie* v. *B.L. Co.* (1881) 8 R. (H.L.) 8; see also *Bain* v. *Assets Co.* (1905) 7 F. (H.L.) 104; *B.L. Co.* v. *Cowan* (1906) 8 F. 704; and as to onus of proof *C.B.* v. *A.B.* (1885) 12 R. (H.L.) 36; *Bosville* v. *Macdonald*, 1910 S.C. 597. But see *Cook* v. *N.B. Ry.* (1872) 10 M. 513.

[51] *Shepherd* v. *Reddie* (1870) 8 M. 619; *Callander* v. *Smith* (1900) 8 S.L.T. 109.

[52] *Steel Co. of Scotland* v. *Tancred Arrol & Co.* (1892) 19 R. 1062. See also *Shepherd* v. *Reddie* (1870) 8 M. 619; *Shiells* v. *Scottish Assce. Corpn.* (1889) 16 R. 1014.

[53] *Clydebank Engineering Co.* v. *Castaneda* (1904) 7 F. (H.L.) 77.

[54] cf. Partnership Act, 1890, S. 14.

[55] *London Joint Stock Bank* v. *Macmillan* [1918] A.C. 777.

[56] *Schofield* v. *L. Londesborough* [1896] A.C. 514.

[57] *Stuart* v. *Potter, Choate & Prentice*, 1911, 1 S.L.T. 337; *Alloa Mags* v. *Wilson*, 1913 S.C. 6; *Bruce* v. *British Motor Trading Corpn.*, 1924 S.C. 908.

The doctrine of res judicata

The doctrine of *res judicata* is recognized to limit vexatious litigation and *ut esset finis litium*.[58] A ground of action heard and determined by a competent court, if rejected, cannot be founded on again. Nor can a second action be brought because the damages in the first one are inadequate.[59] To support a plea of *res judicata* the parties and the subject-matter in the present and the previous decided proceedings must be the same, and the suits must be founded on the same ground of claim, so that the specific point raised in the second has been directly raised and concluded by the judgment in the first suit.[60]

There is no scope for the plea if one if the parties is different,[61] unless the interest of that party were identical with the corresponding party in the earlier action.[62] Nor can the plea be taken if the subject matter of the action is not the same as in the previous action.[63] Nor is the plea open if the latter action is based on a different *medium concludendi* or ground of or substantial basis in law,[64] unless the later action is simply raising again in another guise the question decided in the former action.[65] Hence the dismissal of an action on a point of relevancy can never be *res judicata*,[66] nor is a criminal conviction *res judicata* in a subsequent civil action.[67] An action based on statute may or may not be in substance the same claim as a common law action.[68] Nor does the plea prevent a fresh action if new facts have come to light.[69]

A decree in absence can never found a plea of *res judicata* so as to preclude a subsequent action,[70] but a decree based on a compromise between parties may found such a plea,[71] as may a decree by default.[72] A

---

[58] cf. Stair IV, 40, 16–17; Ersk. IV, 3, 1–4; *Macdonald v. M.* (1842) 1 Bell 819; *Phosphate Sewage Co. v. Molleson* (1879) 6 R. (H.L.) 113; *Edinburgh Water Trs. v. Clippens Oil Co.* (1899) 1 F. 899; *G.S.W. Ry. v. Boyd and Forrest*, 1918 S.C. (H.L.) 14.

[59] cf. *Balfour v. Baird*, 1959 S.C. 64.

[60] *N.B. Ry. v. Lanarkshire Ry.* (1897) 24 R. 564; *Glen v. Dunlop* (1906) 13 S.L.T. 898.

[61] *Harvie v. Stewart* (1870) 9 M. 129; *Scott v. Macdonald* (1885) 12 R. 1123; *D. Atholl v. Glover Incorporation of Perth* (1899) 1 F. 658; 2 F. (H.L.) 57.

[62] *McCaig v. Maitland* (1887) 14 R. 295; *Allen v. McCombie's Trs.*, 1909 S.C. 710.

[63] *Ryan v. McBurnie*, 1940 S.C. 173; *Muir v. Jamieson*, 1947 S.C. 314.

[64] *N.B. Ry. v. Lanarkshire and Dumbartonshire Ry.* (1897) 24 R. 564; cf. *Grahame v. Secretary of State for Scotland*, 1951 S.C. 368.

[65] *Mackintosh v. Weir* (1875) 2 R. 877.

[66] *Russel v. Gillespie* (1859) 3 Macq. 757; *Menzies v. M.* (1893) 20 R. (H.L.) 108; *Cunningham v. Skinner* (1902) 4 F. 1124; *Govan Old Victualling Socy. v. Wagstaff* (1907) 14 S.L.T. 716.

[67] *Wood v. N.B. Ry.* (1899) 1 F. 562; *Faculty of Procurators v. Colquhoun* (1900) 2 F. 1192; *Wilson v. Bennett* (1904) 6 F. 269.

[68] *Edinburgh Water Trs. v. Clippens Oil Co.* (1899) 1 F. 899; *Matuszczyk v. N.C.B.*, 1955 S.C. 418.

[69] *G.S.W. Ry.*, *supra*, 31.

[70] *Mackintosh v. Smith & Lowe* (1865) 3 M. (H.L.) 6; *Paterson v. P.*, 1958 S.C. 141. cf. *Esso Petroleum Co. v. Law*, 1956 S.C. 33.

[71] *Young v. Y's Trs.*, 1957 S.C. 318; *Hynds v. H.*, 1966 S.C. 201; cf. *Boyd & Forrest v. G.S.W. Ry.*, 1918 S.C. (H.L.) 14, 26.

[72] *Forrest v. Dunlop* (1857) 3 R. 15.

decision in the Sheriff Court may be *res judicata* as regards a later action in the Court of Session,[73] and the decision in an action as regards a later arbitration.[74]

Principles

Principles are less general than doctrines but are propositions capable of application to many problems and cases; examples are: a contract confers rights and imposes duties on the parties thereto only, and not on third parties; an employer must take reasonable care for the safety of his employees; a right in security over moveable property can only be constituted by delivery of possession of the property. A principle may be qualified and eroded by exceptions in various circumstances. They may be found stated in institutional writings and major textbooks or are sometimes implied by the *rationes* of decided cases.

Rules

Rules are more detailed and specific than principles and usually relate to a narrow range of cases, or even to one particular category of cases only; examples are: the posting of a letter of acceptance concludes a contract; goods delivered under a contract of sale, if being rejected, must be rejected within a reasonable time. Rules also may be subject to exceptions and qualifications. They are very frequently found stated in legislation.

[73] *Brand* v. *Arbroath Police Commrs.* (1890) 17 R. 790; *Hynds* v. *H.*, 1966 S.C. 201.
[74] *G.S.W. Ry., supra,* 31.

FUNDAMENTAL LEGAL CONCEPTS

The principles and rules of Scottish private law are formulated verbally in statements utilizing legal concepts, that is, general and frequently abstract terms having more or less defined legal connotations, which may and frequently do differ substantially from the connotations of the same words used in non-legal contexts. Some of these concepts require consideration.[1]

The principles and rules of law take the form of statements ascribing to legal persons specified legal rights and legal duties in respect of other persons, conduct or things. Thus the principle: a person must take reasonable care not to harm another person who might foreseeably be injured by his conduct;[2] connotes a legal duty incumbent on the first person, owed to the second person, with regard to certain conduct, vesting the second person with a right not to be harmed by lack of reasonable care in conduct by the first party, and, by implication, with a consequential right to compensation from the first party if he is in fact harmed by the consequences of that party's lack of reasonable care.

Legal persons

The nature, attributes, and characteristics of legal persons are discussed subsequently.[3]

Legal rights

'The proper object [of law] is the right itself, whether it concerns persons, things or actions, and according to the several rights and their natural order, ought to be the order of jurisprudence, which may be taken up in a threefold consideration; first, in the constitution and nature of rights; secondly, in their conveyance or translation from one to another, whether it be among the living, or from the dead; thirdly, in their cognition, which comprehends the trial, decision, and execution of every right by the legal remedies.'[4] Not every alleged social, moral, political, or economic right is

---

[1] See further Salmond, *Jurisprudence*; Paton, *Jurisprudence*.
[2] cf. *Donoghue* v. *Stevenson*, 1932 S.C. (H.L.) 31.
[3] Ch. 3.1, *infra*.
[4] Stair I, 1, 23.

recognized as a legal right, and it is only with legal rights that the legal system is concerned. A legal right is a claim vested in a legal person by virtue of some legal title, availing against another legal person (right *in personam*) or other legal persons generally (right *in rem*), giving a claim to performance of some act or to abstention from some kinds of conduct, in relation to some thing, corporeal or incorporeal, and recognized by the courts by virtue of rules of civil law and normally enforceable by them, if need be, by remedies claimed by civil procedure and enforced by diligence. Some legal rights are imperfect in that they are not directly enforceable, though they may be recognized for certain purposes, such as in defence to a claim. So-called 'human rights' declared by the European Convention on Human Rights 1950 are not enforceable in the municipal law of Scotland, nor as part of the law of the European Communities.[5]

The legal title which vests a person with a right may be original, a fact creating a new right, such as birth or the attainment of majority, the catching of a fish or the painting of a picture, or the grant of a decree of court in his favour, or the operation of some rule of law;[6] or derivative, a fact transferring an existing right, such as purchase, or inheritance, or the operation of some rule of law transferring the right to him from another.

A person may be divested of title to a right by alienative or divestitive facts, such as sale, gift, or bequest on death, or the operation of certain rules of law; or by extinctive facts such as consumption, or destruction, or the satisfaction of a decree, or performance of an obligation or the operation of other rules of law. These classes of facts deal respectively with the creation, transfer to or from a person, and extinction of particular rights.

Titles again may be distinguished into acts of the law, operating by force of rules of law themselves, or juristic acts (acts in the law, acts of the party) operating by force of the expressed will of the party, such as agreement or gifts, to which the law normally attributes force.

Rules of law prescribe what rights do come into existence, are transferred, or disappear, on the occurrence of particular investitive or divestitive facts, and what procedures are necessary in various cases validly to invest or divest a person of particular rights.

The thing in relation to which a right exists, or the object of the right, may be of very many kinds, and the rules of law have to define to what kinds of objects, tangible and intangible, particular rights relate.

Legal duties

A legal duty is a requirement of conduct of a required kind and standard in particular circumstances, incumbent on a legal person, owed to another

---

[5] *Kaur* v. *Lord Advocate*, 1980 S.C. 319.

[6] Rights created in individuals by the treaties establishing the European Communities are enforceable in British courts: *Applications des Gaz* v. *Falks Veritas* [1974] 3 All E.R. 51, 58; *Van Duyn* v. *Home Office* [1975] 3 All E.R. 190, 205.

legal person or to persons generally, requiring particular acts or absten-
tions, compliance with which is legally obligatory and enforceable, and
importing further legal liability, failing compliance. Thus there are legal
duties to adhere to one's spouse, to perform one's undertakings, not to
harm others unjustifiably, and so on.

A duty may become incumbent by voluntarily undertaking it, or by
virtue of a rule of law, but in the latter case persons may sometimes
voluntarily, as by entering into a marriage or an employment, put themselves in a position where certain duties become legally incumbent on
them, which they could otherwise have avoided.

Rights and duties correlative

The concepts of rights and duties are correlative to each other in that the
existence of a right in one person implies a duty on another person or
persons with regard to the same subject. Conversely the fact that a duty is
incumbent on one person implies that some other person or persons have
right to its being implemented. To speak of right or duty is, normally at
least, truly to speak of a right–duty relationship.

Further analysis of rights and duties

The correlative terms 'right' and 'duty' may each be further analysed:[7]
rights may be distinguished into (a) claims, or what one may demand or
exact from another, such as payment of a debt; (b) liberties or privileges,
or what one may do free from legal restraint, such as to criticize a book;
(c) powers, what one may do in relation to another, such as to make a
will, or raise an action; and (d) immunities, what one may do with legal
impunity or freedom from legal retribution, such as in the exercise of the
judicial office to speak what might otherwise be slander.

Duties may be distinguished into (a) duties or burdens, what one must
do to or for another, such as to pay him a debt, or to refrain from
injuring him; (b) inabilities,[8] what one is legally unable to do or to
prevent, such as to make a man stop smoking; (c) liabilities, what one is
legally subjected to perform, such as to pay damages for wrong; and (d)
disabilities, what one cannot legally do, such as to sue a foreign diplomat,
or prevent, such as the use of legal diligence.

Each of the four kinds of rights is correlative to each of the four kinds
of duties, and further logical relationships between the eight terms have
been worked out. But in many cases the terms rights and duties are used
loosely where one or other of the variants would be more accurate, and
the variants are sometimes misused.

---

[7] See further Hohfeld, *Fundamental Legal Conceptions*, Ch. 1; Kocourek, *Jural Relations*,
Chs. 1–3; Salmond, *Jurisprudence*, Ch. 10; Stone, *Legal System and Lawyer's Reasonings*, Ch.
4.

[8] Hohfeld's 'no-right'.

Real and personal rights

Rights, including claims, liberties, powers, and immunities are distinguishable into real rights or rights *in rem*, available against persons generally, often for the protection or vindication of corporeal things or property, arising by virtue of legal dominion, and personal rights or rights *in personam*, available only against particular persons for the performance of some duty which the latter is bound to implement, arising by virtue of legal obligation.[9] Rights *in rem* are generally negative, being commonly rights not to be interfered with, whereas rights *in personam* are commonly positive.[10]

Rights are also distinguished as proprietary and personal, according as they are part of the person's assets, estate, or property, or attach to him as an individual. Hence a right of ownership of land is proprietary, but a right to his reputation, or to custody of his children, is personal.

General and specific duties

Duties similarly may be owed to persons generally, and these are usually negative, such as not to harm anyone else, or to a determinate person only, which are normally positive, such as to perform what one has contractually undertaken to do for that person.

Things

The thing in relation to which a right or duty exists, or the object of the right, may be of very many kinds and the rules of law have to define to what kinds of things particular rights relate. These things comprise, firstly, relationships of obligation giving rise to mutual rights and duties between persons, including both relationships created voluntarily, such as that of buyer and seller, and relationships occurring by chance, such as that of careless driver and injured pedestrian, and, secondly, relationships of rights in and to objects of property, comprising things owned or possessed. Objects of property take many forms and includes both material things, such as buildings and vehicles, and immaterial things having no physical existence, such as copyrights and shares in companies.

Conduct

Conduct includes all human behaviour relevant to the legal issue in question. Conduct may consist of positive acts, of inactivity or neglect or

---

[9] See further Stair I, 1, 22; Ersk. III, 1, 2. On the concept of property see Ch. 5.1, *infra*, and on obligation, see Ch. 4.1. On the terms right *in rem* and *in personam* see Salmond, *Jurisprudence*, 84.

[10] Rights *in rem* and *in personam*, if violated, do not necessarily give rise to actions *in rem* or *in personam* respectively, that is, to actions for recovery of property or against a determinate person respectively.

not-acting, or of omissions or failure to act when the person should have acted. In relation to each of these aspects of conduct the person's state of mind is frequently relevant, and the legal results may depend on whether a person's conduct was voluntary or involuntary, and in the former case whether intentional or deliberate, reckless, or merely careless or inadvertent.[11]

Events

Events are happenings not attributable to nor controlled by human powers or conduct, yet having legal significance. They include such happenings as the lapse of time, birth and death, a person's attaining an age, the occurrence of a storm, and the like. Some happenings, however, such as street accidents are attributable at least indirectly to the prior conduct of some person, and must be treated as the consequences of conduct rather than as pure events.

Other concepts

The examination of other concepts will be made in relation to the branches of the law in which those concepts are important; they include legal personality and persons, obligation, contract, delict, negligence, malice, property, ownership and possession, and so on.

[11] These distinctions are analysed in many books on Jurisprudence.

CHAPTER 1.4

CONSEQUENCES OF MEMBERSHIP OF THE EUROPEAN COMMUNITIES

Many legal consequences for private law follow from British membership of the European Communities. Directly applicable treaty provisions and secondary legislation (regulations and directives) supersede any inconsistent rule of national law.[1] The European Commission may take the U.K. before the European Court of Justice for not properly implementing Community law affecting private persons.[2]

The Court of Justice of the European Communities has jurisdiction to give preliminary rulings on the interpretation of the treaties establishing the Communities, the validity and interpretation of acts of Communities' institutions and the interpretation of the statutes of bodies established by an Act of the Council where those statutes so prescribe. A Scottish court may, and a Scottish court of final appeal must, refer a case for ruling where any of these questions is raised before it and it considers that a ruling is necessary before it can give judgment.[3] Judicial notice must be taken in Scottish courts of any decision of, or expression of opinion by, the Court on any question as to the meaning or effect of any of the treaties or community instruments.[4]

The E.E.C. is based on a customs union and the prohibitions between member states of customs duties and the elimination of quantitative restrictions on import and export. This implies the free movement of goods,[5] persons, services, and capital,[6] the right of nationals of one member state to establish undertakings, agencies, branches, or subsidiaries in another member state,[7] to provide services therein[8] and to move capital freely.[9] Objectives are the adoption of a common policy in agriculture and transport.

---

[1] *Marshall* v. *Southampton Health Authy* [1986] 2 All E.R. 584.
[2] e.g. *E.C. Commission* v. *U.K.*, [1984] 1 All E.R. 353.
[3] E.E.C. Treaty, Art. 177; *Bulmer* v. *Bollinger* [1974] 2 All E.R. 1226; *Geweise* v. *Mackenzie* 1984 S.L.T. 449; [1984] 2 All E.R. 129; see also *Prince* v. *Secretary of State for Scotland*, 1985 S.L.T. 74.
[4] European Communities Act, 1972, S. 3.
[5] E.E.C. Treaty, Arts. 9–37.
[6] Ibid., Arts. 48–51.
[7] Ibid., Arts. 52–8.
[8] Ibid., Arts. 59–66.
[9] Ibid., Arts. 67–73.

A basic principle of the E.E.C is the maintenance of competition[10] and the prohibition of restrictive trade agreements (cartels) and the abuse of a dominant position within the Common Market (monopolies).[11] There are exemptions for agreement for co-operation.

The Council has a duty to issue directives for the harmonization of legal provisions in member states which directly affect the establishment or functioning of the Common Market,[12] of taxation,[13] of provisions which are distorting the conditions of competition in the Common Market[14] and for the harmonization of member states' laws.[15]

Similar objectives are held by the E.C.S.C. and Euratom.

A claim for damages may lie in the event of the government's violation of Community law.[16]

The decisions of the European Court of Human Rights are not of binding legal effect in the United Kingdom, and the rights asserted by the European Convention on Human Rights are not enforceable as part of Scottish municipal law.[17]

[10] Ibid., Arts. 85–94.
[11] Ibid., Arts. 85–6; *Cutsforth* v. *Mansfield Inns Ltd* [1986] 1 All E.R. 577.
[12] Ibid., Art. 100.
[13] Ibid., Art. 99.
[14] Ibid., Art. 101.
[15] Ibid., Art. 235.
[16] *Bourgoin S.A.* v. *Ministry of Agriculture* [1985] 3 All E.R. 585.
[17] *Kaur* v. *Lord Advocate*, 1980 S.C. 319; *Moore* v. *Secretary of State for Scotland*, 1985 S.L.T. 38.

THE CIVIL COURTS AND THEIR JURISDICTION

European Court

In respect of the topics of European Community Law which have direct internal effect on persons and organizations in Scotland the Court of Justice of the European Communities is supreme. Where questions concerning the interpretation of the Community treaties or the validity of interpretation of measures taken by Community institutions are raised before a national court or tribunal, it may, if it considers that a decision on the question is necessary in order to enable it to give judgment, request the European Court to give a preliminary ruling on the question[1] and if the national court or tribunal is one from whose decisions there is no appeal under national law it is bound to make such a reference.[2]

House of Lords

In other respects the supreme civil court of Scotland is the House of Lords, composed, in modern practice, of at least three of the Lord High Chancellor of Great Britain, the eleven Lords of Appeal in Ordinary, and such other peers of Parliament as hold or have held high judicial office.[3] None of these need be Law Lords who have been appointed from the Scottish Bench or Bar though two usually are. Though formerly sittings for judicial business did not differ from sittings for legislative business, non-legal members of the House have long been excluded, and the House now appoints an Appellate Committee consisting of the statutorily qualified persons to hear appeals and report to the House. It may sit as two committees and when the House is not sitting.

It is not certain whether the House functions as a United Kingdom court[4] or as a Scottish, English, or Northern Irish court depending on the

---

[1] For procedure see A.S. (R.C. Amdt. No. 5) 1972 (S.I. No. 1981, 1972) and R.C. 296 A–E. As to registration of order of the European Court see A.S. (R.C. Amdt. No. 6) 1972 (S.I. No. 1982, 1972) and R.C. 296 G. See also *Van Duyn* v. *Home Office* [1974] 3 All E.R. 178; [1975] 3 All E.R. 190; *R.* v. *Henn* [1980] 2 All E.R. 166.

[2] E.C.S.C. Treaty, 1951, Art. 41; Treaty of Rome, 1957, Art. 177; *Bulmer* v. *Bollinger* [1974] 2 All E.R. 1226.

[3] Appellate Jurisdiction Acts, 1876–1947; Administration of Justice Act, 1968.

[4] See *Virtue* v. *Alloa Police Commrs.* (1874) 1 R. 285, 296.

jurisdiction from which the appeal comes,[5] but it has judicial knowledge of the laws of all these systems so that in an appeal from one jurisdiction questions as to the law of another part of the United Kingdom are questions of law before it and not, as in lower courts, questions of fact.[6]

The House exercises appellate jurisdiction only, in respect of any kind of civil case litigated in the Scottish courts, unless such appeal has been excluded by statute,[7] against final judgments of the Inner House of the Court of Session, and against interlocutory judgments of the Inner House if the Division is not unanimous, or it grants leave to appeal.[8] Where leave is necessary, it is sought by petition to the Inner House.[9]

No appeal is competent directly from the decision of a Lord Ordinary,[10] nor against the verdict of a civil jury,[11] but appeal is competent against an interlocutor allowing or refusing a motion for a new jury trial,[12] against interlocutors allowing or refusing bills of exceptions,[11] interlocutors applying a jury verdict,[13] and interlocutors setting aside a jury verdict and entering judgment for the unsuccessful party.[13]

Service of an order by the House of Lords on a petition for appeal stops all further procedure in the Court of Session even where that Court had refused leave to appeal.[14]

Where evidence has been heard in an inferior court, the findings in fact and the law held applicable thereto must be distinguished,[15] and appeal lies on matters of law only.[16] A remit back may be made to make findings on matters of fact not covered already.[17]

The House is very unwilling to disturb inferences drawn from facts by the inferior courts,[18] and will very rarely differ from the view of the judge

---

[5] See *Concha* v. *Murietta* (1889) 40 Ch. D. 543.

[6] *Cooper* v. *C.* (1888) 15 R. (H.L.) 21; *Elliot* v. *Joicey*, 1935 S.C. (H.L.) 57.

[7] e.g. Lands Valuation Appeal Court (Valuation of Lands (Sc.) Amdt. Act, 1867, S. 8). No appeal lies from the High Court of Justiciary (*Mackintosh* v. *H.M. Adv.* (1876) 3 R. (H.L.) 34; Criminal Procedure Act, 1975, S. 281.

[8] Court of Session Act, 1808, S. 15; *Girvan* v. *Leng*, 1919, 2 S.L.T. 29; consent of parties will not evade this rule: *Beattie* v. *Glasgow Corpn.*, 1917 S.C. (H.L.) 22. But see *Orr Ewing's Trs.* v. *Orr Ewing* (1885) 13 R. (H.L.) 1.

[9] cf. *Stewart* v. *Kennedy* (1889) 16 R. 521; *Edinburgh Northern Tramways* v. *Mann* (1891) 18 R. 1140, 1152; *Assets Co.*, v. *Shirres' Trs.* (1897) 24 R. 418; *D. Portland* v. *Wood's Trs.*, 1926 S.C. 640, 653; *Fraser* v. *McNeill*, 1948 S.C. 517, 525.

[10] Court of Session Act, 1808, S. 15.

[11] Jury Trials (Sc.) Act, 1815, Ss. 7 and 9; *Park* v. *Wilsons & Clyde Coal Co.*, 1929 S.C. 679.

[12] Jury Trials (Sc.) Act. 1815; S. 6; Administration of Justice (Sc.) Act, 1972, S. 2.

[13] Jury Trials (Sc.) Act, 1910, S. 2; *Lyal* v. *Henderson*, 1916 S.C. (H.L.) 167. The House may itself exercise this power: 1972 Act, S. 2 (2).

[14] *Edinburgh Northern Tramways*, *supra*.

[15] See *Shepherd* v. *Henderson* (1881) 9 R. (H.L.) 1; *Fleming* v. *Hislop* (1886) 13 R. (H.L.) 43.

[16] Court of Session Act, 1825, S. 40. See also *Strathlorne S.S. Co.* v. *Baird*, 1916 S.C. (H.L.) 134.

[17] *Mackay* v. *Dick & Stevenson* (1881) 8 R. (H.L.) 37; *Gilroy, Sons & Co.* v. *Price* (1892) 20 R. (H.L.) 1; see also *Caird* v. *Sime* (1887) 14 R. (H.L.) 37.

[18] *McIntyre* v. *McGavin* (1893) 20 R. (H.L.) 49; *Rixon* v. *Edinburgh Northern Tramways* (1893) 20 R. (H.L.) 53; *Windram* v. *Robertson* (1906) 8 F. (H.L.) 40.

of first instance on the credibility of the witnesses.[19] The House will not decide hypothetical cases, as where parties agreed not to found on a clause in their contract.[20]

Appeal is taken by petition to the House praying that certain interlocutors of the Court of Session by reviewed and revised, varied, or altered. The effect of an appeal is to open to review all interlocutors in the cause, except any repelling preliminary defences which have been acquiesced in.[21]

After judgment is pronounced in the appeal, it is usually necessary, unless the House merely affirms the judgment and dismisses the appeal,[22] to present a petition to the Court of Session to apply the judgment of the House of Lords.[23] At this stage the function of the Court of Session is purely ministerial.[24]

Court of Session

The superior civil court of Scotland is the Court of Session, which sits permanently in Edinburgh.[25] It is a unitary collegiate court composed now of twenty-four[26] judges, who are styled Senators of the College of Justice or Lords of Council and Session. Formerly the whole Court or at least most of the judges sat together, one or two judges in turn taking preliminary stages of cases in the Outer House. Since 1808[27] and, as further reorganized in 1825,[28] however, it sits as an Inner House of eight judges, mainly exercising appellate jurisdiction, and an Outer House of

[19] *Montgomerie* v. *Wallace-James* (1903) 6 F. (H.L.) 10, 11; *Kilpatrick* v. *Dunlop*, H.L., 1911, noted at 1916 S.C. 631, note; *Strathlorne S.S. Co.* v. *Baird*, 1916 S.C. (H.L.) 134, 135; *Clarke* v. *Edinburgh & District Tramways Co.*, 1919 S.C. (H.L.) 35, 36; *S.S Hontestroom* v. *S.S. Sagaporack* [1927] A.C. 37; *Thomas* v. *Thomas*, 1947 S.C (H.L.) 45. cf. *Dunn* v. *D's Trs.*, 1930 S.C. 131, 144.
[20] *Glasgow Navigation Co.* v. *Iron Ore Co.*, 1910 S.C. (H.L.) 63.
[21] *Alexander* v. *Officers of State* (1868) 6 M. (H.L.) 54.
[22] *Peters* v. *Greenock Mags.* (1893) 20 R. 924; *Reid's Trs.* v. *Dawson*, 1915 S.C. 844.
[23] *Gill* v. *Anderson* (1859) 21 D. 723; *Anstruther* v. *A's Trs.* (1873) 11 M. 955; *Walker* v. *Whitwell*, 1916 S.C. 757.
[24] *Free Church* v. *Lord Overtoun* (1904) 7 F. 202; cf. *Roger* v. *Cochrane*, 1910 S.C. 1. Contrast *Sawers' Exors.* v. *Sawers' Trs.* (1873) 11 M. 451.
[25] See generally Hannay, *College of Justice*; (Stair Society) *Introduction to Scottish Legal History*, Chs. 23–4; Stair IV, 1, 1–69; More's Notes, ccclxvi; Mack. I, 2–4; Bankt. IV, 7, 1–31; Ersk. I, 3, 10–23.
[26] Originally (1532) and for long it was 15; the number was reduced to 13 in 1830 but was restored to 15 in 1948 (Administration of Justice (Sc.) Act, 1948, S. 1(1)) and raised to 19 (Restrictive Trade Practices Act, 1956, S. 32; Criminal Justice (Sc.) Act, 1963, S. 49; Resale Prices Act, 1964, S. 9(2), and Administration of Justice Act, 1968, S. 1) with power by Order in Council further to increase the number. Orders were made in 1973, 1977, and 1986 raising the maximum number to 24. Under the Law Commissions Act, 1965, S. 2, a judge of the Court of Session has been seconded to act as Chairman of the Scottish Law Commission and while so employed does not sit as a judge.
[27] Court of Session Act, 1808, Ss. 4, 6.
[28] Court of Session Act, 1825, S. 1.

sixteen judges,[29] exercising jurisdiction at first instance only. The Inner House is divided into the First Division, composed of the Lord President of the Court of Session and, normally, three Lords of Session, and the Second Division, composed of the Lord Justice-Clerk and, normally, three Lords of Session. The quorum of each Division is, for most purposes, three. An Extra Division may be established from time to time, composed of any three Lords of Session, the senior presiding, to deal with pressure of appellate business.[30] The Divisions have equal status and authority and there is no fixed allocation of work between them. A larger court of five, seven, or more judges may be convened to dispose of particularly important or difficult points,[31] and the decisions of such sittings enjoy greater weight than those of either Division. The decision of a case heard by a Division or larger court is according to the views of the majority in the Division. The Outer House judges sit singly, alone or, in cases prescribed by statute, with a jury of twelve. A Lord Ordinary may report a case to a Division for guidance on disposal[32] and either Division may consult the other Division.[33] Any Inner House judge may sit as a Lord Ordinary, and a Lord Ordinary may sit to make a quorum in a Division. Parties may not now choose their Lord Ordinary or Division.[34]

The Lord President also holds the office of Lord Justice-General of Scotland, and he, the Lord Justice-Clerk, and the other Lords of Session are also the Lords Commissioners of Justiciary who exercise supreme criminal jurisdiction, both appellate and at first instance, in the High Court of Justiciary, and, on appeal from courts-martial, in the Courts-Martial Appeal Court.

Court of Session jurisdiction[35]

In point of area, the Court of Session has jurisdiction over the whole kingdom of Scotland and its territorial waters, and all persons and property therein, and in point of subject-matter, over all kinds of causes connected with Scotland save those expressly excluded from its jurisdic-

---

[29] As at mid-1987 one judge was seconded to the Scottish Law Commission. On re-employment of retired judges see Law Reform (M.P.) (Sc.) Act. 1985, S. 22.

[30] Administration of Justice (Sc.) Act, 1933, S. 2.

[31] See e.g. *Houston* v. *Buchanan*, 1937 S.C. 460 (5 judges) (affd. 1940 S.C. (H.L.) 17); *McElroy* v. *McAllister*, 1949 S.C. 110 (7 judges); *Bell* v. *Bell*, 1940 S.C. 229 (whole court—13 judges) (revd. 1941 S.C. (H.L.) 5). See also *Haldane's Trs.* v. *Murphy* (1881) 9 R. 269.

[32] e.g. *Goold* v. *G.*, 1927 S.C. 177; *Macomish's Exors* v. *Jones*, 1932 S.C. 108; *Kerr* v. *Brown*, 1965 S.C. 144. In such a case the Lord Ordinary does not sit with the Division: *F.* v. *F.*, 1945 S.C. 202; *Borland* v. *B.*, 1947 S.C. 432.

[33] e.g. *Bridges* v. *B.*, 1911 S.C. 250; *Connell* v. *C.*, 1950 S.C. 505.

[34] Administration of Justice (Sc.) Act, 1933, S. 5.

[35] See generally Mackay, *Court of Session Practice* (1877); *Manual of Practice* (1894); MacLaren, *Court of Session Practice* (1917); Thomson and Middleton, *Manual of Court of Session Procedure*; Maxwell, *Court of Session Practice* (1980).

tion. The court must in every case be satisfied that it has jurisdiction before granting decree.[36]

It has exclusive jurisdiction in many actions relating to personal status, including declarator of marriage, of nullity of marriage, of legitimacy, of bastardy, and generally actions the main object of which is to determine the personal status of individuals, actions declarator of putting to silence, certain actions of adjudication, actions of reduction, actions of proving the tenor of a lost document, and in actions against foreigners when they are not subject to the jurisdiction of the sheriff court,[37] and in petitions for the winding up of a company with a paid-up capital exceeding £120,000.

It has concurrent jurisdiction with the sheriff courts in respect of all causes exceeding £500 in value, exclusive of interest and expenses,[38] possessory actions, actions of affiliation and aliment, actions of divorce, separation *a mensa et thoro*, and actions of aliment between husband and wife,[39] actions for custody of children,[40] and petitions for the winding up of a company with a paid-up capital of less than £120,000, and generally all actions not reserved exclusively to one court or the other. The Court of Session may remit any action within concurrent jurisdiction to the appropriate sheriff.[41]

The Court of Session's jurisdiction is excluded in respect of all causes not exceeding £250 in value exclusive of interest and expenses.[42]

The Court's jurisdiction is not excluded by implication.[43]

The court probably has jurisdiction to determine the validity of its own Acts of Sederunt.[44]

By various statutes, various kinds of statutory proceedings cannot be originated in the Court of Session, though may sometimes be appealed thereto. These include certain proceedings under the Heritable Securities (Scotland) Act, 1894, certain applications under the Entail Acts, removings and summary removings of tenants.

Original jurisdiction

In some cases, such as special cases, and petitions relative to companies, procedure must be initiated in the Inner House,[45] but the majority of

---

[36] *Walls' Trs.* v. *Drynan* (1888) 15 R. 359, 363.
[37] *Pagan & Osborne* v. *Haig*, 1910 S.C. 341.
[38] Sheriff Courts (Sc.) Act, 1907, S. 7, amd. Sheriff Courts (Sc.) Act, 1971, S. 31.
[39] Sheriff Courts (Sc.) Act, 1907, S. 5, amd. Divorce Jurisdiction, etc. (Sc.) Act, 1983, S. 1.
[40] *Murray* v. *Forsyth*, 1917 S.C. 721.
[41] Law Reform (M.P.) (Sc.) Act, 1985, S. 14.
[42] Sheriff Courts (Sc.) Act, 1907, S. 7, amd. Sheriff Courts (Sc.) Act, 1971, S. 31.
[43] *Pagan & Osborne* v. *Haig*, 1910 S.C. 341. cf. *Brodie* v. *Ker*, 1952 S.C. 216, 224; *Scotmotors* v. *Dundee Petrosea*, 1980 S.C. 351.
[44] *Carron Co.* v. *Hislop*, 1930 S.C. 1050.
[45] Administration of Justice (Sc.) Act, 1933, S. 6(3).

cases, including all ordinary actions and petitions, are initiated in the Outer House and heard first by a Lord Ordinary alone, or in cases statutorily enumerated,[46] by a Lord Ordinary sitting with a jury of twelve. Where a preliminary defence, such as to the jurisdiction, requires inquiry, this may be taken in a preliminary proof before going into the merits. A judgment of a Lord Ordinary, if not reclaimed, is a judgment of the Court of Session as much as a judgment of a Division or the whole Court.[47] Certain kinds of business are assigned by statute to particular Lords Ordinary. The Court may in any cause on the joint request of the parties summon to its assistance at any hearing a specially qualified assessor.[48]

Parties may on petition have their cause disposed of by a chosen Lord Ordinary by summary trial under such procedure as the parties may agree, from which no appeal lies.[49]

Appellate jurisdiction—reclaiming motion

The Inner House may hear appeals, brought by way of reclaiming motion, from an interlocutor issued by a Lord Ordinary sitting in the Outer House[50] which disposes of the whole, or any part of the merits, of a cause. Reclaiming opens to review all prior interlocutors pronounced by the Lord Ordinary. The appeal is heard by either Division of the Inner House or an Extra Division, and may be reheard before five or seven judges,[51] or the whole court.[52] Evidence is not reheard but in certain cases further evidence may be heard by one of the judges of the Division.[53] The judges of a Division may consult the other Division before giving a judgment.[54] The Divisions are reluctant to differ on a question of fact from the judge who saw and heard the witnesses.[55]

Appellate jurisdiction—motion for new trial

In cases tried by a Lord Ordinary and a jury a motion may be made to the Inner House for the allowance of a new trial on specified grounds.[56]

---

[46] Court of Session Acts, 1825, S. 28 and 1850, S. 49; Evidence (Sc.) Act, 1866, S. 4; *Taylor v. Dumbarton Tramways Co.*, 1918 S.C. (H.L.) 96; *Robertson v. Bannigan*, 1965 S.C. 20.

[47] *Purves v. Carswell* (1905) 8 F. 351, 354; *Macomish's Exrs. v. Jones*, 1932 S.C. 108.

[48] Administration of Justice (Sc.) Act, 1933, S. 13; see also Nautical Assessors (Sc.) Act, 1894; and *Rowan v. West Camak*, 1923 S.C. 316.

[49] Administration of Justice (Sc.) Act, 1933, S. 10. See also *Munro's Trs. v. M.*, 1971 S.C. 280.

[50] Court of Session Act, 1868, Ss. 59–60.

[51] Court of Session Act, 1825, S. 23.

[52] Ibid., S. 24; 1868, S. 60.

[53] Court of Session Act, 1868, Ss. 62, 72; *Pirie v. Leask*, 1964 S.C. 103.

[54] *Connell v. C.*, 1950 S.C. 505.

[55] *Dunn v. D's Trs.*, 1930 S.C. 131, 144; *Ross v. R.*, 1930 S.C. (H.L.) 1; *Jordan v. Court Line*, 1947 S.C. 29; cf. *Thomas v. T.*, 1947 S.C. (H.L.) 45, 54; *Morrison v. Kelly*, 1970 S.L.T. 198; but see *Islip Pedigree Breeding Centre v. Abercromby*, 1959 S.L.T. 161.

[56] Jury Trials (Sc.) Act, 1815, S. 6; *Maltman v. Tarmac, Ltd.*, 1967 S.C. 177.

When hearing the motion the Lord Ordinary who presided at the trial formerly sat with the Division.[57] Such a motion may be reheard by seven judges.[58] The Division may refuse the motion and apply the jury's verdict,[59] or allow a new trial,[60] or enter judgment for the party unsuccessful at the trial.[61] A third trial may similarly be granted.[62]

Appellate jurisdiction—appeals from Sheriff Court

An appeal lies to the Inner House from the decision of a sheriff-principal or sheriff exercising the jurisdiction of the sheriff court,[63] unless statute has excluded appeal or provided a special mode of appeal.[64]

Appeal is competent against final judgments, or interlocutors granting interim decree, sisting an action, refusing a reponing note, or for which leave has been granted.[65] No appeal is competent where the value of the cause does not exceed £250,[66] or the cause is being tried as a summary cause,[67] unless the sheriff-principal after final judgment on appeal certifies the case as suitable for appeal to the Court of Session.[68] There is always right of appeal where the value of the cause is indefinite. An appeal submits to review the whole of the interlocutors pronounced in the cause, but does not prevent immediate execution of certain warrants, nor effect the recall of an interim interdict.[69]

The interlocutor of the sheriff applying the verdict in a case tried by jury in the sheriff court may be appealed, if notes of the evidence have been taken, on specified grounds.[70]

Cases brought in the sheriff court may also, in particular circumstances, be removed to the Court of Session for jury trial,[71] or for further procedure, or be remitted by the sheriff.[72]

---

[57] Court of Session Act, 1868, Ss. 58, 61; *Bicket* v. *Wood* (1893) 20 R. 874; but see *Park* v. *Wilsons & Clyde Coal Co.*, 1928 S.C. 121.

[58] *Park, supra.*

[59] *Kirkland* v. *B.R. Board*, 1978 S.C. 71.

[60] e.g. *Leadbetter* v. *N.C.B.*, 1952 S.C. 19.

[61] Jury Trials (Sc.) Act, 1910, S. 2; e.g. *Mills* v. *Kelvin & White*, 1913 S.C. 521; *West* v. *Mackenzie*, 1917 S.C. 513; *Moyes* v. *Burntisland Shipbuilding Co.*, 1952 S.C. 429.

[62] e.g. *Flood* v. *Caledonian Ry.* (1889) 27 S.L.R. 127; *Watson* v. *N.B. Ry. Co.* (1904) 7 F. 220; *Mitchell* v. *Caledonian Ry.*, 1910 S.C. 546; *McCallum* v. *Paterson*, 1968 S.C. 280; 1969 S.C. 85. The Court is reluctant to allow a third trial: see *McQuilkin* v. *Glasgow District Subway Co.* (1902) 4 F. 462; *Grant* v. *Baird* (1903) 5 F. 459; *McKnight* v. *General Motor Carrying Co.*, 1936 S.C. 17.

[63] Sheriff Courts (Sc.) Act, 1907, S. 28.

[64] *Lanark C.C.* v. *Airdrie Mags.* (1906) 8 F. 802.

[65] 1907 Act, S. 28.

[66] Sheriff Courts (Sc.) Act, 1971, S. 31.

[67] 1971 Act, S. 35.

[68] 1971 Act, S. 38.

[69] Sheriff Courts (Sc.) Act, 1907, S. 29.

[70] Sheriff Courts (Sc.) Act, 1907, S. 31.

[71] 1907 Act, S. 30.

[72] 1907 Act, S. 5 and proviso, as amended 1913.

Other appeals

The Inner House also has jurisdiction in appeals from the Court of Lord Lyon King of Arms,[73] the Restrictive Practices Court,[74] the Sheriff of Chancery, and under numerous statutes which sometimes provide for the form of appeal. The general right to appeal can be taken away only by express words.[75]

It has also a general power, by way of actions for reduction or suspension or petition for judicial review, to review the proceedings and decisions of all inferior courts, tribunals, and persons or bodies entrusted with judicial or administrative powers, on complaint that there has been an excess of jurisdiction, a failure to act, or a defect in procedure so serious as to be a denial of natural justice and to render the decision a nullity.[76]

Nobile officium

The Court of Session has an extraordinary equitable power, the *nobile officium*,[77] which is inherent in it as a supreme court by virtue of which it regulates charitable trusts and settles schemes of administration where the original purposes have failed, makes interim appointments to public offices, grants special powers to trustees, gives directions to trustees, grants remedies for exceptional circumstances in bankruptcy proceedings, and permits rectification of mistakes and *casus omissi* in statutory procedure.

Statute has conferred on the sheriff court also jurisdiction to dispose of certain matters originally falling under the *nobile officium*, sometimes concurrently with, and sometimes to the exclusion of the Court of Session, in such cases as determination of custody and access to children, the appointment of curators, factors, and trustees, grant of their powers, and their removal, and recall of arrestments and inhibitions.

---

[73] See e.g. *Stewart Mackenzie* v. *Fraser Mackenzie*, 1920 S.C. 764; 1922 S.C. (H.L.) 39.
[74] Restrictive Practices Court Act, 1976, S. 10.
[75] *Marr* v. *Lindsay* (1881) 8 R. 784; *Kerr* v. *Hood*, 1907 S.C. 895.
[76] *L.A.* v. *Perth Police Commrs.* (1869) 8 M. 244; *Ashley* v. *Rothesay Mags.* (1873) 11 M. 708; (1874) 1 R. (H.L.) 14; *Dalgleish* v. *Leitch* (1889) 2 White 302; *Moss's Empires* v. *Assessor for Glasgow*, 1917 S.C. 1, 6 per Lord Kinnear; *Brown* v. *Hamilton D.C.*, 1983 S.C. (H.L.) 1; Tribunals and Inquiries Act, 1971, S. 14(2).
[77] Stair IV, 3, 1–2; More's Notes, ccclxxiv; Bankt. IV, 7, 23–8; Ersk. I, 3, 22; Mackay, *Practice*, 1209; *Manual*, 82, 530; Maclaren, *Practice*, 100, 828; see e.g. *Cockburn's Trs.*, 1941 S.C. 187; *Lipton's Trs.*, 1943 S.C. 521; *Sandeman's Trs.*, 1947 S.C. 304; *Dow's Trs.*, 1947 S.C. 524; *Fletcher's Trs.*, 1949 S.C. 330; *Registrar General*, 1949 S.L.T. 385; *Fraser*, 1950 S.L.T. (Notes) 34; *Smart* v. *Registrar General*, 1954 S.C. 81; *Mackay*, 1955 S.C. 361; *Bell's Exor.*, 1960 S.L.T. (Notes) 3; *Kippen's Tr.*, 1966 S.L.T. (Notes) 2; *Fraser*, 1967 S.L.T. 178; *Fife Motor Auctions* v. *Perth Dist. Licensing Bd.*, 1981, S.L.T. 106. The High Court of Justiciary has a similar though more limited power; see *Wylie* v. *H.M. Advocate*, 1966 S.L.T. 149; *Wan Ping Nam* v. *Federal German Republic*, 1972 S.L.T. 220; *Kemp*, 1982 J.C. 29. As to the Court of Teinds see *Cumbernauld* v. *Dumbartonshire*, 1920 S.C. 625.

Inherited jurisdiction

The Court of Session now incorporates, and has assumed the jurisdiction of, the former independent High Court of Admiralty (1681–1830),[78] the Court of Exchequer (1707–1856),[79] and the Jury Court (1815–1830).[80] The inferior Commissary courts (1563) were merged in the sheriff courts in 1876[81] and in 1830 the jurisdiction of the Commissary court of Edinburgh in consistorial matters was transferred to the Court of Session,[82] while it was abolished in 1836.[83] The Bill Chamber was formerly a distinct court within the Court of Session in the hands of the junior Lord Ordinary with responsibilities particularly with regard to diligence, summary remedies, and bankruptcy. It was merged in the Outer House in 1933.[84]

Vacation courts

During vacation the judges, other than the Lord President and Lord Justice-Clerk, act in rotation as vacation judges. The vacation judge can deal with all incidental motions and applications,[85] but is not bound to do so if the matter can more conveniently be postponed till the Court resumes.

Special jurisdictions

Judges of the Court of Session also exercise certain special jurisdictions.

The Lands Valuation Appeal Court consists of three judges of the Court of Session and hears appeals by stated case from local Valuation Appeal Committees on the value set on heritable property for local rating purposes.[86] The Court is a supreme court in its own sphere and its proceedings cannot be set aside by the Court of Session.[87] No appeal lies from this court.

The Court of Teinds consists of the Inner House judges and the second junior Lord Ordinary, five being a quorum,[88] and is not a separate court

---

[78] Court of Session (Sc.) Act, 1830, S. 21. The Sheriff Court also has a limited Admiralty jurisdiction. Between 1681 and 1830 the High Court of Admiralty had exclusive jurisdiction in maritime causes: *Sheaf S.S. Co.* v. *Compania Transmediterranea*, 1930 S.C. 660, 664. For modern Admiralty jurisdiction see Administration of Justice Act, 1956, Ss. 45–50.
[79] Exchequer Court (Sc.) Act, 1856, S. 1; see *Inland Revenue* v. *Barrs*, 1959 S.C. 273; affd. 1961 S.C. (H.L.) 22.
[80] Court of Session (Sc.) Act, 1830, S. 1.
[81] Sheriff Courts (Sc.) Act, 1876, Ss. 35–9.
[82] Court of Session (Sc.) Act, 1830, Ss. 31–3.
[83] Commissary Court of Edinburgh Act, 1836.
[84] Administration of Justice (Sc.) Act, 1933, S. 3.
[85] *Barton* v. *L.M.S. Ry.*, 1932 S.C. 113.
[86] Valuation of Lands (Sc.) Amdt. Act, 1867, S. 8.
[87] *Stirling* v. *Holm* (1873) 11 M. 480.
[88] Court of Session Act, 1839, S. 8; Court of Session Act, 1868, S. 9.

but a function of the Court of Session.[89] The jurisdiction relates to creation and disjunction of parishes, valuation of teinds, augmentation, modification, and locality of stipend, but the law and practice have been greatly modified by the Church of Scotland Act, 1921, and the Church of Scotland (Property and Endowments) Act, 1925. An appeal lies to the House of Lords.[90]

The Election Petition Court consists of two judges and hears petitions challenging the validity of the election of persons as members of Parliament.[91] No further appeal lies.

The Registration Appeal Court, of three judges, deals with appeals from the decision of a registration officer taken to the sheriff and brought before the Court by stated case.[92]

A judge of the Court of Session may be appointed to act as an arbiter or oversman.[93]

The sheriff court

The inferior Scottish civil court, the sheriff court,[94] has jurisdiction in point of area only over its own sheriffdom,[95] and, in point of subject-matter, over all causes save those reserved to the Court of Session or to special courts or tribunals. Neither party can require a case initiated before the sheriff court to be remitted to the Court of Session, save that actions involving questions of heritable right or title where the value of the subject exceeds £50 per annum or £1,000, succession to moveables exceeding £1,000, division of commonty or division or division and sale of common property, where the value in issue exceeds £50 per annum or £1,000, may, within six days of the closing of the record, be required to be remitted,[96] that the sheriff may remit certain actions to the Court of Session,[97] and that certain claims of damages may be required to be remitted for jury trial.[98]

There are excluded from the jurisdiction of the sheriff court consistorial causes other than divorce,[99] but actions relating only incidentally to

---

[89] *Presbytery of Stirling* v. *Heritors of Larbert* (1900) 2 F. 562.

[90] *Presbytery of Stirling, supra*; cf. *Galloway* v. *Earl of Minto*, 1922 S.C. (H.L.) 24.

[91] Parliamentary Elections Act, 1868; Representation of the People Act, 1949, Ss. 107–11; *Grieve* v. *Douglas-Home*, 1965 S.C. 315.

[92] Representation of the People Act, 1949, S. 45(8); *Dumfries Electoral Registration Officer* v. *Brydon*, 1964 S.C. 242; *Edinburgh Electoral Registration Officer* v. *Robertson*, 1946 S.C. 448.

[93] Law Reform (M.P.) (Sc.) Act, 1980, S. 17.

[94] See generally (Stair Society) *Introduction to Scottish Legal History*, Chs. 25–6; Bankt. IV, 14, 1–26; Ersk; I, 4, 1–6; Sheriff Courts (Sc.) Acts, 1907–71.

[95] Sheriff Courts (Sc.) Acts, 1907, S. 4.

[96] 1907 Act, S. 5; *Anderson* v. *McGown*, 1911 S.C. 441.

[97] 1907 Act, S. 5; Sheriff Courts (Sc.) Act, 1971, S. 37; *Butler* v. *Thom*, 1982 S.L.T. (Sh. Ct.) 57.

[98] 1907 Act, S. 30; *Brown* v. *Glenboig Union Fireclay Co.*, 1911 S.C. 179. The Court of Session may remit such a case back to the sheriff court: *Houston* v. *McIndoe*, 1934 S.C. 362; *Armstrong* v. *Paterson*, 1935 S.C. 464.

[99] Divorce Jurisdiction, etc. (Sc.) Act, 1983, S. 1.

status are not excluded.[1] Actions of reduction are also excluded from the jurisdiction,[2] though objections to deeds and writings may be maintained *ope exceptionis* in the sheriff court, and actions of proving of the tenor.[3] Also excluded are exchequer causes, and ecclesiastical causes.

The sheriff court has concurrent jurisdiction[4] with the Court of Session in actions of declarator (except as to status),[5] of divorce,[99] separation, and aliment, aliment between husband and wife, and actions to regulate the custody of children, actions of division of commonty and of division or division and sale of common property, actions relating to questions of heritable right or title[6] (except adjudication and reduction) including declarators of irritancy and removing, and suspension of charges or threatened charges on decrees of the sheriff court or decrees of registration on deeds registered, where the debt does not exceed £50. It has concurrent jurisdiction also in all actions for payment of debt or damages.

It has exclusive jurisdiction in all actions competent in the court where the value of the cause does not exceed £250.[7]

The more important cases in the sheriff court are classed as ordinary actions, proceeding on written pleadings, oral argument, and, where necessary, evidence of disputed facts. Jury trial is not now competent.[8] A 'summary cause' procedure applies to actions for payment of money not exceeding £1,000, or which parties consent shall be tried summarily; pleadings are dispensed with and the evidence is not recorded.[9] A sheriff has a discretion to determine whether an action shall proceed as an ordinary or a summary cause, no matter in which form it was initiated.[10] Some summary causes are prescribed to be dealt with as 'small claims'.[11]

Appeal to sheriff-principal

A ordinary cause heard by a sheriff may be appealed to the sheriff-principal, without leave in the case of final judgments and certain other specified interlocutors,[12] and, in the case of any other interlocutor, if the sheriff grants leave to appeal.[13] Alternatively to appeal to the sheriff-principal, or thereafter, appeal may be taken to the Court of Session.[14]

---

[1] *Wright* v. *Sharp* (1880) 7 R. 460; *McDonald* v. *Mackenzie* (1891) 18 R. 502; *Turnbull* v. *Wilsons & Clyde Coal Co.*, 1935 S.C. 580; cf. *Lamont* v. *L.*, 1939 S.C. 484.

[2] *Donald* v. *D.*, 1913 S.C. 274.

[3] *Dunbar* v. *Scottish County Investment Co.*, 1920 S.C. 210.

[4] Sheriff Courts (Sc.) Act, 1907, S. 5.

[5] A question of mental capacity is not a matter of status: *Mears* v. *M.*, 1969 S.L.T. (Sh. Ct.) 21.

[6] See *Pitman* v. *Burnett's Trs.*, (1882) 9 R. 444; *Anderson* v. *McGown*, 1911 S.C. 441.

[7] Ibid., S. 7, amd. Sheriff Courts (Sc.) Act, 1971, Ss. 31 and 41; *Dickson & Walker* v. *Mitchell*, 1910 S.C. 139.

[8] 1907 Act, S. 31, amd. 1971 Act, S. 40; Law Reform (Misc. Prov.) (Sc.) Act, 1980, S. 11.

[9] Sheriff Courts (Sc.) Act, 1971, Ss. 35–6; S.I. No. 842, 1981.

[10] *Purves* v. *Graham*, 1924 S.C. 477; 1971 Act, S. 37.

[11] Law Reform (M.P.) (Sc.) Act, 1985, S. 18.

[12] 1907 Act, S. 27 (a)–(e), amended 1913.

[13] Ibid., S. 27 (f).

[14] 1907 Act, S. 28; 1971 Act, S. 38.

In summary causes appeal against final judgment lies to the sheriff-principal by way of stated case on a point of law only, with further appeal to the Court of Session on a point of law if the sheriff-principal certifies the cause as suitable for such appeal.[15] Interlocutory judgments may be appealed in the same way as in ordinary causes.

Under various statutes appeal may be taken to the sheriff or sheriff-principal.[16]

Appeal to Court of Session

In causes not exceeding £250 in value no appeal lies unless the case has first been appealed to the sheriff-principal, and he, after final judgment, certifies the cause as suitable for appeal to the Court of Session.[17]

Appeal is competent in other causes in the case of final judgments, certain specified interlocutors, and any interlocutor against which sheriff-principal or sheriff grants leave to appeal.[18] There is no common law right of appeal to the Court of Session where the sheriff has been acting in an administrative capacity.[19]

The Lyon Court

The Lord Lyon King of Arms is the Queen's principal officer of arms in Scotland. He has extensive ministerial duties, particularly the granting of armorial bearings to persons and corporations, the execution of Royal Proclamations, and the conduct of state ceremonials and solemnities, and appointing and controlling messengers-at-arms. The Court of the Lord Lyon consists of Lyon, three heralds, and three pursuivants, but Lyon now always sits alone.[20] Apart from an indefinite common law jurisdiction the court has a statutory jurisdiction to determine entitlement to bear particular arms,[21] but not to determine questions of the chiefship of a clan, or the chieftainship of a branch of a clan.[21] He has no jurisdiction to decide a claim of precedence.[22] Lyon may order the removal of unlawful arms and impose fines.[23] Appeal lies to the Court of Session and to the House of Lords.[24] The Court of Session also has jurisdiction to reduce a decree of the Lyon Court.[25]

---

[15] 1971 Act, S. 38; 1985 Act, S. 18.
[16] e.g. Licensing (Sc.) Act, 1976.
[17] 1971 Act, S. 38.
[18] 1907 Act, S. 28.
[19] *Ross-shire C.C.* v. *Macrae Gilstrap*, 1939 S.C. 808.
[20] Lyon King of Arms Act, 1867.
[21] *Maclean of Ardgour* v. *Maclean*, 1941 S.C. 613.
[22] *Royal College of Surgeons* v. *Royal College of Physicians*, 1911 S.C. 1054.
[23] *Macrae's Trs.* v. *Lord Lyon*, 1927 S.L.T. 285
[24] e.g. *Stewart Mackenzie* v. *Fraser Mackenzie*, 1920 S.C. 764; 1922 S.C. (H.L.) 39.
[25] *Macrae's Trs., supra.*

The Scottish Land Court

The Land Court was created in 1911[26] and assumed the judicial functions of the Crofters Commission of 1885. It is composed of five members,[27] of whom the Chairman has the rank and dignity of a judge of the Court of Session, with a quorum of three,[28] but may delegate its powers to any one member of the court, whose determination may be reviewed by three or more members of the Court.[29] It is a court of law[30] with the usual powers of a court but execution of its decrees requires a decree conform by the sheriff.[31] Its jurisdiction is statutory and includes questions of compensation, grazing rights, succession to crofts, bequest and assignation of crofts, vacant holdings, and questions between landlord and tenant of holdings. An appeal by way of case stated lies from the Court[32] or a member thereof[33] to the Court of Session.

Lands Tribunal for Scotland

The Lands Tribunal for Scotland consists of a legal President and members, some lawyers and some experienced in the valuation of land. Its function is to determine questions of disputed compensation for acquisition of land, variation and discharge of land obligations, allocation of feu-duties and similar disputes.[33] An order of the Tribunal may be recorded for execution in the Books of Council and Session and is enforceable accordingly.[34] The Tribunal may state a case for the opinion of the Court of Session and appeal then lies to the House of Lords.[35]

Buildings authorities

The Secretary of State may provide by regulations for the procedure of local authorities in exercising their jurisdiction and functions as buildings authorities.[36] A person aggrieved by certain decisions of a buildings authority may appeal to the sheriff.[37]

---

[26] Small Landholders (Sc.) Act, 1911, S. 3.
[27] On their positions see *Mackay and Esslemont* v. *L.A.*, 1937 S.C. 860.
[28] cf. *McCallum* v. *Arthur*, 1955 S.C. 188.
[29] *Strachan* v. *Hunter*, 1916 S.C. 901.
[30] *Matheson* v. *Board of Agriculture*, 1917 S.C. 145. As to contempt of court in the Land Court, see *Milburn*, 1946 S.C. 301.
[31] cf. *D. Argyll* v. *Cameron* (1888) 16 R. 139.
[32] e.g. *Kennedy* v. *Johnstone*, 1956 S.C. 39.
[33] Lands Tribunal Act, 1949, Ss. 1, 2; Land Compensation (Sc.) Act, 1963, Ss. 1 and 8; Conveyancing and Feudal Reform (Sc.) Act, 1970, Ss. 1–7, 50; Tenants' Rights (Sc.) Act, 1980, S. 1.
[34] 1970 Act, S. 50(2).
[35] Tribunals and Inquiries Act, 1971, S. 13(6).
[36] Buildings (Sc.) Act, 1959, amd. Local Government (Sc.) Act, 1973, Sch. 15.
[37] 1959 Act, S. 16.

Appeal lay formerly to the Court of Session[38] and now to the sheriff with a further appeal on a question of law to the Court of Session and to the House of Lords.[39]

Sheriff Court of Chancery

The Sheriff Court of Chancery exists to determine competing claims to be declared heir-at-law of a heritable proprietor. If the deceased had no domicile in Scotland the jurisdiction is exclusive. If he had, the jurisdiction was concurrent with that of the sheriff of the county where the lands lay,[40] but is now exclusive also.[41] The Sheriff of Chancery has exclusive jurisdiction in questions of heirship.[42] Appeal lies to the Court of Session and House of Lords. The office of Sheriff of Chancery was united with that of the Sheriff of the Lothians and Peebles on the first vacancy occurring after 1933,[43] and the functions of the court are diminishing in consequence of the reform of the law of succession in 1964.[44]

Church courts

The courts of the Church of Scotland,[45] namely the General Assembly, the Synods, the Presbyteries, and the Kirk Sessions, have a jurisdiction, civil and criminal, supreme in their own sphere and wholly independent of the jurisdictions of the Court of Session and the High Court of Justiciary.[46] But appeal to the civil court lies if a church court acts in excess of jurisdiction or refuses to exercise powers legally conferred on it,[47] and the civil courts may assist the church courts to cite witnesses to attend and give evidence.[48]

The church courts of voluntary churches have no legal status or jurisdiction, but only that conferred by their own constitutions over, and accepted by, their members and adherents,[49] but the civil courts will

---

[38] cf. *Hall* v. *Sinclair*, 1950 S.L.T. (Notes) 69.

[39] Building (Sc.) Act, 1959, S. 16; *Williamson* v. *Purdie*, 1970 S.C. 240.

[40] Service of Heirs (Sc.) Act, 1847, superseded by Titles to Land Consolidation (Sc.) Act, 1868, Ss. 27–55.

[41] Sheriff of Chancery (Transfer of Jurisdiction) Order, 1971 (S.I. 1971, No. 743).

[42] *Bosville* v. *L. MacDonald*, 1910 S.C. 597; *Menzies* v. *McKenna*, 1914 S.C. 272.

[43] Administration of Justice (Sc.) Act, 1933, S. 31(1).

[44] Succession (Sc.) Act, 1964, Ss. 34(2), 35, and Sch. 3.

[45] See generally (Stair Society) *Introduction to Scottish Legal History*, Ch. 27.

[46] General Assembly Act, 1592; Confession of Faith Ratification Act, 1690; Protestant Religion and Presbyterian Church Act, 1706; Church of Scotland Act, 1921; *Lockhart* v. *Presbytery of Deer* (1851) 13 D. 1296; *Wight* v. *Presbytery of Dunkeld* (1870) 8 M. 921; *Ballantyne* v. *Presbytery of Wigtown*, 1936 S.C. 625.

[47] *Sturrock* v. *Greig* (1849) 11 D. 1220.

[48] *Presbytery of Lews* v. *Fraser* (1874) 1 R. 888.

[49] *McMillan* v. *Free Church General Assembly* (1859) 22 D. 290; 23 D. 1314.

interfere only so far as the church courts' decisions are unconstitutional or irregular and affect civil or patrimonial rights.[50]

The Restrictive Practices Court

The Restrictive Practices Court is a United Kingdom court comprising three judges of the High Court in England, one judge of the Court of Session, one judge of the Supreme Court in Northern Ireland, and lay members experienced in industry, commerce, or public affairs. It may sit in one or more divisions, each of one judicial and at least two lay members. It hears cases brought under the Restrictive Trade Practices Act, 1976, the Resale Prices Act, 1976, the Fair Trading Act, 1973, and certain other statutes. Appeal lies to the Court of Session or the Courts of Appeal in England or Northern Ireland.[51]

The Employment Appeal Tribunal

This is a British court comprising judges of the High Court in England, a judge of the Court of Session, and lay members with experience of industrial relations. It hears appeals on questions of law from decisions of industrial tribunals under various statutes. Appeal lies on a question of law with the leave of the Tribunal or the Court of Session or Court of Appeal in England to the Court of Session or Court of Appeal in England.[52]

Special tribunals

Some of the many tribunals established for adjudicating on disputes arising in particular relations operate in fields which impinge on private law. These include local tribunals and the Social Security Commissioners,[53] industrial tribunals,[54] and rent assessment committees.[55] Other special tribunals are more directly concerned with issues arising out of public administration. The Tribunals and Inquiries Act, 1971, S. 13 confers on parties to proceedings before certain tribunals a right to appeal

---

[50] *Smith* v. *Galbraith* (1834) 5 D. 665; *Forbes* v. *Eden* (1867) 5 M. (H.L.) 36; *Wight* v. *Dunkeld* (1870) 8 M. 921; *Brook* v. *Kelly* (1893) 20 R. (H.L.) 104; *Skerret* v. *Oliver* (1896) 23 R. 468; *MacDonald* v. *Burns*, 1940 S.C. 376.

[51] Restrictive Practices Court Act, 1976.

[52] Employment Protection (Consolidation) Act, 1978, Ss. 135–6 and Sch. 11.

[53] Social Security Act, 1980, Ss. 12, 14.

[54] Industrial Training Act, 1964, S. 12; Redundancy Payments Act, 1965, Ss. 9, 44; Equal Pay Act, 1970, S. 2; Contracts of Employment Act, 1972, S. 8; Trade Union and Labour Relations Act, 1974, Sch. 1; Sex Discrimination Act, 1975, S. 63; Employment Protection (Consolidation) Act, 1978; *Gordon District Council* v. *Hay*, 1978 S.C. 327.

[55] Rent (Sc.) Act, 1984, Sch. 4; *Albyn Properties* v. *Knox*, 1977 S.C. 108; *Western Heritable Inv. Co.* v. *Inglis*, 1978 S.C. 304.

to the Court of Session if dissatisfied in point of law,[56] and the Court of Session may set aside *ultra vires* decisions of such tribunals.[57]

The Council on Tribunals

The Council on Tribunals, which has a Scottish Committee, exists to keep under review the constitution and working of many tribunals, but does not act as an appellate body from their decisions.[58]

Contempt of court

Contempt of court may be constituted by rude or disorderly conduct in court, use of improper means to influence the course of justice, conduct which may prejudice the fair administration of justice,[59] conduct which brings the administration of justice into disrepute, and defiance or wilful non-observance of orders of court. Every court has an inherent jurisdiction to punish summarily any conduct amounting to contempt,[60] by admonition, fine, or imprisonment. The question of contempt, and the punishment, may be appealed to the Court of Session[61] or House of Lords.[62] A sentence of imprisonment may be appealed to the Court of Session[63] of High Court of Justiciary.[64]

[56] cf. *Carron Co.* v. *Robertson*, 1967 S.C. 273.
[57] *Watt* v. *L.A.*, 1979 S.L.T. 137.
[58] Tribunals and Inquiries Act, 1971.
[59] *McAlister* v. *Associated Newspapers*, 1954 S.L.T. 14; *Stirling* v. *Associated Newspapers, Ltd.*, 1960 J.C. 5; *Atkins* v. *London Weekend Television Ltd.*, 1978 J.C. 48; *Kemp*, 1982 J.C. 29.
[60] Stair IV, 36–7; Ersk. I, 2, 8; *Johnson* v. *Grant*, 1923 S.C. 789. See also Contempt of Court Act, 1981.
[61] *Hamilton* v. *Anderson* (1858) 3 Macq. 363; *Munro* v. *Matheson* (1877) 5 R. 308.
[62] *Hamilton* v. *Caledonian Ry.* (1850) 7 Bell 272.
[63] *Maclachlan* v. *Bruce*, 1912 S.C. 440.
[64] *Cordiner*, 1973 J.C. 16.

CHAPTER 1.6

ARBITRATION

Arbitration is the adjudication of a dispute or controversy, on fact or law or both, outside the ordinary civil courts by one or more persons to whom the parties who are at issue refer the matter for decision.[1] It has never been the law of Scotland that an agreement to oust the jurisdiction of the courts was invalid as contrary to public policy.[2]

The submission of certain kinds of disputes to arbitration may be required by statute,[3] or provided for in the parties' contract,[4] or may be adopted by parties when dispute arises in preference to resorting to litigation. In the latter two classes of cases the reference depends on agreement of parties[5] and may raise preliminary questions of the capacity of the parties to refer their disputes.[6] Where the arbitration is prescribed or agreed upon either party may object to the other's attempt to resort instead to the courts,[7] though such an attempt may be necessary to determine, failing agreement, whether or not the matter in controversy is among the kinds of issues prescribed or agreed upon to be determined by arbitration. If parties have agreed to arbitrate, they must arbitrate,[8] unless by common consent they depart from this agreement.[9] The court has no power to release parties from their agreement.[8]

A shadowy distinction exists between an arbitration and a valuation[10] but the word 'arbitration' in a statute has been held to include a 'valuation'.[11]

[1] General authorities: Ersk. IV, 3, 29–36; Bell: *Law of Arbitration* (1877); Irons and Melville: *Law of Arbitration in Scotland* (1903).

[2] *Sanderson* v. *Armour*, 1922 S.C. (H.L.) 117, 126.

[3] e.g. Agricultural Holdings (Scotland) Act, 1949, S. 74 ('any question or difference of any kind whatsoever between the landlord and the tenant of an agricultural holding arising out of the tenancy...').

[4] e.g. *Hamlyn* v. *Talisker Distillery* (1894) 21 R. (H.L.) 21.

[5] Ersk. IV, 3, 29; *Brakinrig* v. *Menzies* (1841) 4 D. 274.

[6] See e.g. *Thomson's Trs* v. *Muir* (1867) 6 M. 145; *Aberdeen Town and County Bank* v. *Dean & Son* (1871) 9 M. 842; *McKersies* v. *Mitchell* (1872) 10 M. 861; Bankruptcy (Sc.) Act, 1985, S. 65, Companies Act, 1985, S. 539; Trusts (Sc.) Act, 1921, S. 4.

[7] e.g. *Mauritzen* v. *Baltic Shipping Co.*, 1948 S.C. 646; *Redpath Dorman Long* v. *Tarmac*, 1982 S.C. 14.

[8] *N.B. Ry. Co.* v. *Newburgh, etc. Ry. Co.*, 1911 S.C. 710; *Hegarty & Kelly* v. *Cosmopolitan Ins. Co.*, 1913 S.C. 377, 386; *Sanderson, supra*; *Crawford Bros.* v. *Northern Lighthouses Commrs.*, 1925 S.C. (H.L.) 22.

[9] *Halliburton* v. *Bingham Blades*, 1984 S.L.T. 388.

[10] *Nivison* v. *Howat* (1883) 11 R. 182; *Robertson* v. *Boyd & Winans* (1885) 12 R. 429, 430.

[11] *Graham* v. *Mill* (1904) 6 F. 886; *Stewart* v. *Williamson*, 1909 S.C. 1254, 1258; affd. 1910 S.C. (H.L.) 47. In *Gibson* v. *Fotheringham*, 1914 S.C. 987 the matters in issue in an arbitration were entirely matters of valuation.

Parties to a litigation may be held to have constituted the judge an arbiter, and thereby excluded appeal from him, but only where both parties have agreed and the judge has assented and there has been a complete departure from ordinary procedure.[12]

In course of a litigation a remit or reference may be made to an expert who reports to the court.[13] Consent to a remit does not make him an arbiter and exclude further procedure in court unless the remit is *extra cursum curiae*.[14]

Parties may also by joint minute agree to refer a cause, so far as not disposed of, to a judicial referee, i.e. a person appointed by the court, for decision.[15] A Lord Ordinary or sheriff may thus be made a judicial referee,[16] but a deviation from procedure is not enough to do this.[17]

What matters may be referred to arbitration

Parties may refer to arbitration questions as to any civil right or interest, real or personal, about which they may contract.[18] The questions referred may be questions of fact, or of law,[19] or of discretion, such as of the proper measure of compensation.[20] Questions of public rights or personal status[21] may not be the subject of arbitration,[22] nor criminal matters,[23] nor any illegal or immoral subject. While a submission should be liberally construed,[24] parties cannot be held to have excluded the jurisdiction of the courts except in so far as they have expressly and clearly agreed to do so.[25]

Statutory references

Various statutes provide for the decision of specified issues by arbitration, and provide for the arbiter, his powers, and, sometimes, for reference by

---

[12] *White* v. *Morton's Trs.* (1866) 4M. (H.L.) 53, 58; *Gordon* v. *Bruce* (1897) 24 R. 844. See also *Stark's Trs* v. *Duncan* (1906) 8 F. 429.

[13] *Steel* v. *S.* (1898) 25 R. 715, 720.

[14] *Steel, supra.*

[15] e.g. *Brakinrig, supra; Macrae* v. *Edinburgh Street Tramways Co.* (1885) 13 R. 265.

[16] e.g. *Dykes* v. *Merry & Cunninghame* (1869) 7 M. 603.

[17] *Gordon* v. *Bruce* (1847), 24 R. 844.

[18] Bankt. I, 23, 17; Bell, *Arbitration*, 120.

[19] *N.B. Ry.* v. *Newburgh Ry.*, 1911 S.C. 710, 719.

[20] e.g. *Miller* v. *Edinburgh Corporation*, 1978 S.C. 1.

[21] Bell, 122.

[22] *Ramsay* v. *Hay* (1624) Mor. 16245; but see *E. Kintore* v. *Union Bank* (1863) 1 M. (H.L.) 11. A matter of status may be established, if only incidental to the main issue before the arbiter: *Johnstone* v. *Spencer* 1908 S.C. 1015; *Turnbull* v. *Wilson & Clyde Coal Co.*, 1935 S.C. 580, but the decision probably applies to that case only.

[23] *Stark's Trs.* v. *Duncan* (1906) 8 F. 429. See also *E. Kintore* v. *Union Bank* (1863) 1 M. (H.L.) 11.

[24] Ersk. IV, 3, 32.

[25] *Calder* v. *Mackay* (1860) 22 D. 741, 744; *Holmes Oil Co.* v. *Pumpherston Oil Co.* (1890) 18 R. (H.L.) 52, 55.

him to the civil courts on a question of law.[26] Exclusion of the jurisdiction of the courts requires an express provision in, or a clear implication from, the words of the Act.[27] Such a provision is normally imperative and cannot be waived by agreement or conduct of parties but may be merely enabling.[28] It is always, however, a question of law for the court whether the circumstances which have arisen raise a question of the kinds statutorily required to be determined by arbitration,[29] and the courts may determine any questions precedent to the existence of a statutory claim.[30]

Reference under clause in contract

A contract between two parties may include a provision that disputes of specified kinds are to be decided by arbitration. The scope of such an arbitration clause may give rise to difficulty. When incorporated in a contract dealing with particular matters it is presumed confined to the same subject-matter.[31] It may further be executorial, confined to the determination of questions which may arise during the execution of the contract, or be general, extending to the decision of any claim which may arise from the contract.[32] The scope of a reference clause is more strictly interpreted in the case of an executorial reference.[33]

The existence and validity of the contract must be established before

[26] e.g. Companies Clauses Consolidation (Sc.) Act, 1845, Ss. 127–41; Lands Clauses Consolidation (Sc.) Act, 1845, Ss. 24, 66; Railways Clauses Consolidation (Sc.) Act, 1845, S. 71; Acquisition of Land (Assessment of Compensation) Act, 1919, S. 1; Friendly Societies Acts, 1896, S. 68; 1948; Ss. 21, 25; Agricultural Holdings (Sc.) Act, 1949, Ss. 68, 74; National Health Service (Sc.) Act, 1947, S. 77; Local Govt. (Sc.) Act, 1973, S. 25.

[27] Brodie v. Ker, 1952 S.C. 216, 224.

[28] Houison-Craufurd's Trs. v. Davies, 1951 S.C. 1; Lanark C.C. v. East Kilbride, 1967 S.C. 235.

[29] e.g.Caledonian Ry. v. Greenock, etc. Ry. (1874) 1 R. (H.L.) 8; Mitchell v. Caledonian Bldg. Soc. (1886) 13 R. 918; Glasgow Mags v. Caledonian Ry. (1892) 19 R. 874; Symington's Exor. v. Galashiels Co-operative Store Co. (1894) 21 R. 371; N.B. Ry. v. Lanarkshire and Dumbartonshire Ry. (1895) 23 R. 76; Melrose v. Edinburgh Savings Bank Trs. (1897) 24 R. 483; Lanarkshire Tramways Co. v. Motherwell (1908) 16 S.L.T. 63; Johnstone v. Assoc. Ironmoulders, 1911, 2 S.L.T. 478; McGowan v. City of Glasgow Friendly Socy., 1913 S.C. 991; Caledonian Ry. v. Clyde Shipping Co., 1917 S.C. 107; Picken v. P., 1934 S.L.T. 75; Fairholme's Trs. v. Graham, 1943 S.L.T. 158; Bruce v. Muir, 1944 J.C. 29; Houison-Craufurd's Trs. v. Davies, 1951 S.C. 1; Brodie v. Ker, 1952 S.C. 216; Lanark C.C. v. East Kilbride, 1967 S.C. 235.

[30] Donaldson's Hospital v. Esslemont, 1925 S.C. 199.

[31] Lauder v. Wingate (1852) 14 D. 633. See also Miller v. Howie (1851) 13 D. 608.

[32] Mackay v. Barry Parochial Board (1883) 10 R. 1046; Wright v. Greenock Tramways Co. (1891) 29 S.L.R. 53; N.B. Ry. v. Newburgh & North Fife Ry., 1911 S.C. 710; Sanderson v. Armour, 1922 S.C. (H.L.) 117.

Among references held executorial are: Kirkwood v. Morrison (1877) 5 R. 79; Savile St. Foundry Co. v. Rothesay Tramways (1883) 10 R. 821; Beattie v. Macgregor (1883) 10 R. 1094; Mackay v. Leven Police Commrs. (1893) 20 R. 1093; Aviemore Station Hotel Co. v. Scott (1904) 12 S.L.T. 494.

Among references held general are: Mackay, supra: Wright, supra: McCosh v. Moore (1905) 8 F. 31; N.B. Ry., supra; Scott v. Gerrard, 1916 S.C. 793.

[33] Beattie, supra; Mackay v. Leven, supra.

the arbitration clause can be invoked; if it is doubtful whether the contract exists that is a question for the courts.[34] Similarly whether there is a question to be referred is a question for the courts.[35] Where the clause provides for the appointment of an arbiter by the court, the court will not appoint unless it appears that there is a specific and concrete dispute, prima facie falling within the ambit of the arbitration clause.[36] The court also must determine the scope of the reference clause, and whether it applies in the circumstances.[37]

If there is a general arbitration clause its validity is not affected by allegations that the party invoking it has repudiated the contract, or has been in breach of it.[38] Whether either party has repudiated the contract is a question for the arbiter.[39] But if the contract has been justifiably rescinded by either party, the arbitration clause falls with the rest of the contract.[40]

If external circumstances arise which do, or may, have the effect of terminating the contract and releasing both parties from their obligations, on the grounds of supervening impossibility, illegality, or frustration of the adventure,[41] the better view is that whether the circumstances do terminate the contract or not falls under the arbitration clause also.

If a difference between the parties results in an alleged modification of the contract or an alleged new contract, the question whether this has taken place and has superseded the original contract is probably outwith any arbitration clause in the original contract.[42] A supplementary contract is not governed by an arbitration clause in the main contract unless the intention to incorporate it in the supplementary contract also is evident.

An arbitration clause may bind a person not a party to the contract such as a creditor of one party thereto who has arrested in the hands of the other party thereto and is founding on the contract.[43] An arbitration

---

[34] *Ransohoff & Wissler* v. *Burrell* (1897) 25 R. 284; *Hoth* v. *Cowan*, 1926 S.C. 58, 64.

[35] *Greenock Parochial Board* v. *Coghill* (1878) 5 R. 732; *Mackay* v. *Leven, supra; Woods* v. *Co-operative Ins. Co.*, 1924, S.C. 692.

[36] *Mackay* v. *Leven, supra; Allied Airways (Gandar Dower) Ltd.* v. *Secy. of State for Air,* 1950 S.C. 249.

[37] *Crawford Bros.* v. *Northern Lighthouses Commrs.*, 1925 S.C. (H.L.) 22; *Macdonald* v. *Clark*, 1927 S.N. 6.

[38] *N.B. Ry.* v. *Newburgh & North Fife Ry.*, 1911 S.C. 710; *Sanderson* v. *Armour*, 1922 S.C. (H.L.) 117; *Dryburgh* v. *Caledonian Ins. Co.*, 1922 S.N. 85; cf. *Paterson* v. *United Scottish Herring Drifter Ins. Co.*, 1927 S.N. 141.

[39] *Sanderson, supra.*

[40] *Hegarty & Kelly* v. *Cosmopolitan Ins. Corp.*, 1913 S.C. 377; *Sanderson, supra*, explaining *Municipal Council of Johannesburg* v. *Stewart*, 1909 S.C. (H.L.) 53.

[41] *Scott* v. *Del Sel*, 1923 S.C. (H.L.) 37; *Heyman* v. *Darwins* [1942] A.C. 356; *Mauritzen* v. *Baltic Shipping Co.*, 1948 S.C. 646; *Hirji Mulji* v. *Cheong Yue S.S. Co.* [1926] A.C. 497 is not now followed.

[42] *Tough* v. *Dumbarton Waterworks Commrs.* (1872) 11 M. 236; *Hoth* v. *Cowan*, 1926 S.C. 58.

[43] *Palmer* v. *S.E. Lancashire Ins. Co.*, 1932 S.L.T. 68; *Rutherford* v. *Licences and General Ins. Co.*, 1934 S.L.T. 31, 47; see also *Cant* v. *Eagle Star Ins. Co.*, 1937 S.L.T. 444; contrast *McConnell & Reid* v. *Smith*, 1911 S.C. 635.

clause in a principal contract may be held incorporated in a sub-contract between one of the parties and a third party.[44]

Contract to submit

When a dispute has arisen between two parties they may competently agree to submit it to the decision of an arbiter rather than resort to litigation. All parties who may contract may enter into a contract of submission, and statute has empowered many classes of persons to refer disputes to arbitration.[45] Counsel may,[46] but a solicitor may not, save by express authority,[47] submit a claim. Submission may be made verbally, particularly references regarding marches,[48] or in writing,[49] which, if the subject matter be heritable property, must be probative,[50] or improbative supplemented by *rei interventus* or homologation.[51] In general the rules as to constitution, proof, and extinction apply to the contract to submit as to any other contract.

A submission falls to be interpreted in the same way as any other contract.[52] The scope of any such reference depends on the terms of the submission. A submission should be liberally construed[53] and if ambiguous may be interpreted in accordance with the actings of the parties.[54] If doubts arise during the arbitration the arbiter must form his own opinion thereon,[55] but the ultimate decision lies with the court,[56] but the court will not readily interfere with an arbitration in progress on this ground.[57]

Submissions are distinguished as general, dealing with all disputes between the parties existing at the date of the contract,[58] or special, limited to a particular question, or general-special or mixed, where there

[44] *Goodwins, Jardine & Co. v. Brand* (1905) 7 F. 995.

[45] e.g. Trusts (Sc.) Act, 1921, Ss. 2, 4.

[46] *Forbes v. Duffus* (1837) 12 F.C. 321; *Maclaren v. Ferrier* (1865) 3 M. 833.

[47] *Black v. Laidlaw* (1844) 6 D. 1254.

[48] *Otto v. Weir* (1871) 9 M. 660.

[49] *Maclellan v. Macleod* (1830) 4 W. & S. 157; *Chapman v. Edinburgh Prison Board* (1844) 6 D. 1288; *Fraser v. L. Lovat* (1850) 7 Bell 171; *Dykes v. Roy* (1869) 7 M. 357.

[50] As to what is probative writing, see Ch. 1.7.

[51] *Brown & Colvill v. Gardner* (1739) Mor. 5659.

[52] *Lang v. Brown* (1855) 2 Macq. 93; see also Ersk. IV. 3, 32.

[53] Ersk. IV, 3, 32; but see *Calder v. Mackay* (1860) 22 D. 741, 744; *Holmes Oil Co. v. Pumpherston Oil Co.* (1890) 18 R. (H.L.) 52, 55.

[54] *N.B. Ry. v. Barr* (1855) 18 D. 102; *Orrell v. O.* (1859) 21 D. 554; *Miller v. Oliver & Boyd* (1906) 8 F. 390, 401.

[55] *Bell v. Graham*, 1908 S.C. 1060.

[56] *Adams v. G.N.S. Ry.* (1890) 18 R. (H.L.) 1, 8.

[57] *Dumbarton Waterworks Commrs. v. Blantyre* (1884) 12 R. 115; *Glasgow, Yoker and Clydebank Ry. Co. v. Lidgerwood* (1895) 23 R. 195; *Licenses Ins. Corpn. v. Shearer*, 1907 S.C. 10.

[58] Bell, *Arbitration*, 60; *Hood v. Baillie* (1832) 11 S. 207; even a general submission does not put before the arbiter a plea of compensation: *McEwan v. Middleton* (1866) 5 M. 159; or empower him to assess damages: *Blaikie v. Aberdeen Ry.* (1852) Paterson's App. 119; *N.B. Ry. v. Newburgh & North Fife Ry.*, 1911 S.C. 710.

is a general reference of disputes coupled with the specification of a precise matter in issue. Parties may agree to submit future disputes.[59]

A submission falls on the death of either party,[60] or of the arbiter, or oversman,[61] though a judicial reference is not thus ended,[62] or if by supervening impossibility execution of the arbitration in the mode contemplated is rendered impossible.[63]

Judicial reference

A judicial reference arises when parties to an action in court agree, voluntarily or at the suggestion of the court, with judicial authority to refer the matters in issue to an arbiter. A judicial reference is subject to the same rules as an ordinary submission.[64] It may be to the Lord Ordinary or sheriff, in which case appeal from his judgment is precluded,[65] but a mere deviation from ordinary procedure is not a reference to the judge as arbiter.[66] The jurisdiction of a judicial referee is determined by the minute referring the action.[67] The referee reports to the court which grants decree in terms thereof.[68]

The arbiter

The submission is normally to an arbiter, or to two arbiters, with power to them, unless excluded by the reference, to appoint an oversman in case of dispute.[69] The parties may choose whom they will, ignoring physical and legal disabilities,[70] but an arbiter should have no interest in the matter in dispute not known to or disclosed to the parties.[71] A reference

---

[59] *Robertson* v. *Johnstone* (1835) 13 S. 289.

[60] Ersk. IV, 3, 29; *Ewing* v. *Dewar*, 19 Dec. 1820, F.C.; *Robertson* v. *Cheyne* (1847) 9 D. 599. But the death of one trustee does not have this effect: *Alexander's Trs.* v. *Dymock's Trs.* (1883) 10 R. 1189.

[61] Ersk. IV, 3, 34.

[62] *Watmore* v. *Burns* (1839) 1 D. 743.

[63] *Graham* v. *Mill* (1904) 6 F. 886.

[64] *Brackenrig* v. *Menzies* (1841) 4 D. 274.

[65] *Dykes* v. *Merry & Cunninghame* (1869) 7 M. 603; *Lindsay* v. *Walker's Trs.* (1877) 4 R. 870.

[66] *Gordon* v. *Bruce* (1897) 24 R. 844; contrast *Steele* v. *Steele* (1898) 5 S.L.T. 466.

[67] *Mackenzie* v. *Girvan* (1840) 3 D. 318.

[68] *Gillon* v. *Simpson* (1859) 21 D. 243.

[69] Arbitration (Sc.) Act, 1894, S. 4. On method of choice of oversman see *Smith* v. *Liverpool, etc. Insce. Co.* (1887) 14 R. 931.

[70] See *Gordon* v. *E. Errol* (1582) Mor. 8915 (minor); *Fisher* v. *Colquhoun* (1844) 6 D. 1286 (advocate promoted judge); *Bremner* v. *Elder & Elgin Lunacy Board* (1875) 2 R. (H.L.) 136 (indefinite body of persons); *Dixon* v. *Jones, Heard & Ingram* (1884) 11 R. 739 (firm).

[71] *Mackenzie* v. *Clark* (1828) 7 S. 215; *Tennent* v. *Macdonald* (1836) 14 S. 976; *L.N.W. Ry.* v. *Lindsay* (1858) 3 Macq. 99; *Dixon* v. *Jones, Heard & Ingram* (1884) 11 R. 739; *Smith, supra; McDougall* v. *Laird* (1894) 22 R. 71; *Peckholtz* v. *Russell* (1900) 7 S.L.T. 160; *Riddell* v. *Lanark Ry.* (1901) 8 S.L.T. 330; *Sellar* v. *Highland Ry.*, 1919 S.C. (H.L.) 19; *Fleming's Trs.* v. *Henderson*, 1962 S.L.T. 401.

to a party,[72] or one party's employee[73] is valid, so long as that employee has not given evidence for his employer or otherwise acted partially.[74] An arbiter is disqualified if he has shown bias before accepting the reference.[75] A reference to a person by name, or to an arbiter to be nominated by another, have always been valid.[76] A reference to a person not named, or to the holder of an office for the time being, was formerly ineffectual,[77] with certain exceptions,[78] but is now valid,[79] as is a reference to arbitration in the customary manner of a particular trade.[80] On the failure of one party to an agreement to refer to concur in nominating a single arbiter, or one of two arbiters, the court may appoint.[81] On the failure of two arbiters to agree on an oversman the court may appoint.[82] It has also been held that a party to a contract containing an arbitration clause, notwithstanding that he had left Scotland, had prorogated the jurisdiction of the Scottish court to the effect of entitling it to appoint an arbiter at the instance of the other party, who had claims falling under the arbitration clause.[83]

A Court of Session judge may act as arbiter or oversman in a commercial case.[84]

In commercial arbitrations, in which two arbiters are appointed with power to appoint an oversman, the fact that one arbiter acts as agent for and represents the party appointing him has been recognized and does not invalidate the award.[85]

It is competent for one party to interdict an arbiter before he acts if it is clear that he has no such power as that which he is called on to exercise,[86] or that there is no question for him to decide,[87] or that the

---

[72] *Buchan* v. *Melville* (1902) 4 F. 620.

[73] *Trowsdale* v. *N.B. Ry.* (1864) 2 M. 1334; *Adams* v. *G.N.S. Ry.* (1889) 16 R. 843; 18 R. (H.L.) 1; *Crawford Bros.* v. *Northern Lighthouses Commrs.* 1925 S.C. (H.L.) 22. But see *Halliday* v. *D. Hamilton's Trs.* (1903) 5 F. 800; *Aviemore Station Hotel Co.* v. *Scott* (1904) 12 S.L.T. 494.

[74] *Dickson* v. *Grant* (1870) 8 M. 566; *McDougall, supra*; *McLauchlan & Brown* v. *Morrison* (1900) 8 S.L.T. 279.

[75] *Dickson, supra*; *Peckholtz, supra*; *McLauchlan & Brown, supra*.

[76] *Murdoch* v. *France* (1894) 2 S.L.T. 320; 1894 Act, S. 1.

[77] *Hendry's Trs.* v. *Renton* (1851) 13 D. 1001; *Tancred Arrol & Co.* v. *Steel Co. of Scotland* (1890) 17 R. (H.L.) 31.

[78] See *Smith* v. *Wharton-Duff* (1843) 5 D. 749; *Caledonian Ins. Co.* v. *Gilmour* (1892) 20 R. (H.L.) 13.

[79] Arbitration (Sc.) Act, 1894, S. 1.

[80] *Douglas* v. *Stiven* (1900) 2 F. 575; *United Creameries Co.* v. *Boyd*, 1912 S.C. 617; *Highgate* v. *British Oil and Grant Co.*, 1914 2 S.L.T. 241.

[81] 1894 Act, Ss. 2–3. cf. *Ross* v. *R.*, 1920 S.C. 530.

[82] 1894 Act, S. 4; *Glasgow P.C.* v. *United Collieries* (1907) 15 S.L.T. 232; *Mackay* v. *Robertson*, 1935 S.L.T. 414.

[83] *D. Fife's Trs.* v. *Taylor*, 1934 S.L.T. 76.

[84] Law Reform (Misc. Prov.) (Sc.) Act, 1980, S. 17.

[85] *Scorrier Steamship Coaster's* v. *Milne*, 1928 S.N. 109.

[86] *G.S.W. Ry.* v. *Caledonian Ry.* (1871) 44 S. Jur. 29; *Dumbarton Water Commrs.* v. *Blantyre* (1884) 12 R. 115; *McCoard* v. *Glasgow Corpn.*, 1935 S.L.T. 117.

[87] *Greenock Parochial Board* v. *Coghill* (1878) 5 R. 732; *Low & Thomas* v. *Dunbarton C.C.* (1905) 13 S.L.T. 620.

arbiter would necessarily be disqualified by bias,[88] or at an early stage if he has taken a step which must render an award bad.[89]

The office of arbiter is gratuitous,[90] unless a fee is stipulated for,[91] but a professional person acting as arbiter is entitled to remuneration,[92] as is the arbiter in a statutory arbitration.[93] Each party is liable for half of the fee.[94] Having accepted office an arbiter cannot resign,[95] but may be ordered by the court at the instance of one or both parties to issue an award.[96]

Where an arbiter under the Agricultural Holdings (Sc.) Act, 1949 has been removed and his award reduced it is competent to appoint a second arbiter.[97]

The arbiter's powers

The powers of the arbiter are determined primarily by the terms of the statute or the submission to him, which it is for him, subject to review by the court,[98] to interpret.[99] The Court is slow to interfere with an arbitration in progress.[1] If the arbitration clause does not apply to the dispute which has arisen the arbiter has no power to deal with that dispute.[2]

An arbiter cannot assess damages without express power to do so,[3] but has implied power to award expenses[4] though he must hear parties on the matter.[5]

---

[88] *Caledonian Ry.* v. *Glasgow Corpn.* (1897) 25 R. 74; *Graham House* v. *Environment Secretary*, 1985 S.L.T. 502.

[89] *Birkmyre* v. *Moor & Weinberg* (1906) 14 S.L.T. 702.

[90] *Paul* v. *Henderson* (1867) 5 M. 628; *Murray* v. *N.B. Ry.* (1900) 2 F. 460.

[91] *Fraser* v. *Wright* (1838) 16 S. 1049; *Duff* v. *Pirie* (1893) 21 R. 80.

[92] *Macintyre Bros.* v. *Smith,.* 1913 S.C. 129. As to amount of fee see *Wilkie* v. *Scottish Aviation Ltd.*, 1956 S.C. 198. As to fee where award inept, see *Rutherford* v. *Findochty Mags.*, 1929 S.N. 130.

[93] *Murray, supra.*

[94] *Macintyre, supra.*

[95] Bell, *Arbitration*, 201.

[96] *Marshall* v. *Edinburgh & Glasgow Ry.* (1853) 15 D. 603. See also *Forbes* v. *Underwood* (1886) 13 R. 465; *Watson* v. *Robertson* (1895) 22 R. 362.

[97] *Dundee Corpn.* v. *Guthrie*, 1969 S.L.T. 93.

[98] *Adams* v. *G.N.S. Ry.* (1890) 18 R. (H.L.) 1, 8.

[99] *Calder* v. *Mackay* (1860) 22 D. 741; *Mackay* v. *Leven Police Commrs.* (1893) 20 R. 1093; *Fairholme's Trs.* v. *Graham*, 1943 S.L.T. 158.

[1] *Dumbarton Waterworks Commrs.* v. *L. Blantyre* (1884) 12 R. 115; *Licenses Insce. Corpn.* v. *Shearer*, 1907 S.C. 10.

[2] *Tough* v. *Dumbarton Waterworks Commrs.* (1872) 11 M. 236; *Howden* v. *Dobie* (1882) 9 R. 758; *McAlpine* v. *Lanarkshire and Ayrshire Ry.*, (1889) 17 R. 113; *Allan's Tr.* v. *Allan & Sons* (1891) 19 R. 215.

[3] *Aberdeen Ry.* v. *Blaikie Bros.* (1851) 13 D. 527; (1853) Paters. App. 119; *Mackay* v. *Barry Parochial Board* (1883) 10 R. 1046; *McAlpine* v. *Lanarkshire and Ayrshire Ry.* (1889) 17 R. 113; *Mackay* v. *Leven Police Commrs.* (1893) 20 R. 1093.

[4] *Ferrier* v. *Alison* (1845) 4 Bell 161; *Paul* v. *Henderson* (1867) 5 M. 613; *Pollich* v. *Heatley*, 1910 S.C. 469.

[5] *Islay Estates* v. *McCormick*, 1937 S.N. 28.

Unless limited by statute, an arbiter's powers under a submission blank as to its endurance continue for a year and a day from the submission to him.[6] If they fall by lapse of time parties are restored to their common law rights of action.[7] A submission, blank as to endurance, may be prorogated or extended in duration by writing by the arbiter, if express power were conferred on him,[8] or by express contract by the parties,[9] or even by actings.[10] If the submission contains no blank and imposes no limit his powers last for forty years.[11] If there is a time-limit the submission falls automatically on its expiry, unless extended by the parties, expressly or by conduct;[12] the court probably has no jurisdiction to prolong the reference.[13] If there is a reference to two arbiters and an oversman, and power to prorogate was conferred on the arbiters, it will be inferred in the case of the oversman.[14]

An arbiter is *functus*, the submission discharged and his powers ended once a final award is issued and delivered.[15]

Procedure

The arbiter may fix his own procedure; in informal references no formal procedure is required;[16] he normally orders claims and answers, and hears parties,[17] or their counsel or agents, thereon. A proof,[18] inspection of the subjects in dispute, and the employment of technical assistance may be required. But if skilled assistance is invoked the judgment must be the arbiter's own, though formed after assistance.[19] He has no power to enforce the attendance of witnesses, or obtain production of documents,

---

[6] Ersk. IV, 3, 29; *Dunmore v. McInturner* (1829) 7 S. 595; *Graham v. Mill* (1904) 6 F. 886.

[7] *Graham, supra.*

[8] Ersk. IV, 3, 29; *Lang v. Brown* (1855) 2 Macq. 93; *Graham, supra.*

[9] *Patterson v. Sanderson* (1829) 7 S. 616; *Hill, supra.*

[10] *Fleming v. Wilson & McLellan* (1827) 5 S. 906; *Paul v. Henderson* (1867) 5 M. 613.

[11] Ersk., *supra*; *Fleming v. Wilson & McLellan* (1827) 5 S. 906; *Hill v. Dundee & Perth Ry.* (1852) 14 D. 1034.

[12] *Hill, supra; Paul, supra.*

[13] *Blyth & Blyth's Trs. v. Kaye*, 1976 S.L.T. 67.

[14] *Glover v. G.* (1805) 4 Pat. 655.

[15] Ersk. IV. 3, 32.

[16] *Nivison v. Howat* (1883) 11 R. 182; *Holmes Oil Co. v. Pumpherston Oil Co.* (1890) 17 R. 624, 656; *Hope v. Crookston Bros.* (1890) 17 R. 868; *Paterson v. Glasgow Corpn.* (1901) 3 F. (H.L.) 34; *Gibson v. Fotheringham*, 1914 S.C. 987.

[17] *Scorrier Steamship Coasters v. Milne*, 1928 S.N. 109; he is not always bound to hear parties; *Logan v. Leadbetter* (1887) 15 R. 115; *Paterson, supra; N.B. Ry. v. Wilson*, 1911 S.C. 730. See also *Black v. Williams*, 1924 S.C. (H.L.) 22.

[18] *Mackenzie v. Girvan* (1840) 3 D. 318; *Caledonian Ry. v. Lockhart* (1860) 22 D. (H.L.) 8.

[19] A proof is not essential in a practical matter, so long as the arbiter takes proper means to inform himself of the facts: *Paterson v. Glasgow Corpn.* (1901) 3 F. (H.L.) 34; *N.B. Ry. v. Wilson*, 1911 S.C. 730; *Henderson v. McGown*, 1915, 2 S.L.T. 316; *Cameron v. Nicol*, 1930 S.C. 1. In a reference for valuation to a man of skill a proof is unnecessary and incompetent: *Logan v. Leadbetter* (1888) 15 R. 115.

but the court may, on petition, empower parties to cite witnesses, or to take evidence on commission.[20]

Parties may be barred by failure to do so from objecting to the regularity of proceedings in a statutory arbitration,[21] and an award cannot be set aside for procedural informality if conform to the custom of the place and no substantial injustice has been done.[22]

Once an arbitration has begun the court will interfere with the arbiter proceeding only on strong grounds,[23] but will do so, if it will save parties expense and litigation, if it is plain that the arbiter is going to act *ultra vires*.[24]

The oversman

Where the submission is to two arbiters, an oversman may be nominated or his nomination may be left to the arbiters. Arbiters have implied power in common law submissions, unless excluded, to nominate an oversman.[25] If they cannot agree the court appoints. Appointment may be made before the submission begins.[26]

If the arbiters fail to agree[27] they should devolve the reference on the oversman, by signed minute,[28] or if the oversman has not yet been appointed, have him appointed.[29] It is sufficient to bring the oversman into active operation that there is a difference of opinion amounting to deadlock.[30] The oversman may hear the evidence led before the arbiters, but this does not invoke his jurisdiction.[31] Arbiters may devolve only part of the submission, issuing their award as to the rest, and may from time to time devolve on the oversman questions on which they disagree while keeping in their own hands the decision of questions not yet considered.[32]

[20] *Galloway Water Power Co. v. Carmichael*, 1937 S.C. 135; As to witnesses in England, see *Nimmo & Sons, Ltd.* (1905) 8 F. 173.

[21] *Cameron v. Nicol*, 1930 S.C. 1.

[22] *Hope v. Crookston Bros.* (1890) 17 R. 868.

[23] *Fraser v. Gordon* (1834) 12 S. 887; *Drew v. Leburn* (1853) 18 D. (H.L.) 4; *Farrell v. Arnott* (1857) 19 D. 1000; *Wilson v. Caledonian Ry.* (1860) 22 D. 697.

[24] *G.S.W. Ry. v. Caledonian Ry.* (1871) 44 Sc. Jur. 29; *Sinclair v. Clyne's Tr.* (1887) 15 R. 185; Contrast *Trowsdale v. Jopp and N.B. Ry.* (1865) 4 M. 31.

[25] Arbitration (Sc.) Act, 1894, S. 4, overruling *Merry & Cunningham v. Brown* (1863) 1 M. (H.L.) 14. As to method of choice see *Smith v. Liverpool, London & Globe Ins. Co.* (1887) 14 R. 931.

[26] *Brysson v. Mitchell* (1823) 2 S. 382; *Glasgow P.C. v. United Collieries, Ltd.* (1907) 15 S.L.T. 232.

[27] e.g. *Sinclair v. Fraser* (1884) 11 R. 1139; *Gibson v. Fotheringham*, 1914 S.C. 987.

[28] *Kirkaldy v. Dalgairn's Trs.*, 16 June 1809, F.C. Nomination at the outset does not amount to devolution; *Brysson, supra.*

[29] *McNair's Trs. v. Roxburgh* (1885) 17 D. 445.

[30] *Gibson, supra.*

[31] *Crawford v. Paterson* (1858) 20 D. 488.

[32] *Gibson v. Fotheringham*, 1914 S.C. 987.

Award

An arbiter is not bound to, but frequently issues notes of his proposed findings, and allows parties to make representations thereon and hears them on their representations.[33] It is questionable whether an arbiter, unless expressly authorized, can make an interim or part award.[34] The decision of the arbiters or oversman is final on both fact and law.[35] The final award or decree-arbitral may be formal or informal, as the submission was,[36] but normally and preferably is attested or holograph.[37] Informal submissions and awards, however, suffice in references *in re mercatoria*,[38] valuations or references at the expiry of an agricultural lease.[39] It must be delivered to the parties, or recorded, or delivered to a third party for communication to the parties.[40] While still undelivered it may be altered by the arbiter.[41] It must be final and exhaustive, deciding all matters submitted for decision, unless there is express power to make interim or part awards.[42] Once final award is issued the arbiter's functions are at an end and the submission is closed. An error, other than a clerical error,[43] cannot be corrected.

If two arbiters cannot agree they should by minute devolve the reference on the oversman.[44] In the case of a formal submission the award must indicate how far it represents agreement between the arbiters, and how far it is a decision by the oversman of a matter on which the arbiters could not agree.[45] In informal submissions an award is not vitiated by failure to distinguish between agreed elements of award and elements devolved on the oversman following disagreement.[46]

Where an award is made in an arbitration between parties who are members of an association, as such members, it ceases to be binding on a party ceasing to be such a member.[47]

---

[33] *Baxter* v. *Macarthur* (1836) 14 S. 549; *Islay Estates* v. *McCormick*, 1937 S.N. 28. See also *Wemyss* v. *Ardrossan Harbour Co.* (1893) 20 R. 500.

[34] *Sanderson* v. *Armour*, (1922) S.C. (H.L.) 117.

[35] *Lang* v. *Brown* (1852) 15 D. 38; *E. Hopetoun* v. *Scots Mines Co.* (1856) 18 D. 739; *Dykes* v. *Roy* (1869) 7 M. 357; *Hope* v. *Crookston Bros.* (1890) 17 R. 868.

[36] *Edinburgh & Glasgow Ry.* v. *Hill* (1840) 2 D. 486; *Lyle* v. *Falconer* (1842) 5 D. 236.

[37] *Percy* v. *Meikle*, 25 Nov. 1808. F.C.; *Robertson* v. *Boyd & Winans* (1885) 12 R. 419; *McLaren* v. *Aikman*, 1939 S.C. 222.

[38] *Hope, supra.*

[39] *Robertson, supra.*

[40] *Nivison* v. *Howat* (1883) 11 R. 182; *Cameron* v. *Nicol*, 1930 S.C. 1; *McLaren, supra.*

[41] *Macrae* v. *Edinburgh Street Tramways Co.* (1885) 13 R. 265.

[42] *Macrae, supra; Scott* v. *S.* (1898) 5 S.L.T. 294.

[43] *Mackessock* v. *Drew* (1822) 2 S. 13; *Edinburgh, etc. Ry.* v. *Hill* (1840) 2 D. 486.

[44] *Kerr* v. *Bremner* (1835) 14 S. 180.

[45] *Kirkaldy* v. *Dalgairn's Trs.*, 16 June, 1809, F.C.; *Brysson* v. *Mitchell* (1823) 2 S. 382.

[46] *Cameron* v. *Nicol*, 1930 S.C. 1, 15.

[47] *Bellshill and Mossend Co-operative Socy. Ltd.* v. *Dalziel Co-operative Socy. Ltd.*, 1960 S.C. (H.L.) 64.

An award excludes subsequent consideration of the issues between the parties in the same way as does a decree of court.[48]

Case stated on question of law

Subject to express provision to the contrary in an agreement to refer to arbitration, the arbiter or oversman may, on the application of a party to the arbitration, and shall, if the Court of Session on such an application so directs, at any stage in the arbitration state a case for the opinion of that court on any question of law arising in the arbitration.[49] In certain cases of statutory arbitration the arbiter may, or may be required by either party to, state a case for the opinion of the court on a question of law arising in the course of the arbitration.[50] In such a case the arbiter is bound to apply the law laid down by the court.[51] A request must be made before the arbitration proceedings have terminated.[52]

If arbitration abortive or not exhaustive

A contractual reference to arbitration does not wholly oust the jurisdiction of the courts; if the arbitration from any cause proves abortive, the court's jurisdiction revives to the effect of enabling it to hear and determine the action on its merits.[53] Similarly if the arbitration cannot exhaust all the matters in issue between the parties, the others must be determined by the court.[54]

Enforcement of decree-arbitral

An arbiter has no power to enforce his award, but a submission may contain a clause consenting to registration of the submission and award for preservation and execution, in which case summary diligence may proceed on an extract from the register. Failing this the award may be enforced by action in court for decree conform.[55] Foreign arbitral awards

---

[48] *Fraser v. Lord Lovat* (1850) 7 Bell 171; *Orrell v. O.* (1859) 21 D. 554.

[49] Administration of Justice (Sc.) Act, 1972, S. 3; *Gunac v. Inverclyde D.C.*, 1983 S.L.T. 130. This does not apply to arbitrations under statutes conferring power to appeal or to state a case for a court or tribunal, nor to arbitrations relating to trade disputes within the Industrial Courts Act, 1919, as amended.

[50] *Euman v. Dalziel*, 1912 S.C. 966; *L.M.S. Ry. v. Glasgow Corpn.*, 1940 S.C. 363. It is incompetent by action to have the arbiter ordained to state a case in particular terms: *Forsyth-Grant v. Salmon and Gordon*, 1961, S.C. 54.

[51] *Johnston's Trs. v. Glasgow Corpn.*, 1912 S.C. 300; *Mitchell-Gill v. Buchan*, 1921 S.C. 390.

[52] *Johnson v. Gill*, 1978 S.C. 74.

[53] *Hamlyn v. Talisker Distillery* (1894) 21 R. (H.L.) 21, 25; *Mauritzen v. Baltic Shipping Co.*, 1948 S.C. 646, 651.

[54] *N.B. Ry. v. Newburgh and North Fife Ry.*, 1911 S.C. 710, 721.

[55] *McCosh v. Moore* (1905) 8 F. 31. On defences see *Whitehead v. Finlay* (1883) 11 S. 170.

are, subject to statutory conditions,[56] enforceable by action, or, if the agreement for arbitration contains consent to the registration of the award in the Books of Council and Session and the award is so registered, by summary diligence.[57] An award may be unenforceable if it is in unreasonable restraint of trade.[58]

Challenging award

It is not open to appeal to the courts against an arbiter's decision on fact or law, or against his award on the merits, as this would defeat the object of arbitration.[59] A decision on relevancy cannot be challenged.[60] The Articles of Regulation, 1695,[61] provided that no award of arbiters pronounced on a subscribed submission might be reduced save on the ground of corruption,[62] bribery, or falsehood. Corruption must be actual. An error in law is not challengeable as 'constructive corruption'.[63]

Apart therefrom, at common law reduction of an award may be sought on the ground that the award is improbative,[64] or *ultra vires*, or the arbiter acted *ultra fines compromissi*,[65] or that the award does not exhaust the submission,[66] or that the arbiter refused proof,[67] or refused to hear parties,[68] or heard only one party,[69] or refused to receive a claim tendered by one party,[70] or that the award is uncertain or ambiguous, or has not been delivered, or has been impetrated by fraud or improper influence,[71] or the arbiter has been misled by the improper and unfair

---

[56] Arbitration Act, 1950, Part II, especially S. 37; *Masinimport v. Scottish Light Industries*, 1976 S.C. 102.

[57] Ibid., S. 41.

[58] *Bellshill and Mossend Co-operative Socy. Ltd. v. Dalziel Co-op. Socy. Ltd.*, 1958 S.C. 400.

[59] *Mackenzie v. Girvan* (1840) 2 Bell 43; *Brakinrig v. Menzies* (1841) 4 D. 274 (judicial referee); *Mitchell v. Cable* (1848) 10 D. 1297; *Holmes Oil Co. v. Pumpherston Oil Co.* (1891) 18 R. (H.L.) 52.

[60] *Brown v. Associated Fireclay Companies*, 1937 S.C. (H.L.) 42.

[61] A.S. 2 Nov. 1695, S. 25 (issued by Commissioners under Act, 1693, c. 34); see *Adams v. G.N.S. Ry.* (1890) 18 R. (H.L.) at 7–8.

[62] *Fraser v. Wright* (1838) 16 S. 1055; *Mitchell v. Cable* (1848) 10 D 1297; *Miller v. Millar* (1855) 17 D. 689; *Ledingham v. Elphinstone* (1859) 22 D. 245; *Alexander v. Bridge of Allan Water Co.* (1869) 7 M. 492; *Morisons v. Thomson's Trs.* (1880) 8 R. 147; *Adams v. G.N.S. Ry.* (1890) 18 R. (H.L.) 1. See also *Johnson v. Lamb*, 1981 S.L.T. 300.

[63] *Adams, supra; Robson v. Menzies*, 1913 S.C. (J.) 90, 94.

[64] *McLaren v. Aikman*, 1939 S.C. 222 cf. *Dykes v. Roy* (1869) 7 M. 357.

[65] *Traill v. Coghill* (1885) 22 S.L.R. 616; *Adams, supra; Miller v. Oliver & Boyd* (1903) 6 F. 77; *McIntyre v. Forbes*, 1939 S.L.T. 62.

[66] *Pollich v. Heatley*, 1910, S.C. 469; *Donald v. Shiell's Exrx.*, 1937 S.C. 52; *Dunlop v. Mundell*, 1943 S.L.T. 286.

[67] *Mitchell, supra; Brown v. Assoc. Fireclay Companies*, 1937 S.C. (H.L.) 42.

[68] *Sharp v. Bickerdike* (1815) 3 Dow 102; *Holmes Oil Co. v. Pumpherston Oil Co.* (1891) 18 R. (H.L.) 52; *Black v. Williams*, 1923 S. C. 510; *Islay Estates Co. v. McCormick*, 1937 S.N. 28.

[69] *Sharp, supra;* but see *Black v. Williams*, 1924 S.C. (H.L.) 22.

[70] *Drummond v. Martin* (1906) 14 S.L.T. 365.

[71] *Logan v. Lang*, 15 Nov. 1789, F.C.

conduct of one party.[72] In mercantile arbitrations the court is slow to reduce an award if substantially just, even though the procedure may not have been wholly regular.[73] In a statutory arbitration it is misconduct on the arbiter's part to have taken the court's opinion on a question of law and not to apply it.[76] An award may be reduced in part, if valid and invalid parts can be severed.[75]

An award must stand on its own and speak for itself. It is not competent in a reduction to examine the arbiter, save to explain an ambiguity in his award or to state whether, in making a valuation, he considered matters not included in the submission to him and accordingly outwith his jurisdiction,[76] but it is competent to take the arbiter's note into consideration.[77]

Arbitration excluding later civil action

A civil action is barred by a prior arbitration if the same questions were properly and competently before the arbiter and properly resolved by him; if not, civil action is not excluded.[78]

[72] *Calder v. Gordon* (1837) 15 S. 463.
[73] *Hope v. Crookston Bros.* (1890) 17 R. 868.
[74] *Mitchell-Gill v. Buchan*, 1912, S.C. 390.
[75] *Cox v. Binning* (1867) 6 M. 161; *Adams, supra; Islay Estates Co., supra.*
[76] *Glasgow City Ry. v. Macgeorge, Cowan & Galloway* (1886) 13 R. 609; *Clippens Oil Co. v. Edinburgh Water Trs.* (1901) 3 F. 1113, 1128; *Donald v. Shiell's Exrx.*, 1937 S.C. 52; *Dunlop v. Mundell*, 1943 S.L.T. 286.
[77] *Holmes Oil Co., supra; Farrans v. Roxburgh C.C.*, 1970 S.L.T. 334.
[78] *Crudens v. Tayside Health Board*, 1979 S.C. 142.

CHAPTER 1.7

AUTHENTICATION OF DEEDS

A deed or writ is an expression of a party's meaning in words marked on paper or some similar substance. The words may be in ink or pencil,[1] written, typewritten,[2] printed, or otherwise marked, or partly in one medium, partly in another.[3] The deed or writ may be intended to constitute an offer or undertaking, a conveyance of property, an expression of testamentary desire, or any other lawful communication of meaning. The requisites of authentication are prescribed to determine whether or not the deed can be treated without further evidence as a concluded act or expression of intention by the apparent granter thereof. For the purposes of authentication writs can be distinguished as solemnly attested deeds, holograph writings, writings *in re mercatoria*, and writings statutorily privileged.[4]

SOLEMNLY ATTESTED DEEDS

The formal authentication of deeds has long been regulated by statutes which prescribed solemnities of execution. Originally sealing was necessary,[5] but the Subscription of Deeds Act, 1540 (c. 37) provided that deeds even if sealed should be ineffective without the subscription of the granter or, if he could not write, of a notary.[6] The Subscription of Deeds Act, 1579 (c. 18) (repealed in part) required all 'contracts, obligations, reversions, assignations and discharges or reversions or eiks thereto, and generally all writs importing heritable title, or other bonds and obligations of great importance' to be subscribed and sealed by the principal parties if they could subscribe, otherwise by two notaries before four witnesses, designated by their dwelling places or otherwise that they may

---

[1] *Muir's Trs.* (1869) 8 M. 53; *Simsons* v. *S.* (1883) 10 R. 1247; cf. *Hope* v. *Derwent Rolling Mills* (1905) 7 F. 837.

[2] *Simpson's Trs.* v. *Macharg* (1902) 9 S.L.T. 398.

[3] Titles to Land Consolidation Act, 1868, S. 149.

[4] See generally Stair IV, 42, 1–19; Mack. III, 2, 4–5; Bankt. I, 11, 24–52; Ersk. III, 2, 6–25; Bell, *Comm.* I, 340–5; *Prin.* § 19–21, 2225–32; Duff on *Deeds*; Bell, *Convg.* I, 23–101; Menzies, 77–165; Wood, 66–97; Craigie, *Mov.* 49–97; Dickson I, 339–474; Walkers, 181–217.

[5] Bell, *Convg.* I, 27; Menzies, 82; Craigie, *Mov.* 49.

[6] Bell, *Convg.* I, 28; Menzies, 83; Wood, 68; Craigie, *Mov.* 49.

be known, present at the time.[7] The Act, 1584, c. 11 (later repealed) declared sealing unnecessary in the case of writs agreed to be registered in the Books of Council and Session, and thereafter sealing fell into disuse.[8] The Act, 1593, c. 25 (repealed) required mention of the name and designation of the writer of the deed.[9] The Writs Act, 1672 (c. 16) allowed writs passing the Great or Privy Seals to be written bookwise, each page being signed. The Subscription of Deeds Act, 1681 (c. 5), provided that witnesses must subscribe, that the writer and witnesses must be named and designed in the deed and that these facts could not be supplied by separate condescendence, that no person should subscribe as witness unless he knew the party and saw him subscribe, or saw or heard him give warrant to a notary or notaries to subscribe for him and in evidence thereof touch the notary's pen, or hear him, at the time of the witness's subscription, acknowledge his signature.[10] The Act, 1686, c. 29 (repealed) allowed sasines to be written bookwise, and the Deeds Act, 1696 (c. 15), made it competent to write any deed bookwise, every page to be numbered and signed, and the last page mentioning how many pages are comprised in the writ, and it alone being signed by the witnesses.[11] The requirement of stating of how many pages the deed consisted (Deeds Act, 1696) if written bookwise, was not essential if the deed were on one sheet, even if folded to make four pages,[12] or on sheets battered together to form a roll, in which case it had to be sidescribed at the joins of the sheets.[13] Even where essential, neither an error in stating the number of pages,[14] nor an erasure of part of the word stating the number[15] was fatal to the deed.

The requirement of numbering the pages (Deeds Act, 1696) disappeared with the Form of Deeds (Sc.) Act, 1856.

Mention of the name and designation of the writer under the Act of 1593 and the Subscription of Deeds Act, 1681 (c. 5), continued to be required till 1874, but the requirements were not strictly interpreted.[16] Mention of the designation of the witnesses also continued to 1874 but this also was interpreted reasonably.[17]

---

[7] Bell, *Convg.* I, 29; Menzies, 84; Wood, 68; Craigie, *Mov.* 49.
[8] Ersk. III, 2, 7; Bell, *Convg.* I, 30; Menzies, 85; Wood, 68; Craigie, *Mov.* 50.
[9] Bell, *Convg.* I, 31; Menzies, 85; Wood, 68; Craigie, *Mov.* 50.
[10] Ersk. III, 2, 13; Bell, *Convg.* I, 31–2; Menzies, 85–6; Wood, 68–9; Craigie, *Mov.* 50.
[11] Bell, *Convg.* I, 32; Menzies, 95; Wood, 69; Craigie, *Mov.* 51; *Gardner v. Lucas* (1878) 5 R. (H.L.) 105.
[12] *Robertson v. Ker* (1742) Mor. 16955; *Williamson v. W.* (1742) Mor. 16955; *Macdonald v. M.* (1778) Mor. 16956; *Smith v. B. of Scotland*, 4 July 1816, F.C.
[13] Craigie, *Mov.* 51.
[14] *Smith v. N.B. Ins. Co.* (1850) 12 D. 1132.
[15] *Gaywood v. McEand* (1828) 6 S. 991; *Cassilis's Trs. v. Kennedy* (1831) 9 S. 663.
[16] Bell, *Convg.* I, 59; Menzies, 87–90; *Dronnan v. Montgomery* (1716) Mor. 16869; *Ewing v. Semple* (1739) Mor. 1352; *Macpherson v. M.* (1855) 17 D. 357; *Callender v. C's Trs.* (1863) 2 M. 291; *Johnston v. Pettigrew* (1865) 3 M. 954; but see *Mitchell v. Scott's Trs.* (1874) 2 R. 162.
[17] Menzies, 120.

Later reforms of solemnities

The Form of Deeds (Sc.) Act, 1856, abolished the need to number the pages but preserved the need to state of how many pages the deed consisted. The Titles to Land Consolidation (Sc.) Act, 1868, permitted additional sheets to be added to writs (S. 140) and (S. 149) allowed deeds to be partly written and partly printed or engraved or lithographed,[18] provided that in the testing clause the date, the names and designations of the witnesses, the number of pages of the deed, if specified, and the name and designation of the writer of the written portions of the deed were expressed at length, and abolished the need to name the writer of the written portions of the testing clause.

The Conveyancing (Sc.) Act, 1874, S. 38 made it unnecessary to state the name or designation of the printer or writer, the number of pages, or the names and designations of the witnesses in the body or testing clause of the deed, provided that, if not named and designed in the body or testing clause, their designations should be appended to or follow their subscriptions. This section is not retrospective.[19]

Modern essentials

In consequence, since 1874, the essentials of authentication are (1) subscription by the granter[20] at the end, if the deed consists of only one sheet, even if folded to make four pages,[21] or, if written bookwise, at the foot of each page and also at the end,[22] or, if written on more than one sheet joined into a roll, at each junction and also at the end,[23] save that, in the case of conveyances, deeds, instruments or writings, whether relating to land or not, executed after 28 November 1970, but not wills or other testamentary writings, it is no objection to the probative character of the deed that it is not subscribed or, if appropriate, signed and sealed, on every page other than the last page;[24] (2) authentication in the body of the deed or in the testing clause of deletions, interlineations, marginal additions and erasures; (3) subscription on the last page by two witnesses who know the granter or have credible information that the person

---

[18] Including typewritten: *Simpson's Trs.* v. *Macharg* (1902) 9 S.L.T. 398.

[19] *Gardner* v. *Lucas* (1878) 5 R. (H.L.) 105. For a form of testing clause see Craigie, *Mov.* 53.

[20] *Foley v. Costello* (1904) 6 F. 365; *Taylor's Exces.* v. *Thom*, 1914 S.C. 79; cf. *Bradford* v. *Young* (1884) 11 R. 1135.

[21] *Ferguson*, 1959 S.C. 56; cf. *McLaren* v. *Menzies* (1876) 3 R. 1151.

[22] The requirements of the Deeds Act, 1696, apply only to deeds written on more than one sheet and not to deeds which though written bookwise, are all on one sheet: Menzies, 96; *Smith* v. *Bank of Scotland* (1824) 2 Sh. App. 265; *McCrummen's Trs.* v. *Edinburgh & Glasgow Bank* (1895) 21 D. (H.L.) 3; *Baird's Trs.* v. *B.*, 1955 S.C. 286; *Ferguson, supra.*

[23] Conveyancing and Feudal Reform (Sc.) Act, 1970, S. 44. Plans, inventories, schedules, and other appendices to the deed should also be signed, at the foot of the page thereof, subject to the same saving for deeds executed after 28 Nov. 1970.

[24] Conveyancing and Feudal Reform (Sc.) Act, 1970, S. 44.

signing is the granter, and who see the granter subscribe, or hear him acknowledge his signature; and (4) mention of the designations of the witnesses in the body of the deed, or in the testing clause, or appended to their signatures. The designations may be appended or added at any time before the deed is recorded in any register for preservation, or founded on in court, and need not be written by the witnesses themselves.[25] The essentials are not satisfied by a signature on the front of a one-page document, signed also and witnessed on the back, but with no connecting link between front and back.[26] The requirements of authentication do not apply to Crown writs.[27]

Inessentials

Though usually included, the place of signing[28] and date of signing[29] are inessential, though the date must be given if the validity should depend on the specification of the date.[30] A will or other deed may be written in pencil.[31] A deed executed on a Sunday is valid.[32] The addition of the word 'witness' after a witness's signature has never been essential,[33] though sometimes useful to supplement a defective testing clause.[34] Since 1874 it has not been essential to state the number of pages of which the deed consists, the name and designation of the writer, or the names and designations of the witnesses if their designations are appended to or follow their signatures.

Essential (1)—Subscription by granter

The Sovereign may superscribe; all others must subscribe, at the end of the last page on which the deed is written,[35] and, in the case of wills, at the foot of every page.[36] Signature in the margin is not subscription.[37] By the Lyon King of Arms Act, 1672 (c. 47), noblemen and Anglican bishops

---

[25] Conveyancing Act, 1874, S. 38.

[26] *Baird's Trs.* v. *B.*, 1955 S.C. 286; contrast *Russell's Exor.* v. *Duke*, 1946 S.L.T. 242.

[27] *Catton* v. *Mackenzie* (1874) 1 R. 488.

[28] Ersk. III, 2, 18; Bell, *Convg.* I, 64.

[29] Bell, *Convg.* I, 65.

[30] *Elliot* v. *Faulke* (1844) 6 D. 411.

[31] *Simsons* v. *S.* (1883) 10 R. 1247.

[32] *Elliot, supra.*

[33] *Morison* v. *L. Salton* (1694) 4 B.S. 163; *L. Blantyre* (1850) 13 D. 40.

[34] *Wemyss* v. *Hay* (1825) 1 W. & S. 140; *McDougall* v. *McD.* (1875) 2 R. 814.

[35] *Taylor's Exces., supra; McKillop* v. *Secy. of State for Scotland* (1950) 39 L.C. 17; *McLay* v. *Farrell,* 1950 S.C. 149. Subscription on a blank page following the last page will not suffice: *Baird's Trs.* v. *B.*, 1955 S.C. 286.

[36] Conveyancing and Feudal Reform (Sc.) Act, 1970, S. 44. Initials on each page will not suffice: *Gardner* v. *Beresford's Trs.* (1877) 5 R. (H.L.) 105.

[37] *Robbie* v. *Carr,* 1959 S.L.T. (Notes) 16.

may subscribe by their titles, but all others do so by their Christian names, or the initial or any abbreviation[38] thereof, and surname, adding, if they wish, the designation of their lands.[39] Peers use their title of honour and peers' eldest sons their courtesy titles.[40]

Married women may use their maiden surname,[41] but commonly use their husband's surname.[42] A deletion of a married name and the substitution of the granter's maiden surname has been held irrelevant, where the granter had later been divorced and resumed her maiden name, and it was admitted that there was no intention to revoke the deed.[43]

The subscription must be complete,[44] by the hand of the granter,[45] which may be supported[46] but not guided in whole[47] or in part,[48] and it must be complete.[49] A signature by mark[50] or stamp[51] or cyclostyle[52] or on a tracing by another[53] or typewritten[54] is valueless, though a granter may follow a copy of his signature by another.[55] A signature may be touched up by the granter, even after attestation and outwith the presence of the witnesses.[56] It is valid though wrongly spelled,[57] or illegible,[58] or signed by a blind person.[59] If signed on erasure not declared, it has been held that the onus is on the challenger to show that the signature was not genuine or had not been duly tested.[60]

A signature by initials, if recognizably the initial letters of the granter's name,[61] may be sustained if it be proved that the granter did subscribe the

---

[38] Bell, Convg. I, 37; Menzies, 98; Craigie, Mov. 66.

[39] Any discrepancy between the names in the body of the deed and the signature should be mentioned in the testing clause e.g. 'The said A.B.C.D. subscribing A.D.'.

[40] Bell, Menzies, supra.

[41] Dunlop v. Greenlees' Trs. (1863) 2 M. 1. It is not correct to sign both maiden name and married name, or use the initial of the maiden name before the married surname: see Grieve's Trs. v. Japp's Trs. 1917, 1 S.L.T. 70.

[42] The surname used should be that under which the granter customarily passed at that time.

[43] Fotheringham's Tr. v. Reid, 1936 S.C. 831.

[44] Moncrieff v. Monypenny (1711) Mor. 15936; Rob. App. 26.

[45] Moncrieff, supra.

[46] Noble v. N. (1875) 3 R. 74.

[47] Ballingall v. Robertson (1806) Hume 916; Wilson v. Pringles (1814) Hume 923; Harkness v. H. (1821) 2 Mur. 558.

[48] Moncrieff v. Monypenny (1711) Mor. 15936; Rob. App. 26.

[49] Moncrieff, supra.

[50] Crosbie v. Wilson (1865) 3 M. 870; Morton v. French 1908 S.C. 171; Donald v. McGregor's Exors., 1926 S.L.T. 103.

[51] Stirling-Stuart v. Stirling-Crawfurd's Trs. (1885) 12 R. 610.

[52] Whyte v. Watt (1893) 21 R. 165.

[53] Crosbie v. Pickens (1749) Mor. 16814; cf. Whyte v. Watt (1893) 21 R. 165.

[54] McBeath's Trs. v. McB., 1935 S.C. 471, 476.

[55] Wilson v. Raeburn (1800) Hume 912.

[56] Stirling-Stuart, supra.

[57] Perryman v. McClymont (1852) 14 D. 508.

[58] Stirling-Stuart, supra.

[59] E. Fife v. Fife's Trs. (1823) 1 Sh. App. 498; Ker v. Hotchkis (1837) 15 S. 983.

[60] Brown v. Duncan (1888) 15 R. 511.

[61] Din v. Gillies, 18 June 1812, F.C.; Weirs v. Ralstons, 22 June 1813, F.C.

deed by initials and was accustomed to subscribe by initials only,[62] but it is not probative *per se*.[63] Similarly a signature of a will by Christian name only has been sustained,[64] though not probative without evidence that such was the granter's normal practice. The designation 'Mr.' or 'Mrs.' or 'Miss' followed by a surname is not a valid signature,[65] but the addition of such a prefix to an otherwise valid signature does not affect it.[66]

Deeds executed by mark are null,[67] but certain documents *in re mercatoria* may be so executed,[68] and statute has allowed this,[69] but a mark is not a 'writing under his hand'.[70] The subscription may have preceded the writing of the body of the deed, but the deed is valid if the signature is thereafter acknowledged to the witnesses who then sign.[71] Anything on the deed below the subscription, unless itself subscribed, is not authenticated and invalid.[72] A deed has been held probative though the signature was on erasure not mentioned in the testing clause.[73]

Partnerships sign the firm name, adhibited by one partner, and the signatures of all individual partners. Within the scope of the firm's business the firm name signed by any partner suffices.

Modes of authentication of deeds granted by corporate bodies are prescribed by their constituting Act or charter, or by general legislation.[74]

Essential (2)—Authentication of corrections in deed

At common law deletions, interlineations, marginal additions, and words written on erasure had to be authenticated in the deed itself, usually by having corrections of any of these kinds declared in the testing clause and by having marginal additions signed or initialled as well.[75] Corrections not thus authenticated, if material, are held *pro non scriptis*, possibly with the result of vitiating the whole deed.[76]

---

[62] *Weirs* v. *Ralstons*, 22 June 1813; F.C.; *Speirs* v. *Home Speirs* (1879) 6 R. 1359; Bell, *Convg.* I, 49; Menzies, 100. This does not apply to a witness's signature: *Meek* v. *Dunlop* (1707) Mor. 16806.

[63] *Gardner* v. *Lucas* (1878) 5 R. (H.L.) 105.

[64] *Draper* v. *Thomason*, 1954 S.C. 136; cf. *Rhodes* v. *Peterson*, 1971 S.C. 56.

[65] *Allan and Crichton*, 1933 S.L.T. (Sh. Ct.) 2.

[66] cf. *Ferguson*, 1959 S.C. 56.

[67] *Graham* v. *Macleod* (1848) 11 D. 173; *Crosbie* v. *Wilson* (1865) 3 M. 870; *Donald* v. *McGregor's Exors.*, 1926 S.L.T. 103.

[68] Bell, *Comm.* I, 343; *Bryan* v. *Murdoch* (1827) 2 W. & S. 568.

[69] Marriage Notice (Sc.) Act, 1878, S. 16 (repealed).

[70] *Morton* v. *French*, 1908 S.C. 171.

[71] *Carsewell's Trs.* v. *C.* (1895) 3 S.L.T. 218.

[72] *Taylor's Exces.* v. *Thom*, 1914 S.C. 79; *McLay* v. *Farrell*, 1950 S.C. 149.

[73] *Brown* v. *Duncan* (1888) 15 R. 511.

[74] Local Govt. (Sc.) Act, 1973, S. 193; Companies Act, 1985, S. 36.

[75] Bell, *Convg.* I, 70; Menzies, 138; Wood, 88; Craigie, *Mov.* 59.

[76] See e.g. *Reid* v. *Kedder* (1840) 1 Rob. 183; *Shepherd* v. *Grant's Trs.* (1847) 6 Bell 153; *Kirkwood* v. *Patrick* (1847) 9 D. 1361; *Boswell* v. *B.* (1852) 14 D. 378; *Fraser* v. *F.* (1854) 16 D. 863; *Gollan* v. *G.* (1863) 1 M. (H.L.) 65; *Munro* v. *Butler Johnstone* (1868) 7 M. 250; *Cattanach's Trs.* v. *Jamieson* (1884) 11 R. 972; *Drummond* v. *Peddie* (1893) 1 S.L.T. 189. In

Words deleted will be treated as cancelled if the deletion is authenticated[77] or intent to delete can be inferred from the circumstances.[78] Interlineations and marginal additions must be authenticated even if apparently holograph,[79] though a holograph addition to a deed, above the signature, has been held valid.[80] Words written on erasures, unless authenticated, will be treated *pro non scriptis*; if the words be essential the deed is vitiated, but if not essential the deed stands but the word on erasure is ignored.[81] Where a deed was *ex facie* probative but the signature was written on erasure it was held that the onus of disproof was on the challenger.[82]

In testamentary writings corrections by the testator not properly authenticated do not invalidate the deed *in toto*, if, as altered, it still contains an effectual expression of final testamentary intention.[83] Unauthenticated alterations on a copy of a will are ineffective[84] but authenticated alterations are effective.[85]

By statute[86] no challenge of a notarial instrument by reduction or exception may receive effect, on the ground that any part of the instrument is written on erasure, unless it be proved that such erasures have been made for the purpose of fraud, or the record thereof is not conformable to the instrument as presented for registration. Also[87] no challenge of a deed recorded in the register of sasines may receive effect on the ground that any part of the record thereof is written on erasure unless it be proved to have been made for the purpose of fraud, or the record is not conformable to the deed as presented for registration.

Defects in a testing clause may be rectified at any time before the deed is recorded for preservation or judicially founded upon.[88]

certain cases, e.g. *Milne's Exor.* v. *Waugh*, 1913 S.C. 203; *Allan's Exor.* v. *A.*, 1920 S.C. 732; intention to delete has been inferred from words scored through even though not authenticated. Deletion cannot be effected by pasting a slip of paper over part of a deed: *Dunsire* v. *Bell*, 1909 S.C. (J.) 5, nor by unauthenticated alterations in a copy: *Manson* v. *Edinburgh Royal Institution*, 1948 S.L.T. 196.

[77] *Pattison's Trs.* v. *Edinburgh University* (1888) 16 R. 73.
[78] *Milne's Exor.* v. *Waugh*, 1913 S.C. 203; *Allan's Exor*, v. *A.*, 1920 S.C. 732; see also *Gemmell's Exor.*, v. *Stirling*, 1923 S.L.T. 384.
[79] *Brown* v. *Maxwell's Exors.* (1884) 11 R. 821.
[80] *Gray's Trs.* v. *Dow* (1900) 3 F. 79.
[81] *Gollan* v. *G., supra; McDougall* v. *McD.* (1875) 2 R. 814; *Munro* v. *Butler Johnstone* (1868) 7 M. 250.
[82] *Brown* v. *Duncan* (1888) 15 R. 511. See also *Dowie* v. *Barclay* (1871) 9 M. 726; *Muir* v. *Thompson* (1876) 3 R. (H.L.) 1.
[83] *Robertson* v. *Ogilvie's Trs.* (1844) 7 D. 236; *Richardson* v. *Biggar* (1845) 8 D. 315; *Grant* v. *Stoddart* (1849) 11 D. 860; *Dundee Mags.* v. *Morris* (1858) 3 Macq. 134; *Parker* v. *Matheson* (1876) 13 S.L.R. 405; *Munro's Exors.* v. *M.* (1890) 18 R. 122; see also *Pattison's Trs.* v. *Edinburgh Univ.* (1888) 16 R. 73.
[84] *Manson* v. *Edinburgh Royal Institution*, 1948 S.L.T. 196.
[85] *Thomson's Trs.* v. *Bowhill Baptist Ch.*, 1956 S.C. 217.
[86] Titles to Land Consolidation (Sc.) Act, 1868, S. 144 extending Erasures in Deeds (Sc.) Act, 1836, extended to notices of title by Conveyancing (Sc.) Act, 1924, S. 6.
[87] Conveyancing (Sc.) Act, 1874, S. 54.
[88] Ibid., S. 38.

Essentials (3) and (4)—Subscriptions and designations of witnesses

Custom has long established two as the necessary number of witnesses.[89] Pupils,[90] blind persons,[91] and persons mentally defective or mentally incapable[92] may not act as witnesses, nor may one party to a deed witness the signature of another.[93] Any person, male or female, married or unmarried, not being subject to any legal incapacity, aged fourteen or over, may act.[94] Persons may act as witnesses notwithstanding close relationship to the granter,[95] legal infamy,[96] or having an interest, even beneficial, in the deed.[97]

Each witness must either know the granter, or have credible information that the person signing is the person designed as granter of the deed.[98] Each must see the granter subscribe, or hear him acknowledge his signature, before the witness signs.[99] It is competent for the granter to sign in the presence of one witness and acknowledge his signature to the other, or acknowledge it on separate occasions to the two witnesses.[1] It is not essential that the granter acknowledges his signature by spoken words.[2] Signature as witness before the granter signs is a nullity.[3] A mutual deed signed only by one party before witnesses may be valid *quoad* that party only.[4]

The witnesses sign only at the end of the deed. They must have the express or implied authority of the granter to attest, and sign by his request. Two witnesses suffice for any one or more signatures to the same deed, so long as the witnesses saw, or heard acknowledged, each signature, and they need sign only once;[5] if the granters sign at different places or times the witnesses need sign only once if they saw the parties subscribe.[6] They do not need to sign in presence of the granter[7] and may do so at any time before the deed is founded on or registered for

---

[89] Bell, *Convg.* I, 50; Menzies, 113; Wood, 69.
[90] *Davidson* v. *Charteris* (1738) Mor. 16899.
[91] *Cunningham* v. *Spence* (1824) 3 S. 205.
[92] Menzies, 111.
[93] Bell, *Convg.* I, 51; *Miller* v. *Farquharson* (1835) 13 S. 838.
[94] Titles to Land Consolidation (Sc.) Act, 1868, S. 139; *Hannay* (1873) 1 R. 246.
[95] *Falconer* v. *Arbuthnot* (1750) Mor. 16759; *Simsons* v. *S.* (1883) 10 R. 1247; but see *Brownlee* v. *Robb*, 1907 S.C. 1302, 1310.
[96] *Lockhart* v. *Baillie* (1710) Mor. 8433.
[97] *Mitchell* v. *Miller* (1742) Mor. 16900; *Simsons* v. *S.* (1883) 10 R. 1247.
[98] *Walker* v. *Adamson's Reps.* (1716) Mor. 16896; *Brock* v. *B.*, 1908 S.C. 964.
[99] *Geddes* v. *Reid* (1891) R. 1186; *Forrest* v. *Low's Trs.*, 1907 S.C. 1240; *Boyd* v. *Shaw*, 1927 S.C. 414.
[1] *Robertson* v. *McGraig* (1823) 2 S. 544; *Hogg* v. *Campbell* (1864) 2 M. 848.
[2] *Cumming* v. *Skeoch's Trs.* (1879) 6 R. 540, 963; *Sutherland* v. *Low* (1901) 8 S.L.T. 395; 3 F. 972.
[3] *Smyth* v. *S.* (1876) 3 R. 573.
[4] *Millar* v. *Birrell* (1876) 4 R. 87.
[5] *Hardies* v. *H.*, 6 Dec. 1810, F.C.
[6] *Edmonston* v. *E.* (1749) Mor. 16901; but see *Walker* v. *Whitwell*, 1916 S.C. (H.L.) 75; *Hynd's Tr.* v. *Hynd's Trs.*, 1955 S.C. (H.L.) 1.
[7] *Condie* v. *Buchan* (1823) 2 S. 432; *Thomson* v. *Clarkson's Trs.* (1892) 20 R. 59.

preservation,[8] but a long interval should not be allowed to elapse,[9] and they cannot sign after his death.[10] A witness who only hears a signature acknowledged is not entitled to sign *ex intervallo*.[11] If one witness fails to sign the deed is not validly authenticated.[12] A granter may acknowledge his subscription to two witnesses separately at different times.[13]

By their signatures the witnesses attest the execution only; they have no concern with the substance of the deed[14] and the deed may be so folded or covered that they see only the signature which they attest.[15]

The witnesses adhibit their signatures in the same way as do granters, customarily but not necessarily appending the word 'Witness' thereafter. Their designations, included in the testing clause or following their signatures, customarily comprise the occupations and addresses, business or residential, of the witnesses and need only be sufficient to identify them.[16] They may be added by another hand.[17] A discrepancy between a witness's signature and his name in the testing clause is curable as an informality of execution.[18] An erroneous designation does not vitiate, certainly where the meaning is plain from the context.[19] The want of designations may be supplied before the deed is founded on in any court and is in any event curable as an informality of execution.[20]

The onus on a party challenging a deed *ex facie* solemnly executed is heavy,[21] and a granter seeking to reduce his own deed on the ground of defective attestation may be held barred particularly if third parties have acted on the faith of the deed.[22]

Completion of testing clause

The testing clause though customary is not essential; it is part of the deed and any condition or provision therein which might, and should prefer-

---

[8] *Stewart v. Burns* (1877) 4 R. 427; *Murray* (1904) 6 F. 840.
[9] *Frank v. F.* (1795) Mor. 16842; affd. (1809) 5 Pat. 278; *Thomson v. Clarkson's Trs.* (1892) 20 R. 59; *Stewart v. Burns* (1877) 4R. 427 must now be considered very doubtful.
[10] *Walker v. Whitwell*, 1916 S.C. (H.L.) 75, overruling *Tener's Trs. v. T's Trs.* (1879) 6 R. 1111; see also *Arnott v. Burt* (1872) 11 M. 62; *Beattie v. Bain's Trs.* (1899) 6 S.L.T. 277; *Brownlee v. Robb*, 1907 S.C. 1302.
[11] *Hogg v. Campbell* (1864) 2 M. 848; *Thomson v. Clarkson's Trs.* (1892) 20 R. 59.
[12] *Moncrieff v. Lowrie* (1896) 23 R. 577.
[13] *Hogg, supra.*
[14] Menzies, 113.
[15] *Lady Ormistoun v. Hamilton* (1708) Mor. 16890.
[16] *McDougall v. McD.* (1875) 2 R. 814.
[17] Conveyancing (Sc.) Act, 1874, S. 38.
[18] *Richardson's Trs.* (1891) 18 R. 1131.
[19] *Speirs v. S's Trs.* (1887) 5 R. 923.
[20] *Thomson's Trs. v. Easson* (1878) 6 R. 141; and see *infra; Garrett* (1883) 20 S.L.R. 756; *Nisbet* (1879) 24 R. 411.
[21] *Smith v. Bank of Scotland* (1824) 2 Sh. App. 265; see also *Condie v. Buchan* (1823) 2 S. 432; *Cleland v. Paterson* (1837) 15 S. 1246; *Young v. Paton*, 1910 S.C. 63; *McArthur v. McA's Trs.*, 1931 S.L.T. 463.
[22] *Baird's Tr. v. Murray* (1883) 11 R. 153; *National Bank v. Campbell* (1892) 19 R. 885; *McLeish v. B.L. Bank*, 1911, 2 S.L.T. 168; *Boyd v. Shaw*, 1927 S.C. 414; *Sinclair v. S.*, 1949 S.L.T. (Notes) 16; *Smellie's Trs. v. S.*, 1953 S.L.T. (Notes) 22.

ably, have been in another clause, is valid, though this is not the function of the testing clause,[23] but words in the testing clause can have no effect in altering or adding to the deed.[24]

The testing clause should be completed at once[25] but may be completed at any time,[26] but not after the death of the granter[27] nor after the deed has been registered for preservation or founded on in court,[28] unless it is not founded on by the party producing it.[29] There should be no material error in it, though a mistake or erasure therein is not necessarily fatal.[30] It need not state the names of the witnesses, but only such designations as, taken along with their subscriptions, are sufficient for their identification.[31] Words in the testing clause can have no effect in altering or adding to the provisions of the deed.[32]

Conventional or additional solemnities

Parties may agree or specify that other, greater or less, solemnities than are required by law shall be used in the execution of any deed pursuant to their specification,[33] such as future informal writings supplementary to a will.[34]

Informality of execution

The Conveyancing Act, 1874, S. 39, provides that a deed[35] subscribed by the granter and bearing to be attested by two witnesses subscribing, is not to be deemed invalid or denied effect because of any informality of execution, but the burden of proving that it was subscribed by the granter and by the witnesses lies on the party using or upholding the deed, and proof thereof may be led in any action in which the deed is founded on or objected to, or in a special application to the court to have it declared that

---

[23] *Dunlop* v. *Greenlees' Trs.* (1865) 3 M. (H.L.) 46; *Chambers' Trs.* v. *Smiths* (1878) 5 R. (H.L.) 151; *Gibson's Trs.* v. *Lamb*, 1931 S.L.T. 22.
[24] *Chambers' Trs., supra; Blair* v. *Assets Co.* (1896) 23 R. (H.L.) 36.
[25] Bell, *Convg.* I, 234.
[26] *Blair* v. *E. Galloway* (1827) 6 S. 51 (32 years later); *Stewart* v. *Burns* (1877) 4 R. 427 (4 months later); *sed quaere.*
[27] *Walker* v. *Whitwell*, 1916 S.C. (H.L.) 75; but see *Veasey* v. *Malcolm's Trs.* (1875) 2 R. 748.
[28] Conveyancing (Sc.) Act, 1874, S. 38; *Hill* v. *Arthur* (1870) 9 M. 223; see also *Blair* v. *E. Galloway* (1827) 6 S. 51; *Caldwell* (1871) 10 M. 99.
[29] *Millar* v. *Birrell* (1876) 4 R. 87.
[30] *McDougall* v. *McD.* (1875) 2 R. 814.
[31] *McDougall, supra.*
[32] *Blair* v. *Assets Co.* (1896) 23 R. (H.L.) 36.
[33] *Campbell's Trs.* v. *C.* (1903) 5 F. 366; cf. *Nasmyth* v. *Hare* (1821) 1 Sh. App. 65.
[34] e.g. *Baird* v. *Jaap* (1856) 18 D. 1246; *Crosbie* v. *Wilson* (1865) 3 M. 870; *Lamont* v. *Glasgow Mags.* (1887) 14 R. 603; *Fraser* v. *Forbes' Trs.* (1899) 1 F. 513; *Waterson's Trs.* v. *St. Giles Boys' Club*, 1943 S.C. 369.
[35] See *McLaren* v. *Menzies* (1876) 3 R. 1151; *Brown* (1883) 11 R. 400.

such deed was so subscribed. This section is not retrospective.[36] Informalities of execution include signature on the last page only of a deed consisting of more than one sheet;[37] witnesses who only heard acknowledgement of the granter's signature signing *ex intervallo*;[38] a discrepancy between the witness's signature and his name in the testing clause;[39] a deed subscribed and attested but with the testing clause uncompleted;[40] a deed lacking the designations of the attesting witnesses;[41] subscription of granter or witnesses written on erasures;[42] signature with a docquet of attestation carrying over from the first to the third of four pages formed by a single sheet folded;[43] signature at the end only before witnesses but no testing clause;[44] a codicil partly on the last sheet of a will and unsigned, but continued on a further sheet and signed;[45] a will validly executed by the law of the place of execution, but defective by the rules of Scots law,[46] unauthenticated marginal additions, interlineations, and erasures;[47] a draft signed as principal.[48] Signature neither adhibited nor acknowledged in the presence of one of the subscribing witnesses is a fatal defect, not an informality.[49]

It is no objection to a petition under S. 39 that the particular informality could previously have been cured under S. 38 of the Act, but which remedy was no longer available in the circumstances.[50]

Defects not curable as informalities

The defect was held not curable but radical where a deed without a testing clause bore to be signed by the granter and witnesses, but the granter denied signing and the witnesses had signed but had not seen him sign nor heard him acknowledge his subscription and the person founding on the deed did not prove that the granter had signed it.[51] Nor does the section assist where the witnesses' signatures were adhibited before the granter signed and they neither saw him sign nor heard him acknowledge

---

[36] *Gardner* v. *Lucas* (1878) 5 R. (H.L.) 105; but see *Addison* (1875) 2 R. 457.
[37] *McLaren* v. *Menzies* (1876) 3 R. 1151; *Brown* (1883) 11 R. 400.
[38] *Thomson* v. *Clarkson's Trs.* (1892) 20 R. 59 (within one hour).
[39] *Richardson's Trs.* (1891) 18 R. 1131.
[40] *Addison* (1875) 2 R. 457.
[41] *Thomson's Trs.* v. *Easson* (1878) 6 R. 141; *Garrett* (1883) 20 S.L.R. 756; *Nisbet* (1879) 24 R. 411.
[42] *Brown* v. *Duncan* (1888) 15 R. 511.
[43] *Ferguson*, 1959 S.C. 56 cf. *McNeill* v. *M.*, 1973 S.L.T. (Sh. Ct.) 16.
[44] *Inglis' Trs.* v. *I.* (1901) 4 F. 365.
[45] *Brown* (1883) 11 R. 400.
[46] *Browne* (1882) 20 S.L.R. 76.
[47] *Veasey* v. *Malcolm's Trs.* (1875) 2 R. 748; *Walker* v. *Whitwell*, 1916 S.C. (H.L.) 75; *Elliot's Exors.*, 1939 S.L.T. 69.
[48] *Shiell*, 1936 S.L.T. 317.
[49] *Forrest* v. *Low's Trs.* 1907 S.C. 1240.
[50] *Thomson's Trs.* v. *Easson* (1878) 6 R. 141.
[51] *Geddes* v. *Reid* (1891) 18 R. 1186.

his subscription,[52] nor in a case where subscription was lacking,[53] nor where one witness subscribed *ex intervallo*, after the granter's death,[54] nor where a witness did not sign until after the deed had been judicially founded on or registered for preservation,[55] nor, in a case of notarial execution, if the notarial docquet is not holograph,[56] or was completed outwith the presence of the granter and witnesses,[57] or the notary had a disqualifying interest in the deed.[58]

Petitions under S. 39 for declarator that deeds were duly subscribed have been held unnecessary where there were small discrepancies between the granters' signatures and their names as stated in the body of the deeds.[59]

If the granter's signature is neither adhibited nor acknowledged in the presence of one of the witnesses it is not an informality but a fatal defect.[60] Similarly, for a witness not to sign till after the granter's death is not an informality but a fundamental nullity,[61] as is a deed registered for preservation or founded on in court before the witnesses have signed,[62] and a single sheet signed, and signed on the reverse before two witnesses, but there being no indication of connection between obverse and reverse.[63] A mutual deed signed and witnessed as to the one part and signed only as to the other may be effectual as to the one part and not the other.[64]

The court will set aside a deed *ex facie* perfectly regular and duly tested only on the clearest possible evidence, and not on the unsupported evidence of one attesting witness that the granter's signature had not been adhibited or acknowledged in her presence,[65] but it may do so in face of both witnesses's evidence if persuaded by other cogent evidence.[66] The granters of onerous deeds have been held barred from challenging their

---

[52] *Smyth* v. *S.* (1876) 3 R. 573; *Forrest* v. *Low's Trs.*, 1907 S.C. 1240; cf. *Stewart* v. *Burns* (1877) 4 R. 427.

[53] *Allan & Crichton*, 1933 S.L.T. (Sh. Ct.) 2; *Baird's Trs.* v. *B.*, 1955 S.C. 286.

[54] *Walker* v. *Whitwell*, 1916 S.C. (H.L.) 75.

[55] *Moncrieff* v. *Lawrie* (1896) 23 R. 577; but see *McLaren* v. *Menzies* (1876) 3 R. 1151, 1158; *Todd* v. *Reid* (1883) 20 S.L.R. 382.

[56] *Irvine* v. *McHardy* (1892) 19 R. 458.

[57] *Hynd's Tr.* v. *Hynd's Trs.*, 1955 S.C. (H.L.) 1.

[58] *Finlay* v. *F's Trs.*, 1948 S.C. 16; *Gorrie's Tr.* v. *Stiven's Exrx.*, 1952 S.C. 1; *Crawfurd's Trs.* v. *Glasgow R.I.*, 1955 S.C. 367.

[59] *Grieve's Trs.* v. *Japp's Trs.*, 1917, 1 S.L.T. 70; see also *Dickson's Trs.* v. *Goodall* (1820) Hume 925; *Veasey* v. *Malcolm's Trs.* (1875) 2 R. 748.

[60] *Smyth* v. *S.* (1876) 3 R. 573; *Forrest* v. *Low's Trs.*, 1907 S.C. 1240.

[61] *Tener's Trs.* v. *T's Trs.* (1879) 6 R. 1111, overruled by *Walker's Trs.* v. *Whitwell*, 1916 S.C. (H.L.) 75.

[62] *Moncrieff* v. *Lawrie* (1896) 23 R. 577.

[63] *Baird's Trs.* v. *B.*, 1955 S.C. 286; see also *McLaren* v. *Menzies* (1876) 3 R. 1151; *Russell's Exor.* v. *Duke*, 1946 S.L.T. 242; *Ferguson*, 1959 S.C. 56.

[64] *Millar* v. *Birrell* (1876) 4 R 87.

[65] *Forrests, supra.*

[66] *Young* v. *Paton*, 1910 S.C. 63.

own deeds on the ground that one instrumentary witness had neither seen them sign nor heard them acknowledge their signatures.[67]

Notarial execution

In the case of persons who could not write the Subscription of Deeds Act, 1540 (c. 37), required the subscription of a notary and the Subscription of Deeds Act, 1579 (c. 18), the subscription of two notaries before four witnesses in the case of deeds of great importance, while the Subscription of Deeds Act, 1681 (c. 5), provided that the witnesses should hear the party give warrant to the notaries and in evidence thereof touch their pens.[68] The 1579 Act was held to apply to persons who could write but were blind.[69] The Disqualification of Ministers Act, 1584 (c. 6), entitled a parish minister to act as notary in the execution of testaments of moveable estate, probably within his own parish only.

The Conveyancing Act, 1874, S. 41, provides that, without prejudice to the previous law and practice, any deed, having been read over to the granter, might be validly executed on his behalf if he were from any cause, permanent or temporary, unable to write, by one notary or justice of the peace subscribing for him, without touching the pen, all before two witnesses, and appending a docquet in the form of Sched. I to the Act or in words to the like effect, setting out that the granter authorized the execution and that the deed had been read over to the granter in presence of the witnesses.[70] The Conveyancing (Sc.) Act, 1924, S. 18,[71] authorizes notarial execution by a law agent[72] or notary public or justice of the peace or, as regards wills or other testamentary writings, by a parish minister acting in his own parish, or any minister of the Church of Scotland appointed to a charge to officiate as minister, in any parish in which part of his charge is situated, or his colleague and successor or assistant and successor so acting, subscribing in presence of the granter and by his authority, all before two witnesses who have heard the deed read over to the granter and heard or seen authority given, and a shorter holograph docquet in the form of Sched. I or in any words to the like effect shall precede the signature of such notary or other person acting.

---

[67] *Baird's Tr.* v. *Murray* (1883) 11 R. 153; *MacLeish* v. *B.L. Co.*, 1911, 2 S.L.T. 168; *Boyd* v. *Shaw* 1927 S.C. 414.

[68] Stair III, 8, 34; Ersk. III, 2, 23. For examples of notarial execution under these acts see *Anderson* v. *Tarbat* (1668) Mor. 16836; *Jack* v. *Jacks* (1671) Mor. 16836; *White* v. *Knox* (1711) Mor. 16841; *Birrel* v. *Moffat* (1745) Mor. 16846; *Rollands* v. *R.* (1767) Mor. 16851; *Stoddart* v. *Arkley* (1799) Mor. 16857; *Russel* v. *Kirk* (1827) 6 S. 133; *Ferrie* v. *Ferrie's Trs.* (1863) 1 M. 291; *Henry* v. *Reid* (1871) 9 M. 503. See also for an account of older law *Atchison's Trs.* v. *A.* (1876) 3 R. 388.

[69] *Reid* v. *Baxter* (1837) 16 S. 273.

[70] The reading over is an essential solemnity, even if the granter is deaf: *Hodges* v. *H's Trs.* (1900) 7 S.L.T. 303; *Watson* v. *Beveridge* (1883) 11 R. 40.

[71] Extended by Church of Scotland (Property and Endowments) Amdt. (Sc.) Act, 1933, S. 13.

[72] So long as enrolled, even though not having a current practising certificate: *Stephen* v. *Scott*, 1927 S.C. 85.

Essentials of notarial execution

The essentials of notarial execution are accordingly: The granter must from any cause, temporary or permanent, be blind or unable to write.[73] If blind the granter may either sign personally,[74] or have the deed executed notarially.[75] There must be present a notary public, solicitor,[76] justice of the peace or, in the case of testamentary writings, a parish minister in his own parish or his colleague and successor. The notary or other person acting must know that the person for whom he acts is the person designed as granter of the deed, or have that fact attested by others.[77] There must be present two other persons to act as instrumentary witnesses.[78] The deed must be read over[79] to the granter by the notary in the presence of the two witnesses.[80] The witnesses have to know the granter or have his identity established to them.[81] The notary or other executant must in the presence of the two witnesses obtain the granter's authority to execute the deed.[82] This may be given in any way which can be 'heard or seen'. The notary must sign the deed in his own name on each page and at the end, as the granter would have done, all in presence of the granter.[82] The notary must add the statutory docquet,[83] or words to the same effect,[84] on the last page of the deed.[85] The docquet must be holograph.[86] The notary signs at the end of the docquet adding his designation by virtue of which he is entitled to act, and the two[87] witnesses also sign there opposite his signature.[88] The witnesses may be designed in the testing clause or have their designations added to their signatures. The completion of the docquet and the signatures of the notary and witnesses must be *unico contextu* with the earlier events and in the presence of the granter, and not *ex intervallo*.[88] The witnesses must see or hear every step of the formalities, reading of the deed, authority to sign, writing of the

[73] 1874 Act, S. 41; 1924 Act, S. 18.
[74] E. Fife v. Fife's Trs. (1823) 1 Sh. App. 498.
[75] Reid v. Baxter (1837) 16 S. 273.
[76] He need not hold a practising certificate: Stephen v. Scott, 1927 S.C. 85.
[77] A.S. 21 July, 1688.
[78] cf. Cameron v. Holman (1951) 39 L.C. 14.
[79] cf. Watson v. Beveridge (1883) 11 R. 40; Hodges v. H's Trs. (1900) 7 S.L.T. 303.
[80] 1874 Act, S. 41; 1924 Act, S. 18.
[81] Subscription of Deeds Act, 1681, (c. 5).
[82] 1874 Act, S. 41; 1924 Act, S. 18; Mathieson v. Hawthorns (1899) 1 F. 468. See also Hynd's Tr. v. Hynd's Trs., 1955 S.C. (H.L.) 1. If the end of the deed is on the same page as the notarial docquet the signature to the latter will suffice as the signature for that page: Mathieson, supra; Hynd's Tr., supra.
[83] 1924 Act, Sch. I.
[84] Atchison's Trs. v. A. (1876) 3 R. 388; Cameron v. Holman (1951) 39 L.C. 14; see also Watson v. Beveridge (1883) 11 R. 40; Hynd's Tr., infra.
[85] 1924 Act, S. 18.
[86] Henry v. Reid (1871) 9 M. 503; Irvine v. McHardy (1892) 19 R. 458; Campbell v. Purdie (1895) 22 R. 443.
[87] Cameron, supra.
[88] Kissack v. Webster's Trs. (1894) 2 S.L.T. 172; Hynd's Tr. v. H's Trs., 1955 S.C. (H.L.) 1.

docquet and signature by the notary, and their signing is part of the formalities.[89] The notary also must not, in his private or other capacity, be a party to the deed,[90] nor act for more than one party, certainly if their interests are or may be opposed.[91] The notary must have no interest, direct or indirect, in the deed. Disqualifying interest includes not only direct benefit under the deed, but being thereby appointed,[92] or having his partner appointed,[93] a trustee or to act as solicitor under the deed, but probably does not include being the employee of solicitors so disqualified,[94] nor being the agent of another party to the deed.[95]

If two parties to a deed need to have it executed notarially, particularly if they have conflicting interests, separate notaries should act for each.[96] S. 39 of the Conveyancing (Sc.) Act, 1874, did not, prior to the 1924 Act, apply to notarial execution.[97] A defect, such as a non-holograph docquet, cannot be cured after the granter's death.[98]

HOLOGRAPH WRITINGS

Deeds which are holograph, i.e. entirely or in all substantial parts in the handwriting of the granter, are deemed validly executed if signed at the end by the granter, the signatures and designation of witnesses being unnecessary.[99] The authentication statutes do not apply.[1] A wholly type-written deed signed by the granter with a pen has been held holograph, but only where it was proved or admitted that it had been typed by the granter who had for some time habitually used a typewriter.[2] If a signed holograph deed is witnessed it is the more validly executed, and it remains

---

[89] *Hynd's Tr., supra.*
[90] *Laird of Gormock* v. *The Lady* (1583) Mor. 16874; *Lang* v. *L's Trs.* (1889) 16 R. 590.
[91] *Craig* v. *Richartson* (1610) Mor. 16829; but see *Graeme* v. *G's Trs.* (1868) 7 M. 14.
[92] *Ferrie* v. *F's Trs.* (1863) 1 M. 291; *Newstead* v. *Dansken*, 1918, 1 S.L.T. 136; *Wall's Exors.*, 1939 S.L.T. (Sh. Ct.) 10. See also *Irving* v. *Snow*, 1956 S.C. 257 where notarial execution effected by Scottish notary outside Scotland.
[93] *Finlay* v. *F's Trs.*, 1948 S.C. 16; *Gorrie's Tr.* v. *Stiven's Exrx.*, 1952 S.C. 1; *Crawford's Trs.* v. *Glasgow R.I.*, 1955 S.C. 367. Contrast *McIldowie* v. *Muller*, 1979 S.C. 271.
[94] *Hynd's Tr.* v. *H's Trs.*, 1955 S.C. (H.L.) 1.
[95] *Lang* v. *L's Trs.* (1889) 16 R. 590.
[96] But see *Graeme* v. *G's Trs.* (1868) 7 M. 14.
[97] *Kissack* v. *Webster's Trs.* (1894) 2 S.L.T. 172. See now Conveyancing (Sc.) Act, 1924, s. 18(2).
[98] *Campbell* v. *Purdie* (1895) 22 R. 443. cf. *Walker* v. *Whitwell*, 1916 S.C. (H.L.) 75.
[99] Stair IV, 42, 6; Ersk. III, 2, 22; Bell, *Comm.* I, 341; *Prin.* § 20, 2231; *Lawrie* v. *L.* (1859) 21 D. 240; *Callander* v. *C's Trs.* (1863) 2 M. 291; *Christie's Trs.* v. *Muirhead* (1870) 8 M. 461; *Maitland's Trs.* v. *M.* (1871) 10 M. 79; *Skinner* v. *Forbes* (1883) 11 R. 88; *Goldie* v. *Shedden* (1885) 13 R. 138; *Carmichael's Exors.* v. *C.*, 1909 S.C. 1387; *Bridgeford's Exor.* v. *B.*, 1948 S.C. 416; *Tucker* v. *Canch's Tr.*, 1953 S.C. 270; *Gillies* v. *Glasgow R.I.*, 1960 S.C. 438; cf. *Macnaughton* v. *Finlayson's Trs.* (1902) 10 S.L.T. 322. As to whether a telegram can be holograph see *Mowat* v. *Caledonian Banking Co.* (1895) 23 R. 270.
[1] *Macdonald* v. *Cuthbertson* (1891) 18 R. 101.
[2] *McBeath's Trs.* v. *McB.*, 1935 S.C. 471; distinguished in *Chisholm* v. *C.*, 1949 S.C. 434.

valid if the witnessing is defective.[3] In the case of a testamentary writing in the form of a holograph letter subscription by Christian name only,[4] or by initials,[5] or by the word 'Mum',[6] has been held sufficient, when these were the granters' customary modes of authenticating holograph writings.[7] But a totally unsigned writing, or one superscribed, or one commencing with the granter's name in his own writing, are invalid even though holograph.[8]

A deed or letter written and signed by a partner in the firm name is deemed holograph of the firm.[9] A writ holograph of an authorized agent, and signed in his own name as such agent, is as binding as a writ holograph of the principal.[10] A writ can never be holograph of an incorporated body.

Any holograph deed can be holograph of only one party[11] though it may be holograph of one and adopted as holograph by another. If holograph of only one it will be valid even against him if his being bound does not depend on any other parties also being bound.[12]

A holograph deed of several pages seems not required to be signed on each page.[13]

Holograph deeds superscribed, or merely with the granter's name *in gremio* are invalid, and this informality cannot be cured.[14] But a postscript, though below the signature, may be held authenticated by it, when clearly marked as P.S.[15] Lack of subscription may, however, be cured if the holograph deed is attached to or contained in a signed deed or wrapping.[16] A statement in the text that a writing was written by the

[3] *Yeats* v. *Y's Trs.* (1833) 11 S. 915; *Lorimer's Exors.* v. *Hird,* 1595 S.L.T. (Notes) 8; see also *Gunnell's Trs.* v. *Jones,* 1915, 1 S.L.T. 166; *Harley* v. *Harley's Exor.,* 1957 S.L.T. (Sh. Ct.) 17.
[4] *Draper* v. *Thomason,* 1954 S.C. 136.
[5] *Speirs* v. *Home Speirs* (1879) 6 R. 1359; *Lowrie's J.F.* v. *McMillan's Exrx.,* 1972 S.C. 105.
[6] *Rhodes* v. *Peterson,* 1971 S.C. 56.
[7] Contrast *Russell's Trs.* v. *Henderson* (1884) 11 R. 283, where there was no such proof.
[8] *Foley* v. *Costello* (1904) 6 F. 365; *Shiell,* 1913, 1 S.L.T. 62; *Taylor's Exces.* v. *Thom,* 1914 S.C. 79.
[9] *Nisbet* v. *Neil's Trs.* (1869) 7 M. 1097; *McLaren* v. *Law* (1871) 44 S. Jur. 17.
[10] *Whyte* v. *Lee* (1879) 6 R. 699; *Scottish Lands and Bldgs. Co.* v. *Shaw* (1880) 7 R. 756.
[11] *Goldston* v. *Young* (1868) 7 M. 188.
[12] Bell, *Prin.* s 20; *Sproul* v. *Wilson* (1809) Hume 920; *Millar* v. *Farquharson* (1835) 13 S. 838; *McMillan* v. *McM.* (1850) 13 D. 187.
[13] *Cranston* (1890) 17 R. 410; *Campbell's Exors.* v. *Maudslay,* 1934 S.L.T. 420; *Lorimer's Exors.* v. *Hird,* 1959 S.L.T. (Notes) 8.
[14] Stair IV, 42, 6; *Dunlop* v. *D.* (1839) 1 D. 912; *Skinner* v. *Forbes* (1883) 11 R. 88; *Bradford* v. *Young* (1884) 11 R. 1135; *Goldie* v. *Shedden* (1885) 13 R. 138; *Foley* v. *Costello* (1904) 6 F. 365; *Shiell* v. *S.,* 1913, 1 S.L.T. 62; *Taylor's Exces.* v. *Thom,* 1914 S.C. 79; *McKillop* v. *Secy. of State for Scotland* (1951) 39 L.C. 17. As to signature up the side see *Colvin* v. *Hutchison* (1885) 12 R. 947; *Will's Exrx.* v. *Mackenzie* (1953) 69 Sh. Ct. Rep. 267; *Robbie* v. *Carr,* 1959 S.L.T. (Notes) 16. As to some words below signature see *Burnie's Trs.* v. *Lawrie* (1894) 21 R. 1015; *Harvey's Trs.* v. *Carswell,* 1928 S.N. 96; *McLay* v. *Farrell,* 1950 S.C. 149. As to commencing with testator's name, see *Fraser's Exrx., infra.*
[15] *Fraser's Exrx.* v. *Fraser's C.B.,* 1931 S.C. 536.
[16] *Russell's Trs.* v. *Henderson* (1883) 11 R. 283; cf. *Speirs* v. *Home Speirs* (1879) 6 R. 1359; *Murray* v. *Kuffel,* 1910, 2 S.L.T. 388; contrast *France's J.F.* v. *F's Trs.,* 1916, 1 S.L.T. 126; *Stenhouse* v. *S.* 1922 S.C. 370.

granter is of no value unless the subscription is admitted or proved genuine.[17]

Holograph writings in account books,[18] receipts for partial payments on a bond,[19] and holograph postscripts to a holograph and signed letter[20] have all been held valid though not subscribed.

Corrections in holograph writs

In testamentary holograph writings a marginal addition or interlineation, if holograph of the writer of the main body of the deed, requires no authentication.[21] Deletions are similarly effective though not authenticated.[22] Words written on erasure are similarly effective.[23] The excision of a part of a typewritten will from the copy thereof with a holograph authentication has been held to cancel that part of the principal will,[24] and holograph alterations on a copy will have been held a valid codicil to the principal will.[25]

In *inter vivos* holograph deeds, alterations cannot be presumed made before delivery of the deed even though apparently holograph and require authentication.

Adoption and incorporation

In some testamentary cases an attested or holograph writ has expressly or by implication incorporated an earlier unauthenticated holograph writing and thereby entitled it also to receive effect.[26] The question is one of intention. Even a docquet on an envelope containing the unauthenticated holograph document may have this effect,[27] and a codicil may adopt and thereby validate a defectively executed will.[28] But a holograph title on the

[17] *Harper v. Green*, 1938, S.C. 198.
[18] Stair IV, 12, 6; *Goldie, supra.*
[19] *Currence v. Hacket* (1688) 2 B.S. 121.
[20] *Wauchope v. Niddrie* (1662) Mor. 16965.
[21] *Fraser's Exrx. v. Fraser's C.B.*, 1931 S.C. 536, 542; *Reid's Exors. v. R.*, 1953 S.L.T. (Notes) 52.
[22] *Milne's Exor. v. Waugh*, 1913 S.C. 203; *Allan's Exrx. v. A.*, 1920 S.C. 732; *Gemmell's Exor. v. Stirling*, 1923 S.L.T. 384.
[23] *Robertson v. Ogilvie's Trs.* (1884) 7 D. 236.
[24] *Thomson's Trs. v. Bowhill Baptist Church*, 1956 S.C. 217.
[25] *Manson v. Edinburgh Royal Institution*, 1948 S.L.T. 196; *Lawson v. L.*, 1954 S.L.T. (Notes) 60.
[26] *Baird v. Jaap* (1856) 18 D. 1246; *Speirs v. Home Speirs* (1879) 6 R. 1359; *Cross's Trs. v. C.*, 1921, 1 S.L.T. 244; *Fraser's Exrx. v. F's C.B.*, 1931 S.C. 536.
[27] *Maitland's Trs. v. M.* (1871) 10 M. 79; *Russell's Trs. v. Henderson* (1883) 11 R. 283; *Murray v. Kuffel*, 1910, 2 S.L.T. 388; *Shiell v. S.* 1913, 2 S.L.T. 62; *France's J.F. v. France's Trs.* 1916, 1 S.L.T. 126; *Stenhouse v. S.*, 1922 S.C. 370; *Macphail's Trs. v. M..* 1940 S.C. 560; cf. *Campbell's Exor.*, 1934 S.L.T. 420.
[28] *Liddle v. L.* (1898) 6 S.L.T. 218; *Craik's Exrx. v Samson*, 1929 S.L.T. 592; *Fraser's Exrx. v. Fraser's C.B.*, 1931 S.C. 536.

backing sheet of an unsubscribed will has been held inadequate to validate it.[29]

Sometimes also an authenticated or holograph testamentary writ has
sought to adopt or incorporate by anticipation any future codicil, writ or
notes, even though not themselves authenticated or informally authen
ticated.[30] But a future 'writing under my hand' does not include an unsubscribed writing,[31] and a future 'writing' means a probative writing.[32]
Nor can a testamentary writ be held to incorporate a later document
which is not of a testamentary character.[33]

Incorporation applies also to bilateral contracts[34] and to bonds,[35] and
unilateral acknowledgments of debt.[36]

Deeds partly holograph

The category of holograph writs extends to writs partly printed or otherwise produced and partly in the handwriting of the granter and signed by
him, if the parts which are holograph are the essentials and sufficient by
themselves to convey meaning and capable of receiving effect, the other
parts being inessential or merely formal.[37] The deed is, however, invalid if
the holograph parts do not, taken by themselves, convey meaning or are
incapable of receiving effect, as where they lack executive words.[38] In
later cases, concerned with purported wills, the courts have treated the
deed as holograph if the holograph parts contained the minimum essentials of a will.[30] Holograph words may also be held to adopt prior
non-holograph portions of the document, and validate them as if they
were holograph.[40] A deed partly printed and partly holograph is wholly
valid if solemnly authenticated.

[29] *Shiell* v. *S.*, 1913, 1 S.L.T. 62; *Stenhouse, supra..*
[30] *Crosbie* v. *Wilson* (1865) 3 M. 870; *Pentland* v. *P's Trs.* (1908) 16 S.L.T. 480; see also
Lamont v. *Glasgow Mags.* (1887) 14 R. 603.
[31] *Inglis* v. *Harper* (1831) 5 W. & S. 785; *Wilsone's Trs.* v. *Stirling* (1861) 24 D. 163;
Young's Trs. v. *Ross* (1864) 3 M. 10; *Parker* v. *Matheson* (1876) 13 S.L.R. 405; *Fraser* v.
Forbes' Trs. (1899) 1 F. 513; *Hamilton's Trs.* v. *H.* (1901) 4 F. 266; *Morton* v. *French,* 1908
S.C. 171; *Waterson's Trs.* v. *St. Giles Boys Club,* 1943 S.C. 369, overruling *Gillespie* v.
Donaldson's Trs. (1831) 10 S. 174 and *Ronald's Trs.* v. *Lyle,* 1929 S.C. 104.
[32] Bell, *Prin.* s 1868; *Dundas* v. *Lowis* (1807) Mor. Appx. Writ. 6; *Morton* v. *French,* 1908
S.C. 171; *Waterson's Trs.*; supra, 375.
[33] *Graham's Trs.* v. *Gillies,* 1956 S.C. 437.
[34] *McGinn* v. *Shearer,* 1947 S.C. 334; cf. *Littlejohn* v. *Hadwen* (1882) 20 S.L.R. 5, 7.
[35] *Callender* v. *C's Trs.* (1863) 2 M. 291.
[36] *Christie's Trs.* v. *Muirhead* (1870) 8 M. 461.
[37] *Christie's Trs.* v. *Muirhead* (1870) 8 M. 461; *A's Exors.* v. *B* (1874) 11 S.L.R. 259;
Murdoch's J.F. v. *Thomson* (1896) 4 S.L.T. 155; *Carmichael's Exors.* v. *C.,* 1909 S.C. 1387;
Paterson's Trs. v. *Joy,* 1910 S.C. 1029; *Cameron's Trs.* v. *Mackenzie,* 1915 S.C. 313; *Lowrie's
J.F.* v. *Macmillan,* 1972 S.C. 105.
[38] *Macdonald* v. *Cuthbertson* (1840) 18 R. 101; *Tucker* v. *Canch's Trs.* 1953 S.C. 270;
Campbell Petr., 1963 S.L.T. (Sh. Ct.) 10.
[39] *Campbell's Exor.,* 1934 S.L.T. 420; *Bridgeford's Exor.* v. *B.,* 1948 S.C. 416; *Gillies* v.
Glasgow R.I., 1960 S.C. 438.
[40] *Christie's Trs.* v. *Muirhead* (1870) 8 M. 461.

Deeds adopted as holograph

A deed not holograph of a person may be made holograph of him if he writes at the end the words 'adopted as holograph' or equivalent words and signs it.[41] The signature may be above or below the words of adoption but preferably below.[42] The docquet adopting the deed as holograph must itself be holograph.[43] Exceptionally, the words 'accepted as holograph' typewritten and signed have been sustained.[44] Such a deed may be held not binding if the granter establishes that he did not understand the words.[45]

A writ which should by law be holograph or adopted as holograph may have holograph quality imparted to it, if enclosed with and referred to in a holograph writing,[46] or by holograph and signed writing in the margin referring to the rest of the text.[47]

Date

Holograph writings, unless attested, or *in re mercatoria*, do not prove their own dates against third parties,[48] save that a holograph writing of a testamentary character, in the absence of contrary evidence, is deemed to have been made of the date it bears,[49] and holograph acknowledgements of intimations of assignations prove their own dates, even against an arrester of the debt assigned.[50] Any date stated may be of evidential value, but is not conclusive, and the onus of proof of the date is on the party proponing the deed.[51]

Vicennial prescription

Holograph missive letters, bonds,[52] and subscriptions in account books without witnesses, if not pursued for within twenty years, formerly prescribed unless the pursuer proved the verity of the holograph writing by

---

[41] *Weir* v. *Cuthbertson* (1872) 10 M. 438; *Gavine's Trs.* v. *Lee* (1883) 10 R. 448; cf. *Macdonald* v. *Cuthbertson* (1890) 18 R. 101.

[42] *Gavine's Trs., supra.*

[43] *Maitland's Trs.* v. *M.* (1871) 10 M. 79; *Gavine's Trs.* v. *Lee* (1883) 10 R. 448; *Harvey* v. *Smith* (1904) 6 F. 511.

[44] *McBeath's Trs.* v. *McB.,* 1935 S.C. 471; cf. *Chisholm* v. *C.* 1949 S.C. 434.

[45] *Harvey* v. *Smith* (1904) 6 F. 511.

[46] *Macphail's Trs.* v. *M.,* 1940 S.C. 560; *McGinn* v. *Shearer,* 1947 S.C. 334.

[47] *Liddle* v. *L.* (1898) 6 S.L.T. 218.

[48] Bell, *Prin.* § 20; Dickson, *Evidence,* § 775; Menzies, 150.

[49] Conveyancing Act, 1874, S. 40.

[50] *McGill* v. *Hutchison* (1630) Mor. 12605, *E. Selkirk* v. *Gray* (1708) Rob. App. 1.

[51] *Waddel* v. *W's Trs.* (1845) 7 D. 605; *Dyce* v. *Paterson* (1847) 9 D. 1141.

[52] Including all holograph writs on which an obligation can be founded, e.g. a receipt: *Mowat* v. *Banks* (1856) 18 D. 1093; but not an I.O.U.: *Craig* v. *Monteith's Exor.,* 1926 S.C. 123.

the defender's oath.[53] After twenty years accordingly such holograph writs established nothing creative of obligation.[54] The prescriptive period runs from the date of the document.[55] They probably now subsist till extinguished by the long negative prescription.[56]

WRITINGS *IN RE MERCATORIA*

By long custom formal execution has been allowed to be dispensed with in the case of writings *in re mercatoria*,[57] which include all the variety of engagements or mandates or acknowledgements which the infinite occasions of trade may require.[58] The category includes bills of exchange, cheques and promissory notes,[59] orders for goods, mandates, procurations, guarantees, offers to buy or sell merchandise or to transport it, and acceptances thereof.[60] It has been held to include a guarantee of payment for goods supplied,[61] an arbiter's award in a mercantile reference,[62] an agreement to buy fittings in premises and take over the tenant's obligations[63] an accession by a creditor to a composition by an insolvent,[64] an acknowledgment that bonds were held on account of a particular person,[65] an agreement to apply for shares in a company,[66] an agreement to take advertising space on walls of buildings,[67] a letter explanatory of a bill,[68] submissions to arbitrations, and awards therein in mercantile and agricultural arbitrations.[69]

It has been held not to include a promise to pay an uncertain person,[70]

---

[53] Prescription Act, 1669; *Craig v. Monteith's Exor.*, 1926 S.C. 123; *Baird v. B's Trs.*, 1954 S.C. 290.

[54] *Bank of Scotland v. —* (1747) 5 B.S. 748.

[55] *Home v. Donaldson* (1773) Mor. 10992; *Macadam v. Findlay*, 1911 S.C. 1366; *Dick v. Thomson's Trs.*, 1929 S.L.T. 637.

[56] Prescription and Limitation (Sc.) Act, 1973, S. 7.

[57] Ersk. III 2, 24; Bell, *Comm.* I, 342; *Prin.* s 21; Bell, *Convg.* I, 96; Menzies, 159; Wood, 97; Gloag, 185. The expression should receive wide interpretation: *Beardmore v. Barry*, 1928 S.C. 101, 110; 1928 S.C. (H.L.) 47.

[58] Bell, *Comm*, I, 342.

[59] Bills of Exchange Act, 1882, Ss. 3, 17 and 32. To warrant summary diligence bills and notes must be dated and signed.

[60] Bell, *supra.*

[61] *Paterson v. Wright* (1814) 6 Paton 38.

[62] *Dykes v. Roy* (1869) 7 M. 357.

[63] *Kinnimont v. Paxton* (1892) 20 R. 128.

[64] Bell, *Comm.* II, 398; *Henry v. Strachan & Spence* (1897) 24 R. 1045.

[65] *Stuart v. Potter, Choate & Prentice*, 1911 1 S.L.T. 377.

[66] *Beardmore, supra.*

[67] *U.K. Advertising Co. v. Glasgow Bag Wash Laundry*, 1926 S.C. 303.

[68] *Thoms v. T.* (1867) 6 M. 174.

[69] *Nivison v. Howat* (1883) 11 R. 182; *Hope v. Crookston Bros.* (1890) 17 R. 868; *Cameron v. Nicol*, 1930 S.C. 1; *MacLaren v. Aikman*, 1939 S.C. 222, 228.

[70] *Thomson v. Philip* (1867) 5 M. 679.

a special document framed to raise money,[71] the engagement of a sales-man for longer than a year,[72] an acknowledgement of loan of money,[73] nor a lease of premises.[74]

Docquets of acknowledgment or discharge written on business books or accounts are in the same position as writings *in re mercatoria*.[75] The onus is heavily on the party challenging a docquetted account to prove its inaccuracy.[76]

Doubt exists whether the classes of guarantees within the Mercantile Law Amendment (Sc.) Act, 1856, S. 6, are within the *res mercatoria* category.[77]

A writing *in re mercatoria*, though not attested or holograph, may be authenticated by bare subscription,[78] or even initials[79] or possibly even by cross or mark[80] if that is the party's customary mode of authentication.

Such a writing, if admitted or proved to be signed or initialled by the granter, proves its own date for its mercantile purpose,[81] though not necessarily for any other purpose.[82] Bills and promissory notes, if in-tended to found summary diligence, must be signed and dated.

WRITINGS STATUTORILY PRIVILEGED

Statutes have in certain cases prescribed or permitted special modes of authentication. These include: One witness only: bills of sale or mortgages of ships;[83] Memorandum and Articles of association of companies.[84]

No witness: deeds executed on behalf of a company by the affixing of the seal and subscription by two directors or a director and the secre-tary;[85] transfer of registered securities;[86] testamentary nominations

---

[71] *Commercial Bank* v. *Kennard* (1859) 21 D. 864.
[72] *Stewart & MacDonald* v. *McCall* (1869) 7 M. 544.
[73] *Paterson* v. *P.* (1897) 25 R. 144.
[74] *Danish Dairy Co.* v. *Gillespie*, 1922 S.C. 656.
[75] *McLaren* v. *Liddell's Trs.* (1860) 22 D. 373; *Fell* v. *Rattray* (1869) 41 Sc. Jur. 236. They may be effective even though not subscribed, if holograph: Stair IV, 42, 6; Dickson, *Evidence* s 799. See also *Stephen* v. *Pirie* (1832) 10 S. 279; *Elder* v. *Smith* (1829) 7 S. 656; *Boswell* v. *Montgomerie* (1836) 14 S. 554; *Walker* v. *Drummond* (1836) 14 S. 780; *Laing* v. *L.* (1862) 24 D. 1362. Contrast *Laidlaw* v. *Wilson* (1844) 6 D. 530; *McAdie* v. *McA's Exrx.* (1883) 10 R. 741.
[76] *Laing, supra; Struthers* v. *Smith*, 1913 S.C. 1116.
[77] See *Snaddon* v. *London, etc. Assce. Co.* (1902) 5 F. 182.
[78] Bell, *Comm.* I, 342; *Ramsay and Hay* v. *Pyronon* (1632) Mor. 16963.
[79] Bell, *Comm.* I, 343; *Thomson* v. *Crichton* (1676) Mor. 16968.
[80] Ibid.; *Rose* v. *Johnston* (1878) 5 R. 600.
[81] Ibid.
[82] Dickson, *Evidence* s 794; cf. *Purvis* v. *Dowie* (1869) 7 M. 764.
[83] Merchant Shipping Act, 1894, S. 24(2).
[84] Companies Act, 1985, S. 2.
[85] Companies Act, 1985, S. 36.
[86] Stock Transfer Act, 1963, S. 1(2).

under the rules of trade unions, friendly societies, and industrial and provident societies.[87]

Authentication by mark: certain testamentary nominations.[88]

THE QUALITY OF BEING PROBATIVE

A probative document is one which, in respect that it complies on the face of it with the prescribed legal formalities, is held to prove the verity of the legal *actus* expressed in it as the genuine *actus* of its author.[89] A deed or writing which is probative proves itself in judicial proceedings, its genuineness is assumed until it is judicially reduced, and the evidence of granter and witnesses that they signed as such is unnecessary.[90] The onus is on a party challenging such a deed to prove that, despite appearances, it was not truly the granter's deed,[91] and it is a heavy onus.[92] A deed or writing which is not probative may be valid and legally effectual but if challenged, the onus is on the party relying on it to establish that it is the granter's deed.[93]

A writing which has been authenticated in accordance with the statutory solemnities is deemed probative,[94] as is a deed notarially executed in accordance with the statutory requirements.[95]

A writing containing blanks not completed before the deed is founded on is not probative but may be effectual as to clauses other than those containing the blanks.[96]

A writing suffering from informality of execution curable under the Conveyancing (Sc.) Act, 1874, S. 39, is not probative but is equally valid and effectual when the defects are cured.

Holograph deeds are not probative,[97] but are equally valid as affording

---

[87] Friendly Societies Acts, 1896, Ss. 56–7 and 1955, S. 5; Industrial and Provident Societies Act, 1965, S. 23.

[88] e.g. National Savings Bank Regulations, 1966, reg. 46; see also *Morton* v. *French*, 1908 S.C. 171.

[89] Bell, Prin. § 2223; *McBeath's Trs.* v. *McB.*, 1935 S.C. 471, 476.

[90] Menzies, 80; *Reid* v. *Kedder* (1840) 1 Rob. App. 183; *Grant* v. *Shepherd* (1847) 6 Bell 153; *Boswell* v. *B.* (1852) 14 D. 378; *Ferrie* v. *F's Trs.* (1863) 1 M. 291, 298; *Munro* v. *Butler Johnstone* (1868) 7 M. 250; *Hamilton* v. *Lindsay-Bucknall* (1869) 8 M. 323, 327; *McLaren* v. *Menzies* (1876) 3 R. 1151; *Walker* v. *Whitwell*, 1916 S.C. (H.L.) 75, 90; *McBeath's Trs.* v. *McB.*, 1935 S.C. 471, 476; *Irving* v. *Snow*, 1956 S.C. 257, 261.

[91] *Hamilton, supra*; *Boyd* v. *Shaw*, 1927 S.C. 414.

[92] *Smith* v. *Bank of Scotland* (1824) 2 Sh. App. 265; *Cleland* v. *C.* (1838) 1 D. 254; *Donaldson* v. *Stewart* (1842) 4 D. 1215; *Morrison* v. *Maclean's Trs.* (1863) 1 M. 304; *Baird's Trs.* v. *Murray* (1844) 11 R. 153; *Stirling Stuart* v. *Stirling Crawfurd's Trs.* (1885) 12 R. 610; *Young* v. *Paton*, 1910 S.C. 63; *Boyd, supra*; *McArthur* v. *McA's Trs.*, 1931 S.L.T. 463.

[93] *McIntyre* v. *National Bank*, 1910 S.C. 150.

[94] *Ferrie, supra*; *McLaren* v. *Menzies* (1876) 3 R. 1151.

[95] *Ferrie, supra*; *Hynd's Tr.* v. *H's Trs.* 1954 S.C. 112.

[96] See *E. Buchan* v. *Scottish Widows Fund* (1857) 19 D. 551; Walkers, 198.

[97] *Cranston* (1890) 17 R. 410, 415. See also Bell, *Prin.* § 2231; *Maitland's Trs.* v. *M.* (1871) 10 M. 79.

proof of authenticity and of deliberate undertaking if their authenticity is admitted, or established by the person founding on them, frequently *comparatione literarum*. It must be proved not only that text and signature are in the same hand, but that both are in the hand of the granter.[98] In discharging this onus of proof, it is not sufficient to show that the deed has been accepted as holograph by the commissary court for its own purposes, on the strength of affidavits as to handwriting produced to it.[99] Nor does a declaration *in gremio* that the deed is holograph of the granter relieve the proposer of the deed of the onus of proving its validity.[1]

The Conveyancing Amendment (Sc.) Act, 1938, S. 11, however, provided that any writing of a testamentary character on which confirmation of executors nominate had, before its commencement, been granted should be deemed probative as a link in title, but in subsequent cases the validity of the holograph writing had to be established judicially.

The Wills Act, 1963, S. 5,[2] provided that any testamentary instrument should be treated as probative for the conveyance of heritage if confirmation of executors to property disposed of therein had been issued in Scotland, or a grant of representation made elsewhere had been sealed in Scotland. The Succession (Sc.) Act, 1964, S. 21, now provides that confirmation of an executor to property disposed of in a holograph testamentary disposition is not to be granted unless the court is satisfied by evidence, consisting at least of an affidavit by each of two persons that the writing and signature of the disposition are in the handwriting of the testator. Such a disposition is not accordingly probative. S. 32 substantially re-enacts S. 5 of the 1963 Act but applying it to entitlement to any property, heritable or moveable.

Writings *in re mercatoria* are not probative though valid unless their authenticity is challenged. If challenged, the person founding on the writing must prove its execution and the genuineness of the signature.[3]

Writings statutorily privileged are probably not probative.

[98] *Anderson* v. *Gill* (1860) 3 Macq. 180.
[99] *Frederick* v. *Craig*, 1932 S.L.T. 315.
[1] *Anderson* v. *Gill* (1858) 3 Macq. 180; *Harper* v. *Green*, 1938 S.C. 198. Such a declaration was sufficient to justify the grant of confirmation to carry moveable estate: *Cranston* (1890) 17 R. 410.
[2] This section was in force from 1 Jan. 1964 to 9 Sept. 1964, when it was repealed by the Succession (Sc.) Act, 1964.
[3] Ersk. III, 2, 24; Bell, *Comm.* I, 342; *Prin.* § 21, 2232; *McIntyre* v. *National Bank*, 1910 S.C. 150.

CHAPTER 1.8

INTERPRETATION OF DEEDS AND WRITINGS

Writings include not only formally authenticated deeds but all manner of printed documents, holograph writings, writings *in re mercatoria*, and others. They may constitute, or be intended to constitute contracts, copartneries, assignations, dispositions, wills, or to have other legal effect, and interpretation is frequently necessary to determine what, if any, intention is expressed therein, and what legal effect should be given to the words used.[1]

What documents to be considered

In the case of wills all documents not revoked by a later document must be read together; in so far as they are inconsistent the later is presumed to supersede the earlier.[2] In the case of contracts all communications must be examined to find which provisions have been accepted and which rejected. Only thereafter can the documents be interpreted.

Plain meaning rule

The primary rule is that the granter's intention must be discovered from the expressions used; if the words used are clear and unambiguous they must receive effect, but if they are not, the intention, if discoverable by any reasonable construction, should prevail.[3] In discovering the general intention the deed must be read and interpreted as a whole, so that, if possible, the different parts of the deed are consistent one with another.[4] The words used may be so vague that the court cannot discover any intention with any certainty at all, in which case the deed is unenforceable.[5] A court may find that a writ is a complete nullity.[6]

---

[1] See generally Stair IV, 42, 20–1; Bankt. I, 11, 53; Ersk. III, 3, 87; Bell, *Prin*, § 524, 1871, 1879; See also particularly in relation to contracts and wills Chs. 4, 6, 7.4, *infra*. As to meanings given to words in previous cases see Gibb and Dalrymple, *Scottish Judicial Dictionary*; Stroud, *Judicial Dictionary*; Saunders (ed.), *Words and Phrases Legally Defined*.

[2] e.g. *Morton's Exor.*, 1985 S.L.T. 14.

[3] cf. Stair IV, 42, 21(4) and (5); *N.B. Oil Co.* v. *Swann* (1868) 6 M. 835; *Burnett* v. *G.N.S. Ry.* (1884) 12 R. (H.L.) 25; *Gore-Brown-Henderson's Trs.* v. *Grenfell*, 1968 S.C. 73, 82.

[4] Ersk. III, 3, 87; Bell, *Prin*. § 524; *N.E. Ry.* v. *Hastings* [1900] A.C. 260, 269.

[5] e.g. *McArthur* v. *Lawson* (1877) 4 R. 1134; *Traill* v. *Dewar* (1881) 8 R. 583; *Young* v. *Dougans* (1887) 14 R. 490.

[6] e.g. *Anderson* v. *A.*, 1961 S.C. 59.

Words should prima facie be given their plain, ordinary, and literal meaning,[7] but may be given a special or technical meaning if used in connection with the usage of some trade or profession.[8] Some words such as 'property' in a will, are so indefinite that only consideration of the whole scheme of the will in relation to the testator's known circumstances can render the word definite.[9] If a plain word appears to bear an unusual meaning, it will be presumed to bear that meaning throughout the deed.[10]

The punctuation of a deed may be considered for the purpose of aiding its construction.[11]

Usage of trade or profession

Professional or trade usage may attach a particular meaning to a word or phrase, or may imply a term into a contract, but not fly in the face of plain words in the contract.[12]

Preference for validity

When in doubt the court will prefer the construction which makes the writing valid and effective to one which renders it ineffective.[13] Similarly, the preference should be given to a construction which gives a meaning to each word and phrase of the deed, though redundant or meaningless words may have been incorporated from a style.

Whether writing deliberative or final

Particular in relation to wills a question has frequently arisen whether a writing was intended to be a draft, memorandum, or jotting, or an expression of concluded intention. The decision depends on consideration of the whole circumstances, including the title and words used.[14]

[7] *Buchanan* v. *Andrew* (1873) 11 M. (H.L.) 13; *Caledonian Ry.* v. *N.B. Ry.* (1881) 8 R. (H.L.) 23, 30; *Burnett* v. *G.N.S. Ry.* (1884) 12 R. (H.L.) 25; *Crosse* v. *Banks* (1886) 13 R. (H.L.) 40; *Gatty* v. *Maclaine*, 1921 S.C. (H.L.) 1; *Dunbar Mags.* v. *Mackersy*, 1931 S.C. 180; *Smith* v. *U.M.B. Chrysler (Sc.) Ltd.*, 1978, S.C. (H.L.) 1.
[8] *Thomson* v. *Garioch* (1841) 3 D. 625; *Mackenzie* v. *Dunlop* (1853) 16 D. 129; (1856) 3 Macq. 22; *Hunter* v. *Miller* (1862) 24 D. 1011; *Jack* v. *Roberts* (1865) 3 M 554; *Fleming* v. *Airdrie Iron Co.* (1882) 9 R. 473. In particular words used in the context of charter-parties, bills of lading, or insurance policies must be taken to be used in the sense which such words have long been understood to bear in such contexts: *Salvesen* v. *Guy* (1885) 13 R. 85; *McCowan* v. *Baine & Johnston* (1890) 17 R. 1016; affd. (1891) 18 R. (H.L.) 57; *Lamont, Nisbett & Co.* v. *Hamilton*, 1907 S.C. 628.
[9] e.g. *McLeod's Tr.* v. *McLuckie* (1883) 10 R. 1056; *Oag's Curator* v. *Corner* (1885) 12 R. 1162; *Craw's Trs.* v. *Blacklock*, 1920 S.C. 22.
[10] *Martin* v. *Kelso* (1853) 15 D. 950.
[11] *Turnbull's Trs.* v. *L.A.*, 1918 S.C. (H.L.) 88.
[12] *Tancred Arrol* v. *Steel Co. of Scotland* (1890) 17 R. (H.L.) 31.
[13] Bell, *Prin.* § 524(3); *Brown* v. *Sutherland* (1875) 2 R 615; *Muir* v. *City of Glasgow Bank* (1879) 6 R. (H.L.) 21; *Ainslie's Trs.* v. *Imlach's Exors.*, 1926 S.L.T. 28; *Scottish Farmers Dairy Co.* v. *McGhee*, 1933 S.L.T. 142; cf. *Barr* v. *Waldie* (1893) 21 R. 224, 228.
[14] See Ch. 7.4, *infra.*

Whether document prepared by lawyer or layman

In deeds or documents professionally prepared words and phrases commonly used in legal contexts are presumed to be used in the sense settled by law, and having their technical legal import. Thus such terms as 'heir at law' and 'next of kin' have settled meanings and will be presumed used with those meanings.[15]

But no such presumption can arise where the document was not professionally prepared, as a word or phrase having a technical connotation may have been used in ignorance thereof and with another intention.[16] Similarly a more liberal construction can be given to documents *inter rusticos.*

Blanks

The effect of a blank in a document varies with the circumstances. Bonds blank as to the name of the creditor, and circulating as negotiable instruments, were declared null by statute.[17] The signature of a bill of exchange blank in any material particular is authority to the person in possession to complete the blank in any way he things fit.[18] A signature on blank stamped paper may be authority to the person to whom it is delivered to fill it up as a complete bill of exchange, using the signature for that of the drawer or acceptor or indorser.[18] The onus of proving that the bill was incomplete when delivered, and was completed contrary to his instructions, is on the person who signed the incomplete bill, and it is not for the holder to establish that the bill is in order.[19]

In the case of a feucharter doubts have been expressed as to the competency of filling in from inference from the context a blank in the description of the subjects disponed.[20]

While there is some authority for the view that formal execution of a deed with blanks authorizes its subsequent completion in accordance with the express or implied consent of the granter,[21] it is thought that any part of the deed inserted after the granter's signature can be effective only if the granter is personally barred from challenging its validity. A deed containing blanks is not probative, but may be effectual, depending on the importance of the clause containing the blank. If it is admitted or proved that a deed contained blanks and these have been completed

---

[15] Stair IV, 42, 21; *Inglis* v. *I.* (1869) 7 M. 435; *Glen* v. *Stewart* (1874) 1 R. (H.L.) 48; *Gregory's Trs.* v. *Alison* (1889) 16 R. (H.L.) 10; *Fulton's Tr.* v. *F.* (1900) 8 S.L.T.465; *Rutherford's Trs.* v. *Dickie*, 1907 S.C. 1280; *Murray's Factor* v. *Melrose*, 1910 S.C. 924.
[16] cf. Stair IV, 42, 21.
[17] Blank Bonds and Trusts Act, 1696 (c. 25).
[18] Bills of Exchange Act, 1882, S. 20; cf. *Russell* v. *Banknock Coal Co.* (1897) 24 R. 1009.
[19] *Anderson* v. *Somerville, Murray & Co.* (1898) 1 F. 90.
[20] *Musselburgh Mags.* v. *Musselburgh Real Estate Co.* (1904) 7 F. 308.
[21] *E. Buchan* v. *Scottish Widows' Fund* (1857) 19 D. 551; *Carswell's Trs.* v. *C.* (1896) 3 S.L.T. 218.

subsequent to execution, the deed is probably not probative unless the completion is mentioned in the testing clause;[22] otherwise the presumption is that the blanks were completed later and the onus is on the party founding on the deed to show that they were completed before execution or with the consent of the granter.[23]

If a deed contains blanks when founded on in court the blank may leave the obligation subsisting[24] or render it wholly ineffectual.[25] If when founded on blanks have been completed the words inserted should be ignored.[26]

The Blank Bonds and Trusts Act, 1696, also provides that all bonds, assignations, dispositions, or other deeds, but excepting the bills of exchange or notes of a trading company, subscribed when blank as to the name of the person or persons in whose favour they are conceived, are null, unless the name of the creditor, assignee, or disponee is inserted at the time of subscription or before delivery, in the presence of the witnesses who attested the granter's subscription. The onus of proving that the deed was blank as to the name is on the party challenging the deed; the onus is then on the party founding on the deed to establish that the name was inserted before delivery, and in the presence of the witnesses.[27] Despite the Act it has been held that the nullity affects only the names inserted and the clauses affected thereby.[28]

Clerical error

The court may treat as a mere clerical error, and correct, a word or phrase in a deed, if satisfied that it does not correctly represent the intention of the parties.[29] In one case the court allowed a clerical error in the testing clause of a deed given in for registration in the Books of Council and Session to be corrected, reserving opinions as to the effect of the amendment.[30] In interpreting a will the court has held itself entitled to read one figure for another where this was a manifest error,[31] and to insert, delete, or substitute words if satisfied that that is necessary to give

---

[22] cf. Dickson, *Evidence* 659; Walkers, *Evidence* § 184(b).
[23] cf. E. *Buchan* v. *Scottish Widows' Fund* (1857) 19 D. 551.
[24] *Buchanan* v. *Dickie* (1828) 6 S. 986.
[25] *Ewen* v. *E's Trs.* (1830) 4 W. & S. 346.
[26] *Pentland* v. *Hare* (1829) 7 S. 640; E. *Buchan* v. *Scottish Widows' Fund* (1857) 19 D. 551.
[27] *Donaldson* v. *D.* (1749) Mor. 9080.
[28] *Kennedy* v. *Arbuthnot* (1722) Mor. 1681; *Pentland* v. *Hare* (1829) 7 S. 640; *Abernethie* v. *Forbes* (1835) 13 S. 263; cf. *Robertson* v. *Ogilvie's Trs.* (1844) 7 D. 236.
[29] *Glen's Trs.* v. *Lancashire, etc. Ins. Co.* (1906) 8 F. 915; *Krupp* v. *Menzies*, 1907 S.C. 903; cf. *Carricks* v. *Saunders* (1850) 12 D. 812; *McLaren* v. *Liddell's Trs.* (1862) 24 D. 577; *N.B. Ins. Co.* v. *Tunnock & Fraser* (1864) 3 M. 1, 5.
[30] *Caldwell* (1871) 10 M. 99.
[31] *Reid's Trs.* v. *Bucher*, 1929 S.C. 615; cf. *Yule's Trs.* 1981 S.L.T. 250; contrast *Crawford's Trs.* v. *Fleck*, 1910 S.C. 998.

effect to the testator's intention.[32] In some cases proof that the document contains a clerical error justifies reduction of the whole document.[33]

The court now has power, subject to conditions, where a document fails to express accurately the common intention of the parties, or to give effect to the granter's intention, to order the document to be rectified.[34]

Grammatical error

The court may ignore a grammatical error if it would otherwise nullify the obvious intention of the granter.[35]

Inaccuracy

An inaccurate description does not vitiate if the person or thing designated is recognizable and there is no ambiguity.[36] Similarly an inaccurate enumeration of beneficiaries in a will does not vitiate the gift.[37]

Supplying omission by inference

Where there is an omission or lacuna in a document, the court will rarely supply missing words by inference.[38] But if in the absence of express words the court is judicially convinced that the parties had a particular intention, which by mistake was not expressed, effect may be given to the intention.[39]

Liberal interpretation of testamentary writings

A more liberal interpretation may be given to testamentary writings than to deeds *inter vivos*, particularly if not drafted professionally.[40]

---

[32] *Crawford's Trs. supra; Scott's Trs. v. Bruce*, 1912 S.C. 105; *Robertson's Trs. v. R.*, 1969 S.C. 290.

[33] *Glasgow Feuing Co. v. Watson's Trs.* (1887) 14 R. 610. In *Anderson v. Lambie*, 1954 S.C. (H.L.) 43, the error was not merely clerical, but common error of the solicitors for the parties.

[34] Law Reform (M.P.) (Sc.) Act, 1985, Ss. 8–9.

[35] *Glen's Trs. v. Lancashire and Yorkshire Accident Ins. Co.* (1906) 8 F. 915.

[36] *Wilson's Exors. v. Scottish Socy. for Conversion of Israel* (1869) 8 M. 233 (beneficiary); *Speirs v. S's Trs.* (1878) 5 R. 923 (designation in testing clause); *Jaffrey's Trs. v. S.P.C.A.* (1903) 10 S.L.T. 651; *Allison v. Anderson* (1907) 15 S.L.T. 529; *McGrouther's Trs. v. L.A.* (1907) 15 S.L.T. 653; cf. *Nasmyth's Trs. v. N.S.P.C.C.*, 1914 S.C. (H.L.) 76; *Ormiston's Exor. v. Laws*, 1966 S.C. 47.

[37] *Bryce's Tr.* (1878) 5 R. 722; *Lumsden's Trs. v. L.*, 1921 1 S.L.T. 155.

[38] *Murdoch v. Brass* (1904) 6 F 841; *Crawford's Trs. v. Fleck*, 1910 S.C. 998; contrast *Scott's Trs. v. Bruce*, 1912 S.C. 105.

[39] *Dundee Mags. v. Duncan* (1883) 11 R. 145.

[40] Stair IV, 42, 21(7); Ersk. III, 9, 14.

Presumption for freedom of property

Words restricting or limiting the ordinary rights of property are narowly construed, as imposing no greater restriction than they clearly bear.[41]

Construction contra proferentem

Where a bilateral document has been framed entirely by one of the parties, the court resolves ambiguities in a sense unfavourable to the party who framed the deed.[42] Similarly where a contract framed by one party purports to limit or exclude that party's liability in certain circumstances the exception clause is strictly construed.[43] A clause in a contract under which indemnity was sought against claims by third parties has been held not to extend to claims based on the pursuer's own negligence.[44] A bond of caution framed by the creditor is construed in the sense most unfavourable to him.[45] Similarly private Acts of Parliament fall to be construed *contra proferentem*.[46]

Regard to context

Any particular word or phrase must be read in its context.[47]

Expressio unius est exclusio alterius

The principle expressed by this maxim applies to contracts as well as to statutes.[48]

---

[41] Stair IV, 42, 21; see *Hood* v. *Traill* (1884) 12 R. 362; *Bainbridge* v. *Campbell*, 1912 S.C. 92; *Anderson* v. *Dickie*, 1914 S.C. 706, affd. 1915 S.C. (H.L.) 79.

[42] Stair IV, 42, 21(2); Ersk. III, 3, 8, 7; *Hutchison* v. *National Loan Assce. Socy.* (1845) 7 D. 467; *Life Assoc.* v. *Foster* (1873) 11 M. 351; *Birrell* v. *Dryer* (1884) 11 R. (H.L.) 41; *Sangster's Trs.* v. *General Accident Corpn.* (1896) 24 R. 56; *Reid* v. *Employer's Accident Ins. Co.* (1899) 1 F. 1031; *Hunter* v . *General Accident Corpn.*, 1909 S.C. 344; 1909 S.C. (H.L.) 30; *Dawsons, Ltd.* v. *Bonnin*, 1922 S.C. (H.L.) 156; *Aitken's Trs.* v. *Bank of Scotland*, 1944 S.C. 270.

[43] *L.N.E. Ry.* v. *Neilson* [1922] 2 A.C. 263; *Ballingall* v. *Dundee Ice Co.*, 1924 S.C. 238; *McCutcheon* v. *Macbrayne*, 1964 S.C. (H.L.) 28; *Davidson* v. *G.R.E. Insurance*, 1979 S.C. 192; *Verrico* v. *Hughes*, 1980 S.C. 179; *Ailsa Craig* v. *Malvern*, 1982 S.C. (H.L.) 14.

[44] *N. of S. Hydro-Electric Board* v. *Taylor*, 1956 S.C. 1.

[45] Bell, *Comm.* I, 390; *Prin.* s 251; *Napier* v. *Bruce* (1840) 2 D. 556; affd. (1842) 1 Bell 78; *Bayne* v. *Russell* (1869) 7 S.L.R. 101; *Veitch* v. *National Bank*, 1907 S.C. 554; *Harmer* v. *Gibb*, 1911 S.C. 1341; *Aitken's Trs.* v. *Bank of Scotland*, 1944 S.C. 270.

[46] *Scottish Drainage Co.* v. *Campbell* (1889) 16 R. (H.L.) 16; *Colquhoun* v. *Glasgow Procurators' Widows Fund* (1904) 7 F. 345, revd. 1908 S.C. (H.L.) 10.

[47] *N.B. Oil Co.* v. *Swann* (1868) 6 M. 835.

[48] Ch. 1.1, *supra*; see also *Chaplin's Trs.* v. *Hoile* (1891) 19 R. 237; *Kilwinning P.C.* v. *Cunninghame Combination Board*, 1909 S.C. 829; *Campbell* v. *McCutcheon*, 1963 S.C. 505.

Ejusdem generis

The *ejusdem generis* principle[49] applies to deeds and writings as much as to statutes.[50]

Words of reference

Where words are used referring back to a person or subject previously referred to, prima facie the words refer to the nearest antecedent capable of sustaining the reference.[51]

Implied terms

In interpreting contracts a common problem is to determine whether or not, and, if so, what terms are to be held implied in the contract by virtue of statute, general rules of common law, custom and usage, or the previous actings of parties.[52]

Specialia generalibus derogant

Where there is both a general and a special disposition of property, it is presumed that the property specially mentioned derogates from the general disposition, and to that extent reduces it.[53]

Ambiguity

An ambiguity may be patent, where on the face of the deed there is an uncertainty as to the meaning of word or phrase,[54] or latent, where the deed seems clear, but further information about the background facts reveals that there is ambiguity.[55] If the ambiguty is patent the court must decide which interpretation should be put on the ambiguous phrase.[56]

---

[49] Ch. 1.1, *supra*; cf. Ersk. III, 4, 9.

[50] *Lee* v. *Alexander* (1883) 10 R. (H.L.) 91, 93; *Thamas & Mersey Ins. Co.* v. *Hamilton* (1887) 12 App. Cas. 484; *Lilly* v. *Stevenson* (1895) 22 R. 278; (charter party); *Gore Booth's Tr.* v. *G.B.* (1898) 25 R. 803 (will); *Glasgow Corpn.* v. *Glasgow Tramways Co.* (1898) 25 R. (H.L.) 77; *Admiralty* v. *Burns*, 1910 S.C. 531 (lease); *Abchurch S.S. Co.* v. *Stinnes*, 1911 S.C. 1010 (charter party); *Arden S.S. Co.* v. *Mathwin*, 1912 S.C. 211 (charter party); *Milne's Trs.* v. *Davidson*, 1956 S.C. 81 (will).

[51] *Shepherd's Trs.* v. *S.*, 1945 S.C. 60 ('children of the said J.S.').

[52] See further Ch. 4.6, *infra*.

[53] *Nixon* v. *Rogerson's Exor.* (1882) 20 S.L.R. 10; *Montgomery's Trs.* v. *M.* (1895) 22 R. 824; *Alexander* v. *A.* (1896) 23 R. 724.

[54] e.g. *Watcham* v. *A.G. of S.A. Protectorate* [1919] A.C. 533 (land described by boundaries and by acreage, and discrepancy).

[55] e.g. *Morton* v. *Hunter* (1830) 4 W. & S. 379; *Logans* v. *Wright* (1831) 5 W. & S. 242; *Houldsworth* v. *Gordon Cumming*, 1910 S.C. (H.L.) 49.

[56] Bell, *Prin.* s 524; *Logan, supra; Lee* v. *Alexander* (1882) 10 R. 230; (1883) 10 R. (H.L.) 91.

Extrinsic evidence is, however, admissible as to the background facts to clear up a latent ambiguity.[57] Even in cases of patent ambiguity it has sometimes been held necessary and competent to give evidence of surrounding circumstances so that the court has before it all the information available to the parties when they contracted when it is putting a construction on the deed which they entered into.[58]

Ambiguous expressions construed as obligatory

An ambiguous expression will normally be construed as obligatory rather than as giving a party an avenue of escape.[59] Any exception, or exemption, should be expressed.

Party not to be permitted to benefit from own default.

Ambiguous terms will not generally be construed in a way which permits a party to take advantage from his own default or breach of duty. If a contract is to be void in certain events, a party cannot make it void by his own action to evade loss or to suit his own convenience.[60] Similarly a party may not derogate from his own grant or undertaking.[61]

Presumption against donation

Where words clearly import donation or gratuitous undertaking they should receive effect; but in doubt, they are not to be understood as obliging gratuitously so that an undertaking to deliver imports loan rather than gift,[62] and an unqualified receipt for money implies loan rather than gift or other grounds for payment.[63]

---

[57] *Macdonald v. Newall* (1898) 1 F. 68; *Houldsworth, supra; Robertson's Tr. v. Riddell,* 1911 S.C. 14; *McAdam v. Scott,* 1913, 1 S.L.T. 12; *Hay v. Duthie's Trs.,* 1956 S.C. 511.

[58] *Gray v. G's Trs.* (1878) 5 R. 820; *Welsh's Tr. v. Forbes* (1885) 12 R. 851; *Bank of Scotland v. Stewart* (1891) 18 R. 957; *Stewart v. Shannessy* (1900) 2 F. 1288; *Claddagh S.S. Co. v. Steven,* 1919 S.C. 184; 1919 S.C. (H.L.) 132.

[59] *Menzies v. Barstow* (1840) 2 D. 1317; *Seitz v. Brown* (1872) 10 M. 681; *Ballantine v. Employers Ins. Co.* (1893) 21 R. 305; *Kilmarnock Dist. Cttee. v. Somervell* (1906) 14 S.L.T. 567; *Nelson v. Dundee E. Coast Shipping Co.,* 1907 S.C. 927; *D/S Danmark v. Poulsen,* 1913 S.C. 1043; *Schele v. Lumsden,* 1916 S.C. 709.

[60] *Kinloch v. Mansfield* (1836) 14 S. 905; *Burns v. Martin* (1885) 12 R. 1343, revd. (1887) 14 R. (H.L.) 20; *Bidoulac v. Sinclair's Tr.* (1889) 17 R. 144; cf. *N.Z. Shipping Co. v. Société des Ateliers de France* [1919] A.C. 1, 12; *Maritime National Fish v. Ocean Trawlers* [1935] A.C. 524; *Beresford v. Royal Ins.* [1938] A.C. 586.

[61] *Barr v. Lions* 1956 S.C. 59.

[62] Stair IV, 42, 21(6); Ersk. III, 3, 92; cf. *Thomson v. Geekie* (1861) 23 D. 693; *Gill v. G.,* 1907 S.C. 532.

[63] *Martin v. Crawford* (1850) 12 D. 960; *Fraser v. Bruce* (1858) 20 D. 115; *Robertson v. R.* (1858) 20 D. 371; *Thomson, supra; Christie's Trs. v. Muirhead* (1870) 8 M. 461; *Duncan's Trs. v. Shand* (1873) 11 M. 254; *Gill, supra.* This does not apply to a paid cheque: *Haldane v. Speirs* (1872) 10 M. 537; *Scotland v. S.,* 1909 S.C. 505.

Contemporanea expositio

Where words are ambiguous and equally susceptible of two meanings, if the document has been for long acted on by the parties in a particular sense, such may be held to be the true construction, and may receive effect accordingly.[64] So too where the document is silent as to a matter, it may be interpreted according to the pratice of parties under it.[65] Though *contemporanea expositio* is valuable guide to the interpretation of an old deed[66] it is of little value as to recent contracts.[67]

Demonstrative or taxative

A description in a deed of the subjects of a contract may be demonstrative, i.e. indicating the subjects in question, or taxative, i.e. limiting the subjects to those mentioned. A description limited by the word 'only' is plainly taxative. Thus a description of lands conveyed as being those possessed by the granter or another will usually be held to limit the grant to the lands so possessed.[68] If lands are described by boundaries and their measurements, the latter will normally be held demonstrative only,[69] but otherwise if described by their measurements alone.

Exclusion of prior communings

Where parties after negotiations embody their agreement in a contract or written agreement, the general rule is that it supersedes their prior communings, oral and written, and evidence thereof is incompetent to add to, modify, or qualify the written agreement; the contract must be presumed intended to supersede the earlier negotiations and to record the parties' concluded agreement.[70] Similarly a disposition of heritage in implement

---

[64] *Heriot's Hospital* v. *Macdonald* (1830) 4 W. & S. 98; *Pagan* v. *Macrae* (1860) 22 D. 806; *L.A.* v. *Sinclair* (1867) 5 M. (H.L.) 97; *Russell* v. *Cowpar* (1882) 9 R. 660; *Dundee Mags.* v. *Duncan* (1883) 11 R. 145; *Jopp's Trs.* v. *Edmond* (1888) 15 R. 271; cf. *Hunter* v. *Barron's Trs.* (1886) 13 R. 883; *Mackay* v. *Maclachlan* (1899) 7 S.L.T. 48.

[65] *Hewats* v. *Roberton* (1881) 9 R. 175; *Argyllshire Commrs. of Supply* v. *Campbell* (1885) 12 R. 1255; *Shearer* v. *Peddie* (1899) 1 F. 1201; *Macgill* v. *Park* (1899) 2 F. 272; *Boyd* v. *Hamilton,* 1907 S.C. 912.

[66] *N.B. Ry.* v. *Edinburgh Mags.,* 1920 S.C. 409.

[67] *Scott* v. *Howard* (1881) 8 R. (H.L.) 59; *Borthwick-Norton* v. *Gavin Paul,* 1947 S.C. 659, 680.

[68] *Murray* v. *Oliphant's Wife* (1634) Mor. 2262; *Cunninghame* v. *G.S.W. Ry.* (1883) 10 R. 1173; *Millar's Trs.* v. *Rattray* (1891) 18 R. 989; contrast *Gardner* v. *Scott* (1843) 2 Bell 129; *Critchley* v. *Campbell* (1884) 11 R. 475; *Blyth's Trs.* v. *Shaw Stewart* (1883) 11 R. 99; *Currie* v. *Campbell's Trs.* (1888) 16 R. 237.

[69] *Ure* v. *Anderson* (1834) 12 S. 494; *Fleming* v. *Baird* (1841) 3 D. 1015; *Gibson* v. *Bonnington Sugar Co.* (1869) 7 M. 394; *Blyth's Trs.* v. *Shaw Stewart* (1883) 11 R. 99; *Currie* v. *Campbell's Trs.* (1888) 16 R. 237.

[70] *Forlong* v. *Taylor's Exors.* (1838) 3 S. & McL. 177; *Inglis* v. *Buttery* (1878) 5 R. (H.L.) 87; *Largue* v. *Urquhart* (1881) 18 S.L.R. 491; *Tininver Lime Co.* v. *Coghill* (1881) 19 S.L.R. 7; *Riemann* v. *Young* (1895) 2 S.L.T. 426; *Muller* v. *Weber & Schaer* (1901) 3 F. 401; *Paterson* v. *Inglis* (1902) 10 S.L.T. 449; *McAllister* v. *McGallagley,* 1911 S.C. 112; *Norval* v. *Abbey,* 1939 S.C. 724; *Korner* v. *Shennan,* 1950 S.C. 285.

of a prior contract must be deemed completely to supersede that contract,[71] though it may be otherwise where the deed expressly refers to the prior contract,[72] and parties may agree that this principle shall not apply.[73] Again this rule does not apply where a letter confirming an oral agreement is ambiguous, when evidence as to the original bargain is admissible.[74]

Extrinsic evidence

Extrinsic evidence is admissible, not to help interpret a document,[75] but to inform the court of the meanings which the granter habitually attached to the words in question. Thus translations may be adduced of foreign or dialect words, and explanation of scientific or technical terms,[76] while the meaning of a word or phrase may be shown to have a particular connotation by the custom and usage of a particular trade, or business or place.[77] Similarly extrinsic evidence is admissible to aid in the construction of wills by informing the court of the testators' circumstances and family at the date thereof,[78] or to aid in the construction of a contract by ascertaining the circumstances surrounding the contract.[79]

It is settled that parole evidence is not generally admissible to add to, vary, alter, or contradict the terms of a deed or writing.[80] Similarly where a contract is signed apparently as principal, it is not competent to prove by parole evidence that the party was contracting as agent only.[81]

But parole evidence is admissible if a written contract is admitted or alleged not to express the true agreement between the parties,[82] or if the contract is partly oral and party written,[83] or if the written contract is

---

[71] *Lee v. Alexander* (1883) 10 R. (H.L.) 91; *Orr. v. Mitchell* (1893) 20 R. (H.L.) 27; *Baird v. Alexander* (1898) 25 R. (H.L.) 35; *Butter v. Foster*, 1912 S.C. 1218; but see *Jamieson v. Welsh* (1900) 3 F. 176.

[72] *Inverkeithing Mags. v. Ross* (1874) 2 R. 48; *Smith, Laing & Maitland* (1876) 3 R. 281; see also *Wann v. Gray*, 1935 S.N. 8.

[73] *Young v. McKellar*, 1909 S.C. 1340; *Fraser v. Cox*, 1938 S.C. 506.

[74] *Crondace v. Annandale Steamship Co.*, 1925 S.L.T. 449.

[75] cf. *Miller v. M.* (1822) 1 Sh. App. 308; *Stewart v. S.* (1842) 1 Bell 796; *Davidson v. D.* (1906) 14 S.L.T. 337.

[76] *Sutton v. Ciceri* (1890) 17 R. (H.L.) 40.

[77] *Von Mehren v. Edinburgh Roperie* (1901) 4 F. 232.

[78] *Free Church Trs. v. Maitland* (1887) 14 R. 333; *Craw's Trs. v. Blacklock*, 1920 S.C. 22; *Ormiston's Exor. v. Laws*, 1966 S.C. 47, 51; contrast *Boyd v. B's Trs.* (1906) 13 S.L.T. 875; *Devlin's Trs. v. Breen*, 1943 S.C. 556; 1945 S.C. (H.L.) 27.

[79] *Forlong v. Taylor's Exors.* (1838) 3 S. & McL. 177; *Inglis v. Buttery* (1878) 5 R. (H.L.) 87; *Mackenzie v. Liddell* (1883) 10 R. 705.

[80] *Steuart's Trs. v. Hart* (1875) 3 R. 192; *Tancred Arrol & Co. v. Steel Co. of Scotland* (1890) 17 R. (H.L.) 31; *MacLellan v. Peattie's Trs.* (1903) 5 F. 1031; *Forth Collieries v. Hume* (1904) 11 S.L.T. 576; *Lavan v. Aird*, 1919 S.C. 345; *Norval v. Abbey*, 1939 S.C. 724; *Perdikou v. Pattison*, 1958 S.L.T. 153; *Haigh & Ringrose v. Barrhead Builders*, 1981 S.L.T. 157.

[81] *Gibb v. Cunningham & Robertson*, 1925 S.L.T. 608.

[82] *Grant v. Mackenzie* (1899) 1 F. 889; *Krupp v. Menzies*, 1907 S.C. 903.

[83] *Christie v. Hunter* (1880) 7 R. 729.

challenged on the ground of essential error, fraud, or illegality.[84] or if it is alleged that the writing was not intended truly to record the contract but to conceal some other transaction.[85]

Parole evidence of a testator's intentions is not competent.[86]

By what law transaction is regulated

It is frequently material to determine by what system of law the rights and duties of parties are to be determined. If the parties have a common intention on this they may deal with the point expressly, but failing this an inference as to their intention may be drawn from a provision for arbitration in a particular place,[87] from the use of the technical terms of one legal system rather than another,[88] or from other indications of intention. Similarly a will may declare the testator's domicile.

Meanings of particular words and phrases

The Titles to Land Consolidation (Sc.) Act, 1868,[89] and the Conveyancing (Sc.) Act, 1874,[90] authorize the use in conveyancing deeds of certain short forms of clauses, having prescribed statutory meanings. In many cases the interpretation of particular words and phrases has been considered. In some of these, such as cases of wills, the interpretation may have no application outside the will then construed, but in others, such as cases interpreting words regularly used in common documents, such as charter parties, the interpretation must rule subsequent cases dealing with the same words in another such deed, unless the earlier case is distinguishable on its facts.

[84] *Steuart's Trs., supra; Stewart v. Kennedy* (1890) 17 R. (H.L.) 25; *Bell Bros. v. Aitken,* 1939 S.C. 577.

[85] *Maloy v. Macadam* (1885) 12 R. 431; *Imrie v. I.* (1891) 19 R. 185.

[86] *Fortunato's J.F. v. F.,* 1981 S.L.T. 277.

[87] *Hamlyn v. Talisker Distillery* (1894) 21 R. (H.L.) 21; *Robertson v. Brandes, Schonwald & Co.* (1906) 8 F. 815.

[88] But see *Mackintosh v. May* (1895) 22 R. 345.

[89] Ss. 5–8 and Sch. B., S. 138.

[90] Ss. 4, 26.

THE PUBLIC REGISTERS AND
THE REGISTRATION OF DEEDS

Numerous public registers are maintained under various statutes and registration of various deeds, notices and other writs has in many cases important legal consequences.[1] Under the Public Registers and Records (Sc.) Act, 1948, separate Keepers are appointed of the Registers and of the Records of Scotland. The former is charged with functions in relation to the General Register of Sasines, the Register of Hornings, the Register of Inhibitions and Adjudications, the Register of Entails, the Register of Deeds, and the Land Register of Scotland, and has the powers and duties formerly vested in the Director of Chancery. The latter is charged with the preservation of the public registers, records, and rolls of Scotland, as historical documents. The Registers are grouped under the four offices, Chancery Office, Sasine Office, Horning Office, and Deeds Office, with which they are historically and administratively connected.

THE REGISTERS

Register of the Great Seal

The Secretary of State for Scotland is now Keeper, and the Keeper of the Registers of Scotland is Deputy Keeper, of the Great Seal of Scotland, under which are authenticated charters and grants of land from the Crown, patents of nobility, and commissions to the principal offices of the Crown. In this register are recorded for preservation only writs passing that seal. Extracts of writs from this register are probative.[2]

Register of the Prince's Seal

Grants of lands forming part of the stewartry or principality of Scotland, destined as provision for the eldest son and heir-apparent of the Crown, pass the Prince's Seal and are recorded in this register.

---

[1] See generally M. Livingstone's *Guide to the Public Records of Scotland* (1905).
[2] Public Records (Sc.) Act, 1809, S. 16.

Register of the Quarter Seal

Under this seal pass royal gifts of forfeiture or of *ultimus haeres.*

Register of the Cachet or Privy Seal

The Privy Seal of Scotland is now in abeyance and its registers, now discontinued, were deposited in 1924 and are now in the custody of the Keeper of the Records of Scotland. Grants formerly authenticated by the Privy Seal, such as of gifts of escheat, feudal casualties, personal rights, and presentation of offices in the gift of the Crown, are now made by direct warrant under the Royal Sign Manual.

Register of Crown Writs

By the Titles to Land Consolidation (Sc.) Act, 1868, S. 87, the Director of Chancery[3] is directed to maintain this register and enter in it at full length Crown writs.[4]

Register of Sheriff's Commissions

In this are recorded commissions granted to persons to hold the office of sheriff-principal or full-time sheriff.

Record of Service of Heirs

Service was the process whereby an heir to heritage formerly established the fact of his heirship.[5] Decrees therein were recorded by the Director of Chancery[6] in the manner directed by the Lord Clerk Register,[7] in books known as the Record of Services.[8] By virtue of the Succession (Sc.) Act, 1964, service of heirs is now practically obsolete.

Register of Sasines

In 1617 the Registration Act, replacing earlier legislation from 1540 onwards, provided that all instruments of sasine and writs relating to redeemable rights in land were to be recorded in a public general register in Edinburgh within 60 days of the sasine. The Act also established

---

[3] Office discontinued in 1932 under authority of Reorganization of Offices (Sc.) Act, 1928, S. 7: duties now vested in Keeper of the Registers of Scotland.
[4] As to these see 1868 Act, Ss. 3, 63–79, 83–8, 89, 90, 91.
[5] Titles to Land Consolidation (Sc.) Act, 1868, Ss. 27–35.
[6] Now Keeper of the Registers of Scotland.
[7] Ibid., S. 36.
[8] Ibid., S. 38; The Record of Service was established by the Service of Heirs (Sc.) Act, 1847.

Particular Registers of Sasines throughout the country for the sheriffdoms and districts therein specified; writs might be recorded in either the General or Particular Register. An Act of 1693 made the date of recording the criterion of preference, irrespective of actual possession. The Land Registers (Sc.) Act, 1868, discontinued the old General Register of Sasines, instituted a new General Register with separate divisions for each county in Scotland, and abolished all the Particular Registers from dates specified in the Act.

The Act, 1681, c. 11, brought registration of lands held burgage in burghs, or by booking in Paisley, into line by establishing Burgh Registers of Sasines and the Register of Booking in Paisley. In 1926 the Burgh Registers (Sc.) Act provided for the gradual discontinuance of the Burgh Registers of Sasines and the Register of Booking. This is now complete.

The Register of Interruption of Prescriptions, in which had to be registered all summonses used for interrupting prescription of real rights, with executions thereof, ended in 1868, all entries formerly made in it being thereafter made in the Register of Sasines.[9]

The Court of Session has power to make Acts of Sederunt regarding the General Register of Sasines.[10]

Land Register of Scotland

The Land Register of Scotland was established in 1979;[11] in it are to be registered interests in land by way of feu, long lease, security by way of contract of ground annual, heritable security, liferent or incorporeal heritable right and certain other interests, and transfers of or transactions in any of these interests.[12] Registration vests in the person registered a real right in and to the interest registered and supersedes recording of a deed in the Register of Sasines.[13] Registration is completed by the Keeper preparing a title sheet for the interest in the register and issuing a copy known as a land certificate.[14] A person suffering loss in certain ways is entitled to indemnification by the Keeper.[15] There are not registrable what are called overriding interests in land, such as those of the Crown or a public department, a lessee, the proprietor of the dominant tenement in a servitude, the holder of a floating charge, and certain others.[16] Registration will be introduced over a period, superseding recording in the Register of Sasines, which will ultimately be closed.

[9] Land Registers (Sc.) Act, 1868, S. 15.
[10] Public Registers and Records (Sc.) Act, 1948.
[11] Land Registration (Sc.) Act, 1979, S. 1. See further Ch. 7.2, *infra*.
[12] S. 2.
[13] Ss. 3–4. 'Interest in land' is defined: S. 28.
[14] Ss. 5–6. In the case of securities the creditor will receive a charge certificate.
[15] S. 12. In certain cases there is no entitlement to indemnity.
[16] S. 28.

Register of Entails

The Entail Act, 1685, empowered landowners to entail their lands[17] subject to certain conditions, of which one was that entails should be recorded in a Register opened for the purpose. Later Acts required other writs relating to entails also to be registered.[18] Since the Entail (Sc.) Act, 1914, which prohibited the creation of new entails, the register is open only for the recording of writs relating to existing entails, such as instruments of disentail.

Register of Hornings

The General and Particular Registers of Hornings recorded applications by a creditor against a debtor under which Letters of Horning were issued under the Signet, in pursuance of which the debtor, on failure to pay, was denounced a rebel with four blasts of the horn by a messenger-at-arms. Letters of Horning had by Act of 1579 to be registered in the sheriff court books of the shire in which publication had taken place, but are now in desuetude. By the Debtors (Sc.) Act, 1838, S. 5, a charge on a decree and its execution might be recorded, within a year and a day after its expiry without payment, in the General Register of Hornings, which registration had the same effect as if the debtor had been denounced rebel in virtue of Letters of Horning. Extract sheriff court decrees and execution of charges thereon might similarly (S. 10) be recorded in the Particular Register. The Land Registers Act, 1868, S. 18, preserved the Particular Registers of Hornings.

Register of Inhibitions and Adjudications

The Land Registers Act, 1868, Ss. 16, 18, abolished the Particular Registers of Inhibitions and Interdictions,[19] and the Conveyancing (Sc.) Act,

---

[17] As to this see Ch. 7.8 (Vol. III), *infra*.

[18] See generally Craigie, *Heritable*, 697, 702.

[19] Inhibition is a process whereby a creditor may restrain his debtor from voluntarily alienating or burdening his heritage and follows on Letters of Inhibition passing the Signet. It is ineffective until served on the debtor, and ineffective against persons generally until published at the market cross and pier of Leith, followed by registration within 40 days, formerly in the General Register of Inhibitions (established 1581), in which were recorded notices of inhibitions, letters of inhibition, abbreviates of petitions for sequestration and similar notices, or the appropriate Particular Registers of Inhibitions (established 1600) kept for the counties in which the subjects are situated, and now in the combined Register. The Particular Registers were abolished in 1868. Inhibition is still competent and the Letters or Summons of an action containing warrant to inhibit must be registered to have any effect. Inhibition prescribes in five years: Conveyancing Act, 1924, S. 44. See also Ersk. II, 11, 2; Titles to Land Consolidation (Sc.) Act, 1868, Ss. 145, 156.

Interdiction was the process whereby a person of a facile tendency might be disabled, voluntarily by bond of interdiction, or judicially by the Court of Session, from alienating his heritage gratuitously without the consent of the interdicter. To be effective the bond or decree had to be registered in the General Register of Interdictions or the appropriate Particular Register of Interdictions. See Ersk. I. 7, 54. The process is now incompetent: Conveyancing (Sc.) Act, 1924, S. 44.

1924, S. 44, amalgamated the General Register of Inhibitions and Interdictions and the Register of Abbreviates of Adjudications[20] into the Register of Inhibitions and Adjudications as the sole register for personal diligences. It contains inhibitions, interdictions, adjudications, reductions, notices of litigiosity,[21] abbreviates of petitions for sequestration, statutorily equivalent to inhibitions, abbreviates of the Acts and Warrants of trustees in bankruptcy, statutorily equivalent to adjudications, and adjudication orders and certificates in bankruptcy under the [English] Bankruptcy Act, 1914.

The Registers of Deeds

Until 1809 it was competent by long-standing custom to register writs for preservation or execution in the books of all public courts of record, including the books of the Lords of Council and Session, the books of every sheriff court, commissary courts, and of bailies of royal burghs and burghs of regality. The Public Records (Sc.) Act, 1809, restricted registration to the Books of Council and Session, and sheriff court books. In these are registered marriage contracts, bonds, obligations, (since 1824) wills, and a wide variety of other deeds.

Register of Protests

Under various statutes protests of bills of exchange have been recorded in the Books of Council and Session or sheriff court books. Down to 1811 protests were recorded in the Register of Deeds but a separate Register was commenced in 1812. The town clerks of royal burghs still have the right to receive for recording instruments of protest on bills of exchange where all parties are burgesses or domiciled within the burgh when the deeds are presented for registration.[22]

Record of Edictal Citations

The edictal citation of persons furth of Scotland, formerly done at the market cross of Edinburgh and the pier and shore of Leith,[23] was replaced in 1825 by the delivery of a copy of the summons or charge to the keeper of the records of the Court of Session who registered an abstract thereof in books kept for the purpose.[24]

---

[20] This had superseded the earlier Register of Apprisings (1636). Adjudication is an action, founded on any decree or liquid document of debt, whereby heritable property may be attached for debt. Service of a summons of adjudication, if followed by registration of a notice in statutory form in the Register renders the lands litigious.

[21] Litigiosity is created by registration of a notice of an action of adjudication or reduction. It prescribes in five years: Conveyancing (Sc.) Act, 1924, S. 44(2).

[22] Under Bills of Exchange Acts, 1681 (c. 86), 1696 (c. 38), and 1772, S. 42; see *Sutherland* v. *Gunn* (1854) 16 D. 339. Right preserved by Public Records (Sc.) Act, 1809, S. 1.

[23] See Stair IV, 47, 3; Ersk. I, 2, 18. In certain cases it was also made at the market cross of the county town or head burgh of the county: Act, 1555, c. 6; Ersk. IV, 1. 8.

[24] Court of Session (Sc.) Act, 1825, Ss. 51–2; see also Court of Session (Sc.) Act, 1850, S. 22.

Registers of English and Irish Judgments

By the Judgments Extension Act, 1868, S. 2, a certificate of judgment for debt, damages, or costs obtained in the superior courts of England or Northern Ireland might within twelve months be registered in the Register for English and Irish Judgments in the same way as a bond executed according to the law of Scotland, and had the same force and effect as a decree of the Court.[25] The Inferior Courts Judgments Extension Act, 1882, made similar provision for the judgments of inferior courts being registered by sheriff clerks.

The Administration of Justice Act 1920, Ss. 9–14, provides for reciprocal enforcement by registration of judgments of superior courts of the U.K. and of Commonwealth countries to which it is made applicable by Order in Council. The Foreign Judgments (Reciprocal Enforcement) Act 1933 provides for reciprocal enforcement by registration of judgments of superior courts in the U.K. and of foreign countries to which it is made applicable by Order in Council. The Convention enacted by the Civil Jurisdiction and Judgments Act, 1982, provides for recognition of a judgment given in one contracting state in other contracting states without any special procedure. This will replace registration under the 1868 and 1882 Acts.

Register of Community Judgments

A Register of Community Judgments has been established in which is registered any European Community judgment to which the Secretary of State has appended an order for enforcement or any Euratom inspection order or any order of the European Court that enforcement of a registered Community judgment shall be suspended.[26]

REGISTRATION OF DEEDS

Purposes of Registration

In Scottish practice writs may be recorded for one or more of three purposes, for execution, for preservation, and for publication. Registration for execution is the recording of a deed or probative writ in the Books of Council and Session or sheriff court books so that the grantee may obtain an extract with a warrant for the enforcement by the appropriate diligence of the granters' obligation, the extract and warrant being statutorily equivalent to a decree of court.

Registration for preservation involves the recording of the deed in a

---

[25] See further Ch. 2.4, *infra*.
[26] R.C. 296G added by A.S. 15 Dec. 1972.

public register, the Books of Council and Session or sheriff court books, and its retention in a public office so that it may not be lost or destroyed and an extract may at all times be obtained by a person requiring one.

The registration for publication of writs relating to land in the Registers of Sasines or, where appropriate, the Register of Entails, is intended to make publicly available to persons interested the state of the title to all pieces of land and the burdens affecting it, and to protect the interest of persons interested therein.[27]

Registration for execution[28]

Where a probative deed, such as a bond or contract, includes a clause stating the granter's consent to the deed being registered for execution, it may be registered in the Books of Council and Session, if the granter of the obligation resides anywhere in Scotland or is subject to the jurisdiction of the Court of Session, or in the books of a sheriff court, if the granter is designed as residing within the jurisdiction of that court. The deed must embody a definite obligation enforceable by decree of court. Certain kinds of writs only, particularly protests of bills of exchange,[29] or promissory notes,[30] exchequer bonds,[31] and certain assignations,[32] may be registered for execution without a clause of consent therein.

The creditor may then at any time obtain an authenticated extract in statutory form[33] which concludes by the Court, or sheriff, granting warrant[34] for all lawful execution thereon. This warrant authorizes diligence against the debtor's property in the same way as if the creditor had obtained a decree of court against the debtor.[35]

Where the original debtor has died it is not possible to do diligence on the extract recorded bond,[36] except in the case where the personal obligation in a bond and disposition in security has transmitted against a person taking the security subjects by succession, gift or bequest from the debtor,[37] provided he has signed an agreement to that effect,[38] or where the obligation has been taken over in gremio of a conveyance of the security subjects,[37] provided the purchaser has signed the disposition in

[27] Registration in the Register of Inhibitions and Adjudications is not technically known as a register for publication, but it is so in effect.
[28] See generally Bell, Convg. I, 220; Menzies, 183; Craigie, Heritable, 973; Moveable, 470.
[29] Bills of Exchange Act, 1681, and Inland Bills Act, 1696.
[30] Bills of Exchange (Sc.) Act, 1772, S. 41.
[31] Exchequer Court (Sc.) Act, 1856, S. 38.
[32] Under Transmission of Moveable Property (Sc.) Act, 1862, S. 1.
[33] Writs Execution (Sc.) Act, 1877, S. 5.
[34] Ibid., Sch.
[35] Ersk. II. 5, 54; Bell, Prin. § 68; 1877 Act, S. 3.
[36] Brown v. Binnie (1635) Mor. 14994.
[37] Conveyancing (Sc.) Act, 1874, S. 47; Ritchie and Sturrock v. Dullatur Feuing Co. (1881) 9 R. 358.

his favour.[38] In other cases a decree of constitution of the debt must be obtained.

If a new creditor obtains right from the original creditor and the latter had not obtained decree the new creditor must proceed by letters of horning.

Registration for preservation

Registration of any probative writ for preservation[39] is competent without a clause of consent thereto, but the granter must be subject to the jurisdiction of the court in whose books his writ is registered. An authenticated extract may at any time be obtained, which is equivalent to the principal unless it be challenged on the ground of fraud or forgery.[40] The principal writ is retained and allowed out only by authority of the court and subject to conditions.[41] The court has permitted the correction of a clerical error in the testing clause of a deed given in for registration but not booked,[42] and the chemical examination of a recorded will.[43] There is no power to record only portions of deeds, nor to grant partial extracts only.[44]

Registration for publication[45]

Registration for publication applies to writs affecting land, transferring or burdening or disburdening it. The Registration Act, 1617, which established the Register of Sasines, required sasines to be registered within 60 days of their dates. The Real Rights Act, 1693 (c. 13) provided that writs should have priority according to the dates of their registration,[46] and the Register of Sasines Act, 1693 (c. 14) required the maintenance of a minute book showing the day and hour of the presentation of writs and the names and designations of presenters. The Titles Act, 1858, sanctioned the direct recording of conveyances of land in the Register of Sasines. Writs to be recorded must have endorsed thereon a warrant of registration,[47] stating on whose behalf the deed is to be registered and in

---

[38] Conveyancing (Sc.) Act, 1924, S. 15 and Sch. A, Form 2.
[39] See generally Menzies, 136, 189; Craigie, *Heritable*, 231, 394.
[40] Writs Execution (Sc.) Act, 1877, S. 5.
[41] *Liquidators of Western Bank* (1868) 6 M. 656; *Macdonald* (1877) 5 R. 44; *United Telephone Co.* v. *Maclean* (1882) 9 R. 710; *Inglis* (1882) 9 R. 761; *Walter* (1889) 16 R. 926; *Leigh-Bennett* (1893) 20 R. 787; *Jamieson's Trs.* v. *J.* (1899) 2 F. 96; *Pheysey* (1906) 8 F. 801; *Chevenix-Trench*, 1917 S.C. 168; *Campbell's Trs.*, 1934 S.C. 8.
[42] *Caldwell* (1871) 10 M. 99; *Murray* (1904) 6 F. 840; contrast *Thoms* (1870) 8 M. 857. See also *Mitchell's Trs.*, 1930 S.C. 180.
[43] *Irvine* v. *Powrie's Trs.*, 1915 S.C. 1006.
[44] *B's Exor.* v. *Keeper of the Registers*, 1935 S.C. 745.
[45] See generally Bell, *Convg.* I, 662; Menzies, 555; Wood, 179; Craigie, *Heritable*, 55, 238.
[46] Repeated in Titles to Land Consolidation (Sc.) Act, 1868, S. 142.
[47] Conveyancing (Sc.) Act, 1924, S. 10 and Sch. F.

what division of the General Register, signed by the party or his agent, and they may be recorded at any time in the life of the person on whose behalf they are to be registered. Each writ is recorded in the presentment book, which fixes the date and time of entry, the minute book, which contains the names of the parties and a short description of the property and the record volume, and since 1871 a search sheet has been maintained for every unit of property giving an abstract of all deeds affecting that property. After registration, and being photocopied into the Register, deeds are returned to the presenter for retention, with a certificate of registration endorsed thereon.

Extracts from the Register of Sasines are statutorily declared equivalent to principals, unless the latter should be challenged as forged.[48] but conveyancers have always been reluctant to accept them as such. Extracts of a conveyance, deed, instrument, or other document bearing to have been recorded in the Register of Sasines are to be accepted for all purposes as sufficient evidence of the contents of the original so recorded and of any matter relating thereto appearing on the extract.[49]

The Keeper has a discretion to refuse to register any deed presented to him; deeds are refused particularly if inappropriate to the Register, or incorrect in legal form.[50]

Registration for combined purposes

Registration for execution and for preservation[51] have a common origin and a largely common development, and a deed may be registered for both purposes if an appropriate clause of consent is contained therein. Statute[52] sanctions a short clause of consent with a statutory meaning.

The conjunction of all three purposes of registration is permitted by the Land Registers Act, 1868, S. 12, which provided that a writ registered in the Sasine Register should be held registered in the Books of Council and Session for preservation, or for preservation and execution, provided it has an appropriate warrant of registration[53] endorsed thereon. Such a writ is retained and only an extract delivered. By the Writs Execution (Sc.) Act, 1877, S. 6, a writ registered in the Register of Sasines for preservation only may be afterwards registered for preservation and execution, provided it contains *in gremio* a clause of registration for preservation and execution.[54]

---

[48] Titles to Land Consolidation (Sc.) Act, 1868, S. 142.
[49] Conveyancing and Feudal Reform (Sc.) Act, 1970, S. 45 (applicable to extracts whether issued before or after that Act).
[50] *Macdonald* v. *Keeper of the General Register of Sasines*, 1914 S.C. 854.
[51] See generally Bell, *Convg.* I. 220.
[52] Titles to Land Consolidation (Sc.) Act, 1868, S. 138.
[53] Form in Conveyancing (Sc.) Act, 1924, S. 10 and Sch. F, No. 2.
[54] See further Craigie, *Heritable*, 240.

OTHER REGISTERS

Numerous registers are maintained under various statutes, e.g. of companies, of births, deaths, and marriages, of solicitors, of ships, of trade marks, which are dealt with in their particular contexts.

TIME, AND THE EFFECT OF LAPSE OF TIME

Time is a factor constantly arising in legal issues. The interpretation of words and phrases relating to time frequently has to be considered, and the effect of lapse of time on rights is also frequently material.

Computation of time

Time is normally computed in years, months, weeks, and days. Each common year comprises 365 days, but every fourth year is a leap year comprising 366 days. Hundredth years, except every fourth hundred, are common years.[1] In 1752 eleven nominal days were omitted in September to bring the calendar then in use (Julian Calendar) into line with the Gregorian calendar.[2] The calendar year has since 1600 commenced in Scotland on 1st January.[3]

'Month', by common law,[4] mercantile custom,[5] and statute[6] is a calendar month, in the absence of contrary indications,[7] and 'week' a calendar week of seven days, from Sunday to Saturday.[8]

A 'day' is prima facie the period of twenty-four hours between midnight and midnight, but in certain contexts means the period of light within such twenty-four hours.[9] The time of day or night referred to is to be held as Greenwich Mean Time,[10] but 'sunrise' and 'sunset' are determined by local time, not the time of sunrise or sunset at Greenwich.[11]

According to *naturalis computatio* time is reckoned *de momento in*

---

[1] Calendar (New Style) Act, 1750, S. 2 (amd. Calendar Act, 1751).

[2] Ibid., S. 1.

[3] Ibid., S. 1; *Williamson* v. *Hay* (1855) 17 D. 960. In England until 1752 the year commenced on 25 March.

[4] *Smith* v. *Robertson & Jeffray* (1826) 4 S. 442; *Ashley* v. *Rothesay Mags.* (1873) 11 M. 708; *Farquharson* v. *Whyte* (1886) 13 R. (J.) 29; *McNiven* v. *Glasgow Corpn.*, 1920 S.C. 584.

[5] e.g. in relation to bills of exchange: Bills of Exchange Act, 1882, S. 14(4); sale of goods: Sale of Goods Act, 1979, S. 10(2).

[6] Interpretation Act, 1978, Sch. 1.

[7] *Campbell's Trs.* v. *Cazenove* (1880) 8 R. 21.

[8] *Ferguson* v. *Rodger* (1895) 22 R. 643; *Aberdeen City* v. *Watt* (1901) 3 F. 787; *Roscoe* v. *Mackersy* (1905) 7 F. 761; But see *Fleming* v. *Lochgelly Iron Co.* (1902) 4 F. 890; *McCue* v. *Barclay Curle & Co.* (1902) 4 F. 909.

[9] Night Poaching Act, 1828, S. 12; Day Trespass Act 1832 (Game (Sc.) Act, 1832), S. 3.

[10] Statutes (Definition of Time) Act, 1880, S. 1 (not affected by Summer Time Acts, 1922 to 1947).

[11] *MacKinnon* v. *Nicolson*, 1916, S.C. (J.) 6.

momentum,[12] save that if the exact time is unknown, the period is reckoned from the end of the day, month, or year in question. It does not matter that certain days of the period were *inutiles*.[13]

According to *civilis computatio*, time is computed *de die in diem*. There are no fractions of a day and the day on which time starts to run is normally excluded from the period to run,[14] particularly if so many 'clear days' are specified.[15] Where a period of time is reckoned in days, months or years it is reckoned *de die in diem*. Thus the prescriptive period runs from midnight on the starting day[16] to midnight on the day having the same number in the same month, the requisite number of years later.[17] Exceptionally the day on which time starts to run is included in the period.[18]

Time normally expires at the earliest moment of the final day of the period,[19] but where the loss of rights is in question, only at the last moment of the final day,[20] and where 'clear days' are specified, it does not expire till the earliest moment of the next day.[21] Where the giving of notice is in question it is sufficient if the notice be sent timeously though not received till outwith the time.[22]

Prescribed dates

When something is required to be done by a prescribed date, prima facie the requirement is mandatory.[23]

'From' a date

The primary meaning of 'from' a date is after the expiry of that date.[24]

---

[12] *Drummond v. Cunningham-Head* (1624) Mor. 3465 (attainment of majority); *Greig v. Anderson* (1883) 20 S.L.R. 421.

[13] Ersk. II, 7, 30; cf. *Hutton v. Garland* (1883) 10 R. (J.) 60; *McNiven v. Glasgow Corpn.*, 1920 S.C. 584.

[14] *S. Staffs Tramways Co. v. Sickness and Accident Corpn.* [1891] 1 Q.B. 402. See also Bills of Exchange Act, 1882, S. 14(2); Bankruptcy (Sc.) Act, 1913, S. 3; *Lindsay v. Giles* (1844) 6 D. 771; *Stiven v. Reynolds* (1891) 18 R. 422; *Sickness & Accident Assce. Assocn. v. General Assce. Corpn.* (1892) 19 R. 977; *Lipman & Co's Tr.* (1893) 20 R. 818; *Frew v. Morris* (1897) 24 R. (J.) 50; *McLeod & Sons*, 1969 S.C. 16.

[15] *Wilson* (1891) 19R. 219.

[16] *Simpson v. Marshall* (1900) 2 F. 447, 458, 459.

[17] *Simpson, supra; Cavers Parish Council v. Smailholm Parish Council*, 1909 S.C. 195; cf. *Ashley v. Rothesay Mags.* (1873) 11 M. 708.

[18] *Hough v. Athya* (1879) 6 R. 961; *Mackenzie v. Liddell* (1883) 10 R. 705.

[19] The maxim *dies inceptus pro completo habetur*. Bell, *Prin.*, § 46, note; *Scott v. Rutherford* (1839) 2 D. 206; *Thomson v. Kirkcudbright Mags.* (1878) 5 R. 561; cf. *Lawford v. Davies* (1878) 4 P.D. 61.

[20] Ersk. III, 7, 30; *Thomson, supra*, 563; cf. *Jacobsen v. Underwood* (1894) 21 R. 654; *Simpson v. Melville* (1899) 6 S.L.T. 355.

[21] *Wilson, supra*.

[22] *Charleson v. Duffes* (1881) 8 R. (J.) 34.

[23] *Simpson v. Selkirk Assessor*, 1948 S.C. 270.

[24] *Ashley v. Rothesay Mags.* (1873) 11 M. 708; *Sickness and Accident Assce. Assocn. v. General Accident Assce. Corpn.* (1892) 19 R. 977; *Frew v. Morris* (1897) 24 R. (J.) 50.

'By' a date

'By' a date means not later than the end of that day. A reply called for 'by' a given date has been held timeously given when posted on that date though not received till later.[25]

'At' or 'on' a date

'At' a date or a time means from the period when that date or time begins to run. 'On' a date or day means at any time within that day.[26]

'Within' so many days or months

When something must be done 'within' a number of days, weeks, or months, the number of days runs from the day after the *terminus a quo*, as the first day, to the last moment of the day which completes the prescribed number of days.[27] If the last day is a Sunday and the thing prescribed cannot be done for that day, an extension to the Monday is permissible;[28] similarly the number of months runs from the day after the *terminus a quo* to the day bearing the same number, the prescribed number of months later.[29]

'For' so many weeks or months

Residence 'for' a stated number of weeks, months, or years is reckoned from the day when the period begins to the correspondingly numbered day, the requisite number of calendar divisions later.[30]

Term-days

In leases, lettings frequently commence or terminate at the main term days,[31] namely Whitsunday (15 May) or Martinmas (11 November),[32] but the Removal Terms (Scotland) Act, 1886, S. 4, provides that, in the absence of express stipulation to the contrary, the tenant shall enter to or remove from the house[33] let at noon on 28 May or 28 November, as the case may be, or on the following day if the 28th be a Sunday. But

---

[25] *Jacobsen* v. *Underwood* (1894) 21 R. 654.
[26] *Mackenzie* v. *Liddell* (1883) 10 R. 705, 714.
[27] *Charleson* v. *Duffes* (1881) 8 R. (J.) 34; see also *McDonagh* v. *Maclellan* (1896) 13 R. 1000.
[28] *Russell* v. *R.* (1874) 2 R. 82; *Hutton* v. *Garland* (1883) 10 R. (J.) 60; *Henderson* v. *H.* (1888) 16 R. 5; *McVean* v. *Jamieson* (1896) 23 R. (J.) 25; *Blackburn* v. *Lang's Trs.* (1905) 8 F. 290.
[29] *McNiven* v. *Glasgow Corpn.*, 1920 S.C. 584.
[30] *Cavers Parish Council* v. *Smailholm Parish Council*, 1909 S.C. 195.
[31] The other term (or quarter) days in Scotland are Candlemas (2 Feb.) and Lammas (1 Aug.). See *Scott Chisholme* v. *Brown* (1893) 20 R. 575.
[32] *Fraser's Trs.* v. *Maule* (1904) 6 F. 819; *Hunter* v. *Barron's Trs.* (1886) 13 R. 883.
[33] Defined, S. 3.

warning to remove must be given 40 days before 15 May or 11 November. By the Removal Terms (Scotland) Act, 1886, Amendment Act, 1890, S. 2, the terms for a servant hired by the year or half-year similarly, in the absence of express contrary stipulation, run to 28 May or 28 November.

Need for punctuality

A condition of 'punctual payment' in a contract is strictly enforced.[34] It means paid by the due date.[34] But in the absence of an express condition failure to make payment of the price of heritage on the stipulated day is not a material breach of contract justifying rescission.[35] Unless a different intention appears from the terms of the contract stipulations as to time of payment are not deemed to be of the essence of a contract of sale of goods; whether any other stipulation as to time is of the essence of the contract or not depends on the terms of the contract.[36]

EFFECT OF LAPSE OF TIME ON RIGHTS

The lapse of time may affect rights in different ways. A distinction should be drawn between rules of prescription, substantive rules which exclude challenge of a right or extinguish a right or obligation completely after a period of time, and rules of limitation, procedural rules which after the lapse of a time render an obligation unenforceable, sometimes unless it can be established by special methods of proof.[37] But this terminology has not been strictly followed in Scots law and lapse of time must be considered under the following heads: (a) the statutory positive prescription which precludes challenges and renders a heritable right unchallengeable; (b) the statutory limitations (or prescriptions) which did not extinguish obligations but altered the mode of proof thereof; (c) the statutory prescriptions which do extinguish obligations; (d) statutory limitations on the time within which actions on certain grounds must be raised; (e) conventional limitations; and (f) the effect of *mora* or delay. In relation to the statutory limitations and prescriptions importance attaches to the modes whereby the running of prescription may be interrupted, and the effect thereof, and whether prescription runs against persons *non valentes agere*, such as one in minority.

---

[34] *Scott Chisholme* v. *Brown, supra; Leeds and Hanley Theatre* v. *Broadbent* [1898] 1 Ch. 343; *Gatty* v. *Maclaine*, 1921 S.C. (H.L.) 1.
[35] *Rodgers* v. *Fawdry*, 1950 S.C. 483.
[36] Sale of Goods Act, 1979, S. 10(1).
[37] Bell, *Prin.* § 586, 605. On prescriptions generally see Napier, *Prescription*; Millar, *Prescription*; Walker, *Prescription*. They are fully considered hereafter in the contexts in which each arises.

(a) *Statutory prescription—positive prescription*

The Prescription Act, 1594, c. 218, provided that no one should be compelled to produce the warrants for his sasine of land after forty years' possession, and that the lack thereof should not be a ground of challenge of the infeftment. The Prescription Act, 1617, c. 12, created the rule that uninterrupted and peaceful possession of land for forty years by virtue of heritable infeftment for which charter and instrument of sasine was produced should not thereafter be challengeable.[38] The Conveyancing Act, 1874, S. 34, replaced by the Conveyancing Act, 1924, S. 16, enacted that any *ex facie* valid irredeemable title to an estate in land recorded in the appropriate register of sasines should be a sufficient foundation for prescription and that twenty years' possession should suffice except for servitudes, public rights of way, or other rights. The Conveyancing and Feudal Reform (Sc.) Act, 1970, S. 8 reduced the period to ten years, with exceptions.

The Prescription and Limitation (Sc.) Act, 1973, Ss. 1–5, provides that if an interest in land has been possessed for a continuous period openly, peaceably, and without judicial interruption,[39] and the possession was founded on a recorded deed or decree[40] sufficient in its terms to constitute a title to that interest in the land, the validity of the title is thereafter exempt from challenge except on the ground that the deed is invalid *ex facie*[40] or is forged. The requisite periods are: interests in land generally: ten years:[41] an interest in the foreshore or salmon fishings as against the Crown,[41] an interest in land held on lease or allodially,[42] positive servitudes over land and public rights of way:[43] twenty years. The running of a prescriptive period may be interrupted judicially, by making a claim which challenges the possession.[44]

Decennalis et triennalis possessio

By a rule imported from canon law a churchman was deemed to have a title to any subject as part of his benefice from thirteen years possession, though he could produce no written title to it.[45]

---

[38] Stair II, 12, 15; Ersk III, 7, 8–15; Bell, *Prin.* § 606, 2002.
[39] Defined, 1973 Act, S. 4.
[40] See also 1973 Act, S. 5.
[41] 1973 Act, S. 1.
[42] 1973 Act, S. 2.
[43] 1973 Act, S. 3.
[44] 1973 Act, S. 4.
[45] Ersk. III, 7, 33; *Cochrane v. Smith* (1859) 22 D. 252.

(b) *Statutory limitations (or short prescriptions)*

The statutory limitations (or prescriptions) rendered various kinds of obligations unenforceable after the lapse of various periods of time, but did not wholly extinguish the obligation, and in all cases the obligation could still be enforced by resort to different methods of proof of the obligation.

All these have been replaced with effect from 25 July 1976, by the Prescription and Limitation (Sc.) Act, 1973.[46]

(c) *Statutory prescriptions—negative prescriptions*

The statutory prescriptions proper wholly extinguish the rights or obligations in question after the lapse of the stated time. The individual prescriptions within this class are now:

(i) *the short negative prescription*

Obligations to pay money (including interest, feuduty, ground annual, and rent) and obligations arising from, or by reason of breach of, contract or promise (unless constituted or evidenced by probative writ), from liability to make reparation (other than personal injuries or death), or from obligation of restitution, and of obligations of accounting are extinguished after having subsisted for a continuous period of five years, unless a relevant claim has been made in relation to the obligation within that time, or its subsistence has been relevantly acknowledged within that time, and ignoring certain other specified periods.[47] Liability between wrong doers to make contribution is extinguished after two years.[48]

(ii) *the long negative prescription*

The long negative prescription, created by the Prescription Acts, 1469, c. 28, and 1474, c. 54, and the second portion of the Prescription Act, 1617, c. 12, originally of forty years, and later[49] of twenty years, now replaced by the Prescription and Limitation (Sc.) Act, 1973, Ss. 7–8, extinguishes obligations of any kind (unless a relevant claim has been made in relation thereto, or its subsistence has been relevantly acknowledged),[50] and any right relating to property, heritable or moveable, not being an imprescriptible obligation or right, after twenty years.[51]

---

[46] As to transitional cases, see S. 16.

[47] Prescription and Limitation (Sc.) Act, 1973, S. 6 and Sch. 1, Ss. 9–10, amd. Prescription (Sc.) Act, 1987, S. 1.

[48] 1973, S. 8A., added by Prescription (Sc.) Act, 1984, S. 1.

[49] Conveyancing (Sc.) Act, 1924, S. 17; Conveyancing Amdt. (Sc.) Act, 1938, S. 4.

[50] As defined in 1973 Act, Ss. 9–10.

[51] 1973 Act, Ss. 7–8. Imprescriptible rights which cannot be extinguished by prescription are listed in Sch. 3.

(iii) *other negative prescriptions*

Various other statutes extinguish various rights after the lapse of specified periods of time. The chief individual instances are:[52]

(1) arrestments prescribe in three years.[53]

(2) inhibitions registered in the Register of Inhibitions and Adjudications prescribe after five years but may be renewed for five years.[54]

(3) copyright in a published edition lapses after twenty-five years and an author's copyright after fifty years from his death, or fifty years from the year of first publication.[55]

(4) copyright in a registered design subsists for five years, which may be extended for two further periods of five years.[56]

(5) patents are valid for twenty years.[57]

(6) plant breeder's rights may be granted for fifteen (in certain cases eighteen) years and not exceeding twenty-five years.[58]

(7) registered trade marks subsist for seven years but may be renewed for fourteen years more.[59]

(d) *Statutory limitations on time for bringing actions*

Under various statutes there are statutory limitations on the time for bringing certain actions. They do not extinguish the obligation but merely render claims brought out of time unenforceable by action, so that a sum paid thereafter by way of compromise would be irrecoverable under a *conditio indebiti*. The protection may usually be waived.[60] The main provisions[61] are:

(1) international carriage by air: action against the carrier must be brought within two years of arrival or scheduled arrival.[62]

(2) international carriage by railway: action for injury to or death of a passenger must be brought within three years from the accident, or three years from the death or five years from the accident, whichever is earlier.[63]

(3) international carriage by road: action for loss must be brought

---

[52] Certain extinctive provisions relevant only in public law, taxation, or criminal law are not listed.

[53] Debtors (Sc.) Act, 1838, S. 22; it was formerly five years.

[54] Conveyancing (Sc.) Act, 1924, S. 44

[55] Copyright Act, 1956, Ss. 2, 3, 12–15, 33, 39.

[56] Registered Designs Act, 1949, S. 8

[57] Patents Act, 1977, S. 25.

[58] Plant Varieties and Seeds Act, 1964, S. 3.

[59] Trade Marks Act, 1938, S. 20.

[60] *Burns* v. *Glasgow Corpn.*, 1917, 1 S.L.T. 301.

[61] Provisions applicable in public law or criminal law are not here listed.

[62] Carriage by Air Act, 1961, S. 5 and Sch. I, Art. 29, as replaced by Carriage by Air and Road Act, 1979, Sch.

[63] International Transport Conventions Act, 1983, S. 1.

within one year or, in case of wilful misconduct or equivalent, three years.[64]

(4) international carriage by sea: action must be brought within one year of delivery or the due date of delivery: the period may be extended.[65]

(5) international carriage of passengers by road: action must be brought within three years in case of death or injury, or one year in other cases.[66]

(6) international carriage of passengers by sea: action for injury or death or for loss of or damage to luggage is barred after two years, or in some cases three years.[67]

(7) collisions at sea: a claim for damage or loss of life or for salvage services must be brought within two years, unless the period is extended by the court.[68] A claim to enforce contribution in respect of an overpaid proportion of any damages for loss of life or personal injuries must be brought within one year, unless the period is extended by the court.[69]

(8) compulsory powers of acquiring land: the powers of promoters must be exercised within three years from the passing of the special Act, or any other period prescribed.[70]

(9) defamation actions must be commenced within three years after the right of action accrued.[71]

(10) foreign jurisdiction: actions for any act done in pursuance or execution or intended execution of the Act must be brought within six months.[72]

(11) forestry: claims for compensation on refusal of a felling licence for trees must be brought within ten years of deterioration of the trees or one year from the date of their felling.[73]

(12) merchant seamen: a creditor of a deceased seaman is not entitled to payment unless the debt accrued less than three years before death and action is brought within two years thereafter.[74]

(13) mines and quarries: compensation for damage or disturbance to

---

[64] Carriage of Goods by Road Act, 1965, Sch. Arts. 32, 39.

[65] Carriage of Goods by Sea Act, 1971, Sch. Art. III, para. 6.

[66] Carriage of Passengers by Road Act, 1974, Sch. Art. 22.

[67] Merchant Shipping Act, 1979, Sch. 3.

[68] Maritime Conventions Act, 1911, S. 8. See *Birkdale S.S. Co.*, 1922 S.L.T. 575; *Reresby* v. *Cobetas*, 1923 S.L.T. 492, 719; *Dorie S.S. Co.*, 1923 S.C. 593; *Essien* v. *Clan Line* 1925 S.N. 75.

[69] Maritime Conventions Act, 1911, S. 8.

[70] Lands Clauses Consolidation (Sc.) Act, 1845, S. 116; see also Allotments (Sc.) Act, 1922, S. 13(1).

[71] Prescription and Limitation (Sc.) Act, 1973, S. 18A, added by Law Reform (Misc. Prov.) (Sc.) Act, 1985, S. 12.

[72] Foreign Jurisdiction Act, 1890, S. 13.

[73] Forestry Act, 1967, S. 11.

[74] Merchant Shipping Act, 1894, S. 178.

land resulting from operations must be brought within six years.[75]

(14) nuclear incidents: claims for injury or damage caused by an occurrence involving nuclear matter must be brought within twenty years.[76] Claims for compensation for breach of duty under the Act must be brought within thirty years.[76]

(15) oil pollution: claims for damage resulting from discharge or escape of oil from a ship must be brought within three years after claim arose and six years of occurrence resulting in discharge or escape.[77]

(16) personal injuries or death: action must be brought within three years from the date the injuries were sustained, or the date when the act or omission giving rise to the injuries ceased, or the date on which the pursuer did, or should have, become aware of stated facts, or, in the case of death, the date of death, or the date on which the pursuer became or should have become aware of stated facts, but in certain circumstances an extension of time is allowed.[78]

(17) Post Office: proceedings against the Post Office for loss of or damage to a registered inland packet must be begun within twelve months of posting.[79]

(18) protection of officials: proceedings against various officials for anything done in execution of the licensing acts must be commenced within two months.[80] Action for damages against officials for anything done under the Criminal Procedure Act must be commenced within two months.[81]

(19) recovery of property: a person presumed dead may recover property from one entitled under the Act only if application was made to vary the decree within five years from the date when it was made.[82] An action to recover possession goods, disposed of by a chief constable as found property, must be brought within one year.[83]

(20) sewerage: claims for loss, injury, or damage resulting from exercise of powers under the Act must be brought within twelve months.[84]

(21) social security: rights to benefits under the Social Security Act or

---

[75] Mines and Quarries (Tips) Act, 1969, S. 20.
[76] Nuclear Installations Act, 1965, S. 15.
[77] Merchant Shipping (Oil Pollution) Act, 1971, S. 9.
[78] Prescription and Limitation (Sc.) Act, 1973, Ss. 17–19 as replaced by Prescription (Sc.) Act, 1984, S. 2; L.R. (M.P.) (Sc.) Act, 1980, S. 23, adding new S. 19A; see Walker, *Prescription*.
[79] Post Office Act, 1969, S. 30.
[80] Licensing (Sc.) Act, 1976, S. 130.
[81] Criminal Procedure (Sc.) Act, 1975, S. 456.
[82] Presumption of Death (Sc.) Act, 1977, S. 5.
[83] Civic Government (Sc.) Act, 1982, S. 71.
[84] Sewerage (Sc.) Act, 1968, S. 20.

Family Income Supplements Act must be claimed within twelve months.[85]

(22) standard security: a notice calling up money is effective for five years only.[86] A notice of default authorizes the exercise of certain powers within five years only.[87]

(23) trespass: actions for anything done in pursuance of the Act must be commenced within six months and subject to conditions.[88]

(24) wrongful imprisonment: an action of damages for wrongous imprisonment must be brought within three years of the end thereof.[89]

P,eriods of limitation under certain statutes may be extended in the case of a person within the Limitation (Enemies and War Prisoners) Act, 1945, as amended.

(e) *Conventional limitations*

A conventional limitation may be created by the will of the parties, by a condition in their obligation, such as a guarantee of a debt for six months.[90]

(f) *Mora*

Lapse of time short of the period of the long negative prescription, or a relevant shorter prescription, is not an absolute bar to a party's insistence on the right in question,[91] though delay enhances the onus of proof on the pursuer,[92] and may result in loss of evidence.[93] To support a plea of mora[94] there must be such delay as raises an inference of acquiescence or waiver,[95] or causes prejudice to the other party.[96] Delay has frequently been held a ground for allowing inquiry by way of proof rather than jury trial.[97]

[85] Social Security Act, 1975, S. 81 (2); Child Benefit Act, 1975, S. 6 (5); Family Income Supplements Act, 1970, S. 10.
[86] Conveyancing and Feudal Reform (Sc.) Act, 1970, S. 19.
[87] Ibid., S. 21.
[88] Game (Sc.) Act, 1832, S. 17.
[89] Criminal Procedure Act, 1701 (c. 6.)
[90] Bell, *Prin.* s 587–8.
[91] *Cunninghame* v. *Boswell* (1868) 6 M. 890; *Halley* v. *Watt*, 1956 S.C. 370. But see *Russell* v. *McKnight's Tr.* (1900) 2 F. 520; *Smith* v. *Dixon*, 1910 S.C. 230.
[92] *C.B.* v. *A.B.* (1885) 12 R. (H.L.) 36; *Bain* v. *Assets Co.* (1905) 7 F. (H.L.) 104; *Bosville* v. *Lord Macdonald*, 1910 S.C. 597.
[93] *Jackson* v. *Swan* (1895) 3 S.L.T. 149; cf. *Eliott's Trs.* v. *E.* (1894) 21 R. 858; *McLellan* v. *Western S.M.T. Co.*, 1950 S.C. 112; *Moyes* v. *Burntisland Shipbuilding Co.*, 1952 S.C.429; *Devine* v. *Beardmore*, 1955 S.C.311.
[94] *Lees's Trs.* v. *Dun*, 1912 S.C. 50; 1913 S.C. (H.L.) 12.
[95] *Cook* v. *N.B. Ry.* (1872) 10 M. 513, 516; *Harrison* v. *N. of Scotland Bank* (1890) 28 S.L.R. 162; *Macdonald* v. *Newall* (1898) 1 F. 68; *Gamage* v. *Charlesworth's Tr.*, 1910 S.C. 257; cf. *Macfarlane* v. *M.*, 1956 S.C. 473.
[96] *Devine, supra; Clark* v. *Pryde*, 1959 S.L.T. (Notes) 16.
[97] *McLellan, supra; Milne* v. *Glasgow Corpn.*, 1951 S.C. 340; *Halley* v. *Watt*, 1956 S.C. 370; *Conetta* v. *Central S.M.T. Co.*, 1966 S.L.T. 302; *Graham* v. *A.E.I. Ltd.*, 1968 S.L.T. 81.

BOOK II

INTERNATIONAL PRIVATE LAW

CHAPTER 2.1

CASES INVOLVING FOREIGN ELEMENTS

The principles of the international private law of Scotland or the Scottish principles as to conflict of laws are relevant where a legal problem arising in Scotland involves an element or factor which is non-Scottish, so that reference exclusively to Scots law might be unsatisfactory or unjust.[1] The non-Scottish factor may be such an element as that a party to a marriage is not Scottish, that a contract has been made furth of Scotland, or that a non-Scot dies possessed of property in Scotland and elsewhere. These principles are a branch of Scottish private law, and are not international in the sense of being common to many or all countries with distinct legal systems, though the principles accepted in Scots law show considerable similarity to those accepted in most Anglo-American legal systems and extensive reliance is placed in Scotland on Anglo-American authorities. They constitute the Scottish principles relevant where a private law problem contains an international element, or one involving non-Scottish law as well as Scots law.[2]

The Scottish principles of international private law may be relevant in relation to any of the branches of domestic private law, persons, obligations, property, trusts, and so on. They do not themselves directly solve problems involving a foreign element, but guide the Scots lawyer on three preliminary problems: (1) jurisdiction, whether in the circumstances the Scottish courts can validly exercise jurisdiction to decide the dispute, or must decline;[3] (2) choice of law, whether, if the Scottish courts can validly exercise jurisdiction, the principles of Scots domestic or internal private law, or of some other system of domestic private law, fall to be applied to determine the rights, duties, liabilities, and remedies of parties; and (3) what effect, if any, has to be given in Scotland to any foreign judgment which may already have been granted in relation to the dispute. It follows that, in some cases of problems raising a foreign element, the Scottish courts, having considered their own

---

[1] England and Northern Ireland are non-Scottish or foreign for these purposes, as much as Canada or Germany, cf. *Orr Ewing's Trs.* v. *O.E.* (1885) 13 R. (H.L.) 1, 12.

[2] See generally Stair, More's Note A; Ersk. III, 2, 39–42; Bell, *Comm.* II, 375; *Prin.* s 306, 1537, 1550; Duncan & Dykes, *Civil Jurisdiction*; Anton, *Private International Law*; Dicey and Morris, *Conflict of Laws*; Cheshire and North, *Private International Law*; Morris, *Conflict of Laws*; Graveson, *Conflict of Laws*.

[3] If the Scottish courts can validly exercise jurisdiction the secondary question of jurisdiction may arise, whether the Court of Session, sheriff court, or some other Scottish court or tribunal is the one competent to exercise that jurisdiction. This secondary question is determined purely by Scots internal law.

rules of international private law, must decline to exercise jurisdiction, or, if they exercise it, must apply foreign law, or must recognize an existing foreign judgment as decisive, and give effect to it. It is only if the Scottish courts feel entitled to exercise jurisdiction and when they have selected the appropriate system of law, that they can proceed to ascertain the relevant rules of law and apply them to decide the issue.

Preliminary issues

Before applying Scottish principles of international private law to a situation involving a non-Scottish element the court or legal adviser must be satisfied that the foreign element in the situation is material to the question of jurisdiction or of choice of law. It may be irrelevant; thus the foreign nationality of either or both parties is generally irrelevant to a contract made, and to be performed, or to a delict done, wholly in Scotland.[4] But such a decision itself implies consideration of the possible effect of international private law rules and rejection of them as irrelevant in the circumstances.

Characterization or classification

If, however, the foreign element is deemed material the court must characterize or classify the facts raising the legal problem, or assign the legal question raised thereby to the appropriate legal category.[5] Thus if a young foreigner seeks to marry in Scotland, and the law of the foreigner's country requires parental consent, does the absence of such consent affect his capacity to marry, or is it part of the formalities of marriage?[6] Is a claim for injuries in a railway accident one for breach of contract or for a delict?[7] Such characterization may be differently done in different legal systems. Characterization of a legal question must probably be effected in Scottish courts on the basis of legal concepts and categories recognized in internal Scots law, but sometimes recognizing wider and more general categories to take account of legal concepts and relations unknown to Scots law but analogous thereto. Thus the distinction for purposes of characterization is between immoveable and moveable property rather than between heritable and moveable or real and personal property.[8]

The incidental question

The incidental question is one subsidiary to the main issue in a case raising an issue of international private law, and the question is whether it

---

[4] cf. *Branca* v. *Cobarro* [1947] K.B. 854.

[5] On this problem see Robertson, *Characterisation in the Conflict of Laws*, and chapters in all the textbooks on international private law.

[6] *Bliersbach* v. *MacEwen*, 1959 S.C. 43.

[7] *Horn* v. *N.B. Ry.* (1878) 5 R 1055; *Naftalin* v *L.M.S. Ry.* 1933 S.C. 259. See further such cases as *De Nicols* v. *Curlier* [1900] A.C. 21; *Re Martin* [1900] P.211.

[8] *Re Fitzgerald* [1904] 1 Ch. 573, 588; *Re Hoyles* [1911] 1 Ch. 179, 185; on the distinctions in internal private law, see Ch. 6.1, *infra*.

should be determined also by the law applicable to the main issue, or as if it were a separate issue. If a person domiciled in Scotland leaves moveable property in France to his 'wife', the main issue is determined by Scots law; should the question whether a claimant is his 'wife' also be determined by Scots law, or by the law applicable to the marriage? The matter does not appear to have arisen in any Scottish case but there is much to be said for referring incidental questions also to the system which determines the main issue.

Renvoi

If the Scottish rules provide that a matter is to be determined by the law of another country, the question may arise whether this means the internal or domestic law of that country, or the law of that country including its rules of international private law, which might refer the question back to Scots law, or to a third system. There is no Scottish decision on this matter but a reference to the law of another country should probably be generally understood as one to its internal law only.[9]

CONNECTING FACTORS

In relation both to jurisdiction and to choice of law there must be a connecting factor between the matter in controversy, and, so far as concerns jurisdiction, the Scottish courts or, so far as concerns choice of law, the principles of the system of law applied internally in Scotland or in the territory of another particular legal system, before the Scottish courts are justified in exercising jurisdiction, or in applying the principles of Scottish or another particular system of internal law, as the case may be. In a Scottish court the existence of a connecting factor must be determined by Scots law.[10]

Connecting factors—jurisdiction

In relation to jurisdiction, the main connecting factor in issues of personal status is the pursuer's having Scotland as his domicile or country of permanent home. In issues of obligations or property the general rule is *actor sequitur forum rei*, that the pursuer must seek his remedy in a court having jurisdiction over the defender, at the time when the summons is served,[11] so that the question is whether there is adequate connection between the court chosen and the defender. The principal connecting factor in such cases is the possibility, if the Scottish court exercises

---

[9] cf. *McElroy* v. *McAllister*, 1949 S.C. 110, 126.
[10] *Wilson* v. *W.* (1872) 10 M.573; *Wilson* v. *W.* (1872) L.R. 2 P.& D.435.
[11] *Stewart* v. *North* (1889) 16 R. 927; 17 R. (H.L.) 60.

jurisdiction, of enforcing its decree against the defender by the appropriate diligence—the principle of effectiveness.[12]

The principal circumstances in which a decree can be made effective are where the defender is resident within the territorial area of the court's jurisdiction, or has property, heritable or moveable, situated therein, or has had moveables belonging to him arrested in the hands of a third party therein *jurisdictionis fundandae causa*. Jurisdiction founded by arrestment applies to all personal actions wherein a decree could be made effective by attachment of the property arrested.[13]

Prorogation of jurisdiction

The other main connecting factor in cases of obligations or property is that the defender has expressly or impliedly submitted himself to the jurisdiction of the Scottish courts. This may be done by prorogation of jurisdiction,[14] or voluntary submission to a court's jurisdiction, as by a foreigner.[15] It may be done expressly[16] or impliedly, as by lodging defences without objecting to the jurisdiction.[17] But prorogation is incompetent to confer a jurisdiction which the court could not otherwise exercise.[18]

Reconvention

Submission to the jurisdiction may also be made by reconvention, whereby it is held that one appealing to the courts of this country renders himself subject to the jurisdiction of these courts in a cross-action if arising *ex eodem negotio* or if *ejusdem generis*.[19] This principle also does not extend the court's jurisdiction to include subjects which it could not otherwise have disposed of. It does not amount to reconvention if the appeal to the Scottish courts was in self-defence.[20]

---

[12] Ersk. I, 2, 16; cf. *Henderson v. Patrick Thomson, Ltd.*, 1911 S.C. 246, 249.

[13] *L.N.W. Ry.* v. *Lindsay* (1858) 3 Macq. 99.

[14] Ersk. I, 2, 27.

[15] *Thompson* v. *Whitehead* (1862) 24 D. 331; *Gill* v. *Cutler* (1895) 23 R. 371; cf. *Styring* v. *Mayor of Oporovec*, 1931 S.L.T. 493.

[16] *Longmuir* v. *L.* (1850) 12D. 926; *Lord Macdonald* v. *His Next of Kin* (1864) 2 M. 1194; *Irvine* v. *Hart* (1869) 7 M. 723; *International Exhibition* v. *Bapty* (1891) 18 R. 843; *Elderslie S.S. Co.* v. *Burrell* (1895) 22 R. 389.

[17] *White* v. *Spottiswoode* (1846) 8 D. 952; *Dundee Investment Co.* v. *Macdonald* (1884) 11 R. 537; *Assets Co.* v. *Falla's Trs.* (1894) 22 R. 178; *D. Fife's Trs.* v. *Taylor*, 1934 S.L.T. 76; *Govt. of Spain* v. *National Bank of Scotland*, 1939 S.C. 413; *Grangemouth and Forth Towing Co.* v. *Netherlands E.I. Co.*, 1942 S.L.T. 228.

[18] Ersk. I, 2, 30; *Morton* v. *Gardiner* (1871) 9 M. 548; cf. *Ringer* v. *Churchill* (1840) 2 D. 307.

[19] *Thompson* v. *Whitehead* (1862) 24 D. 331; *Morison & Milne* v. *Massa* (1866) 5 M. 130; *Longworth* v. *Yelverton* (1868) 7 M. 70; *California Redwood Co. Liqdr.* v. *Walker* (1886) 13 R. 810; *Pacific Coast Mining Co. Liqdr.* v. *Walker* (1886) 13 R. 816; *Burrell* v. *Harding*, 1931 S.L.T. 76; *Kitson* v. *K.*, 1945 S.C. 434.

[20] *Davis* v. *Cadman* (1897) 24 R. 297; *Macaulay* v. *Hussain*, 1966 S.C. 204.

Connecting factors—choice of law

In relation to choice of law the main connecting factors between the parties' actings and one or more[21] particular legal systems are: the nationality of the parties; domicile of the parties; residence of the parties; presence of parties; the place of incorporation of a corporation; the intention of parties; the flag of a ship; the *locus* of an act or event, such as the celebration of a marriage, the making or performance of a contract, or the commission of a delict; the *situs* or situation of property; and the *forum* in which proceedings are brought.

INDIVIDUAL CONNECTING FACTORS

Nationality

Nationality is a political relationship between a person and a state, and is only rarely a material connecting factor.[22] Apart from time of war[23] the fact that a party to a legal transaction connected with Scotland is a foreign national is usually irrelevant.[24]

Domicile

A person's domicile is the state, territory, or country having a distinct legal system, which is regarded as the country of his permanent home.[25] No person can be without a domicile.[26] Law attributes to every person one domicile, and only one domicile at any given time.[27] What that domicile is is determined by the same rules in all branches of the law where domicile is relevant, and is a conclusion of law, determined in Scottish cases always by Scots law, on the basis of the facts of the particular case.[28] The Civil Jurisdiction and Judgments Act, 1982, has, however, introduced for the purposes of that Act, which applies in civil and commercial matters, but not to status or capacity, matrimonial property, wills and succession, and certain other cases, a different concept of domicile, requiring only residence and circumstances indicating a substan-

---

[21] Different parts of one controversy may have to be referred to different foreign legal systems.

[22] European legal systems commonly rely on nationality rather than domicile as a connection between a person and a legal system.

[23] cf. *Van Uden* v. *Burrell*, 1916 S.C. 391; *Sovfracht* v. *Van Uden* [1943] A.C. 203.

[24] cf. *Powell* v. *Mackenzie* (1900) 8 S.L.T. 182; But only a British subject can own shares in a British ship (Merchant Shipping Act, 1894, S. 1) or a British aircraft.

[25] *Whicker* v. *Hume* (1858) 7 H.L.C. 124, 160.

[26] *Bell* v. *Kennedy* (1868) 6 M. (H.L.) 69; *Udny* v. *U.* (1869) 7 M. (H.L.) 89.

[27] *Winans* v. *A.G.* [1904] A.C. 287; *Marchioness of Huntly* v. *Gaskell* (1905) 8 F. (H.L.) 4; *Liverpool Royal Infirmary* v. *Ramsay*, 1930 S.C. (H.L.) 83.

[28] *L.A.* v. *Brown's Trs.*, 1907 S.C. 333; *Robinson* v. *R's Trs.*, 1930 S.C. (H.L.) 20.

tial connection with the country in question, which is presumed from three months' residence.[29]

Domicile of origin

Every person has initially a domicile of origin, which is, in the case of a legitimate child, the father's domicile,[30] of the child of a Scottish putative marriage, Scottish,[31] of an illegitimate or posthumous child, the mother's domicile,[32] and of a foundling the country where he is found. It is independent of the place of birth.[33] A domicile of origin may be transmitted through several generations though none of the later generations may have lived in the country of the domicile of origin.[34] On his father's death, a pupil child takes the domicile of his mother, and it changes as her domicile changes.[35] In the absence of evidence of origin there is some presumption that a person is domiciled in a country of long residence.[36]

There is a presumption that a person's domicile of origin continues to be his domicile.[37] Domicile of origin continues to attach to a person despite absences abroad,[38] or involuntary residence, however long, in another state.[39] It is lost only by the acquisition of a domicile of choice,[40] which can only be done *animo et facto*, by settling in another state in circumstances evidencing intention to relinquish connection with the country of origin,[41] and it revives if a domicile of choice be abandoned.[42]

Domicile of choice

A person may acquire a domicile of choice *animo et facto* by residing in another state with the intention of remaining there indefinitely.[43] The court must have regard to the length of residence and any expressed

---

[29] 1982 Act, S. 41, and Sch. I. Arts. 1, 52–3. See Ch. 2.2.

[30] *Udny* v. *U.* (1869) 7 M. (H.L.) 89; *Fairbairn* v. *Neville* (1897) 25 R. 192; this is so even if the child is in the mother's custody after divorce: *Shanks* v. *S.*, 1965 S.L.T. 330.

[31] *Smijth* v. *S.*, 1918, 1 S.L.T. 156.

[32] *Udny* v. *U.*, (1869) 7 M. (H.L.) 89.

[33] *Wylie* v. *Laye* (1834) 12 S. 927; *Corbidge* v. *Somerville*, 1913 S.C. 858.

[34] *Peal* v. *P.* (1930) 46 T.L.R. 645; *Grant* v. *G.*, 1931 S.C. 238.

[35] *Crumpton's J.F.* v. *Fitch-Noyes*, 1918 S.C. 378.

[36] *Watts* v. *W.* (1885) 12 R. 894.

[37] *Fairbairn, supra; Winans* v. *A.G.* [1904] A.C. 287; *Marchioness of Huntly* v. *Gaskell* (1905) 8 F. (H.L.) 4; *Liverpool Royal Infirmary* v. *Ramsay*, 1930 S.C. (H.L.) 83.

[38] *Wilson* v. *W.* (1872) 10 M. 573; *In re Mitchell* (1884) 13 Q.B.D. 418; *Steel* v. *S.* (1888) 15 R. 896; *Hood* v. *H.* (1897) 24 R. 973; *Ross* v. *R.*, 1930 S.C. (H.L.) 1; *Sellars* v. *Sellars*, 1942 S.C. 206; see also *Brown* v. *B.*, 1928 S.C. 542.

[39] *Burton* v. *Fisher* (1828) Milw. 183; *In re Napoleon* (1853) 2 Rob. Eccl. 606 (prisoners); *Hoskins* v. *Matthews* (1856) 8 De G. M. & G. 13 (invalid); *Steel* v. *S.*, (1888) 15 R. 896; *Crumpton's J.F., supra.*

[40] *Bell* v. *Kennedy* (1868) 6 M. (H.L.) 69; *Steel* v. *S.* (1888) 15 R. 896; *Liverpool R.I., supra.*

[41] *Donaldson* v. *McClure* (1857) 20 D. 307; *Aikman* v. *A.* (1861) 3 Macq. 854; *Moorhouse* v. *Lord* (1863) 10 H.L.C. 272; *Steel, supra; Marchioness of Huntly, supra.*

[42] *Udny, supra.*

[43] *Aikman* v. *A.* (1861) 3 Macq. 854; *Bell, supra; Udny, supra; Liverpool R.I.* v. *Ramsay*, 1930 S.C. (H.L.) 83; *McLelland* v. *McL.*, 1942 S.C. 502.

intention,[44] or circumstances evidencing intention to make that his permanent home or otherwise.[45] Long residence abroad evidences acquisition of domicile but is not conclusive.[46] Short residence may suffice if there is clear intention.[47] If there is doubt,[48] or until a domicile of choice has been acquired, the domicile of origin adheres.[49] A person residing in a country by reason of being stationed there may acquire a domicile of choice there, but only if the residence is continued voluntarily.[50] Voluntary residence abroad, even if motivated by health or fiscal reasons, may operate a change of domicile.[51] A move made to facilitate divorce may have the same effect.[52] But illegal residence does not confer domicile of choice.[53]

A domicile of choice may be abandoned *animo et facto*, and a new one acquired. Until then, or if none be acquired, the domicile of origin revives,[54] but mere absence or departure from the country of choice does not at once destroy domicile there.[55] Departure from the country of domicile of choice with ending of intention to return there is sufficient to end that domicile.[56]

The onus is on a person maintaining a change of domicile to prove intention to relinquish the domicile of origin and also the acquisition *animo et facto* of a new domicile.[57]

Domicile of dependants

A wife on contracting a valid or voidable marriage formerly acquired the domicile of her husband,[58] and retained it, even though actually or

[44] cf. *Robinson* v. *R's Trs.*, 1934 S.L.T. 183; *Rankin* v. *R.*, 1960 S.L.T. 308.

[45] *Low* v. *L.* (1891) 19 R. 115; *Marchioness of Huntly* v. *Gaskell* (1905) 8 F. (H.L.) 4; *Tasker* v. *Grieve* (1905) 8 F. 45; *Casdagli* v. *C.* [1919] A.C. 145; *Ross* v. *R.*, 1930 S.C. (H.L.) 1; *McLelland* v. *McL.*, 1942 S.C. 502; *Rankin* v. *R.*, 1960 S.L.T. 308; *Gould* v. *G.*, 1968 S.L.T. 98; *McEwan* v. *M.*, 1969 S.L.Y. 342.

[46] *Jopp* v. *Wood* (1865) 4 De G.J. & S. 616; *Fairbairn* v. *Neville* (1897) 25 R. 192; *Ross* v. *R.* (1899) 1 F. 963; *Winans* v. *A.G.* [1904] A.C. 287; *Brown* v. *B.*, 1928 S.C. 542; *Liverpool R.I.* v. *Ramsay*, 1930 S.C. (H.L.) 83; *Gould* v. *G.*, 1968 S.L.T. 98.

[47] *Bell* v. *Kennedy* (1868) 6 M. (H.L.) 69; *Macphail* v. *M's Trs.* (1906) 14 S.L.T. 388; *Willar* v. *W.*, 1954 S.C. 144.

[48] *Steel* v. *S.* (1888) 15 R. 896.

[49] *Moorhouse* v. *Lord* (1863) 10 H.L.C. 272; *Donaldson* v. *McClure* (1857) 20 D. 307; *Bell* v. *Kennedy* (1868) 6 M. (H.L.) 69; *Hood* v. *H.* (1897) 24 R. 973; *Marchioness of Huntly* v. *Gaskell* (1905) 8 F. (H.L.) 4; *Liverpool R.I.*, supra; *McLelland* v. *McL.*, 1942 S.C. 502.

[50] *Clarke* v. *Newmarsh* (1835) 14 S. 488; *Udny*, supra; *Grant* v. *G.*, 1931 S.C. 238; *Sellars* v. *S.*, 1942 S.C. 206; *Donaldson* v. *D* [1949] P. 363; *Willar* v. *W.*, 1954 S.C. 144.

[51] *Hoskins* v. *Matthews* (1856) 8 De G. M. & G. 13.

[52] *Carswell* v. *C* (1881) 8 R. 901; *Stavert* v. *S.* (1882) 9 R. 519; *Wood* v. *W.* [1957] P. 254.

[53] *Puttick* v. *A.G.* [1980] Fam 1.

[54] *Udny* v. *Udny* (1869) 7 M. (H.L.) 89; *Vincent* v. *Earl of Buchan* (1889) 16 R. 637; *Stewart* v. *S.* (1905) 13 S.L.T. 668; *Re Flynn* [1968] 1 All E.R. 49.

[55] *Hunter* v. *H.* (1893) 30 S.L.R. 915; *Pabst* v. *P.* (1898) 6 S.L.T. 117; *McNeill* v. *McN.*, 1919, 2 S.L.T. 127; *Labacianskas* v. *L.*, 1949 S.C. 280.

[56] *Re Flynn* [1968] 1 All E.R. 49.

[57] *Bell* v. *Kennedy* (1868) 6 M. (H.L.) 69; *Vincent* v. *Earl of Buchan* (1889) 16 R 637; *McLelland* v. *McL.*, 1942 S.C. 502; *Holden* v. *H.* [1968] N.I. 7.

[58] Stair I, 4, 9; *Harvey* v. *Farnie* (1882) 8 App. Cas. 43; *Yelverton* v. *Y.* (1859) 1 Sw. & Tr. 574; *De Reneville* v. *De R.* [1948] P. 100.

judicially separated,[59] and might have it changed by her husband's change of domicile,[60] until her husband's death, when she might by leaving the country revert to her domicile of origin[61] or acquire a fresh domicile of choice.[62] A wife now has an independent domicile.[63] If the marriage is void, she does not thereby acquire her husband's domicile,[64] but may have acquired a domicile of choice in the country of her putative husband's domicile.[65]

A pupil cannot acquire a domicile of choice, but such may be acquired for him by his father,[66] failing whom, by his mother,[67] making a change of domicile, but a minor may acquire a domicile for himself.[68] After majority a person's domicile is not changed merely by his parent's change of domicile. If parents separate, the domicile of a pupil child is that of the mother if he lives with her.[69] A pupil child's domicile may be, but a minor child's domicile is not, changed by his mother's remarriage.[70] After divorce of the parents a pupil child's domicile is determined by the father's domicile, even though the child is in the custody of the mother who has acquired a new domicile.[71] A legitimated child or an adopted child probably takes his father's domicile. An orphan child probably cannot have his domicile changed by his guardian.

A person mentally incapax probably cannot have his domicile changed by himself or by his guardian.[72]

A husband cannot, by seeking to change his domicile after a cause of action has arisen in a matrimonial dispute, subject his wife to the exclusive jurisdiction of a foreign court.[73]

---

[59] *Low v. L.* (1891) 19 R. 115; *Mackinnon's Trs. v. Inland Revenue,* 1920 S.C. (H.L.) 171; *A.G. for Alberta v. Cook* [1926] A.C. 444.

[60] *Mackinnon's Trs. v. Inland Revenue,* 1920 S.C. (H.L.) 171. Many proposals have been made for altering the rules set out in this sentence, e.g. Royal Commission on Marriage and Divorce, 1956.

[61] *In the goods of Raffenel* (1863) 32 L.J.P. & M. 203; *Crumpton's J.F. v. Finch-Noyes,* 1918 S.C. 378.

[62] *Re Wallach* [1950] 1 All E.R. 199.

[63] Domicile and Matrimonial Proceedings Act, 1973, S.1.

[64] *De Reneville v. De R.* [1948] P. 100.

[65] *Administrator of Austrian Property v. von Lorang,* 1927 S.C. (H.L.) 80.

[66] *D'Etchegoyen v. D'E.* (1888) 13 P.D. 132; *Woodbury v. Sutherland's Trs.,* 1938 S.C. 689; *Henderson v. H.* [1965] 1 All E.R. 179.

[67] *Potinger v. Wightman* (1817) 3 Mer. 67; *Johnstone v. Beattie* (1843) 10 Cl. & F. 42, 138; *Arnott v. Groom* (1846) 9 D. 142; *Crumpton's J.F. v. Fitch-Noyes,* 1918 S.C. 378.

[68] *Harvey v. H.* (1860) 22 D. 1198; *Flannigan v. Bothwell Inspector* (1892) 19 R. 909; Clive, 1966 J.R. 1.

[69] *Crumpton's J.F., supra.* See also *Re Beaumont* [1893] 3 Ch. 490. See also *Hope v. H.* [1968] N.I. 1.

[70] Domicile and Matrimonial Proceedings Act, 1973, S. 4, altering *Shanks v. S.,* 1965 S.L.T. 330.

[71] *Shanks v. S.,* 1965 S.L.T. 330. *Sed quaere:* see *Hope v. H.* [1968] N.I. 1.

[72] *Urquhart v. Butterfield* (1887) 37 Ch.D. 357; see also *Crumpton's J.F., supra.*

[73] *Ramsay v. R.,* 1925 S.C. 216; *Hannah v. H.,* 1926 S.L.T. 370; *Lack v. L.,* 1926 S.L.T. 656; *Kelly v. K.,* 1927 S.N. 132; *Crabtree v. C.,* 1929 S.L.T. 675.

Presence of parties

The actual presence of a party in a country is frequently relevant to jurisdiction,[74] but rarely to choice of law as that presence may be explained by extraneous matters.

Residence

Habitual residence and ordinary residence are sometimes referred to[75] as connecting factors. Residence is quite independent of domicile; it connotes physical presence, not necessarily permanent, but at least prolonged and not merely transitory presence. It is entirely a question of fact. A person may have a residence in more than one country, and it is immaterial to a question of residence in Scotland that he is not domiciled in Scotland.[76] By Scots law a person is 'resident' if he is physically present and has resided continuously in Scotland for 40 days.[77] Domicile even along with presence for less than 40 days does not confer jurisdiction on the ground of residence.[78] Residence must be actual; it requires physical presence and it is not sufficient merely to have one's home in Scotland.[79] Jurisdiction based on residence lapses when the person quits Scotland;[80] it does not continue for 40 days thereafter.[81] The Civil Jurisdiction and Judgments Act 1982 bases jurisdiction on 'domicile' defined as residence in circumstances indicating a substantial connection with the U.K. or a part thereof or place therein, and presumed from residence for at least three months.[82]

Nationality, domicile, presence, and residence of unincorporated associations

The domicile of an association is probably determined by the country in which it is established, its residence by having an office, and its presence established by its carrying on business. A friendly society registered in England, carrying on business in Scotland by a branch with rules re-

---

[74] e.g. *Dalziel v. Coulthurst's Exrs.*, 1934 S.C. 564; *Dallas v. McArdle*, 1949 S.C. 481 (need for personal citation in Scotland).

[75] e.g. Wills Act, 1963, S. 1; Adoption Act, 1968, S. 11.

[76] *Marchioness of Huntly v. Gaskell* (1905) 8 F. (H.L.) 4.

[77] *Tasker v. Grieve* (1905) 8 F. 45; *Carter v. Allison*, 1966 S.C. 257.

[78] *Tasker, supra; Hutchison v. H.*, 1912 1 S.L.T. 219.

[79] *Joel v. Gill* (1859) 21 D. 929; *Martin v. Szyszka*, 1943 S.C. 203; *Findlay v. Donachie*, 1944 S.C. 306; *McCord v. McC.*, 1946 S.C. 198; *Nicol v. Bruce*, 1965 S.C. 160.

[80] *Corstorphine v. Kasten* (1898) 1 F. 287; *Carter v. Allison*, 1966 S.C. 257.

[81] It continues for the purposes of the jurisdiction of a particular sheriff court, if the defender has ceased for less than 40 days to reside and has no known residence in Scotland; Sheriff Courts (Sc.) Acts, 1907, S. 6, and 1913, S. 3 and Sch. 1; *Martin, supra; Findlay, supra; McCord, supra.*

[82] 1982 Act, S. 41. This Act applies to contracting states and to civil and commercial causes only.

gistered in Scotland, has been held subject to Scottish jurisdiction.[83] For the purposes of the Civil Jurisdiction and Judgments Act 1982 the seat of an association or corporation is its 'domicile', and its seat is if it was formed under the law of a part of the U.K. and has its registered office or other official address in that part, or its central management and control is exercised in that part, or at least one of these in another contracting state as the case may be.[84]

Nationality, domicile, presence, and residence of corporations

The nationality of a corporation depends on the country of its incorporation.[85] Its domicile is the country in which it is incorporated[86] and that legal system determines its creation and dissolution, attributes and powers.[87] The carrying on of business in Scotland by a corporation is equivalent to the physical presence of a natural person,[88] and its residence is determined by the place where the main controlling power of the corporation is situated.[89] The presence of an agent in Scotland does not make a company resident in Scotland.[90]

Intention of parties

Parties may, particularly in contracts and wills, indicate their intention as to which country's courts are to have jurisdiction and which system of law they desire to regulate their relations. This may be indicated expressly,[91] or impliedly, by the use of the forms or technical terminology of one legal system,[92] by reference to arbitration in a particular place,[93] by the place where the deed was executed[94] or the transaction took place.[95]

---

[83] Sons of Temperance Friendly Socy., 1926 S.C. 418.
[84] 1982 Act, S. 42.
[85] Janson v. Driefontein Consolidated Mines, Ltd. [1902] A.C. 484.
[86] Williams v. R.C.V.S. (1897) 5 S.L.T. 208; A.G. v. Jewish Colonisation Assocn. [1900] 2 Q.B. 556; Lazard Bros, v. Midland Bank [1933] A.C. 289; Gasque v. I.R.C. [1940] K.B. 80.
[87] Risdon Iron works v. Furness [1906] 1 K.B. 49; Banco de Bilbao v. Sancha [1938] 2 K.B. 176; Carse v. Coppen, 1951 S.C. 233.
[88] Thomson v. N.B. and Mercantile Ins. Co. (1868) 6 M. 310; cf. H.M.A. v. Hetherington, 1915 S.C. (J.) 79; O'Brien v. Davies, 1961 S.L.T. 85.
[89] San Paulo (Brazilian) Ry. Co. v. Carter [1896] A.C. 31; De Beers Mines Ltd. v. Howe [1906] A.C. 455; Unit Construction Co. Ltd. v. Bullock [1960] A.C. 351.
[90] Laidlaw v. Provident Plate Glass Ins. Co. [1890] 17 R. 544.
[91] Girvin, Roper & Co. v. Monteith (1895) 23 R. 129; Vita Food Products v. Unus Shipping Co. [1939] A.C. 277.
[92] Corbet v. Waddell (1879) 7 R. 200; Studd v. Cook (1883) 10 R. (H.L.) 53; Brown's Trs. v. Brown (1890) 17 R. 1174; Battye's Trs. v. B., 1917 S.C. 385; Eadie's Trs. v. Henderson, 1919 1 S.L.T. 253; see also Mitchell & Baxter v. Davies (1875) 3 R. 208; Smith v. Smiths (1891) 18 R. 1036; contrast Mackintosh v. May (1895) 22 R. 345.
[93] Hamlyn v. Talisker Distillery (1894) 21 R. (H.L.) 21; Robertson v. Brandes Schonwald & Co. (1906) 8 F. 815; Kwik Ho Tong v. Finlay [1927] A.C. 604.
[94] Shedlock v. Hannay (1891) 18 R. 663.
[95] Scottish Provident Inst. v. Cohen (1888) 16 R. 112.

Flag of a ship

The law of a ship's flag, i.e. of the country in which is situated the port of registry, is a relevant connecting factor in some cases.[96] By the Merchant Shipping Act, 1894, Sec. 265, where in any matter relating to a ship or to a person belonging to a ship there appears to be a conflict of laws then, failing provision in Part II of that Act extending to that ship, the case has to be governed by the laws of the port of registry.'[97]

Locus of fact or event

The place in which a cause of action arises may be a connecting factor with that country's courts or system of law. Thus the solemnizing of a marriage in Scotland,[98] the making or performing of a contract,[99] the commission of a wrong[1] may all be relevant connecting factors. The country in which some act or event happened may be a matter of dispute. It is probably the country where the last event necessary to make the act or event legally significant and, by Scots law, give a complete cause of action in respect thereof.[2]

Situs of property

The situation in Scotland of some property or right, such as land,[3] goods,[4] a debt,[5] or an estate,[6] may also be relevant as a connection. Money in Scotland owed to, or property in Scotland pertaining to, a person, furth of Scotland may be arrested *ad fundandam jurisdictionem*, thereby fixing the locality of the subjects in Scotland and rendering their foreign owner liable to be convened in a Scottish action.[7]

Forum of action

The initiation of legal proceedings in the courts of a particular legal system, if those courts accept jurisdiction, establishes a connection with that legal system, at least in matters of procedure.[8]

---

[96] *R. v. Anderson* (1868) L.R. 1 C.C.R. 161; *R. v. Keyn* (1876) L.R. 2 Ex.D. 63, 94, 98.
[97] Held inapplicable to the facts in *MacKinnon* v. *Iberia Shipping Co.*, 1955 S.C. 20.
[98] *Miller* v. *Deakin*, 1912, 1 S.L.T. 253.
[99] Personal citation of the defender in Scotland is also necessary: *Dallas* v. *McArdle*, 1949 S.C. 481.
[1] e.g. *Parnell* v. *Walter* (1889) 16 R. 917; *Toni Tyres Ltd.* v. *Palmer Tyre Ltd.* (1905) 7 F. 477. Personal citation in Scotland was also necessary: *Dalziel* v. *Coulthurst's Exor.*, 1934 S.C. 546, overruled by Law Reform (Jurisdiction in Delict) (Sc.) Act, 1971.
[2] See *Waygood* v. *Bennie* (1885) 12 R. 651; *Parnell, supra*; *Bata* v. *B.* [1948] W.N. 366.
[3] *Love* v. *L.*, 1907 S.C. 728.
[4] *Hay* v. *Jackson*, 1911 S.C. 876.
[5] *Bank of Scotland* v. *Gudin* (1886) 14 R. 213.
[6] *Kennedy* v. *K.* (1884) 12 R. 275; *Robertson's Tr.* v. *Nicholson* (1888) 15 R. 914; *McGennis* v. *Rooney* (1891) 18 R. 817; *Ashburton* v. *Escombe* (1892) 20 R. 187.
[7] *Cameron* v. *Chapman* (1837) 16 S. 907; *Trowsdale's Tr.* v. *Forcett Ry. Co.* (1870) 9 M. 88; *North* v. *Stewart* (1890) 17 R. (H.L.) 60; *Leggat Bros.* v. *Gray*, 1908 S.C. 67; *Sheaf S.S. Co.* v. *Compania Transmediterranea*, 1930 S.C. 660.
[8] e.g. *McElroy* v. *M'Allister*, 1949 S.C. 110.

Exclusion of foreign law

Scottish courts may decline to recognize a right or legal relationship arising under foreign law if recognition would be inconsistent with the public policy of Scots law. Thus they will not enforce slavery.[9] Nor will they enforce a penal, revenue,[10] or other public law of a foreign country. Similarly statutory provisions of a mandatory character may be held to override the application of foreign law in the Scottish courts.[11]

[9] *Knight* v. *Wedderburn* (1778) M. 14545.

[10] *A.G. for Canada* v. *Schulze* (1901) 9 S.L.T. 4; *Govt. of India* v. *Taylor* [1955] A.C. 491; *Metal Industries Ltd.* v. *S.T. Harle*, 1962 S.L.T. 114. cf. *S.N.O. Society Ltd.* v. *Thomson's Exor.*, 1969 S.L.T. 325.

[11] *Duncan* v. *Motherwell Bridge Co.*, 1952 S.C. 131; *English* v. *Donnelly*, 1958 S.C. 494; *Brodin* v. *A/R Seljan*, 1973 S.C. 213.

JURISDICTION OF THE SCOTTISH COURTS

Jurisdiction is the power of pronouncing a decree resolving an issue between the parties, which will be enforceable by the Scottish court and also be recognized as valid by foreign courts.[1] The question of jurisdiction must be considered by the court at the outset.[2] In general, the Scottish courts will exercise jurisdiction at the instance of any person over any other person, irrespective of the nationality or domicile of either, and without regard to where the cause of action arose or what it concerns, if the court can make the judgment effective within its own territory by its own processes, or if the defender has submitted himself to the jurisdiction of the court.[3]

Persons disabled from suing

The only person disabled from suing in the Scottish courts is an alien enemy, who is for this purpose any person, even a British subject or a neutral, voluntarily[4] residing or carrying on business in another country during the existence of a state of war between the United Kingdom and that country, or a person who adheres to the Queen's enemies, whatever his nationality or residence.[5] His right of action is suspended during hostilities.[6] A person of enemy nationality resident in the United Kingdom in wartime by permission of the Crown, whether interned or not, is fully entitled to sue.[7] Actions may be brought against enemy aliens, who may in such a case defend, counter-claim, and appeal.[8]

---

[1] See generally Duncan and Dykes, *Civil Jurisdiction*; Anton, *Private International Law*, Ch. 5; Maclaren, *Court of Session Practice*; Maxwell, *Court of Session Practice*.

[2] *McLeod v. Tancred Arrol & Co.* (1890) 17 R. 514; *Dallas v. McArdle*, 1949 S.C. 481.

[3] A foreign pursuer will usually, and a foreign defender less usually, be ordained to sist a mandatary, but it is always a matter for the court's discretion: *Ondix v. Landay, Ltd.*, 1963 S.C. 270.

[4] *Vandyke v. Adams* [1942] Ch. 155.

[5] *Daimler Co. v. Continental Tyre Co.* [1916] 2 A.C. 307.

[6] *Janson v. Driefontein Consolidated Mines* [1902] A.C. 484; *Porter v. Freudenberg* [1915] 1 K.B. 957; *Craig Line v. N.B. Storage Co.*, 1915 S.C. 113; *Van Uden v. Burrell*, 1916 S.C. 391; *Rodriguez v. Speyer* [1919] A.C. 59; *Sovfracht v. Van Uden* [1943] A.C. 203. Contrast *The Pamia* [1943] 1 All E.R. 269.

[7] *Robinson v. Continental Insurance Co. of Mannheim* [1915] 1 K.B. 155; *Porter, supra*; *Sovfracht, supra*.

[8] *Schulze, Gow & Co. v. Bank of Scotland*, 1914 2 S.L.T. 455; 1916 2 S.L.T. 207; *Princess*

Persons immune from being sued—sovereigns and states

The sovereigns of independent states outside the United Kingdom are personally immune from action,[9] as are sovereign foreign states which own,[10] or possess,[11] or have effective control of, the subject-matter in issue,[12] or are entitled to an immediate right of possession of the property in issue.[13] A state is not immune if it has submitted to the jurisdiction, nor as to commercial transactions,[14] contracts to be performed in the U.K., contracts of employment, and various other cases.[15] The status of a foreign sovereign or state as independent or otherwise, if in doubt, is determined conclusively[16] by a certificate from the Foreign and Common-wealth Relations Office.[17]

A foreign sovereign, or state, may waive the immunity,[18] or voluntarily submit to, or prorogate, the jurisdiction of the court, expressly, or by implication, as where he enters appearance to defend and takes no plea to the jurisdiction,[19] or himself makes a claim, in which case he lays himself open to a counter-claim,[20] and he may be called where the purpose of so doing is to give notice of a claim.[21] But to lodge a tender under reservation of all rights and pleas does not imply waiver of the claim to immunity.[22]

Persons immune—diplomatic and consular representatives

By the Diplomatic Privileges Act, 1964, members of a diplomatic mission enjoy certain immunity from jurisdiction. Members of the diplomatic staff

---

Thurn and Taxis v. Moffitt [1915] 1 Ch. 58; *Schaffenius v. Goldberg* [1916] 1 K.B. 284; *Schulze*, 1917 S.C. 400; *Johnstone v. Pedlar* [1921] 2 A.C. 262; *Weiss v. W.*, 1940 S.L.T. 467; *Crolla*, 1942 S.C. 21.

[9] *Mighell v. Sultan of Johore* [1894] 1 Q.B. 149; *Kahan v. Pakistan Federation* [1951] 2 K.B. 1003.

[10] *The Parlement Belge* (1880) 5 P.D. 197; *The Porto Alexandre* [1920] P. 30; *The Victoria v. The Quillwork*, 1932 S.L.T. 68.

[11] *The Gagara* [1919] P. 95; *The Cristina* [1938] A.C. 485; *Govt. of Republic of Spain v. National Bank of Scotland*, 1939 S.C. 413.

[12] *The Broadmayne* [1916] P. 64; *The Arantzazu Mendi* [1939] A.C. 256.

[13] *U.S.A. v. Dollfus Mieg and Bank of England* [1952] A.C. 582; *Rahimtoola v. Nizam of Hyderabad* [1958] A.C. 379.

[14] *Trendtex v. Central Bank of Nigeria* [1977] Q.B. 529.

[15] State Immunity Act, 1978, Ss. 2–11; *The Philippine Admiral* [1977] A.C. 373.

[16] *Foster v. Globe Venture Syndicate Ltd.* [1900] 1 Ch. 811; *Duff Development Co. v. Kelantan Government* [1924] A.C. 797.

[17] *Mighell, supra; Sayce v. Armeer* [1952] 2 Q.B. 390; State Immunity Act, 1978, S. 21.

[18] *D. Brunswick v. King of Hanover* (1844) 6 Beav. 1, 37; *Sultan of Johore v. Abubakar Tunku Aris Bendahar* [1952] A.C. 318.

[19] *Rosses v. Bhagvat Sinhjee* [1891] 19 R. 31.

[20] *King of Spain v. Hullet* (1833) 1 Cl. & F. 333; *Rothschild v. Queen of Portugal* (1839) 3 Y. & C. Ex. 594; *Strousberg v. Republic of Costa Rica* (1881) 44 L.T. 199; *Govt. of Republic of Spain v. National Bank of Scotland*, 1939 S.C. 413; *Sultan of Johore v. Abubakar Tunku Aris Bendahar* [1952] A.C. 318.

[21] *Strousberg, supra; Mighell, supra.*

[22] *Grangemouth and Forth Towing Co. v. Netherlands E.I. Co.*, 1942 S.L.T. 228; cf. *S.S. Victoria v. S.S. Quillwork*, 1922 S.L.T. 68.

of a mission and their families have full personal immunity, except in respect of (a) an action relating to private immoveable property; (b) an action relating to succession in which the diplomat is involved as a private person; and (c) an action relating to any professional or commercial activity exercised by the diplomatic agent outside his official functions. A member of the administrative or technical staff of the mission and his family has full immunity for official acts, but is civilly liable for acts outside the course of his duties. A member of the service staff of the mission has immunity for official acts, but is liable civilly and criminally for acts outside the course of his duties.[23] Private servants of members of the mission may enjoy privileges and immunities only to the extent admitted by municipal law, so long as their functions are not unduly interfered with. Diplomatic staff who are British nationals or permanently resident in the U.K. have immunity only in respect of official acts.[24] Whether or not any person is entitled to any privilege or immunity is conclusively determined by a certificate of the Secretary of State.[25]

The head of the mission may expressly waive the immunity, and the initiation of proceedings by a diplomatic agent precludes him from invoking immunity in respect of any counter-claim. A separate waiver is necessary before a decree can be enforced against a person immune.[26]

The Crown may, by Order in Council, restrict the privileges of a mission whose country grants lesser privileges to the British mission in that country.[27]

Similar immunities are granted to representatives of Commonwealth countries and Ireland.[28]

Consular officers and employees are not amenable to the jurisdiction of the judicial or administrative authorities of the receiving state in respect of acts performed in the exercise of consular functions, but the sending state may expressly waive this immunity. Initiation of proceedings precludes invoking immunity in respect of any counter-claim.[29]

Persons immune—international organizations and conferences

The International Organizations Act, 1968,[30] provides that certain privileges and immunities, including immunity from suit, may by Order in Council be conferred on certain international organizations and their officers, and on representatives at international conferences in the United Kingdom. The Diplomatic Immunities (Conferences with Commonwealth

[23] 1964 Act, Sch. I, Arts. 3, 37(2) and (3).
[24] Ibid., Art. 38.
[25] *Engelke* v. *Musmann* [1928] A.C. 433; 1964 Act, S. 4.
[26] Ibid., Art. 32.
[27] 1964 Act, S. 3.
[28] Diplomatic Immunities (Commonwealth Countries and Republic of Ireland) Act, 1952.
[29] Consular Relations Act, 1968, Sch. I, Arts. 43, 45, 53.
[30] Replacing International Organizations (Immunities and Privileges) Act, 1950, and European Coal and Steel Community Act, 1955.

Countries and the Republic of Ireland) Act, 1961, later amended, confers immunities on the representatives of such countries attending conferences in the United Kingdom.[31]

Matters exempted from jurisdiction

The Scottish courts will not entertain actions concerning title to, or possession of, land furth of Scotland,[32] save that these courts may entertain an action arising from a contract relative to foreign land.[33]

Nor will they entertain actions for penalties imposed by the law of other countries,[34] or to enforce foreign revenue laws.[35]

Concurrent jurisdiction—lis alibi pendens

A person may be liable to the jurisdiction of the courts of more than one country and be sued in both.[36] If the Scottish courts have jurisdiction they have no discretion whether to exercise that jurisdiction or not,[37] but may sist the action if the defender is being pursued oppressively and vexatiously by the concurrent actions[38] and they raise the same question.[39] The court is unlikely to sist an action if the defender in one action is pursuer in the other action.[40] The court will not sist an action to preserve the force of arrestments on the dependence until the pursuer raises an action elsewhere.[41] It will normally do so if the action is in breach of a contractual provision referring disputes to the jurisdiction of a foreign court.[42]

---

[31] Similar provision is made by the International Finance Corpn. Act, 1955, the International Development Assocn. Act, 1960, the International Monetary Fund Act, 1979, the Commonwealth Secretariat Act, 1966, the International Organisations Act, 1981, and some other Acts.

[32] Ersk. I, 2, 17; III, 2, 40. See also *British S.A. Co.* v. *Companhia de Moçambique* [1893] A.C. 602; *Cathcart* v. *C.* (1902) 12 S.L.T. 182.

[33] *Ruthven* v. *R.* (1905) 43 S.L.R. 11.

[34] *Huntington* v. *Attrill* [1893] A.C. 150; *A.G. for Canada* v. *Schulze & Co.* (1901) 9 S.L.T. 4; *Banco de Vizcaya* v. *Don Alfonso de Bourbon y Austria* [1935] 1 K.B. 140.

[35] *Govt. of India* v. *Taylor* [1955] A.C. 491; *Metal Industries (Salvage) Ltd.* v. *Owners of Harle*, 1962 S.L.T. 114; cf. *Buchanan and Macharg* v. *McVey* [1955] A.C. 516, n.

[36] e.g. *Hawkins* v. *Wedderburn* (1842) 4 D. 924, on which see *Atkinson & Wood* v. *Mackintosh* (1905) 7 F. 598. The plea of *lis alibi pendens* is a plea not strictly applicable where the other proceedings are in a foreign court; *Martin* v. *Stopford Blair's Exors.* (1879) 7 R. 329.

[37] *Clements* v. *Macaulay* (1866) 4 M. 583, 593, approved *Société du Gaz* v. *Armateurs Français*, 1926 S.C. (H.L.) 13, 19.

[38] *Cochrane* v. *Paul* (1857) 20 D. 178; *Rothfield* v. *Cohen*, 1919 1 S.L.T. 138; see also *McHenry* v. *Lewis* (1882) 22 Ch. D. 397; *Cohen* v. *Rothfield* [1919] 1 K.B. 410; *Logan* v. *Bank of Scotland* [1906] 1 K.B. 141; *Devine* v. *Cementation Co. Ltd.* [1963] N.I. 65.

[39] *Wilson* v. *Dunlop, Bremner & Co.*, 1921 1 S.L.T. 35.

[40] *Rothfield, supra.*

[41] *Atkinson & Wood, supra.*

[42] cf. *The Cap Blanco* [1913] P. 130; *The Eleftheria* [1970] P. 94.

Concurrent jurisdiction—forum non conveniens

The Scottish court may in its discretion decline to exercise jurisdiction where, though it has jurisdiction, a court in another country also has jurisdiction, the parties are the same, and the Scottish court considers that the other forum is more suitable and appropriate having regard to the convenience of the parties and the ends of justice.[43] The court may exercise jurisdiction even though the defender is in Scotland only temporarily if the other forum is less appropriate.[44] Factors weighing in favour of Scottish jurisdiction are the express invocation of Scots law in a deed,[45] the *de quo* being a purely Scottish right such as terce,[46] and Scotland being the domicile of the parties,[47] and the parties to the two actions, or the remedies sought, not being identical.[48] Contrary factors include the need to determine questions of the validity and construction of a will by English law.[49] Priority of initiation of process is important but not conclusive in relation to appropriateness of forum.[50]

JURISDICTION IN PARTICULAR ACTIONS

(a) ACTIONS CONCERNING PERSONAL STATUS

In actions brought to declare or change personal status, such as declarators of legitimacy or of bastardy, of marriage, of nullity of marriage, and actions of divorce, the main ground of the jurisdiction of the Scottish court is that the party or parties are domiciled in Scotland,[51] irrespective of where the parties may be actually resident,[52] and of whether the cause of action would be recognized in a former domicile,[53] but other grounds are recognized in certain cases.

---

[43] *Longworth v. Hope* (1865) 3 M. 1049; *Clements v. Macaulay* (1866) 4 M. 583; *Martin v. Stopford-Blair's Exors.* (1879) 7 R. 329; *Orr Ewing's Trs. v. O.E.* (1885) 13 R. (H.L.) 1; *Sim v. Robinow* (1892) 19 R. 665; *Hine v. McDowall* (1897) 5 S.L.T. 12; *Société du Gaz v. Armateurs Français*, 1926 S.C. (H.L.) 13; *Argyllshire Weavers v. Macaulay*, 1962 S.C. 388; *Balshaw v. B.*, 1967 S.C. 63; *Crédit Chimique v. Scott*, 1979 S.C. 406; see also *Howden v. Powell Duffryn*, 1912 S.C. 920; *Foster v. F's Trs.*, 1923 S.C. 212; *Lawford v. L's Trs.*, 1927 S.C. 360; *Robinson v. R's Trs.*, 1930 S.C. (H.L.) 20. cf. *McShannon v. Rockware Glass* [1978] A.C. 795.

[44] *Prescott v. Graham* (1883) 20 S.L.R. 573.

[45] *Bayley v. Johnstone*, 1928 S.N. 153; cf. *Drummond v. Bell-Irving*, 1930 S.C. 704.

[46] *Robinson, supra.*

[47] *McLean v. McL.*, 1947 S.C. 79.

[48] *Argyllshire Weavers, Ltd. v. Macaulay*, 1962 S.C. 388.

[49] *Jubert v. Church Commrs. for England*, 1952 S.C. 160.

[50] *Thomson v. N.B. and Mercantile Ins. Co.* (1868) 6 M. 310; *Robinson v. R's Trs.*, 1930 S.C. (H.L.) 20; *Woodbury v. Sutherland's Trs.*, 1938 S.C. 689; *Babington v. B.*, 1955 S.C. 115; *Argyllshire Weavers, Ltd. v. Macaulay*, 1962 S.C. 388.

[51] *Le Mesurier v. Le M.* [1895] A.C. 517; *Admin. of Austrian Property v. Von Lorang*, 1927 S.C. (H.L.) 80; *McLelland v. McL.*, 1942 S.C. 502; *Balshaw, supra.*

[52] cf. *Mangrulkar v. M.*, 1939 S.C. 239.

[53] *Carswell v. C.* (1881) 8 R. 901; see also *Stavert v. S.* (1882) 9 R. 519; *Steel v. S.* (1888) 15 R. 896.

Declarator of legitimacy or of bastardy

A declarator of legitimacy or of bastardy may be granted by the Scottish courts if the pursuer is domiciled in Scotland,[54] or seeks to establish rights, such as to property, over which the Scottish courts have jurisdiction.[55]

Declarator of legitimation

Such a declarator may probably be granted if the pursuer is domiciled, or possibly resident, in Scotland, or claims property there.[56]

Declarator of adoption

The Scottish courts probably have jurisdiction to grant declarator of adoption if the pursuer is domiciled, or possibly resident, in Scotland, or claims property there.

Declarator of marriage or of nullity of marriage

The Scottish courts now have jurisdiction if either party is domiciled in Scotland, or habitually resident in Scotland for one year before the action was commenced, or had died and was previously thus qualified.[57]

Divorce, separation, or declarator of freedom and putting to silence

The Scottish court now has jurisdiction only if either party is domiciled in Scotland, or has been habitually resident in Scotland for one year before the action was commenced.[58] Nationality does not give jurisdiction,[59] nor is the place of the marriage or of the matrimonial wrong relevant.[60]

The court's jurisdiction is not excluded by the existence of an order from an English magistrates' court made on a different ground from that in issue before the Scottish court,[61] nor by the existence of a decree of a Roman Catholic ecclesiastical tribunal that the marriage was null under

---

[54] Hume, *Lect.* V, 244; *Balshaw* v. *B.*, 1967 S.C. 63, 82.

[55] *Morley* v. *Jackson* (1888) 16 R. 78; *Smijth* v. *S.*, 1918 1 S.L.T. 156. See also *Shaw* v. *Gould* (1868) L.R. 3 H.L. 55; Law Reform (Parent & Child) (Sc.) Act, 1986, S. 7.

[56] *Dalhousie* v. *McDouall* (1837) 16 S. 18; 1 Rob. 492.

[57] Domicile and Matrimonial Proceedings Act, 1973, S. 7(3), superseding much conflicting older law.

[58] Domicile and Matrimonial Proceedings Act, 1973, S. 7(2). As regards domicile this repeats earlier law; as regards residence it extends a rule recognized only exceptionally. As to separation and aliment in the sheriff court see S. 8.

[59] *Niboyet* v. *N.* (1878) 4 P.D. 1, 19.

[60] *Tulloh* v. *T.* (1861) 23 D. 639; *Mangrulkar* v. *M.*, 1939 S.C. 239.

[61] *Murray* v. *M.*, 1956 S.C. 376; *Richardson* v. *R.*, 1957 S.L.T. (Notes) 45.

canon law.[62] Divorce cannot be effected in the U.K. by any non-judicial process, religious or otherwise.[63]

Property rights arising on divorce

If the Scottish court has jurisdiction as to the marriage it also has jurisdiction as to ancillary and collateral orders[64] but enforcement of any award will be impossible unless the court granting divorce has effective jurisdiction over the defender's property.[65] A Scottish court may entertain an application for financial provision by a party divorced in an overseas country if jurisdictional requirements and stated conditions are satisfied.[66]

Reduction of decree of divorce

The court can reduce its own decree in consistorial proceedings whether or not it has jurisdiction otherwise.[67]

Dissolution on ground of presumed death

The Court of Session now has jurisdiction only if the petitioner is domiciled in Scotland or has been habitually resident there for one year immediately preceding the petition, or the person being presumed dead was so domiciled or resident.[68] Where the husband had acquired a domicile of choice in Scotland but had left Scotland and disappeared it was held that he must be presumed to have retained his Scottish domicile of choice in the absence of evident intention to change.[69]

Polygamous marriages

At common law the Scottish courts had no jurisdiction to grant matrimonial remedies to potentially or actually polygamous marriages.[70] But such

---

[62] Di Rollo v. Di. R., 1959 S.C. 75.

[63] Domicile and Matrimonial Proceedings Act, 1973, S. 16.

[64] Domicile and Matrimonial Proceedings Act, 1973, S. 10.

[65] cf. Fraser v. Fraser and Hibbert (1870) 8 M. 400; Thomson v. T., 1935 S.L.T. 24.

[66] Matrimonial and Family Proceedings Act, 1984, S. 28.

[67] Domicile and Matrimonial Proceedings Act, 1973, S. 9, overruling Longworth v. Yelverton (1868) 7 M. 70; Acutt v. A., 1936 S.C. 386; Jack v. J., 1940 S.L.T. 122; Law Reform (Misc. Prov.) (Sc.) Act, 1980, S. 20.

[68] Domicile and Matrimonial Proceedings Act, 1973, S. 7(4); Presumption of Death (Sc.) Act, 1977, S. 1.

[69] Labacianskas v. L., 1949 S.C. 280.

[70] Hyde v. H. (1866) L.R. 1 P. & M. 30; Mohammed v. Suna, 1956 S.C. 366. A marriage contracted in Britain is monogamous even though either or both parties might by their personal religious law contract polygamous marriage: MacDougall v. Chitnavis, 1937 S.C. 390; Qureshi v. Q. [1971] 1 All E.R. 325. A potentially polygamous marriage may become monogamous if the parties acquire an English or Scottish domicile: Ali v. A. [1968] P. 564.

marriages were not ignored in questions of bigamy,[71] legitimacy of children,[72] succession,[73] and claims for social security.[74] By the Matrimonial Proceedings (Polygamous Marriages) Act, 1972, a court in Scotland may (S. 2) grant decree of divorce, nullity, dissolution of marriage on the ground of presumed death, judicial separation, separation and aliment, adherence and aliment or interim aliment, declarator that the marriage is valid or invalid, or any other decree involving a determination as to the validity of a marriage, and make any ancillary order which it may make in such a case, and is not precluded by reason only that the marriage was entered into under a law which permits polygamy. This applies to both potentially and actually polygamous marriages.

Jurisdiction by virtue of other proceedings

If proceedings are pending in the Scottish courts, they may exercise jurisdiction in other proceedings in respect of the same marriage.[75]

(b) OTHER ACTIONS RELATING TO PERSONAL RELATIONS

Seduction, affiliation and aliment, etc.

In these actions the Scottish courts have jurisdiction only if they can exercise it in respect of a petitory claim.[76]

Judicial separation

An action for judicial separation does not fundamentally affect the status of the parties but only alters the obligations which otherwise flow from that status.[77] Jurisdiction accordingly depends on domicile[78] or habitual residence,[79] or exists if the action is begun when an original action is pending in respect of the marriage.[80] Once events giving a right to

---

[71] *Srini Vasan* v. *S.V.* [1946] P. 67; *Baindail* v. *B.* [1946] P. 122.

[72] *Sinha Peerage Case* [1946] 1 All E.R. 348 n.

[73] *Coleman* v. *Shang* [1961] A.C. 481. See also National Insurance Act, 1965, S. 113(2), and 1971 Acts, S. 12.

[74] *Imam Din* v. *N.A.B.* [1967] 2 Q.B. 213.

[75] Domicile and Matrimonial Proceedings Act, 1973, S. 7(5).

[76] *Bald* v. *Dawson*, 1911 2 S.L.T. 459; *Martin* v. *Szyszka*, 1943 S.C. 203; *Findlay* v. *Donachie*, 1944 S.C. 306.

[77] cf. *Administrator of Austrian Property* v. *Von Lorang*, 1927 S.C. (H.L.) 80; *Jelfs* v. *J.*, 1939 S.L.T. 286; *McCord* v. *McC.*, 1946 S.C. 198.

[78] *Hood* v. *H.* (1897) 24 R. 973; *Eustace* v. *E.* [1924] P. 45; *Ramsay. R.*, 1925 S.C. 216; *Jelfs* v. *J.*, 1939 S.L.T. 286; Domicile and Matrimonial Proceedings Act, 1973, S. 7(2), 8(2).

[79] *Armytage* v. *A.* [1898] P. 178; *Graham* v. *G.* [1923] P. 31; *Jelfs, supra*; *Sim* v. *S* [1944] P. 87; *McCord, supra*; *Matalon* v. *M.* [1952] P. 233; *Sinclair* v. *S.* [1967] 3 All E.R. 882; Domicile and Matrimonial Proceedings Act, 1973, S. 7(2), 8(2).

[80] Domicile and Matrimonial Proceedings Act, 1973, S. 7(2), 8(3).

separation have happened, a husband cannot defeat his wife's right by changing his domicile.[81]

Aliment

A claim for aliment alone is a pecuniary one and the Scottish court can exercise jurisdiction only if it has jurisdiction in petitory actions against the defender,[82] or under the Maintenance Orders Act, 1950.

Jurisdiction under Maintenance Orders Act, 1950

Under this Act (S. 1) a court in England has jurisdiction in proceedings under the Summary Jurisdiction (Married Women) Act, 1895, against a man residing in Scotland if the applicant resides in England and the parties last ordinarily resided together as man and wife in England, or if the woman resides in Scotland against a man residing in England, and may revoke, revise, or vary any such order. By S. 6 the sheriff has jurisdiction in an action by a married woman for aliment for herself and any child of the marriage[83] if the pursuer resides within the jurisdiction and the parties last ordinarily resided together as man and wife in Scotland, and the husband resides in England or Northern Ireland.[84]

A court having jurisdiction where the mother resides in England may grant custody of a child to the mother, with or without an order on the father to make payments for maintenance, against a father residing in Scotland (S. 2). The sheriff court in Scotland has similar power in the converse case (S. 7).

An English court may grant an affiliation order against a man residing in Scotland if the intercourse took place in England, and the mother in Scotland may take proceedings for an affiliation order in a court in England having jurisdiction where the father resides (S. 3). Conversely (S. 8) the sheriff has jurisdiction in an action of affiliation and aliment if the mother resides within his jurisdiction, the intercourse took place in Scotland, and the father resides in England or Northern Ireland.

An English court has by S. 4 jurisdiction in proceedings against a person in Scotland for contribution under the Children and Young Persons Acts, and the Social Security Act; the Scottish courts have corresponding powers (S. 9).

Jurisdiction under Mainenance Orders (Reciprocal Enforcement) Act, 1972

Under the Maintenance Orders (Reciprocal Enforcement) Act, 1972, S. 4, the sheriff has jurisdiction if the pursuer resides within the sheriff's

---

[81] Ramsay v. R., 1925 S.C. 216; Crabtree v. C., 1929 S.L.T. 675.
[82] Hutchison v. H., 1912, 1 S.L.T. 219; McNeill v. McN., 1919, 2 S.L.T. 127.
[83] In Wilson v. W., 1954 S.L.T. (Sh. Ct.) 68, 'child' was held to mean a child under 16.
[84] Plant v. P., 1963 S.L.T. (Sh. Ct.) 58.

jurisdiction, he is satisfied that the defender is residing in a reciprocating country under the Act, and he would not otherwise have jurisdiction, to make a provisional order for payment of aliment, including affiliation and aliment. In such a case the action may proceed without citation of the defender, but decree may be granted only after proof.

Custody of children

The Scottish courts have jurisdiction as to custody of pupils[85] and minors under sixteen.[86] They may determine custody and access if Scotland is the father's domicile,[87] and this is the pre-eminent forum,[88] or if Scotland is the child's domicile, or if there is reason to apprehend immediate danger to a child in Scotland, or to enforce the order for custody of a competent court.[89] It is immaterial that the child has been made a ward of court in England.[90] Under the Guardianship of Children Acts, 1886 to 1973, the Court of Session has jurisdiction if the defender, either father or mother, is resident in Scotland.[91] The Court of Session also has jurisdiction at the instance of either party to an action in Scotland relating to the custody, maintenance, or education of a child, or of the child's guardian, by interim interdict to prohibit the removal of the child furth of Scotland or out of the control of the person having custody.[92]

Under the Conjugal Rights (Sc.) Amendment Act, 1861, extended by the Matrimonial Proceedings (Children) Act, 1958, the court has power in actions for judicial separation, divorce, and nullity of marriage to make orders as to the custody and maintenance of the children of the marriage. It may be that the court having jurisdiction in the principal action also has jurisdiction as to custody and maintenance,[93] or it may be that jurisdiction depends on the same considerations as in other custody cases.[94]

Jurisdiction to appoint guardians to incapaces

The Scottish court has jurisdiction to appoint guardians to persons mentally disordered if the incapax is resident in Scotland, or if he has property

---

[85] At common law.

[86] Family Law Act, 1986, Ss. 8–18.

[87] *Barkworth* v. *B.*, 1913 S.C. 759; *Westergaard* v. *W.*, 1914 S.C. 977; *Ponder* v. *P.*, 1932 S.C. 233; *Kitson* v. *K.*, 1945 S.C. 434; *McLean* v. *McL.*, 1947 S.C. 79; *Babington* v. *B.*, 1955 S.C. 115; see also *Radoyevitch* v. *R.*, 1930 S.C. 619.

[88] *McLean*, *supra*; *Babington* v. *B.*, 1955 S.C. 115; *Oludimu* v. *O.*, 1967 S.L.T. 105.

[89] *McShane* v. *McS.*, 1962 S.L.T. 221; cf. *Oludimu* v. *O.*, 1967 S.L.T. 105.

[90] *McLean*, *supra*; *Babington*, *supra*; *Hoy* v. *H.*, 1968 S.C. 179. See also *Johnstone* v. *Beattie* (1843) 10 Cl. & F. 42; *Stuart* v. *M. Bute* (1861) 9 H.L.C. 440; *Re X's Settlement* [1964] Ch. 44.

[91] 1886 Act, S. 9.

[92] *Low*, 1920 S.C. 351; Matrimonial Proceedings (Children) Act, 1958, S. 13.

[93] *Hamilton* v. *H.*, 1954 S.L.T. 16; *Shanks* v. *S.*, 1965 S.L.T. 330; *Battaglia* v. *B.*, 1966 S.L.T. (Notes) 85.

[94] *McShane*, *supra*; *Robb* v. *R.*, 1953 S.L.T. 44, but on this see *Hamilton*, *supra*.

situated in Scotland,[95] or probably if he is domiciled in Scotland.[96] A person residing outside Scotland will rarely be appointed.[97] A guardian appointed elsewhere will normally be recognized in Scotland, save as to the management of heritable property in Scotland,[98] and the Scottish court will normally assist a guardian lawfully entitled or appointed by other courts having jurisdiction.[99]

Adoption

The Scottish courts may make an adoption order if the applicant is domiciled in the U.K., and applicant and child reside in Scotland,[1] or if the adopter is a U.K. or convention country national and resides in Britain or a U.K. national and resides in a convention country and the child is a U.K. national habitually resident in British territory or a convention country.[2]

(c) IN RELATION TO CORPORATIONS

The Scottish courts have jurisdiction over corporate bodies registered in, centrally managed in, having a place of business in, owning property in, or doing business in Scotland, but such jurisdiction is not necessarily exclusive.[3] They have exclusive jurisdiction in proceedings which have as their object the validity of the constitution, the nullity, or the dissolution of companies or associations if the body has its seat in Scotland.[4]

They may wind up a company registered in Scotland[5] and, in certain circumstances, an unregistered company.[6]

(d) ACTIONS IN PERSONAM

(1) *As between Scotland and England and Northern Ireland*

In this case jurisdiction is determined by the Convention scheduled to the Civil Jurisdiction and Judgments Act, 1982, Titles I and II, as modified in

[95] *Sawyer* v. *Sloan* (1875) 3 R. 271; *Reid* v. *R.* (1887) 24 S.L.R. 281; *Harper*, 1932 S.L.T. 496; *Waring*, 1933 S.L.T. 190.
[96] *Buchan* v. *Harvey* (1839) 2 D. 275; Mental Health Act, 1959, S. 117; Mental Health (Sc.) Act, 1960, S. 93.
[97] *Fergusson* v. *Dormer* (1870) 8 M. 426; *Napier* (1902) 9 S.L.T. 429; *Forsyth*, 1932 S.L.T. 462.
[98] *Buchan* v. *Harvey* (1839) 2 D. 275; *Lamb* (1858) 20 D. 1323; *Sawyer* v. *Sloan* (1875) 3 R. 271; *Ogilvy* v. *O's Trs.*, 1927 S.L.T. 83; *Forsyth*, 1932 S.L.T. 462.
[99] *Stuart* v. *Stuart* (1861) 4 Macq. 1; *Maquay* v. *Campbell* (1888) 15 R. 606; *Marchetti* v. *M.* (1901) 3 F. 888.
[1] Adoption (Sc.) Act, 1978, Ss. 14–17.
[2] Ibid., S. 17.
[3] Civil Jurisdiction and Judgments Act, 1982, Sch. 1, Art. 16; Sch. 4, Art. 16.
[4] Ibid., Sch. 8, rule 2(12).
[5] Companies Act, 1985, S. 515.
[6] Ibid., Ss. 665–9.

Sch. 4 to the 1982 Act. Certain proceedings are excluded from Schedule 4 by Schedule 5. Within the U.K. the rules of *lis alibi pendens* and *forum non conveniens* are preserved by the 1982 Act, S. 49.

(2) *As between Scotland and contracting states (EC countries except Greece, Spain, and Portugal)*

Jurisdiction is determined by the Convention scheduled to the Civil Jurisdiction and Judgments Act, 1982, Titles I and II, set out in Schedule 1 to the 1982 Act. The European Court has jurisdiction to interpret the Convention, there is a 1971 Protocol on Interpretation, and two reports on the Conventions may be considered in interpreting them.[7]

The Convention applies in civil and commercial matters, but not revenue, customs, or administrative matters, nor status or capacity of natural persons, property arising from marriage, wills, and succession, bankruptcy and insolvency, social security, or arbitration.[8]

Persons domiciled[9] in a contracting state shall, whatever their nationality, be sued in the courts of that state, non-nationals being governed by the rules of jurisdiction applicable to nationals of that state.[10] Jurisdiction cannot be founded in a U.K. court against a non-U.K. resident by service of a summons during his temporary presence in the U.K., or on presence of his property in the U.K., or seizure by the pursuer of property in the U.K.[11]

A person 'domiciled' in a contracting state may also be sued in another contracting state, in the courts.

(1) of the place of performance of a contract;

(2) of the place where a maintenance creditor is domiciled or habitually resident or, if ancillary to status, the court having jurisdiction to entertain those proceedings, unless based solely on nationality;

(3) of the place where the harmful event of a delict occurred;

(4) handling a claim for damages or restitution based on an act giving rise to criminal proceedings;

(5) of the place where is situated a branch, agency, or other establishment whose operations gave rise to the dispute;

(6) of the state in which a trust is domiciled, if the party is sued as settler, trustee, or beneficiary;

---

[7] 1982 Act, S. 3.

[8] Art. 1. What follows is a very summary version of the Convention.

[9] Domicile, by 1982 Act, S. 41 and Art. 52, means residence in circumstances indicating that the person has a substantial connection with the U.K. or a jurisdiction thereof or another country. Three months' residence raises a presumption of 'residence'. For domicile of corporations see Ss. 42–3, for trusts S. 45, and for the Crown S. 46. It is therefore different from domicile in relation to status.

[10] Art. 2.

[11] Art. 3.

(7) by whose authority cargo or freight, salvage reward for which is claimed, has been arrested or bail found in lieu.[12]

A person so 'domiciled' may also be sued

(1) if a co-defender, in the courts where any defender is domiciled;
(2) if a third party, in the court seised of the main proceedings;
(3) in a counter-claim, in the court dealing with the main claim.[13]

If a court has jurisdiction in liability arising from use or operation of a ship, that court is also to have jurisdiction over claims for limitation of liability.[14]

In matters relating to insurance, an insurer may be sued in the courts of the state where he is domiciled, or where the policy-holder is domiciled, or if a co-insurer, where the leading insurer is domiciled,[15] or in respect of liability insurance or insurance of immoveables, where the harmful event occurred.[16] These provisions may be departed from by agreement.[17]

In consumer contracts action may be brought in the courts of the state of either party but against the consumer only in the courts of his domicile. These provisions may be altered by agreement.[18]

Exclusive jurisdiction

Courts have exclusive jurisdiction, regardless of domicile, in proceedings:

(1) as to rights *in rem* in or tenancies of immoveable property: the courts where the property is situated;
(2) as to validity of constitution, nullity, or dissolution of companies or other legal persons or associations, or their decisions: courts of the state where the body has its seat;
(3) as to validity of entries in public registers: courts of the state where the register is kept;
(4) as to registration or validity of patents, trade marks, designs, or similar rights: courts of the state where registration applied for;
(5) as to enforcement of judgments: courts of the state in which the judgment is to be enforced.[19]

Prorogated jurisdiction

Courts have exclusive jurisdiction if parties, one or more of whom is domiciled in a contracting state, have agreed in writing, or by agreement

---

[12] Art. 5.
[13] Art. 6.
[14] Art. 6A.
[15] Arts. 7–8.
[16] Arts. 9–11.
[17] Arts. 12–12A.
[18] Arts. 13–15.
[19] Art. 16. See also Art. 19.

evidenced in writing, to settle disputes in the courts of that state. A trust instrument may confer jurisdiction. Entering appearance confers jurisdiction unless solely to contest the jurisdiction.[20]

Refusal of jurisdiction

If a defender domiciled in one state and sued in another does not enter appearance the court must decline jurisdiction unless it has jurisdiction under the Convention.[21]

Lis pendens

If proceedings involving the same or a related cause of action and between the same parties are brought in the courts of different contracting states courts other than that first seised must decline jurisdiction.[22]

Protective measures

Application may be made to the courts of a contracting state for provisional or protective measures available under the law of that state, even if another country's courts have jurisdiction as to the substance of the matter.[23]

(3) As between Scotland and non-Convention states (all other countries not above mentioned)

In these cases common law principles still apply.[24] These are in some respects modified by the 1982 Act, Schedule 8, to avoid inconsistency with the convention in Schedule 1.

Where in any case a Scottish court has no jurisdiction which is compatible with the 1982 Act it must decline jurisdiction.[25]

Jurisdiction in actions *in personam*, such as actions for debt or damages arising *ex obligatione*, depends generally on the ability of the Scottish court to make its decree effective against the defender.[26] It follows that the maxim *actor sequitur forum rei* applies and the pursuer must bring his action in the country where the defender is 'domiciled', i.e. resident for at least 3 months, when action is commenced.[27] The date of citation in the action is the critical date.[28]

---

[20] Arts. 17–18.
[21] Arts. 19–20.
[22] Arts. 21–3.
[23] Art. 24.
[24] Art. 4.
[25] Sch. 8, rule 8.
[26] Ersk. I, 2, 16 and 20.
[27] *Joel* v. *Gill* (1859) 21 D. 929; *North* v. *Stewart* (1889) 17 R. (H.L.) 60; *McLeod* v. *Tancred Arrol & Co.* (1890) 17 R. 514; 1982 Act, Sch. 8 and Ss. 41–2.
[28] *North* v. *Stewart, supra; Smith* v. *Stuart* (1894) 22 R. 130.

Presence

The main ground of this jurisdiction is the defender's personal presence in Scotland,[29] if substantially continuously[30] resident in one locality formerly for forty days,[31] now for three months, and not merely itinerant.[31] This jurisdiction lapses immediately the defender quits Scotland.[32] An itinerant is subject to the jurisdiction only if personally cited in Scotland.[33] A permanent home or address in Scotland does not amount to 'constructive residence'.[34] The defender's domicile is irrelevant.[35] A corporation is subject to jurisdiction if it has a place of business and carries on business in Scotland.[36]

Ratione contractus vel delicti

Another ground of this jurisdiction is in relation to a contract where the place of performance of a contract or in relation to delict or quasi-delict where the occurrence of a harmful event was within the jurisdiction,[37] The defender's domicile in Scotland, even combined with the occurrence of the cause of action in Scotland, does not give jurisdiction, in the absence of personal citation.[38]

Even where the Scottish courts do not have jurisdiction on any other ground they have jurisdiction by interdict to prevent the commission of a wrong in Scotland.[39] They may also, if they have jurisdiction on another ground, interdict the commission of a wrong abroad.[40]

---

[29] *Johnstone* v. *Strachan* (1861) 23 D. 758; *Buchan* v. *Grimaldi* (1905) 7 F. 917; *Kerr* v. *R. & W. Ferguson*, 1931 S.C. 736; *Findlay* v. *Donachie*, 1944 S.C. 306. See also *Young* v. *Harper*, 1970 S.C. 174.

[30] *Ritchie* v. *Fraser* (1852) 15 D. 205; *Prescott* v. *Graham* (1883) 20 S.L.R. 573.

[31] Ersk. I, 2, 16; Kames, H.L.T. 233; *Joel* v. *Gill* (1859) 21 D. 929. The forty days must be complete before citation: *Dallas* v. *McArdle*, 1949 S.C. 481; *McNeill* v. *McN.*, 1960 S.C. 30. For 'three months' see 1982 Act, S. 41(6).

[32] *Johnston, supra; Corstorphine* v. *Kasten* (1898) 1 F. 287; *Buchan, supra; Carter* v. *Allison*, 1966 S.C. 257.

[33] Ersk. I, 2, 16; *Linn* v. *Casadinos* (1881) 8 R. 849; *Martin* v. *Szyszka*, 1943 S.C. 203; 1982 Act, Sch. 8, rule 2(1).

[34] *Nicol* v. *Bruce*, 1965 S.C. 160.

[35] *Tasker* v. *Grieve* (1905) 8 F. 45; *Bald* v. *Dawson*, 1911 2 S.L.T. 459; *Martin* v. *Szyszka*, 1943 S.C. 203.

[36] *Laidlaw* v. *Provident Insce. Co. Ltd.* (1890) 17 R. 544; *Hughes* v. *Stewart*, 1907 S.C. 791; *I.A.* v. *Huron, etc. Co.*, 1911 S.C. 612.

[37] *Sinclair* (1860) 22 D. 1475; *Johnston, supra; Kermick* v. *Watson* (1871) 9 M. 984; *Maxwell* v. *Horwood's Trs.* (1902) 4 F. 489; *Kerr* v. *R. & W. Ferguson*, 1931 S.C. 736; *Dalziel* v. *Coulthurst's Exors*, 1934 S.C. 564; *Dallas* v. *McArdle*, 1949 S.C. 481. The need for personal citation in cases of delict was abrogated by the Law Reform (Jurisdiction in Delict) (Sc.) Act, 1971; *Buchan* v. *Thompson*, 1974 S.L.T. 124. This is now replaced by Civil Jurisdiction and Judgments Act, 1982, Sch. 8, rules 2(2) and (3).

[38] *Kerr, supra,* overruling *Glasgow Corpn.* v. *Johnston*, 1915 S.C. 555; Sch. 8, rule 2(1).

[39] *Campbell* v. *Arnott* (1893) 1 S.L.T. 159; *D. Hamilton* v. *McCracken* (1893) 1 S.L.T. 336; *Gill* v. *Cutler* (1895) 23 R. 371; *Toni Tyres Ltd.* v. *Palmer Tyre Co.* (1905) 7 F, 477; 1982 Act, Sch. 8, rule 2(10).

[40] Cf. *Liqdr. of California Redwood Co.* v. *Walker* (1886) 13 R. 810; *Liqdr. of Pacific Mining Co.* v. *Walker* (1886) 13 R. 816; *Gill* v. *Cutler* (1895) 23 R. 371.

In a civil claim for damages or restitution based on an act giving rise to criminal proceedings jurisdiction is in the court seised of those proceedings to the extent that it has jurisdiction to entertain civil proceedings.[41]

In matters relating to maintenance the courts where the creditor is 'domiciled' or habitually resident have jurisdiction.[42]

In the case of consumer contracts action may be brought by the consumer in the courts of the pursuer's or the defender's 'domicile' but against the consumer only where he is 'domiciled', or under para. 2(9).[43]

Ownership or tenancy of heritage

The ownership[44] or tenancy[45] of heritable property in Scotland confers jurisdiction on the Scottish courts in causes relating to that property,[46] including debts secured over the property,[47] and possibly also in personal claims generally, but not over an owner who is being sued in a representative capacity[48] nor over a claimant on a trust estate including Scottish heritage.[49] The radical right of a disponer in security probably gives jurisdiction,[50] as does a contract to purchase heritage.[51]

This ground of jurisdiction disappears when the owner is feudally divested of the heritage,[52] or even has delivered an absolute conveyance thereof,[53] and does not exist over trustees until they have completed title.[54]

The defender's interest is immaterial so long as it is capable of attachment.[55] Possession as trustee does not give jurisdiction against the trustee as an individual.[56]

---

[41] 1982 Act, Sch. 8, rule 2(4).

[42] 1982 Act, Sch. 8, rule 2(5).

[43] 1982 Act, Sch. 8, rule 3.

[44] Including having the radical right to heritage under a trust: *Smith* v. *Stuart* (1894) 22 R. 130; ownership as trustees: *Charles* v. *C's Trs.* (1868) 6 M. 772; possession of a mid-superiority: *Kirkpatrick* v. *Irvine* (1841) 2 Rob. 475; and even though it has been sold: *Caledonian Stores* v. *Hewson*, 1970 S.C. 168.

[45] *Fraser* v. *F. and Hibbert* (1870) 8 M. 400; *Weinschel*, 1916, 2 S.L.T. 91, 205.

[46] *McArthur* v. *McA.* (1842) 4 D. 354; *Ashburton* v. *Escombe* (1892) 20 R. 187; *Manderson* v. *Sutherland* (1899) 1 F. 621; *Thorburn* v. *Dempster* (1900) 2 F. 583; *Love* v. *L.*, 1907 S.C. 728; *Pagan & Osborne* v. *Haig*, 1910 S.C. 341; *Lawford* v. *L's Trs.*, 1927 S.C. 360. See also *Hastie* v. *Steel* (1886) 13 R. 843; *Buchan* v. *Grimaldi* (1905) 7 F. 917; *Wilson* (1895) 2 S.L.T. 567; *Jubert* v. *Church Commrs. for England*, 1952 S.C. 160; 1982 Act, Sch. 8, rules 2(8)(b), 4(1)(a).

[47] Sch. 8, rule 2(11).

[48] *Mackenzie* v. *Drummond's Exors.* (1868) 6 M. 932.

[49] *Gemmell* v. *Emery* (1905) 13 S.L.T. 490.

[50] *McBride* v. *Caledonian Ry.* (1894) 21 R. 620; *Low* v. *Scottish Amicable Socy.*, 1940 S.L.T. 295.

[51] *Thorburn* v. *Dempster* (1900) 2 F. 583; cf. *Caledonian Stores, supra.*

[52] *Shaw* v. *Dow & Dobie* (1869) 7 M. 449; *Buchan, supra*; *Caledonian Stores, supra.*

[53] *Bowman* v. *Wright* (1877) 4 R. 322; *Dowie* v. *Tennant* (1891) 18 R. 986; *Buchan* v. *Grimaldi* (1905) 7 F. 917; *Lindsay* v. *L's Trs.*, *infra.*

[54] *Lindsay* v. *L's Trs.*, 1922 S.L.T. 363.

[55] *McArthur* v. *McA.* (1842) 4 D. 354; *Smith* v. *Stuart* (1894) 22 R. 130.

[56] *Hastie* v. *Steel* (1886) 13 R. 843.

Similarly executors or trustees may on this ground be sued as such executors or trustees, though not personally.[57]

Presence of moveables

The Scottish courts probably have jurisdiction over a person only where moveables have been legally fixed within Scotland, as by arresting them,[58] and not merely by their presence. In proceedings as to proprietary or possessory rights over moveables, they have jurisdiction if the property is situated there.[59]

Arrestment of moveables ad fundandam jurisdictionem

Another ground of personal jurisdiction over a defender not 'domiciled' in Scotland is where moveable property of some commercial value[60] belonging or owed to the defender has been arrested in the hands of a third party within the jurisdiction.[61] Arrestments do not found jurisdiction if at the time they were laid on, the arrestee was under no liability to account to the defender.[62] The property arrested need not be connected with the subject of the action.[63] A decree based on this ground of jurisdiction may well not be recognized furth of Scotland,[64] and it is probably a good ground of jurisdiction only in actions for debt or damages.[65] A ship may be arrested to found jurisdiction only so long as still in port,[66] and need not be itself connected with the action.[67]

Prorogated jurisdiction

Personal jurisdiction may be conferred where parties prorogate the jurisdiction or submit themselves to it,[68] which may be done expressly,[69] or

---

[57] Robertson's Tr. v. Nicholson (1888) 15 R. 914; Ashurton v. Escombe (1892) 20 R. 187.

[58] Duncan v. Lodijensky (1904) 6 F. 408; cf. Miller v. Ure (1838) 16 S. 1294; Sch. 8, rule 2(8).

[59] Sch. 8, rule 2(9).

[60] Shaw v. Dow & Dobie (1869) 7 M. 449; Trowsdale's Tr. v. Forcett Ry. Co. (1870) 9 M. 88; Ross v. R. (1878) 5 R. 1013; Stenhouse London v. Allwright, 1972 S.L.T. 255.

[61] Cameron v. Chapman (1838) 16 S. 907; L.N.W. Ry. v. Lindsay (1858) 3 Macq. 99; North v. Stewart (1890) 17 R. (H.L.) 60; Leggat Bros. v. Gray, 1908 S.C. 67; O'Brien v. Davies, 1961 S.L.T. 85; Civil Jurisdiction and Judgments Act, 1982, Sch. 8, rule 2(8).

[62] Kerr v. R. & W. Ferguson, 1931 S.C. 736.

[63] Sheaf S.S. Co. v. Compania Transmediterranea, 1930 S.C. 660.

[64] Schibsby v. Westenholz (1870) L.R. 6 Q.B. 155; Emanuel v. Symon [1908] 1 K.B. 302.

[65] Grant v. G. (1867) 6 M. 155; Shaw, supra; Union Electric Co. v. Holman, 1913 S.C. 954.

[66] Carlberg v. Borjesson (1877) 5 R. (H.L.) 215; Administration of Justice Act, 1956, S. 45.

[67] Sheaf S.S. Co. v. Compania Transmediterranea, 1930 S.C. 573.

[68] Thompson v. Whitehead (1862) 24 D. 331; Gill v. Cutler (1895) 23 R. 371.

[69] e.g. International Exhibition v. Bapty (1891) 18 R. 843; Elderslie S.S. Co. v. Burrell (1895) 22 R. 389.

impliedly, as by lodging defences without objection to the jurisdiction,[70] but not in any case where the court could not competently exercise the jurisdiction.[71] It is questionable whether the courts can accept jurisdiction by prorogation where the case has no connection with Scotland or Scots law.[72]

Jurisdiction ex reconventione

It may also be conferred by reconvention, which doctrine holds that a person pursuing in the Scottish courts subjects himself to their jurisdiction in counter-actions[73] arising *ex eodem negotio*[74] or *ejusdem generis*,[75] unless the original action was one purely protective,[76] or he was involved in the actions in different capacities.[77]

Jurisdiction in personal actions cannot be founded on the defender's nationality, or domicile of origin being Scottish.

Jurisdiction in a personal action may be founded against executors, as such, if the executry estate is in Scotland, or both or all executors have been personally cited in Scotland, but not merely because the cause of action has arisen in Scotland.[78]

Jurisdiction in proceedings brought to assert, declare, or determine proprietary or possessory rights or rights in security in or over moveable property, or to obtain authority to dispose of moveable property, may be brought where the defender is resident for 3 months or where the property is situated;[79] in proceedings concerning a debt secured over immoveable property, the courts of the place where it is situated;[80] in proceedings as to a decision of a company or association, the place where the entity has its seat;[81] in proceedings concerning an arbitration in Scotland or under Scots law, the Court of Session;[82] in proceedings concerning the registration or validity in the U.K. of patents, trade marks, designs, or similar rights, the Court of Session.[83]

---

[70] *Assets Co. Ltd.* v. *Falla's Tr.* (1894) 22 R. 178; *Gill, supra.*
[71] *Ringer* v. *Churchill* (1840) 2 D. 307; 1982 Act, Sch. 8, rule 5.
[72] *Styring* v. *Mayor of Oporovec,* 1931 S.L.T. 493.
[73] *Thompson* v. *Whitehead* (1862) 24 D. 331; *Longworth* v. *Yelverton* (1868) 7 M. 70; *Davis* v. *Cadman* (1897) 24 R. 297.
[74] *Burrell* v. *Van Uden,* 1914, 2 S.L.T. 394.
[75] *Morison & Milne* v. *Massa* (1886) 5 M. 130; *Hurst Nelson & Co.* v. *Whatley,* 1912 S.C. 1041; *Munro* v. *Anglo-American Nitrogen Co.,* 1917, 1 S.L.T. 24.
[76] *Davis* v. *Cadman* (1897) 24 R. 297; *Macaulay* v. *Hussain,* 1966 S.C. 204.
[77] *Ponton's Exors* v. *P.,* 1913 S.C. 598.
[78] *Dalziel* v. *Coulthurst's Exors.,* 1934 S.C. 564.
[79] 1982 Act, Sch. 8, rule 2(9).
[80] Ibid., rule 2(11).
[81] Ibid., rule 2(12).
[82] Ibid., rule 2(13).
[83] Ibid., rule 2(14).

(e) ACTIONS IN REM

The only actions *in rem* are Admiralty actions to enable a person having a claim against a ship, its cargo or freight, or against an aircraft,[84] to have it satisfied out of the *res*. Such actions depend on effectiveness and the possibility of arresting the ship or aircraft within the jurisdiction.[85] Under the Administration of Justice Act, 1956, Ss. 45–50, the grounds of Admiralty jurisdiction are defined. The jurisdiction probably exists even though the claim involves land situated abroad.[86] By S. 47(1) arrest may be made of the ship concerned or of a sister ship wholly owned by the defender.[87]

(f) JURISDICTION IN TRUST QUESTIONS

No difficulty arises if all the trustees are in Scotland and the trust property in Scotland. The Scottish courts have jurisdiction over a person as settlor, trustee, or beneficiary of a trust domiciled in Scotland created by statute, written instrument, or evidenced in writing.[88] The Scottish courts have also exercised jurisdiction where the trust is governed by Scots law, and may be said to be domiciled in Scotland, even though the trustees are not otherwise subject to the jurisdiction.[89] They also have jurisdiction over a foreign trust if all the trustees are personally subject to the Scottish jurisdiction,[90] or if it owns heritage in Scotland.[91] The truster's Scottish domicile does not necessarily make his trust a Scottish one so as to give jurisdiction.

Two or more courts may claim jurisdiction[92] and it must be decided which is *forum conveniens*, having regard to the truster's domicile, the residence of his trustees, the language of the trust deed, and the situation of the major part of the trust funds.[93] It is for the court of the domicile of the trust to determine the powers to be exercised by the trustees and to decide any questions with the beneficiaries.[94] The court cannot in the

---

[84] e.g. *The Glider Standard Austria S.H.*, 1964 [1965] P. 463.
[85] *Castrique* v. *Imrie* (1870) L.R. 4 H.L. 414; *Carlberg* v. *Borjesson* (1877) 5 R. (H.L.) 215; 1982 Act, Sched. 9, para 6.
[86] *The Tolten* [1946] P. 135 (ship damaging wharf at Lagos.)
[87] Cf. *The St. Elefterio* [1957] P. 179.
[88] 1982 Act, Sch. 8, rule 2(7).
[89] *Cruikshanks* v. C. (1843) 5 D. 733; *Wick Mags.* v. *Forbes* (1849) 12 D. 299; *Kennedy* v. *K.* (1884) 12 R. 275; *Robertson's Tr.* v. *Nicholson* (1888) 15 R. 914; *Ashburton* v. *Escombe* (1892) 20 R. 187; 1982 Act, Sch. 1, Art. 5(6).
[90] *Peters* v. *Martin* (1852) 4 S. 107; *Hutchison* v. *H.*, 1912 1 S.L.T. 219; cf *Dalziel* v. *Coulthurst's Exors*, 1934 S.C. 564.
[91] *Charles* v. *C's Trs.* (1868) 6 M. 772; *Thomson* v. *Wilson's Trs.* (1895) 22 R. 866; *Mackay* v. *M.* (1897) 4 S.L.T. 337; *Jubert* v. *Church Commrs. for England*, 1952 S.C. 160.
[92] *Ewing* v. *Orr Ewing* (1883) 9 App. Cas. 34; *Orr Ewing's Trs.* v. *Orr Ewing* (1885) 13 R. (H.L.) 1.
[93] *Orr Ewing's Trs.*, supra; *Lawford* v. *L's Trs.*, 1927 S.C. 360.
[94] *Campbell, Petr.*, 1958 S.C. 275; *Campbell-Wyndham-Long's Trs.*, 1962 S.C. 132.

exercise of the *nobile officium* grant foreign trustees any indulgences not available to Scottish trustees.[95]

(g) JURISDICTION IN SUCCESSION

The *forum situs* has jurisdiction to determine whether property is immoveable or moveable in succession,[96] if indeed that distinction is relevant. The succession to immoveable property is governed by the *lex situs*[97] and the *forum situs* is alone competent to determine who is entitled on intestacy, or the validity of bequests, to administer the succession, and to grant the person entitled a legal title.[98] The succession to moveable property is determined by the *lex domicilii* and the *forum domicilii* has jurisdiction to determine who is entitled on intestacy, to adjudicate on the validity of, and interpret, a will[99] and to appoint and confirm executors,[1] but only to the extent of the estate situated within the jurisdiction. Estate situated elsewhere can be administered only under the authority of the courts there.[2]

The Scottish courts have jurisdiction to appoint or confirm an executor if there is property, heritable or moveable, in Scotland vested in the deceased, irrespective of his domicile.[3] The person selected as executor by the *forum domicilii* will normally be confirmed to the assets in Scotland by the Scottish courts.[4] As between Scotland and England or Northern Ireland, confirmation issued by a Scottish court has effect in those countries and has the effect of a grant of probate by the competent courts there.[5] The Scottish courts have jurisdiction in actions against executors if all of them are subject to its jurisdiction in personal actions,[6] or if the deceased's assets are within the jurisdiction[7] but not merely because an executor owns heritage in Scotland,[8] and if Scotland is not the place of the administration of the estate, there may be room for the plea of *forum non conveniens*.[9]

---

[95] *Horne's Trs.*, 1952 S.C. 70.
[96] *Downie* v. *D's Trs.* (1866) 4 M. 1067; *Monteith* v. *M's Trs.* (1882) 9 R. 982.
[97] Stair, More's Note A; Ersk. III, 8, 10.
[98] *Hewit's Trs.* v. *Lawson* (1891) 18 R. 793; *Foster* v. *F's Trs.*, 1923 S.C. 212.
[99] cf. *Elliot* v. *Joicey*, 1935 S.C. (H.L.) 57.
[1] Stair, More's Note A; Ersk. III, 9, 27.
[2] *Preston* v. *Melville* (1841) 2 Rob. App. 88.
[3] Executors (Sc.) Act, 1900, S. 6, amd. Succession (Sc.) Act, 1964, Sch. 2; *Hastings* v. *H's Exor.* (1852) 14 D. 489; *Goetze* v. *Aders* (1874) 2 R. 150.
[4] *Goetze, supra*.
[5] Administration of Estates Act, 1971, S. 1.
[6] *McTavish* v. *Saltoun*, 3 Feb. 1821, F.C.; *Peters* v. *Martin* (1825) 4 S. 107; *Dalziel* v. *Coulthurst's Exors.*, 1934 S.C. 564.
[7] *Grant's Trs.* v. *Douglas Heron & Co.* (1796) 3 Pat. 503.
[8] *Mackenzie* v. *Drummond's Exors.* (1868) 6 M. 932.
[9] *Macmaster* v. *MacM.* (1833) 11 S. 685.

(h) JURISDICTION AS TO CIVIL REMEDIES

If the Scottish courts have jurisdiction to adjudicate on a controversy they have jurisdiction to grant only those remedies which they may grant in cases raising no foreign element. Remedies can be granted, moreover, only subject to the qualifications, limitations, and restrictions applicable in purely Scottish cases. While the rights to awards of damages for particular kinds of losses arising from breach of contract or from delict are matters of substantive law,[10] the measure of the financial compensation, whether it is to be by a lump sum or by instalments, whether it carries interest or not, are matters for the *lex fori* exclusively.[11] Questions of remoteness of damage are matters of substantive law.[12] The Scottish courts can grant decrees for money in the currency in which the pursuer's loss was suffered.[13] Interdict may be sought in the courts where it is alleged that the wrong is likely to be committed.

(j) JURISDICTION IN BANKRUPTCY

By statute Scottish courts have jurisdiction to sequestrate the bankrupt estates of living, or deceased debtors if the debtor had an established place of business in Scotland, or was habitually resident there at any time in the year immediately preceding the presentation of the petition, or the date of death,[14] on their own petition, or on the petition of creditors if the debtor be apparently insolvent, or the petition of the trustee under a voluntary trust deed, and the estates of deceased debtors on the petition of an executor or a qualified creditor or creditors.[15] Scottish domicile does not by itself confer jurisdiction,[16] nor does arrestment *ad fundandam*,[17] but possession of heritage in Scotland may even though the debtor resides elsewhere.[18] Where a bankrupt has been carrying on business in two or more jurisdictions, he may be subject to the bankruptcy jurisdiction of both or all. The jurisdiction in which proceedings are initiated first may be held to exclude that of the other jurisdictions.[19]

A Scottish court in awarding sequestration confers no title to heritable

---

[10] *Kendrick* v. *Burnett* (1897) 25 R. 82; *McElroy* v. *McAllister*, 1949 S.C. 110.

[11] *Kohnke* v. *Karger* [1951] 2 K.B. 670.

[12] *J. D'Almeida Araujo Lda.* v. *Becker* [1953] 2 Q.B. 329.

[13] *Miliangos* v. *George Frank (Textiles) Ltd.* [1976] A.C. 443; *Commerzbank A/G* v. *Large*, 1977 S.C. 375. Under statutes embodying international conventions dates for conversion into sterling are frequently specified.

[14] Bankruptcy (Scotland) Act, 1985, S. 9. cf. *Hughes* v. *Stewart*, 1907 S.C. 791; *O'Brien* v. *Davies*, 1961 S.L.T. 85.

[15] Ibid., S. 5.

[16] *Obers* v. *Paton's Trs.* (1897) 24 R. 719.

[17] *Croil* (1863) 1 M. 509.

[18] *Joel* v. *Gill* (1859) 21 D. 929; *Croil, supra*; *Weinschel*, 1916 2 S.L.T. 91.

[19] *Goetze* v. *Aders* (1874) 2 R. 150; cf. *Young* v. *Buckle* (1864) 2 M. 1077; *Gibson* v. *Munro* (1894) 21 R. 840.

or real property outside Scotland, save in so far as the statute provides,[20] unless the Scottish title of the trustee is recognized by the *forum situs*. Creditors lodging claims thereby submit themselves to the jurisdiction of the Scottish courts in respect of the distribution of the estate.[21]

A discharge in bankruptcy must be granted by the courts which had power to make bankrupt. The effect of such a discharge depends on the *lex fori* of the discharging court;[22] a discharge by a Scottish court operates as a discharge within the United Kingdom of all debts and obligations contracted by him, or for which he was liable at the date of sequestration.[23]

(k) JURISDICTION AS TO ARBITRATIONS

The Court of Session has jurisdiction in proceedings concerning an arbitration conducted in Scotland or in which the procedure is governed by Scots law.[24]

(l) JURISDICTION UNDER INTERNATIONAL CONVENTIONS

Under various statutes giving effect to international conventions provision is made for jurisdiction. These concern actions for damage, loss of life or personal injury arising from ship collision,[25] nuclear occurrences,[26] oil pollution,[27] carriage by air,[28] by road,[29] by railway,[30] of passengers by road[31] and by sea.[32]

---

[20] 1985 Act, S. 31.
[21] *Barr* v. *Smith & Chamberlain* (1879) 7 R. 247.
[22] *Ellis* v. *McHenry* (1871) L.R. 6 C.P. 228.
[23] *Gill* v. *Barron* (1868) L.R. 2 P.C. 157; Bankruptcy (Sc.) Act, 1985, S. 55.
[24] Civil Jurisdiction and Judgments Act, 1982, Sch. 8, rule 2(13).
[25] Administration of Justice Act, 1956, S. 45.
[26] Nuclear Installations Act, 1965, S. 17; Nuclear Installations Act 1969.
[27] Merchant Shipping (Oil Pollution) Act, 1971, S. 13.
[28] Carriage by Air Act, 1961, amd Carriage by Air and Road Act, 1979, Sch. 1, Art. 28; Carriage by Air (Supplementary Provisions) Act, 1962, Sch. Art. VIII; Carriage by Air Acts (Application of Provisions) Order, 1967.
[29] Carriage of Goods by Road Act, 1965, Sch. Art. 31.
[30] International Transport Conventions Act, 1983, S. 1.
[31] Carriage of Passengers by Road Act, 1974, Sch. Art. 21.
[32] Merchant Shipping Act, 1979, Sch. 3, Art. 17.

CHAPTER 2.3

CHOICE OF LAW

Where the Scottish court decides that it can exercise jurisdiction over the defender or in respect of the particular cause of action in issue, it must then determine whether to decide the rights and duties of the parties according to Scots law or the law of some other system involved. The Scottish courts do not necessarily or always apply Scots law to a case before them, nor are all matters in issue in one case necessarily decided by the rules of the same legal system. In many branches of the law the rules for choice of law are vague or uncertain, frequently the decisions are inadequate, ambiguous, or hesitant, and frequently the decisions have been the subject of heavy criticism, so that it is difficult and dangerous to state the rules with any certainty.

The matters in dispute must first be classified or categorized to determine the juridical nature of the question for decision, as relating, e.g. to capacity to contract, or to the formalities of contract.[1] Secondly, the court must consider what legal system is indicated as appropriate by any connecting factors existing and relating the facts of that question and one or more particular systems of law. If the court decides that Scots law is applicable it must determine, if necessary after argument, what the content of the applicable rule is;[2] if it decides that a rule of foreign law is applicable it must ascertain, as a matter of fact, what the relevant rule prescribes.[3] Finally, the court must apply the rule thus revealed to the facts to reach a decision.

THE PROOF OF FOREIGN LAW

When the Scottish choice-of-law rules direct the Scottish court to apply rules of foreign law to determine the rights of parties, the Scottish court must not assume knowledge of the statutes, cases, or rules of that foreign system nor itself look at the textbooks of the foreign legal system.[4] Rules

---

[1] cf. Ch. 2.1, *supra*.
[2] Scots law in a Scottish court is a matter of law.
[3] Non-Scottish law in a Scottish court is a question of fact: see *infra*.
[4] Save that by the Evidence (Colonial Statutes) Act 1907, copies of laws made by the legislature of any British possession can be received in evidence if purporting to be printed by the government printer, without proof that they were so printed: *Papadopoulos* v. *P.* [1930] P. 55.

of foreign law are, in a Scottish case, matters of fact which must be averred as such and proved to the satisfaction of the court.[5] The onus of averment and of proof is on the party founding on the foreign law as being different from Scots law.[6] It is uncertain whether the evidence must be corroborated; probably it must.[7] If he fails to make adequate averments of the foreign law, the case must be decided by Scots law.[8]

The House of Lords, however, has judicial knowledge of all the legal systems of the U.K. and the law of each part of the U.K. is a matter of law, not of fact, in an appeal to it from another part.[9]

Unless parties lodge an agreed statement of the foreign law, or of consent remit to a foreign lawyer for his opinion,[10] or consent to the judge investigating the issue for himself,[11] foreign law must be proved by expert witnesses, who must normally be practising members of the legal profession in the legal system in question,[12] or at least hold an office which requires practical acquaintance with that legal system,[13] giving oral expert opinion evidence, and not, in general, by persons who have only an academic knowledge of that legal system.[14] If the evidence as to foreign law is uncontradicted the court must accept it, unless the result is absurd.[15] If there is a conflict of evidence on the foreign law the court must interpret that law in the light of the evidence,[16] and once foreign law has been proved the court must interpret the evidence as law, not fact.[16] The court may, however, itself interpret an agreed statement of foreign law.[14]

---

[5] *Rosses v. Bhagvat Sinhjee* (1891) 19 R. 31; *Stuart v. Potter, Choate & Prentice*, 1911, 1 S.L.T. 377; *Higgins v. Ewing's Trs.*, 1925 S.C. 440; *Kolbin v. Kinnear*, 1930 S.C. 724, 737; *Faulkner v. Hill*, 1942 J.C. 20; *McElroy v. McAllister*, 1949 S.C. 110.

[6] *Immanuel v. Denholm* (1887) 15 R. 152; *Dynamit A/G v. Rio Tinto Co.* [1918] A.C. 260, 295; *De Reneville v. De R.* [1948] P. 100; *Prawdzic-Lazarska v. P.L.*, 1954 S.C. 98.

[7] It was in *Parnell v. Walter* (1889) 16 R. 917, and *Rosses, supra*. But see *Galbraith v. G.*, 1971 S.C. 65; *Bain v. B.*, 1971 S.C. 146.

[8] *Lloyd v. Guibert* (1865) L.R. 1 Q.B. 115; *Dynamit A/G, supra*; *Rodden v. Whatlings, Ltd.*, 1961 S.C. 132; *Pryde v. Proctor & Gamble*, 1971 S.L.T. (Notes) 18; *Bonnor v. Balfour Kilpatrick*, 1974 S.L.T. 187.

[9] *Stein's Assignee v. Gibson & Craig* (1831) 5 W. & S. 47; *Cooper v. C.* (1888) 15 R. (H.L.) 21; *Municipal Council of Johannesburg v. Stewart*, 1909 S.C. (H.L.) 53; *Elliot v. Joicey*, 1935 S.C. (H.L.) 57. See also *Inland Revenue v. Glasgow Police Athletic Assocn.*, 1953 S.C. (H.L.) 13; *MacShannon v. Rockware Glass Ltd.* [1978] A.C. 795.

[10] *Welsh v. Milne* (1845) 7 D. 213; *Higgins v. Ewing's Trs.*, 1925 S.C. 440.

[11] *Jabbour v. Custodian of Israeli Absentee Property* [1954] 1 W.L.R. 139, 147.

[12] *Parnell v. Walter* (1889) 16 R. 917; (1890) 17 R. 552; *Rosses v. Bhagvat Sinhjee* (1891) 19 R. 31; but see *Said Ajami v. Comptroller of Customs* [1954] 1 W.L.R. 1405.

[13] *Sussex Peerage Case* (1844) 11 Cl. & F. 85; *In bonis Dhost Aly Khan* (1880) 6 P.D. 6.

[14] *Bristow v. Sequeville* (1850) 19 L.J. Ex. 289; *In the goods of Bonelli* (1875) L.R. 1 P.D. 69; contrast *Brailey v. Rhodesia Consolidated Ltd.* [1910] 2 Ch. 95; *In the goods of Whitelegg* [1899] P. 267.

[15] *Buerger v. N.Y. Life Assce. Co.* (1926) 96 L.J.K.B. 930; *Koechlin v. Kestenbaum* [1927] 1 K.B. 616; *Sharif v. Azad* [1967] 1 Q.B. 605.

[16] *Kolbin v. Kinnear*, 1930 S.C. 724; *Lazard Bros. v. Midland Bank* [1933] A.C. 289; *Tallina Laevauhisus v. Estonian State S.S. Line* (1947) 80 Ll.L.R. 99.

Judicial ascertainment of foreign law

Statutory provisions permit Scottish courts to state and remit a case to a foreign court for a statement of its opinion on its own law applicable to the case. The British Law Ascertainment Act, 1859, authorizes a court[17] in one part of Her Majesty's dominions to prepare a case, setting out questions of law on which they desire to have the opinion of another court, and remit it[18] there for opinion.[19] A certified copy of the opinion being returned, the remitting court must apply the opinion on law to the facts. The Privy Council or House of Lords on appeal may reject the opinion if of a court whose judgments are reviewable by it.

The Foreign Law Ascertainment Act, 1861, authorizes superior courts within Her Majesty's dominions to remit a case, with questions of law, to a court of any foreign state with which a convention has been made for the purpose, and conversely.

Exclusion of foreign law otherwise applicable

The court will not, however, give effect to a rule of a foreign system of law which would otherwise be applicable if it conflicts with the policy of Scots law.[20] In at least three sets of circumstances the foreign law will be rejected. These are where the foreign law is of a penal nature, such as confiscatory legislation,[21] where it is part of the foreign revenue system, such as for the recovery of tax,[22] and where the rule of foreign law is contrary to the British concept of public policy,[23] such as a rule permitting what was to British eyes an illegal agreement,[24] or a contract contrary to good foreign relations,[25] or is contrary to British views of morality or the principles of justice.

---

[17] Including a Lord Ordinary: *Hewit's Trs.* v. *Lawson* (1891) 18 R. 793; *Macomish's Exors.* v. *Jones*, 1932 S.C. 108. The court may refuse to settle a case: *MacDougall* v. *Chitnavis*, 1937 S.C. 390.

[18] *Guthrie* (1880) 7 R. 1141.

[19] Cf. *Bradford* v. *Young* (1884) 11 R. 1135; *D. Wellington's Exor.*, 1946 S.C. 32.

[20] *Connal* v. *Loder* (1868) 6 M. 1095, 1110; *Brodin* v. *A/R Seljan*, 1973 S.L.T. 198.

[21] *Banco de Vizcaya* v. *Don Alfonso de Borbon y Austria* [1935] 1 K.B. 140; cf. *Huntington* v. *Attrill* [1893] A.C. 150; *Luther* v. *Sagor* [1921] 3 K.B. 532.

[22] *A.G. for Canada* v. *Schulze* (1901) 9 S.L.T. 4; *Raulin* v. *Fischer* [1911] 2 K.B. 93; *Govt. of India* v. *Taylor* [1955] A.C. 491; *Peter Buchanan Ltd. & McHarg* v. *McVey* [1955] A.C. 516 n.

[23] *Dynamit A/G* v. *Rio Tinto Co. Ltd.* [1918] A.C. 292.

[24] *Grell* v. *Levy* (1864) 16 C.B. (N.S.) 73; *Kaufman* v. *Gerson* [1904] 1 K.B. 591; *Addison* v. *Brown* [1954] 2 All E.R. 213.

[25] *Robson* v. *Premier Oil and Pipe Line Co.* [1915] 2 Ch. 124; *Foster* v. *Driscoll* [1929] 1 K.B. 470; *Regazzoni* v. *Sethia* [1958] A.C. 301.

THE LAW APPROPRIATE IN PARTICULAR QUESTIONS

Status—legitimacy or bastardy

The legitimacy or otherwise of a child must be determined by the *lex domicilii* of the father at the time of the child's birth,[26] or, if the father were unknown or the child posthumous, that of the mother. Hence the children of a man's several polygamous marriages may all be legitimate *lege paterni domicilii*,[27] and the child of a putative marriage is legitimate if the father's or mother's domicile is Scottish.[28]

Whether a child has been legitimated or not, *per subsequens matrimonium* or otherwise,[29] depends on whether the *lex domicilii* of the father at the time of the birth and of the subsequent marriage or other act or events alleged to effect legitimation recognizes that result.[30] The place of birth and of the later marriage are irrelevant.[31] If the father's domicile has changed the domicile at marriage probably rules.[32]

Parent and child

Declarator of legitimacy or of bastardy determines whether a person has the status of legal parent *vis-à-vis* his child or merely that of natural parent, and conversely. The extent of the parent's rights and duties of maintenance, education, and correction, and over the child's property probably depend on the law of the place of residence, or in the case of a child's immoveable property, on the *lex situs* of the property. Hence the rights of all parents residing with their children in Scotland are determined by Scots law, and similarly with the rights of children against parents.

Guardian and ward

Whether a person has been duly constituted guardian of another, and the extent of his rights as such, depends on the law of the country where the ward was domiciled or resident when the guardian was appointed,[33] or

---

[26] *Birtwhistle* v. *Vardill* (1835) 2 Cl. & F. 571; *Fenton* v. *Livingstone* (1859) 21 D. (H.L.) 10; *Beattie* v. *B.* (1866) 5 M. 181; *Re Goodman's Trusts* (1881) 17 Ch. D. 266; *Re Grove* (1888) 40 Ch. D. 216.

[27] *Bamgbose* v. *Daniel* [1955] A.C. 107.

[28] *Smijth* v. *S.*, 1918, 1 S.L.T. 156.

[29] As in *Re Luck* [1940] Ch. 864.

[30] *Shedden* v. *Patrick* (1808) 5 Pat. 194; *Munro* v. *M.* (1840) 1 Rob. 492; *Udny* v. *U.* (1869) 7 M. (H.L.) 89; *Re Grove* (1888) 40 Ch. D. 216; *Blair* v. *Kay's Trs.*, 1940 S.L.T. 464. See also Legitimation (Sc.) Act, 1968, S. 5.

[31] *Munro* v. *M.* (1840) 1 Rob. 492; *Shaw* v. *Gould* (1865) L.R. 3 H.L. 55; *Re Goodman's Trusts* (1881) 17 Ch. D. 266; *Re Andros* (1883) 24 Ch. D. 637; *Blair* v. *Kay's Trs.*, 1940 S.L.T. 464.

[32] *Munro, supra*; *McDouall* v. *Adair* (1852) 14 D. 525; *Aikman* v. *A.* (1859) 21 D. 757.

[33] *Sawyer* v. *Sloan* (1875) 3 R. 271; *Seddon* (1891) 19 R. 101, (1893) 20 R. 675; *Atherstone's Trs.* (1896) 24 R. 39; *Elder* (1903) 5 F. 307; *McFadzean*, 1917 S.C. 142.

where the ward has property requiring protection.[34] The Court of Session is the proper, and probably the only competent, court for deciding any question relating to rights to Scottish heritage.[35]

Engagement to marry

Whether a broken engagement to marry is actionable and, if so, what kinds of loss are relevant for consideration in assessing damages may be determined by the proper law of the contract or possibly by the law of the intended matrimonial domicile.[36]

Marriage

In an action of declarator of marriage or of nullity of marriage, whether as being null *ab initio* or as having been voidable and now being avoided, the existence or not of marriage depends on whether in respect of capacity, each party had capacity by the law of his or her antenuptial domicile,[37] in respect of formalities, such as notice, banns, witnesses, consent, need for parental consent, ceremony, registration,[38] need for personal presence,[39] and the like, the marriage satisfied the requirements of the *lex loci celebrationis*,[40] and in respect of essentials of validity such as legal capacity or disability to marry,[41] consanguinity,[42] monogamous nature,[43] genuine consent,[44] sexual potency,[45] it satisfied the *lex domicilii* of each party,[46] or possibly the law of the matrimonial domicile,[47] unless

---

[34] cf. *Stuart v. Moore* (1861) 23 D. 902; *Nugent v. Vetzera* (1866) L.R. 2 Eq. 704.

[35] *Ogilvie v. O's Trs.*, 1927 S.L.T. 83.

[36] cf. *Hamlyn v. Talisker Distillery* (1894) 21 R. (H.L.) 21; *Hansen v. Dixon* (1906) 23 T.L.R. 56; *Kremezi v. Ridgway* [1949] 1 All E.R. 662; Webb and Brown, 15 I.C.L.Q. 947.

[37] Marriage (Sc.) Act, 1977, Ss. 1–2; *Shaw v. Gould* (1868) L.R. 3 H.L. 55.

[38] *Compton v. Bearcroft* (1767) 2 Hagg. Con. 444, note (Gretna Green runaways); *Dalrymple v. D.* (1811) 2 Hagg. Con. 54; *Simonin v. Mallac* (1860) 2 S. & T. 67; *Ogden v. O.* [1908] P. 46; *Bliersbach v. McEwen*, 1959 S.C. 43. See also *Pease v. P.*, 1967 S.C. 112; *Hoy v. H.*, 1968 S.C. 179. This element would be better classified as an element of essential validity.

[39] *Apt v. A.* [1948] P. 83; *Ponticelli v. P.* [1958] P. 204.

[40] *Warrender v. W.* (1835) 2 S. & MacL. 154; *Cullen v. Gossage* (1850) 12 D. 633; *Macdonald v. M.* (1863) 1 M. 854; *Berthiaume v. Dastous* [1930] A.C. 79; *Di Rollo v. Di R.*, 1959 S.C. 75 (valid notwithstanding ecclesiastical ruling that void).

[41] *Shaw v. Gould* (1868) L.R. 3 H.L. 55; *Chetti v. C.* [1909] P. 67; *Macdougall v. Chitnavis*, 1937 S.C. 390; *Pugh v. P.* [1951] P. 482; *R. v. Brentwood Registrar, ex p. Arias* [1968] 3 W.L.R. 531; Marriage (Sc.) Act, 1977, S. 1.

[42] *Mette v. M.* (1859) 1 S. & T. 416; *Brook v. B.* (1861) 9 H.L.C. 193; *De Thoren v. Wall* (1876) 3 R. (H.L.) 28; *Sottomayor v. de Barros* (1877) 3 P.D. 1; (1879) 5 P.D. 94; *Webster v. W's Tr.* (1886) 14 R. 90; *Martin v. Buret*, 1938 S.L.T. 479; *Cheni v. C.* [1965] P. 85.

[43] *Hyde v. H.* (1866) L.R. 1 P. & D. 130; *Lendrum v. Chakravarti*, 1929 S.L.T. 96; *Ali v. A.* [1968] P. 564.

[44] *Kenward v. K.* [1951] P. 124; *H. v. H.* [1954] P. 258; *Di Rollo v. Di R.*, 1959 S.C. 75.

[45] *De Reneville v. De R.* [1948] P. 100.

[46] *Kenward v. K.* [1951] P. 124; *Pugh, supra.*

[47] *Warrender v. W.* (1835) 2 S. & MacL. 154; *Brook v. B.* (1861) 9 H.L.C. 193; *Mackinnon's Trs. v. I.R.*, 1920 S.C. (H.L.) 171; cf. *Ramsay-Fairfax v. R.F.* [1956] P. 115.

one party only is subject to a domiciliary incapacity of a kind not recognized by Scots law.[48] Whether a particular element belongs to formalities or to essential validity is determined by Scots law as *lex fori*.[49] It is uncertain whether in respect of essential validity a marriage must also satisfy the *lex loci celebrationis*.[50] A marriage may be declared to exist, though Scots law would not declare it null nor dissolve it by divorce.[51]

Compliance in formalities with the *lex loci celebrationis* is not, however, demanded where there is no local form,[52] or it is inappropriate,[53] or the marriage satisfies the Foreign Marriages Acts, 1892 to 1947, the Foreign Marriage Order, 1970[54] and the Foreign Marriages (Armed Forces) Orders, 1964 and 1965.

The court has held that an alleged rule of foreign law that a bigamous marriage was validated by the death of the first wife was not one which the Scottish courts were obliged to recognize.[55]

Judicial separation

The entitlement or not of the pursuer to a decree of judicial separation depends entirely on Scots law, as *lex fori*, because it is for the local system to give protection to a resident, whether or not the wrongs were committed within the jurisdiction, and because the decree does not fundamentally affect the status of the persons as married but only alters their mutual rights and duties.

Nullity of marriage

Whether a marriage is null for incapacity or lack of consent is probably determined by the law of the party's antenuptial domicile, and whether voidable for impotence is probably determined by Scots law.[56]

Divorce

Where the court has jurisdiction, the right of the pursuer to the remedy sought depends on Scots law, as *lex domicilii*, or possibly as *lex fori*,

---

[48] e.g. disability by religion: *Scott* v. *A.G.* (1886) L.R. 11 P.D. 128; *Chetti, supra; Macdougall* v. *Chitnavis*, 1937 S.C. 390. cf. *Sottomayor* v. *De Barros* (1879) 5 P.D. 94.

[49] *Bliersbach* v. *McEwen*, 1959 S.C. 43.

[50] cf. *Breen* v. *B.* [1964] P. 144.

[51] *Baindail* v. *B.* [1946] P. 122; *Muhammad* v. *Suna*, 1956 S.C. 366; *Risk* v. *R.* [1951] P. 50.

[52] *Barclay* v. *B.* (1849) 22 Sc. Jur. 127; *Lauderdale Peerage Case* (1885) 10 App. Cas. 692; *Wolfenden* v. *W.* [1946] P. 61; *Penhas* v. *Tan Soo Eng* [1953] A.C. 304.

[53] *Re Bethell* (1887) 38 Ch. D. 220; *Taczanowska* v. *T.* [1957] P. 301; *Kochanski* v. *K.* [1958] P. 147; *Merker* v. *M* [1963] P. 283.

[54] cf. *Hay* v. *Northcote* [1900] 2 Ch. 262.

[55] *Prawdzic-Lazarska* v. *P.L.*, 1954 S.C. 98.

[56] cf. *Aldridge* v. *A.*, 1954 S.C. 58; *Ramsay-Fairfax* v. *R.F.* [1956] P. 115.

irrespective of the place of marriage, of residence, of the place of the matrimonial breakdown, and of whether the marriage was dissoluble by the *lex loci celebrationis*.[57] The issues fall to be determined as if both parties were domiciled in Scotland, i.e. by Scots law.[58] Dissolution of marriage on the ground of presumed death is regulated by Scots law.

Guardianship

The rights and powers of a guardian are determined by the system of law under which he is appointed, save that a guardian appointed by the *lex domicilii* of a foreign infant has no authority to grant a discharge valid to exonerate trustees transferring Scottish heritage.[59]

Adoption

If the Scottish court has jurisdiction it applies Scots law, save that in the case of a convention adoption[60] some questions may be governed by the legal system of the child's domicile or residence.[61]

Unincorporated associations

Whether an association has any existence or personality distinct from those of its members depends on the legal system of the country where the association has been formed.[62] In the absence of contrary evidence the character of a particular association will be presumed to be like its nearest Scottish counterpart.[63] An association's powers and legal capacities will be determined by the law of its country of creation, save that it probably could not in Scotland be conceded the ability or power to do anything for which no legal facilities exist by Scots law.

Corporations

The nationality of a corporation depends on the country where it is incorporated. The domicile of a corporation is the country by whose laws it is incorporated,[64] and its status, powers, and characteristics are determined by that law,[65] as also are its internal affairs.[66] A corporation may

---

[57] *Warrender* v. *W.* (1835) 2 S. & MacL. 154; *Jack* v. *J.* (1862) 24 D. 467, 475.
[58] Domicile and Matrimonial Proceedings Act, 1973, S. 7.
[59] *Ogilvy* v. *O's Trs.*, 1927 S.L.T. 83.
[60] Children Act, 1975.
[61] *Re. B. (S.)* [1968] Ch. 204.
[62] *Edinburgh and Glasgow Bank* v. *Ewan* (1852) 14 D. 547.
[63] *Reid and McCall* v. *Douglas*, 11 June 1814, F.C.; *Muir* v. *Collett* (1862) 24 D. 1119.
[64] *Leith and Flensburg Shipping Co. Ltd.*, 1925 S.N. 111; *Carse* v. *Coppen*, 1951 S.C. 233.
[65] *Carse, supra; Carl Zeiss Stiftung* v. *Rayner and Keeler* [1967] 1 A.C. 853.
[66] *Branley* v. *S.E. Ry.* (1862) 12 C.B. (N.S.) 63.

be resident in as many countries as it carries on business in. But a corporation formed elsewhere cannot by Scots law do what is illegal by Scots law or anything for which no facilities exist by Scots law.[67] A company incorporated outside Great Britain which carried on business in Scotland but has ceased to do so may be wound up by the Scottish courts, even if it has been dissolved by the law of its place of incorporation.[68]

Promises and contracts

In modern practice it is recognized that one legal system is not necessarily appropriate for application to all matters affecting a contract; the court must select the 'proper law' of the contract, namely that which the parties intended to apply,[69] or would presumably have intended if they had considered the matter,[70] or that with which the contract has the most substantial connection,[71] and this may vary where different parts of the contract are deemed to have been intended to be governed by different laws. Where the parties clearly express their intention, this is normally decisive.[72] Failing that, it has to be inferred from the terms of the contract and concomitant circumstances.[73] Some assistance may be got from presumptions in favour of the *lex loci contractus*,[74] or the *lex loci solutionis*,[75] or the *lex situs* of moveables,[76] or the *lex situs* of immoveables,[77] or the law of the flag of a ship.[78] The choice of arbitration in one country is normally deemed a choice of the arbiter's system of

[67] *Carse, supra;* rule now altered by Companies Act, 1985, S. 462.
[68] Companies Act, 1985, S. 670; *Marshall* (1895) 22 R. 697.
[69] *Lloyd* v. *Guibert* (1865) L.R. 1 Q.B. 115; *Hamlyn* v. *Talisker Distillery* (1894) 21 R. (H.L.) 21; *Mount Albert B.C.* v. *Australian Temperance Socy.* [1938] A.C. 224; *Vita Food Products* v. *Unus Shipping Co.* [1939] A.C. 277.
[70] *Lloyd, supra; Mount Albert B.C.* v. *Australian Life Assce. Socy. Ltd.* [1938] A.C. 224; *The Assunzione* [1954] P. 150.
[71] *Boissevain* v. *Weil* [1950] A.C. 327; *Bonython* v. *Australia* [1951] A.C. 201; *Whitworth Street Estates, Ltd.* v. *Miller & Partners* [1970] A.C. 583.
[72] *Girvin, Roper & Co.* v. *Monteith* (1895) 23 R. 129; *Salt Mines Syndicate* (1895) 2 S.L.T. 489; *Montgomery* v. *Zarifi*, 1918 S.C. (H.L.) 128; *Bayley* v. *Johnstone*, 1928 S.N. 153; *Drummond* v. *Bell-Irving*, 1930 S.C. 704; *Vita Food Products* v. *Unus Shipping Co.* [1939] A.C. 277; *The Assunzione* [1954] P. 150, 175. For a case where it was held not decisive see *English* v. *Donnelly*, 1958 S.C. 494.
[73] *The Metamorphosis* [1953] 1 W.L.R. 543.
[74] The term *locus contractus* may mean the place of making the contract, but in general means the locality of the contract, as ascertained from its nature and what is to be done under it: *Parken* v. *Royal Exchange Assce. Co.* (1846) 8 D. 365, 374; *Valery* v. *Scott* (1876) 3 R. 965, 967.
[75] *Valery, supra.*
[76] *Connal* v. *Loder* (1868) 6 M. 1095; *Todd* v. *Armour* (1882) 9 R. 901; *Shedlock* v. *Hannay* (1891) 18 R. 663; *Inglis* v. *Robertson & Baxter* (1898) 25 R. (H.L.) 70; *Forbes* v. *Receiver in Bankruptcy*, 1924 S.L.T. 522.
[77] *Mackintosh* v. *May* (1895) 22 R. 345; *Bank of Africa* v. *Cohen* [1909] 2 Ch. 129.
[78] *Lloyd* v. *Guibert* (1865) L.R. 1 Q.B. 115; *Immanuel* v. *Denholm* (1887) 15 R. 152; *R.* v. *International Trustee* [1937] A.C. 500, 529; *The Assunzione* [1954] P. 150.

law.[79] The use of the legal terminology of one system may indicate that that system should apply.[80] Other factors, such as the nationality, domicile, or residence of parties, may yield some indication of the proper law.

In relation to capacity to contract, the proper law is normally the *lex loci contractus*,[81] except, probably, in the case of contracts relating to immoveable property, where it is the *lex situs*, and marriage contracts, where it may be the law of the intended matrimonial domicile.[82] What formalities of constitution need to be observed for validity, and whether they have been satisfied, generally falls to be regulated by the *lex loci contractus*[83] or by the proper law.[84]

The proper law also determines the essential validity of the contract,[85] whether there has been consensus or not,[86] and the effect of alleged vitiating factors. Thus English courts have declined to enforce a contract illegal by the *lex loci contractus*,[87] or by the *lex loci solutionis*,[88] and Scottish courts have refused to enforce a contract legal by the *lex loci contractus* but illegal by Scots law,[89] and one to which English law was agreed to be applicable, when it contravened a Scottish Act.[90] In relation to contracts constituted by a bill of exchange, the choice of law to regulate the rights of parties is determined by statute.[91]

The interpretation of the parties' undertakings must probably be according to the proper law of the contract.[92]

Questions as to the due performance, or breach or discharge, of the contract and of remoteness of damages fall to be determined by the

---

[79] *Hamlyn v. Talisker Distillery* (1894) 21 R. (H.L.) 21; *Girvin. Roper & Co., supra*; *Robertson v. Brandes, Schonwald & Co.* (1906) 8 F. 815; *Kwik Hoo Tong v. Finlay* [1927] A.C. 604; *Naamlooze Vennootschap v. A/S Ludwig Mowinckels Rederi* [1938] 2 All E.R. 152; *Tzortzis v. Monark Line* [1968] 1 All E.R. 949. But see *Compagnie d'Armement Maritime v. Compagnie Tunisienne de Navigation* [1970] 3 All E.R. 71.

[80] *Pender v. Commercial Bank*, 1940 S.L.T. 306.

[81] *Male v. Roberts* (1799) 3 Esp. 163; *De Virte v. Macleod* (1869) 7 M. 347; *McFeetridge v. Stewarts and Lloyds*, 1913 S.C. 773.

[82] *Cooper v. C's Trs.* (1888) 15 R. (H.L.) 21.

[83] *Guepratte v. Young* (1851) 4 De G. & Sm. 217.

[84] *Tayler v. Scott* (1847) 9 D. 1504; *Valery v. Scott* (1876) 3 R. 965.

[85] *Corbet v. Waddell* (1879) 7 R. 200; *Todd v. Armour* (1882) 9 R. 901; *Scottish Provident Instn. v. Cohen* (1888) 16 R. 112; *Shedlock v. Hannay* (1891) 18 R. 663; *Forbes v. Official Receiver in Bankruptcy*, 1924 S.L.T. 522; *Pender v. Commercial Bank*, 1940 S.L.T. 306; cf. *Hamlyn v. Talisker Distillery* (1894) 21 R. (H.L.) 21.

[86] *Albeko Schumaschinen v. Kamborian* (1961) 111 L.J. 519.

[87] *Vita Food Products Co. v. Unus Shipping Co.* [1939] A.C. 277.

[88] *Ralli Bros. v. Compania Naviera Sota y Aznar* [1920] 2 K.B. 287; *Boissevain v. Weil* [1950] A.C. 327; cf. *Regazzoni v. Sethia* [1958] A.C. 301.

[89] *Luszczewska v. L.*, 1953 S.L.T. (Notes) 73; cf. *O'Toole v. Whiterock Quarry Co.*, 1937 S.L.T. 521; *Duncan v. Motherwell Bridge Co.*, 1952 S.C. 131; contrast *Clayton v. C.*, 1937 S.C. 619.

[90] *English v. Donnelly*, 1958 S.C. 494.

[91] Bills of Exchange Act, 1882, S. 72; see also *Stewart v. Gelot* (1871) 9 M. 1057.

[92] *Henderson's Trs. v. H.* (1868) 5 S.L.R. 394; *Hamlyn, supra*; *Robertson v. Brandes, Schonwald & Co.* (1906) 8 F. 815; see also *Mackintosh v. May* (1895) 22 R. 345.

proper law, normally *lex loci solutionis*.[93] Procedure, evidence, prescription,[94] and measure of damages are, however, determined by the *lex fori*.[95] Damages may be assessed in foreign currency as at the date of the breach, or the sterling equivalent at the date when the court authorizes enforcement.[96]

Contracts relating to land

In this case the proper law is normally the *lex situs*.[97]

Contracts of employment

Such a contract is regulated by its proper law,[98] but many rules regulative of employment in Scotland will apply whatever the proper law of a contract.[99]

Effect of statutes

Certain statutes applicable to contracts make their own provisions. The Bills of Exchange Act, 1882, contains its own code of conflicts provisions as to bills. Others[1] contain provisions defining the scope of rules of English or Scottish domestic law and a statute may be held applicable to a contract, irrespective of its proper law, to give effect to its policy.[2]

Carriage by Air Act, 1961, and Carriage by Air (Supplementary Provisions) Act, 1962, amended by Carriage by Air and Road Act, 1979

These acts give effect to international conventions, applicable to the carriage of goods, passengers, and luggage by air, and substitute for the law which might be otherwise applicable the rules in the convention.[3]

Carriage of Goods by Road Act

The Carriage of Goods by Road Act, 1965, gives effect to an international convention scheduled to the Act. The convention applies to every

---

[93] *Parken* v. *Royal Exchange Assce. Co.* (1846) 8 D. 365; *Valery* v. *Scott* (1876) 3 R. 965; *Dallas* v. *McArdle*, 1949 S.C. 481; *J. D'Almeida Araujo* v. *Becker* [1953] 2 Q.B. 329.

[94] *Don* v. *Lippmann* (1837) 2 S. & Macl. 682; *Higgins* v. *Ewing's Trs.*, 1925 S.C. 440.

[95] *B.L. Co.* v. *Drummond* (1830) 10 B. & C. 903; *Westminster Bank* v. *McDonald*, 1955 S.L.T. (Notes) 73; *Stirling's Trs.* v. *Legal and General Assce. Soc. Ltd.*, 1957 S.L.T. 73.

[96] *Miliangos* v. *George Frank (Textiles) Ltd.* [1976] A.C. 443.

[97] *Mackintosh, supra; Higgins* v. *Ewing's Trs.*, 1925 S.C. 490; *Whitworth St. Estates Ltd.* v. *Miller & Partners* [1970] A.C. 583.

[98] *Sayers* v. *International Drilling Co.* [1971] 3 All E.R. 163.

[99] *Brodin* v. *A/R Seljan*, 1973 S.C. 213; cf. *Duncan* v. *Motherwell Bridge Co.*, 1952 S.C. 131.

[1] e.g. Carriage of Goods by Sea Act, 1971; Contracts of Employment Act, 1972.

[2] *Duncan* v. *Motherwell Bridge Co.*, 1952 S.C. 131; *English* v. *Donnelly*, 1958 S.C. 494.

[3] See further Ch. 4.19, *infra*. See also Hovercraft (Civil Liability) Order, 1979.

contract for the carriage of goods by road in vehicles for reward, when the place of taking over of the goods and the place designated for delivery are situated in two different countries, of which at least one is a contracting party.[4] It substitutes the rules of the convention for any rules otherwise applicable.[5]

Carriage of Goods by Sea Act, 1971

This Act applies to the carriage of goods by sea from ports in the United Kingdom under a contract providing for the issue of a bill of lading or similar document of title, and where it applies supersedes any rules which might otherwise apply to the contract.[6]

International Transport Conventions Act, 1983

The liability of a railway for damage caused to passengers by an accident on the territory of a state which is a party to the Convention scheduled to the Act is governed by the Convention.[7]

Carriage of Passengers by Road Act, 1974

This Act regulates contracts for international carriage and provides for the legal system to be applied.[8]

Carriage of Passengers and Luggage by Sea

The Merchant Shipping Act, 1979, Sch. 3 gives effect to a convention and regulates the law applicable to claims.

Uniform Laws on International Sales

The Uniform Laws on International Sales Act, 1967, S. 1, gives the force of law in the United Kingdom to the Uniform Law on the International Sale of Goods in Schedule 1 of the Act, being the convention on that topic done at the Hague in 1964. While an Order in Council is in force declaring that a declaration by the United Kingdom has been made[9] the Uniform Law applies to a contract of sale only if chosen by the parties to the contract as the law of the contract.

Section 2 of the same Act gives the force of law also to the Uniform Law on the Formation of Contracts for the International Sale of Goods in Schedule 2 of the Act, also being a convention done at the Hague in 1964,

[4] Art. 1.
[5] See further Ch. 4.17, infra.
[6] See further Ch. 4.18, infra.
[7] See further Ch. 4.17, infra.
[8] Sch. Arts. 10, 12, 23, 24.
[9] None has yet been made.

but not to negotiations before an Order in Council brings the convention into force.

Restitution

A person can probably claim restitution, repayment, recompense, or reward for *negotiorum gestio* if Scots law is the proper law of the relationship giving rise to the claim.[10]

Delicts

A preliminary question, sometimes difficult, may arise of the place where a delict was committed. This is probably where the harm was suffered.[11] A question of a particular pursuer's title to sue depends on whether he could, in that capacity, claim both under Scots law and according to the law under which he claims a particular remedy.[12] The defender's liability similarly depends on his being liable under both systems involved. The rights and liabilities of parties have to be determined by reference to both the *lex loci delicti* and Scots law as *lex fori*; the defender's conduct is actionable in Scotland as a delict only if, and in so far as, it is civilly actionable by both those systems,[13] and not if by either system it is innocent[14] or legalized[15] or subjects to no civil liability[16] or is no longer actionable by reason of lapse of time.[17] If it is so civilly actionable the pursuer's rights are those of the *lex loci delicti*.[18] Questions of remoteness of liability or of injury, or adequacy of causal connection between conduct and harm all fall to be determined by the *lex loci delicti*.[19] Evidence, the effect of lapse of time, measure of damages, remoteness of damage, procedure, and enforcement are determined solely by the *lex fori*.[20] A

---

[10] *Rae v. Wright* (1717) Mor. 4506; *Batthyany v. Walford* (1887) 36 Ch. D. 269; *Cantiere San Rocco v. Clyde Shipbuilding Co.*, 1923 S.C. (H.L.) 105.

[11] *Longworth v. Hope* (1865) 3 M. 1049; *Parnell v. Walter* (1889) 16 R. 917; *Evans v. Stein* (1904) 7 F. 65; *Thomson v. Kindell*, 1910 2 S.L.T. 442. But see *Rosses v. Bhagvat Sinhjee* (1891) 19 R. 31; *Soutar v. Peters*, 1912 1 S.L.T. 111; *Walker v. Ost* [1970] 2 All E.R. 106. See also Civil Jurisdiction and Judgments Act, 1982, Sch. I, Art. 5(3).

[12] *McElroy v. McAllister*, 1949 S.C. 110; cf. *Jones v. Somervell's Tr.*, 1907 S.C. 545.

[13] *Goodman v. L.N.W. Ry.* (1877) 14 S.L.R. 449; *Naftalin v. L.M.S. Ry.*, 1933 S.C. 259; *McElroy, supra*; *McKinnon v. Iberia Shipping Co.*, 1955 S.C. 20. *McLarty v. Steele* (1881) 8 R. 435, has been disapproved.

[14] *The M. Moxham* (1876) 1 P.D. 107; *Rosses v. Bhagvat Sinhjee* (1891) 19 R. 31; *McMillan v. C.N. Ry.* [1923] A.C. 120.

[15] *Phillips v. Eyre* (1870) L.R. 6 Q.B. 1.

[16] *Walpole v. C.N. Ry.* [1923] A.C. 113; *McMillan, supra*.

[17] *McElroy, supra*. See 1950 S.L.T. (News) 209; 63 J.R. 39; 65 L.Q.R. 313; 12 M.L.R. 248. For the view that liability depends on the 'proper law of the tort' see *Boys v. Chaplin* [1971] A.C. 356.

[18] *Naftalin, supra; McElroy, supra*.

[19] *Naftalin v. L.M.S. Ry.*, 1933 S.C. 259; *McElroy, supra; Mitchell v. McCulloch*, 1976 S.C. 1.

[20] *Goodman v. L.N.W. Ry.* (1877) 14 S.L.R. 449; *McElroy, supra; Kohnke v. Karger* [1951] 2 K.B. 670; cf. *J. D'Almeida Araujo v. Becker* [1953] 2 Q.B. 329. As to contractual exclusion of remedy see *Brodin v. A/R Seljan*, 1973 S.L.T. 198.

claim by a spouse or other relative of a deceased for solatium in recognition of grief at the death is a distinct right of action, and not merely a head of damages.[21]

The ordinary principles apply to harms done in territorial waters,[22] but liability for harms done on the high seas is regulated by the law of the ship's flag and by Scots law as *lex fori*: In the special case of collisions at sea the rules applicable are those of the general maritime law, particularly those of the Maritime Conventions Act, 1911.[23]

Property—classification

For the purpose of international private law property is divided into immoveable and moveable property, the former including most things deemed immoveable, real, or heritable by the *lex situs* and the latter most things deemed moveable or personal by the *lex situs*.[24] This division does not always coincide exactly with that drawn between heritable and moveable property by Scottish internal law. Thus a heritable bond, though deemed heritable for certain purposes only by Scots law, is immoveable property for purposes of international private law;[25] a mortgage of English land, being classified by English law as personalty, has been treated as moveable in succession.[26] A lease of land is an immoveable interest both by Scots[27] and English[28] law. In case of doubt the *lex situs* determines the classification.[29] But land is by nature immoveable and rights to land are always rights to an immoveable subject.[30]

Immoveable property

In general the *lex situs* regulates all questions regarding immoveable property, including capacity to hold land,[31] capacity to transfer it,[32] and

---

[21] McElroy, supra.

[22] McKinnon, supra.

[23] Chartered Mercantile Bank of India v. Netherlands India S.N. Co. [1883] 10 Q.B.D. 521; Currie v. McKnight (1896) 24 R. (H.L.) 1; Reresby v. Cobetas, 1923 S.L.T. 719; Sheaf S.S. Co. v. Compania Transmediterranea, 1930 S.C. 660.

[24] Newlands v. Chalmers's Trs. (1832) 11 S. 65; Downie v. D's Trs. (1866) 4 M. 1067; Moss's Tr. v. M., 1916 2 S.L.T. 31; Macdonald v. M., 1932 S.C. (H.L.) 79.

[25] Jerningham v. Herbert (1828) 4 Russ. 388; Allen v. Anderson (1846) 5 Hare 163; Re Fitzgerald [1904] 1 Ch. 573; but see Train v. T's Exrx. (1899) 2 F. 146, sed quaere.

[26] Breadalbane's Trs. v. B. (1843) 15 S. Jur. 389; Monteith v. M's Trs. (1882) 9 R. 982, both doubted in Macdonald, supra; see further In re Hoyles [1911] 1 Ch. 179.

[27] Burns v. Martin (1887) 14 R. (H.L.) 20.

[28] Freke v. Carbery (1873) L.R. 16 Eq. 461; Duncan v. Lawson (1889) 41 Ch. D. 394; Macdonald, supra.

[29] Ross v. R's Trs., 4 July 1809, F.C.; Macdonald, supra.

[30] Macdonald, supra.

[31] Duncan v. Lawson (1889) 41 Ch. D. 394.

[32] Bank of Africa, Ltd. v. Cohen [1909] 2 Ch. 129; Harris's Trs., 1919 S.C. 432; see also Waring, 1933 S.L.T. 190.

the formalities and validity of transfer.[33] But the proper law of a contract to sell or mortgage land in Scotland is not necessarily Scots law,[34] and English courts have long asserted jurisdiction *in personam* in relation to foreign land.[35] The mutual rights of spouses, as regards immoveables, are governed by the *lex situs*.[36] The proprietary and possessory rights attaching to particular interests in land depend on the *lex situs*.

Corporeal moveable property

The nature and extent of the rights which a person has in relation to corporeal moveable property are probably determined by the *lex situs* of the moveables. The capacity of a person to transfer corporeal moveables and matters of the contract are probably governed by the proper law of the transaction, commonly the *lex loci contractus*, the formalities of the transfer by the *lex situs*,[37] and its essential validity and effect by the *lex situs*.[37] So too the validity and effect of a gift is prima facie determined by its *lex situs*.[38] The creation of rights in security over corporeal moveables is probably governed, as to formalities, validity, and effect by the *lex situs*.[39] Thus a purported transfer in security by one foreigner to another in England of a vehicle in Scotland would be void in the absence of *traditio*. The *lex situs* also regulates the kinds of diligence competent against moveables and their effect.

Incorporeal moveable property

Incorporeal moveable property includes a wide variety of rights and the same rules do not necessarily apply to all categories. The validity and enforceability of a claim of debt or a claim of damages probably normally depend on the legal system whereby the duty to pay was created, normally that of the debtor's residence, which is deemed the *lex situs* of the debt.[40] Thus share certificates issued by an English company have been held to be interpreted by English law.[41] The assignability of such a claim

---

[33] Ersk. III, 2, 40; *Adams* v. *Clutterbuck* (1883) 10 Q.B.D. 403; *Hewitt's Trs.* v. *Lawson* (1891) 18 R. 793; cf. *Mackintosh* v. *May* (1895) 22 R. 345; *Re Grassi* [1905] 1 Ch. 584.

[34] *Ogilvy* v. *O's Trs.*, 1927 S.L.T. 83; *Miller and Partners* v. *Whitworth Street Estates, Ltd.* [1970] A.C. 583.

[35] *West & Partners, Ltd.* v. *Dick* [1969] 2 Ch. 424.

[36] *Welch* v. *Tennent* (1891) 18 R. (H.L.) 72; *Love* v. *L.*, 1907 S.C. 728.

[37] *Cammell* v. *Sewell* (1860) 5 H. & N. 728; *Todd* v. *Armour* (1882) 9 R. 901; *Carse* v. *Coppen*, 1951 S.C. 233.

[38] *Re Korvine's Trusts* [1921] 1 Ch. 343.

[39] *Connal* v. *Loder* (1868) 6 M. 1095; *N.W. Bank* v. *Poynter, Son & Macdonalds* (1894) 22 R. (H.L.) 1; *Inglis* v. *Robertson & Baxter* (1898) 25 R. (H.L.) 70; *Hammer and Sohne* v. *H.W.T. Realisations*, 1985 S.L.T. (Sh. Ct.) 21.

[40] *Williamson* v. *Taylor* (1845) 8 D. 156; cf. *Thomson* v. *N.B. and Mercantile Ins. Co.* (1868) 6 M. 310; *Re Queensland Mercantile Agency Co.* [1891] 1 Ch. 536; [1892] 1 Ch. 219; *Dinvoodie* v. *Carruther's Exor.* (1895) 23 R. 234; *Aufhauser* v. *Scotboard*, 1973 S.L.T. (Notes) 87.

[41] *Connell's Trs.* v. *C's Trs.* (1886) 13 R. 1175.

probably depends on the *lex situs*[42] and the formal validity of the assignation probably on the *lex loci contractus*,[43] and whether it has been validly
assigned probably on the *lex situs* of the claim.[44] The rule that intimation
is required to complete an assignation seems to apply to Scottish debts
wherever assigned.[45] Questions between assignor and assignee are probably determined by the rules relating to contracts.

The existence, validity, and extent of any such privileges as right of
copyrights, patents, etc., depends on the system of law by which such
right is alleged to be created, and whether it is recognized by bilateral or
international convention as effective in Scotland also.

Universal assignations of property

Apart from death, universal assignation arises only, in some systems, on
marriage, or on bankruptcy or the granting of a trust deed for creditors.
Whether marriage does or does not operate any general assignation of a
spouse's property depends, so far as concerns moveables, on the law of
the matrimonial domicile at the time of the marriage,[46] and, *quoad*
immoveables, on the *lex situs*.[47] A change of domicile probably does not
subject the rights of the spouses in that property to the rule of the new
domicile.[48]

Marriage contracts

A marriage contract or settlement is generally governed by the proper law
of the transaction, which is prima facie the law of the matrimonial
domicile,[49] capacity to enter into it by the domicile of each party at the
time of the marriage[50] and, so far as concerns immoveables, the *lex situs*,
formal validity by the proper law[51] or the *lex loci actus*,[52] and essential
validity and revocability by the proper law[53] or, so far as concerns

---

[42] *Grant's Trs.* v. *Ritchie's Exors.* (1886) 13 R. 646; *Schumann* v. *Scottish Widows' Fund*
(1886) 13 R. 678; *Pender* v. *Commercial Bank*, 1940 S.L.T. 306.
[43] *Erskine* v. *Ramsay* (1664) Mor. 4502; *Ross* v. *R.* (1806) Hume 187; *Tayler* v. *Scott* (1847)
9 D. 1504.
[44] *Scottish Provident Inst.* v. *Cohen* (1888) 16 R. 112; *Bankhaus H. Aufhauser* v. *Scotboard*,
1973 S.L.T. (Notes) 87.
[45] *Strachan* v. *McDougle* (1835) 13 S. 954; *Donaldson* v. *Ord* (1855) 17 D. 1053.
[46] *Corbet* v. *Waddell* (1879) 7 R. 200; *Welch, infra*; *Re Egerton's Will Trusts* [1956] Ch. 593.
[47] *Welch* v. *Tennent* (1891) 18 R. (H.L.) 72.
[48] *Lashley* v. *Hog* (1804) 4 Paton 581; *De Nicols* v. *Curlier* [1900] A.C. 21.
[49] *Corbet* v. *Waddell* (1879) 7 R. 200; *Re Fitzgerald* [1904] 1 Ch. 573; *Eadie's Trs.* v.
Henderson, 1919, 1 S.L.T. 253; *D. Marlborough* v. *A.G.* [1945] Ch. 78. For cases of express
choice of law see *Stair* v. *Head* (1844) 6 D. 904; *Montgomery* v. *Zarifi*, 1918 S.C. (H.L.) 128;
Drummond v. *Bell-Irving*, 1930 S.C. 704.
[50] *Cooper* v. *C.* (1888) 15 R. (H.L.) 21; *Viditz* v. *O'Hagan* [1900] 2 Ch. 87.
[51] *Re Bankes* [1902] 2 Ch. 333.
[52] *Seafield* v. *S.*, 8 Feb. 1814, F.C.; *Van Grutten* v. *Digby* (1862) 31 Beav. 561.
[53] *Sawrey-Cookson* v. *S-C's Trs.* (1905) 8 F. 157.

immoveables, the *lex situs*.[54] A subsequent change of domicile cannot affect the rights of parties under the settlement.[55]

Trusts

Capacity to create a trust probably depends, *quoad* moveables, on the truster's *lex domicilii* and, *quoad* immoveables, on their *lex situs*.[56] Formal validity, and essential validity[57] and interpretation,[58] probably depend on the proper law of the trust. Where a trust is Scottish in form, particularly if the truster is, or was at death, a domiciled Scotsman, and if the trust estate is situated in Scotland, Scots law must apply to the solution of any questions which arise under the terms of the trust.[59] If the Scottish court exercises jurisdiction over trustees in the management of a trust estate, it must apply Scots law, whatever may be or have been the truster's domicile, or the *situs* of any part of the trust estate.[60] The rights, powers, duties, and liabilities of trustees are probably determined by the domicile of the trust.[61] The Scottish courts have frequently been appealed to to exercise an auxiliary jurisdiction to the effect of granting power in relation to property in Scotland to trustees of English trusts.[62] The capacity of a trust beneficiary to grant a valid discharge has been held determined by his *lex domicilii*.[63]

Intestate succession

Succession on death intestate to property classified by the *lex situs* as immoveable is regulated by the *lex situs* of that property.[64] Succession on death intestate to property classified by the *lex situs* as moveable is regulated by the *lex domicilii* of the deceased.[65] Hence the estate of a

---

[54] *Re de Nicols* [1900] 2 Ch. 410.
[55] *de Nicols* v. *Curlier* [1900] A.C. 21.
[56] *Black* v. *B's Trs.*, 1950 S.L.T. (Notes) 32.
[57] *Boe* v. *Anderson* (1862) 24 D. 732; *Irving* v. *Snow*, 1956 S.C. 257.
[58] *Ferguson* v. *Marjoribanks* (1853) 15 D. 637; *Eadie's Trs.* v. *Henderson*, 1919 1 S.L.T. 253.
[59] *Orr Ewing's Trs.* v. *O.E.* (1885) 13 R. (H.L.) 1, 14; *Betts Brown Trust Fund Trs.*, 1968 S.C. 170.
[60] *Peters* v. *Martin* (1825) 4 S. 107.
[61] *Carruthers' Trs. and Allan's Trs.* (1896) 24 R. 238; *Campbell*, 1958 S.C. 275; cf. *Brower's Exor.* v. *Ramsay's Trs.* 1912 S.C. 1374.
[62] *Allan's Trs.* (1897) 24 R. 718; *Pender's Trs.*, 1907 S.C. 207; *Harris's Trs.*, 1919 S.C. 432; *Lipton's Trs.*, 1943 S.C. 521; *Evans-Freke's Trs.*, 1945 S.C. 382; *Neech's Exors.*, 1947 S.C. 119; *Campbell-Wyndham-Long's Trs.*, 1951 S.C. 685; *Horne's Trs.*, 1952 S.C. 70; *Campbell*, 1958 S.C. 275; *Campbell-Wyndham-Long's Trs.*, 1962 S.C. 132; cf. *Rossmore's Trs.* v. *Brownlie* (1877) 5 R. 201.
[63] *Freeman* v. *Bruce's Exors.* (1905) 13 S.L.T. 97.
[64] *Duncan* v. *Lawson* (1889) 41 Ch. D. 394; *In re Rea* [1902] 1 Ir. R. 451; *Macdonald* v. *M.*, 1932 S.C. (H.L.) 79.
[65] Stair, More's Note A; *Bruce* v. *B.* (1790) 3 Pat. 163; *Hog* v. *Lashley* (1792) 3 Pat. 247; *Orr Ewing's Trs.* v. *O.E.* (1885) 13 R. (H.L.) 1; cf. *Monteith* v. *M's Trs.* (1882) 9 R. 982; *Macdonald, supra*; *Goold Stuart's Trs.* v. *Macphail*, 1947 S.L.T. 221; *In the Estate of Maldonado* [1954] P. 223.

domiciled Scot is divided on intestacy by reference to the statutory rights, legal rights and rights of succession conferred by the Succession (Sc.) Act, 1964, in respect of heritage (immoveables) and moveables in Scotland, and property, wherever situated, which is deemed moveable by the *lex situs*.[66] Conversely heritable estate in Scotland belonging to a person dying domiciled elsewhere devolves by Scots law,[67] and moveable estate in Scotland devolves according to the *lex domicilii* of the deceased.[68]

In each case the designated legal system determines to whom, in what shares, and subject to what conditions, the property descends. But if by the *lex domicilii* property passes to some body as *res nullius*, this is not a rule of succession, and the Scottish courts may treat the property as *bona vacantia*.[69]

Testate succession—testamentary capacity

Capacity to test is determined, *quoad* immoveables, by the *lex situs*[70] and, *quoad* moveables, by the *lex domicilii*,[71] in both cases as the law stood at the time when the will was made.[72] The capacity of a legatee to take is determined by the *lex situs* of the immoveables,[73] or, in the case of moveables, his own *lex domicilii*,[74] as at the date when the bequest vests.

Formal validity of wills—execution

A will is to be treated as properly executed if its execution conforms to the internal law in force in the territory where it was executed, or in the territory where, at the time of its execution or of the testator's death, he was domiciled or had his habitual residence, or in a state of which at either of these times, he was a national.[75] There are also treated as properly executed (a) a will executed on board a vessel or aircraft conforming to the internal law with which the vessel or aircraft is most closely connected; (b) a will, so far as disposing of immoveable property, execution of which conformed to the *lex situs*; (c) a will, so far as

---

[66] *Macdonald, supra.*
[67] *Ross v. R.*, 4 July 1809. F.C.; *Fenton v. Livingstone* (1859) 3 Macq. 497.
[68] *Macdonald, supra.*
[69] cf. *Monteith v. M's Trs.* (1882) 9 R. 982; *Train v. T's Exrx.* (1899) 2 F. 146; *Moss's Trs. v. M.*, 1916, 2 S.L.T. 31.
[70] *Re Hernando* (1884) 27 Ch. D. 284; *Black v. B's Trs.*, 1950 S.L.T. (Notes) 33.
[71] *In the goods of Maraver* (1828) 1 Hagg. Ecc. 498; *In the Estate of Field* [1966] 2 W.L.R. 717.
[72] *Field, supra.*
[73] *Brown's Trs. v. Gregson*, 1920 S.C. (H.L.) 87.
[74] *Seddon* (1891) 19 R. 101; (1893) 20 R. 675; *Freeman v. Bruce's Exors.* (1905) 13 S.L.T. 97; see also *Re Hellman's Will* (1866) L.R. 2 Eq. 363; *Re Schnapper* [1928] Ch. 420.
[75] Wills Act, 1963, S. 1; cf. *Connel's Trs. v. C.* (1872) 10 M. 627; *Macdonald v. Cuthbertson* (1890) 18 R. 101; *Irving v. Snow*, 1956 S.C. 257; see also *Bradford v. Young* (1884) 11 R. 1135.

revoking a will properly executed under the Act or revoking a provision which under the Act would be treated as comprised in a properly executed will, if the execution of the later will conformed to any law by reference to which the revoked will or provision would be so treated; (d) a will, so far as it exercises a power of appointment, if executed conform to the law governing the essential validity of the power. A will so far as exercising a power of appointment, is not treated as improperly executed by reason only that its execution was not in accordance with any formal requirements contained in the instrument creating the power.[76] A law in force outside the U.K. requiring special formalities for particular testators or qualifications for witnesses is to be treated as formal requirements only.[77] A will executed in England by a testator domiciled there but formally invalid by English law has been said to be valid if by the time of his death he had acquired a domicile in Scotland and the will was formally valid by Scots law.[78]

Revocation

Capacity to revoke is normally determined by capacity to test. The validity and effect of a potentially revoking act, such as deletion, depends, *quoad* immoveables, on the *lex situs*[79] and, *quoad* moveables, on the *lex domicilii*. Revocation is not effected by a subsequent change of domicile;[80] whether a subsequent marriage revokes a will depends on the testator's *lex domicilii* as affected by the marriage[81] and whether another rule of law revokes depends on the testator's *lex domicilii* at the time of the alleged revocation.[82]

Essential validity

This includes the non-contravention of restrictions on the creation of liferents, the validity of the extent of dispositions made, and the validity of the exercise of powers by the will. Essential validity is determined *quoad* immoveables by the *lex situs*,[83] and, *quoad* moveables, by the *lex domicilii* at the date of death.[84]

---

[76] Ibid., S. 2.
[77] Ibid., S. 3.
[78] *Chisholm* v. *C.*, 1949 S.C. 434.
[79] *In the estate of Alberti* [1955] 3 All E.R. 730.
[80] Wills Act, 1963, S. 1.
[81] *Westerman's Exor.* v. *Schwab* (1905) 8 F. 132; see also *Battye's Tr.* v. *B.*, 1917 S.C. 385.
[82] *Westerman's Exor., supra.*
[83] *Nelson* v. *Bridport* (1846) 8 Beav. 547; *Keith's Trs.* v. *K.* (1857) 19 D. 1040; *Purvis' Trs.* v. *P's Exors.* (1861) 23 D. 812; *Freke* v. *Carbery* (1873) L.R. 16 Eq. 461; *Studd* v. *Cook* (1883) 10 R. (H.L.) 53; *Hewit's Trs.* v. *Lawson* (1891) 18 R. 793; *Canterbury* v. *Wyburn* [1895] A.C. 89; *Brown's Trs.* v. *Gregson*, 1920 S.C. (H.L.) 87.
[84] *Keith's Trs.* v. *K.* (1857) 19 D. 1040; *Boe* v. *Anderson* (1862) 24 D. 732; *Canterbury, supra; Re Groos* [1915] 1 Ch. 572; *Black* v. *B's Trs.*, 1950 S.L.T. (Notes) 33; cf. *M. Bute* v. *Mss. Bute's Trs.* (1880) 8 R. 191.

Construction of will

In interpreting a will the main consideration is the ascertainment of the testator's intention and the *lex situs* and *lex domicilii* may have to be subordinated to the proper law of the will, or that which the testator apparently intended to apply to his will.[85] This is particularly relevant where there is estate in several countries.[86] The use in the will of the technical terms of any particular system is strongly indicative of that as the proper law of the will.[87] Failing that there is a presumption in favour of the *lex domicilii* at the time the will was made, as being the system which the testator probably knew best,[88] even though the will disposes of interests in immoveables in another country[89] and particularly in the case of moveables.[90] Whether a will executed abroad is intended to carry Scottish heritage is usually treated as a question of Scots law.[91] Where a will bequeathed a legacy to a legatee, whom failing to his 'nearest heirs', it has been held that his nearest heir fell to be ascertained by the law of the legatee's domicile.[92] Special destinations of property fall to be construed according to the *lex situs*.[93] The construction of a will is not altered by reason of any change in the testator's domicile after the execution of the will.[94] Similarly it has been held when interpreting testamentary provisions of a marriage contract in Scottish form that the ascertainment of the deceased's next of kin fell to be made by Scots law, though he had subsequently acquired a domicile of choice in Australia.[95]

Exercise of power of appointment by will

Whether a power of appointment conferred on the testator has been validly exercised by his will is presumed to depend, *quoad* immoveables, on the *lex situs* of the immoveables and, *quoad* moveables, depends as regards capacity to appoint on the law which determines capacity to test, as regards formal validity on the law governing formal validity,[96] and as regards essential validity and interpretation on the *lex domicilii*.[97]

[85] *Ferguson v. Marjoribanks* (1853) 15 D. 637; *Mitchell & Baxter v. Davies* (1875) 3 R. 208; *Smith v. S.* (1891) 18 R. 1036; *Re Gansloser's Will Trusts* [1952] Ch. 30; *McBride's Trs.*, 1952 S.L.T. (Notes) 59.
[86] *Iveagh v. I.R.C.* [1954] Ch. 364; *Philipson-Stow v. I.R.C.* [1961] A.C. 727.
[87] *Rainsford v. Maxwell* (1852) 14 D. 450; *Mitchell & Baxter v. Davies* (1875) 3 R. 208; *Studd v. Cook* (1883) 10 R. (H.L.) 53; *Robinson v. R's Trs.*, 1930 S.C. (H.L.) 20; *Re Allen's Estate* [1945] 2 All E.R. 264.
[88] *Mitchell & Baxter v. Davies* (1875) 3 R. 208; *Smith, supra; Hewit's Trs. v. Lawson* (1891) 18 R. 793; *McBride's Trs.*, 1952 S.L.T. (Notes) 59.
[89] *Philipson Stow v. I.R.C.* [1961] A.C. 727, but see *Nelson v. Bridport* (1846) 8 Beav. 547.
[90] *Re Price* [1900] 1 Ch. 442; *Re Connington* [1924] 1 Ch. 68.
[91] *Griffiths J.F. v. G's Exors.* (1905) 7 F. 470.
[92] *Smith's Trs. v. Macpherson*, 1926 S.C. 983; cf. *Mitchell's Tr. v. Rule* (1908) 16 S.L.T. 189.
[93] *Connell's Trs. v. C's Trs.* (1886) 13 R. 1175; *Cunningham's Trs. v. C.*, 1924 S.C. 581.
[94] Wills Act, 1963, S. 4.
[95] *Smart's Tr. v. Goold's Tr.*, 1947 S.L.T. 221.
[96] Wills Act, 1963, S. 2; *Kennion v. Buchan's Trs.* (1880) 7 R. 570.
[97] *Durie's Trs. v. Osborne*, 1960 S.C. 444. See also *Re McMorran* [1958] Ch. 624; *Re Khan's Settlement* [1966] Ch. 567.

Executors and the administration of estates

The *lex situs* of property must determine whether an executor or administrator of the estate of a deceased need be appointed, if so how and by whom, and what his powers are. In case of conflict, the *forum* where the predominant part of the estate is situated is more appropriate for its main administration.[98] If the estate is heritable the *forum situs* is appropriate.[99] The mode of administration is determined in each country in which a grant of representation has been obtained by that country's rules.[1]

Remedies

An aggrieved person can claim only those remedies which the forum appealed to can grant according to its own law and practice.[2] The actionability of a claim depends on its proper law. The heads of damage for which damages may be claimed are fixed by the proper law of the contract, or the *lex loci delicti*[3]. Remoteness of damage, and other principles excluding certain losses from consideration in quantifying loss are regulated by the proper law of the contract or the *lex loci delicti*.[4] Whether an obligation has been extinguished by prescription depends on the proper law of the obligation.[5] Liability for interest on money depends on the same law.[6] The measure of damages and any liability for interest thereon is, however, a matter for the *lex fori*.[7] So also is the ranking of claimants on a fund.[8]

Evidence and procedure

The evidencing of disputed rights, and all matters of procedure for adjudicating them, fall to be determined solely by the *lex fori*.[9] Procedure for this purpose includes selection of the court appropriate by the internal law, modes of initiation and conduct of proceedings, parties,[10] competency,[11] and relevancy of action, remedies competent,[12] method,

---

[98] *Orr Ewing's Trs.* v. *O.E.* (1885) 13 R. (H.L.) 1.
[99] *Hewit's Trs.* v. *Lawson* (1891) 18 R. 793; cf. Succession (Sc.) Act, 1964, S. 14.
[1] cf. *S.N.O. Society* v. *Thomson's Exor.*, 1969 S.L.T. 325.
[2] *McElroy* v. *McAllister*, 1949 S.C. 110; cf. *Phrantzes* v. *Argenti* [1960] 2 Q.B. 19.
[3] *McElroy, supra.* See also *Boys* v. *Chaplin* [1971] A.C. 356.
[4] *J.D'Almeida Araujo Lda.* v. *Becker* [1953] 2 Q.B. 329.
[5] *Stirling's Trs.* v. *Legal and General Assce. Socy.*, 1957 S.L.T. 73.
[6] *Cochrane* v. *Gilkison* (1857) 20 D. 213; *Price and Logan* v. *Wise* (1862) 24 D. 491.
[7] *Kendrick* v. *Burnett* (1897) 25 R. 82; cf. *Kohnke* v. *Karger* [1951] 2 K.B. 670; *Boys* v. *Chaplin* [1971] A.C. 356.
[8] *Clark* v. *Bowring*, 1908 S.C. 1168.
[9] Ersk. III, 7, 48; *B.L. Co.* v. *Drummond* (1830) 10 B. & C. 903; *Don* v. *Lippmann* (1837) 2 Sh. & MacL. 682; *Jones* v. *Somervell's Tr.*, 1907 S.C. 545.
[10] *McElroy* v. *McAllister*, 1949 S.C. 110.
[11] *Hansen* v. *Dixon* (1906) 23 T.L.R. 56.
[12] *Kendrick* v. *Burnett* (1897) 25 R. 82.

and burden of proof,[13] sufficiency of evidence,[14] appeal, diligence, and expenses. Extinction of an obligation by lapse of time or limitation of time for suing are determined by the system regulating substantive issues, unless that would be inconsistent with public policy.[15]

Bankruptcy

The sequestration by a Scottish court of a person subject to its jurisdiction vests in the trustee the bankrupt's moveables both in Scotland and elsewhere,[16] and possibly also his immoveables elsewhere as well as his Scottish heritage. If a person having assets in Scotland is sequestrated abroad, this has been held to render subsequent sequestration in Scotland incompetent,[17] but this is inaccurate.[18] The Scottish courts are not precluded from appointing a trustee in Scotland[19] but, unless this is done, will normally accept the title of a foreign administrator in bankruptcy to moveables in Scotland,[20] subject to all claims already constituted thereon by diligence under Scots law,[21] provided always that the debtor was only subject to the jurisdiction of the foreign court and was cognizant of the proceedings.[22] As regards immoveable property in Scotland a foreign administrator must petition the court, as *forum situs*, to vest such immoveable property in him and to authorize him to sell it.[23]

Within the United Kingdom the Act and Warrant of a trustee in sequestration appointed by a Scottish court vests in him, *inter alia*, the whole estate of the debtor, wherever situated, a personal right to heritage, and a real right to moveable property.[24] The converse applies in the cases of English and Irish bankruptcies.[25] The rights and powers of a Scottish trustee in bankruptcy to property situated outwith the United Kingdom depend on the recognition granted to such appointment by the *lex situs* of the property.

[13] *Mackenzie v. Hall* (1854) 17 D. 164; *Girvin, Roper & Co. v. Monteith* (1895) 23 R. 129.
[14] *Owners of Immanuel v. Denholm* (1887) 15 R. 152.
[15] Prescription and Limitation (Sc.) Act, 1984, S. 4.
[16] Bankruptcy (Sc.) Act, 1985, S. 31; see also *Lindsay v. Paterson* (1840) 2 D. 1373; *Galbraith v. Nicholson* (1888) 15 R. 914.
[17] *Goetze v. Aders* (1874) 2 R. 150; see also *Phosphate Sewage Co. v. Molleson* (1878) 5 R. 1125; affd. (1879) 6 R. (H.L.) 113; *Okell v. Foden* (1884) 11 R. 906.
[18] *Colville v. James* (1862) 1 M. 41; *Home's Tr. v. H's Trs.*, 1926 S.L.T. 214.
[19] cf. *Queensland Mercantile and Agency Co. v. Australasian Investment Co.* (1888) 15 R. 935; *Gibson v. Munro* (1894) 21 R. 840; *Bank of Scotland v. Youde* (1908) 15 S.L.T. 847.
[20] *Obers v. Paton's Trs.* (1897) 24 R. 719; *Salaman v. Tod*, 1911 S.C. 1214; *Araya v. Coghill*, 1921 S.C. 462.
[21] *Connal v. Loder* (1868) 6 M. 1095; *Goetze, supra; Galbraith v. Grimshaw* [1910] A.C. 508.
[22] *Wilkie v. Cathcart* (1870) 9 M. 168; *Salaman v. Tod*, 1911 S.C. 1214; *Re Anderson* [1911] 1 K.B. 896.
[23] *Salaman v. Tod.*, 1911 S.C. 1214; *Araya v. Coghill*, 1921 S.C. 462.
[24] Bankruptcy (Sc.) Act, 1985, S. 31.
[25] Insolvency Act, 1986. See also *Scrivenor v. Home's Trs.*, 1926 S.L.T. 214.

Any disabilities attaching to the status of bankrupt must be determined by the proper law of the bankruptcy.[26] Questions of competing rights of the trustee and creditors claiming preferences depend on the proper law of the sequestration.[27]

A discharge in bankruptcy granted in one part of the United Kingdom is effective in the others also. Outside that area, a discharge granted in a foreign country will probably be recognized if it is effective under the proper law of the bankruptcy.[28]

Arbitration

The validity, interpretation and effect of an agreement to arbitrate are governed by the proper law of the parties' contract. There is a presumption that the proper law is the law of the country where the arbitration is to be held.[29] The law governing the arbitration proceedings may be stated expressly, but will be presumed to be that of the country where the arbitration is to take place.[30]

[26] *Obers* v. *Paton's Trs.* (1897) 24 R. 719.

[27] *Sc. Provident Instn.* v. *Cohen* (1888) 16 R. 112.

[28] *Ellis* v. *McHenry* (1871) L.R. 6 C.P. 228; *Gibb* v. *Société Industrielle* (1890) 25 Q.B.D. 399.

[29] *Hamlyn* v. *Talisker Distillery* (1894) 21 R. (H.L.) 21; *Tzortzis* v. *Monark Line* [1968] 1 All E.R. 949.

[30] *Miller and Partners, Ltd.* v. *Whitworth Street Estates Ltd.* [1970] A.C. 583.

FOREIGN JUDGMENTS

The problem may arise whether, where some legal issue has already been determined by the courts of another country, that judgment should be accepted by the Scottish courts as decisive, or as valid and enforceable in Scotland. Convenience and international comity require that foreign judgments should only exceptionally be disregarded.

In general a foreign judgment will be recognized (a) if it were pronounced by a court apparently having jurisdiction under the principles of effectiveness or of submission, whether or not the court actually giving the judgment truly had competence, under its own internal law and procedure, to grant that judgment,[1] unless possibly it plainly appeared that the court had no competence by its internal law to do what it has purported to do; (b) if the judgment were final and conclusive, and not interlocutory, nor subject to variation, nor requiring a further order to complete it,[2] though it may be final even though still appealable;[3] and (c) if it is for a definite sum in money, in or convertible into sterling.[4]

A Scottish court will not enforce a decree of a foreign court in a penal or revenue claim.[5]

Foreign judgments affecting status

The judgment determining status is akin to a judgment *in rem*. The general principle is that if a foreign court exercises jurisdiction on grounds accepted by Scots law as adequate, its judgment will be treated as valid by the Scottish courts.[6] Thus a decree of nullity of marriage of the court of the foreign domicile is recognized in Scotland;[7] a decree from the court of the common residence would similarly be recognized[8] but not a

---

[1] *Pick v. Stewart, Galbraith & Co.* (1907) 15 S.L.T. 447; *Geiger v. Macdonald*, 1932 S.L.T. 70; *Scott v. S.*, 1937 S.L.T. 632.

[2] *Nouvion v. Freeman* (1889) 15 App. Cas. I; *Harrop v. H.* [1920] 3 K.B. 386.

[3] *Scott v. Pilkington* (1862) 2 B. & S. 11; *Findlay v. Wickham*, 1920 2 S.L.T. 325.

[4] *Sadler v. Robins* (1808) 1 Camp. 253; *Beatty v. B.* [1924] 1 K.B. 807.

[5] *Huntington v. Attrill* [1893] A.C. 150; *A.G. for Canada v. Schulze* (1901) 9 S.L.T. 4; *Metal Industries (Salvage) Ltd. v. Harle*, 1962 S.L.T. 114; *Govt. of India v. Taylor* [1955] A.C. 491; *Peter Buchanan Ltd. v. McVey* [1955] A.C. 516 n.

[6] cf. Legitimation (Sc.) Act, 1968, S. 5.

[7] *Administrator of Austrian Property v. Von Lorang*, 1927 S.C. (H.L.) 80; cf. *Aldridge v. A.*, 1954 S.C. 58. See now Family Law Act, 1986, Ss. 44–54.

[8] *Ramsay-Fairfax v. R.F.* [1965] P. 115.

decree annulling a marriage by a court of the country where the marriage took place.[9] In divorce cases Scottish courts at common law treated as valid a decree of divorce pronounced by a foreign court if the parties were domiciled within the jurisdiction of that court,[10] or if the courts of the domicile recognize a decree pronounced elsewhere as valid within that domicile.[11]

Legitimacy or legitimation by foreign law

If a person is deemed legitimate by the law of his domicile this will probably be recognized in Scotland. If he is still a pupil the question depends on the domicile of his parents at the time of his birth,[12] but if his parents have different domiciles difficulties arise; probably it depends on the law of the father's domicile at the time of the alleged marriage.[13] But for the purpose of succession to land a person must be legitimate both by the other system involved and by Scots law.[14] The legitimacy in Scotland of a child of a polygamous marriage contracted elsewhere is uncertain.[15]

If a person is deemed legitimated *per subsequens matrimonium* by the law of his father's domicile this will be recognized in Scotland[16] though if the father's domicile has changed between birth and marriage and one of these states does not recognize legitimation it is uncertain which date is material.[17]

Marriage by foreign law

Scots law will normally recognize a marriage contracted elsewhere by persons domiciled there if it satisfies the *lex loci celebrationis*;[18] thus marriage by proxy[19] or polygamous marriage[20] seem likely to be recognized at least for some purposes. Whether Scots law would ever reject on

---

[9] *Casey* v. *C.* [1949] P. 420.

[10] *Shaw* v. *Gould* (1868) L.R. 3 H.L. 55; *Harvey* v. *Farnie* (1882) 8 App. Cas. 43; *Le Mesurier* v. *Le M.* [1895] A.C. 517; *Humphrey* v. *H's Trs.* (1895) 3 S.L.T. 151; *Makouipur* v. *M.*, 1967 S.C. 116. Declarator of the validity of a judicial divorce is unnecessary: *Arnott* v. *L.A.*, 1932 S.L.T. 46; *McKay* v. *Walls*, 1951 S.L.T. (Notes) 6. See also *Sim* v. *S.*, 1948 S.L.T. (Notes) 15.

[11] *Armitage* v. *A.G.* [1906] P. 135; *Perin* v. *P.*, 1950 S.L.T. 51; *McKay* v. *Walls*, 1951 S.L.T. (Notes) 6; cf. *Mather* v. *Mahoney* [1968] 3 All E.R. 223. See also *Galbraith* v. *G.*, 1971 S.L.T. 139; *Bain* v. *B.*, 1971 S.L.T. 141.

[12] *Fenton* v. *Livingstone* (1859) 3 Macq. 497, 547; *Beattie* v. *B.* (1866) 5 M. 181.

[13] *Dalhousie* v. *McDouall* (1840) 1 Rob. 475; *Munro* v. *M.* (1840) 1 Rob. 492; *McDouall* v. *Adair* (1852) 14 D. 525; *Maitland* v. *M.* (1885) 12 R. 899.

[14] *Fenton, supra.*

[15] cf. *Bamgbose* v. *Daniel* [1955] A.C. 107.

[16] *Shedden* v. *Patrick* (1808) 5 Pat. 194; *Munro, supra.*

[17] *Munro, supra; Blair* v. *Kay's Trs.*, 1940 S.L.T. 464.

[18] *Warrender* v. *W.* (1835) 2 S. & MacL. 154.

[19] *Macdonald* v. *M.* (1863) 1 M. 854.

[20] *Baindail* v. *B.* [1946] P. 122.

grounds of public policy a marriage, e.g. a child marriage, validly contracted elsewhere by persons domiciled there is undecided.

Foreign decrees of divorce—statutory recognition

By statute the validity of a decree of divorce or judicial separation granted after 1 January 1972 under the law of Scotland is recognized in England and Wales and conversely, and if granted under the law of Northern Ireland, the Channel Islands, or the Isle of Man, it is recognized in Great Britain.[21] Divorces and legal separations obtained judicially outside the British Isles and effective under the law of the country of granting are recognized in Great Britain if at the date of the institution of the proceedings either spouse was habitually resident, or domiciled, in that country, or either spouse was a national of that country.[22] Divorce or separation obtained non-judicially,[23] if not required to be recognized by Ss. 45–46, is not to be regarded as validly dissolving a marriage if both parties thereto have within the previous year been habitually resident in the U.K.[24] Where there are cross-actions the validity of an overseas divorce or separation obtained either in the original proceedings or in the cross proceedings is recognized if S. 46 is satisfied, and where a separation, the validity of which is entitled to recognition is converted in the country in which it was obtained into a divorce, the validity of the divorce is recognized.[25] In respect of recognition any finding of fact is conclusive evidence of the facts found if both spouses took part in the proceedings, and otherwise sufficient proof unless the contrary is shown.[26] The Act is without prejudice to the recognition of the validity of divorces and legal separations obtained outside the British Isles by virtue of any rule that the spouses had both been domiciled in that other country[27] or that it was recognized as valid under the law of that country,[28] and also if one spouse was domiciled in that country and the divorce or separation was recognized as valid under the law of the other spouse's domicile or, neither spouse being domiciled there, it was recognized as valid under the law of the domicile of each spouse respectively, or by virtue of any other enactment, but no other divorce or legal separation is to be recognized as valid.[29]

---

[21] Family Law Act; 1986, S. 44.
[22] Ss. 45–46; *Broit* v. *B.*, 1972 S.L.T. (Notes) 32; *Cruse* v. *Chittum* [1974] 2 All E.R. 940.
[23] This includes legislative, administrative, e.g. *Nachinson* v. *N.* [1930] P. 217, and religious divorces, e.g. *Qureshi* v. *Q.* [1971] 1 All E.R. 325; *Har-Shefi* v. *H.S.* [1953] P. 220.
[24] S. 46.
[25] S. 47.
[26] Ibid., S. 48.
[27] e.g. *Le Mesurier* v. *Le M.* [1895] A.C. 517.
[28] e.g. *Armitage* v. *A.G.* [1903] P. 135.
[29] Ibid., S. 46. This overrules *Travers* v. *Holley* [1953] P. 246; *Indyka* v. *I.* [1969] 3 A.C. 33.

Neither spouse is precluded from remarrying in Great Britain if the validity of a divorce obtained elsewhere is entitled to recognition under the Act, even though it would not be recognized elsewhere.[30] Recognition is not granted if by Scots law there was no marriage between the parties, and may be refused only if it was granted outside the British Isles and proper notice of the proceedings were not given to the other party,[31] or the other party were not given such opportunity to take part in the proceedings as he should reasonably have been given, or recognition would manifestly be contrary to the public policy.[32] Nothing in the Act requires the recognition of findings of fault made in any proceedings or of any custody or maintenance order made therein.[33]

A decree, if valid under these principles, is a judgment *in rem* binding throughout the world, save that if it also imposes a restriction on remarriage, that might be disregarded in Scotland as being a penalty,[34] and that if it also prevents remarriage until after the lapse of a specified time, the decree may be held not to have finally determined the issue between the parties till that time has elapsed.[35] If such a foreign decree is invalid, it is ineffective to dissolve the marriage, so that a remarriage is adulterous and bigamous, and also ineffective in Scotland as to any consequential matters, such as aliment.[36]

The Scottish courts have refused to accept the decree of an American court presuming the death of a person as valid in Scotland,[37] and a decree of the Rota of the Roman Catholic church as annulling a marriage contracted in Scotland.[38] Decrees of English magistrates' courts for maintenance or permitting non-cohabitation have been held not to bar proceedings in the courts of the domicile determinative of status.[39]

Foreign decrees of judicial separation

Recognition of these is governed by the Family Law Act, 1986, Ss. 44–51.

Foreign decree of nullity

A foreign decree of nullity will be recognized if the conditions set out in the Family Law Act, 1986, Ss. 44–51, are satisfied.

---

[30] Ibid., S. 50.
[31] cf. *Crabtree* v. *C.*, 1929 S.L.T. 675.
[32] cf. *Macalpine* v. *M.* [1958] P. 35; *Meyer* v. *M.* [1971] 1 All E.R. 378.
[33] Ibid., S. 51.
[34] *Scott* v. *A.G.* (1886) 11 P.D. 128; see also *Martin* v. *Buret*, 1938 S.L.T. 479.
[35] *Warter* v. *W.* (1890) 17 P.D. 152.
[36] *Papadopoulos* v. *P.* [1930] P. 55; *Simons* v. *S.* [1939] 1 K.B. 490.
[37] *Simpson's Trs.* v. *Fox*, 1951 S.L.T. 412. cf. *In the Goods of Wolf* [1948] P. 66.
[38] *Di Rollo* v. *D.R.*, 1959 S.C. 75.
[39] *Murray* v. *M.*, 1956 S.C. 376; *Richardson* v. *R.*, 1957 S.L.T. (Notes) 45.

Foreign decree of dissolution by presumption of death

A foreign decree is sufficient evidence if the person was domiciled or habitually resident in the country granting the decree.[40]

Foreign judgments regulating custody or access

An order regulating custody made by the courts of the minor's domicile is treated as made by the court of pre-eminent jurisdiction but can be disregarded if the interest of the minor's welfare appears to demand it.[41] The welfare of the minor is the paramount consideration and the Scottish courts may disregard a foreign order in the interest of the child's welfare.[42]

Foreign judgments appointing guardians

Appointment by a court of a guardian for a minor who is a national of or resident in that country will be recognized in Scotland[43] though the powers of guardian and minor to deal with property in Scotland may be limited.[44]

Foreign adoptions

As the Adoption Acts 1958 and 1968 apply to both Scotland and England English adoptions will be recognized in Scotland. The Adoption Act, 1968, provides for the recognition in Scotland of adoption orders made in Northern Ireland, the Channel Islands, and the Isle of Man. An adoption elsewhere may be recognized if the adoptive parents are domiciled there and the child ordinarily resident there[45] or possibly if recognized by the courts of the adoptive parents' domicile. The 1968 Act allows adoptions in countries specified by order to be recognized if effected under statute in the country concerned. The Adoption (Sc.) Act, 1978,[46] consolidates the law.

Foreign judgments in personam

The common law principle is that a foreign judgment is not enforceable as such, but it has created an obligation which gives a good cause of

---

[40] Presumption of Death (Sc.) Act, 1977, S. 10.

[41] *Barkworth* v. *B.*, 1913 S.C. 759; *Westergaard* v. *W.*, 1914 S.C. 977; *Radoyevitch* v. *R.*, 1930 S.C. 619; *Kelly* v. *Marks*, 1974 S.L.T. 118; *Campbell* v. *C.*, 1977 S.C. 103; see also *Battaglia* v. *B.* 1967 S.L.T. 49; *Hoy* v. *H.* 1968 S.C. 179; *Sergeant* v. *S.*, 1973 S.L.T. (Notes) 27; *Lyndon* v. *L.*, 1978 S.L.T. (Notes) 7; *Thomson*, 1980 S.L.T. (Notes) 29.

[42] Guardianship of Children Act, 1925, S. 1; *Campins* v. *C.*, 1979 S.L.T. (Notes) 41.

[43] *Nugent* v. *Vetzera* (1866) L.R. 2 Eq. 704; *Re Bourgoise* (1889) 41 Ch. D. 310; see also *Johnstone* v. *Beattie* (1843) 10 Cl. & F. 42; *Stuart* v. *Bute* (1861) 9 H.L.C. 440.

[44] *Ogilvy* v. *O's Trs.*, 1927 S.L.T. 83.

[45] *Re Valentine's Settlement* [1965] Ch. 831.

[46] As amended.

action in an action for decree conform, which decree if granted by the Scottish court is enforceable as a Scottish decree. In the absence of statutory warrant for registering a foreign judgment the only method of enforcing it is to bring an action for decree conform in which the foreign decree, if prepared and authenticated according to the practice of the Court granting it,[47] is produced and proved. Such a judgment will be presumed to have been pronounced by a competent court and accordingly to be *res judicata*, but it may be challenged on the grounds that the foreign court did not have jurisdiction over the defender on a ground reasonably consistent with international law,[48] or the defender did not have due notice of the claim made against him,[49] or there was fraud on or by the foreign court,[50] or the decree was not final,[51] or was contrary to British ideas of natural justice,[52] or public policy.[53] A foreign judgment cannot be challenged on the merits, either on fact or law.[54] Apart from direct enforcement a foreign decree may sometimes be founded on as evidencing a debt sued for,[55] or be pleaded in defence as *res judicata*.[56]

Defences to actions on foreign judgments

While it is not open to challenge a foreign judgment on any ground of error in fact or law by the foreign court,[57] certain defences are competent, and render the foreign judgment unenforceable:

(1) Foreign judgment obtained by fraud: this includes collusion by the parties to give the foreign court jurisdiction,[58] or deception of that court and abuse of its procedure.[59]

---

[47] *Robertson v. Gordon*, 15 Nov. 1814 F.C.; cf. *Disbrow v. Mackintosh* (1852) 15 D. 123; *Whitehead v. Thompson* (1861) 23 D. 772; *Cooney v. Dunne*, 1925 S.L.T. 22.
[48] *Waygood v. Bennie* (1885) 12 R. 651; *Schibsby v. Westenholz* (1870) L.R. 6 Q.B. 155; *Sirdar Gurdyal Singh v. Rajah of Faridkote* [1894] A.C. 670; *Pemberton v. Hughes* [1899] 1 Ch. 781; *Carrick v. Hancock* (1895) 12 T.L.R. 59; *Geiger v. Macdonald*, 1932 S.L.T. 70.
[49] *Pemberton v. Hughes* [1899] 1 Ch. 781.
[50] *Vadala v. Lawes* (1890) 25 Q.B.D. 310; *Syal v. Heyward* [1948] 2 K.B. 443.
[51] *Pattison v. MacVicar* (1886) 13 R. 550; *Nouvion v. Freeman* (1889) 15 App. Cas 1; *Delhi and London Bank v. Loch* (1895) 22 R. 849; *Administrator of Austrian Property v. Von Lorang*, 1927 S.C. (H.L.) 80.
[52] *Don v. Lippman* (1837) 2 Sh. & Macl. 682, 745; *Bethell v. Bethell* (1888) 38 Ch. D. 220; cf. *Cooney v. Dunne*, 1925 S.L.T. 22.
[53] *In re Macartney* [1921] 1 Ch. 522.
[54] *Gladstone v. Lindsay* (1868) 6 S.L.R. 71; *Castrique v. Imrie* (1870) L.R. 4 H.L. 414; *Godard v. Gray* (1870) L.R. 6 Q.B. 139; *Nouvion v. Freeman* (1889) 15 App. Cas. I; but see *Meyer v. Ralli* (1876) L.R. 1 C.P. 358.
[55] *Stiven v. Myer* (1868) 6 M. 885; *Phosphate Sewage Co. v. Molleson* (1879) 6 R. (H.L.) 113.
[56] *Phosphate Sewage Co. v. Lawson* (1878) 5 R. 1125; *Comber v. Maclean* (1881) 9 R. 215.
[57] *Castrique v. Imrie* (1870) L.R. 4 H.L. 414; *Godard v. Gray* (1870) L.R. 6 Q.B. 139.
[58] *Shaw v. Gould* (1868) L.R. 3 H.L. 55.
[59] *Boe v. Anderson* (1857) 20 D. 11; *Vadala v. Lawes* (1890) 25 Q.B.D. 310; *Macalpine v. M.* [1958] P. 35; see also *Perin v. P.*, 1950 S.L.T. 51.

(2) Judgment contrary to British public policy: such judgments include foreign judgments of a penal nature,[60] or foreign revenue claims.[61]

(3) Judgment contrary to natural justice: if reached in a manner contrary to natural justice the foreign judgment is unenforceable. This includes failure to hear one party,[62] or failure to give fair notice of the proceedings to a party,[63] but not merely apparent or obvious incorrectness of the judgment.[64]

Statutory enforcement of foreign judgments

(1) Judgments of English and Northern Irish courts

The 1982 Act, S. 18 and Sch. 6, enables any money provisions in a judgment by a court of law in the U.K., any judgment entered in England and Wales or Northern Ireland in the High Court or County Court, any document registered for execution in the Books of Council and Session or the sheriff court books, any award or order made by a tribunal enforceable without an order of court, and an arbitration award given in the same manner as a judgment by a court of law, and also certain kinds of decrees, but not magistrates' courts judgments, nor judgments in other than civil proceedings, or proceedings relating to bankruptcy, winding up, or obtaining a title to administer the estate of a deceased person, to be enforced in another part of the U.K.[65]

A person desiring enforcement may apply for a certificate stating the judgment, and may apply to the superior court in another part of the U.K. to have the certificate registered there.[66] A certificate has the same force and effect, and the registering court has the same powers, as if the certificate had been a judgment given originally in the registering court. In certain cases the registering court may sist or set aside the certificate.[66]

The 1982 Act, S. 18 and Sch. 7, has effect for the purpose of enabling any non-money provisions contained in a judgment of a U.K. court to be enforced in another part of the U.K. An interested party may apply for a certified copy of the judgment to the court which granted the judgment, and then apply to a superior court elsewhere in the U.K. for the judgment to be registered in that court. The non-money provisions of a judgment registered are of the same force and effect and the registering court has the same powers as if the judgment had been originally given in the registering court.

---

[60] *Raulin* v. *Fischer* [1911] 2 K.B. 93; *Re Macartney* [1921] 1 Ch. 522.
[61] *Govt. of India* v. *Taylor* [1955] A.C. 491.
[62] *Don* v. *Lippmann* (1837) 2 S. & Macl. 682; *Det Norske Bjergnings og Dykkercompagni* v. *McLaren* (1885) 22 S.L.R. 861; *Pattison* v. *McVicar* (1886) 13 R. 550.
[63] *Rudd* v. *R.* [1924] P. 72; *Scott* v. *S.*, 1937 S.L.T. 632; *Igra* v. *I.* [1951] P. 404; *Maher* v. *M.* [1951] P. 342.
[64] *Castrique* v. *Imrie* (1870) L.R. 4 H.L. 414.
[65] 1982 Act, S. 18.
[66] Ibid., Sch. 6. All registration must be in the Court of Session.

(2) *Judgments of contracting states (EC countries other than Greece, Spain, and Portugal)*

Recognition

By the Convention scheduled to the Civil Jurisdiction and Judgments Act, 1982, Title 3, which applies in civil and commercial, but not revenue, customs, or administrative matters, nor status or legal capacity of persons, rights arising from marriage, wills, and succession, bankruptcy or winding up, social security or arbitration,[67] a judgment given in a contracting state is to be recognized in another contracting state without special procedure; a party may apply for a decision that the judgment be recognized.[68]

A judgment shall not be recognized

(1) if recognition is contrary to public policy in the recognizing state;
(2) if given in default of appearance, the defendant not having been served with the initiating writ;
(3) if the judgment is irreconcilable with a judgment in a dispute between the same parties in the recognizing state;
(4) if the court giving judgment has decided a preliminary question on status or legal capacity, rights in property arising out of marriage, wills, or succession in a way conflicting with the private international law of the recognizing state;
(5) if irreconcilable with an earlier judgment in a non-contracting state involving the same course of action and between the same parties, provided this fulfils the conditions necessary for recognition.[69]

A judgment is not to be recognized if it conflicts with Arts. 7–18 or 59. The jurisdiction of the court issuing the judgment is not to be reviewed,[70] nor may the judgment be reviewed as to its substance.[71] A court of a contracting state in which recognition is sought may stay the proceedings if appeal against the judgment has been lodged.[72]

Enforcement

A judgment given in a contracting state and enforceable there shall be enforced in another contracting state where an order for enforcement is issued there.[73] The application is submitted to, in Scotland, the Court of Session, save that a maintenance judgment is submitted to the sheriff court on transmission by the secretary of state.[74] The procedure is gov-

---

[67] Sch. Art. 1.
[68] Art. 26.
[69] Art. 27.
[70] Art. 28.
[71] Art. 29.
[72] Art. 30.
[73] Art. 31.
[74] Art. 32.

erned by the enforcing state and must have certain documents attached.[75] The application is to be dealt with without delay and may be refused only for one of the reasons specified in Arts. 27 and 28; the foreign judgment may not be reviewed as to its substance.[76] If enforcement is authorized the person affected may appeal within one month, or in special cases, two months, to the same courts as deal with applications.[77] If enforcement is refused, the applicant may appeal to the same courts and it may be contested only by a single further appeal on a point of law.[78] There may be partial enforcement.[79]

Authentic instruments and court settlements

A document formally drawn up or registered as an authentic instrument and enforceable in one contracting state shall in another contracting state have an order for its enforcement issued there on application under Art. 31. A settlement approved by a court and enforceable in one state is enforceable elsewhere in the same way as authentic instruments.[80]

(3) Judgment of courts in non-contracting states

Recognition and enforcement of these depends on common law.

The Administration of Justice Act, 1920, makes provision for the enforcement within the United Kingdom countries of judgments obtained in a superior court of any part of the British dominions, including any territory under Her Majesty's protection or mandate, with which reciprocal arrangements have been made. Registration is in the discretion of the Court of Session,[81] is competent only if for the payment of money,[82] and is not permitted in certain specified circumstances.[83]

The Foreign Judgments (Reciprocal Enforcement) Act, 1933, provides for the registration of judgments obtained in foreign countries for money, other than sums in respect of taxes, fines, or penalties, if reciprocal arrangements have been made.[84] In certain specified circumstances the judgment must, or may, be set aside.

The Act of Sederunt (Enforcement Abroad of Sheriff Court Judgments),

---

[75] Art. 33.
[76] Art. 34.
[77] Arts. 35–9.
[78] Arts. 40–1.
[79] Art. 42.
[80] Arts. 50–1.
[81] Refused in *Ibbetson*, 1957 S.L.T. (Notes) 15.
[82] Inclusion of an order for costs does not make the judgment one for money: *Platt v. P.*, 1958 S.C. 95.
[83] *Bank of British W. Africa*, 1931 S.L.T. 83.
[84] See *Medinelli v. Malgras*, 1958 S.C. 489; *Jamieson v. Northern Electricity Sy. Corpn.* [1969] C.L.Y. 4189. See also *Black-Clawson v. Papierwerke A/G* [1974] 2 All E.R. 611 and amendments in 1982 Act, Sch. 10.

1962,[85] prescribes procedure whereby Sheriff Court Judgments may be enforced abroad in countries with which the United Kingdom has a convention providing therefor.

The European Communities (Enforcement of Community Judgments) Order, 1972, provides for enforcement by registration of decisions of the European Court and certain other EEC organs.

The State Immunity Act, 1978, provides for the recognition of judgments given against the U.K. in countries parties to the European Convention on State immunity.

Enforcement of Maintenance Orders

Under the Maintenance Orders (Facilities for Enforcement) Act, 1920, and the Maintenance Orders (Reciprocal Enforcement) Act, 1972, orders made outside the U.K. are enforceable in Scotland. By the Maintenance Orders Act, 1950, Sc. 16–18,[86] orders for payment of maintenance, i.e. aliment, to women and children made under specified statutes[87] by a court in any one part of the United Kingdom may be registered in a court in another part of the United Kingdom as if it had been made by the registering court. Such orders may similarly be discharged or varied,[88] and the registration may be cancelled.

Under the Family Law Reform Act, 1969, Ss. 4(5) and 6(7) orders made in England for maintenance of a person up to the age of 21, and orders for the maintenance of a ward of court are enforceable in Scotland under the 1950 Act, S. 16. Under the Matrimonial Proceedings and Property Act, 1970, S. 12, orders made in England for maintenance pending divorce, financial provision on divorce, nullity, or separation, financial provision for children in such cases, and in case of neglect by either party to a marriage to maintain the other or a child of the family, are enforceable in Scotland under the 1950 Act, S. 16. Under the Guardianship of Minors Act, 1971, S. 13, an English court may make an order relating to the custody of a minor, including an order on a father to make payments to the mother towards the minor's maintenance, and this also is enforceable under the 1950 Act, S. 16.

Reciprocal enforcement of maintenance orders

By the Maintenance Orders (Reciprocal Enforcement) Act, 1972, maintenance orders made by courts in the United Kingdom may be transmitted

---

[85] S.I. 1962, No. 1517.
[86] Extended by the Maintenance Orders Act, 1958, S. 20(3) (a).
[87] Listed in S. 16(2), extended by Succession (Sc.) Act, 1964, S. 26, and Social Work (Sc.) Act, 1968, Sch. 8.
[88] *Allum* v. *A.*, 1965 S.L.T. (Sh. Ct.) 26); see also *Thompson* v. *T.* (1953) 69 Sh. Ct. Rep. 193.

to reciprocating countries for enforcement there, and orders made by courts in reciprocating countries may be sent to courts in this country and confirmed or not, or with alterations, registered, and enforced as if made by these courts, and varied or revoked.[89] Provision is made for applications by persons in the U.K. for recovery of maintenance in convention countries[90] and by persons in convention countries for recovery of maintenance in Scotland.[91] Extensive provision is made for transfer, enforcement, variation, and revocation of registered orders.[92]

Foreign judgments in rem

A foreign judgment *in rem*, such as determining title to property, immoveable or moveable, falls to be recognized if proceeding from a court of the country where the property was situated at the date of the action.[93]

Enforcement of orders in company liquidation

An order made by a court in England for or in the course of winding up is enforceable in Scotland and Northern Ireland, if the courts there would have had jurisdiction if the company had been registered there, as if it had been made by them, and conversely.[94]

Enforcement of orders in bankruptcy

At common law the title of a trustee in bankruptcy or equivalent officer appointed by the court of the country where the bankrupt has been residing and carrying on business will be recognized by the Scottish courts.[95] The Scottish courts have held that they will accept the bankruptcy jurisdiction of English courts.[96] The Act and Warrant issued on confirmation of a trustee in bankruptcy vests in him the debtor's whole estate wherever situated; where situated abroad it is for the local law to determine what effect to give to a Scottish sequestration.[97] Orders made by a Scottish court are statutorily enforceable in England and Ireland as if made by the courts there. Similarly orders of a court of bankruptcy in England or Northern Ireland are enforceable in Scotland as if made by the

---

[89] Ss. 1–24; *Killen* v. *K.*, 1981 S.L.T. (Sh. Ct.) 77.
[90] Ss. 25–6, i.e. countries which have acceded to the U.N. Convention on the Recovery Abroad of Maintenance, 1956.
[91] S. 31.
[92] Ss. 32–9.
[93] *Cammell* v. *Sewell* (1858) 3 H. & N. 728; *Castrique* v. *Imrie* (1870) L.R. 4 H.L. 414.
[94] Companies Act, 1985, S. 570; and see R.C. 216; it applies to orders for payment of money only: *Johnstone's Trs.* v. *Roose* (1884) 12 R. 1.
[95] *Obers* v. *Paton's Trs.* (1897) 24 R. 719. See also *Murphy's Tr.* v. *Aitken*, 1983 S.L.T. 78.
[96] *Wilkie* v. *Cathcart* (1870) 9 M. 168; *Salaman* v. *Tod*, 1911 S.C. 1214.
[97] Bankruptcy (Sc.) Act, 1985, S. 31.

court required to enforce them. These courts are to be auxiliary to one another in all matters of bankruptcy.[98]

Foreign appointments of executors

If a deceased person left property in Scotland it can be dealt with only by an executor confirmed by the Scottish courts. By the Administration of Estates Act 1971, S. 3, a grant of probate or letters of administration from the High Court in England or Northern Ireland has, without being resealed, the same force, effect, and operation in relation to property in Scotland as a Scottish confirmation, and conversely. Under the Colonial Probates Act, 1892, a grant of representation made in a country to which the Act applies[99] may be resealed and have the same effect as confirmation. But representatives appointed by decreased persons elsewhere must obtain confirmation in the ordinary way.[1]

Enforcement of judgments under international conventions

Judgments granted by foreign courts under any of the Carriage by Air Act, 1961, the Carriage by Air (Supplementary Provisions) Act, the Carriage of Goods by Road Act, 1965, the Nuclear Installations Act, 1965, the Merchant Shipping (Oil pollution) Act, 1971, the Carriage of Goods by Sea Act, 1971, the International Transport Conventions Act, 1983, the Carriage of Passengers by Road Act, 1974, and the Merchant Shipping Act, 1979, are enforceable under the Foreign Judgments (Reciprocal Enforcement) Act, 1933.

Enforcement of European Community judgments

By the European Communities (Enforcement of Community Judgments) Order, 1972,[2] there may be registered in the Court of Session judgments and orders to which the Secretary of State has duly appended an order for enforcement, so that they are then, subject to the treaties, enforceable as if they were judgments or order of that court.

Enforcement of foreign arbitration awards

At common law the Scottish courts give effect to a final decree-arbitral valid by the proper law of the contract of submission to arbitration,[3] so long as not contrary to natural justice,[4] by decree-conform.

---

[98] Insolvency Act, 1986, S. 213.
[99] This includes most Commonwealth countries.
[1] cf. *New York Breweries Co. Ltd.* v. *A.G.* [1899] A.C. 62.
[2] S.I. 1972, No. 1590.
[3] *E. Hopetoun* v. *Scots Mines Co.* (1856) 18 D. 739; *Hope* v. *Crookston Bros.* (1890) 17 R. 868.
[4] *Hamlyn* v. *Talisker Distillery* (1894) 21 R. (H.L.) 21, 23.

Foreign arbitral awards, as statutorily defined,[5] subject to certain conditions[6] and to being satisfactorily evidenced,[7] are enforceable in Scotland by action, or if the agreement for arbitration contains consent to the registration of the award in the Books of Council and Session for execution and it is so registered, by summary diligence.[8] Certain arbitration awards can be enforced by registration as if they were judgments.[9]

[5] Arbitration Act, 1950, S. 35.
[6] Ibid., S. 37(1).
[7] Ibid., S. 38.
[8] Ibid., S. 41(3).
[9] i.e. those made in countries to which the Administration of Justice Act, 1920, Part II, or the Foreign Judgments (Reciprocal Enforcement) Act, 1933, Part I, has been extended, and certain awards made in pursuance of a contract for the international carriage of goods: Carriage of Goods by Road Act, 1965, Ss. 4, 7.

BOOK III

LAW OF PERSONS

CHAPTER 3.1

PERSONALITY

The law of persons is properly studied first because the legal system operates by ascribing legal rights and duties to legal persons, and obligations exist between legal persons, property is possessed and owned by legal persons, and legal persons claim legal remedies from other legal persons. The concept of the legal person is accordingly fundamental.

Legal personality is the quality, attributed by legal rules, of being a legal person, an entity to which legal rights can attach and on which legal duties may be incumbent. A legal person is a right and duty bearing unit for legal purposes, having *persona standi in judicio*, and only a legal person has rights and duties under the legal system.

The category of legal persons is not confined to natural living persons. Scots law attributes legal personality to all living human beings (natural persons),[1] at least for some purposes to certain kinds of associations of living persons, particularly partnerships (sometimes called quasi-corporations),[2] though for other purposes these groups, and other kinds of groups for all purposes, are deemed merely groups or aggregates of natural persons,[3] and it attributes legal personality for all purposes to certain entities or groups or institutions held to be incorporated by law, and hence known as corporations, such as companies and local authorities.[4] Though in themselves inanimate and incorporeal, corporations (sometimes called artificial or juristic persons) are held in law to be single entities which have legal personality and existence in law quite independently of the legal personalities of all the members or officials thereof.[5] They make contracts, commit harms, sue, and are sued, as entities. Whether the Crown, in the sense of the superior central government of the state, as distinct from the sovereign for the time being, is a corporation for any purpose is uncertain.[6]

---

[1] Chs. 3.2–3.6 *infra*.

[2] Ch. 3.9 *infra*.

[3] Chs. 3.7–3.9 *infra*. Co-proprietors are not a separate legal persona: *Barclay* v. *Penman*, 1984 S.L.T. 376.

[4] Chs. 3.10–3.15 *infra*; cf. Ersk. I, 7, 64; Bell, *Prin.* § 2176–8.

[5] *Salomon* v. *S.* [1897] A.C. 22; *Woolfson* v. *Strathclyde R.C*, 1978 S.C. (H.L.) 90. The Interpretation Act, 1978, Sch. 1, provides that in legislation generally, unless the contrary intention appears, the expression 'person' includes 'a body of persons corporate or unincorporate'. But normally unincorporated groups or associations must be distinguished from incorporated bodies as well as from natural persons.

[6] Ch. 3.12 *infra*.

Animals do not have legal personality; though various rules of law, such as for prevention of cruelty,[7] exist for their benefit these confer no legal rights or duties on the creatures themselves.[8]

Whether legal personality, full or restricted, is attributed to particular categories of human beings is a matter of law, as is the question whether particular kinds of groups or entities can be, or have been, incorporated, and, in the latter event what powers, capacities, duties, and liabilities attach to them thereby. So too the questions whether, and, if so, at what point of time, personality has come into being or terminated, are questions of law.

Distinct from personality are status, which is the legal grouping to which a person belongs, capacity, which is the attribute of personality of being able legally to do certain classes of acts, of having certain classes of rights and duties, and power, which is the quality of being entitled or authorized legally to do particular legal acts. A living being has personality but may have limited capacity[9] and even a being with personality and full capacity may have limited powers or in some respects no power.[10]

---

[7] cf. *Easton* v. *Anderson*, 1949 J.C. 1.
[8] cf. *Re Dean* (1889) 41 Ch. D. 552.
[9] e.g. a pupil child.
[10] e.g. an employed person may have no power to pledge the employer's credit.

PART 1

NATURAL PERSONS

CHAPTER 3.2

NATURAL PERSONS AND THEIR STATUS

Natural persons are living human beings and all are regarded by Scots law as endowed with legal personality. Though by Scots law all living human beings are natural persons, not all have the same legal attributes, capacities, and powers. These vary according to the status of the natural person.

Commencement of personality

Legal personality of natural persons commences at least for certain purposes at conception, provided that the individual is subsequently born alive and has lived, for however short a time. Thus a claim may be open for ante-natal injuries[1] or loss,[2] and in the law of succession a child *in utero* is deemed already born if that will benefit it, under the maxim *nasciturus pro iam nato habetur quando agitur de ejus commodo*, provided it is subsequently born alive.[3] If the child is stillborn he is held never to have been a legal person.

Personality commences generally at birth, though by reason of a child's incapacity he has no legal powers to act on his own behalf so long as he remains a pupil. The precise time of birth is material as the periods of age are computed *de momento in momentum*.[4] Births must be registered under the Registration of Births, Deaths and Marriages (Scotland) Act, 1965, Ss. 13–21.

---

[1] Walker, *Delict*, 96; Atkinson (1904) 20 L.Q.R. 134; Winfield (1942) 8 Camb. L.J. 76; Veitch (1973) 24 N.I.L.Q. 40; see also *Walker* v. *G.N. Ry. of Ireland* (1890) 28 L.R. Ir. 69; *Montreal Tramways* v. *Leveille* [1933] 4 D.L.R. 337.
[2] *Connachan* v. *S.M.T. Co.*, 1946 S.C. 428; *Moorcraft* v. *Alexander*, 1946 S.C. 466; *Leadbetter* v. *N.C.B.*, 1952 S.L.T. 179 (damages to posthumous children for father's death).
[3] *Elliot* v. *Joicey*, 1935 S.C. (H.L.) 57, 70: *Allan's Trs.* v. *A.*, 1949 S.L.T. (Notes) 3; *Cox's Trs.* v. *C.*, 1950 S.C. 117.
[4] Craig II, 12, 14; Stair I, 6, 33; Ersk. I, 7, 36; Fraser, *P. & Ch.*, 200.

Presumption of life

A person once born is presumed to remain alive for a normal and substantial time[5] but at common law the Court may at any time presume his death at a stated date[6] if satisfied by evidence that his death by then is very probable.[7] It is a question of circumstances and it is relevant to consider what the absent person's age would have been, his health, and any circumstances which might shorten his normal expectation of life.[8] The issue may be tried in a multiplepoinding.[9]

Under the Presumtpion of Death (Scotland) Act, 1977, the Court may, where a person has not been known to have been alive for at least seven years, find that he died at a specified date and time or that he is to be presumed to have died seven years after the date on which he was last known to be alive.[10] Action is competent at the instance of anyone having an interest, such as one entitled to succeed to any estate on the death of the absentee,[11] or to any estate the transmission of which depends on the absentee's death, or the fiar of any estate burdened by a liferent in favour of the absentee. The missing person should be called as defender and the Lord Advocate may be called for the public interest.[12] Decree is conclusive and effective against everyone and for all purposes, including dissolution of the person's marriage and the acquisition of rights to or in property belonging to any person.[13] Decree may be varied or recalled by the court, but not to the effect of reviving a marriage dissolved by the decree.[14] On variation or recall within five years the court is to make such further order in relation to rights to or in property acquired as a result of the decree as it considers fair and reasonable in the circumstances, having regard to stated considerations, namely requiring trustees to make over property, and entitling insurers to recover capital sums paid under the original decree.[15] The interests of a person who, in good faith and for

---

[5] Stair IV, 45, 17, (19) mentions 80 or 100 years; Bankt. II, 6, 31; *Bruce* v. *Smith* (1871) 10 M. 130; *Barstow* v. *Cook* (1874) 11 S.L.R. 363; *Stewart's Trs.* v. *S.* (1875) 2 R. 488; *McLay* v. *Borland* (1876) 3 R. 1124; *Secy of State for Scotland* v. *Sutherland*, 1944 S.C. 79, 84.

[6] *Rhind's Trs.* v. *Bell* (1878) 5 R. 527.

[7] *Greig* v. *Edinburgh Merchant Coy.*, 1921 S.C. 76; *Secy of State for Scotland, supra*; contrast *Sharp* v. *S.* (1898) 25 R. 1132.

[8] e.g. *Garland* v. *Stewart* (1841) 4 D. 1; *Fairholme* v. *F's Trs.* (1858) 20 D. 813; *Bruce, supra*; *Rhind's Trs., supra*; *Williamson* v. *W.* (1886) 14 R. 226; *Greig, supra*.

[9] *Tait's Factor* v. *Meikle* (1890) 17 R. 1182.

[10] S. 2; cf. *X.* v. *S.S.C. Socy.*, 1937 S.L.T. 87; *Tait* v. *Sleigh*, 1969 S.L.T. 227. If the absentee is later found to have been alive at a date after he had been presumed dead, a second action is competent: *Andrews* (1901) 9 S.L.T. 117. Other courts or statutory tribunals may determine death as a question incidental to the main issue before such court.

[11] cf. *Shepherd's Trs.* v. *Brown* (1902) 9 S.L.T. 487; *Barr* v. *Campbell*, 1925 S.C. 317; including the case where the heir to a Scottish heritage, who had disappeared, was a domiciled Englishman: *Jones*, 1923 S.L.T. 31.

[12] *Horak* v. *L.A.*, 1984 S.L.T. 201.

[13] S. 3.

[14] S. 4.

[15] S. 5 cf. *Masters and Seamen of Dundee* v. *Cockerill* (1869) 8 M. 278; *North British and Mercantile Insurance* v. *Stewart* (1871) 9 M. 534.

value, acquires property rights from a successor to a missing person are protected. The trustee administering the estate of a missing person must insure against liabilities which may arise as a result of an order under S. 5.[16] The value of rights to or in property acquired under the decree by one whom the missing person would have had a duty to aliment may be declared irrecoverable.[17] Any person having knowledge of the survival or death of the missing person must disclose that information.[18] A decree or judgment of a court of a country furth of Scotland in which a person was domiciled or habitually resident that a person has died or is presumed to have died is, in Scotland, sufficient evidence of the facts so declared.[19] Provision is made for accepting information from various authorities of death or presumed death for the purpose of appointment or confirmation of an executor.[20] A decree and any variation order must be notified by the court to the Registrar of Births, Deaths, and Marriages.[21]

It is frequently important to determine whether one person survived another. At common law there is no presumption that one person survived another in any particular circumstances,[22] and survival has to be proved, but the Succession (Scotland) Act, 1964, S. 31 makes provision for a presumption in certain cases.[23]

Termination of personality

Legal personality terminates with natural death, though it may be said to continue to the extent that a deceased person's wishes for the disposal of his estate, if expressed in a document held to evidence testamentary intention, will be legally enforceable, and rights and liabilities vested in his estate will be exigible by or against his executor, who is accounted as *eadem persona cum defuncto*.[24] But all purely personal rights and liabilities perish with the deceased.[25] Deaths must be registered under the Registration of Births, Deaths, and Marriages (Scotland) Act, 1965, Ss.

---

[16] S. 6.
[17] S. 7.
[18] S. 9.
[19] S. 10, overruling *Simpson's Trs. v. Fox*, 1951 S.L.T. 412.
[20] S. 11.
[21] S. 12.
[22] *Drummond's J. F. v. H.M. Advocate*, 1944 S.C. 298; *Mitchell's Exrx. v. Gordon*, 1953 S.C. 176; *Ross's J. F. v. Martin*, 1955 S.C. (H.L.) 56; see also *Tawse* (1882) 19 S.L.R. 829; *Dear v. Lumgair* (1905) 12 S.L.T. 862; (1906) 13 S.L.T. 850.
[23] Ch. 7.3, *infra*
[24] e.g. right of action for patrimonial loss: *Smith v. Strewart*, 1961 S.C. 91; right to exact payment of money due to deceased, or to recover damages for breach of contract: *Riley v. Ellis*, 1910 S.C. 934; liability to pay: *Gardiner v. Stewart's Trs.*, 1908 S.C. 985; or to perform contract not involving *delectus personae*.
[25] e.g. right of action for solatium: *Smith v. Stewart*, 1960 S.C. 329; liability to perform contract involving *delectus personae*: *Hoey v. McEwan & Auld* (1867) 5 M. 814; *Mitchell v. Mackersy* (1905) 8 F. 198; *Cole v. Handasyde*, 1910 S.C. 68; *Tait's Exrx. v. Arden Coal Co.* 1947 S.C. 100.

22–8. Between the moment of death and the confirmation by the court of an executor, the deceased's property is *haereditas jacens*, vested in nobody, though the executor's confirmation vests it in him, retrospectively to the time of death.

STATUS

Natural persons are grouped for legal purposes according to their status.[26] Status is the legal standing or position of a person and consists in belonging to a particular class of persons to all of whom the law assigns particular legal capacities, powers, liabilities or incapacities. Membership of a particular status-group is in many cases attributed to persons entirely by force of law and independently of their volition; in other cases, such as that of being married, the individual may elect or decline to assume the status, but if he does elect, he cannot assume it without its legal consequences, nor voluntarily divest himself of it. In all cases prescribed rights and duties, capacities and incapacities, attach by force of law to all persons having the particular status, and can be modified by the parties, if at all, only in details. Status is more than, and different from, a mere voluntary relationship between one person and another; it involves a general condition or standing in legal matters, which regulates generally the individual's capacities and incapacities.

A person's status is determined by the totality of various factors each of which has two or more mutually exclusive possibilities, and every person must fall into one or other of the possible classes of each. Each person's total status is determined by the aggregate of the various factors of status which apply in his case, and this totality accordingly determines the aggregate of his legal powers, capacities, immunities, disabilities, and so on. In particular contexts, e.g. as regards capacity to marry, or to contract, one factor of status may be more relevant than others; in many contexts many of the factors are irrelevant.[27] The factors are:

(a) (i) British subjects; (ii) aliens;
(b) (i) patrials; (ii) non-patrials;[28]
(c) (i) unborn child; (ii) pupil; (iii) minor; (iv) adult;
(d) (i) male; (ii) female;[29]

---

[26] On status see Graveson, *Status in the Common Law*; Allen, 'Status and Capacity' in *Legal Duties*, 28; *Admin. of Austrian Property* v. *Von Lorang*, 1927 S.C. (H.L.) 80, 85, 92.

[27] Some of the factors are important primarily in public law, and not in private law.

[28] As defined by Immigration Act, 1971, S. 2.

[29] The hermaphrodite has been said to belong to the sex which he resembles more closely and *in dubio* deemed male: Forbes, p. 18. The transsexual belongs to the sex to which he or she belongs by virtue of chromosomal, gonadal, genital, and psychological factors: *Corbett* v. *C.* [1970] 2 All E.R. 33. If a child's sex is wrongly described when its birth is registered a correction may be made in the Register of Corrected Entries: Registration of Births, Deaths, and Marriages (Sc.) Act, 1965, S. 42. This seems to be the only real case of change of sex.

(e) (i) legitimate; (ii) illegitimate; (iii) legitimated;
     (iv) adopted;
(f) (i) bodily and mentally sound; (ii) bodily or mentally *incapax*;
(g) (i) single;[30] (ii) married;[31]
(h) (i) noble; (ii) commoner;
(j) (i) free; (ii) prisoner;
(k) (i) solvent; (ii) bankrupt;
(l) (i) lay; (ii) cleric;
(m) (i) civilian; (ii) member of one of the armed forces.

For legal purposes the norm or standard natural person is the adult male commoner of British nationality, of sound mind and body, legitimate, unmarried, free and solvent, lay and civilian, and persons of different status have their status described as in some respect variations from that standard. In many respects the variations are insignificant.

Various factors relevant to status at other times or in other legal systems, but irrelevant in modern Scots law, are civil death, heresy, prodigality, serfdom or slavery,[32] outlawry,[33] race,[34] colour,[34] caste, position in the family (whether *sui juris* or *in potestate*), and others. Certain other factors, such as being facile, or under the influence of drink or a drug, may in particular circumstances be relevant to a person's capacity, but do not amount to a distinct element of status. Domicile is the connection between a person and a legal system attributed by law for certain purposes, not a status, and residence is a matter of fact.

Decrees of court altering the status of parties are reported by the court to the Registrar-General and entered by him in the Register of Corrections.[35]

The holding of an official position, or the membership of a particular profession, is sometimes spoken of as a status.[36] This is inaccurate, because any special rights or privileges attach to the individual only so long as he holds the office or is a member of the profession, and only in relation thereto, and does not affect his legal rights, powers, and capacities generally.

Discrimination on ground of sex

The Sex Discrimination Act, 1975, makes it unlawful, subject to limited exceptions, to discriminate against a person on the ground of sex in

---

[30] *Admin. of Austrian Property, supra*, 92.
[31] Including, for all practical purposes, widowed and divorced.
[32] *Knight* v. *Wedderburn* (1778) Mor. 14545.
[33] Criminal Justice (Sc.) Act., 1949, S. 15.
[34] See Race Relations Act, 1976.
[35] Registration of Births, Deaths, and Marriages (Sc.) Act, 1965, S. 48. This deals with Scottish decrees only: *Smart* v. *Registrar General*, 1954 S.C. 81.
[36] cf. *Forbes* v. *Eden* (1865) 4 M. 143, 'a particular status, meaning the capacity to perform certain functions or hold certain offices'.

employment, membership of a trade union or employers' organization, training, education, or the provision of goods, facilities, or services, or to issue an advertisement which indicates an intention to discriminate.[37] An Equal Opportunities Commission has been established with power to conduct investigations.[38] Proceedings may be brought as for breach of statutory duty for declarator or damages.[39] A term in a contract is void if contravening the Act and a court may modify or remove such a term.[40]

Discrimination on grounds of race

It is unlawful, subject to exceptions, for a person to discriminate against another on grounds of colour, race, nationality, or ethnic or national origins by treating him less favourably than other persons in respect of employment, membership of a trade union or employers' organization, education, the provision of goods, facilities, or services, housing accommodation, business premises, or other land, or by displaying any advertisement or notice which indicates intention to discriminate.[41] The Commission for Racial Equality may investigate complaints of discrimination[42] and may bring civil proceedings for declarator, or damages[43] and may have a court revise a discriminatory contract.[44]

Status in general extra-domestic and in domestic relations

The rights, duties, capacities, and incapacities of status-groups must be considered both generally, in relations with everyone, and in respect of domestic relations, with one another within the home and family.[45] The capacities and incapacities or disabilities implied in private law by membership of particular status groups are stated as deviations from the standard of the adult male.

(a) BRITISH SUBJECTS: ALIENS

Nationality denotes the quality of political membership of a state. British subjects include citizens of the United Kingdom and colonies, citizens of various Commonwealth countries, British protected persons, and certain citizens of Ireland. Aliens are persons not British subjects, British pro-

---

[37] Ss. 1–42.
[38] Ss. 53–61.
[39] Ss. 62–76.
[40] S. 77.
[41] Race Relations Act, 1976, Ss. 1–33.
[42] Ss. 43–52.
[43] Ss. 57–62.
[44] S. 72.
[45] Chs. 3.3–3.5, infra.

tected persons, or citizens of Ireland.[46] In the sphere of private law the differences are insubstantial in peace time.[47] Only a British subject by birth or naturalization may own any share in a British ship[48] or aircraft.[49] In most other respects an alien in Britain in peace time has ordinary civil or private rights. He may sue and be sued,[50] hold property, act as trustee, bequeath by will, and take as legatee.

In wartime, however, aliens of enemy nationality in this country may be interned but may still act in a representative capacity[51] and, if domiciled here, bring actions relative to status,[52] sue and be sued and appeal,[53] and contract.[54] Alien enemies outside the realm, including British nationals resident in enemy territory, cannot sue[55] and pending actions must be sisted till peace returns.[56] Save by royal licence a contract with an alien enemy is illegal, but executory contracts become illegal only if performance would involve dealings with or potential benefit to enemies.[57] Property rights are not affected[58] but are suspended and restored when peace returns.[59]

(b) PATRIALS: NON-PATRIALS

Only patrials have the right of abode in the United Kingdom. These are citizens of the United Kingdom and Colonies by birth, adoption, naturalization, or, with exceptions, registration in the U.K., or certain other categories of such citizens, or in certain circumstances Commonwealth citizens. Save as provided by statute a non-patrial may not enter the U.K. unless given leave to do so, which leave may be limited or subject to conditions. They may live, work, and settle in the U.K. by permission only and subject to statutory regulation and control.[60] There appear to be no differences in private law between patrials and non-patrials while in the U.K.

---

[46] See generally Bell, *Prin.* § 2131–60; Status of Aliens Act, 1914, S. 17; Aliens Restrictions Act, 1919; British Nationality Acts, 1948, 1958 and 1965; Naturalization Act, 1870. See now British Nationality Act, 1981.

[47] As defined by British Nationality Acts, 1948, 1958, and 1965.

[48] Merchant Shipping Act, 1894, S. 1. As to pilotage certificates and employment on British Ships, see Aliens Restrictions Act, 1919, Ss. 4, 5.

[49] Air Navigation Order, 1960, arts. 21, 22, and 23.

[50] *Porter* v. *Freudenberg* [1915] 1 K.B. 857; see also *Goldston* v. *Young* (1868) 7 M. 188.

[51] *Schulze*, 1917 S.C. 400; *Rodriguez* v. *Speyer* [1919] A.C. 59; *Crolla*, 1942 S.C. 21.

[52] *Weiss* v. *W.*, 1940 S.L.T. 467.

[53] *Porter* v. *Freudenberg* [1915] 1 K.B. 857.

[54] *Schulze, Gow & Co.* v. *Bank of Scotland*, 1914 2 S.L.T. 455.

[55] *Johnson & Wight* v. *Goldsmid*, 15 Feb. 1809, F.C.; *Sovfracht* v. *van Uden*, [1943] A.C. 203.

[56] *Craig Line* v. *N.B. Storage Co.*, 1915 S.C. 113; *Van Uden* v. *Burrell*, 1916 S.C. 391.

[57] *Stevenson* v. *Cartonnagen Industrie* [1918] A.C. 239; *Ertel Bieber* v. *Rio Tinto* [1918] A.C. 260; *Rodriguez, supra.*

[58] *Halsey* v. *Lowenfeld* [1916] 2 K.B. 707; *Ertel Bieber, supra.*

[59] *Penney* v. *Clyde Shipbuilding Co.*, 1920 S.C. (H.L.) 68.

[60] Immigration Act, 1971, Ss. 1–3.

(c) UNBORN CHILD: PUPIL: MINOR: ADULT

(i) *Unborn child*

The unborn child has legal personality before birth only to the limited extent that, if subsequently born alive, a claim of damages may be brought on his behalf for loss suffered,[61] or ante-natal injuries,[62] and that, for the purposes of inheritance, he will be accounted already born if that would be to his advantage, on the basis of the maxim *nasciturus pro iam nato habetur quando de ejus commodo queritur*.[63] Only to this limited extent has he any legal status. If never born alive he is deemed in law never to have existed.[64]

Age

For the purposes of certain social security legislation a person attains a stated age on the anniversary of the date of his birth.[65]

(ii) *Pupils*

Pupils, that is boys aged under 14 and girls aged under 12 the traditional age of presumed puberty, have, for reasons of their natural incapacity, strictly limited legal personality; indeed they are said to have no person in the legal sense of the word,[66] and to be in a state of absolute incapacity.[67] A pupil must, therefore, have a parent or other person to act as his tutor and administrator-in-law. At common law a pupil cannot marry but if parties continued to cohabit after the age of puberty a marriage was held validly constituted or ratified.[68] A pupil has by himself no contractual capacity, and an attempt to contract is a nullity, and a purported contract is challengeable within the twenty years of the long negative prescription.[69] Any contract must be entered into by his tutor on his behalf, and such contracts are open to challenge by the child until four years after he

---

[61] *Connachan* v. *S.M.T. Co.*, 1946 S.C. 428; *Moorcraft* v. *Alexander*, 1946 S.C. 466; *Leadbetter* v. *N.C.B.*, 1952 S.L.T. 179.

[62] Walker, *Delict; Montreal Tramways* v. *Leveille* [1933] 4 D.L.R. 337; *Pinchin* v. *Santam Ins. Co.*, 1963 (2) S.A. 254.

[63] Dig. I, 6, 7, and 26; Fraser, *P. & Ch.*, 220; *Hardman* v. *Guthrie* (1828) 6 S. 920; *Elliot* v. *Joicey*, 1935 S.C. (H.L.) 57; *Cox's Trs.* v. *C.*, 1950 S.C. 117.

[64] Bankt. I, 2, 7–8.

[65] Social Security Act, 1980, S. 18.

[66] Ersk. I, 7, 14; cf. *Sinclair* v. *Stark* (1828) 6 S. 336.

[67] Bell, *Pr.* § 2067. cf. *McAulay* v. *Renny* (1803) Bell, *Comm.* II, 514; *Calder* v. *Downie*, 11 Dec. 1811, F.C., affd. (1815) 18 F.C. 508; *Hill* v. *City of Glasgow Bank* (1879) 7 R. 68, 74. But a pupil is not a non entity: see *Whitehall* v. *W.*, 1958 S.C. 252, 259.

[68] Ersk. I, 6, 2; Bell, *Pr.* s 1523; Fraser, *H. & W.*, I., 53; *Johnston* v. *Ferrier* (1770) Mor. 8931; *McGibbon* v. *McGibbon* (1852) 14 D. 605.

[69] Ersk., *supra; Bruce* (1577) Mor. 8979.

has attained majority, on proof of lesion.[70] He is said to be able to enforce a contract made on his behalf which is beneficial to himself though it cannot be enforced against him.[71]. Money lent to a pupil may be recovered from him if used beneficially by him,[72] and if necessaries have been sold and delivered to him, he must pay a reasonable price therefor;[73] but these obligations are not contractual but arise *ex lege*, by quasi-contract.

He has no title by himself to sue for wrong done him, nor liability to be sued; the tutor must sue[74] or be called. A pupil can however commit wrong imposing liability on his tutor in reparation,[75] and may be guilty of contributory negligence, if old enough to appreciate the danger.[76] A pupil cannot grant a discharge for damages awarded him and this must be done by his tutor, or a judicial factor be appointed.[77]

Property can be held by a pupil, but must be administered by his tutor for behoof of the pupil.[78] A pupil has no capacity to make a will,[79] nor may he act as a trustee.

An action in name of a pupil without his tutor is incompetent, and a decree against one without his tutor is reducible as a decree in absence, though not wholly null.[80] If a pupil has no legal guardian, or the guardian has an adverse interest, or is incapax, action may be brought in his name and a *curator ad litem* appointed, with whose concurrence the case may proceed.[81] Both the pupil and his tutor should be called as defenders; if the latter is not known the action should be directed against the pupil and his tutors generally.[82] If necessary a *curator ad litem* must be appointed.[83]

---

[70] Ersk. I, 7, 34; Bell, *Prin.* s 2098; *Falconer v. Thomson* (1792) Mor. 16380; *Finlaysons v. F.*, 22 Dec. 1810, F.C. cf. *Patrick v. Baird*, 1927 S.N. 32.

[71] Bank. IV, 45, 13; Ersk. I, 7, 33; Fraser, *P. & Ch.*, 206.

[72] *E. Morton v. Muirhead* (1749) Mor. 8931; *Scott's Trs. v. S.* (1887) 14 R. 1043.

[73] Common law and Sale of Goods Act, 1979, S. 2.

[74] e.g. *Davis's Tutor v. Glasgow Victoria Hospital*, 1950 S.C. 382.

[75] *Somerville v. Hamilton* (1541) Mor. 8905; *Kerr v. Bremner* (1839) 1 D. 618; *Davie v. Wilson* (1854) 16 D. 956.

[76] *Cass v. Edinburgh Tramways*, 1909 S.C. 1068; *Holland v. Lanark C.C.*, 1909 S.C. 1142; *Plantza v. Glasgow Corpn.*, 1910 S.C. 786; *Allison v. Langloan Iron & Chemical Co.*, 1917 2 S.L.T. 162.

[77] *Collins v. Eglinton Iron Co.* (1882) 9 R. 500; *Connolly v. Bent Colliery Co.* (1897) 24 R. 1172; *Boylan v. Hunter*, 1922 S.C. 80; *Fairley v. Allan*, 1948 S.L.T. (Notes) 81; *Falconer v. Robertson*, 1949 S.L.T. (Notes) 57.

[78] Title to heritage is commonly taken in name of a pupil himself without objection; see Titles to Land Consolidation (Sc.) Act, 1868, S. 24, as amended; Bell, *Prin.* s 2084; Bell, *Convg.* I, 117; Fraser, *P. & Ch.*, 205; *Linton v. I.R.*, 1928 S.C. 209, 213. The tutor has no power to alienate or dispose of the heritage without court authority.

[79] Stair III, 8, 37.

[80] Bell, *Prin.* § 2067; *Craven v. Elibank's Trs.* (1854) 16 D. 811; *Dingwall v. Burns* (1871) 9 M. 582.

[81] *M'Conochie v. Binnie* (1847) 9 D. 791; *Ward v. Walker*, 1920 S.C. 80; *Kirk v. Scottish Gas Board*, 1968 S.C. 328. The guardian would be better entitled a *tutor ad litem*.

[82] Fraser, *P. & Ch.*, 211; *Thomson's Trs. v. Livingston* (1863) 2 M. 114.

[83] *Drummond's Trs. v. Peel's Trs.*, 1929 S.C. 484.

(iii) *Minors*

Minors are young persons who have attained 14 (boys) or 12 (girls) but not adulthood. They attain the new status at the time of their birth on the fourteenth or twelfth anniversary thereof.[84]

A minor has legal personality and considerable though limited legal capacity and powers. He cannot be a trustee in sequestration[85] or a tutor, curator, or judicial factor.[86] He is capable of entering into legal transactions, though requiring the protection of the law by reason of his inferior judgment or discretion.[87] He may, but need not, have a parent or other person to act as his curator.

A promise to marry may be made by a minor though his curators do not consent.[88] At common law any minor might marry without consent[89] but since 1929 a marriage is void if either party were under the age of 16.[90] Continuing cohabitation after attaining 16 may however create a marriage by cohabitation with habit and repute.[91]

Contractual powers

A minor's contractual powers vary according as he contracts with or without a curator's consent. A minor without a curator, or forisfamiliated,[92] has the full contractual powers of an adult.[93] But a party paying a capital sum to a minor may demand security for the investment or profitable employment of the money,[94] though he may safely pay a sum of the nature of income or interest, and the minor can grant a valid discharge.[95] A minor who has a curator may, with the consent and concurrence of the curator, enter into any contract,[96] though a contract between the minor and the curator himself is not validated by the latter's consent, and is voidable within the period of the long negative prescription.[97] A minor who has a curator but contracts without the

---

[84] Ersk. I, 7, 36; Bell, *Prin.* § 2091; Fraser, *P. & Ch.*, 201.

[85] Bankruptcy (Sc.) Act, 1985, S.

[86] Ersk. I, 7, 12.

[87] Bell, *Prin.* § 2088; *Harvey* v. *H.* (1860) 22 D. 1198; *Hill* v. *City of Glasgow Bank* (1879) 7 R. 68, 74.

[88] *Whitehead* v. *Phillips* (1902) 10 S.L.T. 577.

[89] Ersk. I, 7, 33; *Bruce* v. *Hamilton* (1854) 17 D. 265.

[90] Marriage (Sc.) Act, 1977, S. 1; Ch. 3.3, *infra*.

[91] *A.B.* v. *C.D.*, 1957 S.C. 415.

[92] On forisfamiliation see Ersk. I, 6, 53; *Anderson* v. *A.* (1832) 11 S. 10; *McFeetridge, infra*.

[93] Ersk. I, 7, 33; Fraser, *P. & Ch.*, 436; *Thomson* v. *Stevenson* (1666) Mor. 8991; *Hill* v. *City of Glasgow Bank* (1879) 7 R. 68; *Brown's Tr.* v. *B.* (1897) 24 R. 962; *McFeetridge* v. *Stewarts & Lloyds*, 1913 S.C. 773.

[94] *Kirkman* v. *Pym* (1782) Mor. 8977.

[95] *Jack* v. *N.B. Ry. Co.* (1886) 14 R. 263.

[96] Ersk. I, 7, 33; Bell, *Prin.* § 2096; Fraser, *P. & Ch.* 483; *Alexander* v. *Thomson* (1813) Hume 411; *Harvey* v. *H.* (1860) 22 D. 1198; *Hill, supra*.

[97] *Mackenzie* v. *Fairholm* (1666) Mor. 8959; *Thomson* v. *Pagan* (1781) Mor. 8985; *Manuel* v. *M.* (1853) 15 D. 284.

latter's consent may bind himself to contracts for necessaries[98] or for, or in the ordinary course of, employment;[99] but apart from those cases a contract without consent is void, and challengeable at any time within the period of the long negative prescription without need for proof of lesion,[1] though it is said to be enforceable by the minor if beneficial to him.[2] A minor contracting without his curator's consent is liable in so far as money obtained by him under the contract has been beneficially employed.[3] The curator by himself has no contractual power at all on behalf of the minor, his function being only to advise and consent, and any contract by him alone is a nullity.[4] Subject to these qualifications, a minor may bind himself to any personal obligation, engage in trade, or become a partner or a shareholder in a company.[5]

Avoidance of contract for minority and lesion

In all cases,[6] following the Roman law,[7] the minor's contracts are voidable at his instance until four years, the *quadriennium utile*, after he has attained majority,[8] on proof of his minority at the time, and of enorm lesion. The plea may also be taken by the minor's heirs, creditors, or assignees.[9] Enorm lesion is consideration for the contract immoderately disproportionate to what might have been got.[10] It must be positive loss, not merely loss of possible gain,[11] and be enorm, or substantial,[12] judged as at the date of the transaction.[13] The transaction will not be reduced if

---

[98] Sale of Goods Act, 1979, S. 2; repeating common law e.g. *Fontaine* v. *Foster* (1808) Hume 409. 'Necessaries' doubtless include food, clothing, and lodging; beyond that it is a question of fact in each case; see *Johnston* v. *Maitland* (1782) Mor. 9036; *Scoffier* v. *Read* (1783) Mor. 8936; cf. *Nash* v. *Inman* [1908] 3 K.B. 1.

[99] Ersk. I, 7, 38; Bell, *Comm.* I, 131; *Stevenson* v. *Adair* (1872) 10 M. 919; *McFeetridge, supra*; *O'Donnell* v. *Brownieside Coal Co.*, 1934 S.C. 534.

[1] Stair I, 6, 33; Bankt. I, 7, 56; Ersk. I, 7, 33; Fraser, *P. & Ch.* 493; *Manuel* v. *M.* (1853) 15 D. 284; see also *Stevenson* v. *Adair* (1872) 10 M. 919; *McFeetridge* v. *Stewarts & Lloyds*, 1913 S.C. 773; *Boyle* v. *Woodypoint Caravans*, 1970 S.L.T. (Sh. Ct.) 34.

[2] Ersk. I, 7, 33.

[3] Stair, *supra*.

[4] Bell, *Prin.* s 2096; Fraser, *P. & Ch.* 471; *E. Bute* v. *Campbell* (1725) Mor. 16338.

[5] *Hill* v. *City of Glasgow Bank* (1879) 7 R. 68, 75.

[6] Even if the curator consented, though a higher degree of lesion must be shown in such a case: Ersk. I, 7, 33; or if the court had authorized the transaction: *Gillam's Curator* (1908) 15 S.L.T. 1043.

[7] D. 4, 4, 1, and see 49 J.R. 50.

[8] Stair I, 6, 44; Ersk. I, 7, 35; Bell, *Prin.* § 2098; Fraser, *P. & Ch.*, 533. Lapse of the time renders the contract unchallengeable, even if the minor were unaware of the privilege: *Hill* v. *City of Glasgow Bank* (1879) 7 R. 68.

[9] Stair I, 6, 44; Ersk. I, 7, 42; *Hamilton* v. *Sharp* (1630) Mor. 8981, 10419.

[10] *Robertson* v. *Henderson* (1905) 7 F. 776, 785; *McGuire* v. *Addie's Collieries*, 1950 S.C. 537.

[11] *Cooper* v. *C.'s Trs.* (1885) 12 R. 473; *Patrick* v. *Baird*, 1927 S.N. 32.

[12] Ersk. I, 7, 36; Bell, *Prin.* § 2100; *Robertson* v. *Henderson* (1904) 6 F. 770; 7 F. 776.

[13] *Cooper, supra*, 486.

in the whole circumstances, it was, in the view of the court, reasonable.[14] A higher degree of lesion must be shown where the minor contracted with his curator's consent,[15] and no proof of lesion is required where a minor, having a curator, contracts without his consent.[16]

Enorm lesion is presumed in the cases of donations,[17] surrenders of rights,[18] cautionary obligations,[19] loans of money made to the minor,[20] or even capital payments to the minor,[21] unless it be shown that the lesion resulted subsequently from mismanagement, or that he had ratified the transaction after attaining majority, in the knowledge of his right to challenge.[22] A person lending money to a minor, or buying property from him, is entitled to demand evidence that the money is profitably employed, for otherwise he cannot recover the money or keep the property unless he can prove that the money was expended *in rem versum* of the minor.[23]

If the minor was engaged in trade or business and contracts in relation thereto,[24] or falsely represented himself to be major and was believed to be such on reasonable grounds,[25] he is not entitled to restitution at all. Reduction may also be barred if the minor has, after attaining full age, in the knowledge of his right of reduction,[26] freely[27] ratified or approbated a transaction inferring liability,[28] but is not barred merely because the minor has ratified a writ by his oath.[29]

A minor seeking reduction on this ground must not only repudiate but bring his action of reduction before expiry of the *quadriennium utile*,[30] or plead minority and lesion as a defence *ope exceptionis* within that period. Reduction for minority and lesion does not apply to marriage, though it

---

[14] *Robertson, supra; Faulds* v. *British Steel Corpn.*, 1977 S.L.T. (Notes) 18.

[15] Ersk. I, 7, 33; *Cooper, supra.*

[16] Stair I, 6, 33; Bankt. I, 7, 56; Ersk. I, 7, 33; Fraser, *P. & Ch.* 493.

[17] Bell, *Prin.* § 2100; *Heriot* v. *Blyth* (1681) Mor. 8935.

[18] *Cooper* v. *C's Trs.* (1885) 12 R. 473; revd. on another point (1887) 15 R. (H.L.) 21.

[19] Stair I, 6, 44; Bell, *Comm.* I, 135; Bell, *Prin.* § 2100; *Wall* v. *Brownlee* (1724) Mor. 9035; *Sutherland* v. *Morson* 19 Jan. 1825 F.C.; *Macmichael* v. *Barbour* (1840) 3 D. 279.

[20] *Harkness* v: *Graham* (1833) 11 S. 760; *Ferguson* v. *Yuill* (1835) 13 S. 886; cf. Consumer Credit Act, 1974, S. 50.

[21] Bell, *Prin.* § 2100; *Jack* v. *N.B. Ry. Co.* (1886) 14 R. 263.

[22] *Dennistoun* v. *Mudie* (1850) 12 D. 613; *Henry* v. *Scott* (1892) 19 R. 545.

[23] *Harkness, supra; Stark* v. *Tennant* (1843) 5 D. 542; *Macara* v. *Wilson* (1848) 10 D. 707; *Gifford* v. *Rennie* (1853) 15 D. 451; *Scott's Trs.* v. *S.* (1887) 14 R. 1043.

[24] Ersk. I, 7, 38; Bell, *Prin.* § 2100; obligations in trade do not include gambling on the Stock Exchange: *Dennistoun, supra.*

[25] Stair I, 6, 44; Ersk. I, 7, 36; Fraser, *P. & Ch.*, 527; *Wemyss* v. *His Creditors* (1637) Mor. 9025; *Kennedy* v. *Weir* (1665) Mor. 11658; see also *Sutherland* v. *Morson* (1825) 3 S. 449; *Harvie* v. *McIntyre* (1829) 7 S. 561.

[26] *McGibbon* v. *McG.* (1852) 14 D. 605.

[27] *Melvil* v. *Arnot* (1782) Mor. 8998; *Leiper* v. *Cochran* (1822) 1 S. 552.

[28] Stair I, 6, 44; Fraser, *P. & Ch.* 531; *Forrest* v. *Campbell* (1853) 16 D. 16; *Adam* v. *A.* (1861) 23 D. 859; *Henry* v. *Scott* (1892) 19 R. 545; *L.A.* v. *Wemyss* (1899) 2 F. (H.L.) 1.

[29] Oaths of Minors Act, 1681.

[30] Bell, *Prin.* § 2099; *Stewart* v. *Snodgrass* (1860) 23 D. 187; *Hill* v. *City of Glasgow Bank* (1879) 7 R. 68, 75; see also *Patrick* v. *Baird*, 1927 S.N. 32.

may to conventional provisions made in a marriage settlement,[31] nor to judicial proceedings.[32] In no case is the minor entitled to any advantage from the reduction, but only to be restored to his former position.[33] If he reduces the transaction he must restore what he received thereunder.[34] The lapse of the *quadriennium utile* does nor preclude a challenge of the contract as being, not voidable, but wholly void, e.g. if the minor contracted without his curator's consent.[35]

Delict

A minor has a title to sue, with the consent of his curator, for wrong done him, and while he may be sued and held liable for delict, his curator, if he any have, must be called as defender with him. By wrongdoing a minor does not automatically render a parent or curator liable. A minor awarded damages can himself grant a valid discharge,[36] but in many cases the court has appointed a factor *loco tutoris* or *curator bonis* to receive and invest the money, and to discharge the defender.[37] Such a discharge is reducible on the ground of minority and lesion within the *quadriennium utile*.[38]

Property

A minor may hold property, heritable and moveable, in his own name and can validly deal with ordinary matters of administration; thus he can receive interest or rent and grant discharges therefor.[39] He may sell land and dispose of the price.[40] But he may not effectually grant a deed whereby he *inter vivos* gratuitously alters the succession to his heritable property,[41] and is deemed incapable of assenting to an arrangement varying trust purposes.[42] He may be made bankrupt.[43] He cannot be called on to defend the right he has to an ancestor's heritage.[44]

---

[31] Bell, *Prin.* § 2100; *Taylor's Trs.* v. *Dick* (1854) 16 D. 529; *Bruce* v. *Hamilton* (1854) 17 D. 265; *Cooper* v. *C's Trs.* (1885) 12 R. 473.

[32] *Anderson* v. *Geddes* (1732) Mor. 9020; *Campbell* v. *Graham* (1752) Mor. 9021.

[33] Bell, *Prin.* § 2100; Fraser, *P. & Ch.* 540.

[34] Ersk. I, 7, 41; Fraser, *P. & Ch.* 540; *Rose* v. *R.* (1821) 1 S. 154.

[35] *Kincaid* (1561) Mor. 8979; *Bell* v. *Sutherland* (1728) Mor. 8985.

[36] *Jack* v. *N.B. Ry.* (1886) 14 R. 263.

[37] *McAvoy* v. *Young's Paraffin Oil Co.* (1882) 19 S.L.R. 441; *Anderson* v. *Muirhead* (1884) 11 R. 870; *Sharp* v. *Pathhead Spinning Co.* (1885) 12 R. 574; *Fairley* v. *Allan*, 1948 S.L.T. (Notes) 81. A curator *ad litem* cannot grant a discharge: *Pratt* v. *Knox* (1855) 17 D. 1006.

[38] *Robertson* v. *Henderson* (1905) 7 F. 776.

[39] *Jack* v. *N.B. Ry. Co.* (1886) 14 R. 263. cf. Building Societies Act, 1962, S. 47.

[40] *Brown's Tr.* v. *B.* (1897) 24 R. 962.

[41] Fraser, *P. & Ch.* 442; *Hunter* (1728) Mor. 8964; *McCulloch* v. *M.* (1731) Mor. 8965.

[42] Trusts (Sc.) Act, 1961, S. 1(2).

[43] *Gray* v. *Purves* (1816) Hume 411; *Miller* v. *Aitken* (1840) 2 D. 1112.

[44] *Minor non tenetur placitare super haereditate*: Stair I, 6, 45; Ersk. I, 7, 43; Bell, *Prin.* § 2101. It is questionable if this principle is still extant.

Trust

A minor may act as a trustee.[45]

Succession

A minor may validly make a will of moveables,[46] and a testamentary disposition or settlement of heritage, though null at common law,[47] is now competent by statute.[48] A minor may challenge the action of the trustees of an estate in which he may be interested as beneficiary *intra quadriennium utile*.[49]

Actions

A minor may sue and be sued alone, but if he has a curator he should himself sue with the consent and concurrence of his curator, and be sued himself and the curator called for his interest. If he has no curator either party may apply for a curator *ad litem* to be appointed.[50] Decree against a minor alone might be set aside as a decree in absence,[51] and, whether he has a curator or not, it is reducible on the ground of minority and lesion within the *quadriennium utile*.[52] A curator cannot sue alone with or without the minor's consent, nor if he disclaims.[53] A minor may himself grant a valid discharge for damages recovered,[54] but where a capital sum is involved the court may direct payment to a trustee to hold and invest the capital until majority.[55] A minor may not grant an effective discharge on receiving a transfer of heritage with which he cannot himself deal.[56] Some of the short statutory prescriptions did not run against a defender so long as he was in minority.[57]

Minors aged 16 or over

While minority continues to the age of 18 various statutes confer particular powers on persons who have attained 16.

---

[45] *Hill v. City of Glasgow Bank* (1879) 7 R. 68.
[46] *Brown's Tr. v. B.* (1897) 24 R. 962.
[47] Ersk. I, 7, 33; Bell, *Prin.* § 2089; *Brand's Trs. v. B's Trs.* (1874) 2 R. 258.
[48] Succession (Sc.) Act, 1964, S. 28.
[49] *McLauchlan v. McL.'s Trs.*, 1941 S.L.T. 43.
[50] *Cunningham v. Smith* (1880) 7 R. 424; see also *Saunders* (1821) 1 S. 115; *Rankine* (1821) 1 S. 118; *McConochie v. Binnie* (1847) 9 D. 791.
[51] Ersk. I, 7, 33.
[52] Ersk. I, 7, 35, and 38; *Cunningham, supra.*
[53] *Allan v. Walker* (1812) Hume 586; Bell, *Prin.* § 2096.
[54] *Jack v. N.B. Ry. Co.* (1886) 14 R. 263.
[55] *Anderson v. Muirhead* (1884) 11 R. 870; *Sharp v. Pathhead Spinning Co.* (1885) 12 R. 574. See also *Boylan v. Hunter*, 1922 S.C. 80.
[56] *Ogilvy v. O's Trs.*, 1927 S.L.T. 83.
[57] Ch. 4.10, *Infra.*

(iv) *Adulthood*

Adulthood or majority is the status of a person who has attained 18,[58] formerly 21, years of age.[59] He attains this age on the eighteenth, formerly twenty-first, anniversary of his birth, at the hour of his birth.[60] He is then *sui juris* and has full legal rights and is subject to all legal liabilities without qualification, and this status is taken as the norm from which all other status are regarded as deviations. It is impossible to enumerate the legal attributes, powers, and capacities, duties, and liabilities of the adult status because the whole of the private law, so far as applicable to natural persons, is stated primarily with reference to the adult or person of full age.

(d) MALE: FEMALE

To which sex a person belongs is a question of fact.[61] An error in stating the sex of a child when registering the birth may be rectified by the Registrar-General causing an appropriate entry to be made in the Register of Corrections.[62] If he refuses, a person claiming that an error has been made may appeal to the sheriff.[63] A hermaphrodite has been said to belong to the sex which he more closely resembles, and *in dubio* to be presumed male.[64] A transsexual belongs to the sex to which he or she belongs having regard to chromosomal, gonadal, genital, and psychological factors. A person may belong to one sex biologically but be advised to belong socially to the other sex.[65] Where a person has elected for psychological reasons to pass as one of the other sex the only formal means of having the fact recognized would probably be a petition to the *nobile officium* of the Court of Session for declarator of change of apparent sex, and possibly of dissolution of marriage by reason thereof, the decree being notified by the court to the Registrar-General.[66]

For the purposes of private law the distinction between the sexes is relevant as to the age at which a pupil child becomes minor,[67] to capacity

---

[58] Age of Majority (Sc.) Act, 1969, S. 1. The change does not affect the meaning of such words as 'majority' in deeds executed before 1 Jan. 1970, or in statutory provisions incorporated in any such deed.

[59] Bankt. I, 2, 11; I, 7, 61; Ersk. I, 7, 1; *Adam* v. *A.* (1861) 23 D. 859.

[60] Stair I, 6, 33; Ersk. I, 7, 36; Fraser, *P. & Ch.* 201; *Drummond* v. *Cunningham-Head* (1624) Mor. 3465.

[61] See Bankt. I, 2, 2.

[62] This is the only true case of 'change of sex'.

[63] Registration of Births, Deaths, and Marriages (Sc.) Act, 1965, S. 42(5). The birth might then be re-registered: S. 20.

[64] Dig. I, 5, 9; Forbes, *Inst.* I, 1, 1, 18; Bankt. I, 2, 8.

[65] *Corbett* v. *C.* [1970] 2 All E.R. 33.

[66] 1965, Act, S. 48; see also X, *Petr.*, 1957 S.L.T. (Sh. Ct.) 61.

[67] Ch. 3.4, *infra.*

to marry,[66] to certain regulations affecting employment, and to certain rules of social security legislation.

At common law no distinction existed between the rights and capacities of adult males and females so long as a woman was unmarried. But when a female married she passed into the curatory of her husband[68] so that she could not sue without his consent, even in actions relating to injuries to her, or to her own property or rights.[69] Curatory now lapses even if, on marriage, she is in minority.[70] She can now acquire a domicile independently of her husband.[71] In modern law a woman, married or not, has full liberty of contract.[72]

A married woman may be liable for delict, independently of her husband; she does not make him liable unless they were acting jointly or she was acting as his agent or servant.[73] She may sue alone for delict done to her, or in the same action, if her husband had also been injured by the same wrong.[74] Husband and wife may sue each other.[75]

At common law by the *jus mariti* a woman's moveable property passed outright to her husband on marriage and by the *jus administrationis* he acquired the right to administer her heritable property. These rights have been abolished,[76] and a married woman has the same rights to own and dispose of property as if she were unmarried. A woman may no longer, by ante-nuptial marriage contract, create an alimentary liferent in her own favour.[77]

A married woman has always had freedom to dispose of property by will,[78] as had an unmarried woman. If judicially separated, or divorced, or carrying on a separate business, a woman has always been entitled to sue and be sued as if unmarried.[79] Since 1920 all women can sue and be sued as if they were unmarried, unless still subject to curatory.[80]

Since the Sex Disqualification (Removal) Act, 1919, no person is disqualified by sex or marriage from holding any appointment or entering any profession, but women may still not be ordained priests or ministers in certain religious denominations.

---

[68] cf. Roman *perpetua tutela mulierum*: Gaius I, 190; Inst. I, 13.

[69] Stair I, 4, 22; Ersk. I, 6, 21; Bell, *Prin.* § 1548.

[70] Law Reform (Husband and Wife) (Sc.) Act, 1984, S. 3.

[71] Ch. 2.1., *supra*.

[72] Married Women's Property (Sc.) Act, 1920, S. 3; *Millar* v. *M.* 1940 S.C. 56; *Horsburgh* v. *H.,* 1949 S.C. 227.

[73] *Barr* v. *Neilsons* (1868) 6 M. 651; *Milne* v. *Smith* (1892) 20 R. 895; *Hook* v. *McCallum* (1905) 7F. 528.

[74] cf. *Finburgh* v. *Moss' Empires, Ltd.*, 1908 S.C. 928.

[75] Law Reform (Husband and Wife) Act, 1962, S. 2.

[76] Conjugal Rights (Sc.) Acts, 1861; Married Women's Property (Sc.) Acts, 1877, 1881, and 1920.

[77] Law Reform (Husband and Wife) (Sc.) Act, 1984, S. 5.

[78] Ersk. I, 6, 28.

[79] Conjugal Rights (Sc.) Amdt. Act, 1861, S. 6; *Cullen* v. *Ewing* (1833) 6 W. & S. 566; *Ritchie* v. *Barclay* (1845) 7 D. 819.

[80] Married Women's Property (Sc.) Act, 1920, S. 3.

Discrimination on grounds of sex or marriage

It is unlawful, subject to certain exceptions, to discriminate against a person on the ground of sex of marriage by treating him less favourably than one would treat a person of the other sex or applying a requirement or condition such that fewer of that sex can comply with it, in relation to employment, save where sex is a genuine occupational qualification, partnership, trade unions, bodies qualifying for a profession or trade, vocational training bodies, employment agencies, and in certain other cases.[81] Discrimination is also generally unlawful in education,[82] the provision of goods, facilities, or services, and premises.[83] Advertisements indicating an intention to discriminate are unlawful.[84] The Equal Opportunities Commission exists to promote equality of opportunity and may make investigations[85] and issue non-discrimination notices.[86] In respect of employment enforcement of the Act is by industrial tribunals[87] and in other cases by the sheriff court, which may grant declarator, interdict, or damages.[88] A term in a contract is void if it makes the contract unlawful under the Act and the court may remove or modify such a term.[89]

(e) LEGITIMATE: ILLEGITIMATE: LEGITIMATED: ADOPTED

In relation to third parties no distinction exists in the capacities and incapacities of these categories of status.[90] A gift by will to the 'children' of a person formerly prima facie included his legitimate children only, but might in particular circumstances have to be construed more widely.[91] In deeds executed after 25 November 1968, words of relationship include illegitimate relations unless the contrary intention appears, and subject to certain exceptions.[92]

(f) BODILY AND MENTAL CAPACITY OR INCAPACITY

The whole private law is stated by reference to the individual who is bodily and mentally *capax*, and every person is presumed *capax*.[93] Bodily incapacity does not in general entail any legal incapacities,[94] though a

---

[81] Sex Discrimination Act, 1975, Ss. 1–21; 43–52.
[82] Ss. 22–8; 43–52.
[83] Ss. 29–36.
[84] Ss. 37–42.
[85] Ss. 53–61.
[86] Ss. 67–70.
[87] S. 63.
[88] S. 66.
[89] S. 77.
[90] cf. *Clarke* v. *Carfin Coal Co.* [1891] 18 R. (H.L.) 63. As regards parents see Ch. 3.4.
[91] *Purdie's Trs.* v. *Doolan*, 1929 S.L.T. 273.
[92] Law Reform (Misc. Prov.) (Sc.) Act, 1968, S. 5, and see also S. 6.
[93] *Lindsay* v. *Watson* (1843) 5 D. 1194.
[94] *Kirkpatrick* (1853) 15 D. 734 (deaf and dumb).

blind person cannot witness a deed[95] and may have a deed executed on his behalf by a notary public.[96] But serious bodily incapacity, such as paralysis, would justify the court, on petition supported by medical evidence, appointing a *curator bonis* to manage the affairs of the incapax and to supersede him therein.[97] Mental incapacity[98] entails total legal incapacity when the court, acting on certificates by two independent medical men that the person is incapable of attending to his affairs or of giving instructions for their management, appoints a *curator bonis* to manage the affairs of the incapax.[99] In this event the capacity to transact legally and to sue is vested in the *curator bonis* alone.[1] Similarly the *curator bonis* alone should be sued.[2] If not under curatory an incapax may sue and be sued himself, his capacity and responsibility in relation to the matter in issue being a question of fact. It is always a question of fact whether the alleged incapax did or did not, at the material time, have the mental capacity to appreciate the legal force of the transaction he was entering into. Thus a will made during a lucid interval may be sustained.[3] Conversely deeds executed while subject to alienation of mind may be reduced on proof of derangement at the time.[4] A contract made by an insane person, though not judicially found so, is void.[5] It is questionable whether an incapax, not under curatory, can be held liable for wrong-doing.

Drunkenness may be so disabling as to render a person temporarily incapax,[6] and if a person was thereby rendered incapable at the time of transacting the kind of business which is in question the transaction is void.[7] The plea that a transaction was reducible because the granter was facile by reason of intoxication has been admitted.[8]

---

[95] Burn's *Conveyancing Practice*, 5.

[96] Conveyancing (Sc.) Act, 1924, S. 18.

[97] *Duncan*, 1915 2 S.L.T. 50.

[98] Ersk. I, 7, 48; Bell, *Prin.* § 2103–22. In *Mears* v. *M.*, 1969 S.L.T. (Sh. Ct.) 21, it was held that a declarator that a person was of sound mind did not come within 'the personal status of individuals' under the Sheriff Courts (Sc.) Act, 1907, S. 5. *Sed quaere.*

[99] *Loudon* v. *Elder's C.B.*, 1923 S.L.T. 226.

[1] Bankt. I, 7, 10; Ersk. I, 7, 50; Fraser, *P. & Ch.*, 685; *Mitchell & Baxter* v. *Cheyne* (1891) 19 R. 324; cf *Cole-Hamilton* v. *Boyd*, 1963 S.C. (H.L.) 1.

[2] *Anderson's Trs* v. *Skinner* (1871) 8 S.L.R. 325.

[3] *Nisbet's Trs.* v. *N.* (1871) 9 M. 937; *Ballantyne* v. *Evans* (1886) 13 R. 652; *Hope* v. *H's Trs.* (1898) 1 F. (H.L.) 1; *Sivewright* v. *S's Trs.*, 1920 S.C. (H.L.) 63; see also *Maitland's Trs.* v. *M.* (1871) 10 M. 79.

[4] Bankt. I, 7, 10; Ersk. I, 7, 51; Bell, *Comm.* I, 133; *Lindsay* v. *Trent* (1683) Mor. 6280; *Currie* v. *Jardine* (1827) 5 S. 838.

[5] Stair I, 10, 13; Ersk. III, 1, 16; *Moncrieff* v. *Maxwell* (1710) Mor. 6286; cf. *Gall* v. *Bird* (1855) 17 D. 1027; *Loudon, supra.* But if necessaries are sold to a person unable to contract by mental incapacity, he must pay a reasonable price therefor: *Ballantyne* v. *Evans* (1886) 13 R. 652; Sale of Goods Act, 1979, S. 2. If money is lent to a lunatic it may be recovered if profitably expended by him.

[6] Stair I, 10, 13; Ersk. III, 1, 18.

[7] *Johnston* v. *Clark* (1854) 17 D. 228; *Taylor* v. *Provan* (1864) 2 M. 1226; *Pollok* v. *Burns* (1875) 2 R. 497; *Harvey* v. *Smith* (1904) 6 F. 511.

[8] *Jardine* v. *Elliot* (1803) Hume 684; *Hunter* v. *Stevenson* (1804) Hume 686; *Jackson* v. *Pollok* (1900) 8 S.L.T. 267; cf. *Taylor, supra.*

(g) SINGLE AND MARRIED

A single person is one who has not been married, or whose marriage has been annulled, or dissolved by death or divorce, whereas a married person is a party to a subsisting valid marriage, even though voidable. A party to a null marriage is single even before the nullity has been declared judicially. As regards third parties a married person cannot validly promise marriage,[9] or enter into a valid marriage,[10] sexual relations constitute adultery,[11] and a child born of such relations is normally illegitimate and until 1968 could not be legitimated.[12] His freedom of testation is limited by the doctrine of the legal rights of his spouse and children,[13] and the division of his estate on intestacy is different.[14] But in other respects this aspect of status makes no difference.

(h) NOBLE AND COMMONER

In private law the only differences of status are that a peer of the realm is exempt from arrest and imprisonment for a civil cause, even though Parliament is not sitting.[15]

(j) FREE AND PRISONER

As regards private law the person lawfully imprisoned now suffers no legal disabilities or incapacities, save the loss of liberty and liability to discipline and training, but may otherwise exercise his civil rights in the same way as a free man. His domestic relations are unaffected, though if in desertion when imprisoned he is presumed to continue to have *animus deserendi*.[16] His property rights are unaffected. He may sue[17] and be sued.[18]

(k) SOLVENT AND BANKRUPT

The insolvent suffers no legal disabilities or incapacities until adjudicated bankrupt. Even then his domestic relations are not affected, nor his capacity to hold private offices such as tutor or factor, though he may be

---

[9] *Spiers* v. *Hunt* [1908] 1 K.B. 720; *Wilson* v. *Carnley* [1908] 1 K. B. 729.

[10] *Ballantyne* v. *B.* (1866) 4 M. 494; *Petrie* v. *Ross* (1894) 4 S.L.T. 63; *Bairner* v. *Fels*, 1931 S.C. 674.

[11] Ch. 3.3, *infra*.

[12] Ch. 3.4, *infra*.

[13] Ch. 7.2, *infra*.

[14] Ch. 7.3, *infra*.

[15] Bell, *Prin.* s 2138–48; *Digby* v. *Lord Sirling* (1831) 8 Bing. 55; *D. Newcastle* v. *Morris* (1870) L.R. 4 H.L. 661.

[16] *Parker* v. *P.*, 1926 S.C. 574; *Anderson* v. *A.*, 1955 S.C. 428.

[17] Including suing the prison authorities for injuries while in prison: *Keatings* v. *Secy. of State for Scotland*, 1961 S.L.T. (Sh. Ct.) 63; cf. *Ellis* v. *Home Office* [1953] 2 All E.R. 149; *Pullen* v. *Prison Commrs.* [1957] 3 All E.R. 470.

[18] *Young* v. *Y.* (1882) 10 R. 184.

superseded in such offices if their interests conflict with those of the creditors in the sequestration.[19] He may carry on his business or commence a new business but may not obtain credit beyond £100 without disclosing that he is an undischarged bankrupt.[20] A mandate to an agent falls, however,[21] No act or deed is effectual without the consent of his trustee, save in certain cases as regards *bona fide* third parties.[22] Though divested of all his property by the award of sequestration, the radical right remains in him,[23] and he can demand an accounting for the trustee's intromissions with the estate.[24]

He may sue alone for personal injuries but may be required to find caution for expenses,[25] and any damages fall to the trustee for behoof of the creditors;[26] he may be sued, and may, exceptionally, be required to find caution as a condition of defending.[27] The trustee may sue for patrimonial loss to the estate[28] but not for solatium to the bankrupt.[28] Once discharged, whether on composition or on payment of dividend, a bankrupt is restored to the position of a solvent person.

(l) LAY AND CLERIC

Persons ordained to the ministry of a branch of the Christian church or the Jewish faith[30] are subject to the jurisdiction of their respective church courts and codes of discipline as well as to the ordinary law, and, as well as superior status in religious matters, have certain legal privileges, such as to perform marriages and, in certain cases, to act in notarial execution of a will.[31]

(m) CITIZEN AND MEMBER OF THE ARMED FORCES

Persons who join one or other of the armed forces of the Crown become subject to the code of discipline of that service and to courts-martial as

---

[19] Bell, *Comm.* I, 121; *Horn* v. *Sanderson* (1872) 10 M. 295; *Sawers* v. *Penney* (1881) 19 S.L.R. 258; *Whittle* v. *Carruthers* (1896) 23 R. 775.
[20] Bankruptcy (Sc.) Act, 1985 S. 67; *Maclean* v. *McCord*, 1965 S.L.T. (Sh. Ct.) 69, *sed quaere*.
[21] *McKenzie* v. *Campbell* (1894) 21 R. 904.
[22] 1985 Act, S. 32.
[23] *Air* v. *Royal Bank of Scotland* (1886) 13 R. 734; *Whyte* v. *Northern, etc. Investment Co.* (1891) 18 R. (H.L.) 37; *Cooper* v. *Frame* (1893) 20 R. 920.
[24] *Burt* v. *Bell* (1863) 1 M. 382.
[25] Bell, *Comm.* II, 324; *Clarke* v. *Muller* (1884) 11 R. 418; *Scott* v. *Roy* (1886) 13 R. 1173.
[26] *Thom* v. *Bridges* (1857) 19 D. 721; *Jackson* v. *McKechnie* (1875) 3 R. 130.
[27] *Taylor* v. *Fairlie* (1833) 6 W. & Sh. 301; *Buchanan* v. *Stevenson* (1880) 8 R. 220; *Lawrie* v. *Pearson* (1888) 16 R. 62.
[28] *Thom, supra; Howden* v. *Rochied* (1868) 6 M. 300; Bankruptcy (Sc.) Act, 1985, S. 39.
[29] *Muir's Tr.* v. *Braidwood*, 1958 S.C. 169.
[30] It is questionable whether, e.g. a Mohammedan imam, is entitled to be treated as a cleric in Scots law. See also *Walsh* v. *Lord Advocate*, 1956 S.C. (H.L.) 126.
[31] Ersk. I, 5, 1–31; Bell, Prin. § 2160; Conveyancing (Sc.) Act, 1924, S. 18.

well as to the ordinary law,[32] but have some legal privileges, in relation to death duties.[33]

OTHER STATUS-DISTINCTIONS

Older authorities refer to other status-distinctions not now of relevance for private law, such as prodigals.[34] Interdiction of lavish and prodigal persons is now abolished.[35]

Representative capacity

Apart from the capacities and powers which a person enjoys by virtue of his status, he may enjoy further powers by virtue of being appointed to act in a representative capacity, such as holding a particular office for the time being, or being agent or trustee for another, or executor of or judicial factor on the estates of another. Such powers and duties are temporary only and affect the person only in so far as he holds the office or represents the other person. They do not amount to a distinct status. There may be a conflict of interest between A as an individual and A as B's trustee.

NAMES[36]

By custom a child when born, if legitimate, is normally given the surname of its father, or, if illegitimate, of its mother, but any name can be given. The surname is that by which the person is designated and identified,[37] and registration of birth by that name initiates a repute normally lifelong. But if the Crown has conferred a name of dignity, descending to heirs, this name is necessarily attached to all within the destination. The designation of a landowner as 'of' his lands was recognized by statute in 1672[38] as part of his name,[39] and a title of dignity is also part of a person's name. Children are also given at baptism one or more Christian names or forenames. Peers subscribe by their titles alone and bishops by their Christian name followed by the abbreviated Latin name of the see. Scottish judges subscribe their personal names, their titles being honorary only. The officers of arms subscribe by their titles only.[40] Commoners subscribe

---

[32] cf. *O'Brien* v. *Strathern*, 1922 J.C. 55.
[33] cf. *Lord Advocate* v. *Mirrielees' Trs.*, 1945 S.C. (H.L.) 1.
[34] Bankt. I, 2; Ersk. I, 7, 54; II, 11, 45; Bell, *Prin.* § 2123–8.
[35] Conveyancing (Sc.) Act, 1924, S. 44 (3) (6).
[36] See generally Seton, *Law and Practice of Heraldry*; Stevenson, *Heraldry in Scotland*.
[37] Bell, *Convg.*, I, 213.
[38] Lyon King of Arms Act, 1672, c. 47.
[39] cf. *Moir of Leckie* (1794) Mor. 15537; *Eliot of Stobs* (1803) Mor. 15542.
[40] Lyon King of Arms Act, 1672, c. 47.

by their forenames, in full or abbreviated, and surname, adding any property or title, or profession. By custom a married woman normally takes her husband's surname, but she is designated for formal legal purposes by her Christian name, maiden surname or married surname or successive married surnames.[41] She may keep her maiden surname or add her husband's surname to her own. A husband may adopt, or be required to adopt, his wife's surname.[42] The misnaming of a party to an action or petition may invalidate the proceedings.[43]

Change of name

A person may assume a new forename or Christian name, or a new surname,[44] or add to or alter it, without the authority of the court.[45] But it is necessary in the case of persons holding public offices or enrolled members of professions to mark the change and establish the identity of the bearer of the former and of the new names by obtaining a private Act of Parliament, or obtaining the authority of the Court of Session on petition to the *nobile officum*,[46] or obtaining a decree or certificate of change of name from the Lord Lyon King of Arms,[47] or by executing and recording in the Books of Council and Session or Lyon Court or sheriff court books a deed stating the change, and by making advertisement in the press. It is questionable whether one parent can change the name of a minor child without the other parent's consent.[48] Where a person is required, as a condition of succeeding to particular lands, to assume a stated surname, it must be assumed exactly as prescribed.[49]

To give as one's name an untrue name or the name of another determinate person and thereby seek to pass oneself off as that other person is personation and may involve criminal sanctions if done fraudulently, and have civil consequences also.[50] To give a false name may also infer criminal penalties.[51] But a person may legitimately practise a profession or business under a name different from his usual name.[52]

---

[41] e.g. Mrs Mary McAlister or Donoghue; see (1933) 49 L.Q.R. 1; (1965) 61 L.Q.R. 109.
[42] *Eliot of Stobs* (1803) Mor. 15542.
[43] *Brown* v. *Rodger* (1884) 12 R. 340; *Overseas League* v. *Taylor*, 1951 S.C. 105. Contrast *Spalding* v. *Valentine* (1883) 10 R. 1092; *Cruickshank* v. *Gow* (1888) 15 R. 326; *Anderson* v. *Stoddart*, 1923 S.C. 755.
[44] *Kinloch* v. *Lourie* (1853) 16 D. 197.
[45] *Young* (1835) 13 S. 262; *Finlayson* (1844) 2 Broun 17; *Kinloch, supra; Johnston* (1899) 2 F. 75; *Robertson* (1899) 2 F. 127; *Clark* v. *Chalmers*, 1961 J.C. 60.
[46] *Forlong* (1880) 7 R. 910; *Robertson, supra; Silverstone*, 1935 S.C. 223.
[47] *M'Donell* v. *M'Donald* (1826) 4 S. 371; *Forlong, supra.*
[48] cf. *Y.* v. *Y.* [1973] 2 All E.R. 574.
[49] *Sir Hugh Munro-Lucas-Tooth*, 1965 S.L.T. (Lyon Ct.) 2; see also *Munro's Trs.* v. *Monson*, 1965 S.C. 84.
[50] *Wilson* v. *Horn* (1904) 11 S.L.T. 702 (nullity of marriage); *Morrisson* v. *Robertson*, 1908 S.C. 332; *MacLeod* v. *Kerr*, 1965 S.C. 253; *Clark* v. *Chalmers*, 1961 J.C. 60.
[51] *Clark, supra.*
[52] e.g. authors, actors, bookmakers. cf. *Galbraith* v. *Provident Bank Ltd.* (1900) 2 F. 1148.

Registration of change of name

The Registrar-General records in the Register of Corrections a change in a child's registered name made within twelve months of the birth, or a name given to it after registration, if a certificate is given him within two years of the birth.[53] Provision is also made for the recording of changes of name or surname of a child under 16,[54] a person between 16 and 21 or over 21[55] or of an alternative name, being the English equivalent of a non-English name.[56] Registration in the Register of Corrections may also be made of a decree or certificate of change of name or surname granted by the Lord Lyon, or a copy of a deed containing a condition that a person shall adopt another name with evidence that it has been so changed, or a decree or certificate of the change of name or surname of a male person following his marriage.[57]

Registration of business names

Under the Business Names Act, 1985, any person who has a place of business in Great Britain and who carries on a business (including a profession) there under a name which (a) in the case of a partnership does not consist of the surnames of all partners who are individuals and the corporate names of all partners who are bodies corporate, or (b) in the case of an individual, does not consist of his surname, or (c) in the case of a company does not consist of its corporate name, without, in all cases, any non-permitted addition,[58] may not without approval carry on business in Great Britain under a name likely to give the impression that the business is connected with the government or any local authority or including any word or expression specified in regulations made under S. 6.[59] Persons affected must, with certain exceptions, state legibly on all business letters, orders for goods or services, invoices and receipts, and written demands for payment the name of each partner of the firm, or the individual's name, or a company's corporate name, and, in relation to each person so named, an address in Great Britain at which service of any document will be effective, and display in premises where business is carried on a notice containing such names and addresses. This information must also be given to anyone doing business and requesting the names and addresses. Contravention of these provisions is an offence.[60] If

---

[53] Registration of Births, Deaths, and Marriages (Sc.) Act, 1965, S. 43(3).
[54] 1965 Act, S. 43(4).
[55] 1965 Act, S. 43(5).
[56] 1965 Act, S. 43(7).
[57] 1965 Act, S. 43(6).
[58] S.1. As to company names see Companies Act, 1985, Ss. 25–34.
[59] S.2. This limits the use of prestigious names. S. 3 empowers specification of words the use of which requires approval.
[60] S. 4. This is important on the question of whom to sue.

a person brings legal proceedings to enforce any right arising out of a
contract made in the course of a business in respect of which he was at
the time the contract was made in breach of S. 4 the proceedings are to be
dismissed if the defender shows that he has a claim against the pursuer
arising out of the contract which he has been unable to pursue by reason
of the pursuer's breach of S. 4, or that he has suffered some financial loss
in connection with the contract by reason of the pursuer's breach thereof,
unless the court is satisfied that it is just and equitable to permit the
proceedings to continue, without prejudice to the right of any person to
enforce such rights as he may have against another person in any proceedings brought by that person.[61]

KINSHIP

Kinsmen are persons related to each other by having a common ancestor.
Their relationship is measured in degrees, each representing the step
between a parent and his child. Two methods of reckoning degrees of
kinship have been recognized. In the Roman law method the degree
between one kinsman and another is reckoned by counting the steps from
one up to the common ancestor and then the steps down to the other;
thus cousins are related in the fourth degree and uncle and niece in the
third degree.[62] In the canon law method the degree is ascertained by
counting up each line to the common ancestor and taking the longer line.
Thus cousins are related in the second degree and uncle and niece in the
second degree.[63] The canon law computation was followed in Scotland
prior to the Reformation and sometimes thereafter[64] but subsequently the
Roman law method has been generally followed.

Agnates and cognates

Agnates are those of a person's kindred who are related to him through
his father;[65] cognates are those who are related to him through his
mother.[66]

Full and half blood

Persons are german or related by full blood who are descended, however
remotely, from the same father and mother,[67] whereas half-blood rela-

---

[61] S. 5.
[62] Inst. III, 6; Dig. 38, 1; Bankt. I, 5, 37–8; Ersk. I, 6, 9; Fraser, *H. & W.* I, 105.
[63] Decretals, IV, 4; Fraser, *H & W.* I. 107.
[64] e.g. Marriage Act, 1567.
[65] Stair, III, 4, 8; Bell, *Prin.* § 2078, 2111. In Roman law agnates were persons related to him through males only.
[66] Ersk. I, 7, 4. In Roman law cognates were persons related to him through one or more females.
[67] Craig II, 17, 11; Stair, III, 3, 47; Ersk. III, 10, 2; Bell, *Prin.* § 1651–2.

tives share the same father or mother but not both. Kinsmen of the half blood consanguinean share the same father, of the half blood uterine the same mother.[68]

Consanguinity and affinity

Persons are related by consanguinity if related by blood, by affinity if related through marriage only.

[68] Bell, *Prin.* § 1653–4.

CHAPTER 3.3

THE DOMESTIC RELATIONS
(1) HUSBAND AND WIFE

The relationship of husband and wife[1] and the status of married persons is constituted by marriage, which is the voluntary union of one man and one woman for the duration of their joint lives, unless earlier terminated judicially.[2] Marriage[3] is based upon agreement by the parties, but is productive of a new status for each, and the contract differs from commercial contracts in respect of personal capacity, formalities, grounds for avoidance or dissolution, and the legal consequences of the contract are fixed by law and unalterable, save in detail, by the will of the parties. Unlike a commercial contract, marriage cannot be discharged by agreement, breach, or frustration. Furthermore the rights and duties of each of the spouses *vis-à-vis* third parties are modified by their marriage.[4]

While Scots law is concerned for the most part with monogamous unions, and provides only for the creation of monogamous unions, a polygamous or potentially polygamous union contracted elsewhere, in a country where such unions are recognized,[5] if deemed valid by the law of the husband's domicile, will be recognized for some purposes,[6] including the grant of divorce, nullity, dissolution on the ground of presumed death, judicial separation, separation and aliment, and aliment and decrees involving determination of the validity of the marriage,[7] succession

---

[1] The Scots law of marriage is based on canon law as administered in ecclesiastical courts prior to the Reformation. At the Reformation jurisdiction was transferred to the Commissary Court of Edinburgh with appeal to the Court of Session, and in 1830 to the Court of Session. The canon law principles have in certain respects been altered by statutes and decisions. See generally Stair I, 4, 1; Mack. 1, 6, 1; Bankt. I, 5, 1; Ersk. I, 6, 1; Hume, *Lect.* I, 19; Bell, *Prin.* § 1506–623; More, *Lect.* 1, 17; Fraser, *H. & W., passim.*

[2] *Hyde* v. *H.* (1866) 1 P. & D. 130; *Lang* v. *L.,* 1921 S.C. 44; *Nachimson* v. *N.* [1930] P. 217.

[3] The word 'marriage' is used both for the ceremony and for the relationship, or state of being married, to which it gives rise.

[4] Fraser, *H. & W.,* I, 155.

[5] Whether a marriage is polygamous or not depends on the *lex loci celebrationis,* whether it recognizes such unions or not; *R.* v. *Hammersmith Registrar ex p. Mir-Anwaruddin* [1917] 1 K.B. 634. It is questionably open to parties to give evidence that their intention was to contract a monogamous union: *Warrender* v. *W.* (1835) 2 Sh. & Macl. 154. See also *Mehta* v. *M.* [1945] 2 All E.R. 690.

[6] cf. *Srini Vasan* v. *S.V.* [1946] P. 67; *Baindail* v. *B.* [1946] P. 122. (legitimacy of children—social welfare legislation).

[7] Matrimonial Proceedings (Polygamous Marriages) Act, 1972, S. 2, overruling *Muhammad* v. *Suna,* 1956 S.C. 366.

by spouses,[8] legitimacy and succession of children,[9] and some social security provisions. It is not essential that either or both parties to a marriage by Scots law should profess Christianity.[10]

ENGAGEMENT

Engagement

Parties contemplating marriage customarily enter first into an engagement or betrothal, *sponsalia per verba de futuro*, an exchange of mutual promises subsequently to contract marriage.[11] This is a bare agreement and by itself does not effect change of status. It now has no effect to create any rights or obligations and breach is not now actionable.[12]

Return of gifts on breaking off of engagement

Gifts given outright by either party to the other are not recoverable,[13] but gifts such as a ring made in contemplation of marriage may be recoverable.[14] The principle probably is that if the man breaks off the engagement without legal justification, the woman may keep the engagement ring, but if he has legal justification he may recover the ring.[15] If the woman breaks off without justification, she must return the ring, but if she has justification she may keep the ring.[16] If the engagement is broken off by mutual consent or by reason of death or disability, all gifts must be returned. Gifts made by third parties should be returned if the marriage does not take place.[17]

CONSTITUTION OF MARRIAGE

For the constitution of a legally valid marriage the parties must each have legal capacity to marry, in that they must be of opposite sexes, of single status, of age to marry, there must be no legal impediments, they must truly consent to contract matrimony, and the requisite formalities must be complied with. A seeming marriage which by reason of some defect is not legally valid may be either void or voidable. A marriage which is void is a

---

[8] *Coleman* v. *Shang* [1961] A.C. 481.
[9] *Bamgbose* v. *Daniel* [1955] A.C. 107.
[10] cf. *MacDougall* v. *Chitnavis*, 1937 S.C. 390.
[11] Ersk. I, 6, 3.
[12] Law Reform (Husband and Wife) (Sc.) Act, 1984, S. 1.
[13] *Gold* v. *Hume* (1950) 66 Sh. Ct. Rep. 85.
[14] *Savage* v. *McAllister* (1952) 68 Sh. Ct. Rep. 11.
[15] *Cohen* v. *Sellar* [1926] 1 K.B. 536.
[16] *Jacobs* v. *Davis* [1917] 2 K.B. 532.
[17] Stair I, 7, 7.

legal nullity and never takes effect in law as a marriage; no declarator of nullity is necessary to set it aside, though such a decree is commonly sought to establish the fact and regularize the position.[18] A marriage which is merely voidable is good and valid but is subject to a resolutive condition in that it contains a flaw entitling either party to have it set aside; if not challenged it continues valid; until declared void by declarator of nullity, it is valid, but once declared null it is deemed void from the start.[19]

The differences between void and voidable marriages are that (i) a void marriage is always a nullity, whereas a voidable marriage is valid until and unless declared null, but when this happens, the decree has retrospective effect: (ii) any person having an interest may challenge a void marriage,[20] but only the parties may challenge a voidable marriage:[21] (iii) a void marriage may be challenged even after the death of one spouse;[20] a voidable marriage becomes unchallengeable if continued till one spouse dies;[21] and (iv) the issue of a void marriage are illegitimate; the issue of a voidable marriage legitimate.[22] But the issue of a putative marriage[23] are also deemed legitimate though the marriage is void.

Capacity to marry

Scots law has adopted from the canon law the distinction between *impedimenta dirimentia* (irritant impediments) and *impedimenta impeditiva* (prohibitive impediments).[24] The former are fundamental and a marriage conflicting with one of them is void. They are sex, prior marriage, nonage, insanity, and relationship.[25] These are disabilities which affect a domiciled Scot, wherever he may wish to marry.[26] The latter include clandestine marriages,[27] and cases where one party lacks parental consent required by the law of his domicile.[28] Impediments of this kind are concerned with the conditions under which marriage may be solemnized and are regulated by Scots law as *lex loci celebrationis*.

---

[18] e.g. *Ballantyne, infra; Aldridge, infra.*
[19] *S.G. v. W.G.*, 1933 S.C. 728. See also Clive, 1968 J.R. 209.
[20] *Fenton v. Livingstone* (1861) 23 D. 366.
[21] *L. v. L.*, 1931 S.C. 477; *F. v. F.*, 1945 S.C. 202.
[22] Law Reform (Misc. Prov.) Act, 1949, S. 4.
[23] See *infra.*
[24] Fraser, *H. & W.*, I, 49; *Administrator of Austrian Property v. Von Lorang*, 1927 S.C. (H.L.) 80, 96; *Bliersbach v. McEwen*, 1959 S.C. 43, 49.
[25] Fraser, *supra*, adds impotency, which is now treated as a resolutive condition, not a condition precedent, and adultery and, in irregular marriages, non-residence, which have been repealed.
[26] *Bliersbach, supra*, citing *Sussex Peerage Case* (1844) 11 Cl. & F. 85; *Sottomayor v. de Barros* (1877) 3 P.D. 1.
[27] Fraser, *supra.*
[28] *Bliersbach, supra.*

Sex

The parties must be biologically male and female respectively. It will not suffice that one appears to be, and dresses and passes as, of one sex if he or she is biologically of the other.[29]

Single status

Both parties must be of single status (whether single, widowed, or divorced) and a marriage is void if either party were already validly married to another,[30] even though that party honestly believed, on reasonable grounds, that he was free to marry.[31] But in the latter event, by the doctrine of putative marriage, the children are accounted legitimate. If the earlier 'marriage' were legally void the later marriage is not invalid by reason thereof.

Age

While by canon law and at common law persons could marry if they had attained the respective ages of puberty (or minority),[32] now by statute no person domiciled in Scotland may marry until he attains 16, and a marriage solemnized in Scotland between persons either of whom is under 16 is void.[33] But though a regular marriage be void by reason of the nonage of one party a valid irregular marriage may be constituted by their subsequent cohabitation and acquisition of the habit and repute of being married.[34]

Persons marrying in Scotland do not require any parental or other consent to their marriage when under 18.[35]

Mental incapacity

A marriage is null if either party was at the time of unsound mind so as to be incapable of understanding the nature of the relation being entered

---

[29] *Corbett* v. *C.* [1970] 2 All E.R. 33.

[30] Ersk. I, 6, 7; *Ballantyne* v. *B.* (1866) 4M. 494; *Petrie* v. *Ross* (1894) 4 S.L.T. 63; cf. *Jack* v. *J.*, 1940 S.L.T. 122; *Aldridge* v. *A.*, 1954 S.C. 58; *Batto* v. *B.*, 1979 S.L.T. (Notes) 7; *Burke* v. *B.*, 1983 S.L.T. 331. Contracting such 'marriage' is the crime of bigamy. An invalid divorce does not permit remarriage: *Van Mebren* v. *V.M.*, 1948 S.L.T. (Notes) 62.

[31] Bell, *Prin* § 1525; *Dalrymple* v. *D.* (1811) 2 Hagg. C.R. 54; *Jolly* v. *McGregor* (1828) 3 W. & S. 85, 202; *Wright* v. *W's Trs.* (1837) 15 S. 767. cf. *Prawdzic-Lazarska* v. *P.L.*, 1954 S.C. 98. But it is a defence to a charge of bigamy that the party concerned had at no time within seven years before the second marriage had reason to believe that the previous spouse was alive: Presumption of Death (Sc.) Act, 1977, S. 13.

[32] Bell, *Prin.* § 1523.

[33] Marriage (Sc.) Act, 1977, S. 1, replacing Age of Marriage Act, 1929, S. 1.

[34] *A.B.* v. *C.D.*, 1957 S.C. 415.

[35] Ersk. I, 6, 6; Bell, *Prin.* § 1523; *Bliersbach* v. *McEwen*, 1959 S.C. 43; *Pease* v. *P.*, 1967 S.C. 112; *Hoy* v. *H.*, 1968 S.C. 179.

into or truly consenting to marry.[36] The onus of proof is on the party seeking to establish the incapacity; the onus is lightened if it be established that the incapax had been of unsound mind shortly before the marriage, and this may cast on the defender the onus of establishing that it took place during a lucid interval.[37] The matter may be raised by either spouse, by the tutor-dative, but not the *curator bonis*, of the insane spouse if placed under guardianship,[38] and by any interested party after the death of either spouse,[39] and even if there has been issue of the marriage.[40] A marriage challengeable on this ground may be approbated if the insane spouse recovers sanity.[41] Intoxication or drugs probably have the same effect in that a marriage is void if either spouse was at that time incapable on that account of understanding the contract being entered into, or of consenting.[42]

Prohibited degrees of relationship

Among the irritant impediments are the existence between the prospective spouses of a degree of relationship deemed to be too close to be permissible, and any such relationship is deemed incestuous.[43] If parties are related within the prohibited degrees of consanguinity or affinity, the marriage will be void, even though they were ignorant of the relationship. The Marriage Act, 1567, c. 16, legalized all marriages not forbidden by the Book of Leviticus, c. 18, verses 6–18, by providing that seconds in degree of consanguinity and affinity,[44] and all more remote degrees not repugnant to the said Biblical prescription, might lawfully marry, and the courts extended the express prohibitions by implication to others of the same degree of relationship.[45]

The Marriage (Sc.) Act, 1977, S. 2, now provides that a marriage between persons related in degrees specified in Sch. 1 of the Act is void if solemnized in Scotland, or when either party is domiciled in Scotland.[46] A

---

[36] Stair I, 4, 6; Ersk. I, 6, 2; Bell, *Prin.* § 1523; Fraser, *H. & W.* I, 55; *Hunter* v. *Edney* (1881) 10 P.D. 93; *Durham* v. *D.* (1885) 10 P.D. 80; *Graham* v. *G* (1907) 15 S.L.T. 33; *Park* v. *P.*, 1914, 1 S.L.T. 88; *Calder* v. *C.*, 1942 S.N. 40; *In the Estate of Park* [1954] P. 112; cf. *Johnston* v. *Brown* (1823) 2 S. 495. As to mental deficiency see *Long* v. *L.*, 1950 S.L.T. (Notes) 32.

[37] *Turner* v. *Meyers* (1808) 1 Hagg. C.R. 414, 417.

[38] cf. *Thomson* v. *T.* (1887) 14 R. 634.

[39] Fraser, *H. & W.* I, 74; *Loch* v. *Dick* (1638) Mor. 6278; *Christie* v. *Gib* (1700) Mor. 6283.

[40] *Jackson* v. *J.* [1908] P. 308.

[41] *Johnstone* v. *Brown* (1823) 2 S. 495.

[42] *Johnstone, supra*; cf. *Gall* v. *G.* (1870) 9 M. 177.

[43] For the reasons for this prohibition see *Philp's Tr.* v. *Beaton*, 1938 S.C. 733, 745. Incest as a crime was governed by the Incest Act, 1567, (c. 15) and refers to the same passage in scripture.

[44] Computed by the canon law method. See Ch. 3.2. Relations by consanguinity are those related by blood; relationship by affinity is that betwen a married person and his spouse's blood-relations.

[45] *Fenton* v. *Livingstone* (1861) 23 D. 366; *Purves' Trs.* v. *P.* (1895) 22 R. 513.

[46] S. 2 (1).

degree of relationship exists, in the case of relationships by consanguinity, whether of the full-blood or the half-blood, and in the case of relationships by consanguinity or by affinity, even where traced through or to a person of illegitimate birth.[47] A person may also not marry his adoptive, or former adoptive, parent or child.[48] Persons related in a degree not listed may lawfully marry, but without prejudice to the effect which a degree of relationship not so specified may have under another legal system where it applies as *lex loci celebrationis* or *lex domicilii*.[49]

Marriage of divorced person with paramour

By statute[50] a marriage between a divorced person and the paramour with whom he committed adultery was null, and the children of such a union could not inherit from their parents. The statute was said to be applicable only if the paramour was expressly named in the decree, which was only done if specially requested.[51] It was long questionable whether the statute was in observance,[52] and it is now repealed.[53]

Consent to marriage

It is essential, however the marriage be contracted, that the parties consent: *consensus non concubitus facit matrimonium*. The parties must give voluntary, real, and genuine consent to marriage, or at least facts must be established from which the exchange of such consent may be inferred. Absence of genuine consent renders the alleged marriage a nullity *ab initio*.[54]

The consent must be to marriage, not to mere betrothal,[55] nor to any other relationship, e.g. concubinage. A marriage for an ulterior motive is void.[56] Consent is not valid if given under essential error as to the identity

---

[47] S. 2 (2).
[48] Sched. 1.
[49] S. 2 (3).
[50] Act 1600, c. 20; Stair I, 4, 7; Ersk. I, 6, 43; III, 10, 9: Bell, *Prin.* § 1526; Ferguson, *Consistorial Law*, 172; Fraser, *H. & W.* I, 140; *Lyle* v. *Douglas* (1670) Mor. 329.
[51] More, Notes, xvi; Riddell, *Peerage Law*, 391, 410.
[52] Bell, *Prin.* § 1526; Fraser *H. & W.* I, 144, 150; *Campbell* v. *C.* (1866) 4 M. 867, 5 M. (H.L.) 115; *Beattie* v. *B.* (1866) 5 M. 181.
[53] Statute Law Revision (Sc.) Act, 1964, Sch. I.
[54] Stair I, 4, 6; More's Notes, xiii; Ersk. I, 6, 2, and 5; Hume, *Lect.* I, 26; Bell, *Prin.* § 1517; Fergusson, *Consist. Law*; Fraser *H. & W.* 1435. Cases of no serious or genuine consent include *Gall* v. *G.* (1870) 9 M. 177; *Steuart* v. *Robertson* (1875) 2 R. (H.L.) 80; *Davidson* v. *D.*, 1921 S.C. 341.
[55] *Ford* v. *Stier* [1896] P. 1; *Hall* v. *H.* (1908) 24 T.L.R. 756; *Kelly* v. *K.* (1932) 49 T.L.R. 99; *Mehta* v. *M.* [1945] 2 All E.R. 690; *Mahmud* v. *M.*, 1977 S.L.T. (Notes) 17; *Akram* v. *A.*, 1979 S.L.T. (Notes) 87; cf. *S.G.* v. *W.G.*, 1933 S.C. 728.
[56] More, Notes, 14; *Browne* v. *B.* (1843) 5 D. 1288, 1295; *Orlandi* v. *Castelli*, 1961 S.C. 113. See also *H.* v. *H.* [1953] 2 All. E.R. 1229; *Buckland* v. *B.* [1967] 2 All. E.R. 300; *Szechter* v. *S.* [1970] 3 All E.R. 905.

of the other party,[57] nor if induced by fraud or deception,[58] (though it is valid if the error relates merely to the chastity or other qualitites or attributes of the other[59]), nor if there is error as to the nature and effect of the ceremony,[60] nor if induced by fear or coercion,[61] nor if not deliberate,[62] nor if parties have a mental reservation, and do not regard themselves as truly married.[63] If consent is obtained by fraud the marriage may still be ratified by the innocent party.[64]

If parties have truly consented, the validity of the marriage is not affected by one party's subsequent erroneous belief that the marriage was invalid for lack of a formality,[65] nor by the fact that one party was disabled by his religion from marrying outside that religion.[66] Consent may be held not to have been given, when, even though statutory formalities had been fulfilled, the marriage was a sham, contracted purely for some ulterior purpose,[67] though it is more difficult to establish absence of true consent in a case of regular marriage,[68] and the court is reluctant to recognize the misuse of marriage for ulterior purposes by allowing parties to controvert the consent exchanged.

Formalities of marriage

The formalities of marriage are determined by the *lex loci celebrationis*. The Scots law was shaped by the canon law as it stood before the Council of Trent (1563) and the pre-Tridentine law was continued in Scotland after and notwithstanding the Reformation. Under this no religious ceremony was necessary, but only acceptance by the parties of each other as husband and wife *per verba de praesenti*, in which case marriage was at once constituted, or *per verba de futuro*, in which case marriage became binding as soon as consummated, or parties might be deemed married if

---

[57] e.g. where there has been personation: *Lang, infra*, 49; cf. *Wilson* v. *Horn* (1904) 11 S.L.T. 702; *McLeod* v. *Adams*, 1920, 1 S.L.T. 229.

[58] Fraser, *H. & W.* I, 457, 461; *Lang, infra*, 50.

[59] *Lang* v. *L.*, 1921 S.C. 44, (wife concealing that she was pregnant by another) overruling *Stein* v. *S.*, 1914 S.C. 903; cf. *Moss* v. *M.* [1897] P. 263.

[60] *Valier* v. *V.* (1925) 133 L.T. 830; *Lendrum* v. *Chakravarti*, 1929 S.L.T. 96; *Kelly, supra*; *Mehta, supra*.

[61] *Cameron* v. *Malcolm* (1756) Mor. 12680; *Jolly* v. *McGregor* (1828) 3 W. & S. 85; *Scott* v. *Sebright* (1886) 12 P.D. 21; *Griffith* v. *G.* [1944] Ir. R. 35.

[62] *Blair* v. *Fairie* (1766) 5 B.S. 921.

[63] *Brady* v. *Murray*, 1933 S.L.T. 534.

[64] *Alexander* v. *A.*, 1920 S.C. 327.

[65] *Courtin* v. *Elder*, 1930 S.C. 68.

[66] *MacDougall* v. *Chitnavis*, 1937 S.C. 390.

[67] *H.* v. *H* [1954] P. 258; *Silver* v. *S.* [1955] 2 All E.R. 614; *Orlandi* v. *Castelli*, 1961 S.C. 113.

[68] See cases of *McInnes* v. *More* (1782) 2 Pat. 598; *Taylor* v. *Kello* (1787) 3 Pat. 56; *Sassen* v. *Campbell* (1826) 2 W. & S. 309; *Stewart* v. *Menzies* (1841) 2 Rob. App. 547; *Lockyer* v. *Sinclair* (1846) 8 D. 582; *Robertson* v. *Steuart* (1874) 1 R. 532, 667; *Imrie* v. *I.* (1891) 19 R. 185; *Lang* v. *L.*, 1921 S.C. 44, 54.

they cohabitated openly and continuously so as to acquire the reputation of being married, but it became common to celebrate marriage *in facie ecclesiae* after publication of banns and with a religious service. Hence until recent times marriage might be constituted in Scotland regularly or irregularly. There are now two modes of regular marriage: (1) before a minister of religion after due notice; and (2) before an authorized registrar after due notice. There were three modes of irregular marriage: (1) by declaration *de praesenti*; (2) by promise *subsequente copula*; and (3) by cohabitation with habit and repute. Since 1 July 1940 contracting marriage in either of the first two irregular modes is incompetent.[69]

Regular marriage—preliminaries

As a preliminary to a regular marriage, each of the parties must submit to the district registrar a marriage notice stating intention to marry, together with his birth certificate, the death certificate of a former spouse or a copy of a decree of divorce, dissolution, or annulment, or a valid certificate for marriage issued in another part of the U.K., or a certificate issued by a competent authority in the state in which he is domiciled to the effect that he is not known to be subject to any local incapacity which would prevent him marrying. The calling of banns of marriage in the parish church has been abolished.[70] The district registrar then enters particulars in a marriage notice book and lists the names of the parties in a list displayed in the registration office. The marriage notice book may be inspected by any person claiming that he may have reason to make objection to an intended marriage.[71] Any person may submit to the district registrar an objection in writing to a proposed marriage. If the objection is merely as to the accuracy of the marriage notice the district registrar must notify the parties and correct the notice, and in other cases must notify the Registrar-General and suspend issue of the marriage schedule; if the Registrar-General believes that there is an impediment to the marriage he must direct the district registrar to ensure that the marriage does not take place.[72]

If there are no objections or any have been disposed of, the district registrar completes a marriage schedule and issues it, not less than fourteen days after the receipt of the marriage notice, save in special cases, nor, unless specially authorized, more than seven days before the date of the intended marriage. A religious marriage may be solemnized only on the date and at the place specified in the marriage schedule. Provision is made for change of date or place.[73]

[69] Marriage (Sc.) Act, 1939, S. 5.
[70] Marriage (Sc.) Act, 1977, S. 3.
[71] S. 4.
[72] S. 5.
[73] S. 6.

Where a person residing in Scotland is to be party to a marriage to be solemnized outside Scotland, he may give notice of intention to marry to the district registrar who may give a certificate that he is not subject to any incapacity to marry.[74]

Religious marriage

A religious marriage may be solemnized only on the date and at the place specified in the marriage schedule,[75] and only by a person who is a minister of the Church of Scotland, or of a religious body prescribed by regulations or recognized by a religious body as entitled to solemnize marriage, or registered under the Act, S. 9, or temporarily authorized under S. 12.[76] Religious bodies other than the major churches may nominate members aged at least 21 to be registered as empowered to celebrate marriages.[77] A person may be temporarily authorized to celebrate a marriage, or marriages, for a period.[78]

The form of a religious marriage is determined by the particular religion,[79] but essential elements are presence of the parties, declaration in the presence of the celebrant, each other and two witnesses, that they accept each other as husband and wife, and subsequent declaration by the celebrant that the parties are then husband and wife.[80]

The marriage schedule must be signed by the parties, the celebrant, and the two witnesses, and delivered within three days to the district registrar, who must enter the particulars in the register of marriages.[81] Once a marriage has been registered its validity is not to be questioned on the ground of failure to comply with a requirement or restriction imposed by the 1977 Act.[82]

Civil marriage

A civil marriage may be solemnized only by a district registrar or assistant registrar appointed under the Act.[83] Marriages are solemnized at the registration office or, exceptionally, at another place in the registration district,[84] and, save exceptionally, not within fourteen days of receipt of the marriage notice. The registrar must have available to him a completed marriage schedule, both parties must be present, and there must be two

---

[74] S. 7.
[75] Marriage (Sc.) Act, 1977, S. 6 (5).
[76] S. 8; Marriage (Prescription of Religious bodies) (Sc.) Regs., S. I., 1977, No. 1670.
[77] Ss. 9–11.
[78] S. 12.
[79] S. 14.
[80] Ss. 9 (3); 13. The celebrant may use an interpreter at the ceremony: S. 22.
[81] Ss. 15–16. The entry is cancelled if the marriage is found or declared void: S. 23.
[82] S. 23A added by the Law Reform (Misc. Prov.) (Sc.) Act, 1980, S. 22.
[83] Marriage (Sc.) Act, 1977, Ss. 8, 17.
[84] S. 18.

witnesses professing to be aged at least 16. After the solemnization of the marriage the schedule must be signed by the parties, the witnesses, and the registrar, and the particulars entered in the register of marriages.[85] It is not provided whether the marriage is affected by the fact that the registrar does not have the schedule available.[86] Once the marriage has been registered its validity is not to be questioned on the ground of failure to comply with a requirement or restriction imposed by the 1977 Act.[87]

Irregular marriage

Though marriage may no longer be contracted either by declaration *de praesenti*, or by promise *subsequente copula*, marriages previously constituted by either of these modes remain valid and questions of their constitution may still arise. Contracting marriage by cohabitation with habit and repute remains competent.

Prerequisite residence

Originally parties could marry irregularly in Scotland without any need for prior residence; hence 'Gretna Green' and other 'runaway' marriages were valid by Scots law.[88] After 1856 no irregular marriage contracted by declaration, acknowledgment, or ceremony[89] is valid unless one of the parties had his or her usual place of residence[90] in Scotland, or had lived in Scotland for twenty-one days[91] next preceding the marriage.[92] This Act was repealed when irregular marriages by declaration after 1 July 1940 were invalidated, but it applies to such marriages prior thereto.

Marriage by declaration de praesenti

This mode of marriage, recognized in canon law, consisted in a mutual declaration of consent there and then [93] to take each other as spouses.[94] If the mutual consent were proved, matrimony was at once thereby constituted, whether concubitus followed or not.[95] The consent might be

---

[85] S. 19. The entry is cancelled if the marriage is found or declared to be void: S. 23.

[86] Contrast S. 13, and see S. 24 (1).

[87] S. 23A added by Law Reform (Misc. Prov.) (Sc.) Act, 1980, S. 22.

[88] On history see *Mackie* v. *Dumfriesshire Assessor*, 1932 S.C. 397, 404; Anton and Francescaskis, 1958 J.R. 253.

[89] This seems to refer to clandestine, not regular, marriages. The Act does not appear to cover marriages by cohabitation.

[90] Interpreted: *Gray* v. *G.*, 1941 S.C. 461; *Cooke* v. *Taylor*, 1941 S.C. 461.

[91] *Lawford* v. *Davies* (1878) 4 P.D. 61.

[92] Marriage (Scotland) Act, 1856 (Lord Brougham's Act); *Miller* v. *Deakin*, 1912, 1 S.L.T. 253; *Bach* v. *B.* (1927) 43 T.L.R. 493; and see *Adamson*, 1958 J.R. 148.

[93] *Brady* v. *Murray*, 1933 S.L.T. 534.

[94] Generally, Stair I, 4, 6; Ersk. I, 6, 5; Bell, *Prin.* § 1508, 1514.

[95] *Dalrymple* v. *D.* (1811) 2 Hagg. C.R. 54; *Walker* v. *Macadam* (1813) 1 Dow 148; *Aitchison* v. *Incorpn. of Solicitors* (1838) 1 D. 42; *Leslie* v. *L.* (1860) 22 D. 993.

proved by witnesses,[96] or by the testimony of one of the parties, if corroborated by facts and circumstances,[97] or by the giving and acceptance of a written declaration or acknowledgment of marriage,[98] if proved to be written, or adopted and signed, by the giver.[99]

Marriage by promise subsequente copula

In the medieval canon law parties were held married if they uttered words denoting a future intention to become man and wife and subsequently had intercourse in reliance thereon; promise to marry became marriage by consummation. This mode of marriage was accepted in Scots law also,[1] prior to 1 July 1940.[2] Probably both promise and *copula* had to take place in Scotland.[3] If both were proved marriage was held constituted at the time of the *copula*.[4] The *copula* was held to imply consent to marriage in implement of the prior promise.[5] There had to be promise to marry, not merely courtship.[6] The promise of subsequent marriage had to be admitted by, or proved by the writ of, the defender, or by reference to his oath.[7] The requisite *copula* must have taken place after the promise and in reliance thereon. It might be proved *prout de jure*. If the promise were established it was usually presumed that subsequent *copula* was in reliance thereon, but this could be rebutted.[8]

Marriage by cohabitation with habit and repute

By an old Act[9] it was provided that a woman who had been reputed to be a man's wife during his lifetime should be entitled to terce from his estate unless it were proved that she was not married to him. From this arose the doctrine that if a couple cohabit openly and constantly as husband and wife so as to produce a general belief that they are married, they will

---

[96] *Craigie v. Hoggan* (1839) Macl. & R. 942.
[97] *Dysart Peerage Case* (1881) 6 App. Cas. 489, 538; *Glass v. G's Trs.* (1907) 15 S.L.T. 716; *Petrie v. P.,* 1911 S.C. 360; *Polack v. Shiels,* 1912, 2 S.L.T. 329.
[98] *Richardson v. Irving* (1785) Hume 361; *Dunn v. D's Trs.,* 1930 S.C. 131; cf. *Strathern v. Stuart,* 1926 J.C. 114; *Reid v. H.M.A.,* 1934 J.C. 7.
[99] *Mackenzie v. Stewart* (1848) 10 D. 611; *Forster v. F.* (1872) 10 M. (H.L.) 68; *Imrie v. I.* (1891) 19 R. 185.
[1] Stair I, 4, 6; Ersk. I, 6, 4; Bell, *Prin.* § 1515; *Dalrymple v. D* (1811) 2 Hagg. C.R. 54.
[2] Marriage (Sc.) Act, 1939, S. 5.
[3] *Yelverton v. Longworth* (1864) 4 Macq. 745, 834, 879, 902.
[4] *Mackie v. M.,* 1917 S.C. 276.
[5] *Stewart v. Menzies* (1841) 2 Rob. 547, 591; *Yelverton, supra*; *N. v. C.,* 1933 S.C. 492.
[6] *Monteith v. Robb* (1844) 6 D. 934.
[7] Competency of reference to oath doubted in *Longworth v. Yelverton* (1867) 5 M. (H.L.) 144. Subsequent cases do not share this doubt: see *Morrison, infra,* 353; *Mackie, supra,* 282, 283; *Lindsay v. L.,* 1927 S.C. 395.
[8] *Morrison v. Dobson* (1869) 8 M. 347; *N. v. C.,* 1933 S.C. 492.
[9] 1503, c. 77 (repealed).

be presumed to have exchanged matrimonial consent.[10] This mode of irregular marriage remains competent. The question in every case is one of fact, whether the proper inference from the evidence is that the parties must have exchanged matrimonial consent.[11] There must be cohabitation at bed and board[12] in Scotland[13] by parties free to marry, or cohabitation continued after they have become free to marry,[14] unless the circumstances of continuance do not imply consent to marry.[15] If the parties knew that their relationship was initially illicit, concubinage,[16] or adultery, no presumption of marriage arises from it, or from its continuance after the impediment has been removed,[17] unless there is clear evidence of matrimonial intent.[18] If, at the commencement of the relationship, one of the parties is proved to have intended to remain single, the onus of proof of marriage is increased.[19] No particular period of cohabitation is requisite, so long as it is sufficient reasonably to support the presumption of exchange of matrimonial consent.[20] The relationship must also have given rise to substantially consistent and unvarying reputation of being married,[21] as evidenced preferably by the opinions of friends and relatives, rather than by the views of servants, shopkeepers, and casual acquaintances.[22] Acknowledgment of marriage to friends is favourable,[23] but concealment of the marriage from friends and connections is unfavourable.[24] Disparity of social position between the parties is also

[10] Stair, I, 46, III, 3, 42; Ersk. I, 6, 6; Bell, *Prin.* § 1516; *Elder v. McLean* (1829) 8 S. 56; *Lapsley v. Grierson* (1845) 8 D. 34; *Campbell v. C.* (1867) 5 M. (H.L.) 115. See also Ashton-Cross, 1961 J.R. 21.

[11] *Low v. Gorman,* 1970 S.L.T. 356.

[12] *Lowrie v. Mercer* (1840) 2D. 953, 963; *Hamilton v. H.* (1842) 1 Bell 736.

[13] *Macdouall v. Lady Dalhousie* (1840) 1 Robin. 475; *Dysart Peerage Case* (1881) 6 App. Cas. 489.

[14] *Campbell, supra; De Thoren v. Wall* (1876) 3 R. (H.L.) 28; *A.B. v. C.D.,* 1957 S.C. 415; *Shaw v. Henderson,* 1982 S.L.T. 211; see also *Secretary of State for Scotland v. Sutherland,* 1944 S.C. 79, 84.

[15] *Bairner v. Fels,* 1931 S.C. 674.

[16] *Mackenzie v. Scott,* 1980 S.L.T. (Notes) 9.

[17] *Cuninghame v. C.* (1814) 2 Dow. 482; *Lapsley v. Grierson* (1845) 8 D. 34; (1848) 1 H.L.C. 498; *Campbell v. C.* (1867) 5 M. (H.L.) 115; *Dysart Peerage Case, supra.*

[18] *Elder v. Maclean* (1829) 8 S. 56; *Wood's Trs. v. Findlay,* 1909, 1 S.L.T. 156; *Cossar v. C.* (1901) 9 S.L.T. 44; *A.B., supra; Low v. Gorman,* 1970 S.L.T. 356.

[19] *Nicol v. Bell,* 1954 S.L.T. 314. cf. *Mackenzie v. Scott,* 1980 S.L.T. (Notes) 9.

[20] Insufficient: *Wallace v. Fife Coal Co.,* 1909 S.C. 682 (10½ mos.); *Mackenzie, supra* (4 years); sufficient; *Shaw v. Henderson,.* 1982 S.L.T. 211 (11 months); *A.B. v. C.D.,* 1957 S.C. 415 (6 years); *Petrie v. P.,* 1911 S.C. 360 (8 years); *Hendry v. L.A.,* 1930 S.C. 1027 (20 years); *Nicol v. Bell,* 1954 S.L.T. 314 (22 years); *Wood's Trs. v. Findlay,* 1909, 1 S.L.T. 156 (38 years). cf. *Low, supra* (10 mos.).

[21] *Petrie v. P.,* 1911 S.C. 360.

[22] *Thomas v. Gordon* (1829) 7 S. 872; *Hamilton v. H.* (1839) 2 D. 89; *Lapsley v. Grierson, supra; Cossar, supra; Lynch v. L.,* 1926 S.N. 172; *Hendry v. L.A.,* 1930 S.C. 1027; see also *Longworth v. Yelverton* (1862) 24 D. 696 and 28 J.R. 38 thereon.

[23] *Inglis v. Robertson* (1787) 3 Pat. 53; *MacGregor v. Campbell,* 28 Nov. 1801, F.C.; *Aitchison v. Incorporation of Solicitors* (1838) 1 D. 42; *Lang v. L.* (1841) 3 D. 980.

[24] *Thomas, supra; Lowrie v. Mercer* (1840) 2 D. 953, 961.

relevant.[25] The registration of children as legitimate suggests marriage.[26] Uncertain or divided repute will not suffice.[27] Marriage may be held not constituted if one party has delayed to have it declared,[28] or has acquiesced in inconsistent conduct, such as the other taking up cohabitation with a third party.[29] If the evidence points to marriage by cohabitation with habit and repute, no regard will be paid to a subsequent writing acknowledging that the parties did not cohabit as man and wife.[30] If the facts justify an inference of an exchange of matrimonial consent, this may be deemed to have taken place at the outset of the cohabitation, or when some event indicative of marriage took place, such as registering a child as legitimate,[31] or when the parties became free to marry.[32]

Registration of irregular marriages

Where decree of declarator that a marriage has been contracted irregularly, by declaration *de praesenti* or by promise *subsequente copula* before 1st July 1940, or by cohabitation with habit and repute at any time, the decree, and the date on which the marriage was held constituted, must be intimated to the Registrar-General for registration.[33]

Clandestine marriage

A clandestine marriage is one celebrated by a person falsely assuming the character of a clergyman,[34] or by a clergyman, without a marriage schedule, issued under the 1977 Act, being available to him.[35] It is an offence to celebrate marriage with religious ceremony but without a marriage schedule,[36] or to personate a clergyman, or without authority to perform a marriage ceremony.[37] Such a marriage is now void; formerly it could have had effect as a marriage by *de praesenti* consent,[38] but it might yet be the basis for marriage by cohabitation with habit and repute.

---

[25] *Hamilton, supra;* cf. *MacGregor* v. *Campbell*, 29 Nov. 1801, F.C.

[26] *A.B., supra.*

[27] *Hamilton, supra.*

[28] *Darsie* v. *Sceales* (1867) 39 Sc. Jur. 191.

[29] *Napier* v. *N.* (1801) Hume 367; *Wright* v. *W's Trs.* (1837) 15 S. 767. Contrast *Reid* v. *Robb* (1813) Hume 378.

[30] *Mackenzie* v. *M.*, 8 Mar. 1810, F.C.

[31] *Nicol* v. *Bell*, 1954 S.L.T. 314.

[32] *Campbell* v. *C.* (1867) 5 M. (H.L.) 115; *A.B.* v. *C.D.*, 1957 S.C. 415.

[33] Marriage (Sc.) Act, 1977, S. 21; for former practice see *Courtin* v. *Elder*, 1930 S.C. 68, 76.

[34] cf. *H.M.A.* v. *Ballantyne* (1859) 3 Irv. 352. *Quaere* as to an adherent of an unrecognized body? See *Walsh* v. *L.A.*, 1956 S.C. (H.L.) 126.

[35] Ersk. I, 6, 11; Bell, *Prin.* § 1514; 1977 Act, S. 24 (1) (c).

[36] Marriage (Sc.) Act, 1977, S. 24 (1) (c); cf. *Strathern* v. *Stuart*, 1926 J.C. 114.

[37] *H.M.A.* v. *Ballantyne, supra*; 1977 Act, S. 24 (1) (d).

[38] Stair, I, 4, 6.

Marriages in England

The formalities of marriage in England are prescribed by the Marriage Act, 1949, as amended.[39]

Marriages in naval, military, and air force chapels

Under the Marriage Act, 1949, Part V, persons at least one of whom is or was a regular member of the forces, or of the women's services, or the daughter of any such person, may marry in a garrison church, subject to certain qualifications of the rules applicable to marriages in England.

Declarator of marriage

Declarator of marriage is the process for seeking to have a doubtful marriage judicially recognized as valid and binding, or to have established a marriage which is denied by the other party.[40] It may be a necessary preliminary to an action of divorce, may be brought by a child of the marriage after the death of one spouse,[41] and may be continued by the pursuer's executor after her death *pendente lite*.[42] An alternative conclusion may be for damages for breach of promise and seduction.[43] The existence of marriage may also be decided incidentally in other actions.[44]

Declarator of freedom and puttting to silence

Declarator of freedom and putting to silence is the process whereby a person, troubled by another falsely calling himself or herself that person's spouse, may have himself declared free of the alleged marriage and the other enjoined to preserve silence as to the false claim.[45] It is a competent defence that marriage was truly constituted.[46]

Declarator of nullity

Declarator of nullity is the process to have declared that an apparent marriage was truly void on any ground on which it is void *ab initio*,[47] or that, being voidable, it should now be declared void.[48] In a declarator

---

[39] As to the notice of intention in Scotland to marry outside Scotland see 1977 Act, S. 7.
[40] e.g. *Steuart* v. *Robertson* (1875) 2 R. (H.L.) 80; *Nicol* v. *Bell*, 1954 S.L.T. 314.
[41] *X.* v. *Y.*, 1921 1 S.L.T. 79.
[42] *Borthwick* v. *B.* (1896) 24 R. 211; cf. *Mackie* v. *M.*, 1917 S.C. 276.
[43] *Borthwick, supra.*
[44] *Wright* v. *Sharp* (1880) 7 R. 460; *Burke* v. *B.*, 1983 S.L.T. 331. But contrast *Lenaghan* v. *Monkland Iron Co.* (1857) 19 D. 975; *Wallace* v. *Fife Coal Co.*, 1909 S.C. 682.
[45] *Williams* v. *Forsythe*, 1909 2 S.L.T. 252; cf. *A.B.* v. *C.D.* (1901) 8 S.L.T. 406.
[46] *H.* v. *R.* (1844) 16 Sc. Jur. 576; *Longworth* v. *Yelverton* (1862) 1 M. 161; (1864) 2 M. (H.L.) 49.
[47] See *infra.*
[48] See *infra.*

of nullity on the ground of prior subsisting marriage which was not registered, it is competent to include a conclusion for declarator that the defender was previously married to another named person.[49]

RELATIONS *STANTE MATRIMONIO*

The constitution of marriage effects substantial changes in the rights and duties of the spouses *inter se*.

Change of name

By modern custom a married woman usually takes the title Mrs and substitutes her husband's surname for her own or adds it to her maiden surname, but there is no obligation to do this.[50] For legal purposes she is designated Mrs [Christian names] [maiden surname] or [married surname]. Her husband's designation, if any, may be assumed with the rest of his name.

Husband's curatory

At common law a married woman fell under her husband's curatory and could sue or be sued only with his concurrence. She is now released from curatory by marriage, even if still a minor.[51] Neither spouse may, as such, represent the other in litigation.[52]

Litigation

Either spouse can sue or be sued alone, and the other incurs no liability merely by reason of marriage, but either may incur liability by taking control of the action.[53]

Obligations inter se

Spouses may contract with one another and sue each other for breach of contract.[54] Either may stand to the other in the relation of landlord to tenant and may eject the other from the house,[55] or the relation of

---

[49] *Courtin* v. *Elder*, 1930 S.C. 68.
[50] This is a modern practice under English influence: Seton, *Law and Practice of Heraldry*, 392.
[51] Law Reform (Husband and Wife) (Sc.) Act. 1984, S. 3.
[52] *Gordon* v. *Nakeski-Cumming*, 1924 S.C. 939.
[53] *Swirles* v. *Isles*, 1930 S.C. 696.
[54] *Horsburgh* v. *H.*, 1949 S.C. 227.
[55] *MacLure* v. *M.*, 1911 S.C. 200; *Millar* v. *M.*, 1940 S.C. 56.

creditor to debtor and sue for repayment,[56] or the relation of employer to employee. Each owes duties of care to the other and may now sue for injury or damage caused by breach thereof.[57] Neither is vicariously liable to a third party for the other's wrong,[58] unless the wrongdoing one were at the time acting as agent or servant of the other. One spouse may steal from the other,[59] or commit assault or any other kind of crime against the other.

Property

At common law, by the *jus mariti*, a wife's whole moveable property passed automatically to her husband on marriage as his absolute property, including all moveables which she might acquire during the marriage, but excluding all items from which the *jus mariti* was excluded by the destination thereof.[60] The husband also acquired the *jus administrationis*, a right of management of the wife's heritable estate springing from his curatorial power over her.[61] Statute intervened in the nineteenth century; now marriage does not of itself affect the respective rights of the parties to the marriage in relation to their property or their legal capacity.[62] Each spouse, that is, continues to own his or her pre-matrimonial property; there is no transfer or presumption of common property. But this is subject to exceptions, notably the presumption of equal shares in household goods acquired in prospect of or during the marriage,[63] and in money and property derived from a housekeeping allowance,[64] occupancy rights in the matrimonial home,[65] and it does not affect the law of succession.[62]

Paraphernalia

At common law a wife's paraphernalia were always her own property.[66] These were her clothing, jewellery, and personal trinkets.[67] The concept is now obsolete.

---

[56] *Aitken* v. *A.*, 1954 S.L.T. (Sh. Ct.) 60.
[57] Law Reform (Husband and Wife) Act, 1962, overruling *Young* v. *Y.* (1903) 5 F. 330; *Harper* v. *H.*, 1929 S.C. 220; *Cameron* v. *Glasgow Corpn.*, 1936 S.C. (H.L.) 26.
[58] *Barr* v. *Neilson* (1868) 6 M. 651; *Milne* v. *Smiths* (1892) 20 R. 95.
[59] *Harper* v. *Adair*, 1945 J.C. 21.
[60] Stair, I, 4, 17; Ersk; I, 6, 12; Bell, *Prin*, § 1547, 1561; Fraser, *H. & W.*, I, 679.
[61] Bell, *Prin.* s 1563.
[62] Family Law (Sc.) Act, 1985, S. 24.
[63] Ibid., S. 25.
[64] Ibid., S. 26.
[65] Matrimonial Homes (Family Protection) (Sc.) Act, 1981.
[66] Ersk. I, 6, 15; Bell, *Prin.* § 1554–9; *Craig* v. *Monteith* (1684) Mor. 5819; *Cameron* v. *McLean* (1876) 13 S.L.R. 278; *Young* v. *Johnson* (1880) 7 R. 760; *Sleigh* v. *S.'s J.F.* (1901) 9 S.L.T. 35.
[67] *Dicks* v. *Massie* (1655) Mor. 5821; *Cameron* v. *McLean* (1870) 13 S.L.R. 278.

Liability for each other's debts

Under the *jus mariti* the husband acquired liability for his wife's ante-nuptial debts, whether or not he benefited from the marriage. Such debts included her liability to aliment her indigent parents,[68] or an illegitimate child.[69] By the 1877 Act, S. 4, this was limited to the value of property received through her,[70] and he is now no longer liable for her ante-nuptial debts at all.[71] By the 1881 Act, S. 1, a wife's moveable property, if placed in her name, was not liable for the husband's debts, but if lent or entrusted to the husband or inmixed with his funds, had to be treated as assets in the husband's bankruptcy, the wife having a claim to a dividend for her property.

Marriage contracts

While the *jus mariti* and *jus administrationis* subsisted, it was common where the wife had, or might inherit, substantial property, for the spouses and their parents to enter into ante-nuptial or post-nuptial marriage contracts whereby property was assigned to trustees to be held for the wife or the survivor of the spouses and the children of the marriage on such terms as might be arranged, exclusive of the husband's rights. The necessity for such arrangements has largely disappeared and they are now much less common. Such contracts commonly provide provisions to a surviving spouse and children in lieu of legal rights.[72] A wife may no longer in an ante-nuptial marriage contract create an alimentary right in her own favour.[73]

Wife as husband's agent

A wife may act as her husband's agent and render him liable on contracts concluded by her, either where she had actual or express authority to act as such, either generally or in regard to particular kinds of transactions only, or where such authority is held implied by a past course of dealings which has led persons to believe that the wife had authority.[74]

Agency of necessity

A wife also has an implied agency in case of necessity. This confers on her an implied power to pledge his credit and render him liable for necessary

---

[68] *Reid* v. *Moir* (1866) 4 M. 1060; *Foulis* v. *Fairbairn* (1887) 14 R. 1088.

[69] *Aitken* v. *Anderson* (1815) Hume 217.

[70] Bell, *Prin.* § 1570–3; *McAllan* v. *Alexander* (1888) 15 R. 863; *Dear* v. *Duncan* (1896) 3 S.L.T. 241.

[71] Married Women's Property (Sc.) Act, 1920, S. 3 (1); Law Reform (Husband and Wife) (Sc.) Act, 1984, S. 6.

[72] On legal rights, see Ch. 7.2, *Infra.*

[73] Law Reform (Husband and Wife) (Sc.) Act, 1984, S. 5.

[74] *Slowey* v. *Robertson and Moir* (1865) 4M. 1.

goods and services supplied to her.[75] It is founded on the husband's obligation to maintain his wife and children and arises if she is living apart, with her husband's consent or with reasonable cause, and is without means.[76] It does not arise if she was in receipt of an adequate allowance,[77] is in desertion of her husband, nor if she has separate estate. 'Necessaries' include food, clothing, lodging, medical care, and legal advice, even for proceedings against the husband,[78] unless the solicitor acted negligently, or knew, or could by ordinary reasonable inquiries, have ascertained that proceedings were unfounded.[79] The husband's liability arises only if the creditor intended to give credit to the husband, and not if he relied on the wife's credit exclusively or she incurred the obligation on her own behalf.[80]

Praepositura

A married woman is not now presumed in law to have been placed by her husband in charge of his domestic affairs so as to make him liable on obligations incurred by her,[81] but she may have actual or ostensible authority to bind him.

Housekeeping allowance

In a question as to the right to money derived from any allowance made by either spouse for their joint household expenses or for similar purposes, or to any property acquired out of such money, the money or property is, in the absence of contrary agreement, to be treated as belonging to each party in equal shares.[82]

Moveable property in matrimonial home

Household goods kept or used at any time during the marriage in any matrimonial home for the joint domestic purposes of the parties, other than money or securities, any motor car, caravan, or other road vehicle, and any domestic animal, if obtained in prospect of or during the marriage other than by gift or succession from a third party, are presumed, unless the contrary is proved, owned by the spouses in equal shares. The

[75] Fraser, H. & W. I, 638.
[76] M.W.P. (Sc.) Act, 1920, S. 3(2).
[77] Star Stores Ltd. v. Joss [1955] C.L.Y. 3288..
[78] McAlister v. McA. (1762) Mor. 4036; Macgregor v. Martin (1867) 5 M. 583; Clark v. Henderson (1875) 2 R. 428; Milne v. M. (1885) 13 R. 304; A.B. v. C.B. (1906) 8 F. 973; Warden v. W., 1962 S.C. 127; Laurie v. L., 1965 S.C. 49.
[79] Robertson v. L. (1881) 6 P.D. 119.
[86] Married Women's Property (Sc.) Act, 1920, S. 3(1).
[81] Law Reform (Husband and Wife) (Sc.) Act. 1984, S. 7.
[82] Family Law (Sc.) Act, 1985, S. 26.

contrary is not proved by reason only that the goods were purchased by either party alone or by both in unequal shares.[83] Goods acquired by gift or succession belong to the spouse to whom they were destined. Excluded goods must be determined in the circumstances of the case.

Heritable property

Where title to heritable property is taken in the joint names of husband and wife they are deemed joint proprietors; if survivorship be expressed, the survivor has the benefit of accretion.[84] The spouse paying the price in such a case has been held entitled by will to evacuate the destination *quoad* his own *pro indiviso* share only.[85] Though title is taken in the name of one spouse only, if the price was borrowed on the security of the obligations of both, each has an equal half-share in the profits on sale.[86] It may be proved, but only by writ or oath, that heritable property in the name of one was held in trust for the other.[87]

Donations between spouses

At common law donations between spouses during the marriage were revocable by the donor; but they are now irrevocable, though any donation made within a year and a day before sequestration of the donor's estate is revocable at the instance of his creditors.[88] In case of dispute the donee has to establish delivery sufficient to evidence gift and circumstances showing *animus donandi*.[89]

Personal allowance

A husband may make a personal allowance to his wife for her own use. Such sums fall to be regarded as periodical donations, and become her absolute property.

Wife's earnings

A wife's earnings are her own absolute property. She is now obliged to aliment her husband,[90] and there may now be a legal duty in other

---

[83] Family Law (Sc.) Act, 1985, S. 25.
[84] *Walker* v. *Galbraith* (1895) 23 R. 347. For more complicated destinations see Fraser, *H. & W.* II, 1428; Craigie, *Heritable*, 567.
[85] *Hay's Tr.* v. *Hay's Trs.*, 1951 S.C. 329.
[86] *McDougall* v. *M.*, 1947 S.N. 102.
[87] *Adam* v. *A.*, 1962 S.L.T. 332; cf. *Galloway* v. *G.*, 1929 S.C. 160; *Weissenbruch* v. *W.*, 1961 S.C. 340.
[88] Married Women's Proeprty (Sc.) Act, 1920, S. 5.
[89] *Donald* v. *D.*, 1953 S.L.T. (Sh. Ct.) 69.
[90] Family Law (Sc.) Act. 1985, S. 1.

circumstances on her to maintain the common home or to contribute to its cost.[91]

Where income pooled

Prima facie the income of each spouse, however earned, remains his or her private property. But if spouses pool the whole or part of their incomes they probably acquire a joint right of property in the fund, irrespective of the amounts contributed by each thereto,[92] the whole accrescing to the survivor on the death of either. Joint property is not, however, necessarily constituted by a bank account in joint names and on which either may draw, as such may be merely a convenient arrangement.[93] Property purchased from a joint fund will belong to the purchaser, unless it appears to be a joint investment, in which case it will be joint property. Thus a house bought by contributions from both spouses may be deemed joint property, each being entitled to half the proceeds on sale.[94]

Life insurance policies

Each spouse has an insurable interest in the life of the other, and may insure the other's life and recover on the other's death without proof of actual loss.[95] Under the Married Women's Policies of Assurance (Sc.) Act, 1880,[96] a policy of assurance effected by a man[97] or woman on his or her own life and expressed to be for the benefit of his or her spouse[98] or children[99] or spouse and children[99] shall be deemed a trust for their benefit, and vest in him or any trustee appointed,[1] and shall not otherwise be subject to his control, or form part of his estate,[2] or be liable to the diligence of his creditors,[3] or be revocable as a donation, or reducible on any ground of excess or insolvency, though if it is proved that the policy was effected and the premiums paid with intent to defraud creditors, or

---

[91] *Preston* v. *P.*, 1950 S.C. 253 may now be superseded.
[92] cf. *Jones* v. *Maynard* [1951] Ch. 572.
[93] *Marshal* v. *Crutwell* (1875) L.R. 20 Eq. 328.
[94] cf. *Rimmer* v. *R.* [1953] 1 Q.B. 63; *Cobb* v. *C.* [1955] 2 All. E.R. 696. See also *Fribance* v. *F.* [1957] 1 All E.R. 357.
[95] *Griffiths* v. *Fleming* [1909] 1 K.B. 805.
[96] As amended by M.W. Policies of Assurance (Amndt.) (Sc.) Act, 1980.
[97] Including a widower: *Kennedy's Trs.* v. *Sharpe* (1895) 23 R. 146. As to man about to be married see *Coulson's Trs.* v. *C.* (1901) 3 F. 1041.
[98] Including future spouse: 1980 Act, S. 1.
[99] Including illegitimate or adopted children but not children of the spouse and another person, unless adopted: 1980 Act, S. 1.
[1] It is a trust under the Trusts (Sc.) Acts: 1980 Act, Ss 2 and 4.
[2] cf. *Walker's Trs.* v. *L.A.*, 1955 S.C. (H.L.) 74. But see *Sharp's Trs.* v. *L.A.*, 1951 S.C. 442, where husband retained contingent interest, and Finance Act, 1968, Ss. 37–8, limiting amounts.
[3] *Chrystal's Trs.* v. *C.*, 1912 S.C. 1003.

the person effecting it be made bankrupt within two years from the date of the policy, the creditors may claim repayment of the premiums from the trustee of the policy out of the proceeds thereof. Such a policy may be surrendered at any time by the trustee with the spouse's concurrence.[4] A beneficiary may assign or renounce his interest whether or not the effect is to make the policy subject to the control of the person effecting it, part of his estate or liable to the diligence of his creditors.[5]

DUTIES TO EACH OTHER

Duties to each other—aliment

Each spouse is bound to aliment the other, i.e. to provide such support as is reasonable in the circumstances, having regard to the needs and resources of the parties, the earning capacities of the parties, and generally to all the circumstances of the case, which may include taking account of any support, financial or otherwise, given by the defender to any person whom he maintains as a dependant in his household, whether or not the defender owes an obligation of aliment to that person and is not to take account of any conduct of a party unless it would be manifestly inequitable to leave it out of account.[6] This obligation is normally satisfied by one maintaining the other in family with him, or by providing a home and money during his necessary absence. It subsists even if one has been guilty of behaviour for which the other has obtained decree of separation,[7] or has committed adultery,[8] or has been put out of the house,[9] or is with just cause living in separation from the other by reason of the desertion or other conduct of the other,[10] so long as the one is willing to adhere[10] but not if he or she has left the other without legal justification and refuses to adhere.[11]

No claim lies against parents[12] or parents-in-law,[13] or children.[14]

---

[4] *Schumann* v. *Scottish Widows Fund* (1886) 13 R. 678; 1980 Act, S. 2.

[5] 1980 Act, S. 3.

[6] Family Law (Sc.) Act, 1985, Ss. 1, 4. Spouses include parties to a valid polygamous marriage.

[7] *Nisbet* v. *N.* (1896) 4 S.L.T. 142.

[8] Fraser, *H. & W.* 644; *Milne* v. *M.* (1901) 8 S.L.T. 375; *Donnelly* v. *D.*, 1959 S.C. 97; *Harkness* v. *H.* (1961) 77 Sh. Ct. Rep. 165.

[9] *Croall* v. *C.* (1832) 11 S. 185; *McMillan* v. *M.* (1870) 9 M. 1067; *MacLure* v. *M.*, 1911 S.C. 200; *Donnelly, supra.*

[10] *Barbour* v. *B.*, 1965 S.C. 158; *Barr* v. *B.*, 1968 S.L.T. (Sh. Ct.) 37.

[11] *Bell* v. *B.*, 22 Feb. 1812, F.C.; *Coutts* v. *C.* (1866) 4 M. 802; *Cameron* v. *C.*, 1956 S.L.T. (Notes) 7; *Beveridge* v. *B.*, 1963 S.C. 572; *Brunton* v. *B.*, 1986 S.L.T. 49.

[12] 1985 Act, S. 1.

[13] 1985 Act, S. 1; *Hoseason* v. *H.* (1870) 9 M. 37; *McAllan* v. *Alexander* (1888) 15 R. 863; *Dear* v. *Duncan* (1896) 3 S.L.T. 241; *Reid* v. *R.* (1897) in 6 F. 935; *Mackay* v. *M.'s Trs.* (1904) 6 F. 936.

[14] 1985 Act, S. 1.

Either spouse may claim aliment by action, which may be made alone, or in proceedings for divorce, separation, declarator of marriage, or nullity of marriage or any other kind if the court consider it appropriate,[15] and even though the claimant is living in the same household as the defender.[15]

Either is entitled to an award of aliment if he or she has obtained decree of aliment,[16] so long as the other refuses to adhere, or decree of separation and aliment, so long as the separation stands unrevoked,[17] or if the spouses have separated by consent, or if either has justification for divorce and has withdrawn from cohabitation,[18] even if no longer willing to adhere.[19] A sufficient answer to the claim is an offer to entertain the other at bed and board, if *bona fide* and reasonable in the circumstances.[20]

When granting decree the court may order periodical payments for a definite or an indefinite period or until a specified event, and alimentary payments of an occasional or special nature, but not a lump sum in lieu of a periodical payment. Awards may be backdated, and may be less than claimed.[21] A decree may be varied or recalled if there has been a material change of circumstances.

Interim awards of aliment may be made to a spouse *pendente lite*,[22] but this is inexpedient in a declarator of marriage where the marriage is denied.[23] Such an award supersedes an existing sheriff court decree for aliment in an action of adherence and aliment.[24]

Interim aliment alone may be claimed by a wife, justifiably expelled from the house by her husband, so long as he refuses to receive her back,[25] but is normally conjoined with a claim for adherence, being due failing adherence and so long as non-adherence continues, or a claim for separation, being due so long as the separation stands unrevoked.[26] Decrees for aliment consequential on the decision of an issue of adherence or separation are permanent, though subject to review at the instance of

[15] Family Law (Sc.) Act, 1985, S. 2.
[16] The onus of proof is on the defender to rebut the presumption of the pursuer's willingness to adhere: *Reid* v. *R.* 1978 S.L.T. (Sh. Ct.) 2.
[17] cf. *Lawson* v. *Bain* (1830) 8 S. 923.
[18] *Scott* v. *Selbie* (1835) 13 S. 278; *McFarlane* v. *McF.* (1844) 6 D. 1220; *Fyffe* v. *F.,* 1954 S.C. 1; *Barr* v. *B.,* 1968 S.L.T. (Sh. Ct.) 37.
[19] *Stirling* v. *S.,* 1971 S.L.T. 322.
[20] *Paterson* v. *P.* (1961) 24 D. 215. For inadequate offers see *Arthur* v. *Gourley* (1769) 2 Pat. 184; *Reid* v. *R.* (1823) 2 S. 468.
[21] 1985 Act, S. 3.
[22] *Macfarlane* v. *M.* (1844) 6 D. 1220; *Borthwick* v. *B,* (1848) 10 D. 1312; *Hoey* v. *H.* (1883) 11 R. 25; *A.D.* v. *W.D.,* 1909, 1 S.L.T. 342; *Pirrie* v. *P.* (1903) 10 S.L.T. 598; *Robertson* v. *R.* (1905) 13 S.L.T. 114; *Barbour* v. *B.,* 1965 S.C. 158; 1985 Act, S. 6.
[23] *Murison* v. *M.,* 1923 S.C. 40.
[24] *Cosgrove* v. *C.* 1980 S.L.T. (Sh. Ct.) 105.
[25] *Pearce* v. *P.* (1898) 5 S.L.T. 338; *Gatchell* v. *G.* (1898) 6 S.L.T. 224; *Hicks* v. *H.* (1899) 6 S.L.T. 261; *Milne* v. *M.* (1901) 8 S.L.T. 375; *Donnelly* v. *D.,* 1959 S.C. 97.
[26] *Williamson* v. *W.* (1860) 22 D. 599; see also *Adair* v. *A.,* 1924 S.C. 798.

either party if financial circumstances change.[27] There is no rule that a
wife earning money must expend the whole of it on her maintenance to
the relief of her husband's obligation under a decree for aliment.[28] Aliment should be calculated by reference to the husband's gross income and
be made 'less tax'.[29] It is incompetent to seek, or for the court to grant,
decree for aliment to be paid in all time coming.[30] The sanction for wilful
failure to pay aliment due under a decree is civil imprisonment at the
instance of the pursuer holding the decree.[31]

Spouses may make an agreement about aliment but an agreement
purporting to exclude future liability or restrict any right to sue for
aliment is ineffective unless the provision was fair and reasonable in all
the circumstances of the agreement at the time it was entered into.
Application may be made for variation of an agreement.[32]

Statutory duty to aliment

By statute, for the purposes of the Act,[33] each spouse is liable to maintain
the other spouse and his or her children, and a man to maintain children
his paternity of whom has been admitted or established, and a woman to
maintain her illegitimate children. It is a criminal offence persistently to
refuse or neglect to do so.[34] Where assistance is given by the Department
of Health and Social Security or a local authority the court may order the
person liable to maintain the person assisted to pay such sum as the court
considers appropriate.[35]

Duties to each other—adherence

The spouses should adhere to each other, and cohabit at bed and board.
Neither spouse has the prior right to determine the place of the matrimonial home, or the prior duty to provide it.[36] It is questionable if either
may insist on the other living in a house provided for her separate use,[37]
and, if he offers aliment, have the other ejected from the house and
interdicted from returning.[38] A wife may now act similarly towards her

---

[27] *Donald* v. *D.* (1862) 24 D. 499; *Christie* v. *C.*, 1919 S.C. 576; *Adair* v. *A.*, 1932 S.N. 47,
69; *Donnelly, supra.*
[28] *Dowswell* v. *D.*, 1943 S.C. 23.
[29] *Thomson* v. *T.*, 1943 S.C. 154.
[30] *Duncan* v. *Forbes* (1878) 15 S.L.R. 371; *Brunt* v. *B.*, 1958 S.L.T. (Notes) 41.
[31] *Macdonald* v. *Denoon*, 1929 S.C. 172; *Brunt* v. *B.*, 1954 S.L.T. (Sh. Ct.) 74; *Cassells* v. *C.*,
1955 S.L.T. (Sh. Ct.) 41; *McWilliams* v. *McW.*, 1963 S.C. 259.
[32] Family Law (Sc.) Act, 1985, S. 7.
[33] Supplementary Benefits Act, 1976, Ss. 17–18.
[34] *Corcoran* v. *Muir*, 1954 J.C. 46.
[35] *Supplementary Benefits Commission* v. *Black*, 1968 S.L.T. (Sh. Ct.) 90; *S.B.C.* v. *Mitchell*,
1982 S.L.T. 389.
[36] Law Reform (Husband and Wife) (Sc.) Act, 1984, S. 4.
[37] *Colquhoun* v. *C.*, (1804) Mor. Appx. Husband and Wife, 5.
[38] *MacLure* v. *M.*, 1911 S.C. 200.

husband if the house is hers.[39] But refusal by either spouse to receive the other into his house, if persisted in without reasonable cause for two years, would be desertion justifying divorce.[40]

If either spouse ceases to adhere without adequate legal justification the other cannot enforce the obligation by action, calling on the other to adhere: No person is liable in delict to any person by reason only of having induced that person's spouse to leave or remain apart from that person.[41]

Either party is relieved of the duty to adhere if the other has been guilty of such conduct as would justify an action of divorce against him or her,[42] or of certain lesser matrimonial wrongs,[43] or if either has obtained a decree of separation. There is no duty to adhere if the marriage were void *ab initio*,[44] and it is ended if a voidable marriage is declared void.[45]

Occupancy of matrimonial home

At common law a spouse who owned,[46] or tenanted, a house might eject the other spouse from the house if the latter were a tenant, or occupier, possibly on condition of paying aliment. If a deserting spouse was tenant of a house subject to the Rent Acts he could not on desertion confer on his spouse any right to remain in occupation.[47]

The Matrimonial Homes (Family Provision) (Sc.) Act, 1981, amended by the Law Reform (M.P.) (Sc.) Act, 1985, S. 13, provides (S. 1) that where one spouse is entitled, or permitted by a third party, to occupy a matrimonial home and the other is not, the latter has the rights, if in occupation, to continue to occupy the home, and if not, to enter into and occupy the matrimonial home, if need be with leave of the court. A non-entitled spouse may renounce occupancy rights in writing only if at the time of renouncing the latter has sworn or affirmed before a notary public that the renunciation was made freely and without coercion of any kind. The rights include (S. 1A) the right to do so with children of the family. A non-entitled spouse may, without the consent of the entitled spouse, pay rent, rates, loan instalments, interest or other outgoings, carry out essential repairs, or with the authority of the court non-essential

---

[39] *MacLure, supra; Millar v. M.,* 1940 S.C. 56.
[40] See *infra.*
[41] Law Reform (Husband and Wife) (Sc.) Act, 1984, S. 2.
[42] *Mackenzie v. M.* (1895) 22 R. (H.L.) 33.
[43] *Hastings v. H.,* 1941 S.L.T. 323; *Hamilton v. H.,* 1953 S.C. 383; *Richardson v. R.,* 1956 S.C. 394; *McMillan v. McM.,* 1962 S.C. 115.
[44] *Jack v. J.,* 1940 S.L.T. 122.
[45] *Allardyce v. A.,* 1954 S.C. 419.
[46] *Millar v. M.,* 1940 S.C. 56; as to spouses' joint title, see *Cairns v. Halifax Bldg. Soc.,* 1951 S.L.T. (Sh. Ct.) 67. See also *Scott v. S.* (1948) 64 Sh. Ct. Rep. 119; *Macpherson v. M.,* 1950 S.L.T. (Sh. Ct.) 24; *McLeod v. McL.,* 1950 S.L.T. (Sh. Ct.) 31.
[47] *Temple v. Mitchell,* 1956 S.C. 267.

repairs, and make payments for hire of furniture and plenishings. Possession by a non-entitled spouse continues possession for the purposes of a tenancy. Either spouse may (S. 3) apply to the court for an order declaring occupancy rights, enforcing occupancy rights, restricting the other spouse's occupancy rights, regulating occupancy rights, and protecting the applicant's occupancy rights. The court must have regard to certain factors.[48] Either spouse may (S. 4) apply for an exclusion order suspending the other's occupancy rights in the home and the court may grant warrant for summary ejection of the non-applicant, interdict him from entering the home without the applicant's permission, and interdict the removal by the non-applicant of furniture and plenishings.[49] Such orders may (S. 5) be varied or recalled but cease on termination of the marriage or the entitled spouse ceasing to be an entitled spouse.

A non-entitled spouse's rights are not prejudiced by reason only of the entitled spouse's dealing with the home and a third party is not thereby entitled to occupy the matrimonial home (S. 6), but this does not apply where the non-entitled spouse in writing consents or has consented to the dealing, or renounces occupancy rights, or the court makes an order under S. 7 dispensing with consent, or the dealing occurred, or implements a binding obligation entered into before the marriage or before the Act, or comprises a sale to a third party who acted in good faith if at or before the dealing there is produced by the seller an affidavit declaring that the subjects of sale are not a matrimonial home in which a spouse has occupancy rights, or the entitled spouse has ceased to be entitled and for at least 5 years thereafter the non-entitled spouse had not occupied the matrimonial home. The court may (S. 7) dispense with the non-entitled spouse's consent if it is unreasonably withheld or cannot be given or the spouse cannot be traced or is a minor.[50] There is provision for protection of the interests of heritable creditors (S. 9) and protection against diligence of creditors (Ss. 10–12).

The court may (S. 13) order transfer of the tenancy of a matrimonial home, with certain exceptions, to a non-entitled spouse on payment of such compensation as is just and reasonable, and this may be done in a divorce or nullity case, or vest a joint or common tenancy in one spouse alone.[51]

Even though spouses are living together a court may (S. 14) grant a matrimonial interdict which restrains or prohibits any conduct by one spouse to the other or a child or prohibits a spouse from entering or

---

[48] *Welsh* v. *W.*, 1987 S.L.T. (Sh. Ct.) 30.
[49] *Bell* v. *B.*, 1983 S.L.T. 224; *Smith* v. *S.*, 1983 S.L.T. 275; *Ward* v. *W.*, 1983 S.L.T. 472; *Colagiacomo* v. *C.*, 1983 S.L.T. 559; *Brown* v. *B.*, 1985 S.L.T. 376; *Matheson* v. *M.*, 1986 S.L.T. (Sh. Ct.) 2; *McCafferty* v. *McC.*, 1986 S.L.T. 650; *Mather* v. *M.*, 1987 S.L.T. 565.
[50] *Longmuir* v. *L.*, 1985 S.L.T. (Sh. Ct.) 33; *Dunsmore* v. *D.*, 1986 S.L.T. (Sh. Ct.) 9; *O'Neill* v. *O'N.*, 1987 S.L.T. (Sh. Ct.) 26, *Fyfe* v. *F.*, 1987 S.L.T. (Sh. Ct.) 38.
[51] *Brown, supra; McGowan* v. *McG.*, 1986 S.L.T. 112.

remaining in a matrimonial home or an area in the vicinity.[52] Power of arrest may (S. 15) be attached to a matrimonial interdict and a constable may arrest without warrant a spouse reasonably suspected of being in breach of the interdict. A spouse arrested may be liberated or detained (S. 16) and further detained for 2 days if there is risk of violence to the applicant spouse (S. 17).

The court may (S. 18) grant occupancy rights to the non-entitled partner of a cohabiting couple for not more than 6 months, extensible for further periods of 6 months, transfer a tenancy, or grant a matrimonial interdict.

Where one spouse brings an action for the division and sale of a matrimonial home owned in common the court may refuse or postpone decree or grant it only subject to conditions (S. 19).[53]

The court has refused to make an order under the Act where the applicant did not disclose her own conduct which was responsible for the marital difficulties.[54]

SEPARATION

Voluntary separation

Parties may by agreement separate and live apart, but the courts will not enforce any contract providing for this,[55] though an agreement to make financial provision for an already agreed separation is enforceable.[56] Any such agreement is at any time revocable by agreement, or by either party calling on the other to adhere,[57] if accompanied by *bona fide* intention to adhere and, if made by the husband, by a genuine offer of a home.[58] Despite separation the husband is still liable to aliment his wife, and this is frequently provided for in a separation agreement.[59] The wife may sue for arrears of aliment due thereunder,[60] and for interim aliment for the future, but the court will not grant decree for the future if the husband *bona fide* offers to take her back,[61] and in such an action may try the

---

[52] *Tattersall* v. *T.*, 1983 S.L.T. 506; *McKenna* v. *McK.*, 1984 S.L.T. (Sh. Ct.) 92; *Brown, supra.*

[53] *Crow* v. *C.*, 1986 S.L.T. 270; *Hall* v. *H.*, 1987 S.L.T. (Sh. Ct.) 15.

[54] *Boyle* v. *B.*, 1986 S.L.T. 656.

[55] *Macdonald* v. *M.'s Trs.* (1863) 1 M. 1065.

[56] *Webster* v. *W's Trs.* (1886) 14 R. 90; *Scott* v. *S.* (1894) 21 R. 853.

[57] Ersk. I, 6, 30, Fraser *H. & W.* II, 911; *A.B.* v. *C.D.* (1853) 16 D. 111; *Macdonald, supra.* cf. *Barr* v. *B.*, 1939 S.C. 696.

[58] *Adair* v. *A.*, 1932 S.N. 47, 69.

[59] *Davidson* v. *D.* (1867) 5 M. 710; *Jameson* v. *J.* (1886) 23 S.L.R. 402; *Thomson* v. *T.* (1890) 17 R. 1091; *Scott* v. *S.* (1894) 21 R. 853; *Campbell* v. *C.*, 1923 S.L.T. 670.

[60] *Malcolm* v. *Mack* (1805) Hume 2.

[61] *Hood* v. *H.* (1871) 9 M. 449; *Bonnar* v. *B.*, 1911 S.C. 854; *Douglas* v. *D.*, 1932 S.C. 680.

issue whether or not a decree of separation would have been warranted, if
the husband pleads that the contract was not binding.[62] The amount of
aliment fixed by agreement may be revised by the court as if it had been
fixed by decree.[63] If aliment exceeds what is necessary for maintenance
the wife may keep the excess.[64] If the parties resume cohabitation the
agreement is revoked unless it provides for resumption of cohabitation.[65]

Judicial separation[66]

The court may on the application of one spouse permit them to cease
cohabitation and order the defender to separate himself from the pursuer.
The effect of such a decree is to leave the marriage standing,[67] but relieve
parties of the obligation of adherence, and the main justification has been
the protection of the pursuer from the defender's conduct.[68] An action by
an insane wife is incompetent.[69] A conclusion for interdict against the
defender molesting the pursuer may be added.[70]

It may be granted on any of the grounds which evidence irretrievable
breakdown justifying divorce, and subject to the same defences.[71] The
pursuer's own adultery does not bar an action,[72] nor does the existence of
a voluntary separation agreement.[73] The grant of judicial separation does
not prejudice a subsequent action for divorce on the same ground and
alleging the same facts,[74] and a separation may be brought while divorce
is pending.[75] It has been held incompetent to refuse separation merely
because the defender had given an undertaking to refrain from further
cruelty.[76] A husband may obtain decree of separation but remains liable
to aliment his wife.[77] A decree lapses if parties resume cohabitation but

[62] Campbell, supra.
[63] Scott, supra; McKeddie v. McK. (1902) 9 S.L.T. 381. But see Smith v. S., 1983 S.L.T. (Sh. Ct.) 83.
[64] Davidson, supra; Henry v. Fraser (1907) 14 S.L.T. 164; Preston v. P., 1950 S.C. 253.
[65] Campbell v. C., 1976 S.L.T. (Sh. Ct.) 69.
[66] This is the old divortium a mensa et thoro or separatio quoad thorum of the canon law which did not admit of divorce a vinculo matrimonii. It was continued after and notwithstanding the Reformation by the Scottish courts.
[67] cf. Shirrefs v. S. (1896) 23 R. 807.
[68] Adair v. A., 1924 S.L.T. 749.
[69] Thomson v. T. (1887) 14 R. 634.
[70] Gunn v. G., 1955 S.L.T. (Notes) 69.
[71] Divorce (Sc.) Act, 1976, S. 4.
[72] Taylor v. T. (1903) 11 S.L.T. 487.
[73] Martin v. M. (1895) 3 S.L.T. 150.
[74] Stewart v. S. (1906) 8 F. 769; Summers v. S., 1935 S.C. 537; Divorce (Sc.) Act, 1976, S. 4; Wilson v. W., 1939 S.C. 102; McFarlane v. McF., 1951 S.C. 530.
[75] Stewart, supra.
[76] Dawson v. D., 1925 S.C. 221.
[77] Nisbet v. N. (1896) 4 S.L.T. 142; see also Hastings v. H., 1941 S.L.T. 323.

the pursuer may later again seek decree of separation if there are fresh grounds.[78]

A claim for separation, if brought by the wife, is normally conjoined with one for aliment for the pursuer and her children.[79] Any such award is *ad interim* and either party may apply for it to be increased or restricted in view of changed circumstances.[80] If the wife has separate income it must be taken into account,[81] and where it was as great as that of the husband aliment has been refused.[82] There is no rule that a wife earning money must spend it all on her maintenance to the relief of her husband's obligation to aliment her.[83] It is incompetent to award aliment for a past period even though the pursuer had had to rely on charity because the wife could have pledged her husband's credit in case of need.[84] The pursuer's conduct before the separation is not relevant to the amount of aliment to be paid.[85]

If the wife is maintaining a child or children of the marriage she is entitled to aliment for them also.[86] The decree will not be recalled by the court on averments by the defender that the pursuer no longer needs the protection it affords,[87] but the decree lapses if cohabitation is resumed by common consent. If one spouse offers to adhere, the other must at least test the genuineness of the offer.[88]

A wife who holds a decree of separation may hold and dispose of all property which she may acquire, as if unmarried, and on her death intestate her property passes to her heirs on intestacy as if her husband were dead.[89]

Rights on death

Each spouse, by marriage, acquires rights to certain proportions of the other spouses's estate on the latter's predecease, testate or intestate, and to provisions from the latter's estate, if dying intestate.[90]

---

[78] *Donachie* v. *D.*, 1965 S.L.T. (Sh. Ct.) 18.

[79] On amount of aliment see *Lang* v. *L.* (1868) 7 M. 24; *Wotherspoon* v. *W.* (1869) 8 M. 81; *Maitland* v. *M.*, 1912 1 S.L.T. 350.

[80] *Hay* v. *H.* (1882) 9 R. 667; *Stewart* v. *S.* (1886) 13 R. 1052; (1887) 15 R. 113; *Purdom* v. *P.*, 1934 S.L.T. 315; *Dowswell* v. *D.*, 1943 S.C. 23. On interim aliment pending sppeal see *Cunningham* v. *C.*, 1965 S.C. 78.

[81] *Overbeck-Wright* v. *O.W.*, 1929 S.L.T. 653.

[82] *Thacker* v. *T.*, 1928 S.L.T. 248.

[83] *Dowswell* v. *D.*, 1943 S.C. 23.

[84] *McMillan* v. *M.* (1871) 9 M. 1067; *Smith* v. *S's Trs.* (1882) 19 S.L.R. 552; *Bruce* v. *B.*, 1945 S.C. 353.

[85] *Malcolm* v. *M.*, 1976 S.L.T. (Sh. Ct.) 10.

[86] cf. *Hay* v. *H.* (1882) 9 R. 667; *Scott* v. *S.* (1894) 21 R. 853.

[87] *Strain* v. *S.* (1890) 17 R. 297.

[88] *Fletcher* v. *Young*, 1936 S.L.T. 572.

[89] Conjugal Rights Amdt. (Sc.) Act, 1861, S. 6 amd. Family Law (Sc.) Act, 1985.

[90] Chs. 7.1–7.3, *infra*.

NULLITY OF MARRIAGE

A petition for declarator of nullity of marriage may be brought either on the ground that the marriage is void, or that it is voidable.[91] In either case the decree declares that a seeming marriage has never had legal existence and that the parties have never had the status of married persons; but a void marriage is, and has been *ab initio*, a nullity and the declarator is necessary only to determine and record that fact, whereas a voidable marriage, despite its inherent flaw, is good until or unless set aside by declarator, which, when granted, has retrospective effect.[92] Decree of nullity of a void marriage makes no change in status, but merely declares authoritatively that the parties have never been married, whereas decree of nullity of a voidable marriage causes the status of married parties to revert to that of single persons. A void marriage cannot be ratified or approbated; a voidable marriage can. A decree of nullity is a judgment *in rem*.[93]

Grounds on which marriage is void ab initio

A marriage may be declared void on any of the following grounds:[94] (a) legal incapacity of either party to marry by reason of nonage;[95] (b) unsoundness of mind;[96] (c) existing marriage;[97] (d) impediment of consanguinity or affinity;[98] (e) failure to comply with formalities of marriage;[99] (f) absence of true consent to marriage by reason of e.g. intoxication, intimidation, or error as to the other party or the nature of the ceremony.[1] It does not follow that any or every failure in the formalities of marriage will result in nullity. Once a marriage has been registered its validity is not to be questioned on the ground of failure to comply with a requirement or restriction imposed by the 1977 Act.[2] In some cases, such as non-registration, the only sanction will be a penalty for non-compliance.[3]

---

[91] *S.G.* v. *W.G.*, 1933 S.C. 728; see also *F.* v. *F.*, 1945 S.C. 202.

[92] Stair I, 4, 6; Bankt. I, 5, 27; Ersk. I, 6, 7; *F.* v. *F. supra*, 211.

[93] *Administrator of Austrian Property* v. *Von Lorang*, 1927 S.C. (H.L.) 80.

[94] cf. Fraser, *H. & W.*, I, 51–79, 105–39.

[95] *Johnstone* v. *Ferrier* (1770) Mor. 8931; *A.B.* v. *C.D.*, 1957 S.C. 415.

[96] *Graham* v. *G.* (1907) 15 S.L.T. 33; *A.B.* v. *C.D.* (1908) 15 S.L.T. 911; *Park* v. *P.*, 1914, 1 S.L.T. 88; *Calder* v. *C.*, 1942 S.N. 40.

[97] *Ballantyne* v. *B.* (1866) 4 M. 494; *Mackenzie* v. *Macfarlane* (1891) 5 S.L.T. 292; *Macdonald* v. *Parkinson* (1905) 12 S.L.T. 710; *Courtin* v. *Elder*, 1930 S.C. 68; *Bairner* v. *Fels*, 1931 S.C. 674; *Martin* v. *Buret*, 1938 S.L.T. 479; *Aldridge* v. *A.*, 1954 S.C. 58; *Balshaw* v. *B.*, 1967 S.C. 63; *Burke* v. *B.*, 1983 S.L.T. 331.

[98] *Purves' Trs.* v. *P.* (1895) 22 R. 513.

[99] *Miller* v. *Deakin*, 1912 1 S.L.T. 253; *Admin. of Austrian Property* v. *Von Lorang*, 1927 S.C. (H.L.) 80; *Bradley* v. *Mochrie*, 1947 S.L.T. (Notes) 27.

[1] *Brebner* v. *Bell* (1904) 12 S.L.T. 2; *McLeod* v. *Adams*, 1920 1 S.L.T. 229; *Brady* v. *Murray*, 1933 S.L.T. 534; *Orlandi* v. *Castelli*, 1961 S.C. 113; *Balshaw* v. *B.*, 1967 S.C. 63.

[2] 1977 Act, S. 23A, added by Law Reform (Misc. Prov.) (Sc.) Act, 1980.

[3] 1977 Act, S. 24 (2).

Ground on which marriage is voidable

The sole ground on which a marriage is voidable is the sexual impotence of either spouse,[4] which consists in total physical incapacity for sexual intercourse, or in invincible repugnance to and revulsion from intercourse with that partner,[5] existing at, and continuously since, the date of the 'marriage', and wholly preventing consummation. Till consummation, by intercourse after the marriage, the 'marriage' is voidable. The defect of impotence is not a flaw making the marriage void *ab initio* but rather a resolutive condition invalidating the marriage retrospectively.[6] Hence the spouses may waive the objection. Either spouse may petition, and on the ground of his or her own,[7] or the other spouse's,[8] impotence or the impotence of either alternatively,[9] but the plea is personal to the spouses and cannot be raised by a third party having a patrimonial interest.[10] A person may be impotent, either physically[11] or psychologically,[12] and *quoad* the present partner only, and not *quoad omnes*. If the ground is physical incapacity, the court must be satisfied that the defect is incurable,[13] and has been so for the whole duration of the 'marriage',[14] or not curable without danger to life or the infliction of unreasonable pain,[15] or that the impotent spouse is unlikely ever to submit to treatment.[16] If the evidence shows that an impotent defender may be cured, the defender, if willing, is entitled to an opportunity to undergo treatment.[17] Absence of evidence of structural defect does not preclude nullity, if the other circumstances indicate incapacity.[18] The petition is barred if the marriage has been consummated at any time since the marriage. Once consummated it is valid, though intercourse be never repeated. There is no matrimonial relief for cases of supervening impotence, whatever its cause. Refusal of sexual relations is not a ground for relief, but may amount to cruelty and justify divorce.[19]

Consummation requires full normal penetration of the female vagina

---

[4] Stair I, 4, 6; Bankt. I, 5, 27, 56; Ersk, I, 6, 7; Bell, *Prin.* § 1524; Fraser, *H. & W.* I, 80; C.B. v. A.B. (1885) 12 R. (H.L.) 36; *L.* v. *L.,* 1931 S.C. 477; *S.G.* v. *W.G.,* 1933 S.C. 728.

[5] *A.B.* v. *C.D.* (1903) 10 S.L.T. 266; C. v. C. [1921] P. 399; G. v. G., 1924 S.C. (H.L.) 42.

[6] Fraser, *H. & W.* I, 83; *Admin. of Austrian Property* v. *Von Lorang,* 1926 S.C. 598, 616.

[7] *F.* v. *F.,* 1945 S.C. 202; *H.* v. *H.,* 1949 S.C. 587. Such a pursuer must prove his or her defect to be irremediable.

[8] Stair I, 4, 6; Ersk. I, 6, 7; *A.B.* v. *C.B.* (1906) 8 F. 603; G. v. G., 1924 S.C. (H.L.) 42.

[9] *M.* v. *M.,* 1967 S.L.T. 157.

[10] Bell, *Prin.* § 1524; Fraser *H. & W.* I, 98.

[11] G. v. G. (1909) 25 T.L.R. 328.

[12] *A.B.* v. *C.D.* (1903) 10 S.L.T. 266.

[13] C. v. M. (1876) 3 R. 693; cf. *L.* v. *L.* (1882) 7 P.D. 16; *H.* v. *H.,* 1949 S.C. 587.

[14] *M.* v. *M.,* 1966 S.L.T. 25.

[15] C. v. M. (1876) 3 R. 693.

[16] *W.Y.* v. *A.Y.,* 1946 S.C. 27; cf. *G.* v. *B.,* 1934 S.L.T. 421.

[17] *W.Y., supra.*

[18] *A.B.* v. *C.D.* (1900) 38 S.L.R. 559; *M* v. *G.* (1902) 10 S.L.T. 264; *A.B.* v. *C.B.* (1906) 8 F. 603; *G.* v. *G.,* 1924 S.C. (H.L.) 42.

[19] *H.* v. *H.,* 1968 S.L.T. 40.

by the male organ, but not necessarily any emission of semen. There is no consummation if there is only partial or imperfect penetration[20] or if one party has an artificial organ.[21] A marriage may be held consummated though the husband practised *coitus interruptus*,[22] though a contraceptive was used,[23] or though ejaculation was impossible.[24] Nullity has been granted in England even though the wife had become pregnant by *fecundatio ab extra*,[25] or by artificial insemination by the husband;[26] the birth of a child accordingly does not necessarily establish consummation. Nullity is not competent if there is merely wilful delay or refusal to consummate,[27] though evidence of such conduct, if prolonged, may suggest an inference of impotence.[28] So too absence of desire or attempt to consummate may be evidence, but is not conclusive. If there is *potentia copulandi* it matters not that there is *impotentia procreandi*: sterility is irrelevant.[29] Parties may each aver that the other is impotent, and one may adopt the other's allegations as alternative to his allegations against the other.[30]

Psychological impotence

Where the ground of action is psychological the pursuer must establish that non-consummation resulted not from indifference or lack of attempt on his part, nor from wilful refusal, nor mere temporary objection to intercourse on the defender's part, but from permanent invincible repugnance to or revulsion from intercourse.[31] The onus is on the pursuer to prove the case on balance of probabilities.[31] The court may infer incapacity if after a reasonable period of cohabitation there has been no intercourse and reasonable attempts have met with resistance or produced mental upsets.[32]

Nullity barred by insincerity

Decree may be held barred where the pursuer's case lacks substantial justification,[33] as where a woman married solely to obtain a settlement

---

[20] *D.E.* v. *A.G.* (1854) 1 Rob. Eccl. 279; *J.* v. *J.,* 1978 S.L.T. 128.
[21] *D.* v. *D.* [1955] P. 42; *Corbett* v. *C.* [1970] 2 All E.R. 33.
[22] *White* v. *W.* [1948] P. 330; *Cackett* v. *C.* [1950] 1 All E.R. 677.
[23] *Baxter* v. *B.* [1948] A.C. 274.
[24] *R.* v. *R.* [1952] 1 All. E.R. 1194.
[25] *Snowman* v. *S.* [1934] P. 186; *Clarke* v. *C.* [1943] 2 All E.R. 540; *L.* v. *L.* [1949] P. 211.
[26] *L.* v. *L* [1949] P. 211.
[27] *Paterson* v. *P.,* 1958 S.C. 141.
[28] *A.B.* v. *Y.Z.* (1900) 8 S.L.T. 253; *A.B.* v. *C.B.* (1906) 8 F. 603; *G.* v. *G.,* 1924 S.C. (H.L.) 42.
[29] Stair I, 4, 6; Ersk. I, 6, 7; *A.B.* v. *C.B., supra,* 607; *G.* v. *G., supra;* cf. *Baxter* v. *B.* [1948] A.C. 274.
[30] *M.* v. *M.,* 1967 S.L.T. 157.
[31] *M.* v. *M.,* 1966 S.L.T. 153.
[32] *A.B.* v. *C.B.* (1906) 8 F. 603; *G,* v. *G.,* 1924 S.C. (H.L.) 42.
[33] *C.B.* v. *A.B.* (1885) 12 R. (H.L.) 36, 45.

for herself and her child.[34] Knowledge at the time of the marriage of the defender's impotence is not *per se* a bar to decree, but may amount to approbation.[35] Decree is not barred, if otherwise admissible, merely because the pursuer wishes to rid himself of liability to aliment the defender,[36] or has another collateral reason for wishing the marriage avoided.[37]

Nullity barred by approbation

Nullity will not be granted where, despite non-consummation, the parties have by their conduct approbated and ratified the marriage, as where the wife has had a child by artificial insemination with the husband's semen,[38] or by *fecundatio ab extra*,[39] or the parties have adopted a child.[40] Nullity may be held barred by the petitioner's knowledge of his own impotence, certainly if the defender does not concur.[41] There can, however, be no approbation where the petitioner is ignorant of the facts or the law,[42] the onus of proof of which is on him.[43] To bring an action for divorce does not imply approbation of the marriage sufficient to bar a subsequent petition for nullity.[44] If the defender is relying on personal bar she must prove facts from which it can be inferred that she has been prejudiced and that justice requires that nullity be refused.[45]

Bar by delay

Delay in seeking nullity is a factor to be considered though no particular lapse of time will automatically bar an action.[46] Delay is ineffective if the pursuer did not have the knowledge of facts and law essential to the decision whether to avoid or approbate the marriage.[47] If delay extends to the death of either spouse, it is too late thereafter to have the marriage avoided.

Consequences of nullity

On decree of nullity being pronounced the court has the same powers to make orders regulating financial provisions for the parties as it has in

---

[34] *L. v. L.*, 1931 S.C. 477.
[35] *L. v. L.*, *supra*; *Nash v. N.* [1940] P. 60; *J. v. J.* [1947] P. 158.
[36] *Allardyce v. A.*, 1954 S.C. 419.
[37] *C.B.*, *supra*.
[38] *A.B. v. C.B.* 1961 S.C. 347; cf. *L. v. L.* [1949] P. 211; *Slater v. S.* [1953] P. 235.
[39] *Pettit v. P.* [1963] P. 177.
[40] *W. v. W.*, 1933 S.N. 73; *W. v. W.* [1952] P. 152.
[41] *Harthan v. H.* [1949] P. 115.
[42] *G. v. M.* (1885) 10 App. Cas. 171.
[43] *Allardyce v. A.*, 1954 S.C. 419.
[44] *M v. M.*, 1966 S.L.T. 25.
[45] *M. v. M.*, 1966 S.L.T. 153.
[46] *C.B. v. A.B.* (1885) 12 R. (H.L.) 36; *W. v. W.*, 1933 S.N. 73.
[47] *Allardyce v. A.*, 1954 S.C. 419; *M. v. M.*, 1966 S.L.T. 153.

actions of divorce. Either party may claim interim aliment in an action for nullity notwithstanding that he denies the existence of the marriage.[48]

DISSOLUTION OF MARRIAGE

Dissolution of marriage is effected only by the death of either spouse or by the decree of a competent court. It differs from nullity in that the marriage is for all purposes good and valid so long as it lasted, and parties acquired married status.

Dissolution by death

On the death of either spouse, the marriage is dissolved and the surviving spouse restored to the status of single person and entitled to remarry. The surviving spouse is entitled to certain rights from the estate of the deceased[49] and may be entitled to payments under the deceased's will or the provision of a marriage contract. *Bona fide* belief in the other spouse's death does not entitle a spouse to remarry.[50]

Dissolution by decree of court

The Court of Session may dissolve a marriage by divorcing one spouse from the other *a vinculo matrimonii*. The principle underlying all the grounds of divorce, except insanity, was formerly that divorce was a remedy granted for the commission of a matrimonial offence, or wrong done to the innocent spouse by conduct contradictory of the fundamental obligations of the matrimonial relationship.[51] Since and by virtue of the Divorce (Sc.) Act, 1976, the underlying principle is to release parties from a marriage which has irretrievably broken down. Even if the action is undefended, the court may not grant decree unless satisfied by evidence of the factual justification for the action.[52]

By the Divorce (Sc.) Act, 1976, the court may grant divorce only if it is established that the marriage has broken down irretrievably, which is taken to be established if (a) since the date of the marriage the defender has committed adultery; or (b) the defender has at any time behaved,

---

[48] Family Law (Sc.) Act, 1985, S. 17.

[49] Ch. 7.2, *infra*.

[50] *Hunter* v. *H.* (1900) 2 F. 771.

[51] See *Report of Royal Commission on Marriage and Divorce*, 1956 (Cmnd. 9678).

[52] Court of Session Act, 1830, S. 36; *Smith* v. *S.*, 1929 S.C. 75; *Macfarlane* v. *M.*, 1956 S.C. 472. Evidence may now be given by affidavit in undefended cases; R.C. 168. Each page of the affidavits requires to be subscribed by the deponent and the notary before whom it is sworn: *Macalister* v. *M.*, 1978 S.L.T. (Notes) 78. In appropriate cases two deponents may depone to the same facts in a single document: *Sanderson* v. *S.* 1979 S.L.T. (Notes) 36.

whether or not as a result of mental abnormality and whether actively or passively, in such a way that the pursuer cannot reasonably be expected to cohabit with the defender; or (c) the defender has wilfully and without reasonable cause deserted the pursuer and during a continuous period of two years immediately succeeding the defender's desertion (i) there has been no cohabitation between the parties, and (ii) the pursuer has not refused a genuine and reasonable offer by the defender to adhere; or (d) there has been no cohabitation for a continuous period of two years preceding the action and the defender consents to the divorce; or (e) there has been no cohabitation for a continuous period of five years preceding the action.[53]

The court may grant divorce notwithstanding a previous grant of separation on the same or substantially the same facts as those averred in the action of divorce, and, save in an action founded on adultery, an extract decree of separation may be lodged as sufficient proof of the facts on which that decree was granted.[54]

Jurisdiction in action

The pursuer must specifically aver and prove facts sufficient to entitle the court to assume jurisdiction.[55]

Proof of marriage

The parties must be proved to be married, normally by production of an extract from the Register of Births, Deaths, and Marriages.[56] If the marriage was irregular it may be necessary to preface the divorce by a declarator of marriage.[57] In defence it may be contended that the 'marriage' was null.[58]

Cross-actions

It is competent for spouses to bring cross-actions, each charging the other with a conduct justifying divorce,[59] and for the court to grant decree in either action, or in both.[60] Decree in one suffices to dissolve the marriage.

---

[53] S. 1.
[54] S. 3.
[55] *Horn* v. *H.*, 1935 S.L.T. 589.
[56] cf. *McDonald* v. *McD.*, 1924 S.L.T. 200.
[57] *Nicol* v. *Bell*, 1954 S.L.T. 314.
[58] *C.B.* v. *A.B.* (1885) 12 R. (H.L.) 36; *Sharp* v. *S.* (1898) 25 R. 1132.
[59] Cross actions each alleging desertion cannot both result in decree. Apart from that both actions may be on the same, or on different grounds.
[60] *Brodie* v. *B.* (1870) 8 M. 854; *Connell* v. *C.*, 1950 S.C. 505. Either spouse may reclaim to obtain a finding that he or she was not in fault: *Connell, supra*.

Divorce for adultery

Adultery consists in voluntary[61] sexual relations[62] between a married person and a person of the opposite sex, other than his or her spouse, during the subsistence of the marriage.[63] A woman raped is not guilty of adultery.[64] It is adultery to have intercourse with one other than one's spouse, notwithstanding separation, voluntary or judicial, desertion by, or reasonable belief in the death of, the other spouse.[65] If *coitus* be admitted, the onus of proving that it was involuntary lies on the party admitting.[66] It has been held that only physical *coitus* amounts to adultery, and not even the birth to a wife of a child conceived by artificial insemination by a donor amounts to adultery.[67] Sexual gratification without penetration of the female is, however, not adultery.[68] Emission need not be proved, still less impregnation. Only the injured spouse has a title to sue and the right of action falls on his death.[69]

The other spouse has title and interest to defend, but not his creditors, nor a child of the marriage. Where the defender cannot be found the summons must be intimated to the children of the marriage, if any, above the age of puberty, and on one or more of the defender's next of kin, any one of whom may appear and lodge defences.[70]

The Lord Advocate may state defences.[71] The paramour with whom adultery is alleged must, if known,[72] have intimation of the action, and he may apply to be sisted as a party to the action, and is then entitled to a decision as to his guilt or innocence.[73] He may be found liable in the expenses of the action,[74] provided he is shown to have known that the

---

[61] *Long* v. *L* (1890) 15 P.D. 218; *Hanbury* v. *H.* [1892] P. 222; *Yarrow* v. *Y.* [1892] P. 92; *Stewart* v. *S.*, 1914 2 S.L.T. 310; *Clarkson* v. *C.* (1930) 46 T.L.R. 623; *S.* v. *S.* [1962] P. 133; Insanity is a defence: Fraser, *H. & W.* II, 1143.

[62] *MacLennan* v. *M.*, 1958 S.C. 105; *sed quaere*; see *Russell* v. *R.* [1924] A.C. 687, 721.

[63] Mack, *Crim. L.* 86; Fraser, *H. & W.* II, 1142; Hume, *Lect.* I, 83. See also *Sands* v. *S.*, 1964 S.L.T. 80.

[64] *Clarkson, supra*; cf. *Black* v. *Duncan*, 1924 S.C. 738.

[65] Ersk. I, 6, 44; *Donald* v. *D.* (1863) 1 M. 741, 749; *Hunter* v. *H.* (1900) 2 F. 771, 774, 775.

[66] *Stewart* v. *S.*, 1914 S.L.T. 310; cf. *Redpath* v. *R.* [1950] 1 All. E.R. 600.

[67] *McLennan, supra*. But the essence of adultery is infidelity, granting the use of the sexual organs to another than one's spouse, whether for gratification or reproduction, and whether or not pregnancy results, though carnal connection is the normal form of this infidelity, cf. Batholomew, 21 M.L.R. 236; Tallin, 34 Can. B.R. 1, 166.

[68] *Sapsford* v. *S.* [1954] P. 394; *Dennis* v. *D.* [1955] P. 153; cf. *Clarke* v. *C.* [1943] 2 All E.R. 540; *L.* v. *L.* [1949] P. 211.

[69] *Clement* v. *Sinclair* (1762) Mor. 337; *Ritchie* v. *R.* (1874) 1 R. 826; but personal representatives have an interest to prosecute a reclaiming motion; *Fenton* v. *Livingstone* (1859) 3 Macq. 497; *Ritchie, supra*.

[70] R.C. 160.

[71] Conjugal Rights (Sc.) Amdt. Act, 1861, S. 8; see *Ralston* v. *R.* (1881) 8 R. 371; *Riddell* v. *R.*, 1952 S.C. 475.

[72] It is competent to charge adultery with a person whose name is unknown: *Smith* v. *S.* (1838) 16 S. 499; *Gray* v. *G.* (1865) 37 S. Jur. 566.

[73] *Raeside* v. *R.*, 1913 S.C. 60.

[74] *Fraser* v. *F. and Hibbert* (1870) 8 M. 400; *Murray* v. *M.* 1944 S.L.T. 46; *Duncan* v. *D.*, 1948 S.C. 666; *Reynolds* v. *R.*, 1965 S.C. 150; *Morrison* v. *M.*, 1970 S.L.T. 116; Divorce (Sc.) Act, 1976, S. 10 (2).

defender was married,[75] or be awarded expenses. His liability does not transmit on his death against his estate.[76]

A pursuer is not barred from suing by his own adultery. It is competent for spouses to bring cross-actions of divorce for adultery.[77]

The averments of time and place, or circumstances giving rise to the inference of adultery, must be as specific as possible, and vague allegations will not be admitted to probation.[78]

Proof of adultery

The onus is on the pursuer and he cannot found on the fact that the defender has abstained from giving evidence.[79] Adultery must be proved on balance of probability,[80] or facts and circumstances be proved from which the court is prepared to infer adultery. Only one act of illicit coitus need be proved, not necessarily a course of adultery or adulterous cohabitation.[81] There may be direct evidence of persons being seen or found *in flagrante delicto*. Failing that, the facts must be inconsistent with innocence before an inference will be drawn,[82] but adultery may be inferred from facts and circumstances without direct proof of any specific act of adultery.[83] An inference of adultery may be drawn if one spouse is proved to have shared a bedroom for the night with a third party.[84] It will not necessarily be drawn, in the absence of other evidence of mutual passion, merely from propinquity, opportunity, or evidence of familiarities.[85] The defender's conviction of rape,[86] or his frequenting a brothel,[87] are factors justifying an inference of adultery. Condoned acts of adultery may not be founded on, but may be proved to cast light on the defender's conduct thereafter.[88]

Adultery may be inferred from proof of the birth of a child to the wife at a time so long after the latest possible opportunity for intercourse with

[75] *Miller* v. *Simpson* (1863) 2 M. 225; *Kydd* v. *K.* (1864) 2 M. 1074; *Laurie* v. *L.*, 1913, 1 S.L.T. 117; *Heggie* v. *H.*, 1917 2 S.L.T. 246; *Forrester* v. *F.*, 1963 S.C. 662.
[76] *Kelly* v. *K.*, 1953 S.L.T. 284.
[77] e.g. *Connell* v. *C.*, 1950 S.C. 505.
[78] *Walker* v. *W.* (1869) 41 S. Jur. 502; *Soeder* v. *S.* (1897) 24 R. 278; *Blakely* v. *B.*, 1947 S.N. 10; *Smith* v. *S.*, 1947 S.N. 80.
[79] *Bird* v. *B.*, 1931 S.C. 731.
[80] Divorce (Sc.) Act, 1976, S. 1(6) overruling *Currie* v. *C.*, 1950 S.C. 10.
[81] e.g. *Smith* v. *S.*, 1930 S.C. 75.
[82] *Wilson* v. *W.* (1898) 25 R. 788; *Bennet Clark* v. *B.C.*, 1909 S.C. 591, 609.
[83] *Walker* v. *W.* (1871) 9 M. 1091; *Fullerton* v. *F.* (1873) 11 M. 720; *McInnes* v. *McI.*, 1954 S.C. 396.
[84] *Hannah* v. *H.*, 1931 S.C. 275; cf. *Smith* v. *S.*, 1929 S.C. 75.
[85] *McIver* v. *M.* (1859) 21 D. 655; *Bennet Clark, supra*; *Ross* v. *R.*, 1930 S.C. (H.L.) 1; *Burnett* v. *B.*, 1955 S.C. 183; *Hall* v. *H.* 1958 S.C. 206.
[86] *Galbraith* v. *G.* (1902) 9 S.L.T. 346. On evidence see Law Reform (Misc. Prov.) (Sc.) Act, 1968, S. 10.
[87] *Marshall* v. *M.* (1881) 8 R. 702; contrast *Edward* v. *E.* (1879) 6 R. 1255; see also *Tennant* v. *T.* (1883) 10 R. 1187.
[88] *Collins* v. *C.* (1884) 11 R. (H.L.) 19; *Robertson* v. *R.* (1888) 15 R. 1001; *Nicol* v. *N.*, 1938 S.L.T. 98.

her husband, or so soon after the first possible opportunity following long absence, that the child must have been begotten by another.[89] While the normal duration of pregnancy is 280 days, no set periods give rise to presumptions and courts have, on the strength of medical evidence, held that unusually long,[90] or short,[91] periods of gestation have not been impossible, so as inevitably to give rise to the inference of adultery, but exceptional periods of gestation go someway to yield an inference of adultery.[92] It is in each case a question of fact and evidence, and the presumption *pater est quem nuptiae demonstrant* has to be overcome.[93] Even where parties lived in the same town, but apart, the presumption *pater est* may be rebutted and adultery inferred.[94] Similarly acknowledgment by a wife that a child is illegitimate is evidence of adultery.[95] It has also been held proved where the alleged paramour had given birth to a child of which the defender acknowledged paternity,[96] or had obtained decree of affiliation and aliment against the defender.[97] The fact that a person has been found guilty of adultery in any matrimonial proceedings or has been found to be the father of a child in affiliation proceedings in any court in the United Kingdom, is admissible evidence to prove that he committed that adultery, or is the father of that child, and in a subsequent case that fact will be held established unless the contrary is proved.[98]

Evidence that the defender had contracted venereal disease is relevant.[99] The court will not ordain a defender and her child, allegedly illegitimate, to submit to blood tests.[1] It is relevant to prove that the defender had had an immoral relationship with the co-defender before the marriage, but not to prove that the co-defender had previously had immoral relations with other women,[2] though it is to prove that the defender was guilty of indecent conduct with another woman at the same period as the alleged adultery.[3]

A judicial admission by the defender is admissible but not conclusive

---

[89] *Pegg v. P.* (1859) 21 D. 820; *Tulloh v. T.* (1861) 23 D. 639.
[90] *Whyte v. W.* (1884) 11 R. 710 (297 days); *Marshall v. M.,* 1934 S.N. 39 (308 days); *McIntosh v. M.,* 1947 S.N. 23 (316 days); *Gaskill v. G.* [1921] P. 425 (331 days); *Gray v. G.,* 1919, 1 S.L.T. 163 (331 days); *Currie v. C.,* 1950 S.C. 10 (336 days); *M.T. v. M.T.* [1949] P. 331 (340 days); *Wood v. W.* [1947] P. 103 (346 days); *Doherty v. D.,* 1922 S.L.T. 245 (348 days); *Hadlum v. H.* [1949] P. 197 (349 days); *Preston-Jones v. P.J.* [1951] A.C. 391 (360 days).
[91] *Clark v. C.* [1937] P. 228 (174 days); contrast *Re S.B.* [1949] Ch. 108 (188 days: no evidence that child premature).
[92] *Currie v. C., supra.*
[93] cf. *Marshall v. M.,* 1934 S.N. 39.
[94] *Steedman v. S.* (1887) 14 R. 1066.
[95] *Fullerton v. F.* (1873) 11 M. 720; *Duncan v. D.* (1893) 30 S.L.R. 435.
[96] *Campbell v. C.* (1860) 23 D. 99; *McDougall v. M.,* 1927 S.C. 666; see also *Stewart v. S.,* 1930 S.L.T. 363.
[97] *Mathieson v. M.,* 1914 1 S.L.T. 511.
[98] Law Reform (Misc. Prov.) (Sc.) Act, 1968, s. 11.
[99] *Kelly v. K.,* 1946 S.L.T. 208; *McRae v. M.,* 1947 S.C. 173.
[1] *Whitehall v. W.,* 1958 S.C. 252; contrast *Borthwick v. B.,* 1929 S.L.T. 596.
[2] *Johnston v. J.* (1903) 5 F. 659.
[3] *Whyte v. W.* (1884) 11 R. 710.

evidence, unless corroborated to eliminate the risk of collusion.[4] A written confession by the defender, even of adultery with the co-defender, is admissible but is not evidence against the co-defender.[5] Judicial admissions by paramours are admissible, but not conclusive.[6] The pursuer cannot found on the fact that the defender, though denying adultery on record, has neither given nor led evidence.[7]

An extra-judicial confession by the defender, made *ante litem motam*, is admissible but requires corroboration.[8] Letters from, or the diaries of, the defender may be interpreted as admissions of adultery.[9] Extrajudicial confessions by the co-defender are not evidence against the defender.[10] No witness in any proceedings instituted in consquence of adultery is liable to be asked or bound to answer any question tending to show that he or she has been guilty of adultery.[11]

An extract conviction of the husband for rape, together with a letter expressing regret, has been held sufficient proof.[12]

Divorce for intolerable behaviour

It is a question of fact whether a defender's behaviour has been such that the pursuer cannot be expected further to cohabit with him. It may take the form of physical or mental cruelty,[13] habitual drunkenness,[14] humiliating behaviour,[15] accusations of immorality.[16]

It may be by abnormal,[17] excessive,[18] or perverted[19] sexual behaviour,

---

[4] *Muirhead* v. M. (1846) 8 D. 786; *Laidlaw* v. L. (1894) 2 S.L.T. 168; *Macfarlane* v. M., 1956 S.C. 472; cf. *Ramsay* v. R. (1880) 17 S.L.R. 793; *Whyte* v. W. (1884) 11 R. 710; *Barnes* v. B., 1935 S.C. 646. See also *Chatman* v. C., 1944 S.C. 494.

[5] *Laidlaw* v. L. (1894) 2 S.L.T. 168; *Ramsay* v. R. (1880) 17 S.L.R. 793; *Smith* v. S., 1929 S.C. 75.

[6] *Sim* v. *Miles* (1834) 12 S. 633; *Barnes, supra; Michlek* v. M., 1971 S.L.T. (Notes) 50.

[7] *Bird* v. B., 1931 S.C. 731.

[8] *Smith* v. S. (1866) 2 S.L.R. 243; *Fullerton* v. F. (1873) 11 M. 720; *Duncan* v. D. (1893) 30 S.L.R. 435; *Stewart* v. S., 1930 S.L.T. 363; *Mackay* v. M., 1946 S.C. 78; *MacColl* v. MacC., 1948 S.C. 500; *Hamilton* v. H., 1953 S.C. 383.

[9] *McNeill* v. M., 1929 S.L.T. 251; *Creasey* v. C., 1931 S.C. 9; *Watson* v. W., 1934 S.C. 374; *Barnes, supra*; *Argyll* v. A., 1962 S.C. (H.L.) 88; see also *Turner* v. T., 1930 S.L.T. 393; *Smith* v. S., 1929 S.C. 75.

[10] *Swapp* v. S., 1931 S.L.T. 199; contrast *Reid* v. R., 1926 S.L.T. 102.

[11] Evidence (Further Amdt.) (Sc.) Act, 1874, S. 2; *Bannatyne* v. B. (1886) 13 R. 619; *McDougall* v. McD., 1927 S.C. 666.

[12] *Galbraith* v. G. (1902) S.L.T. 346. On admissibility of convictions see Law Reform (Misc. Prov.) (Sc.) Act, 1968, S. 10.

[13] Prior to 1977 a substantive ground of divorce. Many cases discussed cruelty; these may now be illustrative of intolerable behaviour, but are not authoritative.

[14] Prior to 1977 a statutory form of cruelty.

[15] cf. *Mackenzie* v. M. (1895) 22 R. (H.L.) 32; *Aitchison* v. A. (1903) 10 S.L.T. 331; *Jamieson* v. J., 1952 S.C. (H.L.) 44.

[16] cf. *Jackson* v. J. (1906) 14 S.L.T. 331; *Duffy* v. D., 1947 S.C. 54.

[17] cf. *White* v. W. [1948] P. 330; *Cackett* v. C. [1950] 1 All E.R. 677; *Scott* v. S., 1960 S.C. 36; *H.* v. H., 1968 S.L.T. 40.

[18] cf. *Holborn* v. H. [1947] 1 All E.R. 32.

[19] cf. *White* v. W., 1966 S.C. 188.

or by homosexuality,[20] or sexual misconduct not amounting to adultery.[21]

It may be by dishonest, selfish, thoughtless, or indifferent conduct,[22] or conduct directed against the pursuer's relatives[23] or the children of the marriage.[24]

The behaviour may not be reprehensible in itself; an obsession with golf or scientific experiments would satisfy the requirement if it were such that the pursuer found it intolerable.

The behaviour may or may not be the result of mental abnormality; accordingly that insanity, mental deficiency, or other mental state caused the behaviour will not be a defence. It may also be either active or passive, so that an idle, shiftless mode of life will suffice.[25]

The words 'in such a way that' indicate that the defender's behaviour must have caused the pursuer to find life intolerable. The court must have regard to the effect of the behaviour on the pursuer, not on a hypothetical reasonable spouse. But 'cannot reasonably be expected' indicates that spouses must be expected to put up with a moderate amount of undesirable behaviour from their partners.

Divorce for desertion[26]

The court may grant divorce where one spouse has wilfully and without reasonable cause deserted the other and persisted in such desertion for not less than two years.[27] Action cannot be brought until the two years have elapsed.[28] The pursuer has then a vested right to divorce,[29] so that the defender's subsequent insanity does not affect the issue.[30] It is constituted by cessation of adherence at bed and board by one spouse *animo deserendi*, the other spouse being willing to adhere, and normally by the departure of one spouse from the matrimonial home. This separation constitutes actual desertion where the deserting spouse leaves the matrimonial home and remains apart, despite the willingness of the other to

---

[20] cf. *Hutchison* v. *H.*, 1945 S.C. 427, 431; *M.* v. *M.*, 1967 S.L.T. 119.

[21] cf. *Richardson* v. *R.*, 1956 S.C. 394; *McMillan* v. *M.*, 1962 S.C. 115.

[22] cf. *Waite* v. *W.*, 1961 S.C. 266; *Hutton* v. *H.*, 1962 S.C. 10; *Rose* v. *R.*, 1964 S.L.T. (Notes) 14; *Kerr* v. *K.*, 1967 S.L.T. (Notes) 77; *Campbell* v. *C.*, 1973 S.L.T. (Notes) 82.

[23] cf. *A.* v. *B.* (1896) 23 R. 588; *Christie* v. *C.*, 1964 S.L.T. 72; *A.B.* v. *C.D.*, 1959 S.C. 27.

[24] cf. *Duffy* v. *D.*, 1947 S.C. 54.

[25] cf. *Fullarton* v. *F.*, 1976 S.L.T. 8.

[26] Introduced by Act 1573, c. 55, and requiring four years' malicious non-adherence. This was reduced to three years by the Divorce (Sc.) Act, 1938. Until the Conjugal Rights Act, 1861, an action of adherence, non-implement of that decree, and an application to the presbytery were necessary preliminaries to an action for divorce for desertion: see Stair I, 4, 8; Ersk. I, 6, 44; Bell, *Prin.* s 1535; Fraser, *H. & W.* II, 1207; *Watson* v. *W.* (1890) 17 R. 736; *Mackenzie* v. *M.* (1895) 22 R. (H.L.) 32.

[27] Divorce (Sc.) Act, 1976, S. 1 (2) (c).

[28] *Ross* v. *R.* (1899) 1 F. 963; *Martin* v. *M.*, 1968 S.C. 205.

[29] *Bell* v. *B.*, 1941 S.C. (H.L.) 5; *Graham* v. *G.*, 1942 S.L.T. 142.

[30] *Scott* v. *S.*, 1908 S.C. 1124.

adhere;[31] or constructive desertion where the deserting spouse, though remaining in the matrimonial home, has put the other out, or made life so intolerable for the other as to have driven that other to leave, though willing to adhere.[32]

There may be desertion though the spouses continue both to occupy the same house, if there are truly separate establishments and no cohabitation, social contact, mutual assistance or services.[33] The refusal of sexual relations not acquiesced in, by itself does not now amount to desertion.[34] Divorce for desertion is not precluded by the pursuer having previously obtained decree of separation and aliment, after which the defender had disappeared,[35] or refused the pursuer's offer to resume cohabitation.[36]

Wilful desertion

The desertion must be wilful or intentional, not mere disappearance,[37] or separation enforced by business, duty, illness, imprisonment, or other overriding compulsion,[38] nor consensual separation.[39] Separation initially consensual becomes wilful desertion when one spouse refuses the other's *bona fide* call to resume co-habitation,[40] or breaks off communication.[41] Similarly a spouse holding a decree of separation may offer to resume cohabitation; the other spouse, if refusing unjustifiably, is thereafter in desertion.[42] If, however, the defender was in desertion when imprisoned and continues to be so on release the triennium is deemed not thereby interrupted.[43] This conclusion will not necessarily be drawn if the trien-

---

[31] e.g. *Bell* v. *B.*, 1941 S.C. (H.L.) 5.

[32] *Winchcombe* v. *W.* (1881) 8 R. 726; *Gow* v. *G.* (1887) 14 R. 443; *Murray* v. *M.* (1894) 21 R. 723; *Mackenzie, supra*; *Munro* v. *M.* (1895) 2 S.L.T. 598; cf. *Bowman* v. *B.* (1866) 4 M. 384; *Forbes* v. *F.* (1881) 19 S.L.R. 118; contrast *Gibson* v. *G.* (1894) 21 R. 470.

[33] *Forbes* v. *F.* (1881) 19 S.L.R. 118; *Goold* v. *G.*, 1927 S.C. 177, 183; *Lennie* v. *L.*, 1950 S.C. (H.L.) 1, 5, 16; *Cooke* v. *C.*, 1946 S.L.T. (Notes) 28; cf. *Smith* v. *S.* [1940] P. 49; *Littlewood* v. *L.* [1943] P. 11; *Wilkes* v. *W.* [1943] P. 41; *Hopes* v. *H.* [1949] P. 227; *Bartram* v. *B.* [1950] P. 1; *Naylor* v. *N.* [1962] P. 253.

[34] *Lennie* v. *L.*, 1950 S.C. (H.L.) 1, overruling *Stair* v. *S.* (1905) 12 S.L.T. 788; *A.* v. *B.* (1905) 13 S.L.T. 532; *Goold, supra*; *Pinder* v. *P.*, 1932 S.L.T. 292; *Burrell* v. *B.*, 1947 S.C. 569; *Macdonald* v. *M.*, 1948 S.L.T. 380; cf. *A.* v. *B.* (1905) 13 S.L.T. 532; *X.* v. *Y.*, 1914, 1 S.L.T. 366; *C.* v. *D.*, 1921, 2 S.L.T. 82; *G.* v. *G.*, 1923 S.C. 175; *Robertson* v. *R.*, 1939 S.L.T. 432.

[35] *Whalley* v. *W.*, 1921 2 S.L.T. 135; *Summers* v. *S.*, 1935 S.C. 537.

[36] *Macdonald* v. *M.*, 1912 2 S.L.T. 14; cf. *Horsley* v. *H.*, 1914 1 S.L.T. 92; *Smellie* v. *S.*, 1914 2 S.L.T. 240.

[37] *Lench* v. *L.*, 1945 S.C. 295; contrast *Lough* v. *L.*, 1930 S.C. 1016.

[38] *Irvine* v. *I.* (1884) 21 S.L.R. 493; *Ross* v. *R.* (1899) 1 F. 963.

[39] *Barrie* v. *B.* (1882) 10 R. 208; *Gibson* v. *G.* (1894) 21 R. 470.

[40] cf. *Barr* v. *B.*, 1939 S.C. 696.

[41] *Mason* v. *M.* (1877) 14 S.L.R. 592; *Muir* v. *M.* (1879) 6 R. 1353; *Jeffrey* v. *J.* (1901) 9 S.L.T. 54; *Smellie* v. *S.*, 1914, 2 S.L.T. 240; *Mitchell* v. *M.*, 1931 S.L.T. 484; cf. *Stair* v. *S.* (1905) 12 S.L.T. 788.

[42] *Irvine* v. *I.* (1884) 21 S.L.R. 493; *Horsley* v. *H.*, 1914, 1 S.L.T. 92.

[43] *Hunter* v. *H.* (1898) 5 S.L.T. 384; *Parker* v. *P.*, 1926 S.C. 574; *Trondsen* v. *T.*, 1948 S.L.T. (Notes) 85; *Anderson* v. *A.*, 1955 S.C. 428; contrast *Young* v. *Y.* (1882) 10 R. 184, where defender still in prison.

nium has expired while the imprisonment continues.[44] If one spouse is in desertion and offers *bona fide* to resume cohabitation but the other refuses, the latter is in desertion,[45] but an offer which is not *bona fide* may be ignored.[46] Wilful desertion may be inferred from conduct inconsistent with willingness to adhere, such as forming an association with another while justifiably abroad. An insane person cannot form *animus deserendi* so that insanity is a defence.[47]

Desertion without reasonable cause

Separation amounts to desertion only if the non-adhering spouse had no reasonable cause for leaving the other spouse or staying apart. That spouse has a good defence if he or she can establish reasonable cause for non-adherence. The defences of being willing to adhere, and of having reasonable cause for non-adherence, are not mutually exclusive.[48] Reasonable cause includes conduct by the pursuer such as would entitle the defender to defend an action for adherence, or himself to bring an action of divorce,[49] such as adultery,[50] cruelty,[51] or sodomy,[52] but not insanity, which is not an offence but an involuntary misfortune.[53] But reasonable cause as a defence also includes circumstances which do not by themselves give any positive remedy, as where the wife was willing to live with the husband only on condition that no marital intercourse took place,[54] or the husband was alleged to have attempted connection with the wife's niece,[55] or where the wife had tricked the husband into marriage by falsely representing that he was the cause of her pregnancy,[56] where the only home the pursuer had offered was with his relatives,[57] or where the pursuer had confessed to adultery,[58] or had committed crime so long as associated with the matrimonial relationship,[59] or conduct such that it would shock the conscience of reasonable men to ordain the

---

[44] *Parker, supra,* 578.

[45] *Forbes* v. *F.* (1881) 10 S.L.R. 118.

[46] *Chalmers* v. *C.* (1868) 6 M. 547.

[47] *Gilfillan* v. *G.* (1902) 10 S.L.T. 295; *Mudie* v. *M.*, 1956 S.C. 318.

[48] *Sinclair* v. *S.*, 1950 S.L.T. (Notes) 65.

[49] *Mackenzie* v. *M.* (1895) 22 R. (H.L.) 32.

[50] *Auld* v. *A.* (1884) 12 R. 36; *Hunter* v. *H.* (1900) 2 F. 771; *Wilkinson* v. *W.*, 1943 S.C. (H.L.) 61.

[51] *Stevens* v. *S.* (1882) 9 R. 730; *Mackenzie* v. *M.* (1895) 22 R. (H.L.) 32; *Anderson* v. *A.*, 1958 S.L.T. (Notes) 31.

[52] *Borland* v. *B.*, 1947 S.C. 432, 444; *Jack* v. *J.*, 1962 S.C. 24, 31.

[53] *Stair* v. *S.* (1905) 12 S.L.T. 788.

[54] *A.* v. *B.* (1896) 23 R. 588.

[55] *Hastings* v. *H.*, 1941 S.L.T. 323; cf. *Lang* v. *L.*, 1921 S.C. 44.

[56] *Young* v. *Y.*, 1947 S.L.T. 5.

[57] *Wilkinson* v. *W.*, 1943 S.C. (H.L.) 61; *Hamilton* v. *H.*, 1953 S.C. 383.

[58] *Brown* v. *B.*, 1955 S.L.T. 48; *A.B.* v. *C.B.*, 1959 S.C. 27.

[59] *Richardson* v. *R.*, 1956 S.C. 394; cf. *McMillan* v. *McM.*, 1962 S.C. 115.

spouses to cohabit again,[60] or was guilty of ill-treatment not amounting to legal cruelty justifying separation or divorce.[60] It is no longer a defence that the pursuer has committed adultery, unless that was a cause of the defender's desertion.[61]

Proceedings taken in good faith, though unjustifiably, for the defender's detention as a person of unsound mind have been held not to be reasonable ground for non-adherence,[62] as has been a wife's refusal to cohabit unless she could bring her grown-up children with her,[63] and a wife's refusal, after a brief cohabitation, to have her husband's sister continue to stay with them.[64] Nor does a wife have reasonable cause because she is employed and her husband (pursuer) is unemployed,[65] nor because she holds a non-cohabitation order granted by magistrates in England,[66] nor because he had formed an association, not adulterous, with another woman.[67] Unhappiness or matrimonial disharmony is not reasonable cause for non-adherence.

Pursuer's willingness to adhere

Desertion is bilateral in involving a spouse who deserts and a spouse who is willing to adhere.[68] This distinguishes it from consensual separation. Offers to adhere, ignored or rejected by the defender, or requests to resume cohabitation, are material evidence in a pursuer's case.[69] The sincerity of the offers must be judged by the court.[70] To raise an action for adherence and aliment during the biennium constitutes an offer to adhere.[71] To allow a spouse to live apart without serious effort to induce her to return suggests consensual separation.[72] The pursuer had formerly to be able to aver, and satisfy the court, in all cases, that he remained willing to adhere to the deserting spouse for at least three years after the date of desertion;[73] this is no longer so, so long as he has not refused any

---

[60] *Jack* v. *J.*, 1962 S.C. 24.
[61] *Muir* v. *M.*, 1967 S.L.T. 264.
[62] *Cathcart* v. *C.* (1900) 2 F. 404; cf. *Gould* v. *G.* (1887) 15 R. 229.
[63] *Inglis* v. *I.*, 1919 1 S.L.T. 184.
[64] *Anderson* v. *A.*, 1928 S.L.T. 199.
[65] *Knox* v. *K.*, 1934 S.C. 240.
[66] *Murray* v. *M.*, 1956 S.C. 376; cf. *Richardson* v. *R.*, 1957 S.L.T. (Notes) 45.
[67] *Richardson*, 1956 S.C. 394.
[68] *Burrell* v. *B.*, 1947 S.C. 569, 578.
[69] *Willey* v. *W.* (1884) 11 R. 815; *Watson* v. *W.* (1890) 17 R. 736; *Gibson* v. *G.* (1894) 21 R. 470; *Murray* v. *M.* (1894) 21 R. 723; *Munro* v. *M.* (1895) 2 S.L.T. 598; *Shaw* v. *S.* (1908) 16 S.L.T. 371; *McEwan* v. *McE.*, 1908 S.C. 1263; *Robertson* v. *R.* (1908) 16 S.L.T. 641; *Farrow* v. *F.*, 1920 S.C. 707; *Woodhouse* v. *W.*, 1936 S.C. 523.
[70] *Lilley* v. *L.* (1884) 12 R. 145; *Mackenzie* v. *M.* (1893) 20 R. 636, 657; *Hutchinson* v. *H.*, 1909 S.C. 148; *Mulherron* v. *M.*, 1923 S.C. 461; *Summers* v. *S.*, 1935 S.C. 537.
[71] *Deans* v. *D.*, 1965 S.L.T. (Notes) 9.
[72] *Barrie* v. *B.* (1882) 10 R. 208.
[73] *Macaskill* v. *M.*, 1939 S.C. 187; *Bell* v. *B.*, 1941 S.C. (H.L.) 5; *Borland* v. *B.*, 1947 S.C. 432.

genuine offer to resume cohabitation.[74] Once desertion is proved, the
pursuer's willingness to adhere is presumed, unless the defender rebuts
that presumption, as by showing the pursuer's refusal of a genuine offer
to adhere.[75] On the expiry of this biennium he acquires a vested right to
divorce,[76] though the right is barred if during the biennium the pursuer
refused a genuine and reasonable offer by the defender to adhere.[77] After
the expiry of the biennium an offer by the defender to adhere comes too
late,[78] and a pursuer is not bound to accept an offer by the defender to
adhere after twenty years' desertion when she refused to give information
about her life in the interval.[79] A spouse is not unwilling to adhere merely
because she declines to join her husband in inadequate or unsatisfactory
accommodation.[80]

The pursuer's adultery during the biennium formerly excluded his
action, since it was inconsistent with willingness to adhere, and absolved
the defender from the duty of adherence,[81] but this is no longer a defence,
unless it appears to the court that the adultery was a cause of the
defender's desertion or persistence in desertion;[82] after the biennium it
has no effect.[83]

Two years' desertion

The two year period runs from the date when the parties finally separated, the pursuer unwillingly, the defender *animo deserendi*,[84] or from
the date when, the parties being already separated, one declares an
intention not to resume cohabitation,[85] or unjustifiably refuses an offer of
a home,[86] or forms a connection with another,[87] or has disappeared and
ceased to communicate with the pursuer.[88] The proved period of deser-

---

[74] *Thomson* v. *T.*, 1965 S.L.T. 343; *Donnelly* v. *D.*, 1969 S.L.T. 52; *Burgess* v. *B.*, 1969
S.L.T. (Notes) 22; *McLean* v. *McL.*, 1969 S.L.T. (Notes) 67; but see *Greenwald* v. *G.*, 1967
S.L.T. (Notes) 97; *Thomson* v. *T.*, 1969 S.L.T. 364.
[75] *Thomson* v. *T.*, 1965 S.L.T. 343.
[76] *Muir* v. *M.* (1879) 6 R. 1353; *Auld* v. *A.* (1884) 12 R. 36; *Forbes* v. *F.* (1900) 8 S.L.T. 51;
Scott v. *S.*, 1908 S.C. 1124; *Bell, supra*; *Graham* v. *G.*, 1942 S.L.T. 142; *Wilson* v. *W.*, 1944
S.L.T. 223; *Wright* v. *W.*, 1966 S.L.T. (Notes) 86, superseding *Bisset* v. *B.*, 1933 S.C. 764.
[77] *Thomson* v. *T.*, 1965 S.L.T. 343.
[78] *Muir, supra*; *Pirie* v. *P.*, 1927 S.N. 124; cf. *Bisset* v. *B.*, 1933 S.C. 764; *Gilfillan* v. *G.*,
1931 S.L.T. 454.
[79] *Forbes* v. *F.* (1900) 8 S.L.T. 51.
[80] *Fletcher* v. *F.* [1945] 1 All E.R. 582; *Young* v. *Y.*, 1947 S.L.T. 5; contrast *Stewart* v. *S.*,
1959 S.L.T. (Notes) 70.
[81] *Wilkinson* v. *W.*, 1943 S.C. (H.L.) 61.
[82] *Muir* v. *M.*, 1967 S.L.T. 264.
[83] *Bell, supra*, modifying principles stated in *Auld* v. *A.* (1884) 12 R. 36; *Hunter* v. *H.* (1900)
2 F. 771; and *Wooler* v. *W.*, 1940 S.L.T. 66; *Graham* v. *G.*, 1942 S.C. 575.
[84] *Tronsden* v. *T.*, 1948 S.L.T. (Notes) 85.
[85] *Belken* v. *B.* [1948] P. 302.
[86] *Darroch* v. *D.*, 1947 S.C. 110.
[87] *Stickland* v. *S.* (1876) 35 L.T. 767.
[88] *Lough* v. *L.*, 1930 S.C. 1076.

tion must be two full years,[89] and continuous. If interrupted, the biennium commences afresh. Interruption is constituted by the resumption of matrimonial cohabitation, but not necessarily by living in the same house, though separately,[90] nor by unsuccessfully suing for separation during the biennium,[91] nor by sharing a bed for one night when there was no intention to resume cohabitation,[92] nor by a brief return with the intention of interrupting the biennium,[93] though the court will not in general inquire into the alleged purpose of resumed cohabitation.[94] No account is to be taken of any period or periods not exceeding six months in all during which the parties cohabited with one another; but such periods do not count as part of the period of non-cohabitation.[95] A brief resumption of cohabitation after the expiry of the biennium, and in ignorance of facts as to the defender's conduct during the biennium does not cancel that desertion.[96] If *currente biennio* the defender became insane, he or she could not be held to be in wilful desertion.[97] If not certified insane, it was a question of fact whether the defender was capable of *animus deserendi*.[98] It is no bar to divorce that, the biennium having expired, the defender has become insane, because the pursuer's right has vested.[99] If during the biennium a period of imprisonment has interposed that does not interrupt the period unless there is evidence of no *animus deserendi* during that period.[1]

Termination of desertion

Desertion is terminated if, before the biennium has expired, the spouses resume cohabitation, or the deserted spouse consents to their living apart, as by coming to an agreement for aliment, or commits some act which justifies the other in living apart, or if the spouse in desertion *bona fide* offers to resume cohabitation; if such an offer is unjustifiably refused the spouse refusing becomes in desertion and a new biennium commences. If the spouse in desertion has also been guilty of adultery, cruelty, or sodomy, the innocent spouse is not bound to take the other back as this

[89] cf. *Darroch, supra*. Action cannot be brought until two years have expired: *Martin* v. *M.*, 1968 S.C. 205.
[90] *McEwan* v. *McE.*, 1908 S.C. 1263.
[91] *Forbes* v. *F.* (1881) 19 S.L.R. 118.
[92] *Crawford* v. *C.*, 1946 S.L.T. 138; cf. *Calder* v. *C.*, 1962 S.L.T. (Notes) 78; contrast *Meiklem* v. *M.*, 1949 S.L.T. 370, where one night's resumption of full cohabitation.
[93] *Wallace* v. *W.*, 1952 S.C. 197.
[94] *Beggs* v. *B.*, 1947 S.N. 182; *Wallace, supra*.
[95] Divorce (Sc.) Act, 1976, S. 2 (4).
[96] *Wilson* v. *W.*, 1944 S.L.T. 223; contrast *Grant* v. *G.*, 1961 S.L.T. 322.
[97] *Williams* v. *W.* [1939] P. 365; *Rushbrook* v. *R.* [1940] P. 24; *Mudie* v. *M.*, 1956 S.C. 318.
[98] *Monckton* v. *M.* [1942] P. 28.
[99] *Scott* v. *S.*, 1908 S.C. 1124; cf. *Bell* v. *B.*, 1941 S.C. (H.L.) 5.
[1] *Hunter* v. *H.* (1898) 5 S.L.T. 384; *Parker* v. *P.*, 1926 S.C. 574; *Tronsden* v. *T.*, 1948 S.L.T. (Notes) 85; contrast *Young* v. *Y.* (1882) 10 R. 184.

would effect condonation of the additional offence and bar the innocent spouse's remedy on that ground.[2] If the spouse in desertion has also been guilty of conduct giving the innocent spouse reasonable ground for non-adherence it is probably a question of circumstances whether the innocent spouse should take the guilty spouse back if the latter, apparently *bona fide*, offers to resume cohabitation.

Divorce for non-cohabitation, defender consenting

Non-cohabitation involves not in fact living together as man and wife.[3] The reason for this is immaterial; it may be consensual, or a result of circumstances, such as employment abroad or imprisonment. Parties may live under one roof and yet not cohabit as man and wife.

The period of two years runs from the first day of separation until its second anniversary and must have expired before this ground for divorce is alleged.[4]

The defender must positively consent, not merely acquiesce or fail to object, and may withdraw consent before decree.

In cases brought under this head, the defender must have been given such information as will enable him to understand the consequences to him of consenting, the steps he must take to indicate his consent, and the manner of indicating consent to the decree and of withdrawing it. If the defender has indicated his consent in the prescribed manner and not withdrawn it, such indication is sufficient evidence of consent.[5]

Divorce for non-cohabitation, defender not consenting

In this case also there must be a state of not in fact living together as man and wife.[6] In this case the period required is a continuous one of five years, and in this case decree may be granted without the defender's consent. This provision is applicable to cases where the defender does not consent, which he can indicate by defending the action,[7] or has disappeared, though there may be no evidence that he intended to desert.[8] It covers also the case where the defender has become permanently of unsound mind.[9]

In this case the court is not bound to grant decree, notwithstanding irretrievable breakdown of the marriage, if in the opinion of the court the

---

[2] *Everitt* v. *E.* [1949] P. 374.
[3] 1976 Act, S. 13 (2).
[4] *Duncan* v. *D.*, 1986 S.L.T. 17.
[5] 1976 Act, S. 1 (4).
[6] 1976 Act, S. 13 (2).
[7] Absence of consent does not bar decree; the defender must rebut allegations of irretrievable breakdown of the marriage.
[8] cf. *Lench* v. *L.*, 1945 S.C. 295.
[9] Previously a distinct ground of divorce.

grant of decree would result in grave financial hardship to the defender, including the loss of the chance of acquiring any benefit.[10]

Encouragement of reconciliation

If, before granting decree, the court thinks that there is a reasonable prospect of a reconciliation between the parties, it must continue the action to enable attempts to be made to effect reconciliation, and if, during such a continuation, the parties cohabit, no account is to be taken of it for the purpose of the action.[11]

Dissolution of marriage by judicial presumption of death

Any person having interest may seek declarator that a person, who is missing and is thought to have died or has not been known to be alive for at least seven years, has in fact died at a stated date and time or at the end of the day seven years after the date on which he was last known to be alive.[12] The court in granting decree may determine the deceased's domicile, determine any question relating to any interest in property arising in consequence of the death, or appoint a judicial factor on the deceased's estate.[13] The decree is effective against all persons and for all purposes including the dissolution of marriage, and such dissolution is not invalidated by the fact that the missing person was in fact alive at the date found as the date of death.[14] The decree may be varied or recalled, but a variation order does not revive a marriage dissolved by the declarator,[15] and in general does not have any effect on rights to or in property acquired as a result of the declarator.[16] It is a defence to a charge of bigamy to prove that at no time within the seven years preceding the purported marriage had the accused any reason to believe that his spouse was alive.[17]

Cross-actions of divorce

It is competent for each spouse simultaneously to seek divorce from the other; the grounds may be the same, or different. Normally such actions

---

[10] 1976, Act, S. 1 (5). Grave financial hardship may consist in the prospective loss of entitlement to a widow's pension linked to the husband's pension, and to a widow's state pension: *Nolan* v. *N.*, 1979 S.L.T. 293.

[11] i.e. it will not interrupt the period for desertion or non-cohabitation.

[12] Presumption of Death (Sc.) Act, 1977, Ss. 1–2. See also Ch. 3.2, *supra*.

[13] S. 2.

[14] S. 3.

[15] S. 4.

[16] S. 5.

[17] S. 13.

will be heard together.[18] Where decree in one action had become final, it has been held that the pursuer in the other no longer had a title to reclaim in the other action, the marriage having been dissolved.[19] If decree is granted in both actions simultaneously either party may reclaim to avoid the finding that he or she was guilty of adultery, and to alter the consequences of the actions so far as concerning property.[20] Similarly there may be cross-actions of divorce and of nullity of marriage, in which case the divorce will be sisted to await the decision of the action for nullity.[21]

Absolute bars to action for divorce

There are three pleas, the establishment of any one of which wholly bars the pursuer from obtaining judicial separation or divorce.

Condonation

Condonation or forgiveness of the offence bars an action of divorce on the ground of adultery or intolerable behaviour or desertion. Adultery[22] cannot be condoned by mere expressions of forgiveness,[23] nor will it be inferred from anything less than a continuance or resumption of full matrimonial relations in the full knowledge of the other spouse's adultery,[24] or at least genuine belief in its having taken place,[25] but not if there is merely suspicion of infidelity.[26] It may be inferred even though the condoner did not have full knowlege of the extent of the other's guilt, if no further inquiry is made.[27] If sexual relations are resumed in the full knowledge of adultery condonation will be held established[28] and this result cannot be escaped by a denial of real forgiveness,[29] or by the imposition of any condition.[27] Even the resumption of cohabitation without sexual relations may amount to condonation[30] and if the parties resume or continue residence in the same house condonation will be presumed unless disproved.[31] Any presumption of condonation arising from the continuance or resumption of marital intercourse may be rebut-

---

[18] *Gray* v. *G.*, 1968 S.C. 185; *Wormsley* v. *W.*, 1977 S.L.T. (Notes) 79.
[19] *Bridges* v. *B.*, 1911 S.C. 250.
[20] *Connell* v. *C.*, 1950 S.C. 505.
[21] *A.B.* v. *C.B.*, 1911 2 S.L.T. 99.
[22] Bell, *Prin* § 1531.
[23] *Ralston* v. *R.* (1881) 8 R. 371; *Annan* v. *A.*, 1948 S.C. 532; *Dick* v. *D.*, 1949 S.C. 66.
[24] *Hunt* v. *H.* (1893) 31 S.L.R. 244; *Edgar* v. *E.* (1902) 4 F. 632; *Steven* v. *S.*, 1919, 2 S.L.T. 239.
[25] *Wemyss* v. *W.* (1866) 4 M. 660; *Paterson* v. *P.*, 1938 S.C. 251.
[26] *Collins* v. *C.* (1884) 11 R. (H.L.) 19.
[27] *A.* v. *B.* (1870) 8 S.L.R. 258; *Smith* v. *S.* (1904) 12 S.L.T. 341.
[28] *Edgar* v. *E.* (1902) 4 F. 632.
[29] *Wemyss* v. *W.* (1866) 4 M. 660; *Collins* v. *C.* (1884) 11 R. (H.L.) 19.
[30] *Edgar*, *supra*; *Dick* v. *D.*, 1949 S.C. 66, 68; but see *Mitchell* v. *M.*, 1947 S.L.T. (Notes) 9.
[31] *Edgar*, *supra*; *McKellar* v. *McK.*, 1977 S.L.T. (Notes) 70.

ted by a pursuer of either sex.[32] Condonation of adultery is not to be inferred by reason only of a continuation or resumption of cohabitation between the parties after the adultery, provided the pursuer did not cohabit with the defender at any time after the end of three months from the date of cohabitation resumed in the knowledge of adultery.[32] If condonation is held proved, the effect is to wipe out all known incidents of adultery prior to the condonation, but not any acts of adultery then unknown to the pursuer.[33] It matters not that there might not have been condonation had they been known.[34] But even condoned adultery may subsequently be referred to, not as a ground of action, but as casting light on subsequent suspicious conduct by the defender.[35] It does not prejudice an action for subsequent adultery, even with the same paramour. Condonation does not bar an action of damages against the paramour for the wrong of interfering with the pursuer's domestic relations.[36] The onus of proof is on the defender pleading condonation.[37]

Condonation of desertion may be inferred if, after the biennium for divorce has run, the pursuer resumed cohabitation with the defender and cohabited with him at any time after the end of three months from the date when the cohabitation was resumed.[38]

Condonation of intolerable behaviour is not to be inferred from refusal or failure to seek a judicial remedy on the occurrence of one or two acts of cruelty.[39] Even where cohabitation has been continued or resumed after e.g. cruelty, those incidents are not excluded from consideration if there is a subsequent incident, because the inquiry must consider the whole married life and determine whether the pursuer can with safety continue to live with the defender.[40] But if there are no subsequent incidents the continuance of cohabitation may yield an inference of forgiveness and suggests that the behaviour was not intolerable.

Connivance or lenocinium

This is a bar to divorce on the ground of adultery. Lenocinium is whoremongering, and in Scotland[41] the substance of the plea is that the

---

[32] Divorce (Sc.) Act, 1976, S. 2 (2).
[33] *Ralston v. R.* (1881) 8 R. 371; *Steven v. S.*, 1919 2 S.L.T. 239.
[34] *Ralston, supra.*
[35] *Robertson v. R.* (1888) 15 R. 1001; *Nicol v. N.*, 1938 S.L.T. 98.
[36] *Macdonald v. M.* (1885) 12 R. 1327.
[37] *Andrews v. A.*, 1961 S.L.T. (Notes) 48.
[38] Divorce (Sc.) Act, 1976, S. 2 (3).
[39] *Richards v. R.*, 1939 S.C. 554.
[40] *Macfarlane v. M.* (1848) 10 D. 962; *Graham v. G.* (1878) 5 R. 1093; *Martin v. M.* (1895) 3 S.L.T. 150; *Smeaton v. S.* (1900) 2 F. 837; *Richards, supra; Adams v. A.*, 1964 S.L.T. (Notes) 101. See also *Watson v. W.* (1874) 12 S.L.R. 78.
[41] The English concept of connivance is different; see *Wemyss v. W.* (1866) 4 M. 660; *Riddell v. R.*, 1952 S.C. 475.

husband was actively accessory to, or participant in, or the direct occasion of, or otherwise promoted or positively encouraged, his wife's adultery.[42] It is not inferred from mere lack of care[43] or indifference[44] or imprudence[45] or acquiescence,[46] or even permission to act when there were grounds of suspicion.[47] The wife's misconduct must be causally connected with her husband's encouragement to adultery, and not too remotely connected in time.[48] It is not lenocinium to have suspicions but conceal them and have the defender watched,[49] nor to say that divorce will be considered if evidence is furnished,[50] nor even to take a wife to a brothel, unless to tempt her to adultery.[51]

Collusion

Collusion is a bar to divorce on the ground of adultery only.[52] It also differs from collusion in English law. It consists not in a common desire to have the marriage ended, nor in allowing an action to pass undefended, nor even in co-operation to secure divorce, as by communicating evidence, but only in permitting a false case to be substantiated or withholding a just defence.[53] It does not strike at an agreement to withdraw defences,[54] or even acting in fulfilment of a promise to divorce if the parties quarrelled.[55]

Pursuer's conduct as bar to divorce

The pursuer's own misconduct is in some cases a bar to divorce. In adultery the pursuer's own adultery or other misconduct is no bar, though it grounds a cross-action.[56] In desertion the pursuer's conduct giving reasonable cause for non-adherence is a bar. In intolerable conduct the pursuer's misconduct of any kind is probably irrelevant.

---

[42] Bell, *Prin.* § 1532; Fraser, *H. & W.*, II, 1184; *Wemyss* v. *W.* (1866) 4 M. 660, 662; (1877) 4 R. 332; *Marshall* v. *M.* (1881) 8 R. 702; *Hunter* v. *H.* (1884) 11 R. 359; *Thomson* v. *T.*, 1908 S.C. 179; *Gallacher* v. *G.*, 1928 S.C. 586; *Hannah* v. *H.*, 1931 S.C. 275; *Riddell* v. *R.*, 1952 S.C. 475. A wife also can probably be guilty of lenocinium.
[43] *Fletcher* v. *F.* (1902) 10 S.L.T. 296.
[44] *Erskine* v. *E.* (1907) 15 S.L.T. 144.
[45] *Hunter* v. *H.* (1883) 11 R. 359.
[46] *McMahon* v. *McM.*, 1928 S.N. 37, 158 (bigamous marriage).
[47] *Thomson* v. *T.*, 1908 S.C. 179.
[48] *Marshall, supra; Hunter, supra; Gallacher* v. *G.*, 1928 S.C. 586; 1934 S.C. 339.
[49] Fraser, *H. & W.* II, 1186; *McIntosh* v. *M.* (1882) 20 S.L.R. 117; *Thomson, supra.*
[50] *Hannah, supra.*
[51] *Donald* v. *D.* (1863) 1 M. 741; *Wemyss, supra.*
[52] Bell, *Prin.* § 1530; cf. *Shaw* v. *Gould* (1868) L.R. 3 H.L. 55.
[53] *Walker* v. *W.*, 1911 S.C. 163, 169; see also *McKenzie* v. *McK.*, 1935 S.L.T. 198.
[54] *Williamson* v. *W.*, 1932 S.N. 65; cf. *Graham* v. *G.* (1881) 9 R. 327.
[55] *McKenzie* v. *M.*, 1935 S.L.T. 198.
[56] *Marchant* v. *M.*, 1948 S.L.T. 143; cf. *Connell* v. *C.*, 1950 S.C. 505.

Discretionary bars to action for divorce

In certain circumstances the court may hold that a pursuer is barred by his own conduct from obtaining divorce, but the court is not obliged in such a case to refuse decree. The grant or refusal of decree is discretionary in the circumstances. The main conditional bar is mora. Lapse of time after adultery before bringing action is not a bar if the pursuer was ignorant of the wrong,[57] and if the wrong were known delay bars only if circumstances suggest condonation or acquiescence.[58] Mora and acquiescence may bar an action though they fall short of condonation.[59] An action of divorce for desertion is not necessarily prejudiced by even long delay after the biennium has expired,[60] but it may be held barred.[61]

EFFECT OF DIVORCE ON PROPERTY RIGHTS

At common law

Decree of divorce on any ground, except incurable insanity,[62] formerly entitled the innocent spouse at once[63] to claim from the estate of the guilty party the legal rights which could have been claimed on death,[64] i.e. a capital payment once and for all, but not any periodical payments of aliment. The innocent wife might accordingly exact terce and *jus relictae*,[65] the innocent husband courtesy (if the requisites for that claim had been satisfied)[66] but not *jus relicti*.[67] The fiction that the guilty spouse was treated as dead was not rigidly applied, and the innocent spouse was held entitled to legal rights out of the capital value of liferent interests enjoyed by the guilty,[68] though not out of capital in which the guilty spouse had only a contingent interest.[69] The innocent spouse might also exact provisions conventionally payable, as under a marriage contract,

---

[57] *Gatchell* v. *G.* (1898) 6 S.L.T. 218; *Robertson* v. *R.* (1901) 9 S.L.T. 332.

[58] *A.B.* v. *C.D.* (1853) 15 D. 976; *Hellon* v. *H.* (1873) 11 M. 290; *Holmes* v. *H.*, 1927 S.L.T. 20; *Johnstone* v. *J.*, 1931 S.C. 60; see also *Cocozza* v. *C.*, 1955 S.L.T. (Notes) 29; *Macfarlane* v. *M.*, 1956 S.C. 472.

[59] *Macfarlane, supra.*

[60] *Mackenzie* v. *M.* (1883) 11 R. 105; *Monahan* v. *M.*, 1930 S.C. 221; see also *Goold* v. *G.*, 1927 S.C. 177.

[61] *Grant* v. *G.*, 1961 S.L.T. 322.

[62] Divorce (Sc.) Act, 1938 S. 1(1)(b).

[63] *Smith* v. *McLean*, 1940 S.L.T. (Sh. Ct.) 22.

[64] For further discussion see Ch. 7.2, *infra.*

[65] Stair I, 4, 20; Ersk. I, 6, 46 and 48; Fraser, H. & W. II, 1216; *Harvey* v. *Farquhar* (1871) 10 M. (H.L.) 26; *Montgomery* v. *Zarifi*, 1918 S.C. (H.L.) 128, 137; *Manderson* v. *Sutherland* (1899) 1 F. 621.

[66] *Fraser, supra.*

[67] Married Women's Property (Sc.) Act, 1881, S. 6.; *Eddington* v. *Robertson* (1895) 22 R. 430.

[68] *Scott* v. *S.*, 1930 S.C. 903; *Selsdon* v. *S.*, 1934 S.C. (H.L.) 24.

[69] *Wright* v. *Bryson*, 1935 S.C. (H.L.) 49.

by the guilty spouse, or any third party on his behalf, on the termination
of the marriage, to the survivor, not only funds actually contributed by
the other and forfeited by him.[70] But the innocent spouse could not exact
payment of testamentary bequests by his or her own relatives conditional
on his or her survivance, unless this intention was apparent,[71] and divorce
was not equivalent to death in relation to the rights of children.[72]

Conversely the guilty spouse on being divorced forfeited all claims to
conventional provisions under marriage contracts.[73] In the case of cross
actions of divorce, if decree were granted, in both actions, neither party
had any claim on the other's property.[74]

Under statute

The Family Law (Scotland) Act 1985, replacing the Divorce (Scotland)
Act, 1976,[75] provides (S. 8) that in an action for divorce either party may
apply to the court for one or more of orders for the payment of a capital
sum or the transfer of property to him by the other party to the marriage,
an order for the making of a periodical allowance, or an incidental order
within S. 14, i.e. one or more of an order for the sale of property, for the
valuation of property, determining a dispute as to property rights, regulating the occupation of the matrimonial home, regulating liability for
outgoings in respect of the matrimonial home, to give security for any
financial provision, to make payments to a *curator bonis* or trustee for the
applicant, setting aside or varying any term in a marriage contract, as to
the date of interest, or any ancillary order required. Such an incidental
order may later be varied or recalled. The court must make an order
which is justified by the principles set out in S. 9 of the Act and reasonable having regard to the resources of the parties. S. 9 provides that the
principles to be applied by the court in deciding on an order for financial
provision are that (a) the net value of the matrimonial property should be
shared fairly; (b) fair account should be taken of any economic advantage
derived by either from contribution by the other and of any economic
disadvantage suffered by either in the interests of the other or the family;
(c) any economic burden of caring after divorce for a child of the marriage under 16 should be shared fairly; (d) a party dependent on the
financial support of the other should be enabled to adjust over not more

[70] *Thom* v. *T.* (1852) 14 D. 861; *Harvey* v. *Farquhar* (1872) 10 M. (H.L.) 26; *Johnstone-Beattie* v. *J.* (1867) 5 M. 340; *Somervell's Tr.* v. *Dawes* (1903) 5 F. 1065; *Fortington* v. *Kinnaird*, 1942 S.C. 239; *Coats's Trs.* v. *Lord Advocate*, 1965 S.C. (H.L.) 45.
[71] *Mason* v. *Beattie's Trs.* (1878) 6 R. 37.
[72] *Harvey's J.F.* v. *Spittal's Curator* (1893) 20 R. 1016; *Dawson* v. *Smart* (1903) 5 F. (H.L.) 24; *Montgomery* v. *Zarifi*, 1918 S.C. (H.L.) 128; *Coats's Trs., supra*.
[73] *Johnstone-Beattie* v. *Dalzell* (1868) 6 M. 333; *Ritchie* v. *R's Trs.* (1874) 1 R. 987; *Hedderwick* v. *Morison* (1901) 4 F. 163.
[74] *Thomson* v. *Donald's Exor.* (1871) 9 M. 1069; *Fraser* v. *Walker* (1872) 10 M. 837.
[75] Replacing Succession (Sc.) Act, 1964, Ss. 25–7.

than three years to the loss of that support on divorce; (e) a party who seems likely to suffer serious financial hardship as a result of the divorce should be given such financial provision as is reasonable to relieve him of hardship over a reasonable period. S. 10 deals further with sharing of the value of matrimonial property. Fair sharing means equal sharing unless there are special circumstances. Valuation of assets and liabilities is at the date when parties ceased to cohabit or the start of divorce proceedings, whichever is earlier. No account is to be taken of any cessation of cohabitation where the parties resumed cohabitation, unless it were for 90 days or more continuously before resuming cohabition for less than 90 days in all. Special circumstances may include agreement between the parties on ownership or division of matrimonial property. In applying the principles in S. 9 various stated factors are to be taken into account (S. 11). By S. 12 an order for payment of a capital sum or transfer of property may be made on granting divorce, or within such period as the court may then specify; it may come into effect at a future date; it may be payable by instalments. On material change of circumstances the court may vary the date or method of payment or of transfer of property.

An order for a periodical allowance may (S. 13) be made on divorce, or within such period as the court may then specify, or after divorce if application is made later and there has been change of circumstances. The order must be justified by stated ones of the principles in S. 9 and the court must be satisfied that payment of a capital sum or transfer of property would be inappropriate or insufficient to satisfy S. 8. An order may be for a definite or indefinite period or till a specified event. An order may be varied or recalled or converted into an order for a capital sum or a transfer of property.[76] An order continues to affect a debtor's estate on his death but lapses on the remarriage or death of the creditor. The court is not (S. 15) to make an order for a transfer of property if the necessary consent of a third party has not been obtained, or without the consent of a creditor in a security over it unless he has been given an opportunity to be heard. An incidental order is not to prejudice the rights of any third party. Where parties have made an agreement as to financial provision to be made on divorce the court may after granting divorce set aside or vary any term as to periodical allowance if the agreement provides for setting aside or variation, or may on granting divorce or within a specified time thereafter set aside or vary the agreement or any term where the agreement was not fair and reasonable when entered into. The court may also set aside or vary an agreement in the event of the debtor's sequestration or executing a trust deed for creditors (S. 16). Transactions having the effect of avoiding liability for aliment or financial provision are challengeable within five years, unless in favour of a third party acting in good faith and for value (S. 18). Inhibition and arrestment on the dependence

[76] *Smith* v. *S.*, 1987 S.L.T. 199; *Collins* v. *C.*, 1987 S.L.T. 224; *Stewart* v. *S.*, 1987 S.L.T. 246; *Wilson* v. *W.*, 1987 S.L.T. 262; *Grindlay* v. *G.*, 1987 S.L.T. 264.

of an action for aliment or divorce may be allowed (S. 19). In an action
for aliment or one including a claim for financial provision or interim
aliment the court may order either party to provide details of his resources or those relating to a child or incapax for whom he is acting (S.
20).

Under the repealed legislation it was held that the question of which
spouse was primarily responsible for the breakdown of the marriage was
relevant to the amount of an award of periodical allowance.[77]

Other provisions

Provisions for children in a marriage-contract, to become operative on
their parents' death, are not rendered payable by divorce,[78] and powers
granted thereunder are still exercisable.[79] The Act 1592, c. 11, enacted
that a wife divorced for adultery who married or openly cohabited with
her paramour could not alienate her heritage to any person to the prejudice of the issue of the dissolved marriage or of her lawful heirs at
law,[80] but this has been repealed.[81]

Reduction of decree of divorce

A decree of divorce may be reduced, as having been granted without
jurisdiction, or by perjured evidence or concealment of known facts.[82]
This necessarily restores the marriage and reinstates the parties in married
status. Hence intercourse by one spouse with a third party, even between
the raising of the action of reduction and decree therein is adultery,[83] and
a fortiori after decree of reduction.

Registration

The Registrar-General maintains a register of decrees of divorce and of
declarators of nullity of marriage, an extract of an entry in which is
evidence of a decree of divorce or nullity. The register may be searched by
any person.[84]

When a decree otherwise altering the status of a person has been

---

[77] *Lambert* v. *L.*, 1982 S.L.T. 144; *Cunningham* v. *C.*, 1985 S.L.T. 304.
[78] *Harvey's J.F.* v. *Spittal's Curator* (1893) 20 R. 1016; *Dawson* v. *Smart* (1903) 5 F. (H.L.)
24.
[79] *McGrady's Trs.* v. *McG.*, 1932 S.C. 191; *Peel's Trs.* v. *Drummond*, 1936 S.C. 786.
[80] Ersk. II, 3, 16; Fraser, *H. & W.* II, 1224; *Irvine* v. *Skeen* (1707) Mor. 6350.
[81] Succession (Sc.) Act, 1964, Sch. 3.
[82] *Campbell* v. *C.*, 1983 S.L.T. 530.
[83] *Sands* v. *S.*, 1964 S.L.T. 80.
[84] Registration of Births, etc. (Sc.) Act, 1965, S. 28A added by Law Reform (Misc. Prov.) (Sc.)
Act, 1985, S. 50.

granted the court notifies the Registrar-General who causes an appropriate entry to be made in the Register of Corrections.[85]

COHABITATION

Where two persons of opposite sexes cohabit as if married but without having been married their relationship does not in general give rise to any of the incidents or consequences of being married, unless it gives rise to the habit and repute of being married and even then only after judicial declarator of that marriage.[86] Neither acquires any rights against the other save that for the purpose of certain rules, particularly in the fields of social security, protected tenancies, and occupancy rights in a home, cohabitants may be treated as belonging to the same family.

[85] Registration of Births, etc. (Sc.) Act, 1965, S. 48. This is concerned only with Scottish decrees; *Smart* v. *Registrar-General*, 1954 S.C. 81.

[86] *Mackenzie* v. *Scott*, 1980 S.L.T. (Notes) 9. As to property disputes see *Prangnell O'Neill* v. *Skiffington*, 1984 S.L.T. 282.

THE DOMESTIC RELATIONS
(2) PARENT AND CHILD

The mutual obligations and legal relations between parent and child are obediential, not voluntary, and are defined by law itself.[1] They vary according as, in the first place, the child is of legitimate, illegitimate, legitimated, or adopted status, and in the second place according to the age of the child. Scots law, following Roman law, distinguishes the status of the pupil (from birth to puberty, fixed as 14 in the case of boys, 12 in the case of girls), from that of the minor (from these ages till the attainment of majority at 18) and of the adult or person of full age.[2] Statute has intervened in many circumstances to modify the common law principles. There is now a general principle of legal equality for all children whether or not their parents have ever been married to each other. The marriage of parents is to be ignored in determining relationship.[3]

Legitimacy or illegitimacy

The issue of legitimacy or illegitimacy if in doubt is determined by an action of declarator of legitimacy or of bastardy. With either may be combined a conclusion for decree of putting to silence, ordaining the defender to desist from asserting falsely that the pursuer was illegitimate, or as the case may be.[4] The competency of combining a declarator of bastardy with a divorce has been doubted.[5] Where a decree altering the status of any person has been granted, its import must be notified to the Registrar-General who will have it entered in the Register of Corrections.[6]

LEGITIMATE CHILDREN

Legitimate children

A legitimate child is one either conceived or born in lawful marriage, or to parties to a putative marriage, i.e. one which, though null, at least one

---

[1] Stair I, 5, 1; Mack. I, 7, 1; Bankt. I, 6, 1; Ersk. I, 6, 49; Hume, *Lect.* I, 191; Bell, *Prin.* § 1624–36; More, *Lect,* I, 78; Fraser, *P. & Ch., passim.*
[2] Stair I, 5, 2; Ersk. I, 7, 1; Bell, *Prin.* § 2066.
[3] Law Reform (Parent and Child) (Sc.) Act, 1986, S. 1.
[4] cf. *Imre* v. *Mitchell*, 1958 S.C. 439.
[5] *Jamieson* v. *J.*, 1969 S.L.T. (Notes) 11. See also *Curran* v. *C.*, 1957 S.L.T. (Notes) 47.
[6] Registration of Births, Deaths, and Marriages (Sc.) Act, 1965, S. 48.

party honestly though erroneously believed to be valid.[7] In accordance with the maxim *pater est quem nuptiae demonstrant* a child born to a married woman, if born sufficiently long after her marriage, or sufficiently shortly after its termination, that it could have been conceived in wedlock,[8] is presumed begotten by her husband and therefore legitimate.[9] The presumption is strong and is not redargued merely by evidence of her adultery, but only by clear and conclusive facts.[10] The presumption is inapplicable if the birth is so shortly after the marriage, or so long after its dissolution, that the child could not have been conceived in wedlock,[11] though if a man has arranged to marry a woman already, to his knowledge, pregnant, and there were opportunities for pre-marital intercourse, a similar presumption arises that he is the father.[12] If he did not know of her pregnancy a presumption will arise if he take no action to repudiate the wife and child when he has ground for suspicion.[13] The presumption does not arise when a man marries a woman who has had an illegitimate child, even shortly before the marriage.[14] The presumption is probably inapplicable if the marriage was irregular,[15] and does not arise if the legal issue in doubt is of the existence of the marriage or otherwise.[16] The fact that parties have registered their child as legitimate is evidence, but by no means conclusive, of that fact, or at least of their belief at the time.[17] The presumption still applies though parties live apart or have separated voluntarily, but may be rebutted by proof of non-access by the husband.[18]

The presumption does not, however, apply if the parties have been judicially separated before the probable date of conception, since after judicial separation a husband is not entitled to access to his wife. The presumption, though strong, may be rebutted by clear evidence of the husband's impotence, or of his not possibly having had access to his wife at or about the date of conception.[19] It is not sufficient by itself to show

---

[7] Ersk. I, 6, 49, 52; Bell, *Prin.* § 1624–5.

[8] *Gardner* v. *G.* (1876) 3 R. 695; 4 R. (H.L.) 56.

[9] Stair III, 3, 42; Ersk. I, 6, 49; Bell, *Prin.* § 1626.

[10] *Routledge* v. *Carruthers* (1816) 4 Dow 392; *Imre* v. *Mitchell*, 1958 S.C. 439.

[11] Stair, *supra*; *Lepper* v. *Watson* (1802) Hume 488; *Aitken* v. *Mitchell* (1806) Hume 489; see also *Jobson* v. *Reid* (1827) 5 S. 715; (1830) 8 S. 343; (1832) 10 S. 594.

[12] *Gardner, supra*; *Reid* v. *Mill* (1879) 6 R. 659; *Kerr* v. *Lindsay* (1890) 18 R. 365; *Imre* v. *Mitchell*, 1958 S.C. 439.

[13] cf. *Lang* v. *L.*, 1921 S.C. 44; *Hastings* v. *H.*, 1941 S.L.T. 323, where in such circumstances the husband left the wife.

[14] *Imre, supra*; *Brook's Exrx.* v. *James*, 1970 S.C. 147; 1971 S.C. (H.L.) 77.

[15] *Baptie* v. *Barclay* (1665) Mor. 8431; *Swinton* v. *S.* (1862) 24 D. 833.

[16] *Dean's J.F.* v. *D.* 1912 S.C. 441.

[17] *Imre, supra*.

[18] *Montgomery* v. *M.* (1881) 8 R. 403; *Colquhoun* v. *C.* (1891) 28 S.L.R. 689; *Marshall* v. *M.*, 1934 S.N. 39; *Ballantyne* v. *Douglas*, 1953 S.L.T. (Notes) 10.

[19] Craig II, 18, 13, and 20; Stair III, 3, 42; IV, 45, 20; Bankt. I, 2, 3; Ersk. I, 6, 50; *Mackay* v. *M.* (1855) 17 D. 494; *Brodie* v. *Dyce* (1872) 11 M. 142; *Steedman* v. *S.* (1887) 14 R. 1066; *Tennent* v. *T.* (1890) 17 R. 1205; *Coles* v. *Homer & Tulloh* (1895) 22 R. 716. Many such cases raise questions of the maximum and minimum possible durations of pregnancy, on which see Ch. 3.3, *supra*, and *infra*.

that the wife was guilty of adultery at or about that time.[20] The presumptive father of the child may consent to the child's blood being tested,[21] as may a tutor or any person having custody or care and custody, or the court may do so.[22] Blood tests alone are insufficient to rebut the presumption.[23] The presumption may also be rebutted by inference, based on evidence of unreasonably short pregnancy after the first cohabitation following the husband's absence, or of unreasonably long pregnancy after the last cohabitation before his absence.[24] There is now a statutory presumption that a man is father of a child if married to the mother at any time between its conception and its birth, or if both have acknowledged paternity and he is regarded as the father.[25]

A married woman may bring an action of affiliation and aliment against a man not her husband and thereby rebut the presumption, even though there had been a possibility of access by him.[26] Evidence by the parents themselves tending to bastardize their child is competent[27] but possibly not sufficient by itself to rebut the presumption.[28] When a man marries the mother of an illegitimate child there is no presumption that he is the father.[29]

The status of legitimacy also attaches, as in canon law, to the children of a putative marriage, i.e. one where one or both parties honestly believed themselves free to marry, though their marriage was in fact null by reason of the existence of an impediment.[30] The marriage may have been irregular[31] but the parties' error must have been one of fact and not of law.[32] If a person has by common reputation enjoyed the status of legitimacy throughout his life this is presumed justified.[33]

Statute[34] has also provided that where a decree of nullity of a voidable

---

[20] Routledge v Carruthers, 19 May 1812, F.C.; Ballantyne, supra.
[21] Docherty v. McGlynn, 1983 S.L.T. 645.
[22] Law Reform (Parent and Child) (Sc.) Act, 1986, S. 6.
[23] Imre v. Mitchell, 1958 S.C. 439. Sed quaere.
[24] Stair II, 3, 42; IV, 45, 20; Ersk. I, 6, 49, and 50; Gray v. G., 1919 1 S.L.T. 163; McIntosh v M., 1947 S.N. 23; Currie v. C., 1950 S.C. 10.
[25] Law Reform (Parent and Child) (Sc.) Act, 1986, S. 5.
[26] Mackay, supra; Brodie, supra; Ballantyne, supra; cf. Reid v. Mill (1879) 6 R. 659.
[27] Burman v. B., 1930 S.C. 262.
[28] Tennent v. T. (1890) 17 R. 1205, 1223; Burman v. B., 1930 S.C. 262; Imre, supra.
[29] Brooks's Exrx. v. James, 1970 S.C. 147; 1971 S.C. (H.L.) 77.
[30] Craig II, 18, 18; Stair III, 3, 42; Ersk. I, 6, 51; Bell, Prin. § 1625; Jolly v. McGregor (1828) 3 W. & S. 85; Petrie v. Ross (1896) 4 S.L.T. 63; Smijth v. S., 1918, 1 S.L.T. 156. See also Purves's Trs. v. P. (1895) 22 R. 513; Kirkcaldy Parish Council v. Traquair Parish Council, 1915 S.C. 1124.
[31] Smijth v. S., 1918, 1 S.L.T. 156.
[32] Fraser, P. & Ch. 33; Purves's Trs. v. P. (1896) 22 R. 513; Philp's Trs. v. Beaton, 1938 S.C. 733.
[33] Brooks's Exrx, supra.
[34] Law Reform (Misc. Prov.) Act, 1949, S. 4. This can in Scotland cover only the case of a child conceived by fecundation ab extra, and possibly also the case of the child conceived by A.I.H., where the marriage has not been consummated naturally; cf. MacLennan v. McL., 1958 S.C. 105.

marriage is granted, any child who would have been legitimate had the marriage been dissolved and not annulled is to be deemed legitimate.

The child of adultery, of concubinage or casual cohabitation, or of a void marriage is not legitimate. Though the artificial insemination of a married woman with the semen of a donor is not adultery,[35] a child by A.I.D., not being begotten by the husband, is presumably illegitimate.

Registration of birth

A parent or the parents or any relative of either having knowledge of the birth, or the occupier of the premises in which the birth takes place, or any person present at the birth or having charge of the child must within 21 days attend personally at the local registrar's office to give information of statutory particulars regarding the birth.[36] An abbreviated extract of the entry is given to the informant and further copies may be obtained.[37]

Name

A legitimate child is normally given a christian or baptismal name and the surname of the parents, or of the father. The right to change a child's surname before majority probably resides primarily in the father, as the natural guardian, and a widowed or divorced mother, having custody of the child and having remarried, is probably not entitled to change the child's name without at least the father's consent, if still alive, and, probably, if the child is a minor, the child's consent.[38]

Parental rights over child

Parental rights and powers are of two kinds, that of guiding and directing the persons of children under full age, and that of legal administration, of managing their property and legal business or advising thereon.

In relation to a pupil or minor and to the administration of any property belonging to or held in trust for a pupil or minor or the application of income of any such property, a mother now[39] has the same rights and authority as a father; the parents' rights and authority are equal and exercisable by either without the other. The mother always has parental rights, and the father rights only if he is or was married to the mother (including in a voidable or void but putatively valid marriage).[40]

---

[35] As held in *MacLennan* v. *McL.*, 1958 S.C. 105, *Sed quaere*.
[36] Registration of Births, Deaths, and Marriages (Sc.) Act, 1965, S. 14. As to registrar's powers to require information, see Ss. 16, 21, 56(1). As to events in institutions, see S. 50.
[37] Ss. 19, 40.
[38] Note, 1949 S.L.T. (News) 95; cf. *Re T.* [1962] 3 W.L.R. 1477; Registration of Births, Deaths, and Marriages (Sc.) Act, 1965, S. 43.
[39] Guardianship Act, 1973, S. 10; Law Reform (Parent and Child) (Sc.) Act, 1986, S. 2.
[40] 1986 Act, S. 2.

An agreement by either to surrender any such rights is unenforceable, save during the parents' separation and even then not if the court is of opinion that it will be for the benefit of the child to give effect to it. If the parents disagree either may apply to the Court of Session or any sheriff court for the court's direction, except in relation to custody or access.

Patria potestas

So long as a child is a pupil, the father had at common law, and now each parent has, the right of custody, and the power and authority to regulate the child's upbringing and discipline and govern its person;[41] this power is diminished but not ended when the pupil child becomes minor,[42] and terminates when the minor child becomes major.[43] During minority the father's authority may be lost by apparent intention to abandon it or by inability or unwillingness to discharge rightly the parental duty towards his child,[44] and in determining such a question the wishes and feelings of the child are entitled to weight.[45] The authority is also lost if the father dies or the child, while minor, is forisfamiliated, i.e. has, with the father's consent, set out on its own by leaving home or taking employment, or, being a daughter, has married.[46]

Older authorities[47] state that the father is entitled to all the profits accruing from children's labour and industry, while they are living in family or maintained by him, but it is questionable if this right would be enforceable today, beyond what is a fair contribution to the expenses of the family home. Donations to children from the father or third parties have always been their own property.[48]

Custody and access

Custody is concerned with control of the physical person of the child only. By virtue of the *nobile officium* the Court of Session has power to deal with all questions of custody,[49] but it and the sheriff court also have power under statute.[50] At common law the father was alone entitled to the custody of a pupil child; the court would in the exercise of its *nobile*

---

[41] Stair I, 5, 13; Ersk. I, 6, 53; Bell, *Prin.* § 1636; *Harvey* v. *H.* (1860) 22 D. 1198; but see *Young* v. *Rankin*, 1934 S.C. 499, 507.
[42] *Fisher* v. *Edgar* (1894) 21 R. 1076; *Greenock* v. *Kilmarnock and Stirling*, 1911 S.C. 570.
[43] The child then becomes *sui juris*.
[44] Stair, *supra*; Ersk. I, 6, 53.
[45] *Harvey, supra; Craig* v. *Greig* (1863) 1 M. 1172.
[46] Erak., *supra*.
[47] Stair I, 5, 8; Ersk. I, 6, 53.
[48] Ersk., *supra*.
[49] *McCallum* v. *McC.* (1893) 20 R. 293; *S.* v. *S.*, 1967 S.C. (H.L.) 46, 51.
[50] Conjugal Rights (Sc.) Amdt. Act, 1861, S. 9; Sheriff Courts (Sc.) Acts, 1907, S. 5; 1913, S. 3; *Brown* v. *B.*, 1948 S.C. 5; *Campbell* v. *C.*, 1956 S.C. 285, 289; cf. *Curran* v. *C.*, 1957 S.L.T. (Notes) 47; *Beverley* v. *B.*, 1977 S.L.T. (Sh. Ct) 3.

officium interfere only if the child's health or morals were in danger.[51] As custodier the father could fix the residence and regulate the upbringing of the child.[52] The court sometimes conferred custody on a factor *loco tutoris* after the father's death rather than leave the child with the mother.[53]

At common law a widowed mother has a legal title to custody, which will usually be enforced against any other custodier.[54] The court has several times refused to give custody of an orphan to a grandparent in preference to leaving him in an institution.[55] The power of the Scottish courts to grant custody is not limited by the fact that the parties are furth of Scotland.[56]

The Guardianship of Children (Scotland) Acts, 1886 to 1973,[57] provide that on all questions of custody or upbringing or administration of any property or application of income thereof the court must regard the welfare of the child as the first and paramount consideration.[58] The claim of the father from any other point of view, is not to be considered.[59] The court may exercise its powers though the parents are living together.[60] Interim custody may be granted pending a consistorial action between the parents.[61]

The Custody of Children (Scotland) Act, 1939, extends the powers of the court to make orders as to the custody, maintenance, or education of, or access to, pupil children, and minor children under 16.[62] After the father's death a minor child can choose his own residence and is not, unless by court order made under statute, subject to regulation as to its person by curators.[63]

---

[51] *A.B.* v. *C.D.* (1847) 10 D. 229; *McIver* v. *M.*(1859) 21 D. 1103; *Harvey* v. *H.* (1859) 22 D. 1198; *Lang* v. *L.* (1869) 7 M. 445; *Nicolson* v. *N.* (1869) 7 M. 1118; *Steuart* v. *S.* (1870) 8 M. 821; *Ketchen* v. *K.* (1870) 8 M. 952; *Symington* v. *S.* (1875) 2 R. (H.L.) 41; 2 R. 974; *Lilley* v. *L.* (1877) 4 R. 397.

[52] Even if he were resident abroad: *Pagan* v. *P.* (1883) 10 R. 1072.

[53] *Gulland* v. *Henderson* (1878) 5 R. 768.

[54] *Macallister* v. *M.*, 1962 S.C. 406.

[55] *Smith* v. *S's Trs* (1890) 18 R. 241; *Flannigan* v. *Bothwell Inspector* (1892) 19 R. 909; *Morrison* v. *Quarrier* (1894) 21 R. 889. Contrast *Low*, 1920 S.C. 351.

[56] *Ponder* v. *P.*, 1932 S.C. 233.

[57] Viz: Guardianship of Infants Acts, 1886 and 1925; Guardianship Act, 1973, Part II. Applicable to legitimate pupil children only: 1886 Act, S. 8; *Brand* v. *Shaw* (1888) 16 R. 315. Extended to children under 16; 1973 Act, S. 10, 13.

[58] 1925 Act, S. 1; *Maquay* v. *Campbell* (1888) 15 R. 606; *Rintoul* v. *R.* (1898) 1 F. 22; *Marchetti* v. *M.* (1901) 3 F. 888; *M.* v. *M.*, 1926 S.C. 778; *Hume* v. *H.*, 1926 S.C. 1008; *Christison* v. *C.*, 1936 S.C. 381; *McLean* v. *McL.*, 1947 S.C. 79; *Brown* v. *B.*, 1948 S.C. 5.

[59] *Sleigh* v. *S.* (1893) 30 S.L.R. 272; *Mackellar* v. *M.* (1898) 25 R. 883; *A.C.* v. *B.C.* (1902) 5 F. 108; *Fairley* v. *F.* (1904) 12 S.L.T. 140; *Campbell* v. *C.*, 1920 S.C. 31.

[60] 1925 Act, S. 3, amd. 1973, Sch. 4.

[61] *Beattie* v. *B.* (1883) 11 R. 85; *McCallum* v. *M.* (1893) 20 R. 293; *Stevenson* v. *S.* (1894) 21 R. (H.L.) 96; *Reid* v. *R.* (1901) 3 F. 330.

[62] In such a case the minor has a right to be heard: *Morrison*, 1943 S.C. 481.

[63] Ersk. I, 7, 14; Bell, *Prin.* s 2090; *Harvey* v. *H.* (1860) 22 D. 1198, 1207; *Flannigan* v. *Bothwell Inspector* (1892) 19 R. 909.

Under all these acts the paramount consideration is the welfare of the child in the whole circumstances of the case.[64] Custody may be regulated pending consistorial proceedings.[65] Factors held to tip the balance in favour of one parent include the provision of a religious upbringing for the child.[66] If considerations of welfare are equally balanced, the father is still preferred.[67] There is no rule that the mother is preferable for a very young child.[68] Where both parents had died the nearest male agnate has been preferred.[69]

In an application under the 1886, 1925, 1939, and 1973 Acts relative to custody, if it appears to the court that there are exceptional circumstances making it impracticable or undesirable for the child to be entrusted to either parent or to anyone else, the court may commit the child to a specified local authority, or award custody to a person but order that the child be under the supervision of a specified local authority, subject to any directions from the court. Any such order lapses when the child attains 16. The parents may be ordered to pay for the child's maintenance.[70] Such an order may be varied or discharged.[71]

Under the Children Act, 1975, S. 47, any relative,[72] step-parent,[73] or foster-parent of a child may be granted custody. Save under the Illegitimate Children (Sc.) Act, 1930, S. 2, a person other than a parent or guardian is not to be granted custody unless

(a) being a relative or step-parent, he has the consent of the parent or guardian and has had care and possession for the three months prior to his application for custody; or

(b) he has the consent of a parent or guardian and has had care and possession for at least twelve months including the three months prior to the application; or

(c) he has had care and possession for at least three years, including the three months prior to the application; or

(d) he can show cause, having regard to the Guardianship of Infants Act, 1925, S. 1, why an order should be made awarding him custody.

An applicant for custody must give notice of his application to each known parent, including the father of an illegitimate child. Such a custody

---

[64] 1925 Act, S. 1. cf. *Zagrodnik* v. *Z.*, 1952 S.C. 258; *Macallister* v. *M.*, 1962 S.C. 406.
[65] *Beattie* v. *B.* (1883) 11 R. 85; *Sleigh* v. *S.* (1893) 30 S.L.R. 272; *Stevenson* v. *S.* (1894) 21 R. (H.L.) 96; *Reid* v. *R.* (1901) 3 F. 330; *B.* v. *B.*, 1907 S.C. 1186.
[66] *Mackay* v. *M.*, 1957 S.L.T. (Notes) 17; *McClements* v. *M.*, 1958 S.C. 286.
[67] *Douglas* v. *D.*, 1950 S.C. 453; *Hannah* v. *H.*, 1971 S.L.T. (Notes) 42.
[68] *Whitecross* v. *W.*, 1977 S.L.T. 225.
[69] *Alexander* v. *McGarrity* (1903) 5 F. 654.
[70] Guardianship Act, 1973, S. 11.
[71] Ibid., S. 12.
[72] e.g. brother: *Morrison* v. *Quarrier* (1894) 21 R. 889; grandparents: *Cochrane* v. *Keys*, 1968 S.L.T. 64; *Klein, Petrs.*, 1969 S.L.T. 53.
[73] cf. *G.* v. *H.*, 1976 S.L.T. (Sh. Ct.) 51.

order may be varied or discharged (S. 48). Notice of an application by a relative, step-parent, or foster-parent must be given to the local authority, which must investigate and report to the court (S. 49). Where custody is awarded to a non-parent, the local authority may make payments towards the child's maintenance (S. 50). There are restrictions on the removal of a child from an applicant for custody if the applicant has provided a home for three years (S. 51). A custody order may be made in favour of an applicant for adoption of the child (S. 53).

Custody of children in separation, nullity, and divorce cases

The Court has jurisdiction in separation, nullity, and divorce cases to regulate the custody, maintenance, and education of any child of the marriage under the age of 16[74] and to decree aliment for such child, liberty being reserved to either party to reapply to the Court on these matters until the date when the child last to attain 16 will do so.[75] The paramount consideration is the welfare of the child or children,[76] and the court will consider the child's wishes, and a child in minority is entitled to be heard on the matter.[77] Accordingly though custody is commonly granted to the innocent party to such proceedings[78] it may be granted to a parent guily of adultery[79] or of desertion.[80] The tender age of a child is a relevant factor, but not conclusive.[81] Where the welfare would be equally regarded, the father still has the superior claim.[82] The court may, in granting decree, declare the culpable spouse unfit to have the custody of the children, and in that event that parent is not entitled to the custody or guardianship of the children as of right on the death of the other.[83] The court may refuse to remove children from the custody of grandparents who have been caring for them.[84]

---

[74] Conjugal Rights (Sc.) Amdt. Act, 1861, S.9; Guardianship of Infants Acts, 1886 and 1925; Custody of Children (Sc.) Act, 1939; Matrimonial Proceedings (Children) Act, 1958. As to jurisdiction see *McShane* v. *M.*, 1962 S.L.T. 221. Under the 1861 Act at least, no order could be made if the court refused separation or divorce: *McArthur* v. *M.*, 1955 S.C. 414; and any order made ceased to apply to each child as it emerged from pupillarity; *Watson* v. *W.* (1895) 23 R. 219.

[75] Where custody was awarded to the mother and she died, it was held incompetent for her parents to apply by minute in the process for custody: *McKenzie*, 1963 S.C. 266; contrast *Smith* v. *S.*, 1964 S.C. 218.

[76] *Symington* v. *S.* (1875) 2 R. (H.L.) 41; *Huddart* v. *H.*, 1961 S.C. 393.

[77] *Morrison* v. *M.*, 1943 S.C. 481.

[78] *Ketchen* v. *K.* (1870) 8 M. 952; *Minto* v. *M.*, 1914 2 S.L.T. 381; *Hume* v. *H.*, 1926 S.C. 1008; *Christison* v. *C.*, 1936 S.C. 381.

[79] *McCurdie* v. *McC.*, 1918 2 S.L.T. 250; *Allan* v. *A.*, 1919 2 S.L.T. 88; *Stewart* v. *S.*, 1914 2 S.L.T. 310; *McCarroll* v. *McC.*, 1937 S.N. 62; *Christie* v. *C.*, 1945 S.L.T. 300; *Johnston* v. *J.*, 1947 S.L.T. (Notes) 26; *Wallace* v. *W.*, 1947 S.L.T. (Notes) 47.

[80] *Gibson* v. *G.* (1894) 2 S.L.T. 71; *Maclean* v. *M.*, 1947 S.C. 79.

[81] *Christison* v. *C.*, 1936 S.C. 381; *McLean, supra; Brown* v. *B.*, 1948 S.C. 5.

[82] *Mackellar* v. *M.* (1898) 25 R. 883.

[83] 1886 Act, S. 7.

[84] *Pow* v. *P.*, 1931 S.L.T. 485; contrast *Klein* v. *K.*, 1969 S.L.T. (Notes) 53.

By the Matrimonial Proceedings (Children) Act, 1958,[85] the power of the court to deal with custody, maintenance, and education applies also[86] in relation to an illegitimate child of both parties,[87] or to the child of one party (including an illegitimate or adopted child) who has been accepted as one of the family by the other party.[88] The court is not to grant divorce, nullity, or separation unless and until satisfied that arrangements have been made for care and upbringing of each child which are satisfactory or are the best which can be devised in the circumstances, or that it is impracticable for the parties appearing to make any such arrangements. Exceptionally the court may grant decree on an undertaking by the parties to bring the arrangements for the children before the court within a specified time.[89] The court may also make provision for custody and maintenance where an action is dismissed or the defender assoilzied,[90] or where one spouse has not obtempered a decree of adherence[91] and may commit the care of a child to a local authority or another person.[92] Probation officers or other persons may be appointed to report on the child's circumstances and the proposed arrangements for its care and upbringing,[93] and a probation officer or local authority may be appointed to supervise a child which is in the care of any person.[94] The court may prohibit removal of a child furth of Scotland or out of the control of a person having custody of it,[95] but may allow the parent having custody to emigrate with the child.[96] There is power to entrust custody to a person other than a parent[97] and one parent may be given *de jure* custody and the other *de facto* custody.[98] The child's views may be taken into account.[99] Access may be regulated though custody is not in issue.[1] All orders may subsequently be varied or revoked. The court may in its discretion allow a third party to lodge a minute in the divorce process relating to the custody of the children.[2]

---

[85] Ss. 7–15.

[86] S. 7.

[87] e.g. a child of a void marriage, not being a putative marriage.

[88] e.g. child by one spouse's previous marriage. Despite denial of such acceptance, the court has awarded a wife interim aliment under this section: *Hart v. H.*, 1960 S.L.T. (Notes) 33; 1961 S.L.T. (Notes) 14.

[89] S. 8.

[90] Overruling *Pringle v. P.*, 1953 S.L.T. (Notes) 49; *McArthur v. McA.*, 1955 S.C. 414. The court has no jurisdiction where a nullity petition is dismissed before proof on the merits: *Gall v. G.*, 1968 S.C. 333.

[91] S. 9; *Driffel v. D.*, 1971 S.L.T. (Notes) 60.

[92] S. 10.

[93] S. 11; *MacIntyre v. M.*, 1962 S.L.T. (Notes) 70; only the court may invoke S. 11; *Wallace v. W.*, 1963 S.C. 256.

[94] S. 12.

[95] S. 13.

[96] *Johnson v. Francis*, 1982 S.L.T. 285.

[97] S. 14 (2); *S. v. S.*, 1967 S.C. (H.L.) 46.

[98] *Robertson v. R.*, 1981 S.L.T. (Notes) 7.

[99] *Fowler v. F.*, 1981 S.L.T. (Notes) 9.

[1] S. 14(2); *Huddart v. H.*, 1960 S.C. 300 (sequel 1961 S.C. 393).

[2] *Smith v. S.*, 1964 S.L.T. 309. Such a minute was incompetent where divorce has been

Where the court has jurisdiction under the Domicile and Matrimonial Proceedings Act, 1973, in a matrimonial dispute it also has jurisdiction to deal with ancillary matters such as custody.[3]

Access

The parent not having or refused custody is normally entitled to reasonable access to the child, by agreement or by order of the court.[4] But the court may decline to allow access if the parent's circumstances, character, or conduct render this undesirable in the child's interests.[5] Access may be granted to a person other than the parent refused custody,[6] and an application for access can be dealt with whether custody is raised or not.[7]

Children in the custody of third parties

A parent or parents may entrust custody to a third party and at common law the father, having the preferable right, could reclaim custody unless he were manifestly unsuitable.[8] By the Custody of Children Act, 1891, the Court of Session[9] may (S. 1) refuse to make an order for the production of a child by a third-party[10] custodier if of opinion that the parent applying has abandoned or deserted the child or so conducted himself that the court should refuse to enforce his right to custody.[11] If it makes a delivery order under the 1891 Act the court may (S. 2) require the petitioner to repay to the custodier money spent on rearing the child.[12]

granted, and the party granted custody has died; *Sutherland* v. *S.*, 1959 S.L.T. (Notes) 61; *McKenzie* v. *McK.*, 1963 S.C. 266; see now R.C. 166(b); *Copeland* v. *C.*, 1969 S.L.T. (Notes) 70.
   [3] *Lyndon* v. *L.*, 1978 S.L.T. (Notes) 7.
   [4] *A.* v. *B.*, (1870) 7 S.L.R. 276; *Symington* v. *S.* (1875) 2 R. (H.L.) 41; 2 R. 976; *Lilley* v. *L.* (1877) 4 R. 397; *Mackenzie* v. *M.* (1881) 8 R. 574; *Bloe* v. *B.* (1882) 9 R. 894; *Bowman* v. *Graham* (1883) 10 R. 1234; *Mackenzie* v. *M.* (1887) 25 S.L.R. 183; *Mackellar* v. *M.* (1898) 25 R. 883; *C.D.* v. *A.B.* (*Kiegler* v. *Hamilton*) 1908 S.C. 737; *McLean* v. *McL.*, 1947 S.C. 79; *Murray* v. *M.*, 1947 S.N. 102. The parent having custody should encourage the children to accept access by the other parent: *Blance* v. *B.*, 1978 S.L.T. 74; *Cosh* v. *C.*, 1979 S.L.T. (Notes) 72; *Brannigan* v. *B.*, 1979 S.L.T. (Notes) 73.
   [5] *McAllister* v. *McA.*, 1947 S.N. 41; *Urquhart* v. *U.*, 1961 S.L.T. (Notes) 56; *Gray* v. *G.*, 1961 S.L.T. (Notes) 83; *Gover* v. *G.*, 1969 S.L.T. (Notes) 78.
   [6] *McCallum* v. *McDonald* (1853) 14 D. 535; *S.* v. *S.*, 1967 S.C. (H.L.) 46.
   [7] *Huddart* v. *H.*, 1960 S.C. 300; *S.* v. *S.*, *supra*, 52.
   [8] *Russell* (1873) 10 S.L.R. 314; *Leys* v. *L.* (1886) 13 R. 1223; *Markey* v. *Colston* (1888) 15 R. 921; *Smith* v. *S's Trs.* (1840) 18 R. 241; *Moncrieff* (1891) 18 R. 1029; *Edgar* v. *Fisher's Trs.* (1893) 21 R. 59; *Fisher* v. *Edgar* (1893) 21 R. 1076. Similarly tutors-nominate under the father's will may claim custody of children from other relatives: *Hogan* v. *McCrossan* (1899) 7 S.L.T. 22. A widowed mother has a primary right to custody in a question with the child's half-sister, subject to the best interests of the child: *Macallister* v. *M.*, 1962 S.C. 406.
   [9] *Campbell* v. *C.*, 1956 S.C. 285; cf. *Mackenzie* v. *Keillor* (1892) 19 R. 963; *Murray* v. *Forsyth*, 1917 S.C. 721; *McLean* v. *Hardie*, 1927 S.C. 344.
   [10] *Murray*, *supra*; *Campbell*, *supra*; *Macallister* v. *M.*, 1962 S.C. 406.
   [11] *Campbell* v. *Croall* (1895) 22 R. 869; *Mitchell* v. *Wright* (1905) 7 F. 568; *McLean* v. *Hardie*, 1927 S.C. 344; *Begbie* v. *Nichol*, 1949 S.C. 158.
   [12] *Soutar* v. *Carrie* (1894) 21 R. 1050; *Begbie* v. *Nichol*, 1949 S.C. 158.

The Court is not (S. 3) to make an order for delivery of a child to a parent if the parent has abandoned or deserted his child or allowed it to be brought up by another at the latter's expense for so long and under such circumstances as to satisfy the Court that the parent was unmindful of his parental duties.[13] If it refuses to order delivery the court may make an order to ensure that the child is brought up in the religion which the parent wishes (S. 4). The welfare of the child, in the whole circumstances of the case, is the paramount consideration of the court.[14]

Enforcement

Orders for the delivery of custody of a child must be obeyed under pain of being in contempt of court. The court may grant warrant to messengers-at-arms to take the child,[15] or to search for and recover the child,[16] and impose imprisonment,[17] or sequestration of estates[18] on the contumacious party. Interdict may be granted against an attempt to remove the child from Scotland.[19]

Divestiture of custody

Where on the trial of an offence under the Sexual Offences (Scotland) Act, 1976, it is proved that the seduction or prostitution of a girl under 16 has been caused, encouraged, or favoured by her parent, guardian, master, or mistress, the court may divest such person of all authority over her and appoint any person or persons willing to take charge of such girl to be her guardian till she is 21, or less as the court may direct. The order may be rescinded or varied by the court.[20]

International child abduction

The Child Abduction and Custody Act, 1985, gives effect to an international convention designed to limit removal of children to other countries.[21]

---

[13] cf. *Gillan* v. *Barony Parish* (1898) 1 F. 183; *Gibson* v. *Hagen*, 1960 S.L.T. (Notes) 24; *Macallister, supra.*
[14] *Fenwick* v. *Hannah's Trs.* (1893) 20 R. 848; *Campbell* v. *Croall* (1895) 22 R. 869; *Alexander* v. *McGarrity* (1903) 5 F. 654; *Pow* v. *P.*, 1931 S.L.T. 485; *Nicol* v. *N.*, 1953 S.L.T. (Notes) 68; *Macallister, supra.*
[15] *Hutchison* v. *H.* (1890) 18 R. 237; *Low*, 1920 S.C. 351.
[16] *Guthrie* v. *G.* (1906) 8 F. 545. The police cannot be ordered to assist: *Caldwell* v. *C.*, 1983 S.C. 137.
[17] *Muir* v. *Milligan* (1868) 6 M. 1125; *Leys* v. *L.* (1886) 13 R. 1223.
[18] *Ross* v. *R.* (1885) 12 R. 1351; *Edgar* v. *Fisher's Trs.* (1893) 21 R. 59, 325; *Fisher* v. *Edgar* (1894) 21 R. 1076.
[19] *Robertson*, 1911 S.C. 1319; cf. *Lumsden* (1882) 20 S.L.R. 240.
[20] 1976 Act, S. 11 (4–5).
[21] cf. *Kilgour* v. *K.*, 1987 S.L.T. 568.

Management of legitimate children's legal affairs

At common law the father was by natural right the tutor and administrator in law of his pupil child and as such managed the pupil's property and acted for him in all legal transactions.[22] When the child became a minor the father became curator, and the child then managed his own property and transacted legally, but with the father's consent and concurrence, unless forisfamiliated, when he might act alone.[23] The curatory terminated when the child became adult, unless the child was bodily or mentally incapax; if a daughter married while a minor the curatory devolved on her husband so long as she remained a minor.[24]

Failing the father, the mother was, by statute,[25] guardian, alone, or jointly with any guardian appointed by the father or by the Court,[26] but her power of administration terminated when the child became a minor; she did not, as mother, automatically become curatrix, nor might she nominate a curator. She might be appointed curatrix by the father's will, and a minor might by petition have his mother appointed as curatrix, in which case she was not subject to the Accountant of Court, nor obliged to find caution.[27]

Since the Guardianship Act, 1973, S. 10, a mother now has the same rights and authority as the father and can hold the offices of tutor or curator, and the rights of each parent are equal and exercisable by either alone. In case of disagreement the court may give directions.

A parent may, appoint guardians of a pupil or minor child in writing after the death of the parents.[28]

Where a conflict of interest arises the court may appoint a factor *loco tutoris* to supersede the parent as a pupil's guardian.[29]

A third party making a gift or bequest to a minor may make it exclusive of the father's administration, nominating a curator for the purpose; if no curator is named, the court may appoint a curator other than the father.[30] Where the child has a claim against the father, the court will appoint a curator *ad litem* to advise in the suit.[31]

---

[22] cf. *Dumbreck* v. *Stevenson* (1861) 4 Macq. 86; *Murray's Trs.* v. *Bloxsom's Trs.* (1887) 15 R. 233.
[23] Ersk. I, 6, 54; Bell, *Prin.* § 2068.
[24] Ersk., *supra*; Married Women's Property (Sc.) Act, 1920, S. 2.
[25] Guardianship of Infants Act, 1925, S. 4. ('Infant' is defined as pupil.) *Willison* (1890) 18 R. 228. She was not disqualified by remarriage: *Campbell* v. *Macquay* (1888) 15 R. 784.
[26] *Martin* v. *Stewart* (1888) 16 R. 185; such an appointment fell on the mother's death, but the tutor has a right and interest to see that a suitable successor is appointed: *Fraser* (1893) 1 S.L.T. 126.
[27] *Maclean, Petr.*, 1956 S.L.T. (Sh. Ct.) 90.
[28] Law Reform (Parent and Child) (Sc.) Act, 1986, S. 4, replacing Guardianship of Infants Act, 1925, S. 5.
[29] *Mann* (1851) 14 D. 12; *Cochrane* (1891) 18 R. 456; *Balfour Melville* (1903) 5 F. 347.
[30] *Robertson* (1865) 3 M. 1077.
[31] Ersk. I, 6, 54.

Powers of parent as tutor

A parent acting as tutor of a pupil at common law or under the Guardianship of Children (Scotland) Acts, 1886 to 1973, is deemed a trustee within the meaning of the Trusts (Scotland) Acts, 1921 and 1961.[32] In the ordinary case he need not find caution,[33] but exceptionally the court may require him to do so, or appoint a factor *loco tutoris*.[34] The pupil may hold property but has no capacity to transact legally and all legal powers are vested in the parent as tutor for behoof of the child. A parent as tutor has power to sue[35] and be sued, to grant a valid discharge of damages paid for the pupil's behoof,[36] and to compromise an action without the court's authority.[37] He may sell the pupil's heritage,[38] or feu it.[39] The court may, on application, grant special powers deemed necessary.[40]

Powers of parent as curator

As curator a parent has no power to deal with the minor's estate, but only the power of consenting to the minor's own transactions therewith. Even if the parent withholds consent that does not nullify or invalidate the minor's actings.[41] The curator is guardian of the estate, not of the minor's person.[42] As curator, the parent cannot compel the minor to take any step, nor to refrain; if the minor be obstinate he may act alone,[43] but deeds by the curator alone are null.[44] The minor's powers of administration, with or without his curator's consent, are unlimited, but all actings are voidable at any time within four years of majority, on proof of minority and lesion.[45] If the parent declines to concur or has an adverse

[32] 1925 Act, S. 10.
[33] Ersk. I, 6, 54; Bell, *Prin.* § 2068.
[34] Bell, *Prin., supra; Stevenson's Trs.* v. *Dumbreck* (1859) 19 D. 462; 4 Macq. 86; *Cochrane* (1891) 18 R. 456.
[35] e.g. *Davis's Tutor* v. *Glasgow Victoria Hospitals*, 1950 S.C. 382. As to expenses see *White* v. *Steel* (1894) 21 R. 649. If the parent is dead: *Ward* v. *Walker*, 1920 S.C. 80; or refuses to sue, the court may appoint a curator *ad litem: McConochie* v. *Dinnie* (1847) 9 D. 791; *Kirk* v. *Scoittish Gas Board*, 1969 S.C. 328.
[36] *Jack* v. *N.B. Ry. Co.* (1886) 14 R. 263.
[37] *Gow* v. *Henry* (1899) 2 F. 48; *Murphy* v. *Smith*, 1920 S.C. 104.
[38] *Logan* (1897) 25 R. 51. Authority of the court is not now requisite in cases within the Trusts Acts; see *Ferrier's Tutrix*, 1925 S.C. 571; *Dempster*, 1926 S.L.T. 157; *Cunningham's Tutrix*, 1949 S.C. 275, explaining *Linton* v. *I.R.*, 1928 S.C. 209.
[39] *Lord Clinton* (1875) 3 R. 62; *Campbell* (1880) 7 R. 1032; *Shearer*, 1924 S.C. 445.
[40] *Hamilton's Tutors*, 1924 S.C. 364; *Brunton*, 1928 S.N. 112.
[41] See further, *infra*.
[42] Bell, *Prin.* § 2090, 2096.
[43] *Stevenson* v. *Adair* (1872) 10 M. 919.
[44] Bell, *Prin.* § 2096.
[45] See further, *infra*.

interest a curator *ad litem* may be appointed. A father as curator is entitled to advise his child against risking a contemplated marriage, and is not liable in damages for preventing it, unless he acted maliciously.[46] A father as curator who takes an active part in litigation on behalf of the minor may render himself liable for expenses.[47]

Aliment

Each parent is bound to aliment his or her child, including a child who has been accepted as a member of the family, i.e. to provide such support as is reasonable in the circumstances, having regard to the needs and resources of the parties, the earning capacity of the parties, and to all the circumstances of the case including any support, financial or otherwise, given by the defender to any person whom he maintains as a dependant in his household, whether or not he owes an obligation of aliment to that person and excluding any conduct of a party unless it would be manifestly inequitable to leave it out of account. A 'child' is a person under 18 or over 18 and under 25 who is reasonably and appropriately undergoing instruction at an educational establishment or training for employment for a trade, profession, or vocation.[48] Where two or more parties owe the obligation, there is no order of liability, but the court must have regard to the circumstances, including an obligation of aliment by any other person.[49] The obligation is normally discharged by maintaining the child in a family home, but may be discharged by making an allowance for the child's support.[50] If not done in either way, the parent will be liable to persons who supply the child with necessaries.[51]

A claim for aliment may be brought by action, or in proceedings for divorce, separation, declarator of marriage, or of nullity of marriage, concerning rights and obligations in relation to children, concerning parentage or legitimacy, or of any other kind. Claims may also be brought by the curator of an incapax minor, or on behalf of a child under 18 by either parent, a pupil's tutor, or a person entitled to, seeking, or having custody or care of a child. A claim may be brought even though the claimant is living in the same household as the defender.[52] A woman, whether married or not, may claim aliment on behalf of her unborn child, but no such claim is to be disposed of prior to the child's birth.[52] The

---

[46] *Findlay* v. *Blaylock*, 1937 S.C. 21.
[47] *Rodger* v. *Weir*, 1917 S.C. 300.
[48] Family Law (Sc.) Act, 1985, Ss. 1, 4(1).
[49] Ibid., S. 4(2).
[50] *Ketchen* v. *K.* (1871) 9 M. 690; *Whyte* v. *W.* (1901) 3 F. 937.
[51] Stair I, 5, 7; Ersk. I, 6, 57.
[52] Family Law (Sc.) Act, 1985, S. 2.

court may order periodical payments, or alimentary payments of an occasional or special nature, but not a lump sum, and may backdate the award.[53] A decree may be varied or recalled.[54]

A claim may also be brought for interim aliment in various actions on behalf of the claimant and any person on whose behalf he is entitled to act.[55]

The parent may discharge his obligation in the way least burdensome to himself, and meet a claim for aliment by an offer to maintain the child in family, unless his conduct to the child has been such as to forfeit this alternative.[56] The court is much less willing to award aliment to a child who has completed education and training than to one who has not, unless the child's need is due to physical or mental incapacity or inability to obtain suitable employment.[57]

On the parent's death a child in need of aliment has a claim against the parent's representatives, postponed to ordinary creditors but preferred to special and general legatees.[8] If the parent has left legacies to the children their aliment must be paid in the first instance from their own income therefrom.[59] But if the parent's estate has passed chiefly to one child, the inheritance carries with it the parent's liability to aliment the other children, so far as *lucratus* by the succession, and in such a case one child may claim aliment from another, *jure representationis* as representing the parent.[60] There is no such claim where all children have succeeded equally.[61] This liability by representation may extend to the representatives of grandparents,[62] certainly where the more distant relative has acknowledged the obligation during his lifetime.[63] A posthumous child has been held entitled to aliment out of the father's trust estate.[64]

Where a child is infirm or incapax, the father's executors or trustees are not bound to set aside funds for that child's maintenance beyond the legal share due to him on the father's death, but may distribute the estate, the other children being bound to give their undertakings to provide for the

---

[53] Ibid., S. 3.
[54] Ibid., S. 5.
[55] Ibid., S. 6.
[56] Ersk. I, 6, 56; Bell. *Prin.* s 1630; *Smith, supra; Westlands v. Pirie* (1887) 14 R. 763; *Bell v. B.* (1890) 17 R. 549.
[57] Ersk., *supra; Reid v. Moir* (1866) 4 M. 1060; *Smith, supra; Watson v. W.*, (1896) 33 S.L.R. 771; *Whyte v. W.* (1901) 3 F. 937; *McKay v. McKay*, 1980 S.L.T. (Sh. Ct.) 111.
[58] *Ker's Trs. v. K.*, 1927 S.C. 52; see also *Hutcheson v. Hoggan's Trs.* (1904) 6 F. 594; Family Law (Sc.) Act, 1985, S. 1.
[59] *Ker's Trs., supra.*
[60] Fraser, *P. & Ch.* 128; *Mackintosh v. Taylor* (1868) 7 M. 67; *Davidson's Trs. v. D.*, 1907 S.C. 16; *Beaton v. B's Trs.*, 1935 S.C. 187; *Hutchison v. H's Trs.*, 1951 S.C. 108; cf *Stevenson v. McDonald's Trs.*, 1923 S.L.T. 451; 1985 Act, S. 1(4).
[61] Fraser, *P. & Ch.* 129; *Beaton, supra.*
[62] Ersk. I, 6, 58; *Spalding v. S's Trs.* (1874) 2 R. 237; *Anderson v. Grant* (1899) 1 F. 484; *Gay's Tutrix v. G's Tr.*, 1953 S.L.T. 278.
[63] *Leslie Parish Council v. Gibson's Trs.* (1899) 1 F. 601.
[64] *Spalding v. S's Trs.* (1874) 2 R. 237.

maintenance of the incapax child.[65] If the child has independent estate the mother certainly,[66] and now even the father, despite the greater duty incumbent on him,[67] may claim reimbursement from the income or capital of that estate. No repayment could formerly be claimed from capital without a contract with the child or his tutor,[68] but there is now no absolute rule forbidding this,[69] though the acquisition of property by the child does not justify a claim for reimbursement of past outlays.[70] A father who has been alimenting his son has no right of recovery against the son's wife.[71]

A father is not obliged to aliment his daughter-in-law,[72] nor a step-mother her step-son,[73] nor a son-in-law his father-in-law,[74] or mother-in-law.[75]

Under the Supplementary Benefits Act, 1976,[76] for the purposes of that Act each parent is liable to maintain his or her spouse and children; the Supplementary Benefits officers may recover from persons liable to maintain the cost of assistance given to an indigent child.[77] It is an offence wilfully to neglect a child of which one has custody.[78]

Where spouses are judicially separated or divorced the wife, if awarded custody, is normally also awarded aliment for the children in her charge, for whose aliment the husband remains primarily liable.[79] The amount of aliment may be altered on change of circumstances.[80] The aliment may be ordered to be paid directly to the child via the custodial parent as *curatrix* or *tutrix*[81].

---

[65] *Mackintosh v. Taylor* (1868) 7 M. 67; *Howard's Exor. v. H's C.B.* (1894) 21 R. 787; *McKenna v. Ferguson* (1894) 1 S.L.T. 599; *Davidson's Trs. v. D.*, 1907 S.C. 16; *Edinburgh Parish Council v. Couper*, 1924 S.C. 139; cf. *Hutchison v. H's Trs.*, 1951 S.C. 108.

[66] *Baird v. B's Trs.* (1872) 10 M. 482; *Douglas v. D's Trs.* (1872) 10 M. 943; *Christie v. C's Trs.* (1877) 4 R. 620; *Fairgrieves v. Henderson* (1885) 13 R. 98; *Ker's Trs. v. K.*, 1927 S.C. 52; see also *Ross v. R.* (1896) 23 R. (H.L.) 67.

[67] *Edmiston v. Miller's Trs.* (1871) 9 M. 987; *Stewart's Trs. v. S.* (1871) 8 S.L.R. 367; *Duke of Sutherland* (1901) 3 F. 761; *Hutcheson v. Hoggan's Trs.* (1904) 6 F. 594; *Ker's Trs., supra*; *Polland v. Sturrock's Exors.*, 1952 S.C. 535.

[68] *Galt v. Boyd* (1830) 8 S. 332; *Milne* (1888) 15 R. 437.

[69] *Polland v. Sturrock's Exors.*, 1952 S.C. 535.

[70] *Fraser, P. & Ch.*, 119.

[71] *Fingzies v. F.* (1890) 28 S.L.R. 6; see now Married Women's Property (Sc.) Act, 1920, S.4.

[72] *Hoseason v. H.* (1870) 9 M. 37; *Reid v. R.* (1904) 6F. 935; *Mackay v. M's Trs.* (1904) 6 F. 936.

[73] *Macdonald v. M.* (1846) 8 D. 830; *Barty's Trs. v. B.* (1888) 15 R. 496.

[74] *Dear v. Duncan* (1896) 3 S.L.T. 241.

[75] *McAllan v. Alexander* (1888) 15 R. 863.

[76] S. 17; cf. *Corcoran v. Muir*, 1954 J.C. 46; *Supplementary Benefits Commission v. Higgins*, 1980 S.L.T. (Sh. Ct.) 20.

[77] Parents' liability is joint and several: *N. A. Board v. Casey*, 1967 S.L.T. (Sh. Ct.) 11.

[78] Children and Young Persons (Sc.) Act, 1937, Ss. 12, 27; *Henderson v. Stewart*, 1954 J.C. 94.

[79] *Foxwell v. Robertson* (1900) 2 F. 932; *Matthew v. M.*, 1926 S.L.T. 723; *Dickinson v. D.*, 1952 S.C. 27.

[80] *Hay v. H.* (1882) 9 R. 667; *Rowat v. R.* (1904) 12 S.L.T. 449; *Maitland v. M.*, 1912 1 S.L.T. 350; *Melvin v. M.*, 1918 2 S.L.T. 209; *Dickinson, supra*.

[81] *Huggins v. H.*, 1981 S.L.T. 179.

Parents' claim against children

Parents who are obliged to aliment a child now have no corresponding claim against their children who are capable of contributing, to be supported and alimented by them in case of need.[82]

Education

Parents are obliged to provide education for their children, normally by ensuring attendance at a local authority or other school till at least the minimum school-leaving age.[83] An education authority is bound to consider but not necessarily to give effect to the wishes of a parent as to which school a child is to attend.[84] At common law the father has the main right to regulate the children's education.[85] A parent is guilty of an offence if the child fails to attend regularly at public school.[86] There is no legal obligation to provide better or further education than that required by statute.[87]

Religious upbringing

Formerly the father had the prior right to dictate in what religion the child was to be brought up.[88] Since the Guardianship of Infants Act, 1925, the parents have equal rights in the matter,[89] and the court has refused to disturb a widow's arrangements for upbringing at the request of the nearest male agnates.[90] The parents' views, though weighty, are not conclusive on the matter.[91] Where the father was an atheist, the court has awarded custody to a mother, though guilty of adultery, on the ground that a child should during its formative years have the opportunity of a religious upbringing.[92] Under the Custody of Children Act, 1891, S. 4, if the court refuses a parent custody, it may make an order to secure that the child be brought up in the religion in which the parent has a legal right that the child be brought up. The child's wishes may be consulted and if old enough to do so, it may exercise its own free choice.

[82] Family Law (Sc.) Act, 1985, S. 1.
[83] Education (Sc.) Act, 1962, S. 31. see *Brown* v. *Lothian R.C.*, 1980 S.L.T. (Sh. Ct.) 14. *Edwards* v. *Lothian R.C.*, 1988 S.L.T. (Sh. Ct.) 107; 1981 S.L.T. (Sh. Ct.) 41.
[84] *Sinclair* v. *Lothian R.C.*, 1981 S.L.T. (Sh. Ct.) 13.
[85] *Pagan* v. *P.* (1883) 10 R. 1072.
[86] Ibid., S. 35–6; 1949 Act, S. 5; 1956 Act, S. 3, 13(1).
[87] Bell, *Prin.* § 1635, 2083.
[88] *O'Donnell* v. *O'D.*, 1919 S.C. 14.
[89] cf. *Re Collins* [1950] Ch. 498; *Barr* v. *B.*, 1950 S.L.T. (Notes) 15; *Zamorski* v. *Z.*, 1960 S.L.T. (Notes) 26.
[90] *Kincaid* v. *Quarrier* (1896) 23 R. 676; *Murray* v. *Maclay* (1903) 6 F. 160.
[91] *Morrison* v. *Quarrier* (1894) 21 R. 1071; *Reilly* v. *Quarrier* (1895) 22 R. 879.
[92] *McClements* v. *M.*, 1958 S.C. 286; see also *Mackay* v. *M.*, 1957 S.L.T. (Notes) 17.

Other relations between parent and child

There is no bar to contractual relations between parent and child, though such a transaction may be reduced if it be shown that the parent had exercised undue influence on the child.[93] Parent may sue child[94] and conversely[95] for damages for delict. The parent is not automatically liable for the child's delicts, but may be if he authorized or ratified them, or if the child were acting at the time as his agent or servant in the course of his employment.

Children's obligations inter se

Children have no legal liability to look after or aliment each other,[96] except in the case where, *jure repraesentationis*, one or more children have inherited the whole or the major part of the father's estate and another child is unable is earn, in which case those who inherit take the estate under burden of alimenting those whom the deceased was under a natural obligation to aliment.[97] This liability subsists until the child not provided for attains majority or, if a girl, marries under that age, or becomes able to earn his own livelihood.

Children have full liberty of transacting legally one with another as if with third parties.

ILLEGITIMATE CHILDREN

Illegitimate children

A natural, illegitimate, or bastard child is one born to a woman who was not at the time of its conception or of its birth or at any time between validly married to the father of the child, or was joined to him in a union deemed legally null.[98] If a man marries a woman who is, to his knowledge pregnant, and there had been opportunities for premarital intercourse, the child is deemed his and legitimate.[99] The relationship between a father and his bastard child is not in any proper civil sense that of parent and child. A bastard is in law *filius nullius*.[1] A bastard child was

---

[93] *Smith Cunninghame* v. *Anstruther's Trs.* (1872) 10 M. (H.L.) 39; *Gray* v. *Binny* (1879) 7 R. 332; *Menzies* v. *M.* (1893) 20 R. (H.L.) 108; *Allan* v. *A.*, 1961 S.C. 200.
[94] *Wood* v. *W.*, 1935 S.L.T. 431.
[95] *Young* v. *Rankin*, 1934 S.C. 499.
[96] Stair I, 5, 10; *Greenhorn* v. *Addie* (1855) 17 D. 860; *Eisten* v. *N.B. Ry.* (1870) 8 M. 980.
[97] Stair, *supra*; Ersk. I, 6, 58; Bell, *Prin.* § 1632; Fraser, *P. & Ch.*, 128; *Marshall* v. *Gourley* (1836) 15 S. 313; *Stuart* v. *Court* (1848) 10 D. 1275; *Mackintosh* v. *Taylor* (1868) 7 M. 67; *Beaton* v. *B's Trs.*, 1935 S.C. 187; *Hutchison* v. *H's Trs.*, 1951 S.C. 108 (adopted child).
[98] Stair III, 3, 43–6; Ersk. I, 6, 51; Bell, *Prin.* § 2058–63.
[99] *Gardner* v. *G.* (1877) 4 R. (H.L.) 56; *Reid* v. *Mill* (1879) 6 R. 659; *Kerrs* v. *Lindsay* (1890) 18 R. 365.
[1] *Corrie* v. *Adair* (1860) 22 D. 897; *Silver* v. *Walker*, 1938 S.C. 595.

entitled at common law to none of the civil rights conferred on legitimate children, but this position has been alleviated by statute. In case of doubt or dispute the child's status must be determined by a declarator of legitimacy,[2] or of bastardy.[3] With the latter may be combined a conclusion putting the defender to silence as to the child's legitimacy.[4]

Foundlings

A living child found exposed, in default of discovery of its parentage, must be deemed illegitimate.[5]

Child of rape

A child conceived by an unmarried woman in consequence of rape is illegitimate,[6] proof thereof being relevant to rebut the presumption *pater est* in the case of a married woman.[7]

Name

An illegitimate child is normally given a christian name and the mother's surname. Where the mother of a bastard proposed to adopt it and give it the name of her late husband who was not the child's father, it was held permissible with the consent of the late husband's relatives.[8]

Registration

An illegitimate child's birth must be registered in the same way as a legitimate one, but the registrar may not register on information supplied by the father alone, nor enter the name of any person as the father unless at the joint request of both parents, in which case the father must attend personally and sign as informant along with the mother. The mother must produce a declaration stating that a particular person is the father and a statutory declaration by him acknowledging himself to be the father. Where the name of the father has not been registered, it may be recorded in the Register of Corrections if decree of paternity has been granted, or

---

[2] e.g. *Tennent* v. *T.* (1890) 17 R. 1205.

[3] The woman's husband must rebut the presumption *pater est quem nuptiae demonstrant.* e.g. *Smith* v. *Dick* (1869) 8 M. 31; *Steedman* v. *S.* (1887) 14 R. 1066; *Whitehall* v. *W.*, 1958 S.C. 252; *Imre* v. *Mitchell*, 1958 S.C. 439; *S.* v. *S.*, 1977 S.L.T. (Notes) 65.

[4] *Imre, supra.*

[5] As to registration of its birth see Registration of Births, etc. (Sc.) Act, 1965, Ss. 15 and 20(1)(b).

[6] cf. *H.M.* v. *W.M.* (1953) 69 Sh. Ct. Rep. 271.

[7] cf. *Black* v. *Duncan*, 1924 S.C. 738.

[8] *Mrs. C. Cn. or Cl.*, 1951 S.L.T. (Sh. Ct.) 83.

declarations are produced by both parents, or, where the mother is dead, he is ordered to do so by the sheriff on application by the father. Where paternity has been established by decree, notice of the import of the decree is sent to the Registrar-General.[9] An abbreviated birth certificate may be obtained containing no mention of parentage.[10]

Determination of paternity

Where paternity is doubtful or disputed,[11] and in order to obtain a contribution to its aliment, and to her inlying expenses, the mother may bring an action of affiliation and aliment against the alleged father.[12] Decree in such an action does not affect the status of the child as illegitimate.[13] A married woman may bring such an action against a man other than her husband, but must discharge the heavy onus of rebutting the presumption *pater est quem nuptiae demonstrant*.[14] A pregnant unmarried woman may bring an action of affiliation and aliment against the alleged father at any time before the child's birth if she produces medical evidence that she is pregnant and evidence sufficient to satisfy the court that the defender is the father, but no declarator of paternity may be pronounced for payment until after the birth, save that if the action is undefended or paternity admitted, the court may before birth grant decree for a payment to account of inlying expenses, and for periodical payments of aliment from the date of birth, and may subsequently grant decree for a further payment for inlying expenses, and review or alter the sums decerned for as aliment.[15]

If the mother has died an action of affiliation and aliment may be brought by the bastard child through its tutor.[16]

In establishing paternity there is frequently *penuria testium*;[17] inferences may be drawn from evidence of courtship about the time of

---

[9] Registration of Births, Deaths, and Marriages (Sc.) Act, 1965, S. 18.

[10] 1965 Act, S. 19.

[11] As to blood test evidence see *Sproat* v. *McGibney*, 1968 S.L.T. 33; *Docherty* v. *McGlynn*, 1985 S.L.T. 237.

[12] Such an action is one for debt and not a declarator of status: *Silver* v. *Walker*, 1938 S.C. 595. The rate of aliment is in the court's discretion and was held not limited by the Affiliation Orders Act, 1952, S. 1 which was held not to apply to Scotland: *Halkett* v. *McSkeane*, 1962 S.L.T. (Sh. Ct.) 59.

[13] cf. *McDonald* v. *Ross*, 1929 S.C. 240, 249.

[14] cf. *Lepper* v. *Brown* (1802) Hume 488; *Aitken* v. *Mitchell* (1806) Hume 489; *Routledge* v. *Carruthers* (1816) 4 Dow 392; *Jobson* v. *Reid* (1827) 5 S. 715; (1830) 8 S. 343; *Mackay* v. *M.* (1855) 17 D. 494; *Brodie* v. *Dyce* (1872) 11 M. 142; *McLachlan* v. *Lewis*, 1925 S.C. 886; *Imre* v. *Mitchell*, 1958 S.C. 439.

[15] Family Law (Sc.) Act, 1985, S. 2. As to right of appeal, see *McDonald* v. *Ross*, 1929 S.C. 240. On factors relevant to expenses and aliment see *Freer* v. *Taggart*, 1975 S.L.T. (Sh. Ct.) 13. Aliment runs from the date of birth: *Findlay* v. *Pallys*, 1977 S.L.T. (Sh. Ct.) 13.

[16] *Robertson* v. *Hutchison*, 1935 S.C. 708.

[17] On evidence generally see *Young* v. *Nicol* (1893) 20 R. 768.

conception,[18] opportunities,[19] familiarities,[20] and suspicious circumstances.[21] If the defender admits intercourse prior to that alleged to have started the child little corroboration of the pursuer's evidence is necessary,[22] but intercourse subsequent thereto requires substantial corroboration.[23] Subsequent marriage raises no presumption that the husband was father of the child.[24]

Evidence by the defender which is disbelieved or proved false may justify an unfavourable inference, particularly if the pursuer's contrary evidence is corroborated.[25] The practice of calling the defender as the pursuer's first witness has been disapproved.[26] If the defender is not called by the pursuer, his failure to give or lead evidence is not an admission, nor corroboration of the pursuer's evidence.[27] Where a woman has been promiscuous she cannot sue both or all her paramours, nor can she elect which one to sue. She must sue the one whom she believes was the father and establish his paternity of her child.[28] Hence proof of intercourse also with another man may throw doubt on a pursuer's case.[29] But if she fails against one man, she may subsequently sue another.

In all cases there must be specific averment of the date and place of the intercourse alleged, and proof at least of circumstances yielding an inference of very probably intercourse then. Blood tests of the parties and the

---

[18] *Lawson v. Eddie* (1861) 23 D. 876; *Harper v. Paterson* (1896) 33 S.L.R. 657.

[19] *Ruddiman v. Bruce* (1863) 2 M. 70; *Costley v. Little* (1892) 30 S.L.R. 87; *Dawson v. McKenzie*, 1908 S.C. 648; but see *Morrison v. Monaghan*, 1969 S.L.T. (Notes) 25.

[20] *Muir v. Tweedie* (1883) 21 S.L.R. 241; *Scott v. Dawson* (1884) 11 R. 518; *Buchanan v. Finlayson* (1900) 3 F. 245.

[21] *Dunn v. Chalmers* (1875) 3 R. 236; *Macfarlane v. Raeburn*, 1946 S.C. 67; cf. *Gray v. Marshall* (1875) 2 R. 907.

[22] *McDonald v. Glass* (1883) 11 R. 57; *Havery v. Brownlee*, 1908 S.C. 424. As to medical evidence see *Sproat v. McGibney*, 1968 S.L.T. 33.

[23] *Muir v. Tweedie* (1883) 21 S.L.R. 241; *Havery, supra; Buchanan v. Finlayson* (1900) 3 F. 245.

[24] *Imre v. Mitchell*, 1958 S.C. 439.

[25] The so-called doctrine of corroboration by contradiction: see *McBayne v. Davidson* (1860) 22 D. 738; *Dunn v. Chalmers* (1875) 3 R. 236; *Harper v. Paterson* (1986) 33 S.L.R. 657; *Macpherson v. Largue* (1896) 23 R. 785; *Dawson v. McKenzie*, 1908 S.C. 648; *McWhirter v. Lynch*, 1909 S.C. 112; *Florence v. Smith*, 1913 S.C. 978; *Lowdon v. McConnachie*, 1933 S.C. 574; *Macfarlane v. Raeburn*, 1946 S.C. 67; *Macpherson v. Beaton*, 1955 S.C. 100; *Roy v. Pairman*, 1958 S.C. 334; *Gormanley v. Knox*, 1983 S.L.T. 477; see also *McWhirter v. Lynch*, 1909 S.C. 122 where false denial was of immaterial circumstances; *Rathmill v. McInnes*, 1946 S.L.T. (Notes) 3; *Clarke v. Halpin*, 1977 S.L.T. (Sh. Ct.) 50. On procedure see *Pirie v. Leask*, 1964 S.C. 103.

[26] *McArthur v. McQueen* (1901) 3 F. 1010; *Darroch v. Kerr* (1901) 4 F. 396; *McWhirter v. Lynch*, 1909 S.C. 112; *Fraser v. Smith*, 1937 S.N. 67; *Finnegan v. Maan*, 1966 S.L.T. (Notes) 47.

[27] *Faddes v. McNeish*, 1923 S.C. 443.

[28] See *Lawson v. Eddie* (1861) 23 D. 876; *Barr v. Bain* (1896) 23 R. 1090; *Butter v. McLaren*, 1909 S.C. 786; *Sinclair v. Rankin*, 1921 S.C. 933; *Robertson v. Hutchison*, 1935 S.C. 708.

[29] *Butter, supra; Sinclair, supra; Robertson, supra.* See also *Scrimgeour v. Stewart* (1864) 2 M. 667.

child may yield relevant evidence.[30] The courts have frequently been faced by the problem of whether certain periods of gestation were too short or too long since any proven intercourse to make paternity probable and have frequently held unusually long or short periods not to be impossible, and therefore not to rebut any normal inference.[31] The defence of total physical incapacity or sterility is relevant.[32]

Obligation to aliment

If paternity is not established the mother must bear the whole expenses of alimenting her child. If paternity is admitted or proved both parents are liable jointly and severally to aliment their child until he is old enough to earn his own living[33] and, if need be, throughout his life.[34] Without prejudice to the common law,[35] statute has provided that this obligation continues until the child attains 16,[36] with possible extension for two years, or further but not beyond 21, if the child is undertaking full-time education.[37] The mother is entitled to constitute her claim for aliment against the father by decree even if he has admitted paternity, if he will not make arrangements for future aliment, but at her own expense.[38] The claim transmits against the parents' representatives.[39] If either parent is unable to contribute, the whole liability falls on the other. If the mother supports the child she has a claim of relief against the father for a share, formerly a half, but now a greater or lesser share depending on the means of the parties and the whole circumstances of the case,[40] of the cost of

---

[30] *Allardyce v. Johnston*, 1979 S.L.T. (Sh. Ct.) 54.

[31] See e.g. *Ritchie v. Cunningham* (1857) 20 D. 35 (228 days inadequate); *Pitcairn v. Smith* (1872) 9 S.L.R. 608 (237 days); *McDonald v. Main* (1897) 4 S.L.T. 252 (244 days); *Whyte. W.* (1884) 11 R. 710 (297 days); *Cook v. Rattray* (1880) 8 R. 217 (305 days); *Boyd v. Kerr* (1843) 5 D. 1213 (306 days); *Williamson v. McClelland*, 1913 S.C. 678 (306 days); *Jamieson v. Dobie*, 1935 S.C. 415 (306 days); *Henderson v. Somers* (1876) 3 R. 997 (311 days impossible); *Gibson v. McFagan* (1874) 1 R. 853 (312 days impossible); *Gray v. G.*, 1919 1 S.L.T. 163 (331 days impossible); *Doherty v. D.*, 1922 S.L.T. 245 (348 days impossible). See also *Grassie v. Couper* (1829) 8 S. 259; Ch. 3.3, *supra*.

[32] *McDonald v. Gilruth* (1874) 12 S.L.R. 43.

[33] *Hardie v. Leith* (1878) 6 R. 115; *Dunnet v. Campbell* (1883) 11 R. 280. Aliment was discontinued in *Purves's Trs. v. P.* (1900) 8 S.L.T. 179, where the child had succeeded to funds sufficient for its support.

[34] Ersk. I, 6, 56; Bell, *Prin.* § 2062; *Oncken's J.F. v. Reimers* (1892) 19 R. 519; *A.B. v. C.D.'s Exor.* (1900) 2 F. 610. But see *Stewart's J.F. v. Law*, 1918, 2 S.L.T. 319. An action for aliment need not contain a conclusion declaratory of paternity but the crave of the writ must include an assertion of the fact: *Silver v. Walker*, 1938 S.C. 595.

[35] *S. v. P's Trs.*, 1941 S.L.T. 35.

[36] Illegitimate Children (Sc.) Act, 1930, S. 4.

[37] Affiliation Orders Act, 1952, S. 3.

[38] *Oncken's J.F., supra.*

[39] *Robbie v. Dawes*, 1924 S.C. 749.

[40] 1930 Act, S. 1; *Shearer v. Robertson* (1877) 5 R. 263; *Mottram v. Butchart*, 1939 S.C. 89; *Terry v. Murray*, 1947 S.C. 10; *Bell v. McCurdie*, 1981 S.L.T. 159. She may claim on the father's bankrupt estate for future aliment as a contingent debt: *Downs v. Wilson's Tr.* (1886) 13 R. 1101. See now Family Law (Sc.) Act, 1985.

upbringing. She can recover unpaid arrears.[41] If the mother deserts the child and the father supports it he may sue her, if she has means, for a share of the cost. A third party having custody of the child may claim aliment.[42] The amount which may be awarded as aliment depends on the means of the parties,[43] the minimum being the amount of support beyond want which must be accorded to an illegitimate child.[44]

The child's claim for aliment was exigible as a debt against the father's executors in preference to the rights in succession of his widow and legitimate children,[45] or against the trustee in the father's sequestration in priority to the bankrupt's family.[46] By the Law Reform (Miscellaneous Provisions) (Sc.) Act, 1968, S. 4, a bastard is to have the same right to aliment from a deceased parent's estate, or from any person who had received property from the estate, *quantum lucratus*, as he would if legitimate. Any agreement for the bastard's aliment after the parent's death may be varied by the court.

When the bastard had reached 7 or, if a girl, 10, the father could formerly, unless in exceptional circumstances, discharge any further claim for aliment by the mother by offering *bona fide* to take the maintenance and upbringing into his own hands,[47] even if he intended to put the child in the custody of a stranger.[48] This is not now competent.[49]

The parents are liable, jointly or in such proportions as the sheriff may determine, for the funeral expenses of a bastard who dies while under 16.[50]

Where assistance is given from social security funds[51] a local authority[52] and supplementary benefits officers[53] have the same right as the mother to bring an action for affiliation and aliment concluding for aliment for a bastard, and the court may order that the sums due under the decree, or

---

[41] *Shearer* v. *Robertson* (1877) 5 R. 263; *Dunnet* v. *Campbell* (1883) 11 R. 280.
[42] 1930 Act, S. 1(3). See now Family Law (Sc.) Act, 1985.
[43] 1930 Act, S. 1(2); *Terry*, supra; but a maximum of £1.50 per week was fixed by the Affiliation Orders Act, 1952, S. 1 (now Affiliation Proceedings Act, 1957, S. 4) and raised to £2.50 by the Matrimonial Proceedings (Magistrates Courts) Act, 1960, S. 15. Query, whether S. I applied to Scotland: held it did not, in *Halkett* v. *McSkeane*, 1962 S.L.T. (Sh. Ct.) 59, 80.
[44] *Fraser* v. *Campbell*, 1927 S.C. 589.
[45] *Oncken's J.F.* v. *Reimers* (1892) 19 R. 519; *Hare* v. *Logan's Trs.*, 1957 S.L.T. (Notes) 49.
[46] *Gairdner* v. *Monro* (1848) 10 D. 650.
[47] *Ballantine* v. *Malcolm* (1803) Hume 424; *Corrie* v. *Adair* (1860) 22 D. 897; *Grant* v. *Yuill* (1872) 10 M. 511; *Shearer*, supra; *Brown* v. *Halbert* (1896) 23 R. 733; *Millar* v. *Melville* (1898) 1 F. 367; *Moncrieff* v. *Langlands* (1900) 2 F. 1111; *Macdonald* v. *Denoon*, 1929 S.C. 172; cf. *Brown* v. *Ferguson*, 1912 S.C. 22, where mother died.
[48] *Corrie* v. *Adair* (1860) 22 D. 897; *Grant* v. *Yuill* (1872) 10 M. 511; *Shearer* v. *Robertson* (1877) 5 R. 263; *Westland* v. *Pirie* (1887) 14 R. 763; *Wilson* v. *Lindsay* (1893) 1 S.L.T. 272; *Oliver* v. *Bayne* (1894) 2 S.L.T. 106; *Moncrieff* v. *Langlands* (1900) 2 F. 1111.
[49] 1930 Act, S. 2(2).
[50] 1930 Act, S. 5.
[51] Under Social Security Act, 1986.
[52] Social Work (Sc.) Act, 1968, S. 81.
[53] Social Security Act, 1980, S. 6.

part thereof, shall be paid to the benefit officer or the local authority or such other person as the court may direct, and such payee may enforce the decree. Such payments are to recompense the authority or benefit officer for assistance given under the Acts.[54,55] Supplementary benefits officers may also seek to recover from the parents of a bastard sums expended on the child's maintenance and the parents are jointly and severally liable therefor.[54]

Where a child maintainable by the local authority is illegitimate, the authority has the same right as the mother to bring an action of affiliation and aliment. If a decree for aliment is in force the local authority may have a court order the payments to be made to the local authority entitled thereto.[55]

Custody and guardianship—illegitimate children

The father of a bastard has no common law right of *patria potestas*, or of custody.[56] Nor has a grandparent.[57] The mother is the natural custodier of her own bastard child and has the primary right to custody.[58] The court may on the application of either parent, or in an action for aliment, make an order regarding custody and the right of access thereto of either parent, having regard to the welfare of the child, to the conduct of the parents, and the wishes of each of them, and may on the application of either recall or vary such order.[59] The paramount consideration is the welfare of the child.[60] The court may commit the care of the child to a local authority.[61] The court may make an order for payment to the person entitled to custody, whether father, mother or a third party, by the father or mother or both, of such aliment as the court thinks reasonable, having regard to the means and position of the parents and the whole circumstances of the case, and may recall or vary any such order.[62] The court's power on divorce to regulate custody, maintenance and education[63] applies to an illegitimate child of the parties, or of one party who

---

[54] N.A.B. v. *Casey*, 1967 S.L.T. (Sh. Ct.) 11. See also *Supplementary Benefits Commn. v. Black*, 1968 S.L.T. (Sh. Ct.) 90.

[55] Social Work (Sc.) Act, 1968, S. 81.

[56] *Corrie v. Adair* (1860) 22 D. 897; *Macpherson v. Leishman* (1887) 14 R. 780; *Greenock Parish Council v. Kilmarnock and Stirling*, 1911 S.C. 570; *A. v. B.*, 1955 S.C. 378; *A. v. N.*, 1973 S.L.T. (Sh. Ct.) 34.

[57] *Brown v. Ferguson*, 1912 S.C. 22.

[58] *Macpherson, supra; Brand v. Shaws* (1888) 15 R. 449; *Kerrigan v. Hall* (1901) 4 F. 10; *Walter v. Cuthbertson*, 1921 S.C. 490; *Duguid v. McBrinn*, 1954 S.C. 105.

[59] 1930 Act, S. 2(1); *Duguid, supra; A. v. B., supra.* Custody awarded to father in *Sutherland v. Taylor* (1888) 15 R. 224; *A.B. v. C.D.*, 1962 S.L.T. (Sh. Ct.) 16; *A. v. G.*, 1984 S.L.T (Sh. Ct.) 65.

[60] *Duguid, supra; Mackenzie v. Hendry*, 1984 S.L.T. 322.

[61] Guardianship Act, 1973, S. 11.

[62] 1930 Act, S. 1(3). See also Family Law (Sc.) Act, 1985.

[63] Matrimonial Proceedings (Children) Act, 1958, Ss. 7–15.

has been accepted as one of the family by the other party. The extended powers to award custody under the Children Act, 1975, Ss. 47–55 apply also to illegitimate children.

Children in care

The provisions for legitimate children apply also to illegitimate children.

Tutory and curatory—illegitimate children

The father has no common law right to the administration of his bastard child's legal affairs.[64] Nor has the mother such a right.[65] Where a bastard pupil sues he may do so in his own name, and the court will appoint a tutor *ad litem*, with whose concurrence the action proceeds.[66]

Relations between parents and natural child

The legal relations between the parents of a bastard and it are limited.[67] A bastard was at common law *filius nullius* and, save under statute, has no reciprocal rights and duties with his parents. Neither parent is deemed a blood relative of the child, and neither has any right to aliment from the bastard in case of need.[68] Nor are different bastards by the same parent or parents deemed in any way connected. Natural parent and natural child may transact with one another as if they were strangers.

At common law no right of succession was recognized in favour of, or through, illegitimate children. By the Succession (Scotland) Act, 1964, S. 4, illegitimate children were entitled on intestacy, failing legitimate issue, to the whole of their mother's estate, and, failing legitimate issue and other relatives of a bastard who died intestate, his mother is entitled to the whole of his intestate estate. By the Law Reform (Miscellaneous Provisions) (Scotland) Act, 1968, S. 1, S. 4 of the 1964 Act is replaced by a new S. 4, which gives legitimate and illegitimate children of an intestate equal rights to his whole estate, and the parents of an illegitimate person, if dying intestate and without issue, have right to his whole estate, it being presumed that the illegitimate was not survived by his father unless the contrary be shown. Apart from these provisions nothing in Part I of the 1964 Act is to be held to import any rule of succession through illegitimate relationship. The 1968 Act, S. 2, enacts a new S. 10 A of the 1964 Act giving an illegitimate child a right to legitim.

---

[64] *Corrie* v. *Adair* (1860) 22 D. 897.
[65] *Jones* v. *Somervell's Tr.*, 1907 S.C. 545.
[66] Mackay, *Manual of Practice*, 148; in *Ward* v. *Walker*, 1920 S.C. 80, the court appointed a curator *ad litem*.
[67] Bell, *Prin.* § 2058.
[68] *Weir* v. *Coltness Iron Co.* (1889) 16 R. 614; *Clarke* v. *Carfin Coal Co.* (1891) 18 R. (H.L.) 63; *Clement* v. *Bell* (1899) 1 F. 924. *Samson* v. *Davie* (1886) 14 R. 113 is overruled by *Clarke, supra*.

LEGITIMATED CHILDREN

Legitimated children

In accordance with the civil and canon law doctrine of *legitimatio per subsequens matrimonium*,[69] a child born out of wedlock was at common law held legitimated if the natural parents were under no legal impediment to marry at the time the child was conceived, and subsequently did marry, and the husband admitted paternity, expressly or impliedly, or if it was proved against him.[70] The place of birth was immaterial.[71] But if there were a legal impediment to marriage, such as a subsisting marriage of either parent to another, legitimation could not take place; hence an adulterine bastard could never be legitimated, nor could the offspring of incest. Declarator of legitimation may be granted long after the death of the person involved at the instance of his descendants.[72] Where the doctrine of legitimation operates it does so independently of the consent of the child.[73] If the mother of a bastard marries it is still competent to prove, even after the deaths of the spouses and of the child, that the child was illegitimate.[74] The marriage by itself does not prove, nor even raise a presumption of, paternity by the husband.[75] A child cannot be legitimated by the marriage of its parents after it has died,[76] but it may be legitimated, though one parent had married a third party and been widowed between the birth of the child and her marriage to the child's other parent.[77] Where the doctrine applies the bastard is retrospectively deemed legitimate from birth and has the same status as a fully legitimate child.[78] It is probable that such a child takes priority over later children born legitimate.[79] A bastard may also be legitimated by royal letters of legitimation.[80] By the Legitimation (Sc.) Act, 1968, S. 1, where the parents of a bastard marry after the commencement of the Act,[81] if the father is then domiciled in Scotland and the bastard is alive, the marriage

---

[69] Stair III, 3, 42; Bankt. I, 5, 54; Ersk. I, 6, 52; III, 10, 7, Bell, *Prin.* § 1627, 2064; Fraser, *P. & Ch.* 37. See also history and authorities cited in *Kerr* v. *Martin* (1840) 2 D. 752.

[70] *Innes* v. *I.* (1837) 2 S. & Macl. 417; *Udny* v. *U.* (1869) 7 M. (H.L.) 89; *Imre* v. *Mitchell,* 1958 S.C. 439, 469.

[71] *Blair* v. *Kay's Trs.,* 1940 S.N. 82.

[72] *Bosville* v. *Lord Macdonald,* 1910 S.C. 597.

[73] *Hume* v. *Macfarlane* (1908) 16 S.L.T. 123.

[74] *Smith* v. *Dick* (1869) 8 M. 31.

[75] *Imre, supra; Brooks's Exrx.* v. *James,* 1970 S.C. 147; cf. *Gaffney* v. *Connerton,* 1909 S.C. 1009.

[76] *McNeill* v. *McGregor* (1901) 4 F. 123; contrast *McLean* v. *Glasgow Corpn.,* 1933 S.L.T. 396.

[77] *Kerr* v. *Martin* (1840) 2 D. 752.

[78] *Crawford's Trs.* v. *Hart* (1802) Mor. 12698; *Kerr, supra;* see also *Munro* v. *Ross* (1827) 5 S. 605.

[79] Ersk. I, 6, 52; Bell, *Prin.* § 1627; *Kerr, supra.*

[80] Ersk. III, 10, 7; Fraser, *P. & Ch.,* 51. cf. legitimation *per rescriptum principis:* Nov. 74, 89.

[81] 8 June 1968.

legitimates the bastard from the date of the marriage. By S. 4, where the parents of a bastard had married each other before the Act, the father was domiciled in Scotland at the date of the marriage, the bastard was alive at the date of the marriage, and by reason of the existence at any time previous to the marriage of an impediment thereto, the marriage did not, at common law, effect legitimation, the marriage does so with effect from the commencement of the Act, or if he had died the Act applies to determine the rights and obligations of persons living thereafter as if the bastard had been legitimated as from that date.

Where a child has been registered as illegitimate entry may be made in the Register of Corrections respecting its legitimation *per subsequens matrimonium* only where such legitimation has been found by decree of court.[82] The Registrar-General may, in case of legitimation, authorize re-registration of the birth, but not where paternity of the bastard had not been registered, unless with the sanction of the sheriff on the application of both parents, or the survivor or of or on behalf of the legitimated bastard, after intimation and inquiry.[83]

Effect of legitimation

Under the Legitimation (Sc.) Act, 1968, S. 2, legitimation under the Act confers no status or right, and imposes no obligation in respect of any time prior to the legitimation.[84] A person is not entitled, by virtue of the legitimation of anyone, to any right in the intestate estate of a person dying after the Act and before the legitimation, nor to legitim from the estate of any such person.[85] A person's legitimation does not affect any right under a deed coming into operation after the Act if the right has become indefeasibly vested in any other person before the legitimation, but,[86] subject to that, a legitimated person is entitled to any right under a deed coming into operation after the Act if his entitlement depends on his legitimacy and another person is entitled if his entitlement depends on the legitimacy of the legitimated person.[87] A reference in a deed coming into operation after the Act to a child or issue of a marriage is to be construed as including a reference to any child legitimated by the marriage.[88] Where a right is conferred or an obligation imposed by law or under a deed operative after the Act by reference to the relative seniority of the members of a class in terms which indicate that the class consists of legitimate

---

[82] Registration of Births, Deaths, and Marriages (Sc.) Act, 1965, Ss. 44, 48.

[83] 1965 Act, S. 20 (1) (c). Re-registration was held incompetent where there was no evidence of legitimation by English law, the father's *lex domicilii: Mr. and Mrs. X.*, 1966 S.L.T. (Sh. Ct.) 86.

[84] 1968 Act, S. 2(1) and (8).

[85] S. 2(2).

[86] S. 2(3).

[87] S. 2(4).

[88] S. 2(5).

persons only, any member of the class who is legitimated ranks as if born on the date of legitimation, and, if two or more, according to the respective times of birth.[89] Subject to these provisions, legitimation enures to the benefit of any other person claiming any right arising after the Act if entitlement depends on the legitimacy of the legitimated person.[90]

Where an illegitimate has died or dies, and would otherwise have been legitimated by the 1968 Act, the rights and obligations of any person living at or after the relevant date are determined by the Act as if legitimation had occurred.[91]

Where the parents of a bastard married before the Act, the father was domiciled in Scotland, the bastard was living, but the marriage did not effect legitimation at common law, marriage legitimates from the date of the Act; if the bastard were not living the Act determines the rights and obligations of any person living after the Act as if legitimation had operated.[92]

Legitimation includes recognition by Scots law of legitimation *per subsequens matrimonium* under the law of another country.[93]

Where the parents of a bastard married and adopted their bastard the adoption may be revoked without prejudice to succession rights acquired before the revocation.[94]

ADOPTIVE CHILDREN

Adoptive children

At common law an arrangement for the adoption of a child so as to make him legally the child of another parent or other parents was not recognized though such arrangements as fostering were permissible contractually.[95] By statute adoption has been introduced,[96] having definite legal consequences and creating the status of adoptive child. Only local authorities and approved adoption societies may make arrangements for the adoption of children.[97] Advertisement relating to adoption and certain payments in relation thereto are forbidden.[98] In reaching any decision on adoption a court or adoption agency staff must have regard above all to the welfare of the child and so far as practicable ascertain the

---

[89] S. 2(6).
[90] S. 2(7).
[91] S. 3.
[92] S. 4.
[93] S. 5.
[94] S. 6.
[95] cf. *Kerrigan* v. *Hall* (1901) 4 F. 10; *Briggs* v. *Mitchell*, 1911 S.C. 765.
[96] Adoption of Children (Sc.) Act, 1930, now replaced by Adoption (Sc.) Act, 1978.
[97] 1978 Act, Ss. 1–5, 8–11. The court will refuse an adoption of a child obtained from an unregistered person: *Mr. and Mrs. S.S.*, 1953 S.L.T. (Sh. Ct.) 29.
[98] Ss. 51–2.

child's feelings and give effect to them,[99] and in placing a child have regard to the wishes of the child's parents and guardians as to religious upbringing.[1]

An adoption order vests parental rights and duties in the adopters and extinguishes parental rights and duties relating to the child previously vested in a parent or guardian, and any duty to or by the child to pay aliment or to make any payment arising out of parental rights. An order may not be made in relation to a child who is or has been married; it may contain terms and conditions, may be made although the child is already adopted[2] and in the case of a minor child requires the child's consent unless the minor is incapable of consenting.[3] Where an applicant for adoption is a parent,[4] step-parent, or relative or the child was placed by an adoption agency, an order may not be made unless the child is nineteen weeks old and has had his home with the applicants for at least thirteen weeks. In other cases the child must be twelve months old and had his home with the applicants all that time. The adoption agency or local authority must have opportunities to see the child with the applicants.[5]

An adoption order may be made on the application of a married couple, each aged at least 21, if at least one is domiciled in the U.K., Channel Islands, or Isle of Man, or it is a Convention adoption order under S. 17.[6] It may be made on the application of one person aged at least 21 and not married, or whose spouse cannot be found, is living apart or is by reason of ill-health incapable of applying, subject to conditions as to domicile, but not on the application of a single parent unless the other parent is dead or cannot be found or there is some other reason justifying the exclusion of the other natural parent.[7] The child must be free for adoption,[8] or each parent or guardian has freely agreed unconditionally to an adoption order,[9] unless his agreement is dispensed with on the grounds that he cannot be found or is incapable of giving agreement, is withholding agreement unreasonably,[10] has persistently

---

[99] S. 6. cf. *A.B. and C.D. Petrs.*, 1963 S.C. 124; *A. and B. Petrs.*, 1971 S.C. (H.L.) 129.
[1] S. 7.
[2] cf. *E. and E.*, 1939 S.C. 165; *F. Petr.*, 1939 S.C. 166.
[3] S. 12. A person over 18 cannot be adopted: S. 65; *M. Petr.*, 1954 S.C. 227. As to child's consent, see *A. Petr.*, 1936 S.C. 255.
[4] The father of an illegitimate child is not a 'parent', but is relative. cf. *A. v. B.*, 1955 S.C. 378.
[5] S. 13. cf. *M. Petr., supra; A. Petrs.*, 1953 S.L.T. (Sh. Ct.) 45; *G. Petr.*, 1955 S.L.T. (Sh. Ct.) 27.
[6] S. 14. The Act does not favour adoptions by relatives or step-parents, though these have been allowed in the past. cf. *B. and B.*, 1936 S.C. 256; *I. and I. Petrs.*, 1947 S.C. 485; *B. and B.*, 1965 S.C. 44.
[7] S. 15. Hence a parent may adopt his or her own illegitimate child. Cf. *D.* 1938 S.C. 223.
[8] Under S. 18. A former parent may make a declaration declining to be further involved with the child, or obtain progress reports on the child (S. 19) or apply for revocation of the freeing order under S. 20.
[9] cf. *H. and H.*, 1976 S.L.T. 80.
[10] cf. *A.B. v. C.D.*, 1970 S.C. 268; *A. and B. v. C.*, 1977 S.C. 27; *A. v. B.*, 1987 S.L.T. (Sh. Ct.) 121.

failed to discharge parental duties, has abandoned or neglected the child, has persistently ill-treated the child, or has seriously ill-treated the child. A mother cannot validly agree within six weeks of the birth.[11] Provision is made for Convention adoption orders, where adopters and child are not all U.K. nationals living in British territory.[12]

An applicant for adopting must give three months' notice to the local authority which shall investigate his suitability and report to the court.[13] An adoption agency must do similarly.[14] The court may not determine an application for adoption where a previous application by the same persons was refused, save exceptionally.[15] The court may postpone determination of the application and grant the applicants custody for a probationary period not exceeding two years.[16] If an adoption order is refused the court may place the child under the supervision of the local authority or commit it to the care of the local authority.[17] There are restrictions on the removal of children awaiting adoption from the prospective adopters.[18] When a person gives notice of intention to apply for an adoption order the child becomes a 'protected child' and must be visited by the local authority; he may be removed from unsuitable surroundings.[19] In prescribed cases the court must appoint a curator *ad litem* to safeguard the child's interests.[20]

A child who is the subject of an adoption order[21] is treated, where the adopters are a married couple as their legitimate child, and in other cases, as if born a legitimate child of the adopter, and not the child of any other person. Adoption of an illegitimate child by one natural parent who later marries the other natural parent renders it the legitimate child of both.[22] Provision is made as to citizenship, and other statutory matters.[23] Since 1964[24] an adopted child has been in the position of a legitimate child for purposes of succession, testate or intestate.

The Registrar-General maintains an Adopted Children Register and registers to link children born and adopted with entries in the Adopted

---

[11] S. 16. The father of an illegitimate child is not a 'parent': *A. v. B.*, 1955 S.C. 378. The agreement of the mother's husband is not required. The parent must have information about the consequences of adoption: *H. and H.*, 1944 S.C. 347; and may know the identity of the adopters; see A.S. (Adoption of Children) 1959; *B. and B. Petrs.*, 1946 S.L.T. (Sh. Ct.) 36. On dispensing with consent see *A.B. and C.B. Petrs.*, 1963 S.C. 124; *A. and B. Petrs.*, 1971 S.C. (H.L.) 129; *A.B. v. C.B.*, 1985 S.L.T. 514.
[12] S. 17. This is pursuant to the Hague Convention on Adoption of 1965.
[13] S. 22.
[14] S. 23.
[15] S. 24.
[16] S. 25.
[17] S. 26.
[18] Ss. 27–31.
[19] Ss. 32–7.
[20] S. 58.
[21] S. 38.
[22] S. 39.
[23] Ss. 40–4.
[24] Succession (Sc.) Act, 1964, S. 23.

Children Register.[25] Where one of the natural parents of an illegitimate child adopted him and then married the other natural parent, or a person adopted by a single parent has become legitimated on the marriage of the two parents, the court may revoke the adoption.[26] There are restrictions on the removal of children for adoption outside Great Britain.[27]

[25] S. 45.
[26] S. 46. An adoption order cannot be reduced on grounds of error or misrepresentation: *J. and J.* v. *C's Tutor*, 1948 S.C. 636.
[27] S. 50.

THE DOMESTIC RELATIONS
(3) GUARDIAN AND WARD

Pupils, minors, and persons physically or mentally incapax require for their own protection and good to be under the guardianship of persons of greater maturity both for physical care, custody, and upbringing, and for advice in business transactions and legal relations.[1] In the case of pupils and minors both custody and guidance are normally provided by the natural parents, or persons nominated by them or designated by law as guardians, failing the parents.[2] Extensive statutory provision is now made for the custody and guidance of children in other cases, and of incapaces.

PUPILS AND MINORS

In its doctrines of guardianship of children Scots law closely resembles Roman law. Corresponding to the two stages of life short of majority, there are two kinds of guardianship, tutory and curatory.

Tutory is a power and faculty to govern the person, and to manage the estate of a pupil; curatory is the power of managing the estate of a minor, or of a major who is incapable of acting for himself through defect of judgment.[3] *Tutor datur personae, curator rei.* Failing a parent, a tutor is essential for a pupil but a curator is not essential to a minor, since he has capacity to act on his own. The rules as to guardianship vary according as the child is legitimate, legitimated, or adopted on the one hand, or illegitimate on the other.

Guardianship of legitimate pupils—tutors testamentary or nominate

At common law, on the father's death, the office of tutor to his pupil children devolves on one or more tutors nominate or testamentary named in his will, to control the pupil's person and manage his estate.[4] The father's testamentary trustees are frequently so named.[5] They need neither

---

[1] See generally Stair I, 6, 1; Ersk. I, 7, 1; Bell, *Prin.* § 2065–128; Fraser, *P. & Ch., passim.*
[2] Ch. 3.4, *supra.*
[3] Stair I, 6, 1; Ersk. I, 7, 1; Bell, *Prin.* § 2065–6, 2088–90.
[4] Ersk. I, 7, 2–3; Bell, *Prin.* § 2071; Fraser, *P. & Ch.,* 239.
[5] e.g. *McCrossan's Trs.* v. *McC.* (1899) 7 S.L.T. 22; see, however, *Walker* v. *Stronach* (1874) 2 R. 120.

take the oath *de fideli administratione,* nor find caution for their intromissions, unless the court had reason to suspect their honesty or their circumstances,[6] but must make up an inventory as a check on administration.

A person devising any property to a pupil may nominate a person to manage it during the pupillarity, but such a person is not tutor for any other purpose.

Tutor of law or tutor-legitim

Failing any tutors-nominate, the office, as in Roman law, devolves by law on the nearest of the male agnates, i.e. kinsmen on the father's side, the one who would by common law be the pupil's heir at law, if aged 25, as tutor-legitim or tutor of law.[7] Even after accepting office a tutor-legitim must relinquish the office if a tutor-testamentary offers to accept.[8] The tutor of law obtains appointment by petition to the sheriff for service as tutor-legitim, after such inquiry as may be necessary. He must take the oath *de fideli,* find caution for his intromissions,[9] and is subject to the supervision of the Accountant of Court.[10] But a tutor-legitim might not be sufficiently careful to preserve the pupil's life so that, while he has the direction of the pupil's education and of the expenses attaching to him, the mother, if still a widow, has the custody, at least till the pupil is 7. If she remarries or her mode of life be bad, the custody is given to the next of the cognates, i.e. all relations by the mother.[11]

Tutor-dative

In default of tutor-legitim, a tutor-dative may be appointed by the court. To enable a tutor-legitim to decide whether to serve or not, no appointment as tutor-dative can be made till a year from the time when the first tutor of law might have served.[12] A tutor-dative must find caution, and is subject to the supervision of the Accountant of Court.[13]

The usual practice is, however, on the petition of any kinsman of the pupil, to appoint a judicial factor *loco tutoris* to the pupil, for the

---

[6] Ersk. I, 7, 1–3; Bell, *Prin.* § 2081; Guardianship of Infants Act, 1886, S. 12.
[7] Ersk. I, 7, 4–5; Bell, *Prin.* § 2078–9; Fraser, *P. & Ch.,* 249; *McLay* v. *Thornton* (1868) 41 S. Jur. 68; *Alexander* v. *McGarrity* (1903) 5 F. 654.
[8] Ersk. I, 7, 4–5.
[9] Ersk. I, 7, 6.
[10] Judicial Factors (Sc.) Act, 1849, Ss. 3, 25, 30.
[11] Ersk. I, 7, 7; Bell, *Prin.* § 2078.
[12] Ersk. I, 7, 8; Bell, *Prin.* § 2080; Fraser, *P. & Ch.,* 258; *Martin* (1859) 22 D. 45; *Urquhart* (1860) 22 D. 932; *Simpson* (1861) 23 D. 1292.
[13] Bell, *Prin.* § 2081–81A; Judicial Factors (Sc.) Act, 1849, S. 26.

management of his affairs.[14] He should be a neutral person.[15] The court may, on cause shown, remove or accept the resignation of any tutor of law or tutor-dative and appoint a factor *loco tutoris* in his place.[16] A father's poverty alone is not a sufficient ground for depriving him of the administration of his pupil child's property,[17] nor the mere possibility of conflict of interest between him and his child.[18] On a father's death a mother cannot be appointed factor *loco tutoris* since she is now, by the Guardianship of Children (Sc.) Acts, 1886 to 1973, guardian.[19] A temporary appointment may be made while the Court is dissatisfied with the administration of a tutor-nominate.[20]

A factor *loco tutoris* who continues to act after the pupil becomes minor becomes a *curator bonis*.[21]

Statutory provisions

In most cases the common law provisions are now superseded by statutory ones. By the Guardianship of Children (Scotland) Acts, 1886 to 1973[22] both parents have equal rights. On the death of either the survivor is to be tutor,[23] alone or jointly with any tutor appointed by the deceased parent. Failing any such appointment the court may appoint a tutor to act jointly with the survivor.[24] If a pupil has no parent or tutor the court may appoint any applicant to be tutor.[25] Either parent may by deed or will appoint any person to be tutor after his death; such a tutor will act jointly with the surviving parent, unless the latter objects. If so, or if the tutor considers the parent unfit to have custody, the tutor may apply to the court, which may make either parent or tutor sole tutor, or make them joint tutors, and may, if making the tutor sole tutor, regulate custody and access to the child by the parent and order the parent to make payments towards maintenance. Where both parents appoint tutors, they act jointly after the death of the surviving parent. A tutor appointed by the court continues to act after the death of the surviving parent and jointly with

---

[14] Ersk. I, 7, 10; *Prin.* § 2068.

[15] *Hutcheon* v. *Alexander*, 1909 1 S.L.T. 71.

[16] Judicial Factors (Sc.) Act. 1849, S. 31.

[17] *Wardrop* v. *Gossling* (1869) 7 M. 532.

[18] *Cochrane* (1891) 18 R. 456; contrast *Allan* (1895) 3 S.L.T. 87.

[19] *Willison* (1890) 18 R. 228.

[20] *Edgar* v. *Fisher's Trs.* (1893) 21 R. 59, 325, 1076.

[21] Judicial Factors (Sc.) Act, 1889, S. 11; *Stiven* v. *Masterton* (1892) 30 S.L.R. 50.

[22] 'Guardian' is defined as 'tutor' and 'infant' as 'pupil'; 1886 Act, S. 8. The Acts apply only to legitimate children: *Brand* v. *Shaws* (1888) 16 R. 315; 1973 Act, S. 10(6).

[23] A mother's tutory is not affected by remarriage: *Campbell* v. *Maquay* (1888) 15 R. 784. In view of the Acts a mother cannot now be appointed factor *loco tutoris*: *Willison* (1890) 18 R. 228.

[24] *Martin* v. *Stewart* (1888) 16 R. 185; *Sim* v. *Robertson* (1901) 3 F. 1027. It is incompetent to seek to have a factor *loco tutoris* appointed to act with the mother: *Speirs*, 1946 S.L.T. 203.

[25] 1925 Act, S. 4.

any tutor appointed by the survivor.[26] Disputes between joint tutors may be settled by the court on application.[27]

Powers of tutors—custody

A tutor, except a tutor of law who is heir-at-law, has custody of the person of the pupil. If the mother be not tutor, she will have the custody of the pupil till 7, unless she is unfit therefor. The tutor may direct the residence and education of the pupil, subject to the control of the Court of Session.[28] A factor *loco tutoris* may be granted custody in preference to the father.[29]

Powers of tutors—estate and actions

A tutor of law, tutor-dative, or factor *loco tutoris* is subject to the Judicial Factors (Scotland) Acts, 1849 to 1889,[30] and a tutor who is administrator-in-law, tutor-nominate, or guardian under the 1886 Act is deemed a tutor within the meaning of the Judicial Factors (Scotland) Act, 1849 and subject to the provisions thereof.[31] A parent acting as tutor at common law or under the 1886 to 1973 Acts is a trustee within the meaning of the Trusts (Scotland) Acts, 1921 and 1961,[32] and any tutor or judicial factor is deemed, and has the powers of, a trustee under those Acts.[33] All such tutors have ordinary powers of administration of the pupil's property.[34] They bring and defend legal proceedings alone, for behoof of the pupil.[35] A tutor *ad litem* may be appointed to a pupil, called as defender, for whom appearance has not been entered.[36] A mother, as tutor under the 1886 Act, has been held entitled to grant a good discharge for damages awarded to her pupil children.[37] In other cases the Court has sometimes *de plano* appointed a factor *loco tutoris*[38]

---

[26] 1925 Act, S. 5, overruling *Fraser* (1893) 1 S.L.T. 126.
[27] 1925 Act, S. 6.
[28] Bell, *Prin.* § 2083.
[29] *Moncrieff* (1891) 18 R. 1029.
[30] 1849 Act, S. 1.
[31] 1886 Act, S. 12.
[32] Guardianship of Infants Act, 1925, S. 10.
[33] Trusts (Sc.) Act, 1921, S. 2.
[34] Bell, *Prin.* § 2082, 2084.
[35] Fraser, *P. & Ch.*, 208; cf. *Craven* v. *Elibank's Trs.* (1854) 16 D. 811; *Davis's Tutor* v. *Glasgow Victoria Hospitals,* 1950 S.C. 382.
[36] *Macdonald's Trs.* v. *Medhurst,* 1915 S.C. 879; *Ward* v. *Walker,* 1920 S.C. 80; *Aitken's Trs.* v. *Milne,* 1921 S.C. 454; *Drummond's Trs.* v. *Peel's Trs.,* 1929 S.C. 484; the court in the last case speaks of a curator *ad litem,* which seems a misnomer.
[37] *Jack* v. *N.B. Ry. Co.* (1886) 14 R. 263.
[38] *Collins* v. *Eglinton Iron Co.* (1882) 9 R. 500; *McAvoy* v. *Young's Paraffin Oil Co.* (1882) 19 S.L.R. 441; *Boylan* v. *Hunter,* 1922 S.C. 80.

and sometimes required a formal petition for such a factor to administer awards of damages.[39]

Expiry of office

The office expires on the death of tutor or pupil, or the pupil's attainment of minority.[40] A tutor may be removed by the Court of Session.[41] Mutual actions lie for an accounting for intromissions with the pupil's estate, and for loss or damage from any transaction against which the pupil cannot be restored,[42] and on the other hand for reimbursement of outlays, relief of engagements undertaken, and discharge. These actions prescribe in five years.[43] A discharge under the 1849 Act is generally conclusive against all parties.[44]

Guardianship of minors—estate and actions

The minor manages his property and transacts legally himself, but with the consent and concurrence of his curator, as his adviser.[45] Transactions by the curator himself are null, and he cannot compel the minor to any course of action; if the minor is obstinate, the curator should apply to be discharged.[46] The minor's powers of administration, with his curator's concurrence, are unlimited. If a minor is a defender in litigation and has no curator, the court may appoint a curator *ad litem* to him.[47]

Powers of curators

A curator is deemed to be, and has the powers of, a trustee under the Trusts (Scotland) Acts, 1921 and 1961.[48] But the function of a curator is not to administer, but to interpose consent and concurrence to the minor's actings. Thus minors can themselves grant a valid discharge for damages,[49] though if the sum is substantial the court may direct it to be paid to a person in trust for the minor.[50]

---

[39] *Connolly v. Bent Colliery Co.* (1897) 24 R. 1172; cf. *Anderson v. Muirhead* (1884) 11 R. 870.

[40] Bell, *Prin.* § 2086.

[41] *Butchart v. B.* (1851) 13 D. 1258; *Dewar* (1853) 16 D. 163, 489; *Fleming v. Craig* (1863) I M. 850; *Mitchell* (1864) 2 M. 1378; see also Judicial Factors (Sc.) Act, 1849, Ss. 25, 31; Guardianship of Infants Act, 1886, S. 6.

[42] *A.B.* (1854) 16 D. 1004; *Guthrie* (1853) 16 D. 214; *Cochrane v. Black* (1855) 17 D. 321; 19 D. 1019; *Laird v. L.* (1855) 17 D. 984; *Acct. of Court v. Geddes* (1858) 20 D. 1174.

[43] Prescription and Limitation (Sc.) Act, 1973, S. 6.

[44] 1849 Act, S. 34.

[45] Ersk. I, 7, 16; Bell, *Prin.* § 2096.

[46] *Mackenzie's Tr. v. M.*, 1908 S.C. 995, 999.

[47] cf. *Drummond's Trs. v. Peel's Trs.* 1929 S.C. 484 (pupil).

[48] 1921 Act, S. 2.

[49] *Jack v. N.B. Ry. Co.* (1886) 14 R. 263; cf. *Macdonald* (1896) 4 S.L.T. 4.

[50] *Sharp v. Pathhead Spinning Co.* (1885) 12 R. 574; *Spring v. Blackhall* (1901) 9 S.L.T. 162; See also *Anderson v. Muirhead* (1884) 11 R. 870; *McIntosh v. Wood.* 1970 S.C. 179.

Guardianship of minors

At common law the father is the natural curator of his minor child,[51] but the minor may by forisfamiliation, i.e. by setting out, with the father's consent, on an independent career,[52] or, if a girl, by marriage, release himself from the father's curatory. With the father's consent, however, or if he has acted in violation of paternal duty, or if there is conflict of interest between father and child, another person may be appointed curator to guide the child in managing his affairs.[53] By the Tutors and Curators Act, 1696, c. 8, fathers while still in health, in *liege poustie*,[54] may nominate curators to their children.[55] Failing the father the mother was not automatically curator, but might be appointed to the office by the father's will. Under the Guardianship Act, 1973, a mother is now curator. A person appointed factor *loco tutoris* automatically becomes curator when the child attains puberty unless the child chooses curators for himself.[56] A minor might, under the Act 1555, c. 35, bring an action for choosing curators for himself.[57] Now, if a minor desires a curator he may have one appointed by petitioning the Court of Session.[58]

A curator may be named to a minor for a special purpose, as where a third party has devised property to the minor, but such is more properly a *curator bonis* than a guardian,[59] and such an appointment does not prejudice a petition for choosing curators.[60]

Also, where a minor is involved in litigation with his curator, or having no curator, with a stranger, a curator *ad litem* must be appointed by the court.[61]

While tutory was at common law *officium virile* which could not be exercised by women, all persons may be appointed curators to minors who are fit to manage an estate. Hence a father may nominate his widow, or any unmarried woman, and doubtless now,[62] any woman at all, to be curatrix.[63]

[51] Ersk. I, 6, 54; Bell, *Prin.* § 2092.
[52] Fraser, *P. & Ch.*, 499; *Thomson* v. *Gibson & Borthwick* (1851) 13 D. 683; *McFeetridge* v. *Stewarts & Lloyds*, 1913 S.C. 773.
[53] Ersk. I, 6, 54; *McNab* v. *McN.* (1871) 10 M. 248.
[54] i.e. *in legitima potestate*.
[55] Ersk. I, 7, 11; Bell, *Prin.* § 2093; Fraser, *P. & Ch.*, 455; see e.g. *Greig* v. *G.* (1872) 11 M. 20.
[56] Judicial Factors (Sc.) Act, 1889, S. 11; *Ferguson* v. *Blair* (1908) 16 S.L.T. 284.
[57] Ersk. I, 7, 11; Bell, *Prin.* § 2095; Fraser, *P. & Ch.*, 459; *Fergusson* v. *Dormer* (1870) 8 M. 426.
[58] Administration of Justice (Sc.) Act, 1933, S. 12; cf. *Thomson* (1881) 19 S.L.R. 105; *Hutchison* (1881) 18 S.L.R. 725.
[59] *Macdonald* (1896) 4 S.L.T. 4; *Perry* (1903) 10 S.L.T. 536.
[60] Ersk. I, 7, 13; Bell, *Prin.* § 2094.
[61] Fraser, *P & Ch*, 466; *Cunningham* v. *Smith* (1880) 7 R. 424; *Young* v. *Rankin*, 1934 S.C. 499. If such a minor later becomes insane the office of *curator ad litem* falls and a *curator bonis* must be appointed: *Moodie* v. *Dempster*, 1931 S.C. 553.
[62] *Chalmers' Trs.* v. *Sinclair* (1897) 24 R. 1047 is probably superseded, at least *quoad* married women over 18, who are not now themselves subject to curatory.
[63] Ersk. I, 7, 12.

A minor need not have a curator at all and may manage his affairs himself without any curatorial guidance.

Guardianship of minors—control of the person

A minor without parents is not subject to custody or control of his person or residence, and may choose his or her own residence.[64] Even where a minor has a curator, the latter has no control of the minor's person or residence. A curator may advise as to education and training for a career, but cannot compel.[65]

Termination of curatory

Curatory terminates by the death of curator or minor, or by the minor's attaining majority[66] or, if a girl, marrying, when she now becomes a minor without curator.[67] The office falls by supervening incapacity, natural or legal. Curators may be removed by the court.[68] If the minor refuses to accept advice, or to sign necessary deeds, the curator should apply to the court to be discharged.[68]

Accounting

On the termination of tutory or curatory, a minor or adult has an *actio directa tutelae vel curatelae* against the guardian for an accounting for intromissions in the management of the ward's affairs, payment of any balance due and restoration of papers in the guardian's possession.[69] Guardians may bring an *actio tutelae vel curatelae contraria* against the minor or adult to obtain discharge from their office and administration, to obtain relief from all engagements undertaken, for reimbursement of outlays and charges, but not for any remuneration or reward for their services.[70]

Administration by tutor, factors loco tutoris, and curators

The main distinction between the offices of tutor and curator is expressed in the maxim *tutor datur personae, curator rei.* The tutor has the governance of the pupil's person and the sole management of his estate; the

---

[64] *Flannigan* v. *Inspector of Bothwell* (1892) 19 R. 909; *Morrison* v. *Quarrier* (1894) 21 R. 889, 1071; *Fisher* v. *Edgar* (1894) 21 R. 1076.
[65] Bell, *Prin.* § 2090; Fraser, *P. & Ch*, 470.
[66] cf. *McIntosh* v. *Wood*, 1970 S.C. 179.
[67] Law Reform (Husband and Wife) (Sc.) Act, 1984, S. 3.
[68] Ersk. *supra.*
[69] Ersk. I, 7, 31; Bell, *Prin.* § 2097.
[70] Ersk. I, 7, 32; Bell, *Prin. supra.*

curator has no power of governance of the minor's person, and cannot prescribe where he may reside, and no power of management, but only of advising, and consenting and concurring with, the minor in the latter's management of his own estate.[71] In most other respects the powers, privileges, duties, and obligations of the offices of tutory and curatory coincide. The offices are gratuitous, though a father may allow a tutor-testamentary and a minor allow his curator an allowance, presumed to be in full of all charges and outlays.[72] Tutors, and factors *loco tutoris* are subject to the Judicial Factors (Scotland) Acts, 1849,[73] 1880, and 1889, and are subject to the supervision of the Accountant of Court. A factor appointed to a pupil automatically becomes a *curator bonis* when the pupil becomes a minor.[74]

No person can be compelled to accept either office and acceptance is not to be inferred by implication.[75] Having accepted, however, tutors and curators are accountable for their intromissions from the time of acceptance.[76] They must first make an inventory of the pupil or minor's whole estate.[77]

Tutors and curators must not be *auctores in rem suam* or act contrary to their trust, as by entering into obligations in which they have an interest, or which favour or benefit them.[78] Thus a curator cannot lend money to the minor, nor purchase anything from the minor, nor employ a firm in which he was a partner to conduct a lawsuit.[79]

The court will not sanction the expenditure of the ward's funds to support a person whom the ward is under no legal obligation to support[80] but expenditure of this kind may be allowed in special circumstances, if the funds are ample,[81] the beneficiary is of kin[82] and the beneficiary be destitute, particularly if the ward would probably have made the expenditure.[83] The court may even sanction it retrospectively.[84]

Pro-tutors and pro-curators

Persons who act as tutors or curators without having a legal title to the office, whether they believe themselves guardians or know that they are

---

[71] Ersk. I, 7, 14; Bell, *Prin.* § 2090. See also *Browning's Factor* (1905) 7 F. 1037.
[72] Ersk. I, 7, 15.
[73] Sometimes called the Pupils' Protection Act, 1849.
[74] 1889 Act, S. 11.
[75] As to modes of express acceptance, see Ersk. I, 7, 20.
[76] Ersk. I, 7, 20.
[77] Ersk. I, 7, 21; Act 1672, c. 2.
[78] Ersk. I, 7, 19; cf. *Dunn* v. *Chambers* (1897) 25 R. 247.
[79] *Mitchell* v. *Burness* (1878) 5 R. 1124.
[80] *Court* (1848) 10 D. 822; *Primerose* (1852) 15 D. 37; *Dunbar* (1876) 3 R. 554; *Balfour* (1889) 26 S.L.R. 268.
[81] *Primerose, supra; Robertson* (1853) 25 Sc. Jur. 554.
[82] But see *Boyle* (1854) 17 D. 790.
[83] *Gardner* (1882) 20 S.L.R. 165; *Blackwood* (1890) 17 R. 1093; *Bowers* v. *Pringle-Pattison's C.B.* (1892) 19 R. 941.
[84] *Hamilton's Tutors*, 1924 S.C. 363.

not, are deemed pro-tutors or pro-curators. They are on the same footing as tutors or curators as to the obligations incumbent on them but have none of the powers competent to those duly appointed, such as to sue third parties for payment or to grant valid discharges.[85]

Guardianship of illegitimate children

The father of a bastard pupil has no common law right of *patria potestas*, of custody or administration, and cannot appoint tutors to the child.[86] The mother is the natural custodier and tutor of her own bastard child, the only person with a legal title to its custody,[87] and probably cannot by agreement deprive herself of the right to its custody.[88] She cannot nominate a guardian to her bastard, either at common law or under the Guardianship of Infants Acts.[89] But in a question between the mother and a person to whom the mother has given the child to be brought up the court must consider the child's welfare and may refuse the mother custody.[90] After the mother's death her expressed wishes may be given effect to,[91] but apart from that the bastard has no tutor but if he litigates a *tutor ad litem* will be appointed.[92] A bastard minor is not subject to his mother's control as to his person, nor is she his curator for business matters. He has no curator, unless he chooses one for himself, but if he litigates a curator *ad litem* may be appointed.[93]

Guardianship of legitimated children

Till legitimation the child is under the mother's guardianship as a bastard. After legitimation it passes into the tutory or curatory of its father and is thereafter regarded as if legitimate from birth.

Guardianship of adopted children

On adoption a child passes into the guardianship of its adoptive parents and falls to be treated as if legitimate from birth.

---

[85] Stair I, 6, 12; Bankt. I, 7, 19; Ersk. I, 7, 28; Bell, *Prin.* § 2098; Fraser, *P. & Ch.*, 561; *Fultons* v. *F.* (1864) 2 M. 893.
[86] Bell, *Prin.* s 2071.
[87] *Sutherland* v. *Taylor* (1887) 15 R. 224.
[88] *Macpherson* v. *Leishman* (1887) 14 R. 780; *Kerrigan* v. *Hall* (1901) 4 F. 10.
[89] *Brand* v. *Shaws* (1888) 16 R. 315.
[90] Custody of Children (Sc.) Act, 1891; *Mackenzie* v. *Keillor* (1892) 19 R. 963; *Campbell* v. *Croall* (1895) 22 R. 869; *Kerrigan, supra; Mitchell* v. *Wright* (1905) 7 F. 586; *Walter* v. *Culbertson*, 1921 S.C. 490.
[91] *Brand, supra.*
[92] *Ward* v. *Walker*, 1920 S.C. 80.
[93] *Young* (1828) 7 S. 220.

Factors loco tutoris *and* curators bonis

Failing tutors or curators appointed under other principles the Court of Session[94] and sheriff court[95] may appoint a judicial factor *loco tutoris*[96] or a *curator bonis*[97] to supply the need. Such factors are officers of the court and subject to the supervision of the Accountant of Court, and must conform to the relevant statutes.[98] A factor *loco tutoris* becomes a *curator bonis* on the ward becoming a minor.[99] He has no control of the person of the pupil.[1]

Appointments have been made where the tutor was acting improperly,[2] to administer sums of damages awarded to pupils[3] or minors,[4] to supersede the father as curator,[5] to enable a minor to sell heritage,[6] to complete title to land in a minor's name and complete sale thereof,[7] to advise in managing inherited estate.[8] A factor *loco tutoris* cannot be appointed to act jointly with a surviving widow.[9]

Protected children

A child placed in the care and possession of a person not a parent, guardian, or relative of his, or of an applicant for an adoption order, is a protected child till he attains 18 or is adopted.[10] Notice must be given to the local authority which may inspect premises and ensure the well-being of protected children.[11] The sheriff may order his removal to a place of safety and he may be taken into the care of a local authority.[12]

Children in care

A local authority must receive into its care a child appearing to be under seventeen, if it appears that he has neither parent nor guardian, or has

---

[94] At common law and under Judicial Factors Acts, 1849 and 1889.
[95] By Judicial Factors (Sc.) Act, 1880, and Law Reform (Misc. Prov.) (Sc.) Act, 1980, S. 14.
[96] Ersk. I, 7, 10; Bell, *Prin.* § 2114.
[97] Bell, *Prin.* § 2121.
[98] Judicial Factors (Sc.) Acts, 1849 (Pupils' Protection Act), 1880 and 1889.
[99] 1889 Act, S. 11; *Stiven v. Masterton* (1892) 30 S.L.R. 50.
[1] *Bryce v. Graham* (1828) 3 W. & S. 323.
[2] *Edgar v. Fisher's Trs.* (1893) 21 R. 59, 325; *Fisher v. Edgar* (1894) 21 R. 1076.
[3] *Collins v. Eglinton Iron Co.* (1882) 9 R. 500; *McAvoy v. Young's Paraffin Oil Co.* (1882) 19 S.L.R. 441; *Anderson v. Muirhead* (1884) 11 R. 870; *Connolly v. Bent Colliery Co.* (1897) 24 R. 1172; *Boylan v. Hunter*, 1922 S.C. 80; *Fairley v. Allan*, 1948 S.L.T. (Notes) 81; *Falconer v. Robertson*, 1949 S.L.T. (Notes) 57; *McIntosh v. Wood*, 1970 S.C. 179.
[4] *Sharp v. Pathhead Spinning Co.* (1885) 12 R. 574; cf. *Jack v. N.B. Ry.* (1886) 14 R. 263.
[5] *McNab v. NcN.* (1871) 10 M. 248.
[6] *Perry* (1903) 10 S.L.T. 536.
[7] *Waring*, 1933 S.L.T. 190.
[8] *Perry, supra.*
[9] *Speirs*, 1946 S.L.T. 203.
[10] Adoption Act, 1978, S. 32.
[11] S. 33.
[12] S. 34.

been and remains abandoned or lost, or that his parent or guardian is prevented from providing for the child's accommodation, maintenance, and upbringing, and that the intervention of the local authority is necessary in the interests of the child's welfare; it must keep the child in care so long as is necessary and the child has not attained 18.[13] It may in prescribed circumstances resolve to vest in it the parental rights and powers with respect to a child in care, or to vest in a voluntary organization the parental rights and powers with respect to a child in the care of that organization.[14] Such a resolution is effective until the child attains 18.[15] It supersedes a prior award of custody to a parent[16] but a relative may thereafter petition for access.[17] The local authority must seek to further the best interests of the child.[18] The cases of such children must be reviewed every six months.[19] The local authority discharges its duty by boarding the child out, or maintaining him in a residential establishment.[20] It may contribute to the maintenance of persons over school age but not 21,[21] and give advice, guidance, or assistance to children formerly in care and under 18.[22] Local authorities must also ensure the well-being of foster-children maintained for reward by persons other than relatives or guardians and may inspect premises and impose conditions.[23] The sheriff may order the removal of a foster-child kept in unsuitable surroundings.[24]

Children in need of compulsory care

A child who has not attained 16, or one between 16 and 18 in respect of whom a children's hearing has made a supervision requirement, or a child whose case has been referred to a children's hearing, may be in need of compulsory measures of care if he is beyond the control of his parent, is falling into bad associations or is exposed to moral danger, or lack of care is likely to cause him unnecessary suffering or to impair his health or

---

[13] Social Work (Sc.) Act, 1968, S. 15.
[14] S. 16 as substituted by the Children Act, 1975, S. 74. cf. *Strathclyde R.C.* v. *T.*, 1984 S.L.T. (Sh. Ct.) 18; *Lothian R.C.* v. *T.*, 1984 S.L.T. (Sh. Ct.) 74; *Lothian R.C.* v. *B.*, 1984 S.L.T. (Sh. Ct.) 83. The power may be delegated to the social work committee: *Central Regional Council* v. *Mailley*, 1977 S.L.T. (Sh. Ct.) 36; *Lothian R.C.* v. *B.*, 1984 S.L.T. (Sh. Ct.) 83 By S. 16 A (1975 Act, S. 75) the local authority may assume parental powers vested in a voluntary organization. S. 17 (amended 1975 Act, S. 76) states the effect of the assumption of parental rights. For Ss. 18 and 18A see 1975 Act, Ss. 77–8.
[15] S. 18.
[16] *Beagley* v. *B.*, 1984 S.L.T. 202.
[17] *MacInnes* v. *Highland R.C.*, 1982 S.L.T. 288.
[18] S. 20 amended 1975 Act, S. 79.
[19] S. 20A added by 1975 Act, S. 80.
[20] S. 21.
[21] S. 26.
[22] Foster children (Sc.) Act, 1984, Ss. 1–7.
[23] 1984 Act, S. 12.
[24] 1975 Act, S. 81.

development,[25] or an offence has been committed against him, or is a
female member of a household and another female has been subjected to
incest, or he has failed to attend school regularly or has committed an
offence or his case has been referred to a children's hearing.[26] Such a
child may be brought before a children's hearing and may be required to
submit to supervision in accordance with conditions,[27] or to reside in a
residential establishment.[28] If the grounds for referral are not accepted
application is made to the sheriff for a finding whether they are established or not.[29] A supervision requirement may be terminated[30] and ends
when the child attains 18.[31] Contributions in respect of a child subject to
a supervision requirement are payable by his parents while he is under 16
and by the child himself if over 16 and engaged in remunerative
employment.[32]

Right of local authority to aliment

Where a maintainable child is illegitimate the local authority has the same
right as the mother to bring an action for affiliation and aliment for
aliment in respect of the child. Where a decree for aliment of an illegitimate child is in force the local authority may have the court order
payments under the decree to be paid to it.[33]

INCAPACES

Persons physically incapacitated

A person physically incapacitated is not thereby deprived of any legal
capacity or power for managing his affairs, but if his incapacity is of such
a nature or gravity that he cannot execute necessary deeds or attend to
affairs, the court may appoint a *curator bonis* on the petition of any
relative or interested person, supported by two medical certificates of
incapacity to manage his affairs.[34]

---

[25] *McGregor* v. *L.,* 1981 S.L.T. 194; *M.* v. *McGregor,* 1982 S.L.T. 41.
[26] Social Work (Sc.) Act, 1968 Ss. 30, 32.
[27] It is competent to impose a condition of residence with one parent though the Court of
Session has awarded interim custody to the other parent: *Aitken* v. *A.,* 1978 S.L.T. 183.
[28] Ibid., S. 44. On access by parent see *D.* v. *Strathclyde R.C.,* 1985 S.L.T. 14. On children's
hearings see Ss. 33–58. On residential establishments see Ss. 59–68.
[29] S. 42; *K.* v. *Finlayson,* 1974 S.L.T. (Sh. Ct.) 51; *H.* v. *Mearns,* 1974 S.L.T. 184. See also
J.F. v. *McGregor,* 1981 S.L.T. 334; *McGregar* v. *H.,* 1983 S.L.T 626.
[30] Ibid., Ss. 47, 52.
[31] Ibid., S. 47.
[32] Ibid., Ss. 78, 83.
[33] Ibid., S. 81.
[34] *Kirkpatrick* (1853) 15 D. 734; *Duncan,* 1915, 2 S.L.T. 50.

Persons mentally incapacitated: care of person

At common law the court may appoint the nearest male agnate as tutor-at-law, or appoint a suitable person as guardian (tutor-dative) of the person of an incapax, without prejudice to administration of his property by a *curator bonis*.[35] If the nearest male agnate were served tutor-at-law he was formerly debarred from custody of the ward's person, because suspicion attached to him as the ward's heir,[36] but little force now attaches to this.[35]

A person suffering from mental disorder i.e. mental illness or mental handicap, may, in pursuance of an application for admission, be detained in hospital if suffering from mental disorder which makes treatment appropriate, or from mental handicap comprising severe mental impairment or treatable mental impairment, and detention for treatment is necessary.[37] Admission and detention requires an application to the hospital management board by the patient's nearest relative or a mental health officer, accompanied by two medical recommendations, and approved by the sheriff[38] Alternatively such a person may receive treatment as a voluntary patient.[39] Guardianship requires a similar application to the local health authority, accompanied by two medical recommendations, and approved by the sheriff, and naming as guardian the local health authority, a person chosen by that authority, or any other person including the applicant, accepted as a suitable person to act in that behalf by that authority.[40] Guardianship may be transferred in case of death or incapacity of the guardian.[41]

Approval of an application for admission is authority for the patient's removal and admission within seven days;[42] approval of a guardianship application confers on the local health authority or the guardian named, to the exclusion of anyone else, the powers to require the patient to reside at a specified place, to attend for treatment or training, and to require access to be given to a doctor, mental health officer, or other specified person.[43] A patient may be transferred from detention to another hospital or to the guardianship of a local health authority or of a person approved by such authority.[44] If a guardian dies or wishes to relinquish the post, guardianship vests in the local health authority.[45]

---

[35] *Dick v. Douglas*, 1924 S.C. 787. Such a person may seek delivery of the person of the ward into his custody.
[36] Ersk. I, 7, 7.
[37] Mental Health (Sc.) Act, 1984, Ss. 17–18.
[38] 1984 Act, Ss. 18–23.
[39] 1984 Act, S. 17 (2).
[40] 1984 Act, Ss. 37–52.
[41] 1984 Act, S. 46.
[42] 1984 Act, S. 22.
[43] 1984 Act, S. 41.
[44] 1984 Act, Ss. 29, 45.
[45] 1984 Act, S. 46.

In a case of urgent necessity an emergency recommendation may be made justifying detention for 72 hours,[46] which may be extended by 28 days in particular circumstances.[47] There is still a common law power to detain in emergency.[48]

A patient who absents himself may be taken into custody but not after 28 days, in the case of a patient liable to be detained or subject to guardianship by reason of mental deficiency, or 72 hours, in the case of a patient liable to be detained under an emergency recommendation, or twenty-eight days in other cases.[49]

Detention or guardianship lasts only for 6 months but may be renewed for a further 6 months and thereafter for periods of a year.[50] A patient aged at least 16 may appeal to the sheriff to order his discharge.[50]

The Mental Welfare Commission for Scotland (replacing the General Board of Control for Scotland) has the duty of exercising protective functions in respect of persons who by reason of mental disorder are incapable of adequately protecting their persons or their interests[52] Various rights of appeal against detention are provided.[53]

Persons mentally incapacitated: care of property

At common law a person found incapax by the process of cognition of the insane was superseded in the management of his property by the nearest male agnate of full age or a near male relative as tutor-at-law,[54] and this is still competent.[55] Alternatively, a person might be appointed tutor-dative to an incapax.[56] Subsequently it became normal for the court on the petition of a relative[57] supported by two medical certificates[58] to appoint a suitable person, frequently the petitioner, to be *curator bonis* to the incapax.[59] The alleged incapax may oppose the petition.[60] Such a

---

[46] 1984 Act, Ss. 34–5.
[47] 1984 Act, S. 26.
[48] *B. v. F.,* 1987 S.C.L.R. 155.
[49] 1984 Act, S. 28.
[50] 1984 Act, S. 30; *W. v. Carstairs State Hospital,* 1967 S.L.T. (Sh. Ct.) 18.
[51] 1984 Act, Ss. 33, 50.
[52] 1984 Act, Ss. 2–6.
[53] 1984 Act, Ss. 35, 52.
[54] Stair I, 6, 25; Bankt. III, 47; Ersk. I, 7, 50; Bell, *Prin.* § 2103–12; Fraser, *P. & Ch.,* 651; *Irving v. Swan* (1868) 7 M. 86; *Larkin v. McGrady* (1874) 2 R. 170; see also *C.B. v. A.B.* (1891) 18 R. (H.L.) 40 (incapax not entitled to insist on cognition): *Simpson v. S.* (1891) 18 R. 1207; *A.B. v. C.B.,* 1937 S.C. 408.
[55] Court of Session Act, 1868, S. 101, replacing Act, 1585, c. 18.
[56] *Urquhart* (1860) 22 D. 932; *Simpson* (1861) 23 D. 1292; *Graham* (1881) 8 R. 996.
[57] Or of the incapax himself: *A.B.* (1908) 16 S.L.T. 557.
[58] On these see *McKechnie* (1890) 27 S.L.R. 261; *Knox* (1894) 2 S.L.T. 388; *Leslie* (1895) 3 S.L.T. 128; *Calderwood v. Duncan* (1907) 14 S.L.T. 777. For remit to neutral medical man see *Davies v. D.,* 1928 S.L.T. 142; *Shand v. S.,* 1950 S.L.T. (Notes) 32; *Brown v. Hackston,* 1960 S.C. 27.
[59] *Johnstone v. Barbe,* 1928 S.N. 86.
[60] e.g. *Dowie v. Hagart* (1894) 21 R. 1052; *Greig,* 1923 S.L.T. 434; *Davies, supra; Shand, supra.*

curator bonis is subject to the Judicial Factors Acts and subject to the supervision of the Accountant of Court.[61] Hence the court will rarely appoint as curator a person residing outwith the jurisdiction.[62] A married woman may be curator.[63] Such an appointment supersedes a factory and commission granted by the ward while capax.[64] Service of a relative as tutor-at-law supersedes the appointment of a tutor-dative or *curator bonis*.[65]

Under the Mental Health (Scotland) Act, 1960, S. 91, a local health authority must, in case of need, petition for such an appointment and under the 1984 Act, S. 28, the Mental Welfare Commission may also do so. Hospital boards of management have limited powers to receive and hold money and valuables.

A *curator bonis* to an incapax supersedes the *incapax* in the management of his estates, but the ward is not divested of those estates;[66] the curator has the powers of a trustee under the Trusts (Scotland) Acts, 1921 and 1961. He has no power over the person of the incapax[67] but may if necessary apply to the court for the ward's protection.[68] He may sue for damages for a delict which caused the ward's incapacity,[69] take legal advice and make inquiries relative to a contemplated action of divorce against the ward's wife.[70] It is incompetent for an incapax to bring an action and have a curator *ad litem* appointed when the action comes into court.[71] When a person becomes insane during the dependence of an action the process should probably be sisted until a *curator bonis* is appointed.[72] A claim against the ward, such as for aliment, must be made against the estate.[73] The curator may be authorized to elect on the ward's behalf between legal and testamentary provisions accruing to the ward on another person's death,[74] to sell heritage,[75] or to compromise an action.[76]

---

[61] Judicial Factors Act, 1880, S. 4; 1889, S. 14.

[62] *Napier* (1902) 9 S.L.T. 439; *Duff*, 1910 2 S.L.T. 202; *Forsyth*, 1932 S.L.T. 462.

[63] *Smith Sligo*, 1914 1 S.L.T. 287.

[64] *Dick* (1901) 9 S.L.T. 177.

[65] Ersk. I, 7, 51; *Young v. Rose* (1839) 1 D. 1242; *Dick v. Douglas*, 1924 S.C. 787.

[66] Bell, *Prin.* § 2121; Irons, 310; *Yule v. Alexander* (1891) R. 167; *Mitchell & Baxter v. Cheyne* (1891) 19 R. 324; *I. R. v. McMillan's C.B.*, 1956 S.C. 142.

[67] *Robertson v. Elphinstone*, 28 June 1814, F.C.; *Bryce v. Graham* (1832) 3 W. & S. 323.

[68] *Robertson, supra; Gardiner* (1869) 7 M. 1130.

[69] *Cole-Hamilton v. Boyd*, 1963 S.C. (H.L.) 1; see also *Calver v. Howard Baker & Co.* (1894) 22 R. 1.

[70] *Thyne's C.B.* (1882) 19 S.L.R. 724.

[71] *Reid v. R.* (1839) 1 D; *Mackenzie* (1845) 7 D. 283; *Moodie v. Dempster*, 1931 S.C. 553.

[72] *Anderson's Trs. v. Skinner* (1871) 8 S.L.R. 325; *Moodie, supra.*

[73] *Latta*, 1977 S.L.T. 127.

[74] *McCall's Tr. v. McCall's C.B.* (1901) 3 F. 1065; *Neave's J.F. v. Neave's Tr.*, 1928 S.L.T. 411; *Burns' C.B. v. Burns' Trs.*, 1961 S.L.T. 166; see also *Skinner's C.B.* (1903) 5 F. 914; *Allan's Exors. v. Allan's Trs.*, 1975 S.L.T. 227.

[75] *Lothian's C.B.*, 1927 S.C. 579; *Cameron's C.B.*, 1961 S.L.T. (Notes) 21; *Barclay, Petr.*, 1962 S.C. 594.

[76] *Tennent's J.F. v. T.*, 1954 S.C. 215.

The *curator bonis* may petition for discharge when the ward recovers,[77] on having his accounts audited by the Accountant of Court and being discharged by the ward, or when the ward dies, on confirmation of the ward's executor and discharge by the latter.

There was formerly a process of interdiction[78] whereby persons liable to be imposed on were restrained from executing any deed, not being rational or onerous, affecting heritage to their prejudice without the consent of the interdictors. It was abolished in 1924.[79]

[77] *Inglis* v. *I.*, 1927 S.N. 181; *A.B.* v. *C.B.*, 1929 S.L.T. 517.
[78] Ersk. II, 7, 53.
[79] Conveyancing (Sc.) Act, 1924, S. 44(3).

CHAPTER 3.6

SOCIAL SECURITY

At common law persons had to support themselves and those having claims to be supported by them, and to provide by savings or insurance against diminution in earnings caused by unemployment, ill-health, accident, or old age. In case of poverty the poor law system made some provision for the diseased and impotent poor, so far as necessary to supply deficiencies in church-door and other contributions, the able-bodied poor being left to private charity.[1] In the twentieth century an extensive system of social security has developed, but without prejudice to private provision by savings or insurance. Though itself a branch of public rather than of private law it overlaps with private law at many points and interacts with many of its rules.

National Health Service

The National Health Service is managed by the Secretary of State for Scotland through Health Boards, local Health Councils, and various committees.[2] Each board provides general medical services, general dental services, general opthalmic services, and pharmaceutical services by persons qualified in these fields.[3] The Secretary of State has responsibility for providing hospital accommodation and related medical, nursing and other services.[4] Provision is also made for vaccination,[5] medical and dental inspection of school children, family planning and other services.[6] All these services are provided free and without contribution, save in so far as charges are expressly authorized.[7] Under certain conditions provision may be made for health service accommodation and services to be used by private patients.[8]

---

[1] Ersk. I, 7, 63; Bell, *Prin.* § 2190–204.

[2] National Health Service (Sc.) Act, 1978, Ss. 1–17.

[3] Ss. 18–35. This includes provision of medicines on prescription, hearing aids, dentures, and spectacles.

[4] S. 36.

[5] The Vaccine Damage Payments Act, 1979, authorizes payment of compensation where severe disablement occurs as a result of vaccination against certain diseases or contact with persons vaccinated against them.

[6] Ss. 37–48.

[7] Ss. 1, 69–75.

[8] Ss. 50–68.

Social security

The numerous kinds of social security benefits are of three main types, National Insurance benefits which can be claimed only by persons who have paid enough contributions, non-contributory benefits, claimable by those who satisfy the conditions, without reference to contributions, and means-tested benefits, claimable by those who satisfy conditions of need, having given evidence of income low enough to qualify but without reference to contributions.

Social security benefits are paid from a National Insurance Fund, built up from contributions by employers, earners, and others and Treasury supplements. Contributions are of four classes:

Class 1, earnings related, paid partly by employees (S. 4);

Class 2, flat-rate, paid weekly by self-employed earners (S. 7);

Class 3, paid voluntarily by earners and others to secure entitlement to benefit, or to make up entitlement (S. 8);

Class 4, paid in respect of the profits or gains of a trade, profession or vocation or equivalent earnings (Ss. 9–10). The amounts of contributions are increased annually.[9]

Contributory benefits[10] comprise:

(a) unemployment benefit (with earnings-related supplement and increase for adult and child dependants) subject to certain disqualifications (Ss. 14, 17–20).

(b) sickness benefit (with earnings-related supplement and increase for adult and child dependants) (Ss. 14, 17), but the first twenty-eight weeks of sickness must be covered by statutory sick pay from the person's employer.[11]

(c) invalidity benefit, comprising:

(i) invalidity pension (with increase for adult and child dependants) (Ss. 15, 17);

(ii) invalidity allowance (Ss. 16, 17).

(d) maternity benefit, comprising:

maternity allowance (with earnings-related supplement and increase for adult and child dependants) (Ss. 22, 23).

(e) widow's benefit, comprising:

(i) widow's allowance (with earnings-related supplement and increase for adult and child dependants) (S. 24);

---

[9] Social Security Act, 1975, S. 1. Class 4 contributions are a tax, exacted by the Inland Revenue, and secure no benefits at all. It is a Government fraud. In certain circumstances individuals belong to two classes and have to contribute under both heads.

[10] The sections of the Act dealing with eligibility for each benefit are noted under each benefit.

[11] Social Security and Housing Benefits Act, 1982, Part I, and. Social Security Act, 1985, Part III.

    (ii) widowed mother's allowance (with increase for child de-
        pendants) (S. 25);
    (iii) widow's pension (S. 26).
(f) retirement pensions of the following categories:

Category A, payable to a person by virtue of his own contributions
(with increase for adult and child dependants) (Ss. 27, 28, 30;
Social Security Act, 1985, S. 9).
Category B, payable to a woman by virtue of her husband's contributions or conversely (with increase for child dependants) (Ss.
27, 29, 30).

(g) child's special allowance (S. 31).

In these cases, except for invalidity benefit, entitlement depends on
satisfaction of contribution conditions, and only certain classes of contributions entitle to certain benefits.[12] In certain cases there is entitlement
for partial satisfaction of contribution conditions.[13] Non-payment of contributions is an offence[14] and unpaid contributions for twelve months
preceding have priority in bankruptcy or liquidation.

Non-contributory benefits[15] comprise:

(a) attendance allowance (S. 35).
(b) severe disablement allowance (with increase for adult and child
dependants) (Ss. 36, 49; Health and Social Security Act, 1984,
S. 11).
(c) Mobility allowance (Social Security Pensions Act, 1975, S. 22).
(d) invalid care allowance (with increase for adult and child dependants) (Ss. 37, 49).
(e) guardian's allowance (S. 38).
(f) retirement pensions of the following categories:

Category C, payable to certain persons who were over pensionable
age on 5 July 1948 and their wives and widows (with increase for
adult and child dependants), and Category D, payable to persons
over the age of 80 (S. 39).

(g) age addition, payable to persons over 80, by way of increase of a
retirement pension of any category or of some other pension or
allowance from the Secretary of State (S. 40).

The rates of benefit are altered from year to year.

Industrial injuries benefits
Where an employed earner suffers personal injury caused after 4 July,
1948, by accident arising out of and in the course of his employment,

---

[12] S. 13.
[13] S. 33. As to increases for dependants see Ss. 41–8.
[14] Ss. 146–52.
[15] S. 34. The sections of the Act dealing with eligibility for each benefit are noted under each
benefit.

being employed earner's employment, there are payable the following benefits:[16]

> (a) sickness benefit, during the period he is, as a result of the injury, incapable of work (Social Security and Housing Benefits Act, 1982, S. 39).
>
> (b) disablement benefit, by way of gratuity or pension if he suffers as a result of the injury from loss of physical or mental faculty, with possible unemployability supplement or reduced earnings allowance (Ss. 57–63; Social Security Act, 1986, Sch. 3).
>
> (c) industrial death benefit, if the earner dies as a result of the injury (Ss. 67–75).

The Act specifies certain circumstances in which injuries are deemed to arise out of and in the course of employment (Ss. 52–5).

Industrial diseases

A person who has been in employed earner's employment is entitled to industrial injuries benefits in respect of any prescribed disease or personal injury due to the nature of that employement and developed after 4 July, 1948. A disease or injury may be prescribed if the Secretary of State is satisfied that it ought to be treated as a risk of the occupation and not as a risk common to all persons and it is such that, in the absence of special circumstances, the attribution of particular cases to the nature of the employment can be established or presumed with reasonable certainty.[17]

Claims of social security benefit

Benefits must in general be claimed in the prescribed manner and within the prescribed time.[18] Benefits cannot be assigned or charged.[19] In the case of industrial injuries benefit accidents have to be notified and claimants have to undergo medical examination from time to time and to submit to medical treatment.[20]

Determination of questions and claims

Certain questions are determined by the Secretary of State, and a question of law arising from some of them may be referred for decision to the Court of Session, or appealed to that Court.[21] Most questions are deter-

---

[16] S. 50. The sections of the Act dealing with eligibility for each benefit are noted under each benefit. There are provisions for increases for dependants.
[17] Ss. 76–8.
[18] Ss. 79–86; Social Security Act, 1985, S. 17.
[19] S. 87.
[20] Ss. 88–92.
[21] Ss. 93–6.

mined by adjudication officers, subject to appeal to social security appeal tribunals and then to Social Security Commissioners.[22] Medical issues are decided by medical boards and medical appeal tribunals.

Child benefit

Under the Child Benefit Act, 1975,[23] a person who is responsible for one or more children in any week is entitled to child benefit for each child, paid by the Secretary of State of Social Services at a weekly rate prescribed by regulations. A child is a person under 16 or under 19 and receiving full-time education, other than advanced education. It is not payable for children in detention, under the care of the local authority, or married. Entitlement to child benefit is determined by an adjudication officer, social security appeal tribunal, or a Social Security Commissioner. Child benefit increase is paid in addition to single parents bringing up children alone and not already receiving widow's or certain other benefits. Child's special allowance is payable to a divorced woman with a child if her ex-husband has been paying, or been liable to pay, aliment for the child, and has died; it ceases on remarriage.

Occupational pensions

Rates of contributions to and benefits from social security are reduced where an occupational pension scheme provides for an earner and his widow the requisite benefits and his employment is contractedout under a certificate granted by the Occupational Pensions Board.[24] An occupational pension scheme must comply with conditions as to financing and assurance of benefits and must in general provide for a pension from the time when the earner attains pensionable age for his lifetime, and for the earner's widow to be entitled to a pension under the scheme. A guaranteed minimum pension may not be assigned or charged for debt.

Income support

Income support, replacing supplementary benefits, provides a basic weekly income determined by age and family responsibilities, with age-related amounts for each child and extra allowances for certain specific groups. A social fund makes discretionary loans or grants for special contingencies such as funerals.[25]

---

[22] Health and Social Services and Social Security Adjudications Act, 1983, S. 25.
[23] Superseding Family Allowance Acts.
[24] Social Security Act, 1973; Social Security Pension Act, 1975.
[25] Social Security Act, 1986, Part II. The scheme replaces the National Assistance scheme under National Assistance Act, 1948 and the supplementary Benefits scheme under the Supplementary Benefit Act, 1976.

Family credit

Family credit is a benefit for any family in Great Britain if the weekly amount of its resources falls short of the prescribed amount. The family resources are the aggregate of the normal gross income of its members, with certain exceptions, calculated in a specified manner.[26]

Housing benefits

The Social Security and Housing Benefits Act, 1982, Part II, authorizes the making of Schemes, administered by local authorities, called statutory rate rebate scheme, statutory rent rebate scheme, and statutory rent allowance scheme, for such rebates and allowances from charges otherwise made for housing, in lieu of provisions formerly made by local authorities. Local authorities may modify the schemes in particular areas.

Housing of homeless persons

The Housing (Homeless Persons) Act, 1977 imposes on housing authorities a duty (S. 4), where a person who has applied to them for accommodation is homeless or threatened with homelessness (S. 1), to furnish him with advice and appropriate assistance, where he does not have a priority need (S. 2) or has, but became homeless or threatened with homelessness intentionally (S. 17), or to secure that accommodation is made available for him for a reasonable period, if he is homeless and they have a duty to him, or to take resonable steps to secure that accommodation does not cease to be available for his occupation, if he is threatened with homelessness and has a priority need but they are not satisfied that he became so threatened intentionally, or to secure that accommodation becomes available for his occupation, if he is homeless and has a priority need but did not become homeless intentionally. In case of dispute it is for the person to aver in what respects the housing authority is not entitled to be satisfied that he became homeless intentionally.[27] A spouse entitled to apply for occupancy rights in a matrimonial home is not homeless.[28] A person who abandons tenancy of a house is not intentionally homeless.[29]

   A housing authority's failure to implement its statutory duty gives rise to a claim of damages.[30]

Other related provisions

Other related provisions include free milk and vitamins for certain mothers and children, paid maternity leave from employment, free

---

[26] Social Security Act, 1986, Part II.
[27] *Mackenzie* v. *W. Lothian D.C.*, 1979 S.C. 433; *Brown* v. *Hamilton D.C.*, 1983 S.C. (H.L.) 1; *Kelly* v. *Monklands D.C.*, 1986 S.L.T. 169.
[28] *McAlinden* v. *Bearsden D.C.*, 1986 S.L.T. 191.
[29] *Hynds* v. *Midlothiam D.C.*, 1986 S.L.T. 54.
[30] *Mallon* v. *Monklands D.C.*, 1986 S.L.T. 347.

school milk and meals, educational maintenance allowance, school uniform and clothing grants, fares to school, students grants and allowances, redundancy payments, employment rehabilitation allowance, training allowance, war disablement pensions, war widows or dependant's pensions, reduced fares on transport, the Legal Aid Scheme,[31] and tax concessions.

The Criminal Injuries Compensation Scheme may compensate a person injured as a result of a crime of violence or when trying to prevent a crime or arrest a suspected criminal.

[31] Legal Aid and Advice (Scotland) Act, 1986.

PART 2

UNINCORPORATED ASSOCIATIONS

Natural persons frequently associate themselves in groups for particular purposes. In some cases these groups are deemed by law to be unincorporated associations in which case the group is not incorporated or treated as a legal entity distinct from the members of the group. In other cases the group is legally incorporated and forms a legal entity quite distinct from the natural persons who are its officials or members.[1]

The main kinds of unincorporated associations are voluntary associations, which include clubs and societies, and churches other than the Church of Scotland, friendly societies, trade unions and employers' associations, and partnerships.[2]

CHAPTER 3.7

VOLUNTARY ASSOCIATIONS

Voluntary associations are groups of natural persons who have voluntarily associated themselves for some common lawful purpose.[3] But the group they form is not recognized by the law as a corporation or legal entity endowed with legal personality, and it has no existence in law distinct from the aggregate of the members, unless it can be, and has been, incorporated as a company.[4] Hence such a body must be represented in legal transactions by its authorized office-bearers,[5] or the office-bearers and authorized representative members may sue jointly,[6] or mandataries specially authorized may sue.[7] It is necessary when suing such an association only to call the society and its office-bearers.[8] A

---

[1] Chs. 3.11–3.15, infra.
[2] For these see Chs. 3.8–3.10, infra.
[3] See generally More, Lect. I, 210.
[4] e.g. St Johnstone F.C. v. S.F.A. Ltd., 1965 S.L.T. 171.
[5] Edinburgh Veterinary Medical Society v. Dick's Trs. (1874) 1 R. 1072.
[6] Renton F.C. v. McDowall (1891) 18 R. 670; Bridge v. South Portland St. Synagogue, 1907 S.C. 1351.
[7] Chapter-General of the Temple v. Mackersey (1903) 11 S.L.T. 516; Pagan & Osborne v. Haig, 1910 S.C. 341.
[8] Somerville v. Rowbotham (1862) 24 D. 1187; Skerret v. Oliver (1896) 23 R. 468; Bridge, supra.

member has no title to sue for a wrong to the association.[9] An unincorporated association carrying on business under a descriptive name may sue and be sued in that name.[10] An association is liable for wrong done by an employee while acting in the course of his employment.[11] Property must be held by one or more trustees, in trust for the association's purposes.

The relations between members of an association are contractual and the courts will intervene to secure a member's contractual rights only if some civil right or patrimonial interest under contract is involved,[12] but not if merely social claims are in issue.[13]

Types of voluntary association

The main types are member's clubs, associations, and societies,[14] churches, other than the Church of Scotland, societies formed for religious or charitable purposes or the promotion of some other serious purpose, some trade associations, and organizations of workers or of employers which are not trade unions or employers' associations.

Clubs, associations, and societies

The relations of members of an unincorporated[15] members' club[16] with one another are determined by principles of contract and the joint ownership of property. Persons who join contract with all the other members on the terms set out in the constitution and rules of the club.[17] The constitution and rules fall to be interpreted in the last resort by the court as a matter of law, and the committee or other managing body cannot validly be made the final arbiter on their interpretation.[18] The constitu-

---

[9] *Campbell* v. *Wilson*, 1934 S.L.T. 249.

[10] Sheriff Courts (Sc.) Act, 1913, Sch. 2, R. 11.

[11] *Ellis* v. *National Free Labour Assocn.* (1904) 7 F. 629.

[12] *McMillan* v. *Free Church* (1862) 24 D. 1282; *Forbes* v. *Eden* (1867) 5 M. (H.L.) 36; *Cocker* v. *Crombie* (1893) 20 R. 954; *Brook* v. *Kelly* (1893) 20 (H.L.) 104; *Murdison* v. *S. Football Union* (1896) 23 R. 449; *Mulcahy* v. *Herbert* (1898) 25 R. 1136; *Anderson* v. *Manson*, 1909 S.C. 838.

[13] *Forbes* v. *Eden* (1867) 5 M. (H.L.) 36; *Skerret* v. *Oliver* (1896) 23 R. 468; *Drennan* v. *Associated Ironmoulders*, 1921 S.C. 151.

[14] Including an unregistered friendly society: *Young* v. *Waterson*, 1918 S.C. 9; or an unregistered trade union: *Wilson* v. *Scottish Typographical Assocn.*, 1912 S.C. 534. See also *Ross* v. *L.A.*, 1986 S.L.T. 602.

[15] A member's club may be incorporated, by registration as a company limited by shares or by guarantee under the Companies Act, in which case the membership rules are contained in, or appended to, the articles of association of the company.

[16] It is otherwise with a proprietary club, owned by a person, where members by joining obtain only the privileges of using the premises for the purposes allowed by their membership. Such a club may be conducted as a limited company.

[17] *Lyttleton* v. *Blackburne* (1875) L.J. Ch. 219.

[18] *Baker* v. *Jones* [1954] 2 All E.R. 553; *Blair* v. *Mackinnon*, 1980 S.L.T. 40.

tion and rules can be altered only with the consent of all the members,[19] unless they contain provisions for alteration by other means, in which case any alteration *bona fide* and validly made is binding on all the members unless it is at variance with the fundamental purposes of the association.[20] Unless the constitution provides for dissolution in that manner, it is *ultra vires* for a majority to dissolve it against the wishes of a dissentient minority.[21]

A member is liable to contribute to the club only the agreed subscription;[22] by membership he incurs no liability to creditors of the club, unless he has acted so as to make himself liable as the club's agent[23] or has otherwise undertaken personal liability. Subject to the rules a member may at any time resign by communicating his wish to do so to the secretary.[24]

In the ordinary administration of the club, the views of the majority normally rule. Elected officers do not incur personal liability to outside creditors unless they have represented themselves as acting in a personal capacity.[25] They act normally as agents for the whole body of members. How far they may bind the members depends on the constitution and rules of the club.[26] Similarly an elected officer may incur liability as an agent for injuries sustained by a member on club property.[27] The whole club may be liable for carrying on a nuisance or causing harm to a third party.[28] A club must be registered if exciscable liquor is to be supplied to members on its premises.[29]

All members have a right of joint or common property in the club property, heritable and moveable.[30] But a member cannot insist on a sale thereof and division of the price, and on his death or resignation his right lapses and does not transmit to anyone.[31] Nor may a majority gratuitously alienate club property against the wishes of a minority.[32] If the club is

---

[19] *Dawkins* v. *Antrobus* (1881) 17 Ch. D. 615; *Harington* v. *Sendall* [1903] 1 Ch. 921. But see *Wilson* v. *Scottish Typographical Assocn.*, 1912 S.C. 534; *Abbatt* v. *Treasury Solicitor* [1969] 3 All E.R. 1175.

[20] *Thellusson* v. *Valentia* [1907] 2 Ch. 1; *Morgan* v. *Driscoll* (1922) 38 T.L.R. 251.

[21] *Peake* v. *Assoc. of English Episcopalians in Scotland* (1884) 22 S.L.R. 3; *Gardner* v. *McLintock* (1904) 11 S.L.T. 654.

[22] *Wise* v. *Perpetual Trustee Co.* [1903] A.C. 139.

[23] *Flemyng* v. *Hector* (1836) 2 M. & W. 172; *Todd* v. *Emly* (1841) 7 M. & W. 427; *Thomson* v. *Victoria Eighty Club* (1905) 13 S.L.T. 399.

[24] *Finch* v. *Oake* [1896] 1 Ch. 409.

[25] *Overton* v. *Hewett* (1886) 3 T.L.R. 246; *McMeekin* v. *Easton* (1889) 16 R. 363; *Thomson supra.*

[26] *Flemying, supra; Draper* v. *Manners* (1892) 9 T.L.R. 73.

[27] *Prole* v. *Allen* [1950] 1 All E.R. 476.

[28] *Castle* v. *St. Augustine's Links* (1922) 38 T.L.R. 615; cf. *Bolton* v. *Stone* [1951] A.C. 850.

[29] Licensing (Sc.) Act, S. 103; *Dick* v. *Stirling Tennis Club*, 1981 S.L.T. (Sh. Ct.) 103.

[30] *Edinburgh Y.W.C.A* (1893) 20 R. 894; *Murray* v. *Johnstone* (1896) 23 R. 981.

[31] *Graff* v. *Evans* (1881) 8 Q.B.D. 373; *Murray, supra.*

[32] *Murray, supra.*

wound up any surplus after meeting liabilities may be distributed among the members at the time.[33] A club can be sequestrated.[34]

A member aggrieved by expulsion may appeal to the courts which will entertain his complaint only if the effect of the expulsion has been to deprive him of his enjoyment of club property or of other patrimonial rights and if the expulsion is not authorized by the rules,[35] or was not arrived at in good faith,[36] or if the proceedings were contrary to natural justice, as where the member was not given notice or permitted to state his case.[37] If the rules make no provision for it, expulsion must be done by the whole membership.[38] If the expulsion were wrongful a claim lies for damages. If the expulsion were authorized and fairly carried through, the courts will not investigate the merits of the decision of the committee or club members.[39]

Religious, charitable, and other similar associations

Such associations are formed for the furtherance of particular objects set out in their constitution or other fundamental documents. The relations of members are contractual, and the courts will intervene only if pecuniary or proprietary issues are involved, such as deprivation of quasi-status,[40] injury to character,[41] or alleged misapplication of property.[42] Their funds and property are held in trust by the members, or persons nominated as trustees, for the objects of the society, and in case of dispute, the funds and property belong, in trust, to those who adhere to the principles of the body,[43] unless the society has the power to modify its principles or objects or has made provision in its constitutional documents for disposal of the property in the kind of event which has happened.[44]

---

[33] *Baird* v. *Wells* (1890) 44 Ch. D. 661; *Re St Andrews Allotment Assocn.* [1969] 1 All E.R. 147.

[34] Bankruptcy (Sc.) Act, 1985, S. 6 (1).

[35] *Labouchere* v. *Earl Wharncliffe* (1879) 13 Ch. D. 346; *Young* v. *Ladies Imperial Club* [1920] K.B. 523; *Bell* v. *The Trustees*, 1975 S.L.T. (Sh. Ct.) 60.

[36] *Tantussi* v. *Molli* (1886) 2 T.L.R. 731.

[37] *Fisher* v. *Keane* (1878) 11 Ch. D. 353; *Labouchere, supra*; *Dawkins* v. *Antrobus* (1881) 17 Ch. D. 615; *Anderson* v. *Manson*, 1909 S.C. 838; *Young* v. *Ladies Imperial Club* [1920] 2 K.B. 523; *Burn* v. *National Amalgamated Labourers' Union* [1920] 2 Ch. 364; *Maclean* v. *Workers' Union* [1929] 1 Ch. 602. The exercise of the power of expulsion of a member from an association, incorporated as a company limited by guarantee, need not conform to the principles of natural justice: *Gainman* v. *National Association for Mental Health* [1970] 2 All E.R. 362.

[38] *Innes* v. *Wylie* (1844) 1 C. & K. 257.

[39] *Dawkins, supra*; *Weinberger* v. *Inglis* [1919] A.C. 606; *Thomson* v. *B.M.A.* [1924] A.C. 764.

[40] *McMillan* v. *Free Church of Scotland* (1861) 23 D. 1314; *Forbes* v. *Eden* (1867) 5 M. (H.L.) 36.

[41] *Dunbar* v. *Skinner* (1841) 11 D. 945.

[42] *Craigdallie* v. *Aikman* (1813) 1 Dow 1; *Smith* v. *Galbraith*, 6 June 1839, F.C.

[43] *Free Church of Scotland* v. *Lord Overtoun* (1904) 7 F. (H.L.) 1; cf. *Ferguson Bequest Fund* (1879) 6 R. 486.

[44] *Kennedy* v. *Morrison* (1879) 6 R. 879.

Donations, contributions, or subscriptions are held in trust by the society for the furtherance of its objects[45] and are not revocable so long as those purposes are capable of fulfilment.[46] A subscription does not, unless the constitution provides therefor, make the subscriber a member.[47] If the purposes cease to be capable of fulfilment but there is an overriding general charitable intent the court will settle a scheme for the administration of the funds *cy près*,[48] but if there is no such intent the funds will be repayable to the subscribers.[49] If a subscriber cannot be traced his share probably falls to the Crown as *bona vacantia*.[50] But subscriptions may have been paid in return for benefits and hence not be returnable.[51]

The relations of a clergyman or member with such an association are contractual and if either be expelled he may recover damages if he has suffered patrimonial loss thereby.[52] The court will not require the church or association to readmit the expelled person.[53]

Trade associations

A trade association is a body of persons formed for the purposes of furthering the trade interests of its members, or persons represented by them.[54] It may be an unincorporated association or a trade union within the definition of the Trade Union Acts, or formed as a company under the Companies Acts.[55] Its functions are normally to put the views of its members before government departments and other bodies, to collect and exchange information, to carry out research, to negotiate on behalf of its members with trade unions, and generally to promote the interests of the trade in question.[56]

---

[45] *Ewing* v. *McGavin* (1831) 9 S. 622; *Connell* v. *Ferguson* (1857) 19 D. 482.

[46] *Ewing, supra; Peake* v. *Assocn. of English Episcopalians* (1884) 22 S.L.R. 3; *Stuart's Exors.* v. *Colclough* (1900) 8 S.L.T. 236.

[47] *Goodall* v. *Bilsland*, 1909 S.C. 1152.

[48] *Clephane* v. *Edinburgh Mags.* (1869) 7 M. (H.L.) 7; *Prestonpans Kirk Session* v. *Prestonpans School Board* (1891) 19 R. 193; *Gibson* (1900) 2 F. 1195; *Anderson's Trs.* v. *Scott*, 1914 S.C. 942; *Clyde International Training Ship Assocn.*, 1925 S.C. 676.

[49] *Bain* v. *Black* (1849) 11 D. 1287; 6 Bell. 317; *Connell* v. *Ferguson* (1857) 19 D. 482; *Mitchell* v. *Burness* (1878) 5 R. 954; *Simpson* v. *Moffat Working Men's Institute Trs.* (1892) 19 R. 389; *Re British Red Cross Balkan Fund* [1914] 2 Ch. 419; *Emslie's Trs.* v. *Aberdeen Female Society*, 1949 S.L.T. (Notes) 61; *E. Kilbride District Nursing Assocn.*, 1951 S.C. 64. See also *Leven Penny Savings Bank*, 1948 S.C. 147.

[50] *Incorporated Maltmen of Stirling*, 1912 S.C. 887; *Anderson's Trs.* v. *Scott*, 1914 S.C. 942; *Caledonian Employees' Benevolent Socy.* 1928 S.C. 633.

[51] *Smith* v. *Lord Advocate* (1899) 1 F. 741.

[52] *Forbes* v. *Eden* (1867) 5 M. (H.L.) 36; *Brook* v. *Kelly* (1893) 20 R. (H.L.) 104; *Skerret* v. *Oliver* (1896) 23 R. 468; *McDonald* v. *Burns*, 1940 S.C. 376. Such loss includes loss of quasi-status, the capacity to hold certain offices and to perform certain functions.

[53] *Skerret, supra; Gall* v. *Loyal Glenbogie Lodge* (1900) 2 F. 1187.

[54] Restrictive Trade Practices Act, 1976, S. 4(1). Cf. *Johnston* v. *Aberdeen Master Plumbers Assocn.*, 1921 S.C. 62.

[55] See Ch. 3.9, *infra*.

[56] See list in P.E.P., *Industrial Trade Associations* (1957).

Organizations of workers and employers' organizations

Organizations of workers[57] and organizations of employers,[58] not registered as trade unions or employers' associations under statute,[59] are voluntary associations having none of the privileges of registered bodies.[60] Such organizations were commonly illegal at common law because their objects were in restraint of trade but were legalized by the Trade Union Act, 1871, S. 3.[61] They are not now illegal merely because their purposes are in restraint of trade.[62]

Relations between the organization and the member, and between members, are contractual, regulated by the rules of the organization.[63] The courts have long sought to protect members from oppression by their organizations of their fellow members, as by expulsion unauthorized by the rules or in manner conflicting with natural justice or by unfair disciplinary action.[64]

The property of such organizations must be held by trustees,[65] but they may sue and be sued in the name of the organization and decrees are enforceable against the property belonging to or held in trust for the organization.[66]

[57] Trade Union and Labour Relations Act, 1974, S. 29.
[58] S. 28.
[59] Ss. 2, 3, 8.
[60] On these see Ch. 3.9, *infra*. The earlier Trade Union Acts, having been repealed, do not apply to non-registered unions, i.e. 'organizations'.
[61] cf. *Bernard* v. *N.U.M.*, 1971 S.L.T. 177.
[62] 1974 Act, Ss. 2, 3.
[63] cf. *Martin* v. *Scottish T. & G. W.U.*, 1952 S.C. (H.L.) 1.
[64] *Gardner* v. *McLintock* (1904) 11 S.L.T. 654; *McDowall* v. *McGhee*, 1913, 2 S.L.T. 238; *Kelly* v. *N.A.T.S.O.P.A.* (1915) 31 T.L.R. 632; *Blackall* v. *N.U. Foundry Workers* (1923) 39 T.L.R. 431; *Abbott* v. *Sullivan* [1952] 1 K.B. 189; *Lee* v. *Showmen's Guild* [1952] 2 Q.B. 329; *Huntly* v. *Thornton* [1957] 1 All E.R. 234; *Lawlor* v. *U.P.O.W.* [1965] 1 All E.R. 353; *Walker* v. *A.U.E.W.*, 1969 S.L.T. 150; *Leary* v. *N.U.V.B.* [1970] 2 All E.R. 713; *Edwards* v. *S.O.G.A.T.* [1970] 3 All E.R. 689.
[65] cf. *Re N.U.R.'s Rules* [1968] 1 All E.R. 5.
[66] 1974 Act, Ss. 2, 3. cf. *Hodgson* v. *N.A.L.G.O.* [1972] 1 All E.R. 15.

FRIENDLY AND OTHER SIMILAR SOCIETIES

Friendly societies are unincorporated societies formed for the provision by voluntary subscriptions of members for the relief or maintenance of members and their relatives, during sickness, old age, widowhood, or minority, for insuring money to be paid on a birth or death, for funeral expenses, for relief when seeking employment, and for other kindred purposes.[1] There are various types; some accumulate their funds, others divide their surpluses periodically, and some societies operate more than one system of benefit. Akin to these are cattle insurance societies, benevolent societies for any benevolent or charitable purpose, working men's clubs, old people's home societies, and specially authorized societies for any purpose which the Treasury may authorize under the Act.[1]

Creation

The Friendly Societies Act, now of 1974, provides for a central office of the registry of friendly societies, with a chief registrar, and an assistant registrar for Scotland.[2] Societies registrable under the Acts are societies formed for the purpose of providing, by voluntary subscriptions of the members, for one or more of the statutory purposes,[3] viz.: relief or maintenance of members or relatives in sickness or old age, insuring money to be paid on a birth or death, relief or maintenance during unemployment, endowment on marriage, and other specified purposes. There are financial limits on permissible assurances.

A society need not register under the Act.[4] If a society consists of at least seven members it may be registered, on submitting an application with copies of its rules containing specified particulars.[5] Certain powers

---

[1] cf. Friendly Societies Act, 1974, S. 7. For origins and development of Friendly Societies see Clapham, *Economic History of Modern Britain*; Cole, *Short History of British Working Class Movement*; Gregg, *Social and Economic History of Britain*; Beveridge, *Voluntary Action*. Statutory authority and regulation dates from 1793.

[2] 1974 Act, Ss. 1–6.

[3] S. 7 (1).

[4] *Jennings* v. *Hammond* (1881) 9 Q.B.D. 225; *Shaw* v. *Benson* (1883) 11 Q.B.D. 563; *Shaw* v. *Simmons* (1883) 12 Q.B.D. 117. There is no legal definition of an unregistered friendly society, but its purposes must be generally similar to those of a registered society. It is an unincorporated association and its property is normally vested in trustees. The Act, in general, applies only to registered societies.

[5] 1974 Act, S. 8–16; see also *Finlay* v. *Royal Liver Friendly Socy.* (1901) 4 F. 34; *Batty* v. *Scottish Legal Life Assce. Socy.* (1902) 4 F. 954; cf. *Mackendrick* v. *Union of Dock Labourers*, 1911 S.C. 83.

are exercisable only if the rules so provide. Amendments of the rules must be registered.[6] The rules must contain all the matters mentioned in Schedule 2 of the 1974 Act. They may permit a minor to be a member.[7] The registrar has discretion to reject an unsuitable name.[8] Societies may have branches, which may have separate trustees and rules, be separately registered and administered, and may secede from the parent society.[9] Every society and branch must have a registered office, specified in the rules and notified to the assistant registrar.[10]

A registered society or branch is excepted from the Unlawful Societies Act, 1799 and the Seditious Meetings Act, 1817, so long as it confines itself to society business.[11] It also has certain priorities on the death or bankruptcy of an officer of the society having money or property of the society in his possession.[12]

Management

The affairs of a society or branch are managed by its officers; the rules must provide for trustees, a secretary, a treasurer, and a committee of management,[13] and two auditors or an approved auditor. There may be other officers. The rules must provide for the removal of officers.[14] Every officer having the receipt or charge of money must, if required by the rules, find security for the rendering of his accounts.[15] All property of a society vests in the trustees thereof for the time being for the benefit of the society, the members thereof, and persons claiming through them.[16] The trustees are liable only for sums of money actually received on account of the society or branch.[17]

A member's subscriptions are not recoverable at law,[18] save that sums payable to a registered cattle insurance society or branch or to such specially authorized societies or branch thereof as the Treasury may allow are recoverable in the sheriff court.[19]

Every registered society and branch must have its accounts audited

---

[6] 1974 Act, S. 18. See also *Davie* v. *Colinton Friendly Socy.* (1870) 9 M. 96 (registration not conclusive of legality of rules).

[7] S. 60.

[8] S. 8; *R.* v. *Registrar of Friendly Societies* (1872) L.R. 7 Q.B. 741; cf. Companies Act, 1985, S. 29.

[9] Ss. 11–14.

[10] S. 7 and Sch. 2.

[11] S. 24.

[12] S. 59.

[13] S. 27.

[14] See *Glasgow District of Ancient Order of Foresters* v. *Stevenson* (1899) 2 F. 14; *Liverpool Victoria Loyal Friendly Socy.* v. *Houston* (1900) 3 F. 42.

[15] S. 27.

[16] S. 54.

[17] S. 54; *Re Cardiff Savings Bank* [1892] 2 Ch. 100, 108.

[18] S. 61.

[19] S. 22.

annually,[20] make an annual return to the registrar,[21] and have its assets and liabilities valued at least quinquennially.[22]

A registered society or branch enjoys certain privileges including exemption from income tax and stamp duty[23] and a priority over diligence and bankruptcy in recovering property from officers having it in their possession.[24]

The trustees may invest the society's funds in specified ways, make advances or loans to members, and hold land and transact with it.[25] All property vests in the trustees,[26] who are liable for their own defaults only.[27] Officers having charge of money must give in accounts to be examined and pay over money on demand by the society.[28]

The trustees of a society or branch may bring or defend legal proceedings concerning any property, right, or claim of the society or branch in their proper names, with the title of their office.[29] In proceedings by a member a society may also be sued in the name of an officer who receives contributions on behalf of the society.[30]

Members

There is no limit on the number of members. The rules may permit minors to be members.[31] The terms and manner of admission must be provided in the rules, and also the rights and liabilities of members. Members also have numerous statutory rights, such as to obtain a copy of the last annual return of the society[32] and to inspect the books.[33] Specified proportions or numbers of members have further statutory rights, such as to apply for appointment of an inspector to investigate the affairs of a society.[34] The amount which a member, or a person claiming through a member, may recover from societies is limited.[35] A member may recover damages from the funds of the society for a wrong done to him through violation of the society's rules by one of the society's

[20] S. 31.
[21] S. 43.
[22] S. 41.
[23] See *Incorporation of Tailors in Glasgow* v. *I.R.C.* (1887) 14 R. 729.
[24] S. 59.
[25] Ss. 46–53. *United Deposit Friendly Relief Socy.* (1903) 11 S.L.T. 85.
[26] S. 54.
[27] S. 54.
[28] S. 28; cf. *First Edinburgh & Leith, etc. Socy.* v. *Munro* (1883) 11 R. 5.
[29] S. 56; *Simpson* v. *Ramsay* (1874) 2 R. 129; *Kelly* v. *Peacock* (1917) 55 S.L.R. 65.
[30] S. 56; *Blue* v. *Pollock* (1866) 4 M. 1042; *General Railways Workers' Union* v. *Macdonald* (1900) 37 S.L.R. 721.
[31] S. 60.
[32] S. 44.
[33] S. 62.
[34] S. 90.
[35] S. 64.

officers.[36] A member may terminate his membership as provided by the rules, or at any time. It is usually provided that membership shall cease if contributions are in arrears for a specified period. A member cannot be expelled unless the rules give power to do so.[37] Any power must be exercised in good faith, in accordance with the rules, and for the benefit of the society.[38]

Meetings

The rules must provide for holding general meetings. The assistant registrar may call a special meeting on the requisition of a number of members.[39] Certain changes require a special resolution.[40]

Accounts

Every society must keep proper books of accounts and comply with statutory requirements as to accounts, balance sheets, and auditors.[41]

Functioning

Members pay their contributions periodically to the society, or collectors call at their homes to collect contributions. Friendly societies which receive contributions for death benefit or other assurances on life by collectors at the homes of members or persons assured at intervals of less than two months are known as collecting societies and subject to the Industrial Assurance Acts, 1923 to 1958. A member's subscriptions are not recoverable at law,[42] save in certain cases.[43]

Property and funds

The rules must provide for the investment of the society's funds, and the trustees may invest in stated ways, including land and trustee securities.[44] Societies have power, if the rules permit, to borrow on the security of land or buildings and to accept deposits made by members to a separate loan fund.[45] There are close restrictions on lending the society's money.[46]

---

[36] *Blue* v. *Pollock* (1866) 4 M. 1042.

[37] *Dawkins* v. *Antrobus* (1881) 17 Ch. D. 615; cf. *Bonsor* v. *Musicians' Union* [1956] A.C. 104.

[38] cf. *Wood* v. *Woad* (1874) L.R. 9 Ex. 190; *Fisher* v. *Keane* (1878) 11 Ch. D. 353; *Burn* v. *Nat. Amalgamated Labourers* [1902] 2 Ch. 364; *Hiles* v. *Amalgamated Woodworkers* [1968] Ch. 440.

[39] S. 90.

[40] S. 86.

[41] Ss. 29–40.

[42] S. 61.

[43] S. 22.

[44] S. 46.

[45] S. 49.

[46] S. 48.

Payments on death

The moneys payable on death may include sums insured on his life, moneys in a loan account, and money accumulated for the member. Save in exceptional cases a death certificate must be produced.[47]

Nominations

A member may, by writing under his hand[48] delivered to the society's registered office or made in a book kept there, nominate a person to whom any money payable by the society on his death, not exceeding £1,500, shall be paid.[49] He may revoke and vary the nomination.[50] Marriage revokes a nomination.[51] On receiving satisfactory proof of the nominator's death the society pays the nominee.[52] Nomination does not imply that the nominee is to have the sole beneficial interest in the money affected.[53] On the member's death, not having made a nomination, the society may pay to those whom it considers entitled without need for confirmation. If an illegitimate member dies, not having made a nomination, the trustees may pay to the person who, in the committee's opinion, would have been entitled if the member had been legitimate.[54] A society may insure the life of a child only to a limited extent, except where the person insuring has an insurable interest in the child's life.[55]

Disputes

Disputes within the society[56] are to be decided as the society rules provide,[57] which may be by arbitration,[58] and are not removable into any court; they may be referred to the assistant registrar or to the sheriff court.[59] A case may be stated on a question of law for the opinion of the

[47] S. 70.
[48] *Morton* v. *French*, 1908 S.C. 171.
[49] S. 66, amd Administration of Estates (Small Payments) (Increase of Limits) Order, 1975.
[50] cf. *Young* v. *Waterson*, 1918 S.C. 9.
[51] S. 66 (7).
[52] S. 67.
[53] *Young, supra*, where nominee had to account to executor under subsequent will for money due.
[54] Ss. 68–71. cf. *Symington* v. *Galashiels Co-operative Store Co.* (1894) 21 R. 371.
[55] S. 71; cf. *Carmichael* v. *C's Exrx.*, 1919 S.C. 636.
[56] *Melrose* v. *Adam* (1897) 34 S.L.R. 346; *Glasgow District A.O.F.* v. *Stevenson* (1899) 2 F. 14; *Lewis* v. *Paulton* (1907) 14 S.L.T. 818; *Catt* v. *Wood* [1910] A.C. 404; see also *Blue* v. *Pollock* (1866) 4 M. 1042; *Davie* v. *Colinton Friendly Socy.* (1870) 9 M. 96; *Symington, supra; Gall* v. *Loyal Glenbogie Lodge* (1900) 2 F. 1187; *McGowan* v. *City of Glasgow Friendly Socy.*, 1913 S.C. 991.
[57] S. 76 (1); *Somerville* v. *Meters of Leith* (1868) 6 M. 796; *McKernan* v. *Operative Masons* (1873) 11 M. 548; *Finlay* v. *Royal Liver Friendly Socy.* (1901) 4 F. 34; *Batty* v. *Scottish Legal Life Assce. Socy.* (1902) 4 F. 954; *Collins* v. *Barrowfield Lodge*, 1915 S.C. 190.
[58] *Galashiels Provident Bldg. Socy.* v. *Newlands* (1893) 20 R. 821; *Rombach* v. *McCormack* (1896) 4 S.L.T. 174.
[59] S. 77; *Leitch* v. *Scottish Legal Burial Socy.* (1870) 9 M. 40; *Davie* v. *Colinton Friendly Socy.* (1870) 9 M. 96.

Inner House.[60] But the jurisdiction of the Court is not excluded where it is alleged that the society has acted in contravention of its rules.[61] The court cannot enforce a decree ordering a branch to reinstate a member, as ordered by a superior court of the society, and a petition for such a decree is therefore incompetent,[62] but declarator of membership is competent.[63]

Change of status

A society may change its name, amalgamate with or transfer its engagements to another society, or convert itself into a company under the Companies Acts, or transfer its engagements to such a company. It may become a branch of another society.[64]

The assistant registrar may, on application by members, appoint an inspector to examine into and report on the affairs of the society or call a special meeting of the society, or may suspend or cancel the society's registration.[65]

Dissolution

A society may dissolve itself on the happening of an event having this effect under the rules, or, with certain consents, by an instrument of dissolution,[66] or by the award of the assistant registrar, following an application by members and investigation.[67] Any surplus assets are, if the society's constitution does not provide for it, distributable to the members in equal shares.[68] If a society fails for lack of members surviving annuitants, are not entitled to appropriate the funds.[69]

---

[60] S. 78; *Manners v. Fairholme* (1872) 10 M. 520; *Smith v. Scottish Legal Life Assce. Socy.*, 1912 S.C. 611.

[61] *McGowan v. City of Glasgow Friendly Socy.*, 1913 S.C. 991; Contrast *Crichton v. Free Gardeners* (1904) 6 F. 398.

[62] *Gall v. Loyal Glenbogie Lodge* (1900) 2 F. 1187.

[63] *Collins v. Barrowfield United Oddfellows*, 1915 S.C. 190.

[64] Ss. 81–6; *Blythe v. Birtley* [1910] 1 Ch. 226; *Wilkinson v. City of Glasgow Friendly Socy.*, 1911 S.C. 476.

[65] Ss. 87–92; *Professional, etc., Supply Assocn. v. Dougal* (1898) 5 S.L.T. 359.

[66] S. 93; *Second Edinburgh, etc., Building Socy. v. Aitken* (1892) 19 R. 603; *Kelly v. Peacock* (1917) 55 S.L.R. 65. As to winding up unregistered societies see *Smith v. Irvine and Fullarton Bldg. Socy.* (1903) 6 F. 99; *Sharp v. Dunbar Sailors Socy.* (1903) 10 S.L.T. 572.

[67] Ss. 95–7.

[68] *Re Bucks Constabulary Fund* [1979] 1 All E.R. 623.

[69] *Mitchell v. Burness* (1878) 5 R. 954; cf. *Smith v. Lord Advocate* (1899) 1 F. 741; *Sharp v. Sailors of Dunbar* (1903) 10 S.L.T. 572.

CHAPTER 3.9

TRADE UNIONS AND EMPLOYERS' ASSOCIATIONS

The law of trade unions is understandable only in the light of the history of the trade union movement and related social and economic conflicts.[1] Associations which have purposes and objects lawful at common law are lawful voluntary associations.[2] A trade combination is, however, unlawful at common law if its objects or rules or practices are in unreasonable restraint of trade,[3] and such combinations are lawful only under statute.[4] A trade combination whose purposes are criminal, or actionable as a conspiracy to injure, is not lawful either at common law or under statute.[5] At common law a trade union was an association of employers, or workmen, or employers and workmen, formed normally to impose restrictions on the conduct of trade or business and normally, therefore, existing for purposes contrary to public policy, as in restraint of trade, and consequently an unlawful association.[6]

The Trade Union Act, 1871, was the first Act which fully recognized and legalized unions even though their objects were in restraint of trade, and for a century it was the basis of the law, materially amended, however, by later Acts. Most of this legislation was superseded by the Industrial Relations Act, 1971, itself replaced by the Trade Union and Labour Relations Act, 1974, as amended.

Under the former Acts unions might be temporary or permanent, registered or unregistered, but were not incorporated bodies, though in some respects they were treated as semi-corporations. Registration was of very limited importance.

Definition of trade union

A trade union is an organization, permanent or temporary, which consists wholly or mainly of workers of one more descriptions and is an organiza-

---

[1] See Webb, *History of Trade Unionism*; Hedges and Winterbottom, *Legal History of Trade Unionism*; Cole, *Short History of the British Working Class Movement*; Pelling, *History of British Trade Unionism*; Clegg, Fox, and Thompson, *History of British Trade Unions*. For modern law see Vester and Gardner, *Trade Union Law and Practice*; Grunfeld, *Modern Trade Union Law*.

[2] *Gozney* v. *Bristol Trade Society* [1909] 1 K.B. 901; *Russell* v. *Amalgamated Carpenters* [1912] A.C. 421.

[3] *Osborne* v. *A.S.R.S.* [1911] 1 Ch. 540, 565, 572.

[4] cf. *Rigby* v. *Connol* (1880) 14 Ch. D. 482; *Yorkshire Miners Assoc.* v. *Howden* [1905] A.C. 256; *Russell, supra*; *Briggs* v. *N.U.M.*, 1968 S.L.T. (Notes) 59.

[5] cf. *Crofter Co.* v. *Veitch*, 1942 S.C. (H.L.) 1.

[6] Bell, *Prin.* § 40, 193; *Osborne* v. *A.S.R.S.* [1911] 1 Ch. 540, 565, 572; *Bernard* v. *N.U.M.*, 1971 S.L.T. 177.

tion whose principal purposes include the regulation of relations between workers and employers or employers' associations, or consists wholly or mainly of constituent or affiliated organizations or representatives thereof with such a principal purpose.[7]

Definition of employers' association

An employer's association is an organization, permanent or temporary, which consists wholly or mainly of employers or proprietors of one or more descriptions and is an organization whose principal purposes include the regulation of relations between employers of that description and workers or trade unions, or consists wholly or mainly of constituent or affiliated organizations or representatives thereof with such a principal purpose.[8]

Status of trade union

A trade union which is not a special register body[9] is not, nor to be treated as, a body corporate,[10] but it is capable of making contracts, all property belonging to it is vested in trustees in trust for the union, it is capable of suing and being sued in its own name and may be prosecuted in its own name, but any judgment or order is enforceable against property held in trust for it as if it were a body corporate. Such a union may not be registered as a company, friendly society, or industrial and provident society.

The purposes of such a trade union and, so far as relating to the regulation of relations between employers and workers, the purposes of any trade union are not, by reason only that they are in restraint of trade, unlawful so as to make any member liable to criminal proceedings for conspiracy or otherwise, or to make any agreement or trust void or voidable, nor is any rule of such a trade union or, so far as it so relates, any rule of any trade union unlawful or unenforceable by reason only that it is in restraint of trade.[11]

Status of employers' association

An employers' association may be a body corporate or an unincorporated association. In the latter case it is capable of making contracts, all property is vested in trustees in trust for the association, it is capable of suing

---

[7] Trade Union and Labour Relations Act, 1974, S. 28 (1). 'Workers' are defined in S. 30.
[8] Trade Unions and labour Relations Act, 1974, S. 28 (2). 'Employers' are defined in S. 30.
[9] 1974 Act, S. 30(1).
[10] Hence held that a union cannot sue in its own name for defamation: *E.E.P.T.U.* v. *Times Newspapers* [1980] 1 All E.R. 1097.
[11] Trade Union and Labour Relations Act, 1974, S. 2. As to trustees of property see also S. 4.

and being sued in its own name and may be prosecuted in its own name, but any judgment or order is enforceable against property held in trust for it as if it were a body corporate.

The purposes of an unincorporated employers' association and, so far as relating to the regulation of relations between employers and workers or unions, of an incorporated association are not, by reason only that they are in restraint of trade, unlawful so as to make any member criminally liable for conspiracy or otherwise or to make any agreement or trust void or voidable, nor is any rule unlawful or unenforceable by reason only that it is in restraint of trade.[12]

Lists of trade unions

The Certification Officer[13] must maintain a list of trade unions, and any organization of workers may apply to be registered on submitting specified particulars.[14] An appeal against refusal to register lies to the Employment Appeal Tribunal.[15]

A trade union on the list of unions under S. 8 may apply to the Certification Officer for a certificate that it is independent,[16] i.e. not under the control of an employer or group or employer's association.[17] Organizations must keep accounting records and make annual returns.[18]

Lists of employers' associations

The Certification Officer[13] must maintain a list of employers' organizations and any organization of employers may apply to be registered on submitting specified particulars.[14] An appeal against refusal to register lies to the Employment Appeal Tribunal.[15] Organizations must keep accounting records and make annual returns.[18]

Relations between unions and members: rule books

Membership of a union is constituted by contract, and the rules of the union are the terms of the contract between the members and between the union and each member.[19] Qualifications for membership may be

---

[12] Trade Unions and Labour Relations, Act, 1974, S. 3. As to trustees of property see also S. 4.

[13] See Employment Protection Act, 1975, S. 7. He appoints an assistant for Scotland.

[14] 1974 Act, S. 8.

[15] S. 8(7).

[16] Employment Protection Act, 1975, S. 8.

[17] 1974 Act, S. 30.

[18] Ss. 10–11 and Sch. 2.

[19] *Martin* v. *Scottish T. & G.W.U.*, 1952 S.C. (H.L.) 1; *Haggarty* v. *Scottish T. & G.W.U.*, 1955 S.C. 109; *Bonsor* v. *Musician's Union* [1956] A.C. 104; *Faramus* v. *Film Artistes Assocn.* [1964] A.C. 925; contrast *Nisbet* v. *Percy*, 1951 S.C. 350. See also *Breen* v. *A.E.U.* [1971] 2 Q.B. 175.

imposed,[20] but contribution to an organization's political fund may not be a condition of membership.[21]

In every contract of membership there is implied a right to a member, on giving reasonable notice and complying with any reasonable conditions, to terminate his membership of the union.[22] Unless there is provision to the contrary a member may resign but may not be expelled.[23] The courts will intervene if necessary to protect a member's rights by ensuring compliance with the rules and the rules of natural justice.[24] The qualifications, powers, rights, and duties of all officials should be defined by the union rules, and they are its agents and bind the union if acting within the scope of their authority.[25] Acts outwith the rules by union, committees, or officials are *ultra vires* and void.[26] The terms of employment of paid union officials, and their dismissal or removal, are regulated by the rules and by the ordinary law of employment.[27]

Closed shops—compulsory membership

A closed shop is a place of employment in which only members of a union, or a particular union, may be employed. A 'union membership agreement'[28] is one between employer and union which has the effect of requiring employees to be or become a member of a union party to the agreement. A union membership agreement must be approved by ballot.[29] Where such an agreement is in force an employee may refrain from joining a union only on the ground of conscience or other deeply held personal conviction against belonging to any union,[30] and has the rights not to have an application for membership unreasonably refused, and not to be unreasonably expelled from it, with a right of complaint to an industrial tribunal.[31] Dismissal of an employee for non-membership of a union where there is a union membership agreement is unfair if he

---

[20] cf. *Russell* v. *D. Norfolk* [1949] 1 All E.R. 109; *Nagle* v. *Fielden* [1966] 2 Q.B. 633.

[21] Trade Union Act, 1913, S. 3(1).

[22] 1974 Act, S. 7, as amd. 1976.

[23] *Luby* v. *Warwickshire Miners* [1912] 2 Ch. 371; *Abbot* v. *Sullivan* [1952] 1 K.B. 189.

[24] *Lee* v. *Showmen's Guild* [1952] 2 Q.B. 329; *Bonsor* v. *Musician's Union* [1956] A.C. 104; *Hiles* v. *Amalgamated Woodworkers* [1968] Ch. 440; *Braithwaite* v. *E.E.T.U.* [1969] 2 All E.R. 713; *Jacques* v. *A.U.E.W.* [1987] 1 All E.R. 621.

[25] cf. *N.U. Bank Employees* v. *Murray*, 1948 S.L.T. (Notes) 51; *Bonsor* v. *Musician's Union* [1956] A.C. 104.

[26] *Yorkshire Miners* v. *Howden* [1905] A.C. 256; *Martin* v. *Scottish T. & G.W.U.*, 1952 S.C. (H.L.) 1; *Thomas* v. *N.U.M.* [1985] 2 All E.R. 1.

[27] See *Byrne* v. *K.R.A.* [1958] 2 All E.R. 579; *Lawlor* v. *U.P.O.W.* [1965] 1 All E.R. 353. cf. *Ridge* v. *Baldwin* [1964] A.C. 40.

[28] Defined, Trade Union and Labour Relations Act, 1974, S. 30.

[29] Employment Act, 1982, S. 3.

[30] Employment Protection (Consolidation) Act, 1978, S. 58, as amd.; on beliefs see *Saggers* v. *B.R. Board*, 1977 I.C.R. 809; 1978 I.C.R. 1111.

[31] Employment Act, 1980, Ss. 4–5.

genuinely objects on grounds of conscience or other deeply-held personal conviction to being a member of any trade union whatsoever or of a particular trade union, or pre-closed-shop employees, or new closed shops not approved through a ballot.[32]

Action short of dismissal relating to trade union membership

An employee has a right not to have action (short of dismissal) taken against him for the purpose of preventing or deterring him from being a member of a union, or penalizing him for doing so, or from taking part in union activities, or compelling him to be or become a member of a union.[33] Such action justifies complaint to an industrial tribunal.[34] Action short of dismissal might cover failure to promote or transfer to other work. Pressure to impose union membership or recognition requirements is not immune from delictual liability under the 1974 Act, S. 13.[35]

Meetings and elections

The occasions for which meetings are required, their calling, composition, procedure, and powers are determined mainly by the rules. Interdict may be granted against an irregularly convened or conducted meeting[36] or against the implement of *ultra vires* resolutions. The conduct of elections, eligibility, candidature, and campaign are also determined by the rules,[37] supplemented by the general law as to elections. By statute every union must arrange for elections to certain offices.[38]

Disciplinary powers over members

A union can suspend, expel, fine, impose forfeitures, exclude from union office, or otherwise discipline a member only by virtue of powers contained in its rules and accepted in the contract between union and member.[39] Such powers may be exercised only by the committee or other body specified in the rules, acting as a domestic tribunal. Rules establishing a domestic tribunal and requiring resort to it before going to

---

[32] Employment Protection (Consolidation) Act, 1978, S. 58, amd. 1982 Act, S. 3.
[33] Employment Protection (Consolidation) Act, 1978, S. 23, amd. Employment Acts, 1980, S. 15, 1982, S. 10.
[34] Ibid., Ss. 24–6.
[35] Employment Act, 1982, S. 14.
[36] The court may ignore an unimportant irregularity: *Cotter* v. *N.U.S.* [1929] 2 Ch. 58.
[37] *Watson* v. *Smith* [1941] 2 All E.R. 725.
[38] Trade Union Act, 1984, Part I.
[39] *Parr* v. *Lancashire Miners* [1913] 1 Ch. 366; *Spowart* v. *T. & G.W.U.*, 1926 S.L.T. 245; *Wolstenholme* v. *Amalg. Musicians' Union* [1920] 2 Ch. 388; *Lee* v. *Showmen's Guild* [1952] 2 Q.B. 329; *Martin* v. *Scottish T. & W.G.U.*, 1952 S.C. (H.L.) 1.

law,[40] and even making it final on questions of fact,[41] are valid. A member would not be held bound by rules deemed by the court unreasonable[42] or wholly withdrawing disputes from the jurisdiction of the courts[43] or excluding the application of the principles of natural justice from a domestic inquiry.[44] Any appeals procedure within the union rules should be utilized but failure to utilize it does not prevent, if appropriate, an appeal to the ordinary courts.[45]

Either party may appeal to the ordinary courts only if it is alleged that the union had no such disciplinary powers as it claimed, or that, if it had, they were not validly exercised[46] or not exercised in conformity with the principles of natural justice. Disciplinary powers must be exercised in good faith,[47] in accordance with the rules of the union,[48] and the proceedings of the domestic tribunal must be conducted in accordance with the requirements of natural justice,[49] and the facts must be reasonably capable of supporting the tribunal's decision.[50] The courts will not inquire whether the decision of the domestic tribunal of the union is correct, or fair,[51] or reasonable;[52] they will not act as court of appeal.[53] In appropriate cases the courts may grant declarator that the discipline was *ultra vires*, or interdict against expulsion, or damages for breach by the union of the contract of membership.[54] Exceptionally, union pressure on a member or former member may justify damages for conspiracy to injure.[55]

[40] *Scott v. Avery* (1865) 5 H.L.C. 811; *White v. Kuzych* [1951] A.C. 585.
[41] *Lee, supra.*
[42] *Baker v. Jones* [1954] 2 All E.R. 553; *Edwards v. S.O.G.A.T.* [1971] Ch. 354.
[43] *Scott v. Avery* (1856) 5 H.L.C. 811; *Lee, supra.*
[44] *Russell v. D. Norfolk* [1949] 1 All E.R. 109; *Lee, supra; Lawlor v. Post Office Workers* [1965] 1 All E.R. 353.
[45] *Annamunthodo v. Oilfield Workers* [1961] A.C. 945.
[46] e.g. *Blackall v. N.U. of Foundry Workers* (1923) 39 T.L.R. 431; *Huntley v. Thornton* [1957] 1 All E.R. 234.
[47] cf. *McDowall v. McGhee*, 1913, 2 S.L.T. 238; *Kelly v. N.A.T.S.O.P.A.* (1915) 31 T.L.R. 632; *Wolstenholme v. Amalg. Musicians' Union* [1920] 2 Ch. 388; *Evans v. N.U. of Printing Workers* [1938] 4 All E.R. 51.
[48] *Spowart v. T. & G.W.U.*, 1926 S.L.T. 245. In this respect the rules must be construed strictly: *Blackall v. N.U. Foundry Workers* (1923) 39 T.L.R. 431; *Huntley v. Thornton* [1957] 1 All E.R. 234.
[49] These are: The member must be informed of the charge and given time to prepare his defence; both sides must be given a fair and equal hearing; and the decision must be reached honestly and without bias: see *Maclean v. Worker's Union* [1929] 1 Ch. 602; *White v. Kuzych* [1951] A.C. 58; *Walker v. A.U. Engineers*, 1969 S.L.T. 150; *Leary v. N.U.V.B.* [1970] 2 All E.R. 713; *Breen v. A.E.U.* [1971] 1 All E.R. 1148; 1974 Act, S. 5.
[50] *Allison v. G.M.C.* [1894] 1 Q.B. 750; *Lee, supra.*
[51] *Maclean v. Workers' Union* [1929] 1 Ch. 602.
[52] *Weinberger v. Inglis* [1919] A.C. 606; *Thompson v. B.M.A.* [1924] A.C. 764.
[53] cf. *Leeson v. G.M.C.* (1889) 43 Ch.D. 615; *Young v. Ladies Imperial Club* [1920] 2 K.B. 523; *Hamlet v. G.M.B.A.T.U.* [1987] 1 All E.R. 631.
[54] *Bonsor v. Musicians' Union* [1956] A.C. 104; *McGregor v. N.A.L.G.O.*, 1979 S.C. 401; *Partington v. N.A.L.G.O.*, 1981 S.C. 299.
[55] *Huntley v. Thornton* [1957] 1 All E.R. 234.

Walfare activities

Benevolent objects, including legal aid,[56] may be provided by a union.[57] The rules must provide for any contributions payable in respect thereof and for the payment of benefits. A member may seek interdict against expenditure on unauthorized objects.[58]

Political activities

Trade unions may apply funds to specified political objects, national or local,[59] provided they have obtained the approval of the specified political objects as objects of the union at a ballot vote of members held under special rules approved by the Certification Officer,[60] have adopted rules providing for the setting up of a separate 'political fund',[61] and make payments only out of the political fund. Periodical ballots must be held on whether to maintain a political fund.[62] A member need not contribute to his union's political fund, but may not be excluded from any union benefits nor placed under any disability for that reason.[63] A member not wishing to contribute may 'contract out' by giving notice in a statutory form.[64] A member aggrieved by breach of any of the political fund rules may complain to the Certification Officer who may make an order for remedying the breach, which is conclusive and not appealable.[65]

Accounts

Trade unions and employers' associations must cause proper accounts to be kept, giving a true and fair view of the union or association's affairs, and maintain a system of control of accounts and money. They must make annual returns to the Certification Officer and send audited accounts, and if maintaining a members' superannuation scheme have it examined by an actuary every fifth year.[66]

---

[56] cf. *Mackendrick v. N.U. Dock Labourers*, 1911 S.C. 83; *McGahie v. U.S.D.A.W.*, 1966 S.L.T. 74; on the extent of the union's duty, see *Buckley v. N.U.G.M.W.* [1967] 3 All E.R. 767; *Cross v. B.I.S.K.T.A.* [1968] 1 All E.R. 250.

[57] Trade Union Act, 1913, S. 1(2); *P.R.S. v. London Theatre of Varieties Ltd.* [1922] 2 K.B. 433.

[58] *Oram v. Hutt* [1914] 1 Ch. 98, *Re National Union of Seamen* [1929] 1 Ch. 216.

[59] Trade Union Act, 1913, S. 3(3), overruling *A.S.R.S. v. Osborne* [1910] A.C. 87 and *Wilson v. Scottish Typographical Assocn.*, 1912 S.C. 534. The definition of trade union is modified by 1974 Act, S. 25, and the section by Trade Union Act, 1984, S. 17.

[60] 1913 Act, S. 4(1).

[61] Ibid., S. 3(1).

[62] Trade Union Act, 1984, Part III.

[63] Ibid., S. 3(1); *Birch v. N.U.R.* [1950] Ch. 602.

[64] Ibid., Ss. 5, 6. From 1927 to 1946, under the Trade Union and Trade Disputes Act, 1927 (repealed 1946), a member had to 'contract-in'.

[65] 1913 Act, S. 3(2); *Forster v. National Shop Assistants* [1927] 1 Ch. 539.

[66] T.U.L.R.A., 1974, Ss. 10, 11 and Sch. 2.

Nominations by members of trade unions

The Secretary of State may make provision by regulation (a) for enabling members of trade unions not under 16 to nominate a person or persons to become entitled, at the death of the nominator, to the whole or part of the moneys payable on his death out of any funds of the union, and (b) for enabling such moneys to an amount not exceeding £1,500 (which sum may be increased) to be paid or distributed on his death without confirmation, probate, or letters of administration. Nominations made under superseded enactments continue to be valid.[67]

Termination of membership

A member is entitled to terminate his membership of a union.[68]

Contracts

A union's contracts, including those with its own members, so long as not objectionable on any other ground, are valid and legally enforceable.[65]

Delicts

A trade union cannot recover damages for any kind of wrong done to it as an entity.[70]

A union is not wholly protected from being sued for delict but is given protection in particular circumstances.

Immunity from actions for delict

Trade unions do not now have immunity from certain actions of delict. Where proceedings in delict are brought on a ground under S. 13 (1) (a) or (b) of the 1974 Act or in respect of an agreement or combination to do what, without such agreement, would be actionable as delict, the act is to be taken as done by the union only if authorized by a responsible person.[71] Damages against unions are limited and recovery is restricted.[72]

---

[67] Trade Unions and Labour Relations Act, 1974, Sch. 1, para. 31. T.U. (Nominations) Regulations, 1977. cf. *Symington* v. *Galashiels Co-op Socy.* (1894) 21 R. 371; *Morton* v. *French*, 1908 S.C. 171.

[68] 1974 Act, S. 7.

[69] *Swaine* v. *Wilson* (1890) 24 Q.B.D. 252; *Gozney* v. *Bristol Trade Society* [1909] 1 K.B. 901; *Osborne* v. *A.S.R.S.* [1911] 1 Ch. 540. Restrictions on the direct enforceability of certain contracts with members under the 1871 Act were repealed by the 1971 Act.

[70] *E.E.T.P.U.* v. *Times Newspapers* [1980] All E.R. 1097; contrast *N.U.G.M.W.* v. *Gillian* [1946] K.B. 81; *Willis* v. *London Compositors* [1947] 1 All E.R. 191.

[71] Employment Act, 1982, S. 15.

[72] Ibid., Ss. 16–17.

Improvement of industrial relations

The Advisory Conciliation and Arbitration Service[73] exists to improve industrial relations, extend collective bargaining, effect conciliation in disputes, refer trade disputes to arbitration, advise, inquire and issue Codes of Practice for the improvement of industrial relations.[74] Such a Code is admissible in evidence before an industrial tribunal or the Central Arbitration Committee, but failure to observe it does not render a person liable to any proceedings.[74]

An employer must disclose information without which a union would be materially impeded in collectively bargaining with him and information which he ought to disclose in the interests of good industrial relations, subject to certain exceptions.[75] If a union believes that an employer is refusing to disclose what he ought to disclose it may complain to the Central Arbitration Committee.[76]

The Secretary of State also is empowered[77] to issue Codes of Practice containing practical guidance for the purpose of promoting the improvement of industrial relations. After consultation with ACAS he is to publish a draft of any proposed Code of Practice and consider representations on it. A Code may be revised and reissued; such a Code may supersede one previously issued by him or by ACAS. Such a Code is admissible in evidence before a Court or industrial tribunal or the Central Arbitration Committee, but failure to observe any provision does not make a person liable to any proceedings.

Collective bargaining

The main function of a trade union are to bargain collectively on behalf of its members with employers or employers' associations about the terms and conditions of employment of the members or groups of them. An employer has a discretion with which of various competing unions he will negotiate.[78] At common law such collective bargains are not enforceable as terms of the contracts of individual employees,[79] unless imported into such contracts by reference, or by custom of trade.[80]

Collective agreements

Any collective agreement made after 31 July 1974 is conclusively presumed not to have been intended to be legally enforceable unless it is in

---

[73] Employment Protection Act, 1975, S. 1 and Sch. 1. Its functions to secure recognition of trade unions were abolished by the Employment Act, 1980.
[74] 1975 Act, S. 6. These are replacing the Code of Practice under T.U.L.R.A. 1974, Sch. I, Part 1; 1975 Act, Sch. 17, para. 4. The texts are in *Butterworth's Employment Law Handbook*.
[75] 1975 Act, Ss. 17–18.
[76] 1975 Act, S. 19.
[77] Employment Act, 1980, S. 3.
[78] *R. v. Post Office* [1981] 1 All E.R. 139.
[79] *Hulland* v. *Saunders* [1945] K.B. 78; *Ford Motor Co.* v. *A.U. Engineers* [1969] 2 Q.B. 393.
[80] *Devonald* v. *Rosser* [1906] 2 K.B. 728.

writing and contains a provision stating that the parties intend it to be a legally enforceable contract. It may be in part not enforceable and in part enforceable.

Terms of a collective agreement which restrict the right of workers to strike or take industrial action do not form part of a contract between worker and employer unless it is in writing, contains a provision expressly stating that those terms may be incorporated in such a contract, is reasonably accessible to the worker, is one where each trade union a party to it is an independent one, and unless the contract with that worker expressly or impliedly incorporates these terms in the contract.[81]

Trade disputes

A trade dispute[82] is a dispute between workers and their employer which relates wholly or mainly to one or more of (a) terms and conditions of employment (b) engagement, non-engagement, termination, or suspension of employment or duties thereof, (c) allocation of work, (d) matters of discipline, (e) membership or non-membership of a trade union, (f) facilities for trade union officials, and (g) machinery for negotiation or consultation, including recognition. It includes disputes between a minister of the Crown and any workers though he is not their employer, in certain cases, and disputes to which a trade union or employers' association is a party.

Strikes and lockouts

In industrial relations pressure by one side on the other may take the form of a threat of, or an actual, strike or lockout. A strike is a concerted stoppage of work by a group of workers, in contemplation or furtherance of a trade dispute, whether they are parties to the dispute or not, whether (in the case of all or any of those workers) the stoppage is or is not in breach of their terms and conditions of employment, and whether it is carried out during, or on the termination of, their employment. A lockout is action which, in contemplation or furtherance of an industrial dispute, is taken by one or more employers, whether parties to the dispute or not, and which consists in the exclusion of workers from one or more factories, offices, or other places of employment or of the suspension of work in one or more such places or of the collective, simultaneous or otherwise connected termination or suspension of employment of a group of workers.

A strike is at common law a breach of each employee's contract of

---

[81] 1974 Act, S. 18.
[82] 1974 Act, S. 29 amd. Employment Act, 1982, S. 18; *Mercury* v. *Scott-Garner* [1984] 1 All E.R. 179. 'Employment' and 'worker' are widely defined in the section. The definition extends also to the Conspiracy and Protection of Property Act, 1875.

employment, justifying dismissal, unless all employees concerned have given due notice of termination of employment.[83] A strike not called by a union or without such due notice is commonly termed an 'unofficial strike'; a strike called by a union and with due notice given is an official strike. A strike of either kind is not illegal, nor criminal.[84] A secret ballot is required before industrial action is taken.[85] Members may interdict their union if it calls a strike in an *ultra vires* way.[86]

No legal compulsion to work

No court may by order of specific implement or interdict compel an employee to do any work or attend at any place for the doing of any work.[87]

Public funds for secret ballots

The Secretary of State may make a scheme providing for payments towards expenditure by independent trade unions in respect of such ballots as may be prescribed, relating to the calling or ending of a strike, carrying out a union election, electing a member of the union to represent other members, amending the union rules, obtaining a decision on amalgamation or transfer of unions. The ballots must be secret. The provision does not make ballots compulsory. Provision is also made for secret ballots on employer's premises.[88]

Liability of unions for harm done while pursuing objectives

A union which calls a strike may be liable at common law for the delict of inducing breach of contract, either directly by procuring parties to the contract not to implement it, or indirectly by inducing others to act so that a party to the contract is driven into the position of breaking his contract.[89] The latter arises only where actionably wrongful means are employed. It may even be wrongful to interfere with performance of a contract without causing actual breach.[90] Or a union may be liable for the delict of intimidation of the employer, or of an employee, or of other

---

[83] N.C.B. v. *Galley* [1958] 1 All E.R. 91; *Rookes* v. *Barnard* [1964] A.C. 1129. In *Morgan* v. *Fry* [1968] 2 Q.B. 710 it was suggested that a strike after notice merely suspended the contract; but there is no unilateral right of suspension. See also *Simmons* v. *Hoover* [1977] I.C.R. 61.

[84] Criminality attaches to breach of the Conspiracy and Protection of Property Act, 1875, S. 5.

[85] Trade Union Act, 1984, Part II; *Monsanto plc.* v. *T.G.W.U.* [1987] 1 All E.R. 358.

[86] *Paterson* v. *N.A.L.G.O.*, 1977 S.C. 345.

[87] 1974 Act, S. 16.

[88] Employment Act, 1980, Ss. 1–2.

[89] D.C. *Thomson* v. *Deakin* [1952] Ch. 646; *Stratford* v. *Lindley* [1965] A.C. 269.

[90] *Torquay Hotels* v. *Cousins* [1969] 2 Ch. 106.

persons (such as the employer) to the harm of the pursuer (such as the employee).[91] What is threatened must be actionable. Or a union may be liable for the delict of conspiracy to injure, if the predominant purpose of a combination is to do unjustifiable harm rather than to promote the interests of members, or if unlawful means are used.[92]

Restrictions on legal liability

Statute has however restricted unions' liabilities in delict. An act done by a person in contemplation or furtherance of a trade dispute is not actionable as a delict in the ground only (a) that it induces another person to break a contract or interferes or induces any other person to interfere with its performance; or (b) that it consists in his threatening that a contract (whether he is a party to it or not) will be broken, or its performance interfered with, or that he will induce another person to break a contract or to interfere with its performance.[93] An agreement or combination by two or more persons to do or procure the doing of any act in contemplation or furtherance of a trade dispute is not actionable as delict if the act, done without any such agreement or combination, would not be actionable as delict.[94]

'Contemplation or futherance of a trade dispute'

This phrase has been broadly interpreted as covering practically anything connected with a trade dispute. Also whether acts are or are not in contemplation or furtherance of a trade dispute is determined by whether the union itself believed that it was so acting, not by an objective test.[95] But S. 13 does not prevent an act from being actionable in delict where the contract is not one of employment and a fact relied on to establish liability is that there has been secondary action not satisfying subsections (3), (4) or (5).[96] There is secondary action only where a person induces another to interfere with its performance, or threatens that a contract of employment under which he or another is employed will be broken or its performance interfered with, or that he will induce another to break a contract of employment or interfere with its performance, if the employer

---

[91] *Rookes* v. *Barnard* [1964] A.C. 1129.

[92] *Crofter Co.,* v. *Veitch*, 1942 S.C. (H.L.) 1.

[93] 1974 Act, S. 13(1) as substituted by T.U. and L.R. (Amdt.) Act, 1976, S. 3. cf. Trade Disputes Act, 1906, S. 3; *Merkur* v. *Laughton* [1983] 2 All E.R. 189; *Mercury* v. *Scott-Garner* [1984] 1 All E.R. 179.

[94] 1974 Act, S. 13(4). S. 13 does not protect picketing not legalized by S. 15, nor secondary action, nor acts to compel trade union membership: Employment Act, 1980, Ss. 16–18.

[95] *N.W.L. Ltd.* v. *Nelson* [1979] I.C.R. 867; *Express Newspapers* v. *McShane* [1980] 1 All E.R. 65; *Duport Steels Ltd.* v. *Sirs* [1980] 1 All E.R. 540.

[96] Employment Act, 1980, S. 17(1), repealing T.U.L.R.A., 1974, S. 13(3); *Hadmor* v. *Hamilton* [1981] 2 All E.R. 724; *Dimbleby* v. *N.U.J.* [1984] 1 All E.R. 751.

is not a party to the trade dispute. Secondary action satisfies the requirements of subsections (3) (4) and (5) only if the purpose of the secondary action was to affect an employer party to the dispute and the action was likely to achieve that purpose, or to affect an associated employer of one party to the dispute and was likely to achieve that purpose, or if it is done in the course of lawful picketing. The effect would appear to be that primary action against an employer is protected, but secondary action involving breach of commercial contracts is no longer protected.

Nor does S. 13 protect an act done to compel workers to become members of a particular trade union or one of several particular unions, if none of them works for the same employer or at the same place as the employee concerned and the contract is one of employment, or not one of employment but a person has induced another to break a contract of employment or interfered or induced another to interfere with its performance, or threatened that a contract of employment will be broken or its performance interfered with, or that he will induce another to break a contract of employment or interfere with its performance.[97]

Criminal actings in relation to industrial disputes

Under the Conspiracy and Protection of Property Act, 1875, S. 3 an agreement or combination by two or more persons to do or procure to be done any act in contemplation or futherance of a trade dispute is not indictable as a conspiracy if such act committed by one person would not be punishable as a crime. By S. 5 it is an offence wilfully and maliciously to break a contract of service or hiring, knowing and having reasonable cause to believe that the consequence will be to endanger human life or cause serious bodily injury or expose valuable property to destruction or serious injury. By the same Act, S. 7, it is illegal to use violence to or intimidate[98] a person to compel him to do or abstain from doing what he is entitled to do, persistently follow him[99] about, hide his tools, clothes, or other property,[1] watch or beset his house or place of work or business, or follow him in a disorderly manner[2] in any street.

Picketing

It is lawful for a person in contemplation or futherance of a trade dispute to attend (a) at or near his own place of work, or (b) if he is a union official, at or near the place of work of a member of that union whom he is accompanying and whom he represents, for the purpose only of peace-

---

[97] Employment Act, 1980, S. 18.
[98] See *Gibson* v. *Lawson* [1891] 2 Q.B. 545; *Currain* v. *Treleaven, ibid.*
[99] *Smith* v. *Thomasson* (1899) 62 L.T. 68.
[1] *Fowler* v. *Kibble* [1922] 1 Cr. 487.
[2] *R.* v. *McKenzie* (1892) 2 Q.B. 519.

fully obtaining or communicating information, or peacefully persuading
any person to work or abstain from working. Place of work includes the
employer's premises from which he works, or a dismissed worker's former place of work.[3] Picketing not made lawful by this provision may infer
criminal liability for e.g. assault, obstruction of the police, or obstruction
of the highway,[4] or civil liability for e.g. nuisance.[5]

Amalgamation and dissolution

Trade unions, if the proposal to do so on the basis of an agreed Instrument of Amalgamation, approved by the registrar, is carried by a simple
majority of the votes recorded by the members of each organization
concerned, may amalgamate.[6] The organizations must apply to the assistant registrar for registration of the Instrument; after a period for challenge it becomes effective. Alternatively an organization may by special
resolution passed by specified majorities transfer its engagements to
another which undertakes to fulfil those engagements. Notice of the
transfer must be registered.[7] An organization may dissolve itself only in
accordance with its own rules, by the unanimous consent of its members,
or by the court finding that the interests of those to whom the funds
belong can no longer be carried into effect under the rules.[8] In such a case
the court will order surplus assets to be distributed to the members at the
date of dissolution in proportion to their contributions. If there are no
surviving members any surplus falls to the Crown as *bona vacantia*.[9]

---

[3] T.U.L.R.A, 1974, S. 15(1) as substituted by Employment Act, 1980, S. 16(1). 'Place of
work' is defined by S. 15(2) and (3) as substituted.
[4] e.g. *Tynan* v. *Balmer* [1967] 1 Q.B. 91; *Kavanagh* v. *Hislop* [1974] 2 All E.R. 177; *Broome*
v. *D.P.P.* [1974] 1 All E.R. 314; *Thomas* v. *N.U.M.* [1985] 2 All E.R. 1.
[5] 1980 Act, S. 16(2). cf. *British Airports Authy* v. *Ashton* [1983] 3 All E.R. 6.
[6] Trade Union (Amalgamations) Act, 1964, S. 1, amd. 1971 Act, Sch. 8.
[7] 1964 Act, S. 1, as amended.
[8] *Re Lead Co's Workmen's Fund* [1904] 2 Ch. 196.
[9] *Braithwaite* v. *A.G.* [1909] 1 Ch. 510.

CHAPTER 3.10

PARTNERSHIPS

The Scottish law of partnerships is based on the Roman *societas* and while the law has been substantially codified by the Partnership Act, 1890, that Act preserves the common law rules except so far as inconsistent with the Act,[1] and makes little change on the common law.

Partnership is the relation which subsists between persons[2] carrying on a business (including every trade, occupation, or profession)[3] in common with a view of profit.[4] Members of a company or other incorporated body are excluded from the definition.[4] Each person must have the legal capacity to enter into the contract of copartnery.[5] The trade or occupation in question must be legal and not contrary to public policy and no rights arise between the parties to partnership for an illegal purpose.[6] In certain cases a partnership with an unqualified person is illegal.[7] By custom the profession of advocate may not be carried on in partnership. Association for purposes other than profit is not partnership but merely voluntary association.[8] Partnership is distinguished from joint adventure, which is a partnership confined to a particular adventure, speculation, course of trade, or voyage,[9] but the incidents of the relation are similar, and in some respect indistinguishable.[10]

---

[1] 1890 Act, S. 46. See generally Stair I, 10, 12; I, 16, I; Bankt. I, 22, 1; Ersk. III, 3, 18; Hume, *Lect.* II, 171; Bell, *Comm.* II. 499; *Prim.* § 350–91; More *Lect.* I, 198; Clark, Bennett Miller, Lindley, and Drake on *Partnership*.

[2] Including natural and also juristic persons; hence a 'consortium' of engineering companies, each of which is a limited company, may be a partnership; cf. *Stevenson* v. *Cartonnagen-Industrie* [1918] A.C. 239. A body of trustees may be a partner: *Beveridge* v. *B.* (1872) 10 M. (H.L.) 1; *Alexander's Trs.* v. *Thomson* (1885) 22 S.L.R. 828.

[3] 1890 Act, S. 45.

[4] S. 1; cf. Stair I, 16, 3; *Keith Spicer* v. *Mansell* [1970] 1 All E.R. 462.

[5] cf. *Blackwood* v. *Thorburn* (1868) 7 M. 318.

[6] *Everet* v. *Williams* (1725) Lindley, 130; (1893) 9 L.Q.R. 197 (highwaymen); *Gibson* v. *Stewart* (1840) 1 Robin. 260; *Foster* v. *Driscoll* [1929] 1 K.B. 470; cf. *Gordon* v. *Howden* (1845) 4 Bell 254; *Fraser* v. *Hair* (1848) 10 D. 1402; *Fraser* v. *Hill* (1853) 1 Macq. 392; *Fraser* v. *Bell* (1854) 16 D. 789; *Lindsay* v. *Inland Revenue*, 1933 S.C. 33. By S. 34 a partnership, initially legal, is dissolved by the happening of any event which makes it unlawful for the business of the firm to be carried on, or for the members of the firm to carry it on in partnership. See e.g. *Esposito* v. *Bowden* (1857) 7 E. & B. 763; *Stevenson, supra*.

[7] e.g. Solicitors (Sc.) Act, 1980, Ss. 26–7; Dentists Act, 1957, Ss. 34, 36, 37; *A.B.* v. *C.D.*, 1912, 1 S.L.T. 44.

[8] cf. *Pitreavie Golf Club* v. *Penman*, 1934 S.L.T. 247.

[9] See *infra*.

[10] *Mair* v. *Wood*, 1948 S.C. 83, 86, 90.

Size of partnership

There must be at least two partners,[11] though a single person trading under a firm name may be a 'firm' for certain provisions of the Act,[12] and not more than twenty,[13] save for partnerships of solicitors, accountants, or stockbrokers, or other kinds of partnerships permitted by Department of Trade and Industry regulations.[14] A partnership exceeding, or by the admission of fresh partners coming to exceed, the permitted size is an illegal association which is debarred from suing, and each member, as a partner, is responsible for all the firm's debts.[15]

Constitution of partnership

Partnership may be constituted by express contract,[16] oral or written, or its existence may be inferred from the conduct and relations of parties.[17] The relationship being contractual questions may arise of capacity to contract, or of error or fraud affecting the contract.[18] Its existence is a question of the intention of the parties as disclosed by the whole circumstances of the case.[19] Not every agreement involving the sharing of the profits of a business amounts to partnership,[20] but partnership may be held to exist in face of the terms of the agreement between the parties,[21] and a person may be held liable as a partner if he be held to have assumed that position, despite his contrary view or even disclaimer.[22] He may be held to have acted as a partner towards third parties though he might not be so held as regards the other partners.[23] Distinguishable from partnership are cases of service,[24] security for repayment of debt,[25] sale,[26] and

---

[11] The phrase 'sole partner' is meaningless: *Wallace* v. *W's Tr.* (1906) 8 F. 558.

[12] e.g. Ss. 14, 17, 18.

[13] Companies Act, 1985, S. 716; Limited Partnerships Act, 1907, S. 4 amd. 1985 Act, S. 717.

[14] 1985 Act, S. 716. Regulations have been made in relation to various professions.

[15] *Shaw* v. *Benson* (1883) 11 Q.B.D. 563; *Shaw* v. *Simmons* (1883) 12 Q.B.D. 117; *Greenberg* v. *Cooperstein* [1926] 1 Ch. 657.

[16] On which see Ch. 4.13, *infra*. The alleged contract must be capable of indicating the partnership terms: *McArthur* v. *Lawson* (1877) 4 R. 1134; *Traill* v. *Dewar* (1881) 8 R. 583.

[17] cf. *Warner* v. *Cuninghame* (1815) 3 Dow 76; *Dundee Ry. Co.* v. *Miller* (1832) 10 S. 269; *Gunn* v. *Ballantyne* (1870) 7 S.L.R. 289; *Aitchison* v. *A.* (1877) 4 R. 899; *Kinnell* v. *Peebles* (1890) 17 R. 416.

[18] *Ferguson* v. *Wilson* (1904) 6 F. 779.

[19] *Morrison* v. *Service* (1879) 6 R. 1158; cf. *Lawrie* v. *L.'s Trs.* (1892) 19 R. 675; *Thomson* v. *Bell* (1894) 1 S.L.T. 433; *Menzies' Trs.* v. *Black's Trs.*, 1909 S.C. 239; *Scott* v. *Dick*, 1909, 2 S.L.T. 118. See also *Clippens Oil Co.*, v. *Scott* (1876) 3 R. 651.

[20] *Cox* v. *Hickman* (1860) 8 H.L.C. 268; *Clark* v. *Jamieson*, 1909 S.C. 132; *Sharpe* v. *Carswell*, 1910 S.C. 391.

[21] *Stewart* v. *Buchanan* (1903) 6 F. 15.

[22] *Adam* v. *Newbigging* (1888) 13 App. Cas. 308; *McCosh* v. *Brown's Tr.* (1899) 1 F. (H.L.) 86; *Charlton* v. *Highet*, 1923 S.L.T. 493.

[23] Bell, *Comm.* II, 511; *Clippens Oil Co.* v. *Scott* (1876) 3 R. 651; *Walker* v. *Hirsch* (1884) 27 Ch. D. 460.

[24] *Geddes* v. *Wallace* (1820) 6 Pat. 643; *Kinnell* v. *Peebles* (1890) 17 R. 416; *Walker* v. *Reith* (1906) 8 F. 381. See also *Gunn* v. *Ballantyne* (1870) 7 S.L.R. 289; *Allison* v. *A's Trs.* (1904) 6 F. 496.

[25] *Eaglesham & Co.* v. *Grant* (1875) 2 R. 960; *Scott* v. *Fender* (1878) 5 R. 1104; cf. *Miller* v. *Downie* (1876) 3 R. 548.

[26] *Moore* v. *Dempster* (1879) 6 R. 930.

carrying on a testator's business.[27] The partners may participate in different ways, some contributing services, others only capital. The same principles apply to all partners, whether active or dormant, known or latent.[28]

Rules for determining existence of partnership

In determining whether partnership does or does not exist regard must be had to the rules laid down in the Act:[29] viz:

(1) Joint tenancy, tenancy in common, joint property, common property or part ownership[30] does not of itself create a partnership as to anything so held or owned, whether the tenants or owners do or do not share any profits made by the use thereof.

(2) The sharing of gross returns does not of itself create a partnership, whether the persons sharing such returns have or have not a joint or common right or interest in any property from which or from the use of which the returns are derived.[31]

(3) The receipt by a person of a share of the profits of a business is prima facie evidence that he is a partner in the business, but the receipt of such a share, or of a payment contingent on or varying with the profits of a business does not of itself make him a partner in the business;[32] and in particular—

(a) the receipt by a person of a debt or other liquidated amount by instalments or otherwise out of the accruing profits of a business does not of itself make him a partner in the business or liable as such.[33]

(b) a contract for the remuneration of a servant or agent of a person engaged in a business by a share of the profits of the business does not of itself make the servant or agent a partner in the business or liable as such.[34]

---

[27] *Paterson's Trs.* v. *Learmont & Co.* (1870) 8 M. 500; *Lawrie* v. *L's Trs.* (1892) 19 R. 675.

[28] *Cameron* v. *Young* (1871) 9 M. 786.

[29] 1890 Act, S. 2, substantially re-enacting Law of Partnership Act, 1865 (Bovill's Act), and stated to make no change in the law: *Davis* v. *D.* [1894] 1 Ch. 393.

[30] *Sharpe* v. *Carswell*, 1910 S.C. 391.

[31] *Clark* v. *Jamieson*, 1909 S.C. 132. The sharing of both profits and losses is indicative of partnership.

[32] *Laing Bros. & Co.'s Tr.* v. *Low* (1896) 23 R. 1105; *Allison* v. *A's Trs.* (1904) 6 F. 496; *Eddie* v. *Crawford*, 1912, 2 S.L.T. 360. But a right to a share in profits and also a right to receive or dispose of partnership assets implies partnership: *McCosh* v. *Brown's Tr.* (1899) 1 F. (H.L.) 86; *Charlton* v. *Highet*, 1923 S.L.T. 493. A share in profits and also a power to control the business may imply partnership: *Stewart* v. *Buchanan* (1903) 6 F. 15. See also *Bolton* v. *Mansfield* (1787) 3 Pat. 70.

[33] cf. *McKinlay* v. *Gillon* (1831) 5 W. & Sh. 468; *Cox* v. *Hickman* (1860) 8 H.L.C. 268; *Stott* v. *Fender* (1878) 5 R. 1104; *Gosling* v. *Gaskell* [1897] A.C. 575.

[34] *Kinnell* v. *Peebles* (1890) 7 R. 416; *Lawrie* v. *L's Trs.* (1892) 19 R. 675; *Gatherer* (1893) 1 S.L.T. 401; *Walker* v. *Reith* (1906) 8 F. 381; *Clark* v. *Jamieson*, 1909 S.C. 132; *Sharpe* v. *Carswell*, 1910 S.C. 391; *A.B.* v. *C.D.*, 1912, 1 S.L.T. 44.

(c) a person being the widow or child of a deceased partner, and receiving by way of annuity a portion of the profits made in the business in which the deceased person was a partner, is not by reason only of such receipt a partner in the business or liable as such.[35]

(d) the advance of money by way of loan to a person engaged or about to engage in any business on a contract with that person that the lender shall receive a rate of interest varying with the profits, or shall receive a share of the profits arising from carrying on the business, does not of itself make the lender a partner with the person or persons carrying on the business or liable as such.[36] Provided that the contract is in writing, and signed by or on behalf of all the parties thereto.

(e) a person receiving by way of annuity or otherwise a portion of the profits of a business in consideration of the sale by him of the goodwill of the business is not by reason only of such receipt a partner in the business or liable as such.[37]

If a debtor who has borrowed money on such a contract as is mentioned in S. 2, or a buyer of goodwill on the terms of paying a share of profits in the business, is adjudicated bankrupt, enters into an agreement to pay his creditors less than the full sum due, or dies insolvent, the lender or seller is entitled to recover nothing in respect of his loan or share of profits respectively, until the claims of the other creditors have been satisfied.[38]

The firm and its quasi-personality

Persons who have entered into partnership form collectively a firm or company,[39] which in Scotland is a legal person distinct from the partners of whom it is composed.[40] The firm is in Scotland not merely a collective name for the individual partners. From this certain consequences follow. It may sue and be sued, and partners may sue the firm and conversely.[41] It

---

[35] cf. *Paterson's Tr.* v. *Learmont* (1870) 8 M. 500; *Thomson* v. *T.*, 1962 S.C. (H.L.) 28.

[36] cf. *Pooley* v. *Driver* (1876) 5 Ch.D. 458; *Re Howard* (1877) 6 Ch.D. 303; *Re Megevand* (1878) 7 Ch.D. 511; *Thomson* v. *Bell* (1894) 1 S.L.T. 433; *Laing Bros. & Co.'s Tr.* v. *Low* (1896) 23 R. 1105; *McCosh* v. *Brown & Co.'s Tr.* (1899) 1 F. (H.L.) 86; *Stewart* v. *Buchanan* (1903) 6 F. 15.

[37] cf. *Alexander* v. *Clark* (1862) 24 D. 323.

[38] S. 3 See *ex p. Mills* (1873) L.R. 8 Ch. 569; *Re Hildesheim* [1893] 2 Q.B. 357; *Re Mason* [1899] 1 Q.B. 810. cf. Married Women's Property (Sc.) Act, 1881, S. 1(4), postponing claim of one spouse on another in bankruptcy where loan made for business.

[39] 'Company' as a term equivalent to firm or partnership must be distinguished from 'company' signifying an incorporated company, usually with limited liability, on which see Ch. 3.13, *infra*.

[40] 1890 Act, S. 4(2); Bell, *Comm.* II, 507; *Prin.* § 357; *Mair* v. *Wood*, 1948 S.C. 83, 86.

[41] e.g. *Forsyth* v. *Hare* (1834) 13 S. 42; *Malcolm* v. *West Lothian Ry. Co.* (1835) 13 S. 887; *Glebe Sugar Co.* v. *Lusk* (1866) 2 S.L.R. 9.

may be debtor or creditor to any partner. It may commit actionable wrong, even a wrong requiring proof of malice,[42] or suffer wrong and sue therefor.[43] A partner cannot sue alone for the enforcement of the firm's obligations, but may be sued, but only if the debt has first been constituted against the firm.[44] In relation to third parties, the firm is the primary debtor, the partners being deemed cautioners for the firm. A firm can be sequestrated without individual partners being sequestrated, and conversely. On the sequestration of a firm and the partners, the creditors rank in the first place on the firm's estate and, if not paid in full, for the balance on the estates of the partners. Creditors of a partner can arrest his share in the hands of the firm.

Though the firm is a legal person it is not a full corporation or legal entity in itself.[45] The fact that it is not a corporation is shown by the facts that it is created by contract, not by charter, statute, or registration, that it can be dissolved by consent, that the firm cannot in the firm name hold heritable property, the title to which must be taken in the name of partners as trustees for the firm,[46] that the firm comes to an end by the death or bankruptcy of any partner of the firm,[47] and that an individual partner may be charged on a decree or diligence directed against the firm, being entitled on payment to relief *pro rata* from the firm and its other members.[48] It is an open question whether a firm can employ one of its partners under a contract of service.[49] The firm has no claim if it loses profits by reason of injuries caused to a partner by a third party.[50]

The firm name

The name under which parties carry on business is the firm name.[51] Persons may carry on business under more than one firm name, and the firms may deal with one another.[52] The firm name may be a social name comprising the names of individual partners, in which case the firm may

---

[42] *Gordon v. British and Foreign Metaline Co.* (1886) 14 R. 75.

[43] *May v. Matthews* (1833) 11 S. 305.

[44] *Johnston v. Duncan* (1823) 2 S. 532; *Geddes v. Hopkirk* (1828) 5 S. 697; *Munnoch v. Dewar*, (1831) 9 S. 487; *Muir v. Collett* (1862) 24 D. 1119; *Neilson v. Wilson* (1890) 17 R. 608, 612.

[45] 'It is a quasi corporation possessing many, but not all the privileges which law confers upon a duly constituted corporation': *Forsyth v. Hare* (1834) 13 S. 42, 47.

[46] Bell, *Prin.* § 357; *Kelly's Tr. v. Moncreiff's Tr.*, 1920 S.C. 461; but a firm is capable of holding a lease: *Dennistoun, Macnayr & Co., v. McFarlane*, 16 Feb. 1808, F.C.; *Cooke's Circus Co. v. Welding* (1894) 21 R. 339.

[47] 1890 Act, S. 33.

[48] 1890 Act, S. 4(2); *Thomson v. Liddell*, 24 July 1812, F.C.; *Wallace v. Plock & Logan* (1841) 3 D. 1047; *Ewing v. McClelland* (1860) 22 D. 1347.

[49] *Fife C.C. v. Minister of Nat. Insurance*, 1947 S.C. 629; but see *Allison v. A's Trs.* (1904) 6 F. 496; *Ellis v. E.* [1905] 1 K.B. 324.

[50] *Gibson v. Glasgow Corpn.*, 1963 S.L.T. (Notes) 16.

[51] 1890 Act, S. 4(1).

[52] *Campbell v. McCreath* 1975 S.L.T. (Notes) 5.

sue and be sued in that name even though the names are not those of the existing partners,[53] or a descriptive name, in which case the firm name is not enough without the addition of the names of the partners, or at least three of them.[54] A firm may use any name it pleases, but may not take such a name, or use partners' names, in such a way as to deceive the public.[55] Where one partner purchased the firm's business and goodwill and subsequently his former partner began to trade in the same business in the same town in partnership with a third party of the same name as the first partner, he was held entitled to interdict against their trading under that name.[56] If a firm's name does not consist of the surnames of all the partners without any non-permitted addition[57] it may not carry on business under a name including a word forbidden by regulations.[58] The names of partners must be disclosed in all business letters and forms with addresses in Great Britain at which service of any document will be effective, and a list of names and addresses displayed at places of business.[59] Contravention is an offence.[60]

Actions by and against firm

As the firm has a separate legal personality it alone has a title to sue for the enforcement of obligations to it. A firm in default in disclosing the names and addresses of the partners is liable to have actions against it dismissed if the other party has been prejudiced thereby.[61] An individual partner cannot sue, though all the partners can, if it clearly appears that they are suing for a debt to the firm.[62] Similarly an action against the firm should be directed against it, not against any individual partner, and even though the firm has been dissolved.[63] A partner can be sued only if the

---

[53] *Forsyth* v. *Hare* (1834) 13 S. 42; *Wallace* v. *Plock & Logan* (1841) 3 D. 1047; *Paton* v. *Neill, Edgar & Co.* (1873) 10 S.L.R. 461; *Brims & Mackay* v. *Pattullo*, 1907 S.C. 1106.

[54] *Culcreugh Cotton Co.* v. *Mathie* (1822) 2 S. 47; *Commercial Bank* v. *Pollock* (1828) 3 W. & Sh. 365; *Kerr* v. *Clyde Shipping Co.* (1839) 1 D. 901; *London Shipping Co.* v. *McCorkle* (1841) 3 D. 1045; *McMillan* v. *McCulloch* (1842) 4 D. 492; *Nat. Exchange Co.* v. *Drew* (1848) 11 D. 179; *Antermony Coal Co.* v. *Wingate* (1866) 4 M. 1017. In the sheriff court a firm may sue by its descriptive name alone: Sheriff Courts (Sc.) Act, 1907 (amd. 1913) R. 11. See also *Gordon* v. *British and Foreign Metaline Co.* (1886) 14 R. 75; *City and Suburban Dairies* v. *Mackenna*, 1918 J.C. 105.

[55] *Croft* v. *Day* (1843) 7 Beav. 84; *Levy* v. *Walker* (1879) 10 Ch. D. 436; *Massam* v. *Thorley's Cattle Food Co.* (1880) 14 Ch. D. 748; *Tussaud* v. *T.* (1890) 44 Ch. D. 678; *North Cheshire and Manchester Brewery Co.* v. *Manchester Brewery Co.* [1899] A.C. 83; *Cowan* v. *Millar* (1895) 22 R. 833 (name attached to premises).

[56] *Smith* v. *McBride and Smith* (1888) 16 R. 36.

[57] Business Names Act, 1985, Ss. 1, 4.

[58] Ss. 2, 3. Regulations may be made under S. 6.

[59] S. 4. In cases of big firms it suffices if a list is available for inspection at the principal place of business.

[60] S. 7.

[61] Business Names Act, 1985, S. 5.

[62] *Plotzker* v. *Lucas*, 1907 S.C. 315.

[63] *McNaught* v. *Milligan* (1885) 13 R. 366; *Brims & Mackay, supra*.

debt has first been constituted against the firm, unless the firm has previously been dissolved.[64]

Diligence against firm

Diligence following on a decree against the firm may proceed against the firm,[65] but also against any individual partner,[66] whether or not he is named in the decree, he being entitled on payment to *pro rata* relief against his partners.[67] But a person not a partner cannot be charged to pay under a decree against the firm, even though it be alleged that he is truly liable, having held himself out to be a partner.[68] A person wrongly charged may bring a suspension of the diligence. Poinding of the ground is competent to attach the property of one partner in buildings owned by the firm when the partners had the sole control of and interest in the firm for which, as trustees, they held the title to the buildings.[69] A creditor of one partner cannot attach the partner's share in the firm by poinding to the prejudice of a creditor of the firm,[70] nor arrest it in the hands of the firm, it not being an ascertained debt,[71] nor arrest a firm debt for a debt of one of the partners.[72]

RELATION OF PARTNERS TO THIRD PARTIES

Contracts with third parties

A firm may bind itself contractually by the act of a partner as agent for the firm, or of a servant or agent as such agent.[73] The authority of any partner, acting as agent for the firm, to bind the firm contractually may, as between the partners themselves, be regulated by the contract of copartnery. As regards third parties his mandate is implied by law.

Implied mandate

Every partner is held to be *praepositus negotiis societatis*, and is an agent of the firm and his other partners for the purpose of the partnership

---

[64] *Johnston v. Duncan* (1823) 2 S. 532; *Geddes v. Hopkirk* (1828) 5 S. 697; *Dewar v. Munnoch*, 23 Feb. 1831, F.C.; *Muir v. Collett* (1862) 24 D. 1119; *Neilson v. Wilson* (1890) 17 R. 608.
[65] *Rosslund Cycle Co. v. McCreadie*, 1907 S.C. 1208.
[66] *Brember v. Rutherford* (1901) 4 F. 62.
[67] *Ewing v. McClelland* (1860) 22 D. 1347; 1890 Act, S. 4(2).
[68] *Brember v. Rutherford* (1901) 4 F. 62.
[69] *Kelly's Tr. v. Moncreiff's Tr.*, 1920 S.C. 461.
[70] *Dawson v. Cullen* (1825) 4 S. 39; *Fleming v. Twaddle* (1828) 7 S. 92.
[71] *Parnell v. Walter* (1889) 16 R. 917, 925.
[72] *Corrie v. Calder's Crs.* (1741) Mor. 14596.
[73] e.g. a salaried manager: the authority of such a person depends on the principles of agency.

business, and the acts of every partner who does any act for carrying on in the usual way business of the kind carried on by the firm bind the firm and his partners, unless that partner has in fact no authority to act for the firm in the particular matter, and the person with whom he is dealing either knows that he has no authority, or does not know or believe him to be a partner.[74] As regards third parties every partner is an unlimited agent of every other in every matter relating to their business, or which he represents as firm business and which is not, in its nature, beyond the scope of the partnership.[75] Hence he normally has implied authority to buy and sell goods, engage staff, receive payment and grant discharges therefor,[76] borrow money[77] and undertake financial transactions,[78] and possibly to litigate for recovery of debts due to the firm even if a copartner disclaims.[79] A partner in a firm of solicitors has implied authority to grant an obligation to clear a title and exhibit clear searches.[80] A document written and signed by a partner in the firm's name is holograph of the firm.[81] When all the partners of a firm grant a bill, the presumption is that it is for firm purposes, but the contrary may be proved.[82] The extent of a partner's implied authority to act as an agent for the firm depends on the nature of the firm business.[83] If the obligation undertaken is in exceptional terms, or the circumstances unusual or suspicious, there may be an onus on the other party to ascertain if the partner undertaking truly had authority to grant the obligation in question.[84] An obligation undertaken in the firm name which is beyond the real or ostensible authority of the partner undertaking and is therefore not binding on the firm is still binding on that partner as an individual.[85] The firm is not bound by an undertaking granted, even in the firm name, by a partner if it is known to be granted in his private interest,[86] or granted outwith the

[74] 1890 Act, S. 5; Stair I, 16, 4; Ersk. III, 3, 20; Bell, *Prin.* § 354; *Nisbet's Trs.* v. *Morrison's Trs.* (1829) 7 S. 307; *Bryan* v. *Butters Bros. & Co.* (1892) 19 R. 490; *Cooke's Circus Building Co.* v. *Welding* (1894) 21 R. 339; *Fortune* v. *Young*, 1918 S.C. 1; *Mercantile Credit Co.* v. *Garrod* [1962] 3 All E.R. 1103; *Mann* v. *D'Arcy* [1968] 2 All E.R. 172.

[75] *Baird's Case* [1870] L.R. 5 Ch. 725, 733.

[76] *Nicoll* v. *Reid* (1878) 6 R. 216; *Powell* v. *Brodhurst* [1901] 2 Ch. 160.

[77] *Bank of Australasia* v. *Breillat* (1847) 6 Moo. P.C. 152, 194; *Cumming* v. *Hay & Stephen* (1879) 17 S.L.R. 207; *Bryan* v. *Butters Bros.* (1892) 19 R. 490.

[78] *Williamson* v. *Johnson* (1823) 1 B. & C. 146; *Garland* v. *Jacomb* (1873) L.R. 8 Ex. 216: including power to agree to a composition arrangement with a debtor to the firm: *Mains & McGlashan* v. *Black* (1895) 22 R. 329; as to cautionary obligation see *Fortune* v. *Young*, 1918 S.C. 1, 6.

[79] *Kinnes* v. *Adam* (1882) 9 R. 698, 700.

[80] *Walker* v. *Smith* (1906) 8 F. 619, 624.

[81] *Nisbet* v. *Neil's Trs.* (1869) 7 M. 1097.

[82] *Rosslund Cycle Co.* v. *McCreadie*, 1907 S.C. 1208; see also *Paterson Bros.* v. *Gladstone* (1891) 18 R. 403.

[83] See *Bryan* v. *Butters* (1892) 19 R. 490; *Cooke's Circus Buildings Co.* v. *Welding* (1894) 21 R. 339; *Mains & McGlashan* v. *Black* (1895) 22 R. 329; *Ciceri* v. *Hunter* (1904) 12 S.L.T. 293.

[84] *Paterson Bros.* v. *Gladstone* (1891) 18 R. 403.

[85] *Fortune* v. *Young*, 1918 S.C. 1.

[86] *Crum* v. *McLean* (1858) 20 D. 751; *Walker* v. *Smith* (1906) 8 F. 619.

ordinary course of the firm's business,[87] or known to be granted without authority.[88]

Partners bound by acts on behalf of firm

A firm and its partners are bound by an act or instrument relating to the business of the firm and done or executed in the firm name, or in any other manner showing an intention to bind the firm, by any person thereto authorized, whether a partner or not,[89] without prejudice to the general rules relating to the execution of deeds or negotiable instruments.[90] If in fact the person was so acting, the firm is bound, though its existence was not disclosed and the other party was unaware that he was dealing with a firm.[91] But the firm is not bound by an act by a partner not in the way of the firm's business.[92]

Partner using firm credit for private purposes

Where a partner pledges the credit of the firm for a purpose apparently not connected with the firm's ordinary course of business, the firm is not bound, unless the partner is in fact specially authorized by the other partners; but this does not affect any personal liability of an individual partner.[93] Where a partner not authorized to sign the firm name adhibited the firm name to bills which he discounted with a moneylender and applied the proceeds to his own use, it was held that the partners were not liable as they were ignorant of the transaction and it was not in the course of the firm's business or for its behoof.[94]

Restriction on power of one to bind firm

If partners have agreed that any restriction be placed on the power of one or more to bind the firm no act in contravention of this binds the firm

---

[87] Ersk. III, 3, 20; *Paterson Bros., supra; Gilmour* v. *Nunn's Trs.* (1899) 7 S.L.T. 292.

[88] *Paterson Bros., supra.*

[89] cf. *Beveridge* v. *B's Trs.* (1872) 10 M. (H.L.) 1.

[90] 1890 Act, S. 6; *Turnbull* v. *McKie* (1822) 1 S. 353; *Edmond* v. *Robertson* (1867) 5 S.L.R. 30; *Bryan* v. *Butters Bros. & Co.* (1892) 19 R. 490. As to execution see *Mellis* v. *Royal Bank,* 22 June 1815, F.C.; *Blair Iron Co.* v. *Alison* (1855) 18 D. (H.L.) 49; *Nisbet* v. *Neil's Tr.* (1869) 7 M. 1097; *Littlejohn* v. *Mackay,* 1974 S.L.T. (Sh. Ct.) 82.

[91] *Beckham* v. *Drake* (1843) 11 M. & W. 315; cf. *Watson* v. *Smith* (1806) Hume 756.

[92] *McNair* v. *Gray, Hunter & Speirs* (1803) Hume 753; *Miller* v. *Douglas,* 22 Jan. 1811, F.C.; *Kennedy,* 22 Dec. 1814, F.C.; *Jardine* v. *McFarlane* (1828) 6 S. 564; *McLeod* v. *Tosh* (1836) 14 S. 1058; *Finlayson* v. *Braidbar Quarry Co.* (1864) 2 M. 1297; *Paterson Bros.* v. *Gladstone* (1891) 18 R. 403.

[93] 1890 Act, S. 7; cf. *McNair* v. *Gray, Hunter & Speirs* (1803) Hume 753; *Kennedy,* 22 Dec. 1814, F.C.

[94] *Paterson Bros.* v. *Gladstone* (1891) 18 R. 403.

with respect to persons having notice of the agreement.[95] But such an agreement is ineffective against third parties ignorant of it.[96]

Liability of firm and partners

The liability of a firm on its obligations, contractual and delictual, is unlimited and in no respect limited to the capital employed in the firm business. The liability of the partners is also unlimited,[97] though secondary to the liability of the firm.

Liability of partners

Every partner is jointly and severally liable for all debts and obligations of the firm, incurred while he is a partner, and after his death his estate remains severally liable.[98] But partners are liable only subsidiarily to the liability of the firm, and are in substance guarantors or cautioners for the firm's obligations, each being entitled on payment to *pro rata* relief from the others.[99] The firm's liability must be constituted first.[1] A latent partner is liable, even though the third party did not know of his existence.[2] A retired partner is still liable for all debts incurred while he was a partner. Any arrangement between him and his partners is ineffectual against a creditor, unless the creditor is a party to the arrangement.[3] This may be implied by a subsequent course of trading but the court is unwilling to infer it, and will not do so merely from the creditor's acceptance of interest or part-payment from the new firm, or from his ranking in their bankruptcy.[4] A retired partner who has not given adequate notice of retiral may be liable on obligations undertaken after his retiral.[5] Once a firm has been dissolved an action for a firm debt cannot be brought against one partner without being constituted against the firm,[6] unless where the firm and the other partners are outwith the jurisdiction.[7]

---

[95] 1890 Act, S. 8.
[96] *Cox v. Hickman* (1860) 8 H.L. Cas. 268, 304; cf. *Paterson Bros. v. Gladstone* (1891) 18 R. 403, 404–5.
[97] All partners except one may have limited liability if the partnership if formed under the Limited Partnership Act, 1907.
[98] 1890 Act, S. 9.
[99] Bell, *Comm.* II, 508; *Prin.* § 356; 1890 Act, S. 4(2); cf. *Clydesdale Bank v. Morison's Tr.*, 1982 S.C. 26.
[1] But if one partner admits the firm's liability, decree may pass against him, reserving his rights of relief, without constituting the debt against the firm: *Elliot v. Aiken* (1869) 7 M. 894; *sed quaere.*
[2] *Cameron v. Young* (1871) 9 M. 786.
[3] 1890 Act, S. 17(3).
[4] *Morton's Trs. v. Robertson's J.F.* (1892) 20 R. 72; *Smith v. Patrick* (1901) 3 F. (H.L.) 14. Contrast *Goldfarb v. Bartlett* [1920] 1 K.B. 639; *Rouse v. Bradford Banking* Co. [1894] A.C. 586.
[5] 1890 Act, S. 36; cf. *Scarf v. Jardine* (1882) 7 App. Cas. 345.
[6] *McNaught v. Milligan* (1885) 13 R. 366.
[7] *Muir v. Collett* (1862) 24 D. 1119.

Liability of firm for wrongs

A partner who, while acting as such in the ordinary course of the firm's business, or with the authority of his copartners, by any wrongful act or omission causes loss or injury to a third party, is personally liable, and the firm is also liable to the same extent.[8] If there are no averments of individual fault by partners the action is against the firm only.[9] The liability of the partners is joint and several.[10] The firm is vicariously liable also for its agents and servants acting within the scope of their authority or course of their employment respectively.[11] But the firm is not vicariously liable for the wrong of one partner, while acting as such and within the scope of his implied mandate, done to another partner; only the wrongdoing partner is liable.[12] Nor, in general, is the firm liable for the fraud of one partner committed outside the ordinary course of the firm's business.[13] One partner who is innocent is entitled to relief against others who have without his knowledge engaged in wrongdoing.[14] It is incompetent to sue a firm for damages for fraud, unless the names of the partners alleged to have committed the fraud are specified, fraud being personal to the individual.[15] A firm may be sued for wrong, even though in the circumstances malice has to be proved.[16]

Misapplication of money or property

The firm is liable to make good the loss where one partner, acting within the scope of his apparent authority, receives the money or property of a third person and misapplies it, and also where a firm in the course of its business receives money or property of a third person, and it is misapplied by one or more of the partners while in the firm's custody.[17] The liability of the partners is joint and several.[18] Thus where a partner had, with the

---

[8] 1890 Act, S. 10; *National Exchange Co.* v. *Drew* (1855) 2 Macq. 103; *Jardine's Trs.* v. *Drew* (1864) 2 M. 1101; *Trail* v. *Smith's Trs.* (1875) 3 R. 770; *Blyth* v. *Fladgate* [1891] 1 Ch. 337; *Rhodes* v. *Moules* [1895] 1 Ch. 236; *Hamlyn* v. *Houston* [1903] 1 K.B. 81; *New Mining Syndicate* v. *Chalmers*, 1912 S.C. 126; *Meekins* v. *Henson* [1962] 1 All E.R. 899; see also *Tully* v. *Ingram* (1891) 19 R. 65; *Kirkintilloch Co-operative Socy.* v. *Livingstone*, 1972 S.C. 111.
[9] *Gordon* v. *British and Foreign Metaline Co.* (1886) 14 R. 75.
[10] 1890 Act, S. 12; cf. *McGee* v. *Anderson* (1895) 22 R. 274.
[11] *Barwick* v. *English Joint Stock Bank* (1867) L.R. 2 Ex. 259; *British Legal Life Assce. Co.* v. *Pearl Life Assce. Co. Ltd.* (1887) 14 R. 818; *Lloyd* v. *Grace Smith & Co.* [1912] A.C. 716.
[12] *Mair* v. *Wood*, 1948 S.C. 83; *Parker* v. *Walker*, 1961 S.L.T. 252; *Blackwood* v. *Robertson*, 1984 S.L.T. (Sh. Ct.) 68.
[13] *Cleather* v. *Twisden* (1884) 28 Ch. D. 340; *Hughes* v. *Twisden* (1886) 34 W.R. 498; *Mara* v. *Browne* [1896] Ch. 199.
[14] *Campbell* v. *C.* (1839) Macl. & R. 387; cf. Law Reform (Misc. Prov.) (Sc.) Act, 1940, S. 3.
[15] *Scott* v. *Napier* (1827) 5 S. 414; *Thomson* v. *Pattison Elder & Co.* (1895) 22 R. 432.
[16] *Gordon* v. *British and Foreign Metaline Co.* (1886) 14 R. 75.
[17] 1890 Act, S. 11; *Dundonald* v. *Masterman* (1869) L.R. 7 Eq. 504; *New Mining and Exploring Syndicate* v. *Chalmers & Hunter*, 1912 S.C. 126.
[18] 1890 Act, S. 12; see e.g. *Devaynes* v. *Noble (Clayton's Case)* (1816) 1 Mer. 529, 572; *Blyth* v. *Fladgate* [1891] Ch. 337.

knowledge of his firm, occupied a fiduciary position towards a company and received promotion money from it, the firm was bound to repay the money.[19]

Improper use of trust property

If a partner who is a trustee improperly employs trust property in the business or on the account of the partnership, no other partner is liable for the trust property to the persons beneficially interested therein; but this rule does not affect any liability incurred by any partner by reason of his having notice of a breach of trust; nor does it prevent trust money being followed and recovered[20] from the firm if still in its possession or under its control.[41]

Liability by holding out

A person who by words or conduct represents himself, or knowingly suffers himself to be represented, as a partner in a particular firm,[22] is liable as a partner to anyone has given credit to the firm on the faith of such representation, whether made to him by or with the knowledge of the apparent partner or not.[23] But the continued use of the old firm name after a partner's death, or of the deceased partner's name as part thereof, does not by itself make his estate liable for any partnership debts contracted after his death.[24] The rule of holding out is an application of the principle of personal bar. It applies also to a partner who has retired but not given notice.[25] It does not apply if a man's name is mentioned as a partner without his knowledge, nor even if he misrepresents himself not knowingly but carelessly,[26] nor if the creditor knows the true facts.[27] The representation need not have been made to the creditor directly. A man whose name is mentioned as a partner without his consent may interdict the misuse thereof.[28] Conversely it has been held that payment of a debt due to a firm to a person who has been held out as a partner therein, and in the *bona fide* belief that he is one, is a good payment.[29]

---

[19] *Scottish Pacific Coast Mining Co.* v. *Falkner, Bell & Co.* (1888) 15 R. 290.

[20] As to following trust property, see Ch. 6.2, *infra*.

[21] 1890 Act, S. 13; *New Mining Syndicate* v. *Chalmers*, 1912 S.C. 126, 133; as to case where other partners implicated see *Blyth* v. *Fladgate* [1891] 1 Ch. 337.

[22] *Brember* v. *Rutherford* (1901) 4 F. 62.

[23] 1890 Act, S. 14(1); cf. *McNair* v. *Fleming* (1812) 5 Pat. 639; *Moyes* v. *Cook* (1829) 7 S. 793; *Gardner* v. *Anderson* (1862) 24 D. 315; *Hosie* v. *Waddell* (1886) 3 S.L.R. 16; *Stocks* v. *Simpson* (1905) 13 S.L.T. 422.

[24] 1890 Act, S. 14(2); *Morrison* v. *Leamont* (1869) 8 M. 500.

[25] 1890 Act, S. 36.

[26] *Tower Cabinet Co.* v. *Ingram* [1949] 2 K.B. 397.

[27] *Mann* v. *Sinclair* (1879) 6 R. 1078.

[28] *Walker* v. *Ashton* [1902] 2 Ch. 282.

[29] *Hosie* v. *Waddell* (1866) 3 S.L.R. 16.

Evidence

An admission or representation made by any partner concerning the partnership affairs, and in the ordinary course of its business, is evidence against the firm.[30] Similarly a letter written and signed by one partner in the firm name is holograph of the firm.[31]

Notice

Notice, i.e. the coming of facts to knowledge, to any partner who habitually acts in the partnership business, of any matter relating to partnership affairs, operates as notice to the firm, except in the case of a fraud on the firm committed by or with the consent of that partner.[32] Hence notice to a sleeping partner is not notice, nor, probably is notice to a man who subsequently becomes a partner notice to the firm.[33]

Liabilities of incoming and outgoing partners

A person admitted as a partner into an existing firm does not thereby become liable to the creditors of the firm for anything done before he became a partner,[34] but a retiring partner does not thereby cease to be liable for partnership debts or obligations incurred before his retirement.[35] A retiring partner may be discharged from any existing liabilities by an agreement to that effect between himself and the members of the firm as newly constituted and the creditors, which may be express or inferred from the course of dealing between the creditors and the firm as newly constituted.[36] A person may be held by his course of dealing with the new firm to have accepted it as his debtor and to have discharged the retired partner.[37] Where the business of an existing partnership is transferred to a new one and the business continues on the same basis as before, the presumption is that the new firm assumes liability for all the liabilities which are taken over with the business,[38] but this may be

---

[30] 1890 Act, S. 15.

[31] *Nisbet* v. *Neil's Tr.* (1869) 7 M. 1097.

[32] 1890 Act, S. 16; Stair III, 1, 10.

[33] cf. *Williamson* v. *Barbour* (1877) 9 Ch. D. 529.

[34] 1890 Act, S. 17(1); *Mercer* v. *Peddie* (1832) 10 S. 405; *Nelmes* v. *Montgomery* (1883) 10 R. 974; cf. *New Mining Syndicate* v. *Chalmers*, 1912 S.C. 126, 135. But see *Miller* v. *Thorburn* (1861) 23 D. 359.

[35] 1890 Act, S. 17(2); *Blacks* v. *Girdwood* (1885) 13 R. 243; *Beveridge* v. *Forbes, Bryson & Carrick* (1897) 5 S.L.T. 115.

[36] 1890 Act, S. 17(3); cf. *Pollock* v. *Murray and Spence* (1863) 2 M. 14; *Smith* v. *Patrick* (1901) 3 F. (H.L.) 14; *Roughead* v. *White*, 1913 S.C. 162.

[37] *Ker* v. *McKechnie* (1845) 7 D. 494; *Pearston* v. *Wilson* (1856) 19 D. 197; contrast *Campbell* v. *Cruickshank* (1845) 7 D. 548; *Muir* v. *Dickson* (1860) 22 D. 1070. cf. *Price & Logan* v. *Wise* (1862) 24 D. 491.

[38] *Miller* v. *Thorburn* (1861) 23 D. 359; *McKeand* v. *Laird* (1861) 23 D. 846; *Heddle's Exrx.* v. *Marwick & Hourston's Tr.* (1888) 15 R. 698; *Thomson & Balfour* v. *Boag*, 1936 S.C. 2; *Miller* v. *McLeod & Parker*, 1974 S.L.T. 99.

rebutted, as where the new partner contributes substantial fresh capital,[39] or the new firm is carried on on the basis that there shall be no liability for prior debts and no right to collect sums due to the old firm or its partners.[40]

Change in firm revokes continuing cautionary obligation

A continuing guarantee or cautionary obligation given to a firm or to a third party in respect of the transactions of a firm is, in the absence of agreement to the contrary, revoked as to future transactions by any change in the constitution of the firm to which, or of the firm in respect of the transactions of which, the guarantee or obligation was given.[41] A similar principle may apply in respect of any contract which involves an element of *delectus personae*.[42]

Ordinary contracts, as of employment, are not revoked by a change in the constitution of the firm,[43] but contracts involving personal service may be terminated thereby.[44] The conversion of a partnership into a limited company dissolves the firm utterly and releases all employees from their contracts,[45] and terminates contracts involving *delectus personae*.[46]

RELATIONS OF PARTNERS INTER SE

Relations fixed by contract or Act, but variable

The relations and mutual rights and duties of partners may be defined by their contract of copartnery,[47] but, whether ascertained by agreement or defined by the Act, these may be varied by the consent of all the partners, express or inferred from a course of dealing.[48] Variations assented to bind a partner's assignees or representatives. Partners are not related as debtor and creditor unless and until an accounting after dissolution has shown that one is indebted to another or others; nor are they trustees for each other or for the firm,[49] unless expressly so designated, as when taking title

---

[39] *Thomson & Balfour v. Boag*, 1936 S.C. 2.
[40] *Stephen's Tr.* v. *Macdougall & Co.'s Tr.* (1889) 16 R. 779; *Tully v. Ingram* (1891) 19 R. 65; *Thomson & Balfour, supra*, 10.
[41] 1890 Act, S. 18, replacing Mercantile Law Amdt. (Sc.) Act, 1856, S. 7; cf. *Speirs v. Royal Bank* (1822) 1 S. 516; *Aytoun v. Dundee Bank* (1844) 6 D. 1409; *Alexander v. Lowson's Trs.* (1890) 17 R. 571.
[42] cf. *Hoey v. McEwan & Auld* (1867) 5 M. 814; *Smith v. Patrick* (1901) 3 F. (H.L.) 14.
[43] *Campbell v. Baird* (1827) 5 S. 335.
[44] *Hoey, supra.*
[45] *Berlitz School v. Duchene* (1903) 6 F. 181; *Garden, Haig-Scott & Wallace v. Prudential Assce. Socy.*, 1927 S.L.T. 393.
[46] *Grierson, Oldham & Co. v. Forbes, Maxwell & Co.* (1895) 22 R. 812; *Brown v. Carron Co.* (1898) 6 S.L.T. 90.
[47] See Ch. 4.15, *infra*.
[48] 1890 Act, S. 19; see also *Const v. Harris* (1824) T. & R. 496; *Coventry v. Barclay* (1864) 3 De G. J. & S. 320; *Ex p. Barber* (1870) L.R. 5 Ch. 687.
[49] *Piddocke v. Burt* [1894] 1 Ch. 343.

to land, or after dissolution of the partnership.[50] Partners owe each other the duty to take the care and show the diligence in firm business which they habitually take and show in their own affairs,[51] and must act honestly and honourably towards each other.[52]

Partnership property

Partnership property, i.e. property and rights and interests in property brought into the partnership stock or acquired on account of the firm, or for the purposes and in the course of the partnership business, must be held and applied by the partners exclusively for the purpose of the partnership and in accordance with the partnership agreement.[53] The title to and interest in any heritable estate belonging to the partnership devolves according to the general rules of law but in trust for the persons beneficially interested therein in the partnership.[54] If co-owners of heritable estate, not itself partnership property, who are partners as to profits made by the use of that land, purchase other land, it belongs to them, failing contrary agreement, not as partners, but as co-owners as in the case of the first land.[55] Disputes have frequently arisen as to whether certain property is firm property or personal property of a partner.[56] A partner may insist on having firm property entered in the balance sheet at a real value, and not one stated in the copartnery.[57] It is competent to prove by parole evidence that certain heritage is partnership property.[58] Property bought with firm money is deemed to have been bought on account of the firm.[59] Land held as partnership property is to be treated, as between partners, their heirs, and representatives, as moveable, not heritable property.[60] A lease may be granted to be held in the firm name,[61] but heritage held feudally is vested the partners as trustees.[62]

---

[50] *Gordon* v. *Gonda* [1955] 2 All E.R. 762.

[51] Ersk. III, 3, 21; if one does not the remedy is the dissolution of the partnership: *MacCredie's Trs.* v. *Lamond* (1886) 24 S.L.R. 114.

[52] *McNiven* v. *Peffers* (1868) 7 M. 181; *Cassels* v. *Stewart* (1881) 8 R. (H.L.) 1.

[53] 1890 Act, S. 20(1); cf. *Pillans Bros.* v. *P.* (1908) 16 S.L.T. 611.

[54] 1890 Act, S. 20(2); *Morrison* v. *Miller* (1818) Hume 720; as to completion of title see *Scott's Trs.*, 1957 S.L.T. (Notes) 45; as to proof see *Adam* v. *A.*, 1962 S.L.T. 332.

[55] 1890 Act, S. 20(3); *Davis* v. *D.* [1894] 1 Ch. 393.

[56] e.g. *Wilson* v. *Laidlaw* (1816) 6 Pat. 222; *Wilson* v. *Threshie* (1825) 4 S. 361; *Cox* v. *Stead* (1834) 7 W. & S. 497; *Mabon* v. *Christie* (1844) 6 D. 619; *McArthur* v. *McBrair & Johnstone's Tr.* (1844) 6 D. 1174; *Ord* v. *Barton* (1846) 8 D. 1011; *Miles* v. *Clarke* [1953] 1 All E.R. 779; *Munro* v. *Stein*, 1961 S.C. 362.

[57] *Noble* v. *N.*, 1965 S.L.T. 415.

[58] *Munro* v. *Stein*, 1961 S.C. 362.

[59] 1890 Act, S. 21.

[60] 1890 Act, S. 22; Bell, *Comm.* II, 501; *Murray* v. *M.*, 5 Feb. 1805, F.C.; *Sime* v. *Balfour* (1811) 5 Pat. 525; *Minto* v. *Kirkpatrick* (1833) 11 S. 632; *Irvine* v. *I.* (1851) 13 D. 1367; *Wray* v. *W.* [1905] 2 Ch. 349.

[61] *Denniston, McNayr & Co.* v. *McFarlane*, 16 Feb. 1808, F.C.

[62] Bell, *Prin.* § 357. Proof of the trust is limited to writ or oath of the partners: *Laird* v. *Laird & Rutherford* (1884) 12 R. 294. But see *Munro* v. *Stein*, 1961 S.C. 362.

Each partner has a *pro indiviso* right in the firm's assets,[63] which is wholly moveable, and may be attached by arrestment in the hands of the firm,[64] but a creditor may not arrest money due to the firm for a partner's debt because the partner has no separate share in the firm assets.[65]

Rights of partners inter se

The interest of partners in the partnership property and their rights and duties in relation to the partnership are regulated by their contract of copartnery or any agreement implied by their conduct, failing which by the rules of the 1890 Act.[66] These are:

(1) All the partners are entitled to share equally in the capital and profits of the business[67] and must contribute equally towards the losses whether of capital or otherwise sustained by the firm.[68]

(2) The firm must indemnify every partner in respect of payments and personal liabilities incurred by him—

(a) in the ordinary and proper conduct of the business of the firm; or
(b) in or about anything necessarily done for the preservation of the business or property of the firm.[69]

(3) A partner making, for the purpose of the partnership, any normal payment or advance beyond the amount of capital which he has agreed to subscribe, is entitled to interest at 5 per cent p.a. from the date thereof.[70]

(4) A partner is not entitled, before the ascertainment of profits, to interest on the capital subscribed by him.[71]

(5) Every partner may take part in the management of the partnership business.[72]

(6) No partner shall be entitled to remuneration for acting in the partnership business.[73]

---

[63] As to the difference between the interest of a partner in a firm and that of a shareholder in a company see *Dove* v. *Young* (1868) 7 M. 304; see also *Arthur* v. *Baird* (1868) 7 M. 308.

[64] Ersk. III, 3, 24.

[65] *Parnell* v. *Walter* (1889) 16 R. 917, 925.

[66] 1890 Act, S. 24; Stair I, 16, 4.

[67] Stair I, 16, 3; Ersk. III, 3, 19; *McWhirter* v. *Guthrie* (1823) 1 S. 319; *Fergusson* v. *Graham's Trs.* (1836) 14 S. 871; *Campbell's Trs.* v. *Thomson* (1831) 5 W. & Sh. 16; *Aberdeen Town & County Bank* v. *Clark* (1859) 22 D. 44; *Aitchison* v. *A.* (1877) 4 R. 899.

[68] *Binney* v. *Mutrie* (1886) 12 App. Cas. 160; *Garner* v. *Murray* [1904] 1 Ch. 57.

[69] *Stroyan* v. *Milroy*, 1910 S.C. 174.

[70] *Bate* v. *Robbins* (1863) 32 Beav. 73;

[71] *Kerr, Duff & Co.* v. *Cossar* (1902) 10 S.L.T. 27. If there is provision in the copartnery for interest it ceases to be payable when the partnership is dissolved: *Barfield* v. *Loughborough* (1872) 8 Ch. App. 1.

[72] *Dickson* v. *D.* (1823) 2 S. 462; *Fleming* v. *Campbell* (1845) 7 D. 935; contrast *Duff* v. *Corsar* (1902) 10 S.L.T. 27.

[73] *Geddes* v. *Hamilton* (1801) 4 Pat. 657; *McWhirter* v. *Guthrie* (1821) Hume 760; *Pender* v. *Henderson* (1864) 2 M. 1428; *Faulds* v. *Roxburgh* (1867) 5 M. 373; *Lawrie* v. *L's Trs.* (1892) 19 R. 675.

(7) No person may be introduced as a partner without the consent of all existing partners.[74]

(8) Any difference arising as to ordinary matters connected with the partnership business may be decided by a majority of the partners,[75] but no change may be made in the nature of the partnership business without the consent of all existing partners.[76]

(9) The partnership books are to be kept at the place of business of the partnership (or the principal place, if there is more than one) and every partner may, when he thinks fit, have access to and inspect and copy any of them.[77]

It is incompetent for one partner of a dissolved company to use summary diligence against a copartner on a decree acquired from a creditor of the firm.[78]

Expulsion of partner

No majority of partners can expel any partner unless a power to do so has been conferred by express agreement between the partners.[79] Such a power is very narrowly interpreted.[80] Even then the court may decline to give effect to such a provision if convinced that the expulsion is not in the interests of the firm but for a private reason.[81] But a partner may be prevailed on to agree to leave the partnership; such an agreement may be attacked as impetrated by undue influence,[82] but is not necessarily objectionable.[83]

Retirement from partnership at will

Where no fixed term has been agreed upon for the duration of the partnership, any partner may determine it at any time on giving notice of his intention to all the other partners. If the partnership was entered into by deed, written notice, signed, is sufficient.[84]

---

[74] cf. *Hill* v. *Wylie* (1865) 3 M. 541; cf. *Thomson* v. *T.*, 1962 S.C. (H.L.) 28.

[75] Mere questions of disputed management and general disagreement do not justify an action of damages between partners: *Ferguson* v. *Mackenzie* (1870) 8 S.L.R. 273. cf. also *Hutcheon* v. *Hutcheon*, 1977 S.L.T. (Sh. Ct.) 61.

[76] *Maxton* v. *Brown* (1839) 1 D. 367.

[77] He may call on an accountant or solicitor for assistance: *Fife Bank* v. *Halliday* (1831) 9 S. 693; *Cameron* v. *McMurray* (1858) 17 D. 1142; *Bevan* v. *Webb* [1901] 1 Ch. 724.

[78] *Pearson* v. *Lockhart* (1867) 5 M. 301; *Hamilton* v. *Steele* (1871) 9 M. 805.

[79] 1890 Act, S. 25; cf. Stair I, 16, 4; *Carmichael* v. *Evans* [1904] 1 Ch. 486.

[80] *Clarke* v. *Hart* (1858) 6 H.L.C. 633, 650.

[81] *Blisset* v. *Daniel* (1853) 10 Hare 493; *Wood* v. *Woad* (1874) L.R. 9 Ex. 190; *Green* v. *Howell* [1910] 1 Ch. 495. See also *Montgomery* v. *Forrester* (1791) Hume 748; *Cunninghame* v. *Warner* (1824) 2 Sh. App. 225.

[82] *Tennent* v. *T's Trs.* (1870) 8 M. (H.L.) 10.

[83] *McKirdy* v. *Paterson* (1854) 16 D. 1013.

[84] 1890 Act, S. 26.

Continuance of partnership—tacit relocation

If a partnership is entered into for a fixed period[85] it determines without notice on the expiry of that period. But if after the expiry of the period, without express new agreement, or agreement to prolong the term, the business is continued for a substantial period[86] by the partners who habitually acted in the firm affairs without any settlement or liquidation of the partnership affairs, the court will infer an intention to continue the partnership as a partnership at will, on the terms and conditions, so far as still applicable, obtaining at the end of the former partnership.[87] Continuance by tacit relocation requires that at least two partners survive the term; it will not suffice that only one survives and carries on the business.[86]

A partnership at will may be terminated by any partner giving reasonable notice to the others,[88] or in any event by the death of the second last surviving partner.

Duty to account

Partners are bound to render true accounts and full information of all things affecting the partnership to any partner or his legal representatives.[89] A partner must also account to the firm for any benefit derived by him without the consent of the other partners from any transaction concerning the partnership,[90] or from any use by him of the partnership property, name, or business connection, including transactions undertaken after a partnership has been dissolved by the death of a partner and before the affairs thereof have been completely wound up, either by a surviving partner or by the deceased partner's representatives.[91] A partner may accordingly not make any private profit or benefit from the firm business, but may make private profit outside the scope of, and not competing with the firm business.[92] The same principle applies where a

---

[85] cf. *Gracie* v. *Prentice* (1904) 12 S.L.T. 15.

[86] *Wallace* v. *Wallace's Trs.* (1906) 8 F. 558.

[87] 1890 Act, Ss. 27, 32; *Marshall* v. *M.*, 23 Feb. 1816, F.C.; *Neilson* v. *Mossend Iron Co.* (1886) 13 R. (H.L.) 50; *Browns* v. *Kilsyth Police Commrs.* (1886) 13 R. 515; *McGown* v. *Henderson*, 1914 S.C. 839.

[88] 1890 Act, S. 26(1).

[89] 1890 Act, S. 28; *Law* v. *L.* [1905] 1 Ch. 140; *Smith* v. *Barclay*, 1962 S.C. 1. See also *McIntyre* v. *Maxwell* (1831) 9 S. 284; *Pollock, Gilmour & Co.* v. *Ritchie* (1850) 13 D. 640; *McLaren* v. *Liddell's Trs.* (1862) 24 D. 577; *Lawson* v. *L's Trs.* (1872) 11 M. 168.

[90] Not including the purchase by one partner of a second's share in the firm without the knowledge of the third partner: *Cassels* v. *Stewart* (1881) 8 R. (H.L.) 1; see also *Lister* v. *Marshall's Tr.*, 1927 S.N. 55.

[91] 1890 Act, S. 29; cf. Ersk. III, 3, 20; Bell, *Comm.* II, 522; *Marshall* v. *M.*, 23 Feb. 1816, F.C.; *Bayne* v. *Fergusson & Kyd* (1817) 5 Dow 151; *Wallace, Hamilton & Co* v. *Campbell* (1824) 2 Sh. App.; *Pender* v. *Henderson* (1864) 2 M. 1428; *McNiven* v. *Peffers* (1868) 7 M. 181; *Manners* v. *Raeburn & Verel* (1884) 11 R. 899; *Sc. Pacific Coast Mining Co.* v. *Falkner, Bell & Co.* (1888) 15 R. 290.

[92] *Aas* v. *Benham* [1891] 2 Ch. 244; *Trimble* v. *Goldberg* [1906] A.C. 494.

partner dissolves the partnership to obtain for his private benefit a con-tract which the firm might have obtained.[93]

Profits of competing business

If a partner without the consent of the other partners carries on a business of the same nature as and competing with that of the firm, he must account for and pay over to the firm all profits made by him in that business.[94] If there is no competition there is no obligation to account, even though the position of profit would not have been achieved without connection with the partnership.[95]

Assignation of interests

The partnership relation demands full mutual confidence, so that no partner can, without the consent of all the others, assign his interest to the effect of making the assignee a partner in the firm,[96] except under the provisions of the Limited Partnership Act, 1907.[97] But a partner may assign his interest, either absolutely or in security.[98] The assignee acquires thereby no right to interfere in the management of the firm, to require accounts, or inspect the partnership books, but only the right, so long as the firm continues, to receive the share of profits to which his cedent was entitled, and he must accept the account of profits to which the partners have agreed.[99] He has no power to dissolve the firm, but if it is dissolved, he is entitled to receive the share of the partnership assets which the cedent would have been entitled to receive, and for this purpose, he is entitled to an account as from the date of the dissolution.[1] Similarly a partner may, if the copartnery permits, nominate a relative to his share in the partnership, but this confers only an interest in the partnership assets and does not make the relative a partner.[2]

DISSOLUTION OF PARTNERSHIP

Subject to any agreement between the partners, a partnership is dissolved (a) by the expiry of any fixed term for which it was entered into,[3] or (b)

---

[93] Bell, *Comm.* II, 522; *McNiven, supra.*
[94] 1890 Act, S. 30; *Stewart* v. *North* (1893) 20 R. 260; *Pillans Bros.* v. *P.* (1908) 16 S.L.T. 611.
[95] *Aas* v. *Benham* [1891] 2 Ch. 244.
[96] 1890 Act, S. 31; cf. Ersk. III, 3, 22.
[97] See further, *infra.*
[98] See *Lonsdale Hematite Iron Co.* v. *Barclay* (1874) 1 R. 417; *Cassels* v. *Stewart* (1881) 8 R. (H.L.) 1.
[99] S. 31(1).
[1] S. 31(2).
[2] *Thomson* v. *T.*, 1962 S.C. (H.L.) 28.
[3] *Wallace's Trs.* v. *W.* (1906) 8 F. 558. If continued after the expiry of the fixed term it subsists as a partnership at will: S. 27(1). Bell, *Comm.* II, 521; *Neilson* v. *Mossend Iron Co.* (1886) 13 R. (H.L.) 50.

by the termination of any single adventure or undertaking for which it was entered into,[4] or (c) if entered into for an undefined time, by any partner giving notice to the other or others of his intention to dissolve the partnership,[5] in which case the partnership is dissolved as from any date fixed in the notice as the date of dissolution or, if no date is mentioned, from the date of the communication of the notice.[6] It is also dissolved, in the absence of agreement to the contrary,[7] by the death or bankruptcy of any partner,[8] or by the happening of any event which makes it unlawful for the business to be carried on or for the members of the firm to carry it on in partnership,[9] and may, at the option of the other partners, be dissolved if any partner suffers his share of the partnership property to be charged under the Act for his separate debt.[10] The executor of a predeceasing partner has been said to be absolutely entitled to insist on a public sale of the business, to ascertain the deceased's share.[11]

Dissolution by the Court

The Court may dissolve a partnership on the application of a partner on the following grounds:[12]

(a) When a partner is found a lunatic by cognition, or is shown to the satisfaction of the Court to be of permanently unsound mind, application being competent by the incapax partner's *curator bonis* or by another partner:

(b) When a partner, other than the partner suing, becomes in any other

---

[4] *Gracie* v. *Prentice* (1904) 12 S.L.T. 15.
[5] Ersk II, 3, 26; cf. *Marshall* v. *M.*, 26 Jan. 1815, F.C.; notice given cannot, save by consent, be withdrawn: *Jones* v. *Lloyd* (1874) L.R. 18 Eq. 265.
[6] 1890 Act, S. 32.
[7] e.g. *Hill* v. *Wylie* (1865) 3 M. 541; cf. *Sclater* v. *Clyne* (1831) 5 W. & S. 625; *Beveridge* v. *B's Trs.* (1872) 10 M. (H.L.) 1; *Alexander* v. *Lowson's Trs.* (1890) 17 R. 571.
[8] S. 33(1); Stair I, 16, 5; Ersk. III, 3, 25; *Aitken's Trs.* v. *Shanks* (1830) 8 S. 753; *Christie* v. *Royal Bank* (1840) 2 Robin. 118; *Aytoun* v. *Dundee Bank* (1844) 6 D. 1409; *Hoey* v. *McEwan & Auld* (1867) 5 M. 814; *Oswald's Trs.* v. *City of Glasgow Bank* (1879) 6 R. 461; *Hannan* v. *Henderson* (1879) 7 R. 380; see also *Fleming's Trs.* v. *Henderson*, 1962 S.L.T. 401; *Inland Revenue* v. *Graham's Trs.*, 1971 S.L.T. 46; *Thomson* v. *T.*, 1962 S.C. (H.L.) 28; *Jardine-Paterson* v. *Fraser*, 1974 S.L.T. 93.
[9] S. 34; *Esposito* v. *Bowden* (1857) 7 E. & B. 763; *Stevenson* v. *Cartonnagen Industrie* [1918] A.C. 239; *Hudgell Yeates & Co.* v. *Watson* [1978] 2 All E.R. 363 (member of firm of solicitors becoming unqualified).
[10] S. 33(2); this is ineffective in Scotland by reason of S. 23.
[11] *McKersies* v. *Mitchell* (1872) 10 M. 861.
[12] 1890 Act, S. 35; application may be made by petition or action of declarator: *McNab, Petr.*, 1912 S.C. 421; *Thomson, Petr.*, 1923, 1 S.L.T. 73; cf. *Gordon* v. *Howden* (1854) 4 Bell 254; *Russell* v. *R.* (1874) 2 R. 93; a summary application under this section is not always convenient or competent: *Wallace* v. *Whitelaw* (1900) 2 F. 675; this statutory power does not exclude a provision in the copartnery for arbitration as to dissolution: *Hackston* v. *H.*, 1965 S.L.T. (Notes) 38.

way permanently incapable of performing his part of the partnership contract:[13]

(c) When a partner, other than the partner suing, has been guilty of such conduct as, in the opinion of the Court, having regard to the nature of the business, is calculated prejudicially to affect the carrying on of the business:[14]

(d) When a partner, other than the partner suing, wilfully or persistently commits a breach of the partnership agreement, or otherwise so conducts himself in matters relating to the partnership business that it is not reasonably practicable for the other partner or partners to carry on the business in partnership with him:[15]

(e) When the business of the partnership can only be carried on at a loss:[16]

(f) Whenever in any case circumstances have arisen which, in the opinion of the Court, render it just and equitable that the partnership be dissolved.[17]

If the partner suing cannot do so the court will appoint a judicial factor to wind up the partnership business.[18]

Rights against apparent partners

A person who deals with a firm after a change in its constitution is entitled to treat all apparent members of the old firm as still being members of the firm until he has notice of the change.[19] Hence express notice of change to parties dealing with the firm is prudent. An advertisement in the *Edinburgh Gazette*, in respect of a firm whose principal place of business is in Scotland, is notice to all persons who had no prior dealings with the firm.[20] Direct intimation, by circular or obvious change in the firm name, is necessary in the case of persons who have had dealings with the firm,[21] advertisement or notice in the *Gazette* is insufficient unless the third party can be shown to have had actual knowledge of the change.[21] The estate of a partner who dies, or becomes bankrupt,

[13] cf. *Eadie* v. *McBean's C.B.* (1885) 12 R. 660; *Cleghorn* (1901) 8 S.L.T. 409.

[14] e.g conviction for dishonesty though not affecting the firm: *Carmichael* v. *Evans* [1904] 1 Ch. 486; see also *McCredies' Trs.* v. *Lamond* (1886) 24 S.L.R. 114; *Macnab* v. *M.*, 1912 S.C. 421; *Tomkins* v. *Cohen*, 1951 S.C. 22.

[15] cf. *A.B.* (1884) 22 S.L.R. 294; *Thomson* (1893) 1 S.L.T. 59. See observations on this in *Elder* v. *Elder & Watson*, 1952 S.C. 49.

[16] *Miller* v. *Walker* (1875) 3 R. 242.

[17] *Oliver* v. *Hillier* [1959] 2 All E.R. 220.

[18] e.g. *Allan* v. *Gronmeyer* (1891) 18 R. 784; *Carabine* v. *C.*, 1949 S.C. 521.

[19] 1890 Act S. 36(1); *Campbell, Thomson & Co.* v. *McLintock* (1803) Hume 755; *Kay* v. *Pollock*, 27 Jan. 1809, F.C.; contrast *Dunbar* v. *Remmington Wilson & Co.*, 10 Mar. 1810, F.C; *Blacks* v. *Girdwood* (1885) 13 R. 243.

[20] S. 36(2); *McMillan* v. *Walker* (1814) Hume 755; *Mann* v. *Sinclair* (1879) 6 R. 1078.

[21] Bell, *Comm.* II, 530; *Prin.* § 384; cf. *Dunbar* v. *Remmington, Wilson & Co.*, 10 Mar. 1810, F.C.; *Sawers* v. *Tradestown Victualling Socy.*, 24 Feb. 1815, F.C.; *McMillan* v. *Walker* (1814) Hume 755.

or who retires, not having been known to third parties to be a partner, is not liable for partnership debts contracted after his death, bankruptcy, or retirement respectively.[22]

Right to notify dissolution

On the dissolution of a firm or retirement of a partner any partner may publicly notify the fact and may require the other partner or partners to concur for the purpose in all necessary or proper acts which cannot be done without their concurrence.[23]

Effect of dissolution

The authority of each partner to bind the firm, and the other rights and obligations of the partners, continue notwithstanding dissolution so far as necessary to complete business in progress at the date of dissolution and to wind up the partnership affairs.[24] But the firm is in no case bound by the acts of a partner who has become bankrupt, without prejudice to the liability of any one who after the bankruptcy represented himself or knowingly suffered himself to be represented as a partner of the bankrupt.[25]

Dissolution by the death of one partner terminates contracts of personal service with employees, but is not breach of contract with them,[26] but probably does not terminate other contracts. It may terminate a partnership obligation to pay an annuity to a former partner's widow.[27] On dissolution followed by the creation of a new firm obligations with the old firm may be held novated into obligations with the new one, as by a course of dealing with the new firm and acceptance of it as the debtor.[28] But, in the absence of express or implied agreement to the contrary, a new firm incurs no liability for prior trade debts.[29]

---

[22] S. 36(3). cf. Bell, *Comm.* II, 529.

[23] 1890 Act, S. 37.

[24] 1890 Act, S. 38; *Gordon* v. *Douglas Heron & Co.* (1795) 3 Pat. 428; *Paul* v. *Taylor* (1826) 4 S. 572; *Wotherspoon* v. *Henderson's Trs.* (1868) 6 M. 1052; *Dickson* v. *National Bank*, 1917 S.C. (H.L.) 50; *Goldfarb* v. *Bartlett* [1920] 1 K.B. 639; *Public Trustee* v. *Elder* [1926] Ch. 776; cf. *Muir* v. *Dickson* (1860) 22 D. 1070; *Goodwin* v. *Industrial and General Trust* (1890) 18 R. 193; *Welsh* v. *Knarston*, 1972 S.L.T. 96.

[25] S. 38, proviso.

[26] *Hoey* v. *McEwan & Auld* (1867) 5 M. 814.

[27] *Menzies' Trs.* v. *Black's Trs.*, 1909 S.C. 239.

[28] *Ker* v. *McKechnie* (1845) 7 D. 494; *Price & Logan* v. *Wise* (1862) 24 D. 491; contrast *Campbell* v. *Cruickshank* (1845) 7 D. 548; *Pollock* v. *Murray & Spence* (1863) 2 M. 14; *Heritable Securities Investment Assocn.* v. *Wingates* (1891) 29 S.L.R. 904; *Morton's Trs.* v. *Robertson's J. F.* (1892) 20 R. 72; cf. *Mackintosh* v. *Gibb & Co's Trs.* (1828) 6 S. 992.

[29] *Nelmes* v. *Montgomery* (1883) 10 R. 974.

Assets and liabilities of firm

What the assets and liabilities of the firm at the time of dissolution are, are questions of fact, frequently involving interpretation of any relevant provisions in the contract of copartnery.[30] In the absence of contrary agreement a deceased partner's share of capital depends on valuation of assets at the date of his death.[31] It is a question of fact whether a firm has any goodwill accountable as an asset.[32]

Application of property

Every partner is entitled to have the partnership property applied in payment of the debts and liabilities of the firm, and the surplus assets applied in payment of what may be due to the partners respectively after deducting what may be due from them as partners to the firm; for this purpose any partner or his representative may apply to the Court to wind up the business and affairs of the firm.[33] In dividing firm property among the partners any one can insist on public sale.[34]

Appointment of judicial factor

The court may at common law sequestrate the estate of a partnership and appoint a judicial factor thereon,[35] not to carry on the business but normally only to protect the assets pending dissolution, or where the partners are at loggerheads.[36] An interim appointment may be made.[37] The court may appoint a judicial factor to wind up the estate if a partner has been guilty of misconduct,[38] all the partners have died,[39] or any surviving partners are unfit to, or incapable of winding up the affairs,[40] or

---

[30] See *Forrester* v. *Robson's Trs.* (1875) 2 R. 755; *Glass* v. *Haig* (1877) 4 R. 875; *Charlton* v. *C.* (1894) 2 S.L.T. 61; *Eadie* v. *Crawford*, 1912, 2 S.L.T. 360 (assets); *Clark* v. *Watson*, 1982 S.L.T. 450; *Thom's Exrx.* v. *Russel & Aitken*, 1983 S.L.T. 335. *MacCredie's Trs.* v. *Lamond* (1886) 24 S.L.R. 114; *Menzies' Trs.* v. *Black's Trs.*, 1909 S.C. 239 (liabilities).

[31] *Clark, supra.*

[32] *Mackenzie* v. *Macfarlane*, 1934 S.N. 16; *Reid* v. *R.*, 1938 S.L.T. 415; cf. *Ventisei* v. *V.'s Exors.*, 1966 S.C. 21. Under the National Health Service the goodwill of a medical practice cannot be sold. See also *Smith* v. *McBride & Smith* (1888) 16 R. 36.

[33] 1890 Act, S. 39; Ersk III, 3, 27; *thomson* (1839) 1 S.L.T. 59; *Robertson* (1902) 10 S.L.T. 417; *Elliott* v. *Cassils* (1907) 15 S.L.T. 190.

[34] *Stewart* v. *Simpson* (1835) 14 S. 72; *Mackersies* v. *Mitchell* (1872) 10 M. 861. See also *Marshall* v. *M.*, 23 Feb. 1816, F.C.; *Aitken's Trs.* v. *Shanks* (1830) 8 S. 753; *McWhannell* v. *Dobbie* (1830) 8 S. 914.

[35] A petition for appointment of a judicial factor must contain a crave for sequestration of the estate; *Booth* v. *MacKinnon* (1908) 15 S.L.T. 848.

[36] *Carabine* v. *C.*, 1949 S.C. 521; *McCulloch* v. *McC.*, 1953 S.C. 189.

[37] *McCulloch, supra.*

[38] *Macpherson* v. *Richmond* (1869) 6 S.L.R. 348.

[39] *Dixon* v. *D.* (1832) 6 W. & S. 229.

[40] *Dickie* v. *Mitchell* (1874) 1 R. 1030; *Russell* v. *R.* (1874) 2 R. 93; *Miller* v. *Walker* (1875) 3 R. 242; *Gow* v. *Schulze* (1877) 4 R. 928; *Gatherer* (1893) 1 S.L.T. 401; *Paterson* (1894) 1 S.L.T. 564; *Robertson* (1902) 10 S.L.T. 417.

there is danger of a partner not obtaining his due rights on dissolution,[41] but not if there are surviving partners not prevented by fault or incapacity from winding up their affairs,[42] or if the differences between the partners relate to accounting only,[43] or it is otherwise unnecessary.[44] Minor differences between partners do not justify the appointment of a factor.[45] A petition for appointment of a factor is not a suitable process for determining substantive issues such as whether a partnership existed,[45] the construction of the partnership deed,[46] or whether there was goodwill to be sold.[47]

Where a partnership is prematurely dissolved, the Court may order repayment in whole or in part of any premium paid by one partner to another on entering into partnership, unless the dissolution is wholly or chiefly due to the misconduct of the partner who paid the premium, or the partnership has been dissolved by an agreement containing no provision for return of any part of the premium.[48]

Where a partnership contract is rescinded on the ground of the fraud or misrepresentation of one of the parties,[49] the party rescinding is, apart from any other right, entitled—

(a) to a lien on the surplus of partnership assets after satisfying liabilities, for any money paid by him for a share in the partnership and for any capital contributed by him; and
(b) to stand in the place of the firm creditors for any payments made by him in respect of partnership liabilities; and
(c) to be indemnified by the person guilty of the fraud or making the representation against all the debts and liabilities of the firm.[50]

Where a member of a firm has died or otherwise ceased to be a partner[51] and the surviving or continuing partners carry on business without any final settlement of accounts, failing contrary agreement, the outgoing partner or his estate is entitled in his option to such share of the profits made since dissolution as the Court may find attributable to the use of his share of the partnership assets, or to interest on the amount of his share at 5 per cent.[52] But where the survivors have an option to

[41] *Allan* v. *Gronmeyer* (1891) 18 R. 784; *Carabine, supra.*
[42] *Young* v. *Collins and Feely* (1853) 15 D. (H.L.) 35; 1 Macq. 385; *Russell, supra; Thomson* (1893) 1 S.L.T. 59.
[43] *Gow* v. *Schulze* (1877) 4 R. 928; *Elliott* v. *Cassils* (1907) 15 S.L.T. 190.
[44] *Eadie* v. *MacBean's C.B.* (1885) 12 R. 660.
[45] *Anderson* v. *Blair*, 1935 S.L.T. 377.
[46] *Blake's Trs.* v. *Jolly*, 1920 1 S.L.T. 304.
[47] *Mackenzie* v. *M.*, 1934 S.N. 16.
[48] 1890 Act, S. 40.
[49] *Adam* v. *Newbigging* (1888) 13 App. Cas. 308; *Manners* v. *Whitehead* (1898) 1 F. 171; *Ferguson* v. *Wilson* (1904) 6 F. 779.
[50] 1890 Act, S. 41; and see further *infra.*
[51] Including ceasing by reason of becoming an alien enemy on the outbreak of war: *Stevenson* v. *Cartonnagen Industrie* [1918] A.C. 239.
[52] 1890 Act, S. 42(1); *Vyse* v. *Foster* (1874) L.R. 7 H.L. 318; *Yates* v. *Finn* (1880) 13 Ch. D. 839.

purchase his share and exercise it, he is not entitled to any further or other share of the profits unless there is material non-compliance with the terms of the option.[53] The amount due to an outgoing partner in respect of his share is a debt accruing at the date of dissolution or death.[54]

Priority of payments in final settlement

In the absence of contrary agreement the following rules apply in settling the accounts of a partnership after dissolution:

(a) losses, including losses and deficiencies of capital, are paid first out of profits, next out of capital, and lastly, if necessary, by the partners individually in the proportion in which they were entitled to share profits:

(b) assets including such contributions, fall to be applied (1) in paying debts and liabilities of the firm to non-partners;[55] (2) in paying each partner rateably which is due him for advances,[56] and (3) for capital;[57] (4) the residue is divided among the partners in the proportion in which profits are divisible.[58]

The doqueted accounts of a mercantile firm must be taken as conclusive in the absence of anything casting doubt on their accuracy, but are open to correction at the instance of a representative of one of the partners.[59] They may be challenged on the ground of *error calculi*.[60]

Liability of partners after dissolution

When a firm has been dissolved the partners remain jointly and severally liable for the firm's debts, but no one partner can be sued without calling all the others, so far as that is possible, unless the firm obligation has been previously constituted by writing or decree.[61]

Bankruptcy

The law relating to the bankruptcy of a firm or of the individual partners thereof in Scotland is regulated by the Bankruptcy (Sc.) Act, 1985.[62]

---

[53] 1890 Act, S. 42(2).
[54] 1890 Act, S. 43.
[55] Liabilities include the legal and accountancy fees incurred in winding up the firm's affairs, but these are postponed to business creditors.
[56] *Potter* v. *Jackson* (1880) 13 Ch. D. 845.
[57] 1890 Act, S. 44.
[58] *Garner* v. *Murray* [1904] 1 Ch. 57.
[59] *Findlay, Bannatyne & Co.'s Assignee* v. *Donaldson* (1865) 2 M. (H.L.) 86; cf. *Russel* v. *Glen* (1827) 5 S. 221; *Blair* v. *Russell* (1828) 6 S. 836.
[60] *McLaren* v. *Liddell's Tr.* (1862) 24 D. 577.
[61] *Johnston* v. *Duncan* (1823) 2 S. 625; *Geddes* v. *Hopkirk* (1828) 5 S. 747; *Dewar* v. *Munnoch* (1831) 9 S. 487; *Muir* v. *Collett* (1862) 24 D. 1119; *Neilson* v. *Wilson* (1890) 17 R. 608, 612, 614.
[62] S. 46. See Ch. 10.1, *infra*.

JOINT ADVENTURE

Joint adventure is a co-operative enterprise confined to a particular adventure, speculation, course of trade, or voyage in which the partners use no firm or social name and incur no responsibility beyond the limits of the adventure.[63] It may be of some duration, such as the lease of a farm[64] but is differentiated from partnership by its limited purpose and duration.[65] It is established by contract, express or implied, and evidenced by the same kind of evidence as partnership, but is not necessarily to be inferred from the joint ownership of a ship, unless there has been participation in the mercantile employment of the ship in which the joint adventure is said to have consisted,[66] nor necessarily from taking shares in a company to which one sells property.[67]

It is doubtful whether a joint adventure creates any body having a quasi-persona as does a firm.[68] There can be no contract by the joint adventure as such,[69] and one joint adventurer can sue another or an agent of the adventure for an accounting.[70] A company can be party to a joint adventure.[71]

Each adventurer is *praepositus negotiis societatis* and has an implied mandate in dealing with the limits of the adventure, but not to bind the partners generally.[72] When goods are purchased or money borrowed for the joint adventure, and adventurers are jointly and severally liable therefor.[73] There is no such liability for goods purchased previously by any one and subsequently brought into the stock of the adventure.[74] Each adventurer's liability is limited to that adventure.[75]

---

[63] Ersk. III, 3, 29; Hume *Lect.* II, 194; Bell, *Comm.* II, 538; *Prin.* § 392; More, *Lect.* I, 199; *Wilkie* v. *Johnstone, Bannatyne & Co.* (1808) 5 Pat. 191; *Logan* v. *Brown* (1824) 3 S. 15; *Ferguson* v. *Graham's Trs.* (1836) 14 S. 871; *Venables* v. *Wood* (1839) 1 D. 659; *Orr* v. *Pollock* (1840) 2 D. 1902; *White* v. *McIntyre* (1841) 3 D. 334; *Baxter* v. *Aitchison* (1841) 3 D. 391; *B.L. Co.* v. *Alexander* (1853) 15 D. 277; *Clements* v. *Macaulay* (1866) 4 M. 583; *Aitchison* v. *A.* (1877) 4 R. 899; *Pyper* v. *Christie* (1878) 6 R. 143; *Young* v. *Dougans* (1887) 14 R. 490; *Cooke's Circus Building Co.* v. *Welding* (1894) 21 R. 338; *Livingstone* v. *Allans* (1900) 3 F. 233; *Clayton* v. *C.*, 1937 S.C. 619; *Parker* v. *Walker*, 1961 S.L.T. 252; *Adam* v. *A.*, 1962 S.L.T. 332.

[64] *Cameron* v. *Young* (1871) 9 M. 786.

[65] *Mair* v. *Wood*, 1948 S.C. 83, 86.

[66] Bell, *Prin.* § 392; *Logan, supra; Fergusson, supra*

[67] *Moore* v. *Dempster* (1879) 6 R. 930; see also *Beresford's Tr.* v. *Argyll Assessor* (1884) 11 R. 818; *Clark* v. *Jamieson*, 1909 S.C. 132; *Sc. Ins. Commrs.* v. *McNaughton*, 1914 S.C. 826.

[68] Bell, *Comm.* II, 539, says there is no firm; cf. *Livingstone* v. *Allans* (1900) 3 F. 233, 237; but see *Mair* v. *Wood*, 1948 S.C. 83, 89.

[69] Ersk. III, 3, 29.

[70] *Manners* v. *Raeburn & Verel* (1884) 11 R. 899.

[71] Bell, *Prin.* § 394.

[72] Bell, *Prin,* § 396; *Cameron* v. *Young* (1871) 9 M. 786.

[73] Bell, *Prin.* § 395; *Cameron, supra; Lockhart* v. *Moodie* (1877) 4 R. 859; *Lockhart* v. *Brown* (1888) 15 R. 742; *Mollison* v. *Noltie* (1889) 16 R. 350; *Fowler* v. *Paterson's Trs.* (1896) 3 S.L.T. 305; *Hay* v. *Douglas*, 1922 S.L.T. 365. As to bills given for the price see Ersk. III, 3, 29.

[74] *Venables* v. *Wood* (1839) 1 D. 659; *White* v. *McIntyre* (1841) 3 D. 334; *Lockhart* v. *Brown* (1888) 15 R. 742.

[75] *Jardine* v. *Macfarlan* (1828) 6 S. 564.

Each joint adventurer is jointly and severally liable for wrongs done to third parties in pursuance of the joint adventure.[76] The shares of the adventurers are presumed equal. Their stock is common property and held in trust for the creditors.[77]

The duration of a joint adventure may be evident from the circumstances. Any one adventurer may end it if it comes to be attended with greater risk than when the contract was entered into, or if there be no reasonable belief that profit will be made for either party.[78] It is also terminable at will on reasonable notice.[79] In partnership proper the firm is a separate persona and subsists in that capacity for winding up, while a joint adventure, when completed, is resolved into its elements and each person may maintain his own interests in the common funds by direct action in his own name without the co-operation of the rest. Each joint adventurer is proprietor of his share of the funds, and may vindicate them from anyone in whose hands they are and who holds them on his account.[80]

LIMITED PARTNERSHIPS

By the Limited Partnerships Act, 1907 it is permissible to create a partnership of one or more general partners, liable for all the debts and obligations of the firm, and one or more limited partners, who contribute to the firm capital or property valued at a stated amount and are not liable for the debts or obligations of the firm beyond that amount.[81] A corporate body may be a limited partner. The general law and the 1890 Act apply, save in so far as the 1907 Act makes special provisions.[82] During the continuance of the partnership a limited partner may not, directly or indirectly, withdraw any part of his contribution, on pain of liability for firm debts up to the amount so drawn out.[83] Limited partnerships must be registered as such[84] in the manner provided,[84] failing which it shall be deemed a general partnership and every limited partner deemed a general partner.[85]

---

[76] *McGee* v. *Anderson* (1895) 22 R. 274; *Mair* v. *Wood*, 1948 S.C. 83.
[77] Bell, *Prin.* §396; *McCaul* v. *Ramsay & Ritchie* (1740) Mor. 14608; *Fergusson* v. *Graham* (1836) 14 S. 871; *Buchanan* v. *Lennox* (1838) 16 S. 824; *Keith* v. *Penn* (1840) 2 D. 633; *Livingstone* v. *Allans* (1900) 3 F. 233.
[78] *Miller* v. *Walker* (1875) 3 R. 242, 249.
[79] *Young* v. *Dougans* (1887) 14 R. 490.
[80] *Pyper* v. *Christie* (1878) 6 R. 143.
[81] As to number of partners see 1907 Act, S. 4(2), amd. Companies Act, 1985, S. 717.
[82] 1907 Act, S. 7; see also *Re Barnard* [1932] 1 Ch. 269.
[83] 1907 Act, S. 4.
[84] 1907 Act, Ss. 5, 14–16. Duty must be paid on the amount contributed by the limited partners: S. 5, 11.
[85] 1907 Act, Ss. 8–9. Changes must be notified: S. 9. Notice of a general partner becoming a limited partner or of assigning a share must be given: S. 10.

A limited partner may not take part in the management of the partnership business and has no power to bind the firm, but he may inspect the firm books and examine the state and prospects of the partnership business and advise with the partners thereon. If he takes part in the management he is liable for all debts and obligations of the firm incurred while doing so as if he were a general partner.[86] A limited partnership is not dissolved by the death or bankruptcy of a limited partner, and his lunacy is not a ground for dissolution by the Court unless his share cannot otherwise be ascertained and realized.[87] In the event of dissolution the affairs of a limited partnership are wound up by the general partners unless the court otherwise orders.[88] A petition by a partner for dissolution may be brought under the Bankruptcy (Sc.) Act, 1985, S. 6, but it is competent for the Court to appoint a judicial factor to wind up.[89]

Subject to any agreement expressed or implied between the partners (a) any difference arising as to ordinary matters connected with the partnership business may be decided by a majority of the general partners; (b) a limited partner may, with the consent of the general partners, assign his share in the partnership;[90] (c) the other partners are not entitled to dissolve the partnership by reason of any limited partner suffering his share to be charged for his separate debt; (d) a person may be introduced as a partner without the consent of the existing limited partners; and (e) a limited partner is not entitled to dissolve the partnership by notice.[91]

The winding up of an insolvent limited partnership may be conducted under the Bankruptcy (Sc.) Act, 1985, S. 6, or by a judicial factor.[92]

UNINCORPORATED COMPANIES

It was formerly common, and is still competent, to form a joint stock company with transferable shares, not incorporated[93] in any of the ways by which corporate status can be obtained.[94] Such a company was in effect a large partnership, and the members were personally liable to an unlimited extent to the company's creditors. The maximum number of members of such an association is now restricted to twenty,[95] otherwise the association is illegal. This form of association is accordingly now unimportant.

---

[86] 1907 Act S. 6(1).
[87] 1907 Act, S. 6(2).
[88] 1907 Act, S. 6(3).
[89] *Muirhead* v. *Borland*, 1925 S.C. 474.
[90] This must be advertised in the *Gazette*: S. 10.
[91] 1907 Act, S. 6(5).
[92] *Muirhead, supra.*
[93] An example was The Western Bank of Scotland, on which see *Western Bank* v. *Addie* (1867) 5 M. (H.L.) 80. See history set out in *Muir* v. *City of Glasgow Bank* (1878) 6 R. 392, 399. On the different interests of a partner in an unincorporated company and in one incorporated, see *Dove* v. *Young* (1868) 7 M. 304. See also Bell, *Prin.* § 398.
[94] On these see Ch. 3.11, *infra.*
[95] Companies Act, 1985, S. 716.

PART 3

JURISTIC PERSONS: INCORPORATED BODIES

CHAPTER 3.11

CORPORATIONS

A corporation or corporate body is a juristic person or legal entity capable of existing, of sustaining legal rights and duties, and of suing and being sued, by itself, wholly independently of the natural persons who are for the time being officers or members of the group incorporated.[1] It is not a collective name for the members, nor any aggregate of them, but a separate legal entity. In every Act of Parliament since 1890 the expression 'person', unless a contrary intention appears, includes any body of persons corporate or unincorporate.[2] But a corporation cannot be a 'person' practising certain professions.[3]

A corporation in Scots law is an incorporated aggregate or group of co-existing persons; English law knows also the corporation sole, where a person as the holder of his office is deemed incorporated.[4] Bell[5] states that a parish minister is a corporation sole but this seems unwarranted and the concept of the corporation sole seems unknown in Scots law.

The characteristics of a corporation are: it is incorporated, or created a corporation under a corporate name,[6] by, or in accordance with, some State authority, and not wholly by the acts of private individuals;[7] once created it has perpetual succession[8] and continues in being indefinitely

---

[1] Stair II, 3, 39; II, 4, 20; Bankt. I, 2, 18–27; Ersk. I, 7, 64; Bell, *Comm.* II, 157; *Prin.* § 2176. See also history in *University of Glasgow* v. *Faculty of Physicians and Surgeons* (1834) 13 S. 9; (1835) 2 S. & McL. 275; (1837) 15 S. 736; (1840) 1 Rob. 397.

[2] Interpretation Act, 1978, S. 5 and Sched. 1.

[3] e.g. solicitors: Solicitors (Sc.) Act, 1980.

[4] In English law the sovereign is a corporation sole; *quaere* as to Scots law. Some Ministers of the Crown have been created corporations sole, e.g. Minister of Transport (Ministry of Transport Act, 1919, S. 26(3), and Ministers of the Crown (Transfer of Functions) Act, 1946, S. 6). As to the position of such a Minister in Scots law, *quaere*.

[5] *Prin.* § 2176.

[6] As to protection of names see Chartered Associations (Protection of Names and Uniforms) Act, 1926.

[7] Ersk. I, 7, 64; *Crawford* v. *Mitchell* (1761) Mor. 1958, 14553.

[8] Stair II, 3, 41; exceptionally a corporation may be created for a limited time; e.g. the B.B.C., the charter of which (1927) was for ten years, but has been subsequently renewed for further periods.

until dissolved by or under State authority; it exists wholly independently of the natural persons who are at any time its officers or members[9] and exists though they change or even though all the officers and members die; all rights and property are vested in the corporation itself, and no member has a claim on any identifiable part thereof,[10] nor is any member liable for the liabilities of the corporation but only for any obligation he has undertaken to contribute to its funds;[11] the members have implied power to elect their own officers, and to make by-laws and regulations for the management of the internal affairs of the corporation; and it possesses a common seal the use of which is necessary to authenticate deeds binding the corporation and expressing its will.

Kinds of corporations

Corporations are established for numerous purposes; public corporations exist to manage public utilities and social services;[12] local authorities to administer local government functions;[13] companies to conduct businesses;[14] building societies to lend money for house purchase;[15] industrial and provident societies to improve the conditions of members of the community;[16] and corporations of many kinds and titles to further academic, professional, charitable, and other purposes. The last class include universities, royal colleges of practitioners of particular professions, learned societies, and similar institutions. Whether a particular kind of association is, or can be, incorporated or not may be as much a matter of legal history as of the wish of the persons composing it.[17] The functions and powers of public corporations and local authorities are deter-

---

[9] cf. *G.E. Ry.* v. *Turner* (1872) L.R. 8 Ch. 152; *Flitcroft's Case* (1882) 21 Ch. D. 519, 536; *Salomon* v. *S & Co.* [1897] A.C. 22, 51; *Woolfson* v. *Strathclyde Regional Council*, 1977 S.C. 84.

[10] *Short* v. *Treasury Comms.* [1948] 1 K.B. 116, 122.

[11] *Muir* v. *City of Glasgow Bank* (1878) 6 R. 392, 401, 405; 6 R. (H.L.) 21, 39. This obligation might, and may, be unlimited; but a creditor's claim is against the corporation, not against all or any members. In the case of public and municipal corporations, and, possibly, chartered and statutory companies, the members are under no liability to the corporation at all, unless and so far as the charter or statute so provides: cf. *Elve* v. *Boyton* [1891] 1 Ch. 501, 507.

[12] e.g. The National Coal Board; the Scottish Gas Board; the Clyde Port Authority; on such bodies see *London T.A.F.A* v. *Nichols* [1949] 1 K.B. 35; *Tamlin* v. *Hannaford* [1950] 1 K.B. 18; *Glasgow Corpn.* v. *Central Land Board*, 1956 S.C. (H.L.) 1; and generally Robson, *Nationalized Industry and Public Ownership*; Friedmann, *Law and Social Change*, Ch. 9; Chester, *The Nationalized Industries*. Many of the principles of law applicable to corporations generally cannot be easily applied to these public corporations.

[13] See Bennett Miller, *Outline of Administrative and Local Government Law in Scotland*, Ch. 4. As to burghs in private law see *Banff Mags.* v. *Ruthin Castle*, 1944 S.C. 36; *McDougal's Trs.* v. *L.A.*, 1952 S.C. 260.

[14] Ch. 3.13, *infra*.

[15] Ch. 3.14, *infra*.

[16] Ch. 3.15, *infra*.

[17] Thus friendly societies may be registered but are not and cannot be incorporated. Many societies and bodies remain unincorporated, their property vested in trustees.

mined mainly by public law, but these and all other corporations transact in spheres of private law, when they contract, commit wrongs, hold property, sue and are sued, in much the same way as private persons of full age and capacity.

Modes of creation

A corporation may be created only by public authority,[18] the modes recognized being: by Royal Charter,[19] by letters patent,[20] by special public Act of Parliament,[21] by public general Act of Parliament,[22] by private Act,[23] by registration under and in terms of a public general Act,[24] by the grant by a common law chartered corporation of subordinate corporate powers by grant of a seal of cause,[25] and by long recognition at common law as a corporate body.[26] The three oldest Scottish universities were founded, and probably impliedly incorporated, by Papal bulls, though subsequently regulated also by statute.[27] Some corporations may act under powers conferred by more than one of these creative acts. Registration of a body under the appropriate legislation does not automatically incorporate it.[28]

---

[18] Hence a body of trustees is not a corporation: *Martin* v. *Wight* (1841) 3 D. 485; *Muir* v. *City of Glasgow Bank* (1879) 6 R. (H.L.) 21, 33, 38, 39; nor is a kirk-session; *Kirk Session of North Berwick* v. *Sime* (1839) 2 D. 23.

[19] e.g. The Royal Bank of Scotland; Carron Company (see *I.R.C.* v. *Carron Co.*, 1968 S.C. (H.L.) 47); The National Trust for Scotland; The University of Strathclyde. In the case of Royal Charter the grant of privileges may imply incorporation, though there be no express grant thereof nor bestowal of a corporate name: *University of Glasgow* v. *Faculty of Physicians and Surgeons* (1840) 1 Rob. 397. As to the term 'chartered banks' see *Sanders* v. *S's Trs.* (1879) 7 R. 157.   [20] e.g. S.S.P.C.K; *Bonar* v. *S.S.P.C.K* (1846) 8 D. 660.

[21] e.g. The Bank of Scotland (Act 1695; see Bell, *Comm.* I, 102 and *Sanders* v. *S's Trs.* (1879) 7 R. 157, 165); The National Coal Board (Coal Industry Nationalization Act 1946, S. 1); The Law Society of Scotland (Solicitors (Sc.) Act, 1980, Sch. 1).

[22] e.g. regional councils and district councils: Local Government (Sc.) Act, 1973, S. 2.

[23] e.g. Clyde Navigation Trust (Clyde Navigation Acts, 1858–99: see 1927 S.C. 626) and railway companies in the nineteenth century; see e.g. *Clouston* v. *Edinburgh & Glasgow Ry.* (1865) 4 M. 207; such statutes latterly incorporated provisions of the Companies Clauses Consolidation (Sc.) Act, 1845, or other Clauses Acts.

[24] e.g. Companies registered under Companies Act, 1985: see Ch. 3.13, *infra.*

[25] See Kames, *Elucidations*, 53; *Ritchie* v. *Cordiners of Edinburgh* (1823) 2 S. 565; *Mowat* v. *Tailors of Aberdeen* (1825) 4 S. 52; *Fleshers of Canongate* v. *Wight* (1835) 14 S. 135; *Anderson* v. *Wrights of Glasgow* (1865) 3 M. (H.L.) 1; *Morris* v. *Guildry of Dunfermline* (1866) 4 M. 457; *Tailors of Edinburgh* v. *Muir's Tr.*, 1912 S.C. 603. The exclusive privileges of trading in burghs were abolished by the Burgh Trading Act, 1846.

[26] See Bell, *Prin.* s 2177; *Skirving* v. *Smellie*, 19 Jan. 1803 F.C.; *Dempster* v. *Masters and Seamen of Dundee* (1831) 9 S. 313; e.g. The Dean and Faculty of Advocates. As to whether the W.S. Society is a corporation see *Writers to the Signet* v. *Grahame* (1823) 2 S. 214, 456, 765; (1824) 3 S. 237; (1825) 1 W. & Sh. 538; *Solicitors* v. *Clerks to the Signet*, 25 Feb. 1800, F.C. and observations in 15 S. 744; *Writers to the Signet* v. *Inland Revenue* (1886) 14 R. 34. Bankton I, 2, 25, states that the Established Church is a great corporation.

[27] cf. *University of Glasgow* v. *Faculty of Physicians* (1840) 1 Rob. 397; Universities (Sc.) Acts, 1858 (esp. S. 25), 1889 (esp. S. 5(3) and 1966. Their University Courts are incorporated: 1889 Act, S. 5(3). These Acts apply also to the fourth oldest (Edinburgh).

[28] *Muir* v. *City of Glasgow* (1878) 6 R. 392, 401; cf. registration of friendly societies.

Officers

The constitutive charter or Act normally provides for the existence of certain officers to administer and manage the corporation's affairs and for their appointment or election, tenure of office, powers, and duties.[29] Though a corporation has full legal personality by itself it can act only through the agency of natural persons appointed as its officers, exercising powers conferred on them by the corporation. The members are not necessarily the only persons beneficially interested in the corporation; thus a council performing local government functions must do so for the general benefit of the whole community in its area of responsibility; a company must have regard to the interests of its employees, though they are not members of the company.

Meetings

A corporation may act as such, unless the constitutive document directs otherwise, only by corporate meeting duly convened at which the head of the corporation and a majority, or other specified quorum, of members is present, and a majority approves a resolution to do the act in question. But the everyday execution of policy and the routine administration of the corporation's affairs may be delegated to committees and officers. These may act only within the scope of the remit or authority given them, and any act beyond such limits is *ultra vires* and void, though it may be adopted and ratified by the corporation,[30] unless it is of a kind *ultra vires* not merely of the officer but of the corporation itself, in which case it cannot be adopted or ratified at all.[31]

Powers of corporations

All kinds of corporations have power to sue, and liability to be sued, as entities, by the corporate name,[32] power to elect or admit new members and to appoint officers for the administration of the corporate affairs,[33] to have and use a common seal, to hold property, heritable and moveable,[34] to act in accordance with the views of a majority of the managers or members in any matter within the scope of the purposes of

---

[29] e.g. Local Government (Sc.) Act, 1973, Ss. 2–4, 64.

[30] *Irvine* v. *Union Bank of Australia* (1877) 2 App. Cas. 366.

[31] *Ashbury Ry. Carriage Co.* v. *Riche* (1875) L.R. 7 H.L. 653; *Mann* v. *Edinburgh Northern Tramways Co.* (1892) 20 R. (H.L.) 7.

[32] Bell, *Prin.* § 2178; *Eadie* v. *Clasgow Corpn.*, 1908 S.C. 207; but they must be represented in litigation by counsel and agents, not by directors: *Equity, etc. Life Assce. Socy.* v. *Tritonia, Ltd.*, 1943 S.C. (H.L.) 88; nor employees; *Scottish Gas Board* v. *Alexander*, 1963 S.L.T. (Sh. Ct.) 27.

[33] Ersk. I, 7, 64; see also *London* v. *Tailors of Ayr* (1891) 18 R. 549.

[34] *Thomson* v. *Incorpn. of Candlemakers* (1855) 17 D. 765; *Webster* v. *Tailors of Ayr* (1893) 21 R. 107.

the corporation as fixed by Charter or Act,[35] and to make by-laws, ordinances, or regulations for the administration of its affairs within the limits of the constitution and purposes of the corporation.[36] What other powers a particular corporation has depends on its constitution and statutes empowering it to do certain things. Exercise of powers outwith these limits is *ultra vires* and void.[37] A corporation incorporated by Royal Charter cannot, by its own rules, confer on itself powers wider than those given by the charter and the general law.[38]

Contractual powers

The contractual powers of a corporation depend in the first place on its constitutive deed. Corporations created by Royal Charter have power to do any act or enter into any contract not expressly forbidden by their charter, as interpreted by usage, though certain kinds of conduct may be challengeable as a breach of trust on its members or contrary to public policy.[39] Corporations created by statute have only those powers expressly or impliedly conferred by the statute and powers implied as necessarily incidental thereto, and any act exceeding those powers is *ultra vires* and void.[40] Corporations incorporated under the Companies Acts have only those powers which they have expressly taken in their Memorandum and Articles of Association and powers reasonably incidental thereto, and any act or contract outwith those powers is *ultra vires* and void.[41] Where an act or contract is *ultra vires* of the corporation even the unanimous ratification of all the members thereof cannot validate it,[42] and a corpora-

---

[35] *Gray v. Smith* (1836) 14 S. 1062; *Howden v. Goldsmiths* (1840) 2 D. 996; *Rodgers v. Tailors of Edinburgh* (1842) 5 D. 295; *Balfour's Trs. v. Edin. & Northern Ry.* (1848) 10 D. 1240; *Wedderburn v. Sc. Central Ry.* (1848) 10 D. 1317; *Galloway v. Ranken* (1864) 2 M. 1199; *Clouston v. Edin. & Glasgow Ry.* (1865) 4 M. 207; but see *Baird v. Dundee Mags.* (1865) 4 M. 69; *Morrison v. Fleshers of Edinburgh* (1853) 16 D. 86.

[36] Ersk. I, 7, 64; *Gray v. Smith* (1836) 14 S. 1062; *University of Glasgow v. Faculty of Physicians and Surgeons* (1840) 1 Rob. 397; *Tailors of Glasgow v. Trades' House of Glasgow* (1901) 4 F. 156. See also *Dinning v. Procurators of Glasgow* (1817) Hume 166; *Hill v. Fairweather* (1823) 2 S. 569; *Freight Transport Assocn. v. Lothians R.C.*, 1977 S.C. 324.

[37] *Malloch v. Aberdeen Corpn.*, 1971 S.C. (H.L.) 85; 1973 S.C. 227; *Stornoway Town Council v. Macdonald*, 1971 S.C. 78.

[38] *S.S.A.F.A. v. A.G.* [1968] 1 All E.R. 448.

[39] *Sanderson v. Lees* (1859) 22 D. 24; *Baroness Wenlock v. River Dee Co.* (1885) 10 App. Cas. 354; *Kesson v. Aberdeen Wrights Incorpn.* (1898) 1 F. 36; *A.G. v. Manchester Corpn.* [1906] 1 Ch. 643; *Conn v. Renfrew Corpn.* (1906) 8 F. 905; *Kemp v. Glasgow Corpn.*, 1920 S.C. (H.L.) 73; *Graham v. Glasgow Corpn.*, 1936 S.C. 108.

[40] *Ashbury Ry. Carriage Co. v. Riche* (1875) L.R. 7 H.L. 653; *Caledonian & Dumbarton Ry. v. Helensburgh Mags.* (1856) 2 Macq. 391; *Scottish N.E. Ry. v. Stewart* (1859) 3 Macq. 382; *A.G. v. G.E. Ry.* (1880) 5 App. Cas. 473; *Mann v. Edinburgh Northern Tramways* (1892) 20 R. (H.L.) 7; *Newburgh & N. Fife Ry. v. N.B. Ry.*, 1913 S.C. 1166; *Nicol v. Dundee Harbour Trs.*, 1915 S.C. (H.L.) 7; *Grieve v. Edinburgh Water Trs.*, 1918 S.C. 700; *B.T.C. v. Westmorland C.C.* [1958] A.C. 126; *Roberts v. B.R. Board* [1964] 3 All E.R. 651.

[41] *Ashbury, supra; Shiell's Trs. v. Scottish Property Investment Co.* (1884) 12 R. (H.L.) 14. See further Ch. 3.13, *infra*.

[42] *Ashbury, supra; Mann, supra*.

tion cannot be barred from pleading that its own acts were *ultra vires*.[43] All corporations have by legal implication contractual powers essential to their existence and operation, such as to open a bank account and operate thereon, to employ staff, to lease premises, and to purchase necessaries.[44] No particular form is essential for a contract by a corporation,[45] unless the relevant charter or Act provides otherwise.

Liabilities of corporation and members

If a corporation is created at common law, it has its own property and liabilities and the members are not liable for its debts, but only to it within the limit of the obligation they have undertaken to subscribe to its funds, unless the charter of incorporation expressly makes the corporators liable without limitation for its debts.[46] The liability of corporations established by statute and of their members are determined by the relevant Act. Companies may be incorporated under the Companies Acts with unlimited or limited liability of members. A corporation may be rendered notour bankrupt and sequestrated[47] though special provision is made for companies.

Title to sue for delict

A corporation may sue for harm done to it or its rights or property in its corporate capacity.[48]

Delictual liability

A corporation is liable for unjustifiable harm done by an agent acting within the scope of his authority, or by an employee acting in the course of his employment,[49] both where intention or malice is a necessary element of the wrong[50] and where the agent or employee has been merely negligent.[51]

---

[43] *General Property Inv. Co.* v. *Matheson's Trs.* (1888) 16 R. 282.

[44] Ersk. I, 7, 64; Bell, *Prin.* s 2178.

[45] *Park* v. *Glasgow University* (1675) Mor. 2535; cf. *Cook* v. *N.B. Ry.* (1872) 10 M. 513.

[46] *Muir* v. *City of Glasgow Bank* (1878) 6 R. 392, 401, 405; *Sanders* v. *S's Trs.* (1879) 7 R. 157, 162, 168.

[47] *Wotherspoon* v. *Linlithgow Mags.* (1863) 2 M. 348.

[48] *North of Scotland Bank* v. *Duncan* (1857) 19 D. 881; *Glebe Sugar Refining Co.* v. *Lusk* (1866) 3 S.L.R. 33; *Thorley's Cattle Food Co.* v. *Massam* (1880) 14 Ch. D. 763; *South Hetton Coal Co.* v. *N.E. News Assocn.* [1894] 1 Q.B. 133. Some delicts, from their nature, e.g. assault, cannot be committed against a corporation.

[49] e.g. *Beaton* v. *Glasgow Corpn.*, 1908 S.C. 1010; *Riddell* v. *Glasgow Corpn.*, 1911 S.C. (H.L.) 35; *Percy* v. *Glasgow Corpn.*, 1922 S.C. (H.L.) 144; contrast *Aiken* v. *Caledonian Ry.*, 1913 S.C. 66.

[50] *Gordon* v. *British and Foreign Metaline Co.* (1886) 14 R. 75; *Citizens Life Assce. Co. Ltd.* v. *Brown* [1904] A.C. 423; *Finburgh* v. *Moss's Empires, Ltd.*, 1908 S.C. 928.

[51] e.g. *O'Hanlon* v. *Stein*, 1963 S.C. 357.

Criminal liability

A corporation may be incapable of incurring liability for some common law crimes,[52] but it may be held liable for statutory offences[53] and be responsible for the misdeeds of its executives.[54]

Dissolution of corporations

A corporation can be dissolved only by public authority, by expiry, surrender, or forfeiture of its charter, by Act of Parliament, by dissolution in accordance with the provisions of an Act of Parliament,[55] or by the lapse of time, in the case of a creation for a limited time.[56]

[52] *R.* v. *I.C.R. Haulage* [1948] K.B. 551; *Dean* v. *Menzies*, 1981 J.C. 23.

[53] *Galbraith's Stores* v. *McIntyre* (1912) 6 Adam 461; *Clydebank Coop* v. *Binnie*, 1937 J.C. 17; *D.P.P.* v. *Kent and Sussex Contractors* [1944] K.B. 146. *Lennard's Carrying Co.* v. *Asiatic Petroleum Co.* [1915] A.C. 705; *Sarna* v. *Adair*, 1945 J.C. 141; *Tesco* v. *Nattrass* [1971] 2 All E.R. 127; *Reader's Digest* v. *Pirie*, 1973 J.C. 42.

[54] *Tesco, supra.*

[55] Including, in the case of a company, dissolution by liquidation, which may follow on insolvency.

[56] Ersk. I, 7, 64; Bell. *Prin.* § 2179; *Thomson* v. *Candlemakers of Edinburgh* (1855) 17 D. 765; *Wrights of Leith* (1856) 18 D. 981.

CHAPTER 3.12

THE CROWN

The term, the Crown, is applied both to the sovereign for the time being[1] in her public capacity and used as the title for Her Majesty's Government, including the executive, departments of state, and crown servants. The Crown, in the latter sense is, if not a corporation, a body analogous thereto.[2] It is not always clear which aspect of the Crown has certain rights. Specialities, moreover, arise from the fiction that Ministers and their departments and crown servants are still the personal servants of the sovereign, and entitled to the privileges which attached to the sovereign personally at common law.

It may be a matter of doubt whether a particular person or body is a department of state, or crown servant, or acting on behalf of the Crown, in such a way as to be entitled to the privileged position of the Crown. Thus Crown privileges attach to the (former) Central Land Board,[3] and custodians of enemy property,[4] and to the Lord Advocate as head of the criminal administration,[5] but not to the British Transport Commission,[6] the B.B.C.,[7] nationalized industries generally, local authorities, health boards,[8] the police,[9] or other public bodies,[10] still less to private bodies, though acting for the public benefit.[11] In all civil litigation and other private law contexts the Crown and public departments are represented by the Lord Advocate.[12]

---

[1] Whether, as in English law, the sovereign is a corporation sole, is a difficult question. It is submitted that in Scots law she is not.

[2] cf. Walker, 65 J.R. 255; *Smith* v. *L.A.*, 1979 S.C. 384; 1980 S.C. 227.

[3] *Glasgow Corpn.* v. *Central Land Board*, 1956 S.C. (H.L.) 1.

[4] *Bank Voor Handel* v. *Admin. of Hungarian Property* [1954] A.C. 584.

[5] *McKie* v. *Western S.M.T.*, 1952 S.C. 206.

[6] *Tamlin* v. *Hannaford* [1950] 1 K.B. 18.

[7] *B.B.C.* v. *Johns* [1964] 1 All E.R. 923.

[8] National Health Service (Sc.) Act, 1972, S. 13 (10).

[9] The chief constable is liable: Police (Sc.) Act, 1967, S. 39.

[10] *London T. & A.F.A.* v. *Nicholls* [1948] 2 All E.R. 432.

[11] *Whitehall* v. *W.*, 1957 S.C. 30.

[12] Crown Suits (Sc.) Act, 1857, S. 1; Law Officers Act, 1944, S. 2. For development see *King's Advocate* v. *Lord Dunglas* (1836) 15 S. 314; see also *Lord Advocate* v. *Meiklam* (1860) 22 D. 1427; *Macgregor* v. *Lord Advocate*, 1921 S.C. 847; *Cameron* v. *L.A.*, 1952 S.C. 165; *Gibson* v. *Lord Advocate*, 1975 S.C. 136.

Subjection to jurisdiction

At common law the Crown could be impleaded only in the Court of Session,[13] but by the Crown Proceedings Act, 1947, S.44, subject to that Act and to any Act limiting the jurisdiction of the sheriff court, civil proceedings against the Crown may be instituted in the sheriff court as if against a subject, but may be remitted to the Court of Session at the Lord Advocate's instance.

Contractual powers and capacity

The Crown, acting through the agency of departments of state or Crown officials, may contract in the same way as any other corporation and sue for[14] or be liable for breach of contract.[15] But any undertaking to pay money, or damages, is impliedly subject to the condition that Parliament provides funds for that particular purpose.[16] A department or official, in contracting, is presumed to act in his official capacity and subject to the constitutional limits of his authority, but may so contract as to incur personal liability.[17] Certain exceptions and qualifications arise from the Crown's unique position. Save under statute[18] all Crown employees hold office at the Crown's pleasure only, and have no civilly enforceable contract of employment.[19] Nor does a Crown servant engaging a lower employee warrant his authority to do so, or bind the Crown, though he may bind himself.[20] It is also established that the Crown or its agents cannot by contract restrict the future freedom of action of the executive.[21]

Title to sue for delict

The Crown can sue for delict done to it as a corporation, as by damage done to one of H.M. ships.[22]

[13] *Somerville v. L.A.* (1893) 20 R. 1050, 1067, 1073.
[14] *Ministry of Supply v. B.T.H. Co.* [1943] 1 All E.R. 615.
[15] *Windsor & Annapolis Ry. v. The Queen* (1886) 11 App. Cas. 607; *Parkinson v. Commrs. of Works* [1949] 2 K.B. 632 (building contract); *Cameron v. L.A.*, 1952 S.C. 165 (civilian employment).
[16] *Churchward v. The Queen* (1865) L.R. 1 Q.B. 173; *Auckland Harbour Bd. v. The King* [1924] A.C. 318; *A.G. v. Great Southern Ry.* [1925] A.C. 754.
[17] *Dunn v. Macdonald* [1897] 1 Q.B. 555; *Commercial Cable Co. v. Govt. of Newfoundland* [1916] 2 A.C. 610.
[18] e.g. *Gould v. Stuart* [1896] A.C. 575; *Leaman v. The King* [1920] 3 K.B. 663; Employment Protection (Consolidation) Act, 1978, S. 138.
[19] *Shenton v. Smith* [1895] A.C. 229; *Dunn v. The Queen* [1896] 1 Q.B. 116; *Smith v. L.A.* (1897) 25 R. 112 (pay); *Mackie v. L.A.* (1898) 25 R. 769 (pension); *Mulvenna v. The Admiralty*, 1926 S.C. 842 (pay); *Griffin v. L.A.*, 1950 S.C. 448 (pension); *Riordan v. War Office* [1960] 3 All E.R. 774; see also Crown Proceedings Act, 1974, S. 46.
[20] *Dunn v. Macdonald* [1897] 1 Q.B. 555; *Kenny v. Cosgrove* [1926] I.R. 517.
[21] *The Amphitrite v. The King* [1921] 3 K.B. 500.
[22] *Admiralty Commrs., v. S.S. Chekiang* [1926] A.C. 637; *Admiralty Commrs. v. S.S. Sus-*

Delictual liability

It is probable that the Crown in Scotland has never enjoyed any exemption from delictual liability[23] though certain cases, on English analogy, held the Crown exempt from liability.[24] The actual wrongdoer seems never to have been protected.[25] The Crown Proceedings Act, 1947, provides (S. 2(1)) that, subject to the Act, the Crown shall be subject to all those liabilities in reparation for delict to which, if it were a private person of full age and capacity, it would be subject: (a) in respect of delicts committed by its servants or agents;[26] (b) in respect of any breach of those duties which a person owes to his servants or agents[26] at common law by reason of being their employer; and (c) in respect of any breach of the duties attaching at common law to the ownership, occupation, possession, or control of property.[27] Provided that no proceedings shall lie against the Crown by virtue of para. (a) unless the servant's act or omission would have given rise to an action of delict against the servant or agent or his estate apart from the Act. Statutory duties incumbent on the Crown and also on private persons give rise to delictual liability.[28] The Crown is liable for delict committed by an officer while performing functions conferred or imposed on him by common law or statute as if the functions had been imposed by Crown instructions.[29] The Crown can rely on enactments negativing or limiting the liability of any government department or officer of the Crown in respect of delict committed by it or him as if the proceedings had been against it or him.[30] No proceedings lie against the Crown under S. 2 in respect of anything done or omitted by any person in the discharge of duties of a judicial nature or responsibilities in connection with the execution of judicial process.[31] No proceedings lie against the Crown under S. 2 in respect of any act, neglect, or default of any officer of the Crown unless he has been directly or indirectly appointed by the Crown and was at the material time paid wholly out of the Consolidated Fund, moneys provided by Parliament, the Road Fund, or any other Fund certified by the Treasury

quehanna [1926] A.C. 655; *Admiralty* v. *S.S. Divina* [1952] P. 1.

    See also *Officers of State* (1849) 6 Bell 847; *Cameron & Gunn* v. *Ainslie* (1848) 10 D. 446; *Alexander* v. *Officers of State* (1868) 6 M. (H.L.) 54, 67; *Agnew* v. *L.A.* (1873) 11 M. 309; *Young* v. *N.B. Ry.* (1887) 14 R. (H.L.) 53; *Boy Andrew* v. *St Rognvald*, 1947 S.C. (H.L.) 70.

[23] *Hay* v. *Officers of State* (1832) 11 S. 196; *Macgregor* v. *L.A.*, 1921 S.C. 847, 850, argument; Philip, 40 J.R. 238.

[24] *Smith* v. *L.A.* (1897) 25 R. 112; *Wilson* v. *Edinburgh City R.G.A. Volunteers* (1904) 7 F. 168; *Macgregor, supra,* 852, 853, which goes too far.

[25] *Wilson, supra; Macgregor, supra.*

[26] Including, by S. 38 (2), an independent contractor employed by the Crown; but see S. 40 (2) (d).

[27] The Occupiers Liability (Sc.) Act, 1960, binds the Crown: S. 4 thereof.

[28] S. 2 (2) e.g. Factories Act, 1961, which by S. 173, binds the Crown.

[29] S. 2 (3).

[30] S. 2 (4).

[31] S. 2 (5), cf. *Smith* v. *L.A.* (1897) 25 R. 112 where said that no action lay against the War Department for wrongful acts of a court-martial; cf. *Hester* v. *Macdonald*, 1961 S.C. 370.

for the purposes of the subsection, or was at the material time holding an office in respect of which the Treasury certify that the holder thereof would normally be so paid.[32] Civil proceedings lie against the Crown for infringement of patent, registered trade mark, copyright, or registered design, by a servant or agent with the authority of the Crown.[33] The rules as to indemnity,[34] contribution,[34] joint and several wrongdoers,[35] and contributory negligence[36] are enforceable by or against the Crown as if it were a private person.[37] The limitation of liability of shipowners[38] limits the liability of the Crown in respect of H.M. ships,[39] as do the rules as to division of loss.[40] The limitation of the liability of the owners of docks and canals limits the liability of the Crown as such owner.[41] The law relating to civil salvage[42] applies, with certain exceptions, to salvage services to H.M. ships and to Crown claims to salvage.[43] No act or omission by a member of the armed forces of the Crown while on duty as such subjects him or the Crown to delictual liability for causing the death of another person, or for causing personal injury to another person, in so far as the death or personal injury is due to anything suffered by that person while he is a member of the armed forces of the Crown if he was either on duty or was on premises used for armed forces purposes and the death or injury falls to be treated as attributable to service for pension purposes.[44]

The Crown is not vicariously liable for public services provided by corporations and persons who are not Crown departments or servants.[45] Nothing in the 1947 Act authorizes or applies to proceedings against the Queen in her private capacity.[46]

The Lord Advocate as head of the public system of criminal prosecution is immune from delictual liability, and this extends also to his deputies, procurators-fiscal, and their deputies acting in trials on indictment.[47]

---

[32] S. 2 (6).

[33] S. 3.

[34] Law Reform (Misc. Prov.) (Sc.) Act, 1940, S. 3; Ch. 4.27, *infra*.

[35] At common law: see Ch. 4.27, *infra*.

[36] Law Reform (Contributory Negligence) Act, 1945; Ch. 4.27, *infra*.

[37] S. 4.

[38] Merchant Shipping Act, 1894, S. 503, and M.S. (Liability of Shipowners and Others) Act, 1958; Merchant Shipping Act, 1979, Ss. 17–19.

[39] S. 5; *The Admiralty* v. *S.S. Divina (H.M.S. Truculent)* [1952] P. 1.

[40] S. 6; Maritime Conventions Act, 1911, Ss. 1–3; see also S. 30.

[41] S. 7.

[42] Ch. 4.27, *infra*.

[43] S. 8.

[44] S. 10; *Adams* v. *War Office* [1955] 3 All E.R. 245.

[45] Its former limited liability for the Post Office (1947 Act S. 9; *Triefus* v. *Post Office* [1957] 2 Q.B. 352) disappeared with the Post Office Act, 1969.

[46] S. 40.

[47] *Hester* v. *Macdonald*, 1961 S.C. 370.

Crown property

The sovereign personally owns certain property in Scotland. The Crown, originally personally, holds the ultimate radical right to all land in Scotland held on feudal tenure,[48] and has a reserved right to certain minerals, salmon-fishings, forests, and other subjects.[49] Treasure, and property not inherited by anyone on the owner's death, fall to the Crown.[50] Where the Crown, in the exercise of the prerogative, takes the property of a subject, compensation must be paid.[51]

Remedies against the Crown

Under the 1947 Act[52] the court may make all such orders as it may in proceedings between subjects, save that it may not grant interdict or specific implement[53] but may in lieu thereof make an order declaratory of the rights of the parties,[54] and may not make an order for the recovery of land or the delivery of property, but may in lieu declare the pursuer's entitlement thereto: nor may it grant interdict or make an order against an officer of the Crown if the effect would be to give any relief against the Crown not directly obtainable. Proceedings *in rem* against the Crown are excluded.[55] Proceedings by or against the Crown are not affected by the demise of the Crown.[56]

Special pleas

By the Crown Proceedings Act, 1600, c. 14, the Crown cannot be prejudiced by the negligence of its servants in litigation to which it is a party and may accordingly state a plea formerly omitted by its servants by exception or reply.[57] A plea of bar founded on the error of Crown servants does not lie against the Crown.[58] Both positive[59] and negative[60]

---

[48] cf. *Burmah Oil Co.* v. *Lord Advocate*, 1964 S.C. (H.L.) 117, 127; as to sea-bed see *Crown Estate Commrs.* v. *Fairlie*, 1976 S.C. 161.

[49] Chs. 5.2–5.3, *infra*.

[50] *Lord Advocate* v. *Aberdeen University*, 1963 S.C. 533.

[51] *Burmah Oil Co.* v. *L.A.*, 1964 S.C. (H.L.) 117.

[52] S. 21, as applied by S. 43.

[53] This restricts the remedies, in that interdict against the Crown was formerly competent: *Bell* v. *Secretary of State*, 1933 S.L.T. 519; cf. *Carlton Hotel Co.* v. *L.A.*, 1921 S.C. 237.

[54] A final declaration only. There is no jurisdiction to make an interim declaration: *Underhill* v. *Ministry of Food* [1950] 1 All E.R. 591; *Griffin* v. *L.A.*, 1950 S.C. 448; *Ayr Mags.* v. *Secretary of State for Scotland*, 1965 S.C. 394.

[55] S. 29.

[56] S. 32.

[57] Mack. *Observations*, 311; Stair IV, 35, 1; Ersk. I, 2, 27; *Crawford* v. *Kennedy* (1694) Mor. 7866.

[58] *L.A.* v. *Meiklam* (1860) 22 D. 1427; *L.A.* v. *Miller's Trs.* (1884) 11 R. 1046; *L.A.* v. *D. Hamilton* (1891) 29 S.L.R. 213; *Alston's Trs.* v. *L.A.* (1896) 33 S.L.R. 278.

[59] Prescription and Limitation (Sc.) Act, 1973, S. 1; Stair II, 3, 33; Ersk. III, 7, 31; Bell, *Prin.* § 2025; H.M.A. v. *Graham* (1844) 7 D. 183; *L.A.* v. *Hunt* (1867) 5 M. (H.L.) 1.

[60] *E. Fife's Trs.* v. *Commrs. of Woods and Forests* (1849) 11 D. 889; *Deans of Chapel Royal* v. *Johnstone* (1869) 7 M. (H.L.) 19.

prescription run against the Crown, but an action of warrandice will not lie against the Crown.[61] The Crown is not bound by statute unless the intention that it to be so bound is expressed[62] but may take advantage of provisions of a statute though not named therein.[63]

[61] Ersk. II, 3, 27.
[62] *Edinburgh Mags.* v. *L.A.*, 1912 S.C. 1085. See, however, *Somerville* v. *L.A.* (1893) 20 R. 1050.
[63] Crown Proceedings Act, 1947, S. 31.

CHAPTER 3.13

COMPANIES

A company is a group of persons incorporated by legal authority for the carrying on of some form of business.[1] The incorporated company was developed out of partnerships and common law joint stock companies, incorporation being appropriate when the need for greater capital required a larger membership than could be managed in the form of a partnership. The effect of incorporation is to create the company a legal person or entity wholly distinct from the personalities of any or all of the persons who for the time being are its members, and capable itself of sustaining legal rights and duties.[2]

An incorporated company may be created by Royal Charter,[3] by special Act of Parliament,[4] by private Act,[5] by letters patent,[6] but, most commonly today, by registration in accordance with the provisions of the Companies Act in force at the time. Since 1856 incorporation by registration may include provision for limiting the liability of members to the amount, if any, still unpaid on the nominal value of their shares, or to the amount they guarantee to pay in the event of the company being wound up. The major Act now in force is the Companies Act, 1985. Companies are also affected by many general principles of law, particularly of contract, agency, and trust, and by other statutes,[7] and there is a large volume of case law. Companies formed under older Companies Acts, now repealed, continue in existence.

Formation

Any two or more persons associated for a lawful purpose may form an incorporated company by subscribing a memorandum of association and

[1] The term 'company' is sometimes used as part of an individual or partnership business name; such a body is not incorporated.
[2] *Henderson* v. *Stubbs* (1894) 22 R. 51; *Grierson, Oldham & Co.* v. *Forbes, Maxwell & Co.* (1895) 22 R. 812; *Wilson* v. *Inland Revenue* (1895) 23 R. 18; *Salomon & Co. Ltd.* [1897] A.C. 22; *Woolfson* v. *Strathclyde R.C.*, 1978 S.C. (H.L.) 90.
[3] e.g. The Royal Bank of Scotland; Carron Company.
[4] e.g. The Bank of Scotland (Act 1695; see Bell, *Comm.* I, 102).
[5] Normally incorporating the provisions of the Companies Clauses Consolidation (Sc) Acts, 1845, 1863, and 1869, or other appropriate Clauses Act. See e.g. *Campbell* v. *Edinburgh & Glasgow Ry* (1855) 17 D. 613; *Newburgh & North Fife Ry.* v. *N.B. Ry.*, 1913 S.C. 1166; as to interpretation see *Scottish Drainage and Improvement Co.* v. *Campbell* (1889) 16 R. (H.L.) 16.
[6] Under Chartered Companies Acts, 1837 and 1884. Such letters patent do not incorporate the company but confer corporation privileges.
[7] See generally Charlesworth, *Company Law*; Gower, *Principles of Modern Company Law*; Palmer, *Company Law*; Pennington, *Company Law*.

otherwise complying with the Act.[8] Such a company may be either (a) limited by shares, with the liability of members limited to the amount, if any, unpaid on their shares, or (b) limited by guarantee, with the liability of members limited to such amount as the members undertake to contribute to the company's assets in the event of it being wound up,[9] or (c) unlimited, not having any limit on the liability of its members. A limited company must also be a public company or a private company. A public company is one limited by shares or guarantee and having a share capital the Memorandum of which states that it is to be a public company and which has complied with the registration provisions of the Act as to public companies; other companies are private companies.[10] The name of a public company ends with the words 'public limited company' abbreviated to 'plc'; a private company's name ends with the word 'Limited' or 'Ltd.' The name of an unlimited company does not include the word 'Limited'.

Memorandum of association

The Memorandum of association is the company's basic constitutional document. It must state (a) the company's name;[11] (b) whether the registered office is to be in England or Scotland; (c) the company's objects.[12] The importance of stating the objects if that this defines what the company may or may not lawfully do; contracts for purposes outwith its objects are *ultra vires* and void.[13] Various objects may be stated as independent objects and not restricted by other objects. Objects are distinct from powers, which are things authorized to be done to achieve the objects.[14] (d) If the company is limited by shares or by guarantee the Memorandum must so state, and also (e) the amount of share capital and its division into shares of fixed amount, or the undertaking of each member to contribute to the assets if the company is wound up while he is a member. If the company is public the Memorandum must say so. The Memorandum must be signed by each subscriber in the presence of at

[8] 1985 Act, S. 1.

[9] The amount agreed to be contributed cannot be assigned by the company in security so long as it is a going concern: *Robertson v. B.L. Co.* (1890) 18 R. 1225; *Lloyd's Bank Ltd. v. Morrison*, 1927 S.C. 571.

[10] About 97% of companies are private companies. An unlimited company cannot be a public company. There is a separate classification of private companies for certain accounting requirements: S. 247 and Sch. 8.

[11] There are restrictions on the use of certain names: Ss. 26–9. A misleading name may be interdicted: *Dunlop Tyre Co. v. Dunlop Motor Co.*, 1907 S.C. (H.L.) 15. Certain companies are exempt from the need to use the word 'limited' as part of the company name: Ss. 30–1. A company may be required to abandon a misleading name: S. 32; it is an offence to trade under a misleading name: Ss. 33–4.

[12] 1985 Act, S. 2.

[13] *Ashbury Ry. Carriage Co. v. Riche* (1875) L.R. 7 H.L. 653; *Life Assoc. of Sc. v. Caledonian Heritable Socy.* (1896) 13 R. 750; *Re Jon Beauforte Ltd.* [1953] 1 Ch. 131; *Thompson v. Barke* 1975 S.L.T. 67.

[14] *John Walker & Sons Ltd.*, 1914 S.C. 280.

least one witness. A company may only alter the conditions in its memorandum as permitted by the Act.[12] Forms of Memorandum must be as specified by regulations.[15] By registration the Memorandum becomes public and all persons dealing with the company are presumed to have knowledge of its contents.

A company may by special resolution alter its objects (a) to carry on its business more economically or efficiently;[16] (b) to attain its main purpose by new or improved means;[17] (c) to enlarge or change the local area of its operations;[18] (d) to carry on a business which can advantageously be combined with the company's business;[19] (e) to restrict or abandon any objects;[20] (f) to sell or dispose of the whole or part of the undertaking;[21] (g) to amalgamate with another company.[22] Certain members may object to the alteration in which case the alteration is ineffective unless confirmed by the court.[23] Other alterations to the Memorandum are incompetent.

Articles of association

A company limited by shares may, and a company limited by guarantee or unlimited must, register with the Memorandum Articles of association signed by each subscriber in the presence of at least one witness.[24] The Articles provide the rules for the internal management of the company. A company may as its Articles adopt Table A set out in regulations,[25] in whole or in part; a company limited by shares is deemed to adopt Table A if it does not register Articles or in so far as Table A is not modified or excluded. Companies limited by guarantee and not having a share capital, limited by guarantee and having a share capital, and unlimited having a share capital must have articles following the forms in Tables C, D, or E respectively.[26] Articles may be altered by special resolution,[27] even retrospectively,[28] or in a way affecting existing rights,[29] or in breach of

---

[15] S. 3; Companies (Tables A–F) Regulations, 1985 (S.I. 1985, No. 805).
[16] cf. *J. & P. Coats, Ltd.* (1900) 2 F. 829; *N. of S.S.N. Co.*, 1920 S.C. 633.
[17] cf. *Kirkcaldy Cafe Co. Ltd.*, 1921 S.C. 681.
[18] cf. *Scottish Veterans Garden City Assoc.*, 1946 S.C. 415.
[19] cf. *Hugh Baird & Sons, Ltd.*, 1932 S.C. 455; *Dundee Aerated Water Co.*, 1932 S.C. 473.
[20] cf. *Strathspey Public Hall Co. v. Anderson's Trs.*, 1934 S.C. 385.
[21] cf. *Tayside Floorcloth Co. Ltd.*, 1923 S.C. 590.
[22] S. 4.
[23] Ss. 5–6.
[24] S. 7.
[25] Companies (Tables A–F) Regs. 1985 (S.I. 1985, No. 805).
[26] S. 8.
[27] S. 9; see also Ss. 16–17. cf. *Caledonian Ins. Co. v. Forth and North Sea Steamboat Ins. Assoc.* (1893) 21 R. (H.L.) 1; *McArthur Ltd. Liqdr. v. Gulf Line*, 1909 S.C. 732; *Crookston v. Lindsay Crookston & Co.*, 1922 S.L.T. 62.
[28] *Allen v. Gold Reefs of W. Africa* [1900] 1 Ch. 656; but see *Moir v. Duff* (1900) 2 F. 1265; *McArthur v. Gulf Line*, 1909 S.C. 732.
[29] *Sidebottom v. Kershaw, Leese & Co.* [1920] 1 Ch. 154; see also *Moir, supra; McArthur, supra; Crookston v. Lindsay Crookston & Co.*, 1922 S.L.T. 62; *Caledonian Ins. Co. v. Scottish American Inv. Co.*, 1951 S.L.T. 23.

contract,[30] so long as done *bona fide* for the benefit of the company as a whole and not to defraud or oppress a minority of shareholders.[31] Power to alter the Articles is subject to the Act and to the conditions in the Memorandum, and must not conflict with either. A provision in the Articles is not binding if it is contrary to public policy.[32] A third party, such as a non-member, cannot generally found on an alleged contravention of the Articles.[33]

Relation of Articles to Memorandum

The Memorandum contains the fundamental constitutional provisions and the Articles are subordinate thereto[34] and cannot authorize anything inconsistent with the Memorandum, still less contrary to the Act or the general law, but they may explain an ambiguity in the Memorandum.

Registration

The Memorandum and Articles must be delivered to the appropriate registrar of companies with a statement of the names and particulars of the first director or directors and the first secretary or secretaries, signed by or on behalf of the subscribers and containing the consents of each director or secretary to act, and of the intended situation of the company's registered office.[35] If the memorandum states that the company is to be a public one, the amount of share capital must be at least the authorized minimum, defined in S. 118.[36] If the registrar is satisfied that the statutory requirements have been complied with, which must be evidenced by a statutory declaration in the prescribed form, he retains and registers the Memorandum,[37] and issues a certificate that the company is incorporated and, if it be the case, is limited and, if it be the case, is a public company. From the date of incorporation stated in the certificate the subscribers and members of the company become a body corporate under the name in the Memorandum, which is capable of exercising all the functions of an incorporated company. The certificate is conclusive evidence that the requirements of the Act have been complied with, that the association is registered, and, if it be the case, that it is a

---

[30] *Shirlaw* v. *Southern Foundries* [1940] A.C. 701.

[31] *Burland* v. *Earle* [1902] A.C. 83; *Shuttleworth* v. *Cox* [1927] 2 K.B. 9; *Greenhalgh* v. *Arderne Cinemas* [1951] Ch. 286.

[32] *St. Johnstone F.C.* v. *S.F.A.*, 1965 S.L.T. 171.

[33] *National Bank* v. *Adamson*, 1932 S.L.T. 492; *Scottish Fishermen's Organisation* v. *McLean*, 1980 S.L.T. (Sh. Ct.) 76.

[34] *Ashbury Ry. Carriage Co.* v. *Riche* (1875) L.R. 7 H.L. 653, 671; *Oban and Aultmore-Glenlivet Distilleries Ltd.* (1903) 5 F. 1140; *Humboldt Redwood Co.* v. *Coats*, 1908 S.C. 751; *Scottish National Trust Co.*, 1928 S.C. 499; *Marshall Fleming & Co.*, 1938 S.C. 873; *Re Duncan Gilmour & Co.* [1952] 2 All E.R. 871.

[35] S. 10.

[36] S. 11.

[37] S. 12.

public company.[38] When registered the Memorandum and Articles bind the company and its members as if signed and sealed by each member and containing covenants by each to observe all the provisions thereof.[39] Alterations to a company's Memorandum or Articles must be registered.[40] A member is entitled to a copy on payment.[41]

Until the date of incorporation the company has no existence and at common law cannot contract by itself or through an agent.[42] Once incorporated it is a full corporation or juristic person distinct from all its members, even though one person owns all but one share and entirely controls the company.[43] It can then sue and be sued in its own name,[44] make contracts, commit wrongs, own property, and continues in being indefinitely until dissolved on winding up. It has a commercial reputation which may be impugned by defamation.[45] By reason of its distinct personality third parties have rights against the company, not the members, and members can sue the company and conversely.

Lifting the veil

Only exceptionally does the law look behind the screen of corporate personality at those persons who actually compose or control the company.[46] This happens when the number of members falls below the minimum,[47] where there has been fraudulent trading,[48] where the Department of Trade is making an investigation of related companies, where the company is acting as agent of the shareholders,[49] when it is necessary to determine whether persons controlling a company are alien enemies or not,[50] when companies stand in the relationship of holding and subsidiary companies to one another,[51] and in various matters relating to stamps, taxation, and death duties.[52]

---

[38] S. 13. It is not conclusive of the legality of the company's objects.
[39] S. 14. As to company limited by guarantee see S. 15.
[40] S. 18; see also S. 20.
[41] S. 19.
[42] *Tinnevelly Sugar Co.* v. *Mirrlees Watson & Co.* (1894) 21 R. 1009. This is modified by S. 36. See also *Young* v. *Gowans* (1902) 10 S.L.T. 85; *Neale* v. *Vickery*, 1973 S.L.T. (Sh. Ct.) 88.
[43] *Salomon* v. *Saloman & Co.* [1897] A.C. 22; *Woolfson* v. *Strathclyde R.C.*, 1978 S.C. (H.L.) 90. cf. *Thompson* v. *Barke*, 1975 S.L.T. 67.
[44] But it must appear in court by counsel: *Equity and Law Life Assce. Socy.* v. *Tritonia*, 1943 S.C. (H.L.) 88.
[45] *South Hetton Coal Co.* v. *N.E. News Assocn.* [1894] 1 Q.B. 133; *D. & L. Caterers* v. *D'Ajou* [1945] K.B. 364.
[46] *Woolfson*, *supra*.
[47] S. 116.
[48] *Re F. G. Films Ltd* [1953] 1 All E.R. 615. cf. *Glasgow D.C.* v. *Hamlet Textiles*, 1986 S.L.T. 415.
[49] *Smith, Stone & Knight, Ltd.* v. *Birmingham Corpn.* [1939] 4 All E.R. 116.
[50] *Daimler Co.* v. *Continental Tyre & Rubber Co.* [1916] 2 A.C. 307.
[51] S. 239.
[52] *Unit Construction Co., Ltd.* v. *Bullock* [1960] A.C. 351.

Statutory and common law powers

A company established by Royal Charter has all the powers of a natural person, unless these are expressly or impliedly excluded or abridged by the Charter.[53] A company established by statute has its powers limited by the purposes of incorporation defined by the statute.[54] A company incorporated under the Companies Act has only those powers expressly or impliedly taken as necessary to attain its declared objects, and powers necessarily incidental thereto.[55] Formerly Memoranda tended to state a main object or objects, other powers being deemed merely incidental thereto, but today Memoranda usually state a large number of independent main objects.[56] Memoranda may possibly empower the pursuit of any objects approved by the directors.[57] A company incorporated under the Companies Act also has numerous powers conferred on it by the Act, independently of those taken in the Memorandum of Association, some of which can be exercised only if the company's Articles so permit, other powers conferred, exercisable subject to confirmation by the court, and other powers again expressly withheld entirely or unless conditions are satisfied. It has also, at common law, though these are frequently also expressly taken in the Memorandum, power to enter into the ordinary kinds of contract and to do the kinds of things naturally and normally incidental to its kinds of business, such as to employ staff, open bank accounts, and bring legal proceedings.

The ultra vires rule

The deduction from the rule that a company's objects define and limit its powers is that any transaction outwith those powers is wholly void and expenditure thereon is unwarranted, and neither can be ratified by the shareholders.[58] The company cannot lawfully do anything outside the powers given it in its Memorandum or fairly incidental thereto,[59] or by the Act. The question is of the nature of the transaction, not of the means

[53] *Ellis* v. *Henderson* (1844) 1 Bell 1; *Sanderson* v. *Lees* (1859) 22 D. 24; *Kesson* v. *Aberdeen Wrights Incorpn.* (1898) 1 F. 36.

[54] *Ashbury Ry. Carriage Co.* v. *Riche* (1875) L.R. 7 H.L. 628, 653; *Baroness Wenlock* v. *River Dee Commrs.* (1885) 10 App. Cas. 354; *Mann* v. *Edinburgh Northern Tramways Co.* (1892) 20 R. (H.L.) 7.

[55] *Ashbury, supra; Shiell's Trs.* v. *Scottish Property Investment Socy.* (1884) 12 R. (H.L.) 14; *Life Assocn.* v. *Caledonian Heritable Security Co.* (1886) 13 R. 750.

[56] e.g. *Cotman* v. *Brougham* [1918] A.C. 514; *Anglo Overseas Agencies, Ltd.* v. *Green* [1961] 1 Q.B. 1.

[57] *Bell Houses Ltd.* v. *City Wall Properties Ltd.* [1966] 2 Q.B. 656. But see *Introductions Ltd.* v. *N.P. Bank* [1970] Ch. 199.

[58] *Ashbury Ry. Carriage Co.* v. *Riche* (1875) L.R. 7 H.L. 653; *General Property Co.* v. *Matheson's Trs.* (1888) 16 R. 282.

[59] *Foster* v. *L.C. & D. Ry. Co.* [1895] 1 Q.B. 711; *Waverley Hydropathic Co.* v. *Barrowman* (1895) 23 R. 136; *Life Assoc. of Scotland* v. *Caledonian Heritable Security Co.* (1896) 13 R. 750; *L.C.C.* v. *A.G.* [1902] A.C. 165.

adopted to achieve it.[60] The plea is personal to parties to the transaction.[61] An alteration of the Memorandum cannot retrospectively validate earlier *ultra vires* actings. Moreover, since the Memorandum and Articles are registered and public documents, third parties dealing with the company were at common law deemed to have notice of the company's objects and powers, and had no remedy if they transacted innocently with the company in what was held to be an *ultra vires* transaction.[62] But in favour of a person dealing with the company in good faith,[63] any transaction decided on by the directors shall be deemed to be one which it is within the capacity of the company to enter into, and the power of the directors to bind the company shall be deemed to be free of any limitation under the memorandum or articles of association, and a party to a transaction so decided on shall not be bound to enquire as to the capacity of the company to enter into it or as to any such limitation on the powers of the directors, and shall be presumed to have acted in good faith unless the contrary is proved.[64] But members may still challenge the company's power to enter into *ultra vires* transactions. The *ultra vires* rule does not, moreover, prevent a company being held liable for delicts[65] or crimes.[66]

Contractual powers

Prior to incorporation the company has no contractual powers,[67] and is not bound by a contract,[68] nor can anyone contract as agent for it,[69] but an agreement may be made by a person as trustee for the company, and adopted by it once it is incorporated.[70] Where a contract purports to be made by a company, or by a person as agent for a company, at a time when the company has not been formed, then subject to any agreement to the contrary the contract has effect as one entered into by the person purporting to act for the company or as agent for it, and he is personally

---

[60] *Thompson* v. *Barke*, 1975 S.L.T. 67.
[61] *Clyde Steam Packet Co.* v. *G.S.W. Ry.* (1897) 4 S.L.T. 327.
[62] *Re Jon Beauforte (London) Ltd.* [1953] Ch. 131.
[63] This provision does not apply in favour of the company.
[64] S. 35; *International Sales and Agencies Ltd.* v. *Marens* [1984] 3 All E.R. 551.
[65] *Mersey Dock and Harbour Board* v. *Gibbs* (1866) L.R. 1 H.L. 93; *Barwick* v. *English Joint Stock Bank* (1867) L.R. 2 Ex. 259; *Houldsworth* v. *City of Glasgow Bank* (1880) 7 R. (H.L.) 53.
[66] *R.* v. *I.C.R. Haulage Ltd.* [1944] K.B. 551; *Lott* v. *Macdonald*, 1963 J.C. 57; *Dean* v. *John Menzies (Holdings) Ltd.*, 1981 J.C. 23.
[67] *Newborne* v. *Sensolid (G.B.) Ltd.* [1954] 1 Q.B. 45. Contrast mere change of name: *Lin Pac Containers* v. *Kelly*, 1982 S.L.T. 50.
[68] *Molleson and Grigor* v. *Fraser's Trs.* (1881) 8 R. 630; *Re English and Colonial Produce Co., Ltd.* [1906] 2 Ch. 435.
[69] *Kelner* v. *Baxter* (1866) L.R. 2 C.P. 174; *Tinnevelly Sugar Refining Co.* v. *Mirrlees Watson & Yaryan Co.* (1894) 21 R. 1009; *Cumming* v. *Quartzag*, 1980 S.C. 276. See also *Struthers Patent Co.* v. *Clydesdale Bank* (1886) 13 R. 434.
[70] *James Young & Sons Ltd.* v. *James Young & Sons' Trs.* (1902) 10 S.L.T. 85.

liable on the contract accordingly.[71] Once incorporated, a company has, within the limits of the *ultra vires* rule, full contractual powers, though contracts must be in fact negotiated and signed by persons acting within the scope of their express or implied authority as agents for the company. Authority is normally conferred in the Articles on directors, managers, and others, and this power may be delegated to others. An act by a manager in excess of authority may be ratified by the person entitled to authorize him. A third party dealing with a company cannot assume that an officer has authority to contract unless the company has held him out as having such authority or, possibly, unless the act would be within the ordinary scope of the officer's duties. Contracts which are *intra vires* the company but *ultra vires* the directors may be ratified by the company.[72] Contracts are made in the same form as those by a private person, orally on behalf of the company by any person acting under its authority, express or implied, or in writing signed on behalf of the company by such a person.[73] Where formal writing is required a contract is validly executed if executed in accordance with the provisions of the Act or sealed with the common seal and subscribed by two directors or by a director and the secretary, witnesses being unnecessary.[74] A bill of exchange or promissory note is deemed made, accepted, or endorsed on behalf of the company if that is done in the name of, or by or on behalf or on account of, the company by a person acting under its authority.[75] A company may empower a person to execute deeds abroad,[76] may have an official seal for use abroad,[77] and may have an official seal for sealing share certificates.[78] A document or proceeding requiring authentication by a company may be signed by a director, secretary, or other authorized officer and need not be under the common seal.[79]

The doctrine of notice

Persons dealing with the company should satisfy themselves that the company has power to enter into the proposed transaction, and that the agent for the company is authorized to act in that respect on its behalf. The Memorandum and Articles and special resolutions of the company,

---

[71] S. 36; *Phonogram Ltd.* v. *Lane* [1981] 3 All E.R. 182.
[72] *Gillies* v. *Craigton Garage Co., Ltd.*, 1935 S.C. 423; *Bamford* v. *B.* [1968] 2 All E.R. 655.
[73] S. 36; *Phonogram Ltd.* v. *Lane* [1981] 2 All E.R. 182; the Articles may prescribe the manner of affixing the common seal: *Clydesdale Bank (Moore Place) Nominees, Ltd.* v. *Snodgrass*, 1939 S.C. 805.
[74] *Mahony* v. *East Holyford Co.* (1875) L.R. 7 H.L. 869; *Oakbank Oil Co.* v. *Crum* (1882) 10 R. (H.L.) 11.
[75] S. 37; cf. *Brebner* v. *Henderson*, 1925 S.C. 643; *Scottish and Newcastle Breweries* v. *Blair*, 1967 S.L.T. 72; *McLean* v. *Stuart*, 1970 S.L.T. (Notes) 77.
[76] S. 38.
[77] S. 39.
[78] S. 40.
[79] s. 41.

being registered, are public documents and everyone dealing with the company is deemed to have notice of their contents, including the extent of the company's powers and any limitations imposed by the Articles on the directors' powers.[74] This rule operates only in the company's favour, not against it.[80] Hence even an innocent person who in ignorance transacts with a company to do something *ultra vires* the company has no remedy against it. Fraud, is however, an exception.[81] If the transaction is *intra vires* the company but *ultra vires* the directors and the latter fact is not disclosed by the public documents, a person who innocently transacts in ignorance of that limitation may assume that all matters of procedure internal to the company, such as conferring the requisite authority on the directors with whom he deals, have been duly complied with, and he need not inquire into the company's internal management,[82] on the basis that *omnia praesumuntur rite ac solemniter esse acta*. The other person has no protection if the agent purporting to act on behalf of the company purports to make a contract not within the powers ordinarily or ostensibly possessed by such an agent,[83] nor, probably, if he did not have actual knowledge of the public documents.[84] Reliance on the rule in *Turquand's case*[85] is not possible where the person transacting with the company was ignorant of the contents of the Articles,[86] or knew of the irregularity in internal matters,[87] or had been put on his inquiry and should have investigated further,[88] or if the transaction is based on a forged document.[89]

Delictual liability

As a juristic person a company cannot by itself commit wrongs, but it can be held vicariously liable[90] for wrongs committed by its agents acting within the scope of their authority, or by its servants acting in the course of their employment,[91] even where intention, malice, or other mental

---

[80] *Rama Corpn. Ltd.* v. *Proved Investments Ltd.* [1952] 2 K.B. 147.
[81] *Venezuela Central Ry.* v. *Kisch* (1867) 2 H.L.C. 99; cf. *Heiton* v. *Waverley Hydropathic Co.* (1877) 4 R. 830.
[82] This is 'the rule in *Royal British Bank* v. *Turquand* (1856) 6 E. & B. 327'. See *Mahony, supra; Re County Life Assce. Co.* (1870) L.R. 5 Ch. App. 288; *Heiton* v. *Waverley Hydropathic Co.* (1877) 4 R. 830; *Duck* v. *Tower Galvanizing Co., Ltd.* [1901] 2 K.B. 314; *Gillies* v. *Craigton Garage Co.*, 1935 S.C. 423. Contrast *Irvine* v. *Union Bank of Australia* (1877) 2 App. Cas. 366. See also *National Bank Glasgow Nominees Ltd.* v. *Adamson*, 1932 S.L.T. 492.
[83] *Houghton* v. *Nothard, Lowe & Wills, Ltd.* [1927] 1 K.B. 246; *Rama Corpn., supra.*
[84] *Rama Corpn. Ltd.* v. *Proved Investments Ltd.* [1952] 2 K.B. 147.
[85] (1856) 6 E. & B. 327.
[86] *Rama Corpn. Ltd., supra; Hely Hutchinson* v. *Brayhead, Ltd.* [1967] 3 All E.R. 98.
[87] *Houghton* v. *Nothard, Lowe & Wills* [1928] A.C. 1; *Morris* v. *Kanssen* [1946] A.C. 459.
[88] *Underwood* v. *Bank of Liverpool* [1924] 1 K.B. 775; *Houghton, supra;* E.B.M. Co. v. *Dominion Bank* [1937] 3 All E.R. 555.
[89] *Ruben* v. *Great Fingall Consolidated* [1906] A.C. 439; *Kreditbank Cassel* v. *Schenkers, Ltd.* [1927] 1 K.B. 826; *South London Greyhound Racecourses* v. *Wake* [1931] 1 Ch. 496.
[90] On vicarious liability see Ch. 5.29, *infra.*
[91] *Barwick* v. *English Joint Stock Bank* (1867) L.R. 2 Ex. 259; *Houldsworth* v. *City of*

element is of the essence of the wrong.[92] It is questionable whether the company is liable if the agent or servant, when doing wrong, was acting *ultra vires*.[93] An act is not, however, automatically *ultra vires* merely because the agent, in doing it, is committing delict.

Power to hold property

If authorized by its Memorandum and Articles a company may hold any kind of property in its corporate name.

Change of status by re-registration

By re-registration a private company may become public,[94] a limited company became unlimited,[95] an unlimited company become limited,[96] and a public company become private.[97]

PROMOTERS AND FLOTATION

The promoters of a company are those who participate, in other than a professional capacity,[98] in bringing a company into being, as by raising capital, placing shares, or negotiating with a seller of a business or other interest.[89] The promoters stand in a fiduciary relation to the nascent company and consequently may not make any direct or indirect profit from the promotion without the knowledge of the company.[1] They may not sell their own property to the company without disclosing their interest.[2] Any transaction not adequately disclosed may be reduced by the

---

Glasgow Bank (1880) 7 R. (H.L.) 53; *Wright* v. *Dunlop & Co.* (1893) 20 R. 363; *Citizens Life Assce. Co.* v. *Brown* [1904] A.C. 423; *Finburgh* v. *Moss's Empires*, 1908 S.C. 928; *Power* v. *Central S.M.T. Co.*, 1949 S.C. 376.

[92] *Gordon* v. *British and Foreign Metaline Co.* (1886) 14 R. 75.

[93] *Poulton* v. *L.S.W. Ry.* (1867) L.R. 2 Q.B. 534; *Campbell* v. *Paddington Corpn.* [1911] 1 K.B. 869.

[94] Ss. 43–8.

[95] Ss. 49–50.

[96] Ss. 51–2.

[97] Ss. 53–5.

[98] *Re Great Wheal Polgooth Co.* (1883) 53 L.J. Ch. 42 (solicitors); *Mann* v. *Edinburgh Northern Tramways Co.* (1896) 23 R. 1056; *Muir* v. *Forman's Trs.* (1903) 5 F. 546; *Mason's Trs.* v. *Poolex Robinson* (1903) 5 F. 789.

[99] *Lindsay Petroleum Co.* v. *Hurd* (1874) L.R. 5 P.C. 221; *Twycross* v. *Grant* (1877) 2 C.P.D. 469; *Emma Silver Mining Co.* v. *Lewis* (1879) 4 C.P.D. 396; *Whaley Bridge Printing Co.* v. *Green* (1879) 5 Q.B.D. 109; *Gluckstein* v. *Barnes* [1900] A.C. 240.

[1] *Henderson* v. *Huntington Copper & Sulphur Co.* (1877) 5 R. (H.L.) 1; *Erlanger* v. *New Sombrero Phosphate Co.* (1887) 3 App. Cas. 1218; *Mann* v. *Edinburgh Northern Tramways* (1892) 20 R. (H.L.) 7; (1896) 23 R. 1056.

[2] *Henderson* v. *Huntington Copper Co.* (1877) 5 R. (H.L.) 1.

company[3] and any secret profit may be recovered by the company.[4] Promoters may be legitimately remunerated by receiving certain shares allotted as fully paid, or obtaining an option to take unissued shares, or selling a business or asset to the new company at a profit.[5] But if a promoter is selling his own property to the company he must furnish it with an independent board of directors and disclose his interest in the sale.[6] Payments to a firm of which the promoter is a partner must equally be disclosed.[7] A promoter may recover preliminary expenses only where he has established a contract by the company to pay.[8] The remuneration or benefit, whatever its nature, must be disclosed in the prospectus if paid within the past two years or intended to be paid at any time.[9]

Capital issues

Shares or debentures may be offered to the public by direct invitation to the public, or by an offer for sale by a merchant bank or other issuing house to the public, or by a placing with an issuing house which then invites clients to buy shares from it. A company which seeks capital from the public and quotation on the Stock Exchange must issue an advertisement complying with the listing rules of the Stock Exchange as to matters to be stated, and reports to be set out, in the advertisement, and it must with certain exceptions be registered with the registrar.[10] If there are changes, supplementary listing particulars must be published. If listing is not sought the advertisements must comply with the Financial Services Act, 1986, Part V. There is also a general duty of disclosure. A contract to take shares may at common law be rescinded for material misrepresentation in the advertisement[11] and damages recovered if the misrepresentation were made negligently or fraudulently.[12] The challenge must be made without delay.[13] Rescission is precluded by the liquidation of the company.[14]

---

[3] *Erlanger v. New Sombrero Phosphate Co.* (1878) 3 App. Cas. 1218; *Jubilee Cotton Mills, Ltd. v. Lewis* [1924] A.C. 958.

[4] *Lagunas Nitrate Co. v. Lagunas Syndicate* [1899] 2 Ch. 392; *Re Leeds and Hanley Theatre of Varieties* [1902] 2 Ch. 809; *Jubilee Cotton Mills v. Lewis* [1924] A.C. 958.

[5] cf. *Mason's Trs. v. Poole & Robinson* (1903) 5 F. 789.

[6] *Erlanger, supra.*

[7] *Scottish Pacific Coast Mining Co. v. Falkner, Bell & Co.* (1888) 15 R. 290.

[8] *Mason's Trs., supra; English and Colonial Produce Co.* [1906] 2 Ch. 435; *National Motor Mail Coach Co.* [1908] 2 Ch. 515. See also *Scott v. Money Order Co. of G.B.* (1870) 42 S. Jur. 212; *Robertson v. Beatson, McLeod & Co. Ltd,* 1908 S.C. 921.

[9] Ss. 56, 57; *Henderson v. Huntington Copper and Sulphate Co.* (1877) 5 R. (H.L.) 1.

[10] Financial Services Act, 1986, Ss. 144, 158. Certain exceptions are allowed by S. 161.

[11] *Edinburgh Brewery Co. v. Gibson's Trs.* (1869) 7 M. 886; *Chambers v. Edinburgh & Glasgow Aerated Bread Co.* (1891) 18 R. 1039; *Blakiston v. London and Scottish Banking and Discount Corpn.* (1894) 21 R. 417.

[12] *Davidson v. Tulloch* (1860) 22 D. (H.L.) 7; *Honeyman v. Dickson* (1896) 4 S.L.T. 150; *Mair v. Rio Grande Rubber Estates* 1913 S.C. (H.L.) 74.

[13] *Caledonian Debenture Co. v. Bernard* (1898) 5 S.L.T. 392.

[14] *Houldsworth v. City of Glasgow Bank* (1880) 7 R. (H.L.) 53.

An advertisement is addressed only to those who subscribe on the faith of it, and only they can sue for reduction on the ground of mis-representation.[15] In many cases individuals who subscribed for shares, induced by material mis-statements[16] in the advertisement, have had their contracts set aside by the court and their money returned,[17] or recovered damages from the company or the directors for loss caused if they can prove fraud.[18] They must prove that they were induced by the advertisement and applied for shares on the faith of the advertisement.[19] The right to rescind the contract to take shares will be lost if the contract has been ratified expressly or impliedly, as by delaying to challenge,[20] or trying to sell the shares, receiving dividends,[21] or otherwise acting as a member.[22] It is lost when winding up commences, as the interests of creditors then intervene,[23] or if restitutio *in integrum* cannot be made.[24]

Damages may also be recovered at common law from the promoters or directors or experts for fraud, if the misleading statements were made by them knowingly, or without belief in their truth, or recklessly, careless whether they were true or false, but not merely because they were made without care or without reasonable grounds for belief in their truth.[25] Damages may be recoverable at common law for negligent mis-statement in a prospectus.[26]

A person induced by misrepresentation to take shares may apply to have the register of members rectified by removal of his name therefrom, and the return of his money with interest,[27] but must not have acted as a

---

[15] *Peek v. Gurney* (1873) L.R. 6 H.L. 337; *McMorland's Trs. v. Fraser* (1896) 24 R. 65.

[16] *City of Edinburgh Brewery Co. v. Gibson's Tr.* (1869) 7 M. 886.

[17] *Western Bank of Scotland v. Addie* (1867) 5 M. (H.L.) 80; *Central Ry. of Venezuela v. Kisch* (1867) L.R. 2 H.L. 99; *Reese River Co. v. Smith* (1869) L.R. 4 H.L. 64; *Aaron's Reefs Ltd. v. Twiss* [1896] A.C. 273.

[18] e.g. *National Exchange Co. of Glasgow v. Drew* (1855) 2 Macq. 124; *Houldsworth v. City of Glasgow Bank* (1880) 7 R. (H.L.) 53; *Arnison v. Smith* (1889) 41 Ch. D. 348; *Lagunas Nitrate Co. v. Lagunas Syndicate* [1899] 2 Ch. 392; *Mair v. Rio Grande Rubber Estates Ltd.*, 1913 S.C. (H.L.) 74.

[19] *McMorland's Trs. v. Fraser* (1896) 24 R. 65.

[20] *Caledonian Debenture Co. v. Bernard* (1898) 5 S.L.T. 392.

[21] *Scholey v. Venezuela & Central Ry.* (1868) L.R. 9 Eq. 266 n.

[22] *Ex p. Briggs* (1866) L.R. 1 Eq. 483; *Scholey, supra; Sharpley v. Louth Co.* (1876) 2 Ch. D. 663; *Caledonian Debenture Co. v. Bernard* (1898) 5 S.L.T. 392.

[23] *Oakes v. Turquand* (1867) L.R. 2 H.L. 325; *Western Bank v. Addie* (1867) 5 M. (H.L.) 80; *Tennant v. City of Glasgow Bank* (1879) 6 R. (H.L.) 69.

[24] *Houldsworth v. City of Glasgow Bank* (1880) 7 R. (H.L.) 53.

[25] *Lees v. Tod* (1882) 9 R. 907; *Derry v. Peek* (1889) 14 App. Cas. 337; cf. *Tulloch v. Davidson* (1858) 3 Macq. 783; *Cullen v. Thomson's Trs.* (1862) 4 Macq. 424; *Western Bank, supra; New Brunswick Ry. v. Conybeare* (1862) 9 H.L. Cas. 724; *City of Edinburgh Brewery Co. v. Gibson's Tr.* (1869) 7 M. 886; *Smith v. Chadwick* (1883) 9 App. Cas. 187; *Chambers v. Edinburgh & Glasgow Aerated Bread Co.* (1891) 18 R. 1039; *Blakiston v. London, etc. Discount Corpn.* (1894) 21 R. 417; contrast *Honeyman v. Dickson* (1896) 4 S.L.T. 150.

[26] *Hedley Byrne & Co. v. Heller & Partners* [1964] A.C. 465.

[27] S. 359; *Anderson's Case* (1881) 17 Ch. D. 373; *Re London and Staffordshire Fire Ins. Co.* (1883) 24 Ch. D. 149. See also *Blaikie v. Coats* (1893) 21 R. 150; *Colquhoun's Tr. v. B.L. Co.* (1900) 2 F. 945; *Sleigh v. Glasgow and Transvaal Options, Ltd.* (1904) 6 F. 420; *Gowans v. Dundee S.N. Co.* (1904) 6 F. 613.

shareholder after discovering the misrepresentation.[28] Rectification may also be ordered in an action of reduction.[29]

Criminal liability may also be incurred.[30]

Under the Financial Services Act, 1986, Ss. 150–2 and Ss. 166–8, a statutory remedy is also provided for persons suffering in consequence of misrepresentations or omissions in listing particulars or a prospectus respectively. There is liability for loss as a result of any untrue or misleading statement in the particulars or the omission of anything required to be included by virtue of the duty of disclosure or the duty to publish new matter or change,[31] or for loss as a result of the failure to issue supplementary listing particulars when required to do so,[32] but six defences are provided,[33] namely reasonable belief in truth, reasonable belief in an expert's competence, reasonable steps to correct a defect, reliance on an official statement or document, the pursuer's knowledge, and reasonable belief that any change did not call for supplementary listing. Certain categories of persons are deemed responsible for the listing and hence for misrepresentations or omissions.

A private company may not offer to the public shares in or debentures of the company, or allot shares or debentures with a view to their being offered to the public, but obtains its initial capital from the promoters and persons whom they induce to contribute capital, such as banks.

Allotment

Allotment of shares or debentures requires the authority of the company in general meeting or of the Articles, which is valid for not more than 5 years but may be renewed.[34] A private limited company may not offer shares or debentures to the public.[35] No allotment may be made or action taken on applications for them until the beginning of the third day after that on which the prospectus was first issued or a later specified day,[36] nor unless there has been subscribed the amount stated as the minimum required for preliminary expenses and setting the company going. If these conditions have not been satisfied 40 days after the first issue of the prospectus applicants' money must be returned to them without interest.[37] No allotment may be made of any share capital of a public company offered for subscription unless that capital is subscribed for in full or the offer stated that there might be allotment even if the capital is

[28] *First National Reinsurance Co. Ltd.* v. *Greenfield* [1921] 2 K.B. 260.
[29] *Kinghorn* v. *Glenyards Fireclay Co.* (1907) 14 S.L.T. 683.
[30] cf. *R.* v. *Kylsant* [1932] 1 K.B. 442.
[31] 1986 Act, Ss. 146–7, 163–4.
[32] Ss. 147, 164.
[33] Ss. 151, 167.
[34] S. 80. Allotment is competent only to persons who have applied: *Mason* v. *Benhar Coal Co.* (1882) 9 R. 883.
[35] S. 81.
[36] S. 82.
[37] S. 83.

not subscribed in full.[38] An allotment irregular under Ss. 83 or 84 is voidable by an applicant within one month,[39] and damages can be recovered from a director who has knowingly contravened. Allotment of shares to be dealt in on the Stock Exchange is void if permission to deal has not been applied for or been refused by specified dates, and money is repayable.[40] A return as to allotments must be made to the registrar.[41] A company proposing to allot equity securities must first offer them proportionately to existing holders on the same or more favourable terms.[42] Commissions and discounts are prohibited save where permitted.[43] Shares may be paid for in money or money's worth, including goodwill and know-how, but not by undertaking to do work or perform services for the company or any other person. Shares may not be allotted at a discount,[44] nor unless paid up at least as to a quarter of nominal value and the whole of any premium, unless in pursuance of an employees' shares scheme.[45] A public company may not allot shares as fully or partly paid otherwise than in cash if the consideration is to be or may be performed more than 5 years later. Any non-cash consideration must be valued before allotment.[46]

A public company cannot do business or exercise borrowing powers unless it has obtained a certificate from the registrar that the nominal value of the company's allotted share capital is not less than the authorized minimum[47] and the registrar has received a statutory declaration stating that fact, the amount paid up on the allotted share capital, specifying the amount of the company's preliminary expenses, and any amount paid to any promoter of the company and the consideration therefor.[48]

MANAGEMENT OF THE COMPANY

Directors

The members of a company are usually too numerous all to participate in managing its affairs and to act as agents for the company. The Articles normally therefore name the first directors[49] and provide thereafter for

---

[38] S. 84.
[39] S. 85.
[40] S. 86–7.
[41] S. 88.
[42] Ss. 89–96.
[43] Ss. 97–8.
[44] cf. *Klenck* v. *East India Exploration Co.* (1888) 16 R. 271.
[45] Ss. 97–101.
[46] Ss. 102–16.
[47] £50,000 or a larger sum specified: S. 118.
[48] Ss. 117–20.
[49] Nomination is valid only if the condition of S. 13 are satisfied. Failing nomination the first

the election by the members of directors to manage the affairs of the company. The Articles may prescribe qualifications for appointment, such as holding a certain number of shares.[50] Every public company must now[51] have at least two directors, and every private company at least one director. There must also be a secretary and a sole director cannot also be secretary.[52] A statement of the first directors and the secretary must be delivered with an application for registration of a company.[53] A register of directors and secretaries must be maintained at the registered office showing specified particulars of all directors.[54] Similar particulars must be sent to the Registrar of Companies.[54] A register must also be maintained of directors' service contracts[55] and their holdings of shares or debentures in it or associated companies.[56] The names, former names, and nationality of directors must be published in trade catalogues, trade circulars, showcards and business letters in which the company's name appears.[57]

Directors may be agents of the company and the principles of agency apply to their relationship.[58] They are not by election as directors employees of the company, but an employee may be a director.[59]

Directors are also trustees for the company, in that they must act in good faith for the benefit of the general body of members,[60] though not for individual shareholders,[61] may not, as directors, transact with themselves as individuals,[62] must account to the company for any profit made,[63] must show diligence and care in the execution of their duties, and not abuse their powers.[64] A director of a parent company may contract

---

directors are appointed by the subscribers to the Memorandum: *John Morley Building Co.* v. *Barras* [1891] 2 Ch. 386.

[50] *Consolidated Copper Co. of Canada* v. *Peddie* (1877) 5 R. 393; See also *Galloway S.P. Co.* v. *Wallace* (1891) 19 R. 320; *Elliot* v. *Mackie*, 1935 S.C. 81.

[51] S. 282.

[52] S. 282.

[53] Ss. 10, 13.

[54] Ss. 288, 711.

[55] S. 318.

[56] Ss. 324–6.

[57] S. 305.

[58] *Ferguson* v. *Wilson* (1866) L.R. 2 Ch. App. 77; *McLintock* v. *Campbell*, 1916 S.C. 966, 980; *Hely-Hutchinson* v. *Brayhead Ltd.* [1968] 1 Q.B. 549. They may be personally liable under Ss. 348–50.

[59] *Lee* v. *Lee's Air Farming Ltd.* [1961] A.C. 12.

[60] *Aberdeen Ry.* v. *Blaikie Bros.* (1854) 1 Macq. 461; *G.E. Ry.* v. *Turner* (1872) L.R. 8 Ch. App. 149; *Smith* v. *Anderson* (1880) 15 Ch. D. 247; *Re Faure Electric Accummulator Co.* (1888) 40 Ch. D. 141; *Cook* v. *Barry Henry & Co.* 1923 S.L.T. 692; *Re City Equitable Fire Ins. Co.* [1925] Ch. 407; *Harris* v. *H.*, 1936 S.C. 183; *Selangor Rubber Estates* v. *Cradock* [1968] 2 All E.R. 1073.

[61] *Percival* v. *Wright* [1902] 2 Ch. 421; *Wilson* v. *Dunlop, Bremner & Co.*, 1921, 1 S.L.T. 354.

[62] *Aberdeen Ry., supra; Jacobus Marler Estates* v. *Marler* (1916) 85 L.J.P.C. 167; *Hely-Hutchinson* v. *Brayhead* [1968] 1 Q.B. 549.

[63] *Allen* v. *Hyatt* (1914) 30 T.L.R. 444; *Regal (Hastings) Ltd.* v. *Gulliver* [1942] 1 All E.R. 378; See also *McNaughtan* v. *Brunton* (1882) 10 R. 111; *Marmor Ltd.* v. *Alexander*, 1908 S.C. 78.

[64] *Punt* v. *Symons & Co.* [1903] 2 Ch. 506; *Brenes & Co.* v. *Downie*, 1914 S.C. 97; *Piercy* v. *Mills & Co.* [1920] 1 Ch. 77.

with a subsidiary which has an independent board of directors.[65] They may not delegate their powers or duties save in so far as power to do so is expressed or implied in the Articles.[66] A director may incur liability for breach of trust, either personally or by concurring in conduct by fellow-directors of that nature.[67]

Directors must act honestly towards the company,[68] not contract with the seller of a business to the company for their own benefit,[69] nor accept bribes or private benefits or otherwise make secret profits,[70] exercise diligence and care in the company's affairs,[71] and in appropriate circumstances take and act on independent skilled advice.[72] They are not liable for errors of judgment[73] but are for gross negligence. They may rely on information furnished by senior officers of the company.[74]

Directors must also have regard in the performance of their functions to the interests of the company's employees as well as of the members.[75]

A director owes a duty of care to third parties and must exercise reasonable care and diligence in his acts as director.[76]

A director who is in breach of duty is liable to an action by the company to recover the profit made by him or the loss sustained by the company.[77] On winding up the liquidator or a creditor may apply to the court[78] to examine the conduct of a director or past director and require repayment by him.[79] The court has a discretion, whether to grant relief and how much.[80] The Articles may contain provisions for indemnifying directors from liability,[81] but only so far as permitted by S. 310, but S. 727 empowers the court, in proceedings against a director for negligence,

[65] *Lindgren v. L. & P. Estates Co.* [1968] 1 All E.R. 917.
[66] *Cobb v. Becke* (1845) 6 Q.B. 930; *Leeds Estate Co. v. Shepherd* (1887) 36 Ch. D. 787; *Mahony v. East Holyford Mining Co.* (1875) L.R. 7 H.L. 869; *Allison v. Scotia Motor and Engineering Co.* (1906) 14 S.L.T. 9.
[67] *Caledonian Heritable Security Co. v. Curror's Tr.* (1882) 9 R. 1115.
[68] *Industrial Development Consultants, Ltd. v. Cooley* [1972] 2 All E.R. 162.
[69] *Henderson v. Huntington Copper Co.* (1877) 5 R. (H.L.) 1; cf. *G.N.S. Ry. v. Urquhart* (1884) 21 S.L.R. 377.
[70] *Re George Newman & Co.* [1895] 1 Ch. 674; *Laughland v. Millar Laughland & Co.* (1904) 6 F. 413; *Industrial Development Consultants, supra.*
[71] *Rance's Case* (1870) L.R. 6 Ch. App. 104; *Re City Equitable Fire Ins. Co.* [1925] 1 Ch. 407.
[72] *Re Faure Electric Accumulator Co.* (1888) 40 Ch. D. 141.
[73] *Overend & Gurney Co. v. Gibb* (1872) L.R. 5 H.L. 480; *Liqrs. of City of Glasgow Bank v. Mackinnon* (1882) 9 R. 535.
[74] *Addie v. Western Bank* (1865) 3 M. 899; *Lees v. Tod* (1882) 9 R. 807.
[75] S. 309.
[76] *Western Bank v. Douglas* (1860) 22 D. 447; *Addie v. Western Bank* (1865) 3 M. 899, 901, revd. on other grounds, 5 M. (H.L.) 80; *Caledonian Heritable Secy. Co. v. Curror's Tr.* (1882) 9 R. 1115; *Brenes v. Downie,* 1914 S.C. 97; *Oliver v. Douglas* , 1981 S.C. 192.
[77] *Joint Stock Discount Co. v. Brown* (1869) L.R. 8 Eq. 381; *Western Bank v. Baird's Trs.* (1872) 11 M. 96; *Industrial Development Consultants, supra.*
[78] S. 637; *Re Forest of Dean Mining Co.* (1878) 10 Ch. D. 450; *Cavendish-Bentinck v. Fenn* (1887) 12 App. Cas. 652; *Re City Equitable Fire Insce. Co.* [1925] Ch. 407.
[79] *Liqr. of Caledonian Heritable Security Co. v. Curror's Tr.* (1882) 9 R. 1115.
[80] *Sunlight Incandescent Gas Lamp Co.* (1900) 16 T.L.R. 535.
[81] *Tomlinson v. Liqrs. of Scottish Amalgamated Silks, Ltd.,* 1935 S.C. (H.L.) 1.

default, breach of duty, or breach of trust, to relieve him from liability, wholly or partly, if in the opinion of the court he acted honestly and reasonably and in the circumstances ought fairly to be relieved.[82]

Appointment of directors

First directors are usually named in the Articles, failing which all or a majority of the subscribers may by writing appoint them. Thereafter directors are elected at a general meeting. Casual vacancies may be filled by co-option, subject to ratification at the next general meeting. No qualification is required save that an undischarged bankrupt may not act unless authorized by the court[83] and a person guilty of fraud or breach of duty may be disqualified by the court.[84] A director need not be a share-holder but the Articles may provide that he hold a specified number of shares, in which case he must acquire the qualifying holding within two months.[85] Subject to certain exceptions a person cannot be elected a director of a public company, or a private company which is a subsidiary of a public company, when over the age of 70, unless he is appointed in general meeting in terms of an ordinary resolution of which special notice has been given, stating the director's age.[86] The Articles may provide for permanent directors[87] but frequently provide for directors retiring in rotation, and frequently for re-election unless the general meeting resolves not to fill the vacancy or a resolution for his re-election has been lost. A director may resign at any time or sell his qualification shares and vacate office in consequence.[88] There are restrictions on the terms of the employ-ment with the company of persons who are directors.[89]

Disqualification of directors

A director becomes disqualified if he loses any qualification required by the Articles or does anything which is thereby stated to be a disqualification.[90] A director who becomes bankrupt cannot act as a director without leave of the court.[91] A director must retire after he has attained 70, unless his continuance in office is approved by a general

---

[82] cf. *National Trustee Co. of Australia* v. *General Finance Co.* [1905] A.C. 373; *Re Claridges Patent Asphalte Co.* [1921] 1 Ch. 543; *Re City Equitable Co., supra; Gibson's Exor.* v. *G.*, 1978 S.C. 197.
[83] S. 302.
[84] S. 295.
[85] S. 291; cf. *Brown's case* (1874) L.R. 9 Ch. 102; *Kingsburgh Motor Construction Co.* v. *Scott* (1902) 10 S.L.T. 424.
[86] S. 293.
[87] e.g. *Bersel* v. *Berry* [1968] 2 All E.R. 552.
[88] *Gilbert's Case* (1870) L.R. 5 Ch. App. 559.
[89] S. 319.
[90] See e.g. Table A, Art 81.
[91] S. 302.

meeting, special notice having been given.[92] The Articles may modify the rule, which does not apply to private companies unless they are subsidiaries of public companies.[92] A court may make a disqualification order that a person shall not without leave of the court be a director, liquidator, or receiver of a company, or take part in the promotion, formation, or management of a company, if he is convicted of an indictable offence, has persistently defaulted under the Act, has been guilty of fraud in a winding up, and in certain other circumstances. An undischarged bankrupt may not act as director or liquidator or be concerned in formation or management of a company.[93]

Fair dealing by directors

A company may not pay a director tax free[94] or, without the knowledge and approval of the company, make payment in compensation for loss of office or in connection with retirement.[95] In the case of a take-over a director must disclose any payment to be made for loss of office or in connection with retirement.[96] Directors interested in a contract or proposed contract with the company must declare their interest to the board.[97] Copies of directors' service contracts must be kept at designated places.[98] Directors' contracts of employment for, or continuable beyond, 5 years require approval of the company in general meeting.[99] Substantial property transactions involving directors are with exceptions excluded unless approved in general meeting.[1] It is an offence for directors, their spouses, or children to purchase options to buy or sell shares or debentures of the company.[2] A director must on appointment notify the company of shareholdings in the company or related companies,[3] and every company must keep a register of directors' interests[4] and, if a listed company, notify the stock exchange.[5]

Subject to exceptions, a company may not make a loan or quasi-loan to, or guarantee or provide security for a loan to, a director, or enter into a credit transaction as creditor for a director, or otherwise make an arrangement benefiting a director.[6] Such an arrangement is voidable by the company and an offence by the director.[7]

---

[92] S. 293.
[93] Ss. 295–302.
[94] S. 311.
[95] Ss. 312–13. cf. *Gibson's Exor. v. G.*, 1978 S.C. 197.
[96] Ss. 314–16.
[97] S. 317.
[98] S. 318.
[99] S. 319.
[1] Ss. 320–2.
[2] S. 323, 327–8.
[3] S. 324.
[4] S. 325–6.
[5] S. 329.
[6] Ss. 330–40, 345–7.
[7] Ss. 341–4.

Benefits to directors

Loans by a company to a director or director of its holding company are prohibited, nor may a company guarantee or provide security for a loan to a director by anyone, subject to limited exceptions.[8] A director may not, unless permitted by the Articles, contract with the company as this might result in conflict between his interest and his duty of trust, not even if the contract were perfectly fair.[9] Any interest in a contract or proposed contract with the company must be disclosed.[10] It is an offence for a director to deal in options on the company's shares.[11] Transfers of property over stated values between directors and their companies are not permitted unless sanctioned by a general meeting.[12] A director who obtains any secret benefit by virtue of his position must account to the company for it,[13] and the company may rescind the contract[14] or recover from a third party any benefit it has obtained by bribing a director.[15] Directors have, as such, no claim to remuneration[16] but the Articles normally authorize such remuneration as shall be voted in general meeting.[17] Expenses are frequently also authorized.[18] To take unauthorized remuneration is breach of trust and directors are liable to refund the amount paid.[19] Unless authorized by the Articles directors cannot vote themselves remuneration or appoint one of themselves to a salaried office.[20] All sums paid must be shown in the accounts.[21] They are also entitled to be indemnified for all liabilities properly incurred in managing the company's affairs, including legal expenses,[22] but not for wrongful or *ultra vires* actings.[23] A company must keep at an appropriate place a copy of every written contract of service with a director or, if it is not in writing, a memorandum setting out its terms, and these must be open to public inspection.[24] Directors must notify the company of any acquisition of company's shares.[25]

---

[8] Ss. 163–7. See also *Baird* v. *J. Baird & Co.*, 1949 S.L.T. 368.

[9] *Aberdeen Ry.* v. *Blaikie Bros.* (1854) 1 Macq. 461; *Bray* v. *Ford* [1896] A.C. 44.

[10] Ss. 232–4.

[11] S. 323.

[12] Ss. 320–1.

[13] *Boston Co.* v. *Ansell* (1888) 39 Ch. D. 339; *Eden* v. *Ridsdale Co.* (1889) 23 Q.B.D. 368.

[14] *Shipway* v. *Broadwood* [1889] 1 Q.B. 369.

[15] *Mayor of Salford* v. *Lever* [1891] 1 Q.B. 168; *Grant* v. *Gold Exploration Syndicate* [1900] 1 Q.B. 233.

[16] *McNaughtan* v. *Brunton* (1882) 10 R. 111; *Hutton* v. *West York Ry. Co.* (1883) 23 Ch. D. 654. See also *Fife Linoleum Co.* v. *Lornie* (1905) 13 S.L.T. 670; *Tomlinson* v. *Sc. Amalgamated Silks*, 1935 S.C. (H.L.) 1.

[17] *Woolf* v. *East Nigel Co.* (1905) 21 T.L.R. 660.

[18] *Marmor* v. *Alexander*, 1908 S.C. 78.

[19] *Leeds Estate Co.* v. *Shepherd* (1887) 36 Ch. D. 787.

[20] *Kerr* v. *Marine Products, Ltd.* (1928) 44 T.L.R. 292.

[21] Ss. 231, 237.

[22] *James* v. *May* (1873) L.R. 6 H.L. 328; *Re Famatina Development Corpn.* [1914] 2 Ch. 271; but see *Tomlinson* v. *Scottish Amalgamated Silks, Ltd.*, 1935 S.C. (H.L.) 1.

[23] *Moxham* v. *Grant* [1900] 1 Q.B. 88; *Re Claridge's Patent Asphalte Co., Ltd.* [1921] 1 Ch. 543.

[24] S. 318.

[25] Ss. 328–9.

Removal of directors

The general meeting may by ordinary resolution requiring special notice remove a director, notwithstanding any agreement with him or anything in the Articles.[26] Special notice must be given of the resolution and the director may have circulated to the members written representations, or may make them at the meeting. A director removed from office is not thereby deprived of any claim for compensation or damages which he might have.[26] Compensation for loss of office or in connection with retirement must be disclosed to the shareholders and approved by the company.[27]

Directors' powers

The directors' powers are limited to those acts which the company, their principal, is empowered to do, so that they cannot do anything *ultra vires* of the company, and further limited to those powers which the company has by the Articles delegated to them and anything fairly incidental thereto. Acts intra vires of the company but *ultra vires* of the directors may be ratified by the members in general meeting,[28] failing which the directors will be personally liable to the parties with whom they have dealt for breach of warranty of authority.[29] Persons transacting with the company are entitled to assume that the directors have the authority they claim to have and that the internal rules of management of the company have been complied with.[30] A general conferment of powers by the Articles is valid.[31] Unless they have express or implied powers to do so, they may not delegate their powers,[32] but power of delegation is common. Directors must, in exercising their powers, have regard to the benefit of the company and may not abuse a power or use it unfairly.[33] Directors, as agents, are not personally liable on contracts made professedly on behalf of the company,[34] but may render themselves personally liable, deliberately, or by contracting without disclosing that they are acting as agents for the company, or without purporting to bind the

[26] Ss. 303–4; *Read v. Astoria Garage (Streatham) Ltd.* [1952] Ch. 637; *Yetton v. Eastwoods Froy, Ltd.* [1966] 3 All E.R. 353. But see *Bushell v. Faith* [1970] 1 All E.R. 53.

[27] Ss. 312–13.

[28] *Grant v. U.K. Switchback Ry.* (1888) 40 Ch. D. 135; *Re Oxted Motor Co.* [1921] 3 K.B. 32.

[29] *Firbank's Exors. v. Humphreys* (1886) 18 Q.B.D. 54; *Starkey v. Bank of England* [1903] A.C. 114.

[30] *Royal British Bank v. Turquand* (1856) 6 E. & B. 327; *Gillies v. Craigton Garage Co.*, 1935 S.C. 423; *Freeman & Lockyer v. Buckhurst Park Properties* [1964] 2 Q.B. 480; *Hely-Hutchinson v. Brayhead* [1968] 1 Q.B. 549.

[31] *Re Patent File Co.* (1870) L.R. 6 Ch. App. 83; *Re Anglo-Danubian Co.* (1875) L.R. 20 Eq. 339.

[32] *Leeds Estate Co. v. Shepherd* (1887) 36 Ch. D. 787; *Dunn v. Banknock Coal Co.* (1901) 9 S.L.T. 51.

[33] *Alexander v. Automatic Telephone Co.* [1900] 2 Ch. 56; *Punt v. Symons* [1903] 2 Ch. 506; *Cook v. Barry, Henry & Cook*, 1923 S.L.T. 692.

[34] *Ferguson v. Wilson* (1866) L.R. 2 Ch. App. 77.

company.[35] They are not personally liable for wrongs committed by the company, unless personally parties to the wrong; they may be liable along with the company.[36] The acts of a director or manager are valid despite any defect later discovered in his appointment.[37] If at any time there are no directors power rests in the general meeting and the company may retify acts done without authority on its behalf.[38]

Board meetings

The directors in general act as a body at board meetings, but the Articles may authorize the appointment of one or more as managing directors who take day-to-day decisions,[39] or the delegation of powers to committees. The Articles fix, or authorize the directors to fix, the quorum who may act for the whole board. If no quorum is fixed a majority can act.[40] Unless meetings are held at fixed times due notice must be given calling a meeting a reasonable time beforehand.[41] Decisions are reached in the form of resolutions, and minutes of all directors' proceedings must be recorded in a book kept for the purpose.[42] A managing director is usually an employee of the company as well as a director and his dismissal may be a breach of his contract of employment.[43] A director is entitled to a court order for inspection of the minutes of board meetings.[44]

Secretary

Every company must have a secretary and a sole director cannot also be secretary.[45] The office may be held by a person, a firm, or, subject to qualifications, another company.[46] Qualifications are specified.[47] He is appointed and removed by the directors and is a servant of the

[35] *McCollin* v. *Gilpin* (1880) 5 Q.B.D. 390; *Dermatine Co.* v. *Ashworth* (1905) 21 T.L.R. 510.

[36] *Cullen* v. *Thomson's Trs.* (1862) 4 Macq. 424.

[37] S. 285; *Dawson* v. *African Consolidated Co.* [1898] 1 Ch. 6; contrast *Morris* v. *Kanssen* [1946] A.C. 459.

[38] *Ward* v. *Samyang Navigation Co.*, 1975 S.C. (H.L.) 26.

[39] On their position see *Allison* v. *Scotia Motor Co.* (1906) 14 S.L.T. 9; *Hindle* v. *John Cotton, Ltd.* (1919) 56 S.L.R. 625; *Kerr* v. *Walker*, 1933 S.C. 458; *Anderson* v. *James Sutherland (Peterhead) Ltd.*, 1941 S.C. 203; *Caddies* v. *Harold Holdsworth & Co. (Wakefield) Ltd.*, 1955 S.C. (H.L.) 27; *Shindler* v. *Northern Raincoat Co.* [1960] 1 W.L.R. 1038. See also *Nelson* v. *James Nelson & Sons, Ltd.* [1914] 2 K.B. 770; *Southern Foundries Ltd.* v. *Shirlaw* [1940] A.C. 701; *Read* v. *Astoria Garage (Streatham) Ltd.* [1952] 1 Ch. 637.

[40] *York Tramways Co.* v. *Willows* (1882) 8 Q.B.D. 685.

[41] *Browne* v. *La Trinidad* (1887) 37 Ch. D. 1; see also *Re Homer Gold Mines* (1888) 39 Ch. D. 546.

[42] S. 382; *City of Glasgow Bank Liqrs.* (1880) 7 R. 1196.

[43] See note 39.

[44] *McCusker* v. *McRae*, 1966 S.C. 253.

[45] S. 283.

[46] S. 286.

[47] S. 286.

company.[48] His functions are administrative, not managerial; he has power to bind the company contractually in matters within his ostensible anthority[49] but not to make representations on behalf of the company unless express or implied authority is given him,[50] but may have ostensible authority in administrative matters.[51] His duties include notices, correspondence, board and company meetings, the register of members, share transfer procedure, and numerous statutory duties, but not advice on law.[52] Apart from showing due care, skill, and diligence in the performance of his duties he is, like a director, in a fiduciary position to the company and must not let his interest conflict with his duty, or make a secret profit.[53] Particulars of the secretary must be given in the register of directors and secretaries.[54] A provision that something be done by or to a director and the secretary is not satisfied by one person acting as director and as, or in place of, the secretary.[55]

Registered office

The registered office must be notified in the statement delivered prior to incorporation and changes notified.[56]

Company administration

Every company must have its name displayed outside every office or place where its business is carried on,[57] mention its name in all business letters, notices, bills of exchange, cheques, orders, invoices, receipts, and letters of credit,[58] have its name engraved on its seal,[59] and state in all business letters and order forms the company's place of registration and number, the address of its registered office, the fact if it be the case, that it is an investment company, and, if exempt from the obligation to have the word limited as part of the name, the fact that it is a limited company.[60]

Every company must maintain a register of its members stating specified particulars[61] at its registered office or elsewhere in the same

---

[48] *Scottish Poultry Journal Co.* (1896) 4 S.L.T. 167.
[49] *Panorama Developments v. Fidelis Furnishings* [1971] 3 All E.R. 16.
[50] *Barnet, Hoares & Co. v. South London Tramways Co.* (1887) 18 Q.B.D. 815; *Houghton v. Nothard Lowe & Wills Ltd.* [1928] A.C. 1.
[51] *Panorama Developments v. Fidelis Furnishings* [1971] 3 All E.R. 16.
[52] *Niven v. Collins Patent Lever Gear Co.* (1900) 7 S.L.T. 476.
[53] cf. *Regal (Hastings) Ltd. v. Gulliver* [1942] 1 All E.R. 378.
[54] S. 288-9.
[55] S. 284.
[56] Ss. 10, 287, 711.
[57] S. 348.
[58] S. 349.
[59] S. 350.
[60] S. 351.
[61] S. 352. As to the modes of keeping the register see Ss. 722-3.

country,[62] with an index.[63] Enrolment on the register is the member's document of title to his shares.[64] When a share warrant is issued the member's name must be removed from the register.[65] The register is open to inspection and may be copied,[66] but may on notice given by press advertisement be closed for not more than 30 days a year.[67] If the name of a person is, without sufficient cause, entered on or omitted from a company's register or default is made in removing a name from the register, the person, or any member of the company, or the company, may apply to the court for rectification of the register, which the court may order and also payment by the company of damages sustained by any party aggrieved.[68] No notice of any trust is entered on the register in the case of companies registered in England and Wales.[69] The register is prima-facie evidence of any matters directed or authorized by the Act to be inserted therein.[70] An overseas branch register may be maintained in certain cases.[71]

Annual return

Companies having, or not having, a share capital must at least once every year, within 42 days after the A.G.M., make a return in the prescribed form giving prescribed information required by Sch. 15 and S. 364 respectively.[72]

Meetings and resolutions

Every company must in each year, in addition to any other meetings in that year, hold an A.G.M. not more than 15 months after the last A.G.M.[73] If default is made the Secretary of State may call or direct the calling of a general meeting.[74] Members holding one-tenth of the paid-up

---

[62] Ss. 353, 357. A creditor cannot exercise a lien over the register: *Garpel Haematite Co.* v. *Andrew* (1866) 4 M. 617.

[63] S. 354.

[64] *I.R.C.* v. *Wilson*, 1927 S.C. 733, 737.

[65] S. 355.

[66] S. 356.

[67] S. 358.

[68] S. 359. cf. *Blaikie* v. *Coats* (1893) 21 R. 150; *Blakiston* v. *London and Scottish Banking Corpn.* (1894) 21 R. 417; as to appropriateness of this procedure in complicated cases see *Colquhoun's Tr.* v. *B.L. Co.* (1900) 2 F. 945; *Sleigh* v. *Glasgow and Transvaal Options Ltd.* (1904) 6 F. 420; *Kinghorn* v. *Glenyards Fireclay Co.* (1907) 14 S.L.T. 683.

[69] S. 360. Trust holdings are registered in the name of the trustees or the first four of them as joint owners. In Scotland trustees may be registered as such but this is to identify trust property only and does not affect the holders' liability: *Muir* v. *City of Glasgow Bank* (1878) 6 R. 392.

[70] S. 361.

[71] S. 362.

[72] Ss. 363–5.

[73] S. 366.

[74] S. 367.

capital with voting rights, or representing one-tenth of the total voting rights of members having right to vote, may require the directors to call an extraordinary general meeting. The requisition must state the objects of the meeting.[75] If the directors do not call the meeting half of the requisitionists may themselves convene a meeting at the directors' expense.[76]

The minimum periods of notice for meetings are: A.G.M., 21 days' notice in writing; meetings other than A.G.M. or for the passing of a special resolution, 14 days' notice in writing, or 7 days' notice in the case of an unlimited company. A meeting called on shorter notice is deemed duly called if so agreed, at an A.G.M., by all the members entitled to attend and vote, and in other cases by a majority of the members together holding 95 per cent in nominal value of the shares giving a right to attend and vote, or representing 95 per cent of the total voting rights at that meeting of all the members.[77]

Unless the Articles make contrary provision notice of meeting must be served on every member in the manner required by Table A; two or more members holding at least 10 per cent of the issued share capital, or at least 5 per cent in number of the members, may call a meeting. Two members personally present are a quorum. Any member elected by those present may be chairman. Every member has one vote for each share or £10 of stock held; in other cases every member has one vote.[78] The court may in special circumstances order a meeting to be called and conducted in any manner the court thinks fit.[79] For a quorum the required number of members must be present not only at the commencement but when the business is transacted.[80] A quorum is not made by a person present in more than one capacity.[81] 'Present' means personally present, not represented.[82]

Proxies

A member may appoint another person, who need not be a member, to attend and vote in his place, and in the case of a private company the proxy may speak. Unless the Articles otherwise provide this does not apply in the case of a company not having a share capital, a member of a

---

[75] Business is not confined to that specified in the requisition: *Bell* v. *Metal Industries Ltd.*, 1957 S.C. 315.

[76] S. 368. See *Thyne* v. *Lauder*, 1925 S.N. 123.

[77] S. 369. See also *Aberdeen Comb Works Co. Ltd.* (1902) 10 S.L.T. 210; *Neil McLeod & Sons Ltd.*, 1967 S.C. 16.

[78] S. 370.

[79] S. 371; cf. *Edinburgh Workmen's Houses Co.*, 1935 S.C. 56. *Re El Sombrero* [1958] Ch. 900.

[80] *Henderson* v. *Louttit* (1894) 21 R. 674. But see *Hartley Baird Ltd.* [1955] Ch. 142.

[81] *James Prain & Sons Ltd.*, 1947 S.C. 325.

[82] *M. Harris Ltd.*, 1956 S.C. 207.

private company is not entitled to appoint more than one proxy for one occasion, and a proxy may vote on a poll only. Notice that a member may appoint a proxy must appear in notices calling meetings.[83] The Stock Exchange requires that limited companies issuing forms allowing nomination of a proxy should give the member authority to instruct the proxy to vote For or Against particular resolutions.

The articles may not exclude the right to demand a poll at a general meeting on any question other than the election of chairman or the adjournment, or nullify a demand for a poll by not less than 5 members, or a member or members representing not less than 10 per cent of the total voting rights or by a member or members holding shares with a paid-up value not less than 10 per cent of the total sum paid up.[84] On a poll, a member entitled to more than one vote need not cast all his votes the same way.[85]

A corporation which is a member of a company may authorize any person it thinks fit to act as its representative at a company meeting or a creditors' meeting with the same powers as an individual shareholder or creditor.[86]

Resolutions

Decisions at meetings are reached by members voting on resolutions proposing that something be authorized or done. Resolutions are frequently proposed by the board of directors. On the requisition in writing of stated numbers of members and at their expense, unless the company otherwise resolves, it is the company's duty to give members notice of any resolution intended to be moved at the A.G.M. and to circulate to members any statement of not more than 1,000 words with respect to the matter referred to in a proposed resolution or the business to be dealt with at that meeting. The requisition must be made in statutory form. The company is not bound to circulate the statement if the court is satisfied that the statutory right is being abused to secure needless publicity for defamatory matter.[87]

Most ordinary decisions can be reached by an ordinary resolution passed by a majority. A resolution is an extraordinary resolution when passed by a majority of not less than three-quarters of such members as vote in person or, where allowed, by proxy at a general meeting of which notice specifying the intention to propose the resolution as an extraordinary resolution has been given.[88]

A resolution is a special resolution when passed by the same majority at

---

[83] S. 372.
[84] S. 373.
[85] S. 374.
[86] S. 375.
[87] Ss. 376–7.
[88] S. 378; *Rennie* v. *Crichton's (Strichen) Ltd.*, 1927 S.L.T. 459.

a general meeting of which 21 days' notice, specifying the intention to propose the resolution as a special resolution, has been given. A specified majority may allow less than 21 days' notice.[88] Voting is normally by show of hands, but anyone may demand a poll or count of heads. If the Articles require a show of hands this must be done, and the minutes must record the fact.[89]

At a meeting at which an extraordinary or special resolution is submitted, the declaration by the chairman that the resolution is carried is, unless a poll is demanded, conclusive without proof of the number or proportion of votes in favour of or against the resolution.[90]

Where under the Act special notice is required of a resolution, it is ineffective unless notice of the intention to move it was given at least 28 days before the meeting. The company must give notice of such resolution in the notice calling the meeting or otherwise at least 21 days before.[91]

A copy, printed or in otherwise approved form, of the various resolutions and agreements must within 15 days be sent to the registrar and embodied in or annexed to every copy of the articles issued thereafter. This applies to (a) special resolutions; (b) extraordinary resolutions; (c) resolutions or agreements agreed to unanimously but which would otherwise have been ineffective unless passed as special or extraordinary resolutions; (d) resolutions or agreements agreed to unanimously by members of a class of shareholders but otherwise ineffective unless passed by a particular majority or in a particular manner; (e) a resolution passed to comply with a Secretary of State's direction as to change of name; and certain other specified resolutions.[92]

A resolution passed at an adjourned meeting is treated as passed on the date of actual passing.[93]

Majority rule

In general a majority of the members can bar a claim by a minority if the majority could lawfully approve or ratify the conduct objected to.[94] Directors are not liable to account to individual shareholders; an aggrieved shareholder must complain to the company.[95]

---

[89] *Citizens Theatre Ltd.*, 1946 S.C. 14. But see *Fraserburgh Commercial Co. Ltd.*, 1946 S.C. 444.

[90] S. 378; *Grahams' Morocco Co. Ltd.*, 1932 S.C. 269. This is not so if the declaration shows on its face that the resolution was not carried, as where it referred to proxy votes who could not vote on a show of hands: *Re Caratal New Mines* [1902] 2 Ch. 498; or the figures do not give the required majority: *Cowan* v. *Scottish Publishing Co.* (1892) 19 R. 437; *J. T. Clark & Co., Ltd.*, 1911 S.C. 243.

[91] S. 379.

[92] S. 380.

[93] S. 381.

[94] *Foss* v. *Harbottle* (1843) 2 Hare 461.

[95] *Orr* v. *Glasgow, etc. Ry. Co.* (1860) 22 D. (H.L.) 10; *Cameron* v. *Glenmorangie Distillery Co.* (1896) 23 R. 1092; *Brown* v. *Stewart* (1898) 1 F. 316.

Exceptions arise where the thing done is *ultra vires* of the company,[96] where the conduct is an infringement of the personal rights of shareholders, or where the activity may be called a fraud on the minority.[97]

Accounts and audit

The 1985 Act makes detailed provision for the keeping of accounting records. Every company must cause accounting records to be kept, sufficient to show and explain the company's transactions and to disclose with reasonable accuracy at any time the financial position of the company at that time.[98] The directors must prepare a profit and loss account for the financial year and a balance sheet as at the last day thereof.[99] Accounts must comply with Sch. 4; the profit and loss account and the balance sheet must respectively give a true and fair view of the profit or loss of the company for the financial year and of the state of affairs of the company at the end thereof.[1] There are detailed provisions as to group accounts of holding companies.[2] A report must be prepared by the directors for each financial year containing a fair review of the development of the business of the company and its subsidiaries during the financial year, and stating numerous prescribed matters.[3]

Auditors

A company must at each general meeting at which accounts are laid under S. 241 appoint an auditor or auditors to hold office till the next general meeting; if this is not done the Secretary of State may do so. Their remuneration is also fixed in general meeting.[4] A company may remove its auditors by ordinary resolution.[5] The auditors are entitled to attend any general meeting, to receive the same notices as members, and to be heard on any part of the business which concerns them as such.[6] Special notice is required for a resolution (a) appointing an auditor other than the retiring one; (b) filling a casual vacancy as auditor; (c) reappointing an auditor appointed to fill a casual vacancy; (d) removing an auditor from office before expiry of his term.[7]

---

[96] *Rixon* v. *Edinburgh Northern Tramways Co.* (1889) 16 R. 653; *Dunn* v. *Banknock Coal Co.* (1901) 9 S.L.T. 51.
[97] *Rixon* v. *Edinburgh Northern Tramways Co.* (1890) 18 R. 264; (1893) 20 R. (H.L.) 53; *Hannay* v. *Muir* (1898) 1 F. 306.
[98] Ss. 221–6.
[99] S. 227.
[1] S. 228.
[2] S. 229–34.
[3] S. 235.
[4] Ss. 384–5.
[5] S. 386.
[6] S. 387.
[7] S. 388.

A person is qualified for appointment as auditor only if he is a member of a recognized body of accountants, and is not an officer or servant of the company or an associated company.[8] An auditor may resign,[9] in which case he may requisition a meeting of the company.[10] The auditors of a subsidiary company must give the auditors of a holding company such information and explanation as they reasonably require as auditors.[11] An officer of a company commits an offence if he knowingly or recklessly makes to the auditors a statement which conveys any information required which is misleading, false, or deceptive in a material particular.[12]

The company's auditors must report to the members on the accounts examined by them and on every balance sheet and profit and loss account and on all group accounts, copies of which are to be laid before the company in general meeting. The report must state whether in the auditors' opinion the balance sheet and profit and loss account have been properly prepared in accordance with the Act, and whether in their opinion a true and fair view is given of the state of the company's affairs, of its profit or loss for the year, and, in the case of group accounts, of the affairs of the company and its subsidiaries.[13] It is the duty of the company's auditors to carry out such investigations as will enable them to form an opinion on whether proper accounting records have been kept and whether the balance sheet and profit and loss account are in agreement with the accounting records and returns. If they are not satisfied they should say so in their report. Every auditor has a right of access at all times to the company's books, accounts, and vouchers, and is entitled to require from the company's offices such information and explanations as he thinks necessary for the performance of the auditor's duties.[14] They should be conversant with their duties under the Act and seek to ascertain the true financial position of the company not merely check the accuracy of the figures.[15] They must act honestly and with reasonable skill and care.[16] But they are not concerned with the company's policy nor with whether it is well or badly managed.[17] They owe a duty of care also to persons who are foreseeably likely to act in reliance on the accounts.[18]

---

[8] S. 389.
[9] S. 390.
[10] S. 391.
[11] S. 392.
[12] S. 393.
[13] S. 236.
[14] S. 237.
[15] *Leeds Estate Co.* v. *Shepherd* (1887) 36 Ch. D. 787, 802; *Republic of Bolivia Exploration Syndicate Ltd.* [1914] 1 Ch. 139; *Fomento* v. *Selsdon Pen Co.* [1958] 1 W.L.R. 45.
[16] *Re London and General Bank* [1895] 2 Ch. 673; *Re Kingston Cotton Mill Co.* [1896] 2 Ch. 279.
[17] *Re London and General Bank, supra.*
[18] *JEB Fasteners* v. *Marks, Bloom & Co.* [1983] 1 All E.R. 583.

A company's balance sheet and copies laid before the company in general meeting must be signed by two directors.[19] Copies of the company's accounts must be sent to every member of the company, every debenture holder, and all other entitled persons at least 21 days before the annual general meeting, at which the accounts must be laid, the auditors report read and be open to inspection, and copies be sent to the registrar.[20] In certain cases modified or abridged accounts may be delivered.[21] The Secretary of State may alter the requirements as to annual accounts.[23] Accounts of special category companies, i.e. banking companies, insurance companies, and shipping companies, may be prepared under special accounting regulations.[23]

Distribution of profits and assets

A company may make a distribution of assets only out of profits available for the purpose; a distribution of assets includes dividends, but not an issue of shares as fully or partly paid bonus shares, redemption or purchase of any of the company's own shares out of capital or unrealized profits, reduction of share capital by reducing liability on shares not paid up or by paying off share capital, and a distribution of assets on winding up. Available profits are accumulated, realized profits less accumulated realized losses not previously written off.[24] A public company may make a distribution only if its net assets exceed its called-up share capital and undistributable reserves, i.e. share premium account, capital account, capital redemption reserve, excess of unrealized profits over its unrealized losses, and any other reserve which the company is prohibited from distributing, and the distribution does not reduce the assets below that standard.[25] The amount which may be distributed has to be justified by reference to the company's accounts.[26]

Unless the articles provide to the contrary[27] a company cannot be compelled to declare a dividend and the directors may transfer all profits to reserve.[28] Prima-facie dividends are payable in proportion to the amounts paid up on the shares.[29]

[19] Ss. 238–9.
[20] Ss. 240–6.
[21] Ss. 247–55.
[22] S. 256.
[23] Ss. 257–62 and Sch. 9.
[24] S. 263.
[25] S. 264. As to investment companies and insurance companies, see Ss. 265–9.
[26] Ss. 270–81.
[27] Paterson v. R. Paterson & Sons Ltd., 1917 S.C. (H.L.) 13.
[28] Wemyss Collieries Trust v. Melville (1905) 8 F. 143.
[29] Hoggan v. Tharsis Sulphur Co. (1882) 9 R. 1191.

MEMBERSHIP

Members of the company

The members collectively do not compose the company, which is a separate entity, but they own it by virtue of owning shares therein.[30] A person becomes a member by subscribing the Memorandum,[31] by signing and delivering to the Registrar an undertaking to take and pay for qualification shares as a director,[32] by agreeing to take shares on allotment and being registered,[33] by taking a transfer of shares and being registered, by taking the estate of a deceased or bankrupt member and being registered,[34] or by otherwise allowing his name to be on the register or holding himself out to be a member.[35] A minor may be a member;[36] an executor is not a member unless the becomes registered in his own name,[37] nor is a trustee in bankruptcy,[38] or *curator bonis*.[39] A person holding shares as trustee is a member.[40] A corporate body, if authorized by its constitution, may be a member.[41] A subsidiary company cannot be a member of its holding company save in prescribed circumstances.[42] If a company carries on business without at least 2 members and does so for more than 6 months, a person who is thereafter a member and knows that he is sole member is liable jointly and severally with the company for the company's debts contracted during the period.[43] A person ceases to be a member if he has the contract of membership rescinded for error or

[30] As to the difference between a member and a partner, see *Dove* v. *Young* (1868) 7 M. 304.

[31] S. 22; *Migotti's Case* (1867) L.R. 4 Eq. 238; *Re London and Provincial Coal Co.* (1877) 5 Ch. D. 525; *Nicol's Case* (1885) 29 Ch. D. 444; *Alexander* v. *Automatic Telephone Co.* [1900] 2 Ch. 63.

[32] S. 181.

[33] *Miln* v. *N.B. Fresh Fish Supply Co.* (1887) 15 R. 21.

[34] *McEwen* v. *City of Glasgow Bank* (1879) 6 R. 1315; *Gordon* v. *City of Glasgow Bank* (1879) 7 R. 55; *Galloway Saloon S.P. Co.* v. *Wallace* (1891) 19 R. 330.

[35] *Sewell's case* (1868) L.R. 3 Ch. 138; *Macdonald* v. *City of Glasgow Bank* (1879) 6 R. 621.

[36] *Hill* v. *City of Glasgow Bank* (1879) 7 R. 68; *I.R.C.* v. *Wilson* 1928 S.C. (H.L.) 42.

[37] *Buchan* v. *City of Glasgow Bank* (1879) 6 R. (H.L.) 44; *Macdonald* v. *City of Glasgow Bank* (1879) 6 R. 621.

[38] *Myles* v. *City of Glasgow Bank* (1879) 6 R. 718.

[39] *Lindsay's Curator* v. *City of Glasgow Bank* (1879) 6 R. 671.

[40] *Lumsden* v. *Buchanan* (1865) 3 M. (H.L.) 89; *Muir* v. *City of Glasgow Bank* (1879) 6 R. (H.L.) 21; *Cuninghame* v. *City of Glasgow Bank* (1879) 6 R. (H.L.) 98; *Roberts* v. *City of Glasgow Bank* (1879) 6 R. 805; *Smith* v. *City of Glasgow Bank* (1879) 6 R. 1017; *McEwen* v. *City of Glasgow Bank* (1879) 6 R. 1315. As to resigning trustees see *Alex. Mitchell* v. *City of Glasgow Bank* (1879) 6 R. (H.L.) 60; *Ker* v. *City of Glasgow Bank* (1879) 6 R. (H.L.) 52; *Sinclair* v. *City of Glasgow Bank* (1879) 6 R. 571; *Tochetti* v. *City of Glasgow Bank* (1879) 6 R. 789; *Dalgleish* v. *Land Feuing Co.* (1885) 13 R. 223. A trustee is entitled to relief from the trust estate: *Cunningham* v. *Montgomerie* (1879) 6 R. 1333, unless his holding was *ultra vires*: *Brownlie* v. *B's Trs.* (1879) 6 R. 1233. Trust beneficiaries are not members: *Gillespie* v. *City of Glasgow Bank* (1879) 6 R. (H.L.) 104.

[41] S. 375.

[42] S. 23.

[43] S. 24.

misrepresentation, or has the register rectified to the effect of removing his name, or by transferring his shares to another and the other person being registered, or by death, when another person receives a transfer from his executor and is registered, or if he is adjudicated bankrupt and his trustee disclaims the shares, or if his shares are forfeited, or sold by the company under a provision in the articles and the purchaser is registered in his place, or surrendered.

The register of members

Every company must keep a register of members at its registered office containing stated particulars of each member,[44] and changes in particulars must be registered. Companies registered in Scotland may, but those registered in England may not, record notice of any trust.[45] The register must be open for public inspection[46] but may be closed for not more than thirty days each year on notice given in the press.[47] The register is prima-facie evidence of any matter directed or authorized to be inserted therein.[48] A person must notify the company if he becomes interested in or acquires the shares of a company carrying unrestricted voting rights and quoted on a stock exchange if his holding thereby amounts to 5 per cent or more of the nominal value of the issued share capital of that class, and also if his holding ceases to amount to 5 per cent.[49] The company must keep a register of such information.[50]

The court may, on application by the person aggrieved or any member of the company or the company, rectify the register where the name of any person is without sufficient cause[51] entered in or omitted from the register of members, or where default is made or unnecessary delay takes place in entering on the register the fact that any person has ceased to be a member.[52] A person claiming to have his name removed should claim without delay after discovering that fact, or otherwise may be held to have approbated his registration.[53] Application may be made on such grounds as that the applicant had been induced to take shares by misrepresentation,[54] that the company had neglected to register a

---

[44] Ss. 352, 354, 722–3. The register is the document of title to shares: *I.R.C.* v. *Wilson*, 1927 S.C. 733.
[45] S. 360. See *Muir* v. *City of Glasgow Bank* (1879) 6 R. (H.L.) 21; contrast *Simpson* v. *Molson's Bank* [1895] A.C. 270.
[46] S. 356, *Garpel Haemetite Co.* v. *Andrew* (1866) 14 M. 617.
[47] S. 358. See *Oakes* v. *Turquand* (1867) L.R. 2 H.L. 325, 366.
[48] S. 361; *Reese River Silver Mining Co.* v. *Smith* (1869) L.R. 4 H.L. 80. It is not conclusive in questions between husband and wife: *Thomas* v. *City of Glasgow Bank* (1879) 6 R. 607; *Steedman* v. *Same* (1879) 7 R. 111; *Carmichael* v. *Same* (1879) 7 R. 118.
[49] Ss. 198–210.
[50] Ss. 211–19.
[51] *Elliot* v. *Mackie*, 1935 S.C. 81.
[52] S. 359; *Re Sussex Brick Co.* [1904] 1 Ch. 598.
[53] *Re Scottish Petroleum Co.* (1883) 23 Ch. D. 434; *Property Investment Co. of Scotland* v. *Duncan* (1887) 14 R. 299; *Linz* v. *Electric Wire Co. of Palestine* [1948] A.C. 371.
[54] *Stewart's Case* (1866) L.R. 1 Ch. App. 574; *City of Edinburgh Brewery Co.* v. *Gibson's Tr.*

transfer,[55] that shares had been improperly forfeited,[56] that the company, acting on a forged transfer, had removed the applicant's name.[57] An action of declarator is also competent.[58] It is questionable whether rectification by way of reduction *ope exceptionis* is competent.[59] Some cases are however too complicated for investigation under the rectification procedure.[60]

The rights of members

Members are entitled to numerous rights under statute, the Articles, and the general law, including the rights to annual reports from the directors on the affairs of the company and annual accounts, to payment of dividends as provided by the Articles and resolved on by the company and to repayment on winding up and possibly to participate in surplus assets then. They may sue the company to restrain deviations from the company's purpose, without needing to show that the thing done is hurtful to the company's interests.[61]

Liabilities of members

A member is liable, if the company is limited by shares, to pay if called on, the amount, if any, remaining unpaid of the nominal value of his shares.[62] If the company is limited by guarantee he is liable to have to pay the amount which he has undertaken by the Memorandum to contribute to the company's assets in the event of it being wound up.[62] If the company is unlimited, he is liable, jointly and severally with the other solvent members, for the whole debts of the company.[62] If at any time the number of members is reduced below the legal minimum, and the company carries on business for more than six months while so reduced, every member thereafter cognizant of the fact is severally liable for the whole debts of the company.[63] A shareholder who transfers his shares

---

(1869) 7 M. 886; *Anderson's Case* (1881) 17 Ch. D. 373; *Chambers v. Edinburgh and Glasgow Aerated Bread Co.* (1891) 18 R. 1039; *Blakiston v. London. etc., Discount Corpn.* (1894) 21 R. 417; *Gowans v. Dundee S.N. Co.* (1904) 6 F. 613; *Mair v. Rio Grande Rubber Estates,* 1913 S.C. (H.L.) 74. Contrast *Blaikie v. Coats* (1893) 21 R. 150; see also *Scottish Amalgamated Silks Ltd. v. Macalister,* 1930 S.L.T. 593.

[55] *Re Stranton Iron & Steel Co.* (1873) L.R. 16 Eq. 559.
[56] *Re Ystalyfera Gas Co.* [1887] W.N. 30.
[57] *Re Bahia etc. Ry. Co.* (1868) L.R. 3 Q.B. 584.
[58] *Kinghorn v. Glenyards Fireclay Co.* (1907) 14 S.L.T. 683.
[59] *National Bank of Scotland Glasgow Nominees Ltd. v. Adamson,* 1932 S.L.T. 492.
[60] *Blaikie, supra; Colquhoun's Tr. v. B.L. Co.* (1900) 2 F. 945; *Sleigh v. Glasgow and Transvaal Options Ltd.* (1904) 6 F. 420; *Kinghorn v. Glenyards Fireclay Co. Ltd.* (1907) 14 S.L.T. 683.
[61] *Smith v. G.S.W. Ry.* (1897) 4 S.L.T. 327; *Dunn v. Banknock Coal Co.* (1901) 9 S.L.T. 51.
[62] S. 502.
[63] S. 24.

within one year before the company is wound up is liable to be put on the
'B' list of contributories, and liable to the amount unpaid on his shares if
debts exist incurred while he was a member, and members on the 'A' list
cannot satisfy the contributions required from them.[64]

Meetings

The members of any company must be summoned to a general meeting
within 18 months of incorporation, and thereafter every year and not
more than 15 months from the previous one.[65] The usual business is to
hear an address on the state of the company's business, to consider and
approve the accounts, authorize a dividend, elect or re-elect directors, and
vote the auditors' remuneration. On default the Board of Trade may call
a meeting.[65] A quorum must be present throughout.[66] Extraordinary
general meetings may be called at any time, and must be called when a
proportion of the members request one.[67] Meetings of classes of shareholders have to be held when the Act or Articles or the terms of issue of
shares require, particularly when it is proposed to vary the rights of some
class of shareholders. Meetings require 14 days' notice (21 days for
A.G.M.), and notice must be given of resolutions proposed.[68] Voting at
general meetings is by show of hands,[69] without regard to number of
shares held or proxies held. Any member may demand a poll[70] and the
Articles frequently provide that in such a case each member has a vote for
each share held.[71] The Act gives the right of voting by proxy; i.e. by a
member appointing another person, not necessarily a member, to vote for
him.[72]

Resolutions

Decisions are expressed by resolutions; for most purposes an ordinary
resolution[73] passed by a simple majority of those present and voting is

[64] S. 502.
[65] Ss. 366–7.
[66] *Henderson* v. *Louttit & Co.* (1894) 21 R. 674; as to quorum see S. 370 and *M. Harris, Ltd.*, 1956 S.C. 207; *Neil McLeod & Sons Ltd.*, 1967 S.C. 16. One person does not make a 'meeting': *Prain & Sons*, 1947 S.C. 325. See also *Edinburgh Workmen's Houses Improvement Co.*, 1935 S.C. 56.
[67] S. 368. The requisition for such a meeting must state the objects of calling it but other competent business can be dealt with: *Ball* v. *Metal Industries, Ltd.*, 1957 S.C. 315.
[68] S. 369; see *Aberdeen Comb Works Co.* (1902) 10 S.L.T. 210; *Neil McLeod & Sons, Ltd.*, 1967 S.C. 16.
[69] Even if there is no opposition failure to call for a show of hands may be fatal: *Citizens Theatre*, 1946 S.C. 14; see also *Fraserburgh Commercial Co.*, 1946 S.C. 444.
[70] S. 378.
[71] S. 370.
[72] Ss. 372–3.
[73] See *Bushell* v. *Faith* [1970] 1 All E.R. 53.

enough. An extraordinary resolution is one passed by a three-fourths majority of those voting in person or by proxy at a general meeting of which notice specifying the intention to propose the resolution as an extraordinary resolution has been duly given.[74] Such resolutions are frequently required to sanction winding up or voluntary liquidation or to obtain the sanction of a class of shareholders. A special resolution requires the same majority and at least 21 days notice must have been given of intention to propose it as a special resolution.[74] Special resolutions are required for important business such as altering the Memorandum or Articles or reducing capital.[75] Unless a poll is demanded, a declaration by the chairman that the resolution is carried is conclusive.[76] A resolution requiring special notice requires that prior notice must be given to the company, and by the company to the shareholders when calling the meeting.[77] A resolution cannot receive effect if the Minute of Meeting shows that it had not been passed by the requisite majority.[78] Printed copies of extraordinary and special resolutions and those binding on classes of shareholders must be registered with the Registrar.[79]

Minutes

Companies must keep minutes of proceedings of general meetings and when signed by the chairman they are evidence of the proceedings,[80] but not conclusive evidence.[81] A shareholder is entitled to a court order for inspection of the minutes of general meetings.[82]

SHARE CAPITAL, SHARES, AND DIVIDENDS

Every company having a share capital, whether limited by shares or by guarantee, must have a nominal or authorized capital with which it is incorporated.[83] It need not, however, issue shares to this full extent; the issued capital is the amount of shares actually issued to shareholders, the remainder being unissued capital. The full nominal value of the shares issued is not always fully paid-up and there may be liability on the

---

[74] S. 378; see *N. of Scotland, etc. S.N. Co.*, 1920 S.C. 94; *Rennie* v. *Crichton's Ltd.*, 1927 S.L.T. 459; *Neil McLeod & Sons, Ltd, supra.*

[75] Special resolutions are required by Ss. 4, 9, 135.

[76] S. 378.

[77] S. 379.

[78] *Cowan* v. *Scottish Publishing Co.* (1892) 19 R. 437; *J.T. Clark & Co.*, 1911 S.C. 243; *Graham's Morocco Co., Ltd.*, 1932 S.C. 269; *Citizen's Theatre, Ltd.*, 1946 S.C. 14; *Fraserburgh Commercial Co.*, 1946 S.C. 444.

[79] Ss. 380, 572.

[80] S. 382.

[81] cf. *Fraserburgh Commerical Co., supra.*

[82] *McCusker* v. *McRae*, 1966 S.C. 253.

[83] S. 2(5).

shareholders for the amount uncalled on each share; hence there may be paid-up and uncalled capital. Reserve capital is any part of the uncalled capital which the company has determined may be called up only if the company is being wound up.[84] Shares are designated as of stated nominal values but their true economic and exchange values may be more or less than the nominal values, depending on the company's assets, record, earnings, and prospects.

Shares

A share is an incorporeal right of ownership of a determinate fraction of the company.[85] It carries the rights to receive reports and accounts from the directors, to attend and vote at meetings, to receive a dividend in accordance with the company's prosperity and the conditions attaching under the Articles to the class of shares, and, on winding up, to a proportionate share of the capital and other realized assets of the company. It carries the liability on call to pay to the company any proportion of the nominal value of the share as yet uncalled and on winding up to be put on the B list of contributories.[86] It is arrestable in security or in execution,[87] save that stock of the Royal Bank of Scotland is, by the bank's charter, adjudgeable only.

The company may, if authorized by its Articles,[88] create different classes of shares having different rights, particularly in relation to voting, dividends, and winding up. The Articles may contain provisions for the variation of the rights of the classes of shares. Preference shares may have a preference as to capital or dividend, or both, or carry other preferential rights. Preference shares may be redeemable on conditions.[89] If preference shares carry a preferential right to dividend, the dividend is prima facie cumulative,[90] but may be non-cumulative.[91] Prima facie a preferential dividend[92] of specified percentage excludes further participation in

---

[84] *Re Mayfair Property Co.* [1898] 2 Ch. 28.

[85] Not of the company's assets; the shareholders own the company; the company owns its property and assets. See also *Borland's Tr.* v. *Steel Bros.* [1901] 1 Ch. 279; *I.R.C.* v. *Crossman* [1937] A.C. 26.   [86] Ss. 502–3.

[87] *Sinclair* v. *Staples* (1860) 22 D. 600; *Valentine* v. *Grangemouth Coal Co.* (1897) 35 S.L.R. 12; *Harvey's Yoker Distillery, Ltd.,* v. *Sinclair* (1901) 8 S.L.T. 369; *American Mortgage Co. of Scotland* v. *Sidway*, 1908 S.C. 500.

[88] If the Memorandum expressly provides for equality or specifies the classes of shares, this cannot be altered by the Articles: *Campbell* v. *Rofe* [1933] A.C. 91; *Marshall, Fleming & Co. Ltd.*, 1938 S.C. 873, 878. If the Memorandum does not provide for equality preferential rights may be conferred by the Articles, there being no implication in the Memorandum that all shares shall be equal: *Humboldt Redwood Co. Ltd.* v. *Coats*, 1908 S.C. 751.

[89] Ss. 159–61.

[90] *Webb* v. *Earle* (1875) L.R. 20 Eq. 556; *Partick, etc. Gas Co.* v. *Taylor* (1888) 15 R. 711; *Miln* v. *Arizona Copper Co.* (1899) 1 F. 935; *Ferguson & Forrester, Ltd.* v. *Buchanan*, 1920 S.C. 154.

[91] *Staples* v. *Eastman Photographic Co.* [1896] 2 Ch. 303; *Thornycroft & Co. Ltd.* v. *T.* (1927) 44 T.L.R. 9.

[92] *Will* v. *United Lankat Plantations Co. Ltd.* [1914] A.C. 11.

profits, and gives no priority to repayment of capital in winding up.[93] Non-privileged shares are usually designated ordinary shares. There may also be deferred shares, or shares of other categories with particular rights and conditions attached to them. Shares may carry no, or only restricted, voting rights. The right of preference shareholders to vote at meetings is usually restricted to occasions when their rights are being varied or their dividend in arrears.

Variation of rights of shareholders

If the Articles permit, the rights of any class of shareholders may be varied or abrogated by the consent of a specified proportion of the holders of shares of that class or by a resolution passed at a separate meeting of the holders of those shares, but the holders of at least 15 per cent of the issued shares of that class may apply to the court to have the variation cancelled, and the variation is then ineffective until confirmed by the court.[94] The company may validly pay money to the shareholders to secure their acquiescence.[95]

Partly paid shares: calls

When shares are issued the full nominal value thereof is normally paid up at once or by instalments over a short period, but it is competent to have the shares only partly paid and the balance liable to be called up when the company so decides. The power to make a call must be exercised for the general benefit of the company[96] and is exercised by resolution of the directors in accordance with the Articles.[97] Payment may be enforced. Shares may be issued at a premium, the excess receipts over nominal value being carried to a special share premium account,[98] or with the sanction of the court and on conditions, at a discount,[99] and either for cash or for consideration other than cash, such as fully paid up shares in another company, or the goodwill of a business.

---

[93] *Monkland Iron Co. Ltd.* v. *Henderson* (1883) 10 R. 494; *Williamson-Buchanan Steamers,* 1936 S.L.T. 106.

[94] Ss. 125–7; *Oban and Aultmore-Glenlivet Distilleries Ltd* (1903) 5 F. 1140; *Marshall Fleming & Co. Ltd,* 1938 S.C. 873; *White* v. *Bristol Aeroplane Co. Ltd.* [1953] Ch. 65.

[95] *Caledonian Ins. Co.* v. *Scottish American Investment Co. Ltd.,* 1951 S.L.T. 23.

[96] *Alexander* v. *Automatic Telephone Co.* [1900] 2 Ch. 56.

[97] *Odessa Tramways* v. *Mendel* (1878) 8 Ch. D. 235; *Universal Corpn. Ltd.* v. *Hughes,* 1909 S.C. 1434.

[98] S. 130; prior to 1948 premiums could be distributed as dividends; cf. *Cameron* v. *Glenmorangie Distillery Co.* (1896) 23 R. 1092.

[99] Ss. 100, 112; prior to 1929 this was generally incompetent: see *Klenck* v. *E.I. Co. for Exploration and Mining* (1888) 16 R. 271; *Newburgh and N. Fife Ry.* v. *N.B. Ry.,* 1913 S.C. 1166; *Penang Foundry Co.* v. *Gardiner,* 1913 S.C. 1203.

Share premiums

If a company issues shares at a premium, the total premium must be transferred to a share premium account which may be used to pay up unissued shares to be allotted to members as fully paid bonus shares, or in writing off preliminary expenses or expenses of any issue of shares or debentures, or in providing for the premium payable on redemption of debentures of the company.[1]

Redeemable Shares

A company limited by shares or by guarantee and having a share capital may, if authorized by its articles, issue redeemable shares. No such shares may be issued if there are no issued shares which are not redeemable. Redeemable shares may not be redeemed unless fully paid.[2] There are restrictions on financing of redemption.[3] Such a company may also purchase its own shares by following one of the procedures set out in Ss. 163–70.[4] Private companies may redeem or purchase their own shares out of capital but certain members or creditors may object and the court may cancel the transaction.[5]

Acquisition of shares

Shares are acquired by application and allotment when an issue of shares is made, or subsequently by purchase, gift, or bequest from an existing holder. If an application for an allotment of shares is accepted, the applicant may be entered on the register of members.[6] Allotment letters may be subject to conditions.[7] In the case of a public company, on first allotment of shares offered to the public for subscription, no allotment may be made unless the minimum subscription has been subscribed and the sum payable on application therefor has been received by the company.[8]

Share certificates and share warrants

Share certificates issued under the seal of the company, specifying the shares held by the member, are the shareholder's prima facie evidence of

---

[1] S. 130. Certain reliefs are allowed: Ss. 131–4.
[2] S. 159.
[3] Ss. 160–1.
[4] S. 162, overruling *Trevor* v. *Whitworth* (1887) 12 App. Cas. 409.
[5] Ss. 171–81.
[6] See *Mason* v. *Benhar Coal Co.* (1882) 9 R. 883; *Goldie* v. *Torrance* (1882) 10 R. 174; *Chapman* v. *Sulphite Pulp Co.* (1892) 19 R. 837; *Nelson* v. *Fraser* (1906) 14 S.L.T. 513.
[7] *Liqr. of Consolidated Copper Co. of Canada* v. *Peddie* (1877) 5 R. 393; *National House Property Investment Co.* v. *Watson*, 1908 S.C. 888.
[8] S. 83.

title to his shares in the company.[9] Certificates must be completed by the company and ready for delivery within two months after allotment.[10] A share certificate is not negotiable and confers no right by being handed to another. The company is barred from maintaining that a share certificate, accepted in good faith, untruly represents what it states, e.g. that the shares are fully paid.[11] but a company is not liable on a forged certificate.[12] Share warrants to bearer can be issued only if the shares are fully paid up and the Articles so authorize, and only by public companies.[13] Where issued, they are customarily treated as negotiable instruments,[14] and are transferred by the delivery of the warrant. Subject to the Articles, the bearer of a warrant is entitled to surrender it and be registered as a member.

Transfer and transmission of shares

Shares are incorporeal moveable property and may be transferred voluntarily, unless restricted by the Articles, mortgaged, or transferred in security of debt, and are transmitted on death or bankruptcy. Shares are freely transferable in pursuance of a contract of sale entered into privately or through the intervention of stockbrokers, or by way of gift. The sale or gift is effected by completion of a share transfer form in the form authorized by the Articles, or a stock transfer form in the form introduced by the Stock Transfer Act, 1963, the lodging of it with the share certificate at the company's transfer office, and the securing of the entry of the new owner's name on the register.[15] Until registration the transferor holds as quasi-trustee for the transferee.[16] The company is not concerned with objections to the transferee's right.[17] The directors of private companies normally have under the Articles a discretion to refuse to register transfers, which will not be interfered with by the court unless the directors have acted corruptly or capriciously.[18] The power will be pre-

---

[9] S. 186; see also *Woodhouse & Rawson v. Hosack* (1894) 2 S.L.T. 279.
[10] S. 185.
[11] *Re Bahia and San Francisco Ry.* (1868) L.R. 3 Q.B. 584; *Clavering, Son & Co. v. Goodwins, Jardine & Co. Ltd.* (1891) 18 R. 652; *Penang Foundry Co. v. Gardiner*, 1913 S.C. 1203; cf. *Balkis Consolidated Co. v. Tomlinson* [1893] A.C. 396; *Bloomenthal v. Ford* [1897] A.C. 156.
[12] *Clavering, Son & Co. v. Goodwins, Jardine & Co.* (1891) 18 R. 652; *Ruben v. Great Fingall Consolidated* [1906] A.C. 439; *South London Greyhound Racecources, Ltd. v. Wake* [1931] 1 Ch. 496.
[13] S. 188.
[14] *Webb, Hale & Co. v. Alexandria Water Co.* (1905) 21 T.L.R. 572.
[15] *Morrison v. Harrison* (1876) 3 R. 406; *National Bank Glasgow Nominees Ltd. v. Adamson*, 1932 S.L.T. 492.
[16] *Stevenson v. Wilson* 1907 S.C. 445; *Tennant's Trs. v. Tennant*, 1946 S.C. 420.
[17] *Shaw v. Caledonian Ry.* (1890) 17 R. 466.
[18] *Re Coalport China Co.* [1895] 2 Ch. 404; *Stewart v. James Keiller & Sons* (1902) 4 F. 657; *Stevenson v. Wilson*, 1907 S.C. 445; *Kennedy v. N.B. Wireless Schools*, 1916 1 S.L.T. 407; *Re Bede S.S. Co.* [1917] 1 Ch. 123; *Lyle & Scott v. Scott's Trs.*, 1959 S.C. (H.L.) 64; *Safeguard*

sumed to have been properly exercised, for the company's benefit.[19] So, too, the Articles may require a shareholder first to offer his shares to the company or other shareholders therein.[20] The directors must refuse to register a transfer when the company has stopped payment or ceased to be a going concern, although liquidation has not commenced.[21] A forged transfer is a nullity and a company which has removed the holder's name in reliance on a forged transfer must replace it.[22] The Forged Transfers Acts, 1891 and 1892, empower a company to make pecuniary compensation for any loss arising from a transfer of shares or stock in pursuance of a forged transfer, or of a transfer under a forged power of attorney.

A company may not acquire its own shares by subscription, purchase, or otherwise, save that a company limited by shares may acquire any of its own fully paid shares otherwise than for valuable consideration and any company may acquire its own shares in a reduction of capital and in certain other stated cases.[23]

On death shares pass as moveable property to the member's executor, who may be registered[24] but may[25] transfer the deceased's shares without himself being registered. If the executor becomes registered, he becomes a shareholder for all purposes.[26] So long as the deceased's name remains on the register his estate is liable in connction with the shares.[27] A creditor may do diligence against shares by arrestment.[28] On bankruptcy shares are vested in the trustee in bankruptcy by the Act and Warrant,[29] and he may thereby become registered,[30] but may transfer them without so doing. Certification of an instrument of transfer is to be taken as a representation by the company to any person acting on the faith of the certification that there have been produced documents showing a prima-facie title to the shares or debentures in the transferor, but not that he has any title to the shares or debentures. A company is under the same

---

Industrial Investments v. *Nat. Westminster Bank* [1980] 3 All E.R. 849. The refusal must be exercised by resolution: *Shepherd's Trs.* v. *S.*, 1950 S.C. (H.L.) 60.

[19] *Berry* v. *Tottenham Hotspur F.C.* [1936] 3 All E.R. 554; *Re Smith and Fawcett, Ltd.* [1942] Ch. 304.

[20] *Smith Ltd.* v. *Colquhoun's Tr.* (1901) 3 F. 981; see also *Shepherd's Trs.* v. *S.*, 1950 S.C. (H.L.) 60; *Lyle & Scott* v. *Scott's Trs.*, 1959 S.C. (H.L.) 64.

[21] *Nelson Mitchell* v. *City of Glasgow Bank* (1879) 6 R. (H.L.) 66; *Dodds* v. *Cosmopolitan Ins. Corpn., Ltd.*, 1915 S.C. 992.

[22] *Sheffield Corpn.* v. *Barclay* [1905] A.C. 392.

[23] S. 143.

[24] *Trotter* v. *B.L. Bank* (1898) 6 S.L.T. 213; *Craig* v. *Caledonian Ry.* (1905) 13 S.L.T. 643.

[25] S. 183.

[26] *Buchan* v. *City of Glasgow Bank* (1879) 6 R. (H.L.) 44; *Bell* v. *Same* (1879) 6 R. (H.L.) 55; *McEwen* v. *Same* (1879) 6 R. 1315; *Gordon* v. *Same* (1879) 7 R. 55.

[27] cf. *Stewart's Trs.* v. *Evans* (1871) 9 M. 810; *Heritable Securities Investment Assocn. Ltd.* v. *Miller's Trs.* (1893) 20 R. 675.

[28] *Sinclair* v. *Staples* (1860) 22 D. 600; *American Mortgage Co. of Scotland* v. *Sidway*, 1908 S.C. 500.

[29] Bankruptcy (Sc.) Act, 1985, S. 31; *Lindsay* v. *City of Glasgow Bank* (1879) 6 R. 671; *Myles* v. *City of Glasgow Bank* (1879) 6 R. 718.

[30] *Lumsden* v. *Peddie* (1866) 5 M. 34.

liability to a person action on the faith of a false certification made negligently as it would if made fraudulently.[31]

Disclosure of interests in shares

Sections 198 to 220 impose on individuals in certain circumstances duties to notify the company of the interest they have, or have had, in its shares. The aim is disclosure of substantial interests in voting shares so as to make known who controls companies and to avoid underhand take-overs. The obligation to disclose may arise from an agreement which includes provision by one or more parties to acquire interests in shares of a particular public company.

Every public company must keep a register for the purposes of Sections 198 to 202 and enter disclosed information therein.[32] It may by notice require a person to confirm or deny that he has been interested in shares, and must register interests disclosed.[33]

Transfer of shares in security

Shares may be transferred in security of a loan or other obligation. The shares may be transferred outright to the lender who becomes registered, but is under an obligation to retransfer the shares when his debt is repaid.[34] Or the shares may be transferred to a nominee who holds them in trust for the lender till the debt is repaid, and then for the borrower and, it may be, for the lender again for another advance. A deposit of the share certificate by itself creates no right of security whatever in Scotland,[35] but it may be accompanied by a transfer signed by the borrower, enabling the lender at any time to have himself registered, or to hand back the certificate and destroy the transfer when his loan is repaid. Such a transfer may be void under the Blank Bonds and Trusts Act 1696, c. 25,[36] and an uncompleted transfer could be defeated by another creditor's diligence or by the debtor's obtaining a duplicate certificate from the company and selling the shares to an innocent purchaser who has himself registered. If valid, the borrower must do nothing to prevent the lender having himself registered.[37]

---

[31] S. 184.
[32] S. 211.
[33] S. 212–3.
[34] *Morrison* v. *Harrison* (1876) 3 R. 406; *Guild* v. *Young* (1884) 22 S.L.R. 520; *Siemens Bros.* v. *Burns* [1918] 2 Ch. 324.
[35] *Christie* v. *Ruxton* (1862) 24 D. 1182; *Scottish Provident Inst.* v. *Cohen* (1888) 16 R. 112; *Robertson* v. *B.L. Co.* (1891) 18 R. 1225.
[36] cf. *Shaw* v. *Caledonian Ry.* (1890) 17 R. 466, 478; see also *Guild* v. *Young* (1884) 22 S.L.R. 520; *Gourlay* v. *Mackie* (1887) 14 R. 403.
[37] *Hooper* v. *Herts* [1906] 1 Ch. 459.

Calls on shares

Where shares have not been fully paid up the directors may call up part
or all of the amount still unpaid on each share. The power to make calls
must be exercised for the benefit of the company[38] and normally on all
the shareholders *pari passu*.[39] Any limitations on calls,[40] and the procedure therefor, provided in the Articles must be adhered to. A member is
entitled to notice stating when, where and to whom the call is payable.[41]
The sum called up may be enforced by action[42] or, if authorized, by
forfeiture of the shares.[43] The member may be able, in defence, to plead
that he was induced by misrepresentation to become a member,[44] or that
the call was not validly made.[45] A call may be made to equalize the values
of shares prior to liquidation.[46] In a liquidation the court may make and
enforce payment of calls.[47]

Increase of capital

A limited company may in general meeting increase its share capital,
consolidate and divide its share capital into shares of larger amount,
convert paid-up shares into stock and reconvert stock into shares, subdi-
vide its shares, or cancel shares and thereby diminish the share capital.[48]

Share capital may be divided into different classes, e.g. preference,
ordinary, and deferred shares; the rights of each class must be stated in
the articles.[49]

Where share capital is divided into shares of different classes, the rights
of holders of a class of shares may be varied only by compliance with
conditions and procedural requirements, always involving the consent of
the holders of that class of shares. In certain circumstances some shareholders may apply to the court to have the variation cancelled.[50]

---

[38] *Alexander* v. *Automatic Telephone Co.* [1900] 2 Ch. 56.
[39] *Galloway* v. *Hallé Concerts Society* [1915] 2 Ch. 233.
[40] *Universal Corpn.* v. *Hughes*, 1909 S.C. 1434.
[41] *Ferguson* v. *Central Halls Co.* (1887) 8 R. 997; *Re Cawley and Co.* (1889) 42 Ch. D. 209.
[42] *Mitchell* (1863) 1 M. 1116; *Galloway Saloon S.P. Co.* v. *Wallace* (1891) 19 R. 330.
[43] *Ferguson* v. *Central Halls Co.* (1887) 8 R. 997; *Re Cawley and Co.* (1889) 42 Ch. D. 209.
[44] *City of Edinburgh Brewery Co.* v. *Gibson's Tr.* (1867) 7 M. 886; *Scottish Amalgamated
Silks* v. *Macalister*, 1930 S.L.T. 593.
[45] *Ferguson, supra.*
[46] *Paterson* v. *MacFarlane* (1875) 2 R. 490; *Stewart* v. *Liqr. of Scoto-American Sugar
Syndicate, Ltd.* (1901) 3 F. 585.
[47] Ss. 553, 569.
[48] Ss. 121–4.
[49] The dividend on preference shares is prima facie cumulative: *Partick Gas Co.* v. *Taylor*
(1888) 15 R. 711; *Miln* v. *Arizona Copper Co.* (1889) 1 F. 935; *Ferguson and Forrester Ltd.* v.
Buchanan, 1920 S.C. 154. As to priority for repayment see *Monkland Iron Co.* v. *Henderson*
(1883) 10 R. 494. *Williamson-Buchanan Steamers*, 1936 S.L.T. 106. *Wilsons & Clyde* v.
Scottish Ins. Corpn., 1949 S.C. (H.L.) 90.
[50] Ss. 125–9.

Reduction of share capital

A company having a share capital must maintain its capital as the fund to which creditors look for payment of their debts. But a company may, if authorized by its Articles,[51] by special resolution reduce its share capital in any way, as by reducing liability on any shares not paid up, cancelling paid-up share capital lost or not represented by assets, or paying off capital in excess of the company's wants. The proposal requires the confirmation of the court.[52] The court will not ratify a reduction effected without its approval.[53] If a reduction brings the nominal value of its allotted share capital below the authorized minimum the reduction cannot be registered unless the court so orders or the company is re-registered as a private company.[54]

If a public company's assets fall to half of its called-up share capital the directors must call an extraordinary general meeting to consider what steps should be taken.[55]

In general a company having a share capital may not acquire its own shares, by purchase, subscription, or otherwise, but a company limited by shares may acquire its own fully paid shares otherwise than for valuable consideration, by redemption or purchase of shares under Ss. 159–81, by acquisition in a reduction of capital, by purchase in pursuance of an order of the court, or by forfeiture of shares.[56] A company may not acquire its own partly paid shares through a nominee, subject to exceptions.[57] In cases not covered by S. 143 or S. 144, Ss. 146–50 provide for the treatment of shares acquired by a public company.

In general it is not lawful for a company to give financial assistance to a person acquiring or proposing to acquire or who has acquired shares in the company,[58] but there are excepted cases where the principal purpose is not for the acquisition and it is given in good faith in the interests of the company, nor to reduce or discharge any liability for the acquisition of shares and it is given in good faith, and the section does not prohibit various ordinary acts such as payment of dividends or an allotment of bonus shares.[59]

---

[51] *Avery & Co. Ltd.* (1890) 17 R. 1101.
[52] Ss. 135–8, 140; e.g. *Balmenach-Glenlivet Distillery v. Croall* (1906) 8 F. 1135; *Stevenson, Anderson & Co.,* 1951 S.C. 346; *Caldwell v. C.,* 1916 S.C. (H.L.) 120; *Wm. Dixon Ltd.,* 1948 S.C. 511; *Wilsons & Clyde Coal Co. v. Scottish Insurance Corpn.,* 1949 S.C. (H.L.) 90; *Westburn Sugar Refineries Ltd.,* 1951 S.C. (H.L.) 57; *David Bell Ltd.,* 1954 S.C. 33.
[53] *Alexander Henderson, Ltd.,* 1967 S.L.T. (Notes) 17.
[54] S. 139.
[55] S. 142.
[56] S. 143.
[57] Ss. 144–5.
[58] Ss. 151–2; and see *Belmont v. Williams Furniture* [1980] 1 All E.R. 393.
[59] S. 153. There is a special restriction for public companies in S. 154, and a relaxation for private companies in Ss. 155–8.

Lien on shares

A company has at common law,[60] and commonly by its Articles also reserves for itself,[61] a lien on a mcmber's shares for his debts and liabilities to the company,[62] for such debts as money due under a call or other claims. Liens not authorized by the Acts are void.[63] The lien is enforceable according to the Articles, usually by power to sell the shares on default. It is doubtful if a lien can be enforced by forfeiture of shares.[64]

Forfeiture and surrender of shares

The Articles commonly provide for the forfeiture of shares for non-payment of calls.[65] The power must be exercised bona fide and for the benefit of the company,[66] and in strict accordance with the Articles.[67] If exercised the shareholder ceases to be a member[68] and the shares may be sold by the company. Forfeiture prima facie prevents a claim for unpaid calls, but the Articles may provide that such liability continues, and such an obligation is enforceable.[69] The court may set aside a forfeiture as invalid[70] and give damages for an irregular forfeiture,[70] but will not relieve a shareholder from a forfeiture if duly incurred and properly effected.[71] The company may have power to, and in fact, annul a forfeiture but only with the consent of the former member.[72] A forfeited share may normally, under the Articles, be sold to a third party, who acquires a good title thereto from the company, free from liability for past calls. If the Articles empower the company to accept surrender, shares may be surrendered to it in lieu of forfeiture,[73] but surrender is incompetent as a means of avoiding liability for uncalled capital, as this would amount to

[60] *Bell's Tr.* v. *Coatbridge Tinplate Co.* (1886) 14 R. 246.
[61] As to changing the Articles to create a lien, see *Liqr. of McArthur, Ltd.* v. *Gulf Line, Ltd.*, 1909 S.C. 732.
[62] *Re General Exchange Bank* (1871) L.R. 6 Ch. App. 818; *Bradford Banking Co.* v. *Briggs* (1887) 2 App. Cas. 29; *Stark* v. *Fife and Kinross Coal Co.* (1899) 1 F. 1173; *Paul's Tr.* v. *Thomas Justice & Sons*, 1912 S.C. 1303.
[63] S. 150.
[64] *General Property and Investment Co.* v. *Matheson's Trs.* (1888) 16 R. 282; *Salt* v. *Marquis of Northampton* [1892] A.C. 1.
[65] *Ferguson* v. *Central Halls Co.* (1881) 8 R. 997; *Allen* v. *Gold Reefs of W. Africa* [1900] 1 Ch. 656; *Hopkinson* v. *Mortimer, Harley & Co.* [1917] 1 Ch. 646.
[66] *Clarke* v. *Hart* (1858) 6 H.L.C. 633; *Garden Gully Mining Co.* v. *McLister* (1875) 1 App. Cas. 39; *In re Esparto Trading Co.* (1879) 12 Ch. D. 191.
[67] *Clarke, supra; Ferguson, supra.*
[68] *Liqrs. of Mount Morgan (West) Gold Mine* v. *McMahon* (1891) 18 R. 772.
[69] *Mount Morgan, supra; Ladies Dress Assocn.* v. *Pulbrook* [1900] 2 Q.B. 376.
[70] *Re New Chile Co.* (1890) 45 Ch. D. 598.
[71] *Sparks* v. *Liverpool Waterworks Co.* (1807) 13 Ves. 428.
[72] *Taylor* v. *Union Heritable Securities Co.* (1889) 16 R. 711; *Lackworthy's Case* [1903] 1 Ch. 711.
[73] *General Property Investment Co. and Liqr.* v. *Craig* (1891) 18 R. 389; *Trevor* v. *Whitworth* (1887) 12 App. Cas. 409; *Gill* v. *Arizona Copper Co.* (1900) 2 F. 843.

an unauthorized reduction of capital.[74] If surrender is valid, the shares can be re-issued. Unless the shares are previously disposed of the company must within three years cancel the shares and diminish the share capital.[75]

Rights issues and bonus issues

When an existing company wishes to raise further capital it may make a fresh issue of shares by the same means as an initial issue, but frequently makes a 'rights' issue, giving existing shareholders the right to acquire new shares in a fixed proportion to their existing holdings, e.g. one for every five held, or it may make a bonus issue, in which shares are paid for out of profits and distributed free to the existing shareholders in proportion to their holdings, in lieu of or in addition to dividend. Issues to existing members, including rights issues and bonus issues, have to satisfy the requirements of a prospectus, though it may be abridged.[76]

Profits and dividends

Unless restricted by its Memorandum or Articles a company has implied power to distribute some of its profits to its members as dividend.[77] It is in the discretion of the directors to recommend how much of any year's divisible profits shall be resolved by the members to be distributed as dividend. No dividend may be paid out of capital;[78] this is completely *ultra vires*[79] and directors who are parties thereto are jointly and severally liable to repay the sum.[80] Dividends may be paid only out of profits available for the purpose, which includes reserves of past trading profits and realized capital profits but requires provision out of profits for the depreciation or loss of circulating capital.[81] In the absence of provision in the Articles dividend falls to be distributed in proportion to amounts of nominal rather than paid-up capital.[82] On declaration a dividend be-

---

[74] *Bellerby* v. *Rowland and Marwood's SS. Co.* [1902] 2 Ch. 14.
[75] Ss. 146–9.
[76] Ss. 56, 66.
[77] See *Paterson* v. *R. Paterson & Sons*, 1917 S.C. (H.L.) 13.
[78] Ss. 263, 275.
[79] *Beaumont* v. *G.N.S. Ry.* (1868) 6 M. 1027; *Flitcroft's case* (1882) 21 Ch. D. 519; *Trevor* v. *Whitworth* (1887) 12 App. Cas. 409.
[80] *Flitcroft's case, supra; Liqrs. of City of Glasgow Bank* v. *Mackinnon* (1882) 9 R. 535.
[81] *Lee* v. *Neuchatel Asphalte Co. Ltd.* (1889) 41 Ch. D. 1; *Niddrie & Benhar Coal Co.* v. *Hurll* (1891) 18 R. 805; *Lubbock* v. *British Bank of S. America* [1892] 2 Ch. 198; *Verner* v. *General and Commercial Investment Trust Ltd.* [1824] 2 Ch. 239; *Wilmer* v. *McNamara & Co. Ltd.* [1895] 2 Ch. 245; *City Property Investment Trust Corpn.* v. *Thorburn* (1897) 25 R. 361; *Cadell* v. *Scottish Investment Trust Co.* (1901) 8 S.L.T. 480; 9 S.L.T. 299; *Foster* v. *New Trinidad Lake Asphalt Co. Ltd.* [1901] 1 Ch. 208; *Bond* v. *Barrow Haematite Steel Co.* [1902] 1 Ch. 353; *Ammonia Soda Co. Ltd.* v. *Chamberlain* [1918] 1 Ch. 266.
[82] *Oakbank Oil Co.* v. *Crum* (1882) 10 R. (H.L.) 11; *Birch* v. *Cropper* (1889) 14 App. Cas. 525; contrast *Hoggan* v. *Tharsis Sulphur & Copper Co.* (1882) 9 R. 1191.

comes a debt by the company to the shareholders.[83] Where shares are
entitled by the Articles to a preferential rate of dividend, prima facie this
is cumulative.[84] Profits not distributed as dividend may, subject to the
Memorandum and Articles, be put in reserve, or capitalized for redemption of redeemable preference shares, or otherwise applied as permitted
by the Act.[85] Certain assets are treated as undistributable reserves.[86]

BORROWING AND DEBENTURES

Borrowing

A company may borrow money only if it has power to do so; such a
power is incidental to the company's objects in the case of a trading
company.[87] A non-trading company must have the power in its
constitution.[88] A company with power to borrow has power to charge its
property and give security for repayment;[89] power to borrow may include
power to assign in security uncalled capital.[90] The Articles usually authorize the directors to exercise the borrowing powers, sometimes subject to
the sanction of a general meeting, and may impose a limit on amount, any
borrowing beyond which is *ultra vires*. If borrowing is *ultra vires* of the
directors it may be ratified by the company.[91] If borrowing is *ultra vires*
of the company, securities given are void, and the lender may recover
damages for the directors' breach of warranty that they had power to
borrow.[92]

A company having power may borrow in any way competent to a
natural person, by bank overdraft, unsecured loan, or by granting bills or

---

[83] *Carron Co. v. Hunter* (1868) 6 M. (H.L.) 106; *Re Seven and Wye and Severn Bridge Co.*
[1896] 1 Ch. 559.
[84] *Webb v. Earle* (1875) L.R. 20 Eq. 556.
[85] S. 58; see *Arizona Copper Co. v. London Scottish American Trust* (1897) 24 R. 658;
Cadell v. Scottish Investment Trust (1901) 9 S.L.T. 299; *Wemyss Collieries Trust, Ltd. v.
Melville* (1905) 8 F. 143.
[86] Ss. 264, 275.
[87] *General Auction Co. v. Smith* [1891] 3 Ch. 432; *Re Badger, Mansell v. Cobham* [1905] 1
Ch. 568.
[88] *Wenlock v. River Dee Co.* (1885) 10 App. Cas. 354.
[89] *Paterson's Trs. v. Caledonian Heritable Security Co.* (1886) 13 R. 369; *General Auction
Co. v. Smith* [1891] 3 Ch. 432.
[90] *Newton v. Anglo-Australian Co's Debenture Holders* [1895] A.C. 244; *Liqr of Ballachulish Slate Quarries Co. v. Malcolm* (1908) 15 S.L.T. 963; *Liqr. of Union Club v. Edinburgh Life
Assce. Co.* (1906) 8 F. 1143; contrast *Bank of South Australia v. Abrahams* (1875) L.R. 6 P.C.
265. A company limited by guarantee cannot hypothecate the guarantee obligation of its
members, prestable only on winding up: *Robertson v. B.L. Co.* (1891) 18 R. 1225, but can
assign a guarantee from a third party, not enforceable only on winding up: *Lloyds Bank v.
Morrison*, 1927 S.C. 571.
[91] *Irvine v. Union Bank of Australia* (1877) 2 App. Cas. 366.
[92] *Weeks v. Propert* (1873) L.R. 8 C.P. 427; *Firbank's Exors. v. Humphreys* (1886) 18
Q.B.D. 54; see also *Neath Building Socy. v. Luce* (1889) 43 Ch. D. 158; *Re Wrexham, Mold and
Connah's Quay Ry. Co.* [1899] 1 Ch. 440; *Re Introductions* [1969] 1 All E.R. 887.

promissory notes. In security for repayment a company may grant any security over its heritage or moveables which a natural person could. Uncalled share capital may, if the Articles permit, be assigned to creditors in security, but this must be intimated to each shareholder.[93] It may also issue debentures or grant a floating charge over its undertaking.

Debentures

Debentures are bonds or instruments acknowledging the company's indebtedness for a fixed sum and providing for payment of interest.[94] Debentures may be redeemable,[95] or perpetual, i.e. repayable only on notice or winding up, or convertible, containing an option to the holder to convert his claim against the company into shares at stated times and rates of exchange. They may be made payable to bearer,[96] or to registered holder, or be a combination of these forms. Debentures redeemed may be reissued.[97] They are often issued as a series,[98] all of the same date and ranking *pari passu*, and may be unsecured, or may create a charge or security over company assets, frequently by way of floating charge. Debenture stock or loan stock is generally constituted by a trust deed transferring assets to, or granting a floating charge over property in favour of, named persons as trustees for the debenture-holders, providing for payment of interest, and issuing, for cash, stock which gives the holder a claim, against the trust fund, or the debenture or loan stock may be unsecured and contain only a personal obligation to repay. A sinking fund may be established to enable debentures to be paid off after a time.[99] Debentures are transferable only as units, whereas debenture stock is evidenced by certificates and transferable in units of convenient amounts such as £1, a register of holders of debenture stock being maintained by the company. A register of debenture-holders, if kept, must be kept in the country of registration.[1] It is open to inspection by members and debenture holders and, at a fee, to others.[2]

A provision in a debenture trust deed is void if it exempts a trustee from, or indemnifies him prospectively against, liability for breach of

---

[93] *Union Club* v. *Edinburgh Life Assce. Co.* (1906) 8 F. 1143; *Ballachulish Slate Quarries Co.* v. *Malcolm* (1908) 15 S.L.T. 963.

[94] *British India S.N. Co.* v. *I.R.C.* (1881) 7 Q.B.D. 165; *Knightsbridge Estates Trust* v. *Byrne* [1940] A.C. 613.

[95] e.g. *United Collieries* v. *L.A.*, 1950 S.C. 458.

[96] Expressly legalized for Scotland, notwithstanding the Blank Bonds and Trusts Act 1696, c. 25, by S. 197. Such debentures are negotiable instruments; *Goodwin* v. *Robarts* (1876) 1 App. Cas. 476; *Bechuanaland Exploration Co.* v. *London Trading Bank* [1898] 2 Q.B. 658.

[97] S. 194.

[98] An example of a single debenture is *Tennant's Trs.* v. *T.*, 1946 S.C. 420.

[99] *Arizona Copper Co.* v. *London Scottish American Trust* (1897) 24 R. 658.

[1] S. 190.

[2] S. 191.

trust, but he may in certain circumstances be released from liability incurred.[3]

A debenture or deed for securing debentures is not invalid merely because the debentures are made irredeemable or redeemable only on a remote contingency or after a long period.[4] Redeemable debentures may be reissued with the same priority rights.[5] A contract to take up and pay for debentures is enforceable by an order for specific implement.[6] Debentures to bearer in Scotland are valid and binding.[7]

Issue of debentures

Statutory provisions as to prospectuses apply also to the offering for sale of debentures,[8] but they may be issued at a discount,[9] though not if convertible into paid-up shares of the same amount as the face value of the debentures.[10]

Transfer of debentures

A debenture payable to bearer is transferable by mere delivery and conveys a good title to a holder who has taken in good faith, for value and without notice of any defect or limitation thereon.[11] A debenture to registered holder is transferable as specified therein, but there must be an instrument of transfer.[12] Normally a register of debenture-holders is maintained, transfers are registered, and a note of the registration endorsed on the debenture. The rules applicable to transfer of shares in security apply equally to transfer of debentures.

Remedies of debenture-holders

A debenture-holder is a creditor, not a member, of the company. Where the debenture is not secured the holder may, as an unsecured creditor, sue thereon and do diligence on the decree, or petition for winding up, or claim in the winding up. If the debenture is secured it is usually provided that the debenture-holders, or the trustee for them, may on default by the company take possession of the security subjects and sell them for the benefit of the debenture-holders. Debentures of a company registered in

---

[3] S. 192.
[4] S. 193.
[5] S. 194.
[6] S. 195.
[7] S. 196. This counters the argument that they are invalid under the Blank Bonds and Trusts Act, 1696.
[8] Ss. 56–61; see also *Dunnett* v. *Mitchell* (1885) 12 R. 400.
[9] *Campbell's Case* (1876) 4 Ch. D. 470.
[10] *Mosley* v. *Koffyfontein Mines, Ltd.* [1904] 2 Ch. 108.
[11] *Bechauanaland Exploration Co.* v. *London Trading Bank* [1898] 2 Q.B. 658.
[12] S. 183; *Re Rhodesia Goldfields, Ltd.* (1880) 14 Ch. D. 859.

Scotland can now contain power to appoint a receiver or manager on the company's property in specified events, as can debentures of a company registered in England, and the trustees may be authorized to take possession of and carry on a company's business. A debenture-holder, or the trustee, may petition for winding up.

Floating charges

An incorporated company, to secure any debt or other obligation, incurred or to be incurred by or binding on the company or any other person, may create in favour of the creditor a floating charge over all or any part of the property, including uncalled capital, which may from time to time be comprised in its property and undertaking. This may be done only by the execution under seal of an instrument or bond which purports to create such a charge. A floating charge has effect in relation to heritable property notwithstanding that the instrument is not recorded in the Register of Sasines or registered on the Land Register.[13] While the company is solvent the floating charge does not attach to any particular items of the property charged not prevent them being sold or dealt with. On commencement of winding up a floating charge attaches to the property then comprised in the company's property and undertaking or the part thereof affected, but subject to the rights of any person who (a) has effectually executed diligence[14] on the property or any part of it, or (b) holds a fixed security over the property or any part of it ranking in priority to the floating charge, or (c) holds over the property another floating charge so ranking. Interest accrues until payment of the sum due under the charge is made.[15]

An instrument creating a floating charge may contain provisions prohibiting or restricting the creation of any fixed security or other floating charge having priority over, or ranking *pari passu* with, the floating charge, or regulating the order in which the floating charge should rank with any subsisting or future floating charges or fixed securities. Where all or part of a company's property is subject both to a floating charge and a fixed security the latter has priority. Where the order of ranking is not regulated by the instrument, (a) a fixed security, constituted as a real right before a floating charge has attached, has priority; (b) floating charges rank according to time of registration under Ss. 410–24; (c) floating charges received for registration by the same post rank equally. Where the holder of a floating charge has received intimation of the subsequent

---

[13] S. 462, overruling *Carse* v. *Coppen*, 1951 S.C. 233. See also *L.A.* v. *Royal Bank*, 1977 S.C. 153; *Forth & Clyde Construction Co.* v. *Trinity Timber & Plywood Co.*, 1984 S.L.T. 94. Old floating charges are validated by S. 465.

[14] See *L.A.* v. *Royal Bank*, 1977 S.C. 153; *Gordon Anderson Plant* v. *Campsie Construction Ltd.*, 1977 S.L.T. 7; *Cumbernauld* v. *Mustone*, 1983 S.L.T. (Sh. Ct.) 55; *Forth and Clyde, supra*.

[15] S. 463; *National Commercial Bank* v. *Telford Grier McKay & Co., Liqdrs.*, 1969 S.C. 181; *Royal Bank* v. *Williamson*, 1972 S.L.T. (Sh. Ct.) 45.

registration of another floating charge over the same property or part thereof the preference of the first floating charge is restricted to security for (a) the holder's present advances; (b) future advances he may be required to make under the instrument creating the floating charge or any ancillary document; (c) interest due or to become due on all such advances; (d) expenses and outlays.[16]

The instrument creating a floating charge may be altered by an instrument of alteration executed by the company, the holder of the charge, and the holder of any other charge affected by the alteration.[17]

Floating charges created within 12 months prior to the commencement of winding up or the presentation of a successful petition for an administration order are invalid unless the company was solvent immediately after the charge was created, with certain exceptions.[18]

Registration of charges

Every charge created by a company registered in Scotland is void against the liquidator and any creditor of the company unless the prescribed particulars and a certified correct copy of the instrument creating the charge are delivered to the registrar of companies within 21 days of creation. This is without prejudice to any contract or obligation for repayment, and when a charge is avoided under the section the money secured immediately becomes repayable. This applies to[19] (a) a charge on land or any interest in such land (save for rent; ground annual or other periodical sum);[20] (b) a security over the uncalled share capital of the company;[21] (c) a security over any of (i) the company's book debts;[22] (ii) calls made but not paid;[23] (iii) goodwill;[24] (iv) a patent or licence thereunder;[25] (v) a trade mark;[26] (vi) a copyright or licence thereunder;[27]

---

[16] S. 464.

[17] S. 466.

[18] Insowency Act, 1986, S. 245. See also *Libertas-Kommerz Gmbh.* v. *Johnston*, 1977 S.C. 191.

[19] S. 410.

[20] Including a charge over properties in England owned by a Scottish company: *Amalgamated Securities Ltd.*, 1967 S.C. 56. But holding debentures entitling to a charge on land is not an interest in land: S. 413. See also *Archibald Campbell, Hope & King*, 1967 S.C. 21; *S. & N. Breweries* v. *Rathburne*, 1970 S.C. 215.

[21] Effected by assignation in security intimated to all shareholders on whom a call could be made.

[22] Effected by assignation of the debts in security, intimated to the debtors. It excludes (S. 412) deposit of a negotiable instrument as security.

[23] Effected by assignation in security intimated to all shareholders on whom calls have been made.

[24] Effected by assignation in security.

[25] Effected by assignation in security under Patents Act, 1977, S. 31 and registered with the Comptroller-General of Patents, Designs and Trademarks.

[26] Effected by assignation in security under Trade Marks Act, 1938, S. 22 and S. 25, and registered with the Comptroller-General.

[27] Effected by assignation in security under Copyright Act, 1956, S. 36.

(d) a security over a ship[28] or aircraft[29] or any share in a ship; (e) a floating charge. In the case of a charge created out of the U.K. comprising property situated outside the time for registration is 21 days after the date when the copy of the instrument could in due course of post and dispatched with due diligence have been received in the U.K.

Where a series of debentures containing or giving by reference to another instrument any charge, to the benefit of which the debenture-holders of that series are entitled *pari passu*, is created, it is sufficient if there is delivered to the registrar within 21 days stated particulars in the prescribed form, together with a copy of the deed containing the charge or one of the debentures in the series.[30] Where a charge is created by *ex facie* absolute disposition or assignation qualified by a back letter, or by standard security qualified by an agreement, S. 410 does not by itself make the charge unavailable as security for later indebtedness. Where the amount secured is increased by a further back letter or agreement, a further charge is held created and the provisions of the Act apply to the further charge as if references were to the further charge.[31]

It is the company's duty to send for registration particulars of every charge created by the company and of the issues of debentures of a series requiring registration, but it may be done on the application of any person interested, at the expense of the company.[32]

When a company acquires any property subject to a charge of a kind registrable, the company must send the prescribed particulars and a copy of the instrument for registration.[33]

The registrar must keep for each company a register of all charges requiring registration and enter in the case of debentures particulars specified in S. 413, and in the case of other charges specified particulars with respect to such charges.[34] He issues a certificate of registration of any charge registered, which is conclusive of compliance with the requirements of the Act as to registration.[34] On being satisfied that a debt has been paid or that part of the property charged has been released or ceased to form part of the company's property, the registrar may enter on the register a memorandum of satisfaction. A company is not required to submit particulars where it disposes of part of the property subject to the floating charge.[35] If there is an omission or misstatement the court may rectify the register.[36] A company must keep a copy of every instrument

[28] Effected by mortgage under Merchant Shipping Act, 1894, Ss. 31–8, and registered with Registrar of Shipping at the port of registry.
[29] Effected by Mortgaging of Aircraft Order, 1972 (S.I. 1972, No. 1268) art. 16, entered in the Register of Aircraft Mortgages kept by Civil Aviation Authority.
[30] S. 413.
[31] S. 414; see *S. & N. Breweries v. Rathburne Hotel Co.*, 1970 S.C. 215.
[32] S. 415.
[33] S. 416.
[34] S. 418.
[35] S. 419.
[36] S. 420.

creating a charge requiring registration to be kept at the registered office,[37] and keep a register of charges showing all charges specifically affecting property of the company and floating charges.[38] Copies of instruments and floating charges are open to inspection.[39] These provisions extend to charges on property in Scotland created, or on property in Scotland acquired, by a company incorporated outside Great Britain which has a place of business in Scotland.[40]

Receivers

The office of receiver, unknown at common law, was introduced into Scotland in 1972. It is now competent for the holder of a floating charge over property comprised in the property and undertaking of an incorporated company to appoint a receiver of the part of the property subject to the charge. The court may also appoint on the application of a holder. A body corporate, an undischarged bankrupt, and a firm may not act.[41]

A receiver may be appointed by the holder of a floating charge on the occurrence of any event which by the instrument entitles the holder to appoint, and on the occurrence of any of (a) the expiry of 21 days after demanding payment of any of the principal sum secured by the charge without payment made; (b) the expiry of 2 months during which all interest due and payable has been in arrears; (c) the making of an order or passing of a resolution to wind up; (d) appointment of a receiver by virtue of any other floating charge. A receiver may be appointed by the court on the occurrence of an event which by the instrument entitles the holder to make that appointment and also where the court on the application of the holder is satisfied that the position of the holder is likely to be prejudiced if no appointment is made, or on the occurrence of any of (a) to (c) above.[42]

The mode of appointment by the holder is by instrument of appointment, a copy to be sent to the registrar. On appointment the floating charge attaches to the property subject to the charge and this has effect as if the charge was a fixed security.[43] The court may on petition served on the company make an appointment on such terms as to caution as it may think fit. A copy of the interlocutor is delivered to the registrar for registration. On appointment the floating charge has effect as if it were a fixed charge.[44]

The receiver has in relation to property attached by the floating charge

---

[37] S. 421.
[38] S. 422.
[39] S. 423.
[40] S. 424; cf. *L.A.* v. *Huron and Erie Loan Co.*, 1911 S.C. 612, 616.
[41] Insolvency Act, 1986, S. 51.
[42] S. 52.
[43] S. 53.
[44] S. 54.

the powers given him by the instrument creating the charge and also, so far as not inconsistent, wide statutory powers.[45] These powers are subject to the rights of any person who has effectually executed diligence on the company's property prior to appointment of the receiver,[46] and to the rights of anyone who holds over all or part of the property a fixed security charge having priority over or ranking *pari passu* with the floating charge. A person transacting with a receiver is not concerned to inquire whether any event has happened to authorize the receiver to act.[47]

Provision is made as to precedence among receivers.[48]

A receiver is deemed to be the agent of the company in relation to the property attached by the relevant floating charge. He is personally liable on any contract entered into by him in the performance of his functions unless the contract otherwise provides, but is entitled to be indemnified out of the property. A contract entered into by or on behalf of the company prior to the receiver's appointment continues in force but the receiver docs not by virtue only of his appointment incur any personal liability on any such contract. A contract entered into by a receiver in the performance of his functions continues in force although the receiver's powers are later suspended.[49]

The receiver's remuneration is determined by agreement or by the Auditor of the Court of Session.[50]

If the company is not being wound up the debts to be paid by the receiver in priority to any claim for principal or interest by the holder are those which in a winding up have to be paid in priority to other debts, and those which after six months after advertisement for claims have been intimated or become known to him.[51]

Subject to S. 61 and the rights of any of (a) the holder of a fixed security over the same property and ranking prior to or *pari passu* with the floating charge; (b) all persons who have effectually executed diligence on any part of the company's property subject to the charge; (c) creditors in respect of all liabilities, charges, and expenses incurred by or on behalf of the receiver; (d) the receiver in respect of his liabilities, expenses, and remuneration; and (e) the preferential creditors entitled under S. 59, the receiver pays money received by him to the holder of the floating charge in or towards satisfaction of the debt thereby secured. Any balance is to be paid to (a) any other receiver; (b) the holder of a fixed security over property subject to the floating charge; (c) the company or its liquidator.

---

[45] S. 55; He and not the directors may sue: *Imperial Hotel* v. *Vaux*, 1978 S.C. 86. Whether he should sue in his own name or the company's name is uncertain: see *McPhail* v. *Lothian R.C.*, 1981 S.C. 119; *Taylor* v. *Sc. & Univ. Newspapers*, 1981 S.C. 408.

[46] S. 55; *L.A.* v. *Royal Bank*, 1977 S.C. 155.

[47] S. 55.

[48] S. 56.

[49] S. 57.

[50] S. 58.

[51] S. 59.

Where disputes arise as to payment the sum must be paid into a bank in name of the Accountant of Court pending settlement.[52]

The court may exercise certain powers in relation to receivers, as by giving directions. Where a receiver wishes to sell property and is unable to obtain the consent of a creditor or a person who has executed diligence, the court may, on the application of the receiver, authorize the sale or disposal of the property free of the security or burden or diligence.[53]

A receiver must give notice of his appointment on business forms, obtain information about the company's affairs, and report on his dealings with the company's affairs.[54]

Arrangements and reconstructions

Where a company proposes a compromise or arrangement with its creditors, or its members, or any class of either, the court may order a meeting of those affected to be held. With the notice calling the meeting a statement must be sent explaining the effect of the arrangement. If the arrangement is agreed to by a majority in number representing three-quarters in value of those affected, present and voting at the meeting, the arrangement if sanctioned by the court is binding on the group concerned and on the company or its liquidator and contributories.[55] When application is made for the court's sanction the court may make provision for stated matters.[56] Where a scheme involves the transfer of shares in a company to another company and has been approved by the holders of nine-tenths in value of the shares involved, the transferee company may give notice to any dissenting shareholder that it desires to acquire his shares and it is then, unless the court orders otherwise, bound to acquire these shares on the terms of the scheme; this does not apply if the dissenters hold more than one-tenth in value of the shares involved unless the transferee company offers the same terms to all holders of the shares concerned and those approving the scheme hold nine-tenths of the shares and are also three-fourths in number of the holders of the shares.[57] A dissenter may require the transferee company to acquire his shares.[58]

Amalgamation

If a company has power under its Memorandum to sell its business, it may sell its whole undertaking to another company for shares in the other company, which are distributed among the members in proportion to

[52] S. 60.
[53] S. 61.
[54] Ss. 64–7.
[55] Ss. 425–6; *Singer Mfg. Co.* v. *Robinow*, 1971 S.C. 11.
[56] S. 427.
[57] Ss. 428, 430.
[58] S. 429–30.

their rights. The selling company may then be wound up, or continue in being as a wholly owned subsidiary of the other company, all its shares being held by the other company. Any agreement to sell must make proper provision for the rights of dissentient shareholders.[59]

Take-overs

Where one company wishes to acquire all the shares of another company, or the whole of any class of shares, it makes an offer to the shareholders to acquire their shares, normally conditional on acceptance by the holders of a stated percentage of shares, sufficient to give the acquiring company full control. If this is achieved the offer becomes unconditional. If acceptances are received from holders of 90 per cent of the shares concerned within four months of the offer, the acquiring company may within two months of the expiry of the period for acceptance of the offer intimate to any dissenting shareholder that it desires to acquire his shares.[60] Such a shareholder may apply to the court to declare that the terms are not fair, the onus of proof of unfairness being on him.[61] Unless there is dissent, the fairness of the scheme need never come before the court.[62] The directors of an offeree company must be honest and not mislead their shareholders in advising them whether to accept the offer to buy their shares or not.[63]

Investigation of companies

The Secretary of State may appoint competent inspectors to investigate the affairs of a company and report thereon. Investigation may be made on the application of 200 members or holders of one-tenth of the shares issued, or of one-fifth of persons on the register, or of the company, supported by evidence of good reason for the investigation.[64] He may also order investigation if the court declares that its affairs ought to be investigated, or there are circumstances suggesting fraud on creditors or conduct unfairly prejudicial to some part of its members, or the persons concerned with management have been guilty of fraud, misfeasance, or

---

[59] *Bisgood v. Henderson's Transvaal Estates, Ltd.* [1908] 1 Ch. 743.

[60] S. 428–30; *Musson v. Howard Glasgow Associates. Ltd.*, 1960 S.C. 371; *Nidditch v. C.P.A., Ltd.*, 1961 S.L.T. 282.

[61] *Re Press Caps* [1949] Ch. 434; *Re Sussex Brick Co. Ltd.* [1961] Ch. 289; *Re Grierson Oldham and Adams, Ltd.* [1967] 1 All E.R. 192; *Gething v. Kilner* [1972] 1 All E.R. 1166.

[62] The requirements of disclosure and fairness in take-over bids are controlled not so much by law as by 'The City Code on Takeovers and Mergers' formulated by the London Stock Exchange, issuing houses, bankers, and others in 1968 and operating through a Panel on Takeovers and Mergers. A company contravening the code would find it practically impossible to get professional guidance or assistance, and quotation on the Stock Exchange might be suspended. Certain mergers might be referred to the Monopolies Commission under the Monopolies and Mergers Act, 1965.

[63] *Gething v. Kilner* [1972] 1 All E.R. 1166.

[64] S. 431.

misconduct towards the company or its members, or that the members have not been given all the information they might reasonably expect.[65] Inspectors have extensive statutory powers.[66] They may, and may be directed to, make interim reports, and are bound to make a final report.[67] The Secretary of State may bring civil proceedings on behalf of any body corporate arising from the report,[68] and may petition that the company be wound up.[69] He also has powers to investigate the ownership of a company[70] and dealings in shares,[71] require production of documents,[72] seek warrant to enter, and search premises.[73]

Restrictions on dealing in shares

The Secretary of State and the court have power to impose restrictions on any use of or dealing with shares consequent on failure to disclose interests in shares (S. 210), to disclose information relating to share acquisitions or disposals (S. 216), during or following on an investigation into the ownership of a company (S. 442) and where the Secretary of State seeks information relating to persons interested in shares (S. 444), but application may be made to the court to relax or remove the restrictions.[74]

Fraudulent trading

If any company business is carried on with intent to defraud creditors or for any fraudulent purpose, everyone knowingly a party thereto is liable criminally.[75]

Protection of members against unfair prejudice

A member may apply to the court for an order on the ground that the company's affairs are being or have been conducted in a manner unfairly prejudicial to the interests of some part of the members including himself, or that any proposed conduct would be so prejudicial.[76] The Secretary of

---

[65] Ss. 432, 439.
[66] Ss. 433–6.
[67] Ss. 437, 441.
[68] S. 438.
[69] S. 440.
[70] Ss. 442–5.
[71] S. 446.
[72] S. 447.
[73] Ss. 448–53.
[74] Ss. 454–7. cf. *Re Westminster Property Group plc.* [1984] 1 W.L.R. 1117.
[75] S. 458.
[76] S. 459. cf. *Elder* v. *Elder & Watson Ltd.*, 1952 S.C. 49; *Re Harmer, Ltd.* [1958] 3 All E.R. 689; *Meyer* v. *S.C.W.S.*, 1958 S.C. (H.L.) 40; *Re Jermyn St. Turkish Baths* [1971] 3 All E.R. 1184.

State may also apply.[77] The court may make such order as it thinks fit for giving relief in respect of the matters complained of, including regulating the conduct of the company's affairs in the future, requiring the company to refrain from certain conduct, authorizing a minority shareholder to sue in the company's name, and providing for the purchase of members' shares by other members or by the company.[78]

INSOLVENCY

Insolvency arises when a company's assets do not balance its liabilities. In such a case any one of three procedures may be resorted to: a voluntary arrangement, an administration order, and liquidation, of which the last leads to the dissolution of the company. Liquidation is also invoked when it is desired to bring a company to an end even though it is not insolvent.

It is criminal for anyone to act as liquidator, administrator, administrative receiver, or supervisor of a composition with creditors unless he is qualified to act as an insolvency practitioner.[79] A person so qualified may be qualified by membership of one of certain recognized professional bodies or by direct authorization from the relevant body set up by the Secretary of State and must have provided the necessary security for the proper performance of his functions.[80] This is done by a single-premium insurance policy from a reputable insurance company.

COMPANY VOLUNTARY ARRANGEMENTS

A company voluntary arrangement is a procedure to enable a company which is nearly or actually insolvent to resolve its financial affairs less formally than by liquidation. The directors or a liquidator or administrator may make a proposal to the company and its creditors for a composition in satisfaction of its debts or a scheme of arrangement of its affairs, by a person who is qualified to act as an insolvency practitioner acting as trustee or otherwise to supervise its implementation. If the company is subject to an administration order or the company is being wound up the proposal may be made by the administrator or liquidator.[81] The nominee must report to the court whether meetings should be held to discuss the proposal. The proposer must give information on the state of the company and what the proposal is.[82] The nominee must call meetings of the

---

[77] S. 460.
[78] S. 461.
[79] Insolvency Act, 1986, Ss. 338, 389–90.
[80] Ss. 391–2. The recognized bodies include solicitors and accountants.
[81] Insolvency Act, 1986, S. 1.
[82] S. 2.

company and its creditors, and these must decide whether to approve the proposed voluntary arrangement with or without modifications; the outcome of the meetings is reported to the court.[83] If each of the meetings approves the voluntary arrangement, it takes effect as if made by the company at the creditors' meeting and binds every creditor as if he were a party thereto. The court may discharge any administration order in force or sist a winding up, or give directions to facilitate implement of the voluntary arrangement.[84]

The decisions at the meetings may be challenged on the grounds of unfair prejudice to a creditor, member, or contributory of the company, or of material irregularity at or in relation to the meetings.[85]

Once a voluntary arrangement has been put into effect the nominee becomes supervisor of the arrangement. The court may, on application by a dissatisfied person, confirm, reverse, or modify a decision of the supervisor, give him directions, or make such other order as it thinks fit. The supervisor may seek directions from the court, and apply for an administration order or for winding up.[86]

ADMINISTRATION ORDERS

An administration order is an order of the court that, while it is in force, the affairs, business, and property of the company are to be managed by an administrator appointed by the court. The purpose is to provide an alternative to liquidation by rehabilitating the company or rescuing it from its difficulties. The court may make an order if satisfied that the company is or is likely to become unable to pay its debts, or if it considers that the making of an order would be likely to secure the survival of the company, the approval of a voluntary arrangement,[87] the sanctioning of a compromise or arrangement between the company and its creditors or members,[88] or a more advantageous realization of assets than obtainable on winding up.[89] An order must specify the purpose for which it was made. Application may be made by any or all of the company, its directors, and a creditor or creditors.[90] Notice must be given to anyone entitled to appoint a receiver and other prescribed persons.

If an administration order is made winding up may not be sought or ordered, a receiver must vacate office, and no steps may be taken to

---

[83] Ss. 3–4.
[84] S. 5.
[85] S. 6.
[86] S. 7.
[87] Under Insolvency Act, 1986, Part I.
[88] Under Companies Act, 1985, S. 425.
[89] 1986 Act, S. 8.
[90] S. 9.

enforce security over the company's property without the administrator's consent.[91]

The administrator must be qualified as an insolvency practitioner; he has power to do all things necessary for the management of the affairs, business, and property of the company, and numerous specific powers.[92] He has power also to remove or appoint directors, call meetings, and apply to the court for directions, and must assent to the exercise of any power conferred on the company or its officers if its exercise would interfere with his powers. He is deemed to act as the company's agent and a person dealing with him in good faith and for value is not concerned to inquire whether he is acting within his powers or not.[93] He may dispose of secured property free of a charge subject, in the case of a floating charge, to giving the holder the same priority as he would otherwise have had, and in other cases to satisfying the court that disposal would be likely to promote one of the purposes of the administration order.[94]

The administrator has many statutory duties, particularly to take into custody all property to which the company is entitled, manage the affairs of the company in accordance with the court's directions, and then within 3 months state his proposals to the registrar and all known creditors.[95] The meeting of creditors may approve his proposals, or modify them, or reject them, in which case the court may discharge the administration order.[96] The creditors may appoint a creditors' committee[97] and creditors or members may apply to the court if they fear prejudice.[98] Provision is made for removal of the administrator from office, his resignation, and release.[99] Many provisions of the 1986 Act applicable to liquidations, including setting aside certain charges and other transactions involving the company, apply also to administrators.[1]

LIQUIDATION

A company's existence is normally ended by its being wound up or liquidated[2] under the Insolvency Act, 1986.[3] This is so whether it is

---

[91] Ss. 10–11.
[92] S. 14 and Sch. 1.
[93] S. 14.
[94] Ss. 15–16.
[95] Ss. 17, 21–4.
[96] S. 24.
[97] S. 26.
[98] S. 27.
[99] Ss. 19–20.
[1] Ss. 233–46.
[2] It may also be dissolved without winding up, by order of the court: S. 427; or if defunct be struck off the register by the registrar and then dissolved: S. 652.
[3] Hereafter referred to as '1986 Act'. Its provisions are not confined to insolvent companies.

insolvent or not. There are three modes of winding up, a members' voluntary winding up, a creditors' voluntary winding up, and a winding up by the court.[4] A company cannot be sequestrated under the Bankruptcy (Sc.) Act, 1985.[5]

Voluntary winding up

A company may be wound up voluntarily where the period, if any, of its duration has expired, or the event on the occurrence of which it is to be dissolved has occurred, and the company has passed an ordinary resolution to wind up, or if it passes a special resolution to wind up voluntarily, or if it passes an extraordinary resolution to the effect that it cannot by reason of its liabilities continue its business and that it is advisable to wind up. The commencement of voluntary winding up is the time of passing the resolution.[6]

The consequence is that the company continues in being but it ceases to carry on business, save so far as required for beneficial winding up, transfer of shares is void, and the powers of directors are superseded on the appointment of a liquidator, unless the company in general meeting, or the liquidator, or the liquidation committee, or the creditors, sanction continuance of directors' powers.[7]

Members' voluntary winding up

A majority of the directors may within 5 weeks make a statutory declaration, containing a statement of assets and liabilities, that they have inquired into the company's affairs and formed the opinion that it will be able to pay its debts in full within a period not exceeding 12 months from winding up.[8] It is filed with the registrar. If this is made it is a members' voluntary winding up; if not, it is a creditors' voluntary winding up.

In a members' voluntary winding up the company appoints a liquidator who is an agent of the company[9] and summons general meetings at the end of each year from the commencement of winding up to report on the winding up during the year.[10] When the winding up is completed the liquidator makes up an account and calls a general meeting, laying the account before it, and sends a copy to the registrar who registers the accounts and return of the meeting; after three months the company is deemed dissolved.[11] If the liquidator is at any time of opinion that the

---

[4] 1986 Act, Ss. 73, 90.
[5] 1985 Act, S. 6; cf. *Standard Property Investment Co.* v. *Dunblane Hydro Ltd.* (1884) 12 R. 328.
[6] Ss. 84–6.
[7] Ss. 87–91, 103.
[8] S. 89.
[9] *Taylor* v. *Wilson's Trs.*, 1975 S.C. 146. See also *Highland Dairy Farms, Liqdr.*, 1964 S.C. 1.
[10] Ss. 91–3.
[11] Ss. 94, 201.

company will not be able to pay its debts in full within the period stated in the declaration of solvency, he must summon a meeting of creditors, make a statement as to the affairs of the company, and lay it before the meeting; and from that date the winding up becomes a creditors' voluntary winding up.[12]

Creditors' voluntary winding up

If no declaration of solvency has been filed the company must cause a meeting of its creditors to be summoned and advertised, stating either the name and address of an insolvency practitioner who will furnish creditors with information concerning the company's affairs or a place where a list of the creditors can be inspected.[13] The directors must make out a statement as to the company's affairs, cause it to be laid before the meeting and appoint one of themselves to preside at the meeting.[14] Both creditors and company at their meetings may nominate a liquidator; if they do not agree the creditors' nominee prevails; if the creditors do not nominate the members' nominee is appointed.[15] The creditors may at any meeting appoint not more than five persons to be a liquidation committee; if they do, the company may add not more than five persons, though the creditors may object to any of the company's nominees.[16] The liquidator must call general meetings of both the company and the creditors annually and report on the conduct of the winding up during the preceding year,[17] and call a final meeting and report to the registrar. Three months later the company is deemed dissolved.

The court has power to appoint a liquidator if there is not one acting, or to remove a liquidator on cause shown.[18] He must publish in the *Gazette* and deliver to the registrar a notice of his appointment.[19] In a voluntary winding up a liquidator may be removed only by order of the court, or by a general meeting of the members, or of the creditors, summoned specially for the purpose, save that if he was appointed under S. 108 a meeting to replace him can be summoned only if he thinks fit or the court directs or the meeting is requested by members representing at least half of the voting rights or creditors of half in value. In certain circumstances he must vacate office or may resign.[20] He is released from liability in certain circumstances.[20]

Liquidators' powers in both kinds of voluntary winding up

The liquidator may apply to the court to determine any question arising in the winding up or exercise any of the powers the court could exercise

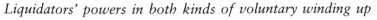

[12] Ss. 95–6.   [13] S. 98.   [14] S. 99.
[15] S. 100   [16] S. 101.   [17] S. 105.
[18] S. 108.   [19] S. 109.   [20] S. 171.

in a winding up by the court.[21] He has powers with the sanction of an extraordinary resolution of the company, or, in a creditors' winding up, of the court or the liquidation committee, to pay any class of creditors in full, to make any compromise or arrangement with creditors, and to compromise all calls, debts, and liabilities and all claims between the company and a contributory or other debtor and all questions relating to the winding up of the company.[22] He may without sanction bring or defend any action or legal proceeding in the name and on behalf of the company, and carry on the business of the company so far as may be necessary for its beneficial winding up,[23] and exercise any of the general powers set out in Schedule 4, Part III. He may also settle a list of contributories, make calls, and summon general meetings of the company to obtain its sanction by special or extraordinary resolution or for any other purpose he may think fit.[24] When exercising his powers he disposes of any property to a person 'connected' with the company he must notify the liquidation committee of the fact.[25] In a creditors' voluntary winding up, during the period between being nominated by the company and the creditors' meeting the liquidator requires the sanction of the court for the exercise of most of his powers.[26] He may sell the property of the company for shares in another company.[27]

He may summon general meetings of creditors or contributories to ascertain their wishes, and must do so when they by resolution direct him to do so or when one-tenth in value of either group request him in writing to do so.[28]

Winding up by the court

A company may be wound up by the court[29] if (a) it has passed a special resolution to that effect; (b) a public company registered as such has not been issued with a certificate under S. 117, Companies Act, 1985, within a year from registration; (c) the company does not commence business within one year from incorporation or suspends business for a whole year; (d) the number of members is reduced below two; (e) the company is unable to pay its debts;[30] (f) the court is of opinion that it is just and

---

[21] S. 112. cf. *N.B. Locomotive Co.* v. *L.A.*, 1963 S.C. 272; *Smith*, 1969 S.L.T. (Notes) 94; *Highland Eng. Co. Liqdrs.* v. *Thomson*, 1972 S.C. 87.
[22] S. 165 and Sch. 4, Part I.
[23] S. 165 and Sch. 4, Part II.
[24] S. 165.
[25] Ss. 165, 249, 435.
[26] S. 166.
[27] Ss. 110–11.
[28] S. 168.
[29] S. 122. The Court of Session always has jurisdiction; if the paid-up capital does not exceed £120,000 the sheriff court also has jurisdiction.
[30] As defined by S. 123, viz.: if a creditor for more than £750 has demanded payment and the company has for 3 weeks neglected to pay or to secure or compound for it to his satisfaction; or

equitable that the company should be wound up;[31] or (g) in the case of a Scottish company there subsists a floating charge over property comprised in the company's property and undertaking and the court is satisfied that the creditor's security is in jeopardy.[32]

A petition to wind up may be presented by the company, if it has passed a special resolution; the directors; a creditor, including a contingent or prospective creditor; a contributory, including a holder of fully paid shares, subject to certain conditions; the Secretary of State in certain cases.[33] These rules do not exclude petition by other persons who can bring themselves within the category of creditors, such as a holder of bearer debentures.

Contributories

A contributory is every person liable to contribute to the assets of the company in the event of its being wound up; this includes the present members and past members who ceased to be members within one year before winding up. The liability of contributories is limited to any amount still unpaid on their shares.[34]

Further procedure

After presentation of a petition an application may be made to the court for appointment of a provisional liquidator and an appointment may be made at any time before the first appointment of liquidators,[35] particularly if assets are in danger[36] or to avoid possible prejudice.[37] The provisional liquidator takes all the company's property into his custody or under his control[38] and he supersedes the directors in managing the company.

The court may dismiss the petition, or adjourn the hearing, or make

a charge for payment has expired without payment; or it is proved that the company is unable to pay its debts as they fall due; or the value of the company's assets is less than its liabilities, allowing for its contingent and prospective liabilities. See *Cunningham* v. *Walkinshaw* (1886) 14 R. 87; *Pollok* v. *Gaeta*, 1907 S.C. 182; *Landauer* v. *Alexander*, 1919 S.C. 492.

[31] This power is purely discretionary and the words are not restricted to particular instances, nor by the previous clauses, nor to cases involving *mala fides*, nor to cases where the petitioner is wronged as a shareholder. The power has been exercised in cases where the main object of the company had failed: *Re German Date Coffee Co.* (1882) 20 Ch. D. 169; there was a deadlock in management; *Re Yenidje Tobacco Co.* [1916] 2 Ch. 426; the company had never had any property or business; a director had control but refused to hold meetings or produce accounts: *Loch* v. *Blackwood* [1924] A.C. 783; *Baird* v. *Lees*, 1924 S.C. 83; where directors were at loggerheads: *Symington* v. *S's Quarries Ltd.* (1905) 8 F. 121; *Ebrahimi* v. *Westbourne* [1973] A.C. 360.

[32] S. 122.
[33] S. 124.
[34] S. 74.
[35] s. 135.
[36] cf. *Levy* v. *Napier*, 1962 S.C. 468.
[37] cf. *McCabe* v. *Middleton*, 1969 S.L.T. (Sh. Ct.) 29.
[38] S. 144. On legal proceedings see S. 130.

any order that it thinks fit, but must not refuse to make an order merely because the assets have been fully mortgaged or there are no assets at all.[39] If the petition is presented by members on the 'just and equitable' ground the court must make an order unless it is of opinion that the petitioners have some other remedy available and that they are acting unreasonably in not pursuing it.[40]

The consequences of a winding-up order date from the commencement of winding up, which is the time of presentation of the petition, or, if the company was then in voluntary liquidation, the time of passing the resolution to wind up.[41] The consequences are that (1) any disposition of the property of the company and any transfer of shares or alteration in the status of members thereafter is void unless the court otherwise orders.[42] This is to prevent improper alienation of the company's property, but the court can sanction transactions in the ordinary course of business;[43] (2) a winding up is equivalent to an arrestment in execution and decree of furthcoming and to a completed poinding and to a decree of adjudication of heritage for payment of the company's debts;[44] (3) after a winding-up order has been made or a provisional liquidator appointed, no action can be commenced or proceeded with save by leave of the court;[45] (4) most of the directors' powers cease and are assumed by the liquidator; (5) the company's employees are automatically dismissed, but an employee may be held to have continued to work for the liquidator[46] or be re-engaged by the liquidator.[47]

The liquidator or provisional liquidator may apply to the court for appointment of a special manager if the nature of the business or property or the interests of creditors, members, or contributories require it; he must find caution for his intromissions and prepare and produce accounts.[48]

Interim liquidator

When the winding-up order is made an interim liquidator is appointed. He must within 28 days summon separate meetings of creditors and contributories to choose himself or another person to be liquidator save that, if the ground for winding up is inability to pay debts, the interim

---

[39] But see *Re Chesterfield Catering Co. Ltd.* [1977] 1 Ch. 373.
[40] *Charles Forte Investments* v. *Amanda* [1964] Ch. 240.
[41] S. 129.
[42] S. 127.
[43] *Re Wiltshire Iron Co.* (1868) L.R. 3 Ch. App. 443; *Millar* v. *National Bank* (1891) 28 S.L.R. 884; *U.D.T. Ltd.*, 1977 S.L.T. (Notes) 56; *Site Preparations* v. *Buchan*, 1983 S.L.T. 317.
[44] S. 185; *Allan* v. *Cowan* (1892) 20 R. 36; *Radford & Bright* v. *Stevenson* (1904) 6 F. 429; *Johnston* v. *Cluny Trs.*, 1957 S.C. 184.
[45] *Langley* v. *Wells* [1969] 1 W.L.R. 503.
[46] *Day* v. *Tait* (1900) 8 S.L.T. 40; *Laing* v. *Gowans* (1902) 10 S.L.T. 461.
[47] *Smith* v. *L.A.*, 1978 S.C. 259.
[48] S. 177.

liquidator need summon only a meeting of creditors. If no person is appointed the court appoints.[49] The meetings of creditors and contributories (or creditors only) may appoint a liquidation committee; if there is none its functions are vested in the Secretary of State.

The liquidator

The liquidator must be a qualified insolvency practitioner,[50] but his acts are valid notwithstanding defect in his appointment, nomination, or qualifications.[51] He is an officer of the court. He is entitled to be treated as a new customer by public utilities.[52]

The liquidator is an agent of the company, not a trustee for individual creditors or contributories,[53] but he may be liable to a creditor or contributory for loss caused by breach of his statutory duties.[54] He should make provision for known contingent claims,[55] and may be liable to refund to the assets money paid away wrongly or on an unfounded claim if he has not taken advice or the directions of the court,[56] but is not liable if he pays an unfounded claim if he took advice and exercised all due care before paying.[57] If he pays money under error of general law, e.g. as to liability for tax, he cannot recover it from the payee.[58]

A person resident outwith the jurisdiction will only exceptionally be appointed.[59] It is not a bar that the liquidator has been a director,[60] secretary,[61] or auditor[62] of the company but, certainly if creditors object, joint liquidators should not both be connected with the company.[63] It is an offence to give or offer any member or creditor any valuable consideration to secure or prevent the appointment of anyone as liquidator.[64]

The court may order anyone who possesses any property, books, papers, or records apparently belonging to the company to transfer them to the liquidator.[65] Any person who may be asked to furnish a statement of affairs must give such information as the liquidator may require.[66] The

---

[49] S. 138.
[50] S. 230.
[51] S. 232.
[52] S. 233.
[53] *Knowles* v. *Scott* [1891] 1 Ch. 717; cf. *U.C.S. Ltd. Liqdr.*, 1975 S.L.T. 39, 40.
[54] *Pulsford* v. *Devenish* [1903] 2 Ch. 625.
[55] *Smith* v. *Goodman* [1936] Ch. 216; *Armstrong Whitworth Securities Ltd.* [1947] Ch. 673.
[56] *Re Windsor Steel Co. Ltd.* [1929] 1 Ch. 151.
[57] *Re Home and Colonial Insurance Co. Ltd.* [1930] 1 Ch. 102.
[58] *Taylor* v. *Wilson's Tr.*, 1975 S.C. 146.
[59] *Brightwen* v. *City of Glasgow Bank* (1878) 6 R. 244; *Barberton Development Ltd.* (1898) 25 R. 654; *Bruce Peebles & Co.* v. *Shiells*, 1908 S.C. 692.
[60] *Sanderson & Muirhead* (1884) 21 S.L.R. 766; *Bruce Peebles, supra.*
[61] *Gilmour's Trs.* v. *Kilmarnock* (1883) 10 R. 1221.
[62] *Argylls Ltd.* v. *Ritchie & Whiteman*, 1914 S.C. 915.
[63] *Argylls Ltd., supra.*
[64] S. 164.
[65] S. 234.
[66] S. 235.

liquidator has powers to apply to the court to have persons required to attend and produce information.[67] The court may require any officer of the company to attend any meeting of creditors or contributories or a liquidation committee to give information on the trade, dealings, affairs, or property of the company.[68]

Duties

The liquidator's duties are to secure that assets are ingathered, realized, and the proceeds distributed to the company's creditors and, if there be a surplus, to the persons entitled to it. He must take all the property of the company into his custody as soon as possible and perform such duties as will enable the court to exercise its functions.[69] The liquidation comittee or a member of it may apply to the court for an order on the liquidator to summon a meeting of creditors or contributories, and he must summon a final meeting.[70]

Powers

A liquidator, including a provisional liquidator,[71] in a winding up by the court has powers,[71] (1) with the sanction of the court or the liquidation committee, to bring or defend actions and legal proceedings in the name and on behalf of the company, subject to personal liability in costs if unsuccessful,[72] to carry on the business of the company so far as necessary for beneficial winding up,[73] to pay any classes of creditors in full, to make any compromise or arrangement with creditors, and to compromise all calls and liabilities to calls and other debts and liabilities. He has power (2)at his own hand to sell the company's property, to do all acts and execute all deeds and documents on behalf of the company, to prove, rank, and claim in the bankruptcy, insolvency, or sequestration of any contributory, to draw, accept, make, and indorse any bill of exchange or promissory note in name and on behalf of the company, to raise money on the security of the company's assets, to do what is necessary to obtain payment of money from a contributory or his estate, to appoint an agent to do business which he cannot do himself, and to do all such other things as are necessary for winding up the affairs of the company and distributing its assets. The exercise of powers is subject to the control of the court and any creditor or contributory may apply to the court as to their

---

[67] S. 236.
[68] S. 157.
[69] Ss. 143–4, 148, 154.
[70] S. 146.
[71] *Wilsons Ltd.*, 1912, 2 S.L.T. 330.
[72] *Re Wilson Lovatt & Sons* [1977] 1 All E.R. 274. He must himself decide what to do: *S.S. Camelot Ltd. Liqdr.* (1893) 1 S.L.T. 358.
[73] *Burntisland Oil Co.* v. *Dawson* (1892) 20 R. 180; *McIntyre* (1893) 30 S.L.R. 386.

exercise.[74] The liquidator has, subject to Rules of Court, the same powers as a trustee on a bankrupt estate.[75]

Contracts

The liquidator may adopt contracts made by the company and complete them, or repudiate them, in which case the company is liable in damages for breach of contract; if he does not adopt within a reasonable time he will be deemed to have abandoned a contract.[76] He may adopt one contract with a party and repudiate another, and the other party may not withhold money due under the first in security of claims under the repudiated contract.[77] The other party may require the liquidator to decide within 28 days of being given notice to do so.[78]

Custody of company's property

When a winding-up order has been made or a provisional liquidator appointed, the liquidator must take into his custody or under his control all the property to which the company is or appears to be entitled. So long as there is no liquidator, the company's property is deemed in the custody of the court.[79] But the company's property remains vested in it;[80] the liquidator has to get it into his possession. The court may however make an order vesting any of it in him in his official name.[81]

The winding up is, at the date its commencement, equivalent to (a) an arrestment in execution and decree of furthcoming and to a completed poinding, and no arrestment or poinding executed on or after the sixtieth day before that date is effectual against the liquidator save that an arrester or poinder thus deprived of the benefit of his diligence is entitled to a preference for the expense *bona fide* incurred in his diligence;[82] (b) a decree of adjudication of heritage for the whole debts of the company, subject to any preferable rights and securities which are valid and unchallengeable and to the right to poind the ground;[83] (c) a poinding of the ground not carried into execution by sale of the effects 60 days before the commencement of winding up is ineffective in a question with the liquidator unless the poinder holds a heritable security preferable to the rights of

[74] S. 167.
[75] S. 169.
[76] *Crown Estate Commrs. v. Highland Eng. Co.*, 1975 S.L.T. 58.
[77] *Asphaltic Limestone Co. v. Glasgow Corpn.*, 1907 S.C. 463.
[78] Bankruptcy (Sc.) Act, 1985, S. 42; Insolvency Act, 1986, S. 169.
[79] S. 144.
[80] *Queensland Mercantile Co. v. Australiasian Investment Co.* (1888) 15 R. 935; *Ward v. Samyang*, 1975 S.C. (H.L.) 26, 47.
[81] S. 145; see also S. 234.
[82] *Johnston v. Cluny Trs.*, 1957 S.C. 184.
[83] *Turnbull v. Sc. County Investment Co. Ltd.*, 1939 S.C. 5; *U.D.T. Ltd.*, 1977 S.L.T. (Notes) 56.

the liquidator, in which case it is available for the interest for the current half-year and arrears of interest for the preceding year, but no more.[84]

Resignation, removal, and release of liquidator

A liquidator must vacate office if he ceases to be a qualified insolvency practitioner, may resign on giving notice to the court,[85] and may be removed by the court or a meeting of creditors.[86] A meeting to replace the liquidator may be called by the liquidator, the court, or a quarter in value of the creditors. If the Secretary of State appointed the liquidator only he can remove him.[87]

He is released if he has died, or been removed by a creditors' meeting which did not resolve against his release; if it did, he must apply to the Accountant of Court for release; or he has resigned or vacated office having called the final meeting of creditors, unless the meeting resolves to the contrary, in which case he must apply to the Accountant of Court. The effect of release is to discharge him from all liability in respect of his acts or omissions as liquidator.[88]

Final meeting and dissolution

In a winding up by the court the liquidator, when satisfied that the winding up is for practical purposes complete, calls a final general meeting of creditors, and reports to them. The meeting must then decide whether to release him. He must give notice then or at an adjourned meeting of any final distribution of assets.

When the liquidator gives notice that the final meeting has been held and he has vacated office, the company will be automatically dissolved three months thereafter unless the court defers that date on the application of any interested party. Subject to any order made by the courts under the Companies Act, 1985, Ss. 651 or 652, any property vested in or held on trust for the company immediately before dissolution vests in the Crown as *bona vacantia*,[89] but the Crown may disclaim such property by notice given by the Queen's and Lord Treasurer's Remembrancer.

The court may within 12 years declare the dissolution void on the application of the liquidator or any person interested. In that event property vested in the Crown remains so vested but the company receives cash in lieu. Grounds are discovery of unsatisfied claims by creditors, or of undistributed assets,[90] or to enable the liquidator to convey a title to

---

[84] S. 185, applying Bankruptcy (Sc.) Act, 1985, S. 37.
[85] cf. *Jamieson* (1877) 14 S.L.R. 667.
[86] e.g. *Lysons* v. *Miraflores Gold Syndicate* (1895) 22 R. 605; *Skinner* (1899) 6 S.L.T. 388. Contrast *McKnight* v. *Montgomerie* (1892) 19 R. 501; *Ker* (1897) 5 S.L.T. 126.
[87] S. 172.
[88] S. 174.
[89] 1985 Act, S. 654.
[90] 1985 Act, Ss. 656–7.

COMPANIES   473

property sold since the dissolution.[91] Dissolution cannot be voided for a
limited purpose only.[92]

Exceptionally the Court of Session may under the *nobile officium*
declare a dissolution void.[93]

Early dissolution

If after a meeting or meetings under S. 138 it appears to the liquidator
that the realizable assets are insufficient to cover the expenses of winding
up, he may apply to the court for early dissolution if it appears appropriate to the court.[94] If an order is made the liquidator forwards a copy to
the registrar and the company is dissolved three months from the date of
registration, though it may order deferment of the date of dissolution on
the application of any person who appears to have an interest.

Provisions applicable to all modes of winding up

The court must settle a list of contributories and cause the assets of the
company to be collected and applied in discharge of the company's
liabilities.[95] Every present and past member who was a member less than
one year before the commencement of winding up is a contributory, but
the liability is limited to the amount if any, unpaid on partly paid
shares;[96] these are known as the A and B lists and the B list is not settled
unless it appears necessary to do so.[97] Where necessary, calls are made by
the court.[98]

Creditors are distinguishable as secured, i.e. holding a fixed security,
charge, or lien, for a debt due to them by the company, or unsecured,
holding no such security. A secured creditor may realize his security and
claim as an unsecured creditor for any balance still due to him, or value
his security and claim as an unsecured creditor for the balance, or surrender his security and claim for the whole debt, or rely on his security and
make no claim.

If the company is solvent claims may be made for all debts payable on a
contingency, and all claims against the company, present or future, certain or contingent, ascertained or sounding only in damages including
unliquidated claims. If it is insolvent claims are competent for all debts
and liabilities, present and future, certain or contingent, owing at the date

---

[91] *McCall & Stephen Ltd.* (1920) 57 S.L.R. 480.
[92] *Champdany Jute Co. Ltd.*, 1924 S.C. 209.
[93] *Collins Bros. & Co.*, 1916 S.C. 620; see also *Kerr*, 1924 S.C. 163; *Forth Shipbreaking Co.*,
1924 S.C. 489.
[94] S. 204.
[95] S. 148.
[96] S. 74; *Paterson* v. *McFarlane* (1875) 2 R. 490.
[97] S. 148.
[98] S. 150.

of commencement of the liquidation, except demands in the nature of unliquidated damages arising otherwise than by reason of contract, promise, or breach of trust. A claim of damages for delict may be made if the company is solvent.

Once a winding up has commenced any creditor whose debt was incurred on or before the date of winding up, or the liquidator, may challenge an alienation by which any part of the company's property has been transferred or by which any claim or right of the company has been discharged or renounced, provided the alienation has become completely effectual, if it favours an 'associate'[99] on a day not earlier than 5 years before the commencement of winding up, or favours any other person not earlier than 2 years before such commencement. If challenged the court must grant reduction of or decree for restoration of the property to the company's assets, unless the person seeking to uphold the alienation establishes that at any time after the alienation the company's assets were greater than its liabilities, or that the alienation was made for adequate consideration, or that it was a reasonable alienation by way of gift, or gift for a charitable purpose.[1]

A liquidator also has the same right to challenge a gratuitous alienation as a creditor has at common law. For that the creditor would have to prove that the company was absolutely insolvent at the date of the transaction or was made so thereby, and continued to be absolutely insolvent at the date of the challenge, and that the transaction was gratuitous and to the prejudice of lawful creditors. Such challenge is not restricted to alienations to associates, nor to those within 2 years before winding up.

Any creditor whose debt was incurred on or before the commencement of winding up, or the liquidator, may challenge transactions entered into by a company which have the effect of creating a preference in favour of creditors to the prejudice of the general body of creditors, provided the preference had become completely effectual not less than 6 months before winding up, but excepting transactions in the ordinary course of business, payments in cash of debts due, unless the transaction was collusive with the purpose of prejudicing the general body of creditors, transactions by which both parties undertook obligations unless collusive, and any mandate granted by the company authorizing an arrestee to pay over arrested funds to an arrester where there had been a decree for payment or a warrant for summary diligence and the decree or warrant had been preceded by an arrestment on the dependence of the action or followed by an arrestment in execution. If challenge is made, the court must grant reduction or restoration of property to the company's assets.[2]

---

[99] Defined by Bankruptcy (Sc.) Act, 1985, S. 74, amd. Bankruptcy (Sc.) Regs. 1985 (S.I. 1985, No. 1925).
[1] S. 242.
[2] S. 243.

The liquidator has the same right to challenge a preference created by the debtor company as a creditor has at common law. At common law a creditor has to prove that the debtor was insolvent at the date of the transaction and continuously thereafter till the date of challenge, that he was aware of that fact, that the transaction was voluntary and in satisfaction or further security of a prior debt, and that the transaction was to the prejudice of the other creditors.[3] A preference is challengeable whether given directly or indirectly.[4] But not reducible are cash payments of debts actually due, transactions in the ordinary course of trade, and *nova debita* or new debts arising out of new transactions, unless there is proof of fraudulent collaboration between debtor and creditor.[5]

Floating charges created within 12 months prior to the commencement of winding up or the successful presentation of a petition for an administration order are invalid unless the company was solvent immediately after the charge was created, except in so far as money was paid or goods or services supplied to the company or a debt of the company reduced or discharged in consideration of and at the same time as or after the creation of the charge with interest if appropriate.[6]

A liquidator can also apply to the court to set aside a credit transaction with the company entered into within 3 years prior to winding up if the terms are extortionate having regard to the risk involved or which otherwise contravenes the ordinary principles of fair dealing.[7]

Application of assets to liabilities

In winding up assets are applied successively to (1) discharging charges and expenses properly incurred in the winding up, including the liquidator's fee, (2) claims of preferential creditors, and (3) claims of unsecured or ordinary creditors.

Preferential debts rank equally among themselves and must be paid in full in priority to unsecured claims, unless the assets are insufficient to satisfy them, in which case they abate in equal proportions.[8] Preferential debts include (a) VAT referable to 6 months next before the relevant date; car tax, betting, and gaming duties which became due within 12 months next before the relevant date. The relevant date is the date of appointment of a provisional liquidator or the date of the winding-up order, or the

---

[3] *Nordic Travel Ltd.* v. *Scotprint Ltd.*, 1980 S.C. 1. A transaction is not voluntary if the debtor was doing what he was bound to do, as by implementing a subsisting obligation to grant a specific security, so long as that was part of the original contract: *Taylor* v. *Farrie* (1855) 17 D. 639; *T.* v. *L.*, 1970 S.L.T. 243.

[4] *Walkcraft Paint Co.* v. *Lovelock*, 1964 S.L.T. 103; *Walkcraft Paint Co.* v. *Kinsey*, 1964 S.L.T. 104.

[5] *Nordic Travel, supra.*

[6] S. 245.

[7] Consumer Credit Act, 1974, Ss. 137–9.

[8] S. 175 (2).

date of passing of the resolution for voluntary winding up, or the discharge of an administration order.[9] (b) Sums due to the Inland Revenue in respect of deductions under PAYE.[10] (c) Remuneration to an employee for services within 4 months next before the relevant date, not exceeding £800 each.[11] (d) National Insurance contributions due from the company as Class 1 or 2 payments under the Social Security Act 1975 for 12 months before the relevant date and certain Class 4 contributions due to the Inland Revenue for the preceding tax year. (e) Accrued holiday remuneration payable to an employee on the termination of employment before or by the effect of the winding-up order or resolution. (f) Debts due under Sch. 3 of the Social Security Pensions Act, 1975.

Unsecured or ordinary debts, including claims of secured creditors in excess of what they have recovered by realizing their right in security, rank equally and if the assets are insufficient abate in proportion.

If there is a surplus after payment of costs and the company's debts the liquidator must adjust the rights of contributories among themselves and distribute any surplus among the persons entitled thereto.[12] Frequently under the Articles preference shareholders are entitled to return of capital in priority to ordinary shareholders.

UNREGISTERED COMPANIES

An unregistered company is any associated or company other than a company registered under the Joint Stock Companies Acts[13] or any of the Companies Acts or a railway company incorporated by statute.[14] It is deemed to be registered where its principal place of business is situated and may be wound up by the court there if it is dissolved, or has ceased business, or is carrying on business only for the purpose of winding up, or is unable to pay its debts, or the court is of opinion that it is just and equitable that it should be wound up.[15]

[9] Ss. 386–7.
[10] This is the only priority for debts to the Crown.
[11] The meaning of employee must be determined by the criteria used in contracts of employment. Older cases are not necessarily helpful.
[12] S. 154.
[13] As defined in 1985 Act, S. 735.
[14] S. 220.
[15] Ss. 221–4.

CHAPTER 3.14

BUILDING SOCIETIES

A building society is a society whose purpose or principal purpose is that of raising, primarily by the subscriptions of the members, a stock or fund for making to them advances secured on land for their residential use. If formed in compliance with the Building Societies Act, 1986, it is incorporated under the Act from the date of its registration.[1]

The Building Societies Commission

There is established by the 1986 Act[2] a Commission with the general functions of promoting the protection by each building society of the investments of its shareholders and depositors, promoting the financial stability of building societies generally, securing that their principal purpose remains that of raising, primarily from their members, funds for making advances to members secured upon land for their residential use, administering the system of regulation of societies provided for by or under the Act, and advising government departments on any matter relating to building societies. It must report annually to Parliament. The Commission has extensive powers of control, may determine a society's powers, grant or revoke authorizations, subject to appeal, control advertising, obtain information, investigate the state and conduct of a society, appoint inspectors, and generally supervise societies.[3]

Establishment

A building society may be established by any ten or more persons agreeing on the society's purpose and its powers in a memorandum and rules for the regulation of the society complying with Schedule 2, Part 1, and sending four signed copies to the central office, i.e. the assistant

---

[1] Building Societies Act, 1986, S. 5. Building Societies originated in the 18th century and developed as one facet of the Victorian drive for thrift and self-help. Originally they were temporary and only later became permanent and continuing large-scale organizations. The first statutory regulation was in 1836. Until 1986 they were supervised by the Registrar of Friendly Societies, who still has certain powers. Societies incorporated under repealed enactments are deemed registered and incorporated under the 1986 Act. The Treasury may modify the Act to assimilate the law to that governing companies.

[2] Ss. 1–4 and Sch. 1.

[3] Ss. 36–57. cf. *R v. Chief Registrar of Friendly Societies* [1984] 2 All E.R. 27.

registrar of friendly societies for Scotland. If satisfied with the memorandum and rules and that the intended name of the society is not undesirable the central office registers the society and issues it with a certificate of incorporation.[4] The central office maintains a public file relating to each society, which may be inspected by members of the public.[5]

The memorandum must specify the society's name and address and purpose or principal purpose, the adoptable powers, and the restrictions on their extent which it has assumed under the Act.[6]

The provisions of the memorandum, as read along with the Act, are binding on each of the members and officers of the society and all persons claiming on account of a member or under the rules, and all such persons are taken to have notice of those provisions.[7]

The rules must provide for the matters specified in para. 3(4) of Schedule 2. These are binding on each of the members and officers of the society and on all persons claiming on account of a member or under the rules, and all such persons are taken to have notice of the rules.[8] A society may by special resolution alter its purpose or principal purpose, powers, and rules.[9] It must have a common seal bearing its registered name and may not use any other name; it may change its name by special resolution without affecting the rights and obligations of the society or its members.[10]

No person, other than a building society, may use a name suggesting that he is a building society, or connected with one, save in limited circumstances.[11] The Commission may require a society to change a misleading name.[12]

Membership

Schedule 2 makes provision for membership, liability of members, joint shareholders, and joint borrowers.[13] Societies must supply copies of the society's memorandum and rules to members and, on payment, to others; they must maintain a register of members.[14]

---

[4] Sch. 1, para. 1.
[5] S. 106.
[6] There are restrictions on certain names: Ss. 107–8.
[7] Sch. 2, para. 2.
[8] Sch. 2, para. 3. cf. *Auld* v. *Glasgow Working Men's Building Socy.* (1887) 14 R. (H.L.) 27; *Galashiels Provident Building Socy.* v. *Newlands* (1893) 20 R. 821.
[9] Sch. 2, para. 4.
[10] Sch. 2, paras. 9–11.
[11] S. 107.
[12] S. 108.
[13] Sch. 2, paras. 5–8.
[14] Sch. 2, paras. 12–15.

Meetings

Societies must hold annual general meetings; provision is made for resolutions, voting, proxies, and postal ballots.[15]

Raising funds and borrowing

A society may raise funds by the issue of shares to members or borrow money and receive deposits from any person to be applied for the purposes of the society. There may be different classes of shares and funds raised by shares may be repaid when no longer required for the purposes of the society.[16] The amount of sums deposited must not exceed 50 per cent of the aggregate of that amount and the value of shares in the society.[17] A society may raise funds and borrow money only if it has an authorization of the Commission.[18]

Shares of designated building societies are 'wider-range' investments for trustees under the Trustee Investments Act, 1961, Sch. 1.[19]

A receipt given to a society by a minor in respect of the payment to him of a sum due in respect of a deposit is not invalid on the ground of his minority.

Advances

A society may make advances to members secured by heritable security over land in Scotland (or the equivalent in England).[20] They are distinguished into class 1 advances (advances to individuals for the borrower's residential use and satisfying certain other conditions) and class 2 advances (where the society is not satisfied under the foregoing conditions).[21] There are requirements as to assessing the adequacy of security for advances.[22] Societies may make mobile home loans, and lend money to individuals, including by way of overdraft, may hold and develop land as a commercial asset, invest in subsidiaries, in companies, or industrial and provident societies.[23] There are extensive controls over assets held by societies.[24]

The terms of interest and repayment of capital are settled in each case

[15] Sch. 2, paras. 20–36.
[16] S. 7. Unlike a company a building society has no fixed share capital: *Irvine and Fullarton Building Socy.* v. *Cuthbertson* (1905) 8 F. 1.
[17] S. 8.
[18] S. 9 and Sch. 3.
[19] cf. *R.* v. *Chief Registrar of Friendly Societies* [1894] 2 All E.R. 27.
[20] S. 10. Societies use standard forms of a standard security over land.
[21] Ss. 11–12.
[22] S. 13 and Sch. 4.
[23] Ss. 14–19.
[24] Ss. 20–3.

though in practice standard terms and conditions are used. The rate of interest may be varied. In practice instalments of repayment include elements of both interest and capital. The sum to be repaid may be index-linked to the real value of the advance to take account of inflation provided the amount repayable is not less than the amount initially advanced.[25]

Protection of investors

There is a Building Societies Investor Protection Board which manages a fund from which to compensate investors if a building society becomes insolvent.[26]

Members or depositors dying

Where a member of or a depositor with a building society dies, testate or intestate, domiciled in any part of the U.K., leaving money in a society not exceeding £5,000 the society may, without requiring confirmation, pay the sum of money to a person claiming to be beneficially entitled under the will or the law of intestacy on his providing satisfactory evidence of the death and making a statutory declaration that the member or depositor has died and that the claimant is beneficially entitled under the will or the law of intestacy to receive it. Such payment is valid and effectual against any other claimant but without prejudice to that other person's claim against the first claimant.[27]

Services

A society may, subject to certain restrictions, provide other services, particularly money transmission services, provision of credit, unit trust schemes, pension schemes, insurance, estate agency services, surveys and valuations of land, and conveyancing services.[28]

Management

Every society must have at least two directors, a chief executive, and a secretary.[29] Directors must be elected at the A.G.M. or by postal ballot, must normally retire at 70, and may be required to hold shares.[30] Tax-free payments to directors are prohibited and they must disclose interests

---

[25] *Nationwide Building Socy.* v. *Registry of Friendly Societies* [1983] 3 All E.R. 296.
[26] Ss. 24–33 and Sch. 5 and 6.
[27] Sch. 7. The sum of £5,000 may be altered by order.
[28] S. 34 and Sch. 8. On conveyancing services, see also S. 124 and Sch. 21.
[29] Ss. 58–9.
[30] Ss. 60–1.

in contracts and other transactions; there are restrictions on loans to them; they must disclose income received in related businesses.[31]

Accounts and audit

Every society must maintain accounting records which explain its transactions, disclose the state of the society's business at any time, and enable the directors and the society properly to discharge their duties under the Act. There must be a system of control of business and records and of inspection and report.[32] There must be prepared annually an income and expenditure account, a balance sheet at the end of the year, and a statement of the source and application of funds during the year.[33]

The annual accounts must conform to the Act and regulations.[34] The directors must also prepare an annual business statement and a report on the society's business, and a summary financial statement for members and depositors.[35] Auditors must be appointed who must report to the members on the annual accounts,[36] and report to the Commission.[37]

Officers and auditors may not be exempted by the rules from liability for negligence, default, breach of duty, or breach of trust, nor indemnified against such liability,[38] but it is a defence in criminal proceedings that a person took all reasonable precautions and exercised all due diligence to avoid such an offence.[39]

Complaints and disputes

An individual has the right against a society to have any complaint about action by the society investigated under a recognized scheme for investigation of complaints.[40]

Dissolution

A society may be dissolved by consent of members, by an instrument of dissolution,[41] or be wound up voluntarily,[42] or wound up by the court on stated grounds.[43] In either of the latter two cases parts of the Insolvency

[31] Ss. 62–72 and Sch. 9.
[32] S. 71.
[33] S. 72.
[34] s. 73.
[35] Ss. 74–6.
[36] Ss. 77–81 and Sch. 11.
[37] S. 82.
[38] S. 110.
[39] S. 112.
[40] Ss. 83–5 and Schs. 12–14.
[41] Ss. 86–7.
[42] S. 88.
[43] s. 89.

Act, 1986, apply with modifications.[44] When wound up voluntarily a society is dissolved 3 months after the liquidator has made his return of the final meetings; when wound up by the court it is dissolved 3 months after the filing of the liquidator's final notice.[45] The court may declare a dissolution void in certain circumstances.[46]

Mergers

Societies desiring to amalgamate may do so by establishing a society as their successor after agreeing on the purposes and rules of the successor and each approving the terms of the amalgamation and making a joint application to the Commission for confirmation of the amalgamation.[47]

Transfer of engagements

A society may transfer its engagements to another society, subject to passing the requisite resolutions. The extent of transfer is to be recorded in an instrument of transfer of engagements. Transfer must be confirmed by the Commission.[48]

Transfer of business to commercial company

A society may transfer the whole of its business to a company, subject to approving the transfer and obtaining the Commission's confirmation.[49]

[44] S. 90 and Sch. 15.
[45] Sch. 15, para. 56.
[46] S. 91.
[47] Ss. 93, 95–6 and Sch. 16.
[48] Ss. 94–6 and Sch. 16.
[49] Ss. 97–102.

CHAPTER 3.15

INDUSTRIAL AND PROVIDENT SOCIETIES

A society for carrying on any industry, business, or trade (including dealings with land) wholesale or retail, specified in its rules, may be registered unde the Industrial and Provident Societies Act, 1965 to 1978,[1] if it is a *bona fide* co-operative society or, being conducted for the benefit of the community, there are special reasons why the society should be registered under the Act rather than as a company, and the rules contain provisions as to the matters contained in Schedule 1 and the registered office is to be in Great Britain or the Channel Islands.[2]

Registration

Registration is effected by application to the Assistant Registrar of Friendly Societies by seven members and the secretary of the society with two printed copies of the society's rules. A society may be formed by two or more registered societies. An acknowledgment of registration is conclusive evidence that the society is duly registered.[3] By virtue of registration a society is a body corporate with limited liability and may sue and be sued by its registered name.[4] The assistant registrar may reject an undesirable name; the name must contain 'Limited' as its last word unless the assistant registrar dispenses with this, where the objects are wholly charitable or benevolent; the name may be changed, and must be used on all premises, publications, and documents.[5] Change in the situation of the registered office must be notified to the assistant registrar.[6] Registration may be cancelled or suspended;[7] an appeal lies from refusal to register, cancellation or suspension, to the chief registrar and to the Court of Session.[8] A registered society may by special resolution convert itself into a company registered under the Companies Acts,[9] and conversely.[10]

---

[1] The first legislation dealing with such societies was in 1852; but such societies had been established under a Friendly Societies Act of 1834.
[2] 1965 Act, S. 1. A society for constructing or improving housing accommodation may be registered under this head.
[3] S. 2. Societies registered under previous Acts are deemed registered under the 1965 Act, S. 4.
[4] S. 3. As to carrying on business also in England, see S. 8.
[5] S. 5.
[6] S. 10.
[7] Ss. 16–17.
[8] S. 18.
[9] S. 52.
[10] S. 53; Companies Act, 1985, S. 378.

Rules

Every society must have rules,[11] and acknowledgment of registration of
the society is conclusive evidence of the registration of its rules.[12] Amendments thereof must be registered.[13] The registered rules bind the society
and all members and all persons claiming through them as if each member had subscribed them and undertaken to conform thereto.[14] Any
person may on demand and on payment receive a copy of the rules.[15] The
rules must provide for entrusting the management of the society's affairs
to a committee.[16] They may be challenged as being in unreasonable
restraint of trade,[17] or illegal, though some illegal rules does not make the
society an illegal association.[18] A society carrying on the business of
banking cannot provide in its rules for its shares being withdrawable.[19]

Management

The rules must make provision for the appointment of a committee of
management and of managers and other officers. Where under the rules
the control of the society's affairs is vested in the committee the members
cannot exercise that control.[20] It has statutory functions in connection
with transfers of property[21] and the general function of carrying on the
business in accordance with the Act.

Members

Individuals or other registered societies or corporate bodies may be members. The rules must set out the terms of admission of members; members
become shareholders, and a register of members must be maintained.
Members have various statutory rights and limited liability for the society's debts.[22]

---

[11] Schedule 1 lists matters to be provided for in a society's rules.
[12] S. 9.
[13] S. 10. Further provisions as to rules are in Ss. 11–13. As to amendment see *Auld* v.
Glasgow, etc., Bldg. Soc. (1887) 14 R. (H.L.) 27; *Strohmenger* v. *Finsbury Bldg. Soc.* [1897] 2
Ch. 469.
[14] S. 14. The section provides certain exceptions; see also *Hole* v. *Garnsey* [1903] A.C. 472.
[15] S. 15.
[16] As to the powers of a committee see *Alexander* v. *Duddy*, 1956 S.C. 24.
[17] *McEllistrim* v. *Ballymacelligott Co-operative Socy.* [1919] A.C. 548; *Bellshill and Mossend
Co-operative Socy., Ltd.* v. *Dalziel Co-operative Socy. Ltd.*, 1958 S.C. 400; affd. on other
points, 1960 S.C. (H.L.) 64.
[18] *Swaine* v. *Wilson* (1889) 24 Q.B.D. 252.
[19] S. 7.
[20] *Alexander* v. *Duddy*, 1956 SC. 24.
[21] Ss. 23–7.
[22] Ss. 44, 57.

Meetings

The rules must provide for the mode of holding meetings and for voting thereat and the mode of making, altering, or rescinding rules.[23]

Capital

The share capital is not usually fixed; it consists normally of withdrawable or transferable shares, and possibly of other classes as provided by the rules. No member, with certain exceptions, may have an interest in the shares of the society exceeding £1,000.[24] A society with withdrawable share capital may not carry on the business of banking.[25] The rules may provide for shares being paid up in full when issued, or paid by instalments or on call. Subject to the rules a corporate body may hold shares, as may a minor over 16.[26] There is no requirement of issuing share certificates and provision therefor is unusual. The rules must provide whether and, if so, by what authority and in what manner any of the society's funds may be invested.[27] A society's borrowing powers depend on its rules. It may grant security for money borrowed in any way competent to a natural person and also, like an incorporated company, grant a floating charge over its property, heritable and moveable, in accordance with the Industrial and Provident Societies Act, 1967, Part II and Schedule, amended by Companies (Floating Charges & Receivers) (Sc.) Act, 1972, S. 10, and subject to compliance with the requirements of the 1967 Act, Part II.

Accounts

Every society must keep proper books of accounts and comply with statutory requirements as to accounts, balance sheets, and auditors.[28]

Application of profits

The rules must provide for the mode of application of the society's profits including, if authorized, the furtherance of political objects.[29]

Loans

The society's rules may provide for advances of money to members on the security of heritable or moveable estate or, if registered to carry on

[23] Sch. 1, para. 5.
[24] S. 6.
[25] S. 7, amd. 1978 Act.
[26] Ss. 19–20.
[27] Sch. 1, para. 14.
[28] Ss. 37–40, partly replaced by Friendly and Industrial Provident Societies Act, 1968.
[29] *Cahill* v. *London Co-operative Socy. Ltd.* [1937] Ch. 265. See also *Lafferty* v. *Barrhead*

banking, in any manner customary in such business.[30] Debts due by members are recoverable in the sheriff court where the registered office is situated or the member resides. The society has a lien on the member's share for any debt due by the member to the society and may set off any sum credited to the member thereon towards the debt.[31]

Nominations

A member may[32] by signed writing,[33] delivered at or sent to the society's registered office or made in a book kept at that office, nominate a person[34] or persons to become entitled on his death to the whole part of the property in the society (shares, loans, deposits, etc.) which he may have at the time of his death, to the extent of £1,500.[35] A nomination may be varied or revoked by a subsequent nomination but not by the nominator's will or codicil. Marriage revokes a nomination.[36] The committee of the society may, on receiving satisfactory proof of the death of the member, transfer or pay the value of the property to which the nominee is entitled.[37] On a member's death with property in the society not exceeding £500 and not the subject of any nomination, the committee may, without confirmation being expede, [38] distribute that property among such persons as appear to the committee on such evidence as they deem satisfactory to be entitled by law to receive it.[39] In so deciding the committee may dispense with evidence of title and relationship, but may not alter the title or select one of the next of kin as payee even with the consent of the majority.[40] If the deceased member were illegitimate and left no widow, widower, or issue and was not survived by his mother, the committee must deal with his property as the Treasury shall direct.[41] If a claiming member is mentally incapable the society may pay to any person whom they judge proper to receive the property on his behalf.[42] Such payments are valid and effectual against demands by other persons.[43]

Co-operative Soc., 1919, 1 S.L.T. 257; *Warburton* v. *Huddersfield Industrial Soc.* [1892] 1 Q.B. 817 (strike fund).
[30] S. 21.
[31] S. 22; see also *Lloyd* v. *Francis* [1937] 4 All E.R. 489.
[32] S. 23.
[33] See *Morton* v. *French*, 1908 S.C. 171 (authentication by mark only).
[34] Not an officer or servant of the society save in special cases: S. 23(2).
[35] S. 23(3)(c) amd. Administration of Estates (Small Payments) Act, 1965, S. 2 and orders thereunder.
[36] S. 23 (4)–(6).
[37] S. 24.
[38] The society can demand production of confirmation: *Escritt* v. *Todmorden Coop. Soc.* [1896] 1 Q.B. 461.
[39] S. 25(1).
[40] *Symington's Exor.* v. *Galashiels Co-op. Store Co. Ltd.* (1894) 21 R. 371.
[41] S. 25(2).
[42] S. 26.
[43] S. 27.

Powers and duties

A registered society may contract, grant bills, purchase, lease, and transact with land, and invest its funds in any security authorized by its rules.[44] It must have its accounts audited and make an annual return to the assistant registrar.[45] Officers may be required to find caution for intromissions, and must account for monies handled.[46] It must maintain a register of members showing shares and property held; a member may inspect his own account and the assistant registrar may on the requisition of ten members have the books inspected, or require the production of books, accounts, and documents.[47] The assistant registrar may on application appoint an inspector to examine into and report on the affairs of the society, or call a special meeting of the society.[48]

Amalgamation and dissolution

Societies may amalgamate or one may transfer its engagements to another, or a society may convert itself into or amalgamate with or transfer its engagements to a company under the Companies Acts. A company may convert itself into a registered society.[49] A society may be dissolved on being wound up by order or resolution as under the Companies Act, 1985,[50] or by instrument of dissolution signed by three-fourths of the members.[51]

Disputes

Disputes between a society or an officer and a member,[52] an aggrieved ex-member or person claiming through him, or any person claiming under the rules of the society, are to be decided in the manner provided by the rules, which may be by arbitration[53] or referred to the assistant registrar, whose decision is enforceable on application to the sheriff court, or referred to the sheriff. At the request of either party the assistant registrar or sheriff may state a case for the opinion of the Court of Session.[54] The courts' jurisdiction is not ousted if the dispute has not been

---

[44] Ss. 28–35. As to execution of deeds see S. 36.
[45] Ss. 37–40.
[46] Ss. 41–3.
[47] Ss. 44–8.
[48] S. 49.
[49] Ss. 50–4.
[50] Ss. 55–7, 59.
[51] S. 58.
[52] *Municipal, etc. Soc.* v. *Richards* (1888) 39 Ch.D. 372.
[53] *Judson* v. *Ellesmere Port Ex-Servicemen's Club* [1948] 1 All E.R. 844; *Birtley Co-op. Socy.* v. *Windy Nook Co-op Socy.* [1959] 1 All E.R. 623; *Bellshill and Mossend Co-op Socy.* v. *Dalziel Co-op Socy.*, 1960 S.C. (H.L.) 64.
[54] S. 60.

decided according to the rules,[55] or if the dispute relates to a matter *ultra vires* of the society.[56] The Court of Session may overrule the sheriff if he has erred in determining whether or not a dispute is one to be decided in accordance with the rules of the society.[57]

[55] *Andrews* v. *Mitchell* [1905] A.C. 78.

[56] *McEllistrim* v. *Ballymacelligott Co-op. Soc. Ltd.* [1919] A.C. 548; *Todd* v. *Kelso Co-op. Soc. Ltd.*, 1953 S.L.T. (Sh. Ct.) 2.

[57] cf. *Gall* v. *Loyal Glenbogie Lodge* (1900) 2 F. 1187; *Collins* v. *Barrowfield United Oddfellows*, 1915 S.C. 190.

CREDIT UNIONS

A society may be registered as a credit union under the Industrial and Provident Societies Act, 1965, subject to modifications, if its objects are only the promotion of thrift among members, the creation of sources of credit, the control of members' savings, and the education of members in the management of money, and membership is limited to persons following a particular occupation, residing or employed in a particular locality, employed by a particular employer, or being a member of an organization or associated for another purpose.[1] The name must contain the words 'credit union'.[2] The rules of a credit union must contain specified matters.[3] Only individuals may be members and there is an upper limit on the shares which may be held.[4] There must be at least twenty-one members and, generally, not more than five thousand.[5] A union operates by accepting deposits from members as subscription for its shares, lending money to members for a provident or productive purpose, on such terms and security as its rules provide, and for limited times.[6] It may invest surplus funds only in approved ways[7] and must insure against loss.[8] Provision is made for cancellation of registration, winding up, amalgamation, and transfer of engagements.[9] A credit union may not be converted into a company, but a company may, on conditions, be converted into a credit union.[10] The Assistant Registrar of Friendly Societies has a general supervisory responsibility.[11]

---

[1] Credit Unions Act, 1979, S. 1. By virtue of the Act, S. 3, it is a corporate body with limited liability.
[2] S. 3. By the 1965 Act, S. 5, the name must end with the word 'Limited'.
[3] S. 4.
[4] S. 5.
[5] S. 6.
[6] Ss. 7–11.
[7] s. 13.
[8] S. 14.
[9] Ss. 20–1.
[10] Ss. 22–3.
[11] Ss. 4, 15, 17–20.

INDEX